RECOVERY OF DAMAGES FOR BAD FAITH

FIFTH EDITION
Volumes 1 & 2

John C. McCarthy

Supplement • May 2021

Supplement Editors
Sharon C. Rutberg, J.D., LL.M.
Wendy Janis Malkin, J.D.

D1300218

LAWPRESS

www.lawpresscorp.com

Library of Congress Catalog Card Number 90-060926
International Standard Book Number 0-915544-21-0

Published by: Lawpress Corporation
               P.O. Box 468
               Tiburon, CA 94920–0468
               www.lawpresscorp.com
E-mail: info@lawpresscorp.com

Printed in the United States of America

Contents

Introduction to 2021 Supplement

This annual cumulative supplement to the Fifth Edition of John C. McCarthy's *Recovery of Damages for Bad Faith* retains the material from the preceding supplements, with updated citations, and summarizes some 50 cases representing another eventful year's worth of developments. Important decisions of the past 16 months have included:

—A decision of a California appellate court denying summary judgment to a medical insurer that refused to authorize full amount of treatment for an autistic child on grounds of failure to fully investigate the claim. See §§1.9–1.10, 1.19A, 1.33.

—A federal court decision under California law denying summary judgment for an insurer on claims related to coverage sought for computer hacking on grounds of failure to investigate. See §§1.10, 1.19A, 1.66.

—The Minnesota Supreme Court's opinion upholding awards to an insured of $100,000 in taxable costs and $97,940.50 in attorney fees under Minn. Stat. §604.18 where her underinsured motorist insurer failed to adequately investigate her claim, disregarding a mountain of medical evidence that her accident caused severe headaches requiring costly Botox treatment. See §§1.10, 1.20, 1.26–1.27, 1.34, 1.59, 4.15.

—The Iowa Supreme Court's holding in a workers' compensation case that the insurer's delay of 1.5 years in determining that the insured was permanently and totally disabled supported an award of $58,452.42 in compensatory damages and $500,000 in punitive damages. See §§1.11, 1.28, 1.57, 1.59, 1.66.

—The Supreme Court of Louisiana's holding that first-party bad faith claims against an insurer under La. Stat. Ann. §22:1973 arise out of an insurer's contractual obligations, and therefore are governed by the 10-year prescriptive period under La. C.C. art. 3499 and not the 1-year prescriptive period for delictual actions. See §§1.25–1.26, 1.33.

—The Hawaii federal district court's dismissal of claims by property owners alleging fraudulent and misleading conduct of surplus lines insurance agents and brokers, where plaintiffs were denied coverage for lava damage following the 2018 eruption of the Kilauea Volcano, holding that the claims failed to satisfy Fed. R. Civ. P. 9(b) and 8(a) but noting that circumstances of the case were "concerning" and granting leave to amend. The court also held that the Insurance Code, Haw. Stat. §431:13–102, does not preempt actions under the Unfair and Deceptive Acts or Trade Practices Act (UDAP), Haw. Stat. §480–2. See §§1.26, 1.33, 1.37, 2.24, 3.30, 3.48, 3.49, 3.52.

—A case from the Massachusetts federal district court addressing a claim of breach of the implied covenant of good faith and fair dealing in the insurance context. See §§1.33, 1.37.

—A holding of the Massachusetts high court that denial of coverage did not breach the insurer's duty of good faith and fair dealing under Mass. Gen. Laws §93A where the coverage decision was supported by a "plausible, reasoned legal position" in case law, although the case was very old and the insurer's position turned out to be wrong. See §1.37.

—The Tenth Circuit's holding under Kansas law that insurer did not breach its duty to defend by negligent hiring of defense counsel, concluding that the attorney's reputation for causing delays in litigation was not sufficient evidence of incompetence, and also rejecting vicarious liability claim. See §§2.7, 2.9, 2.31, 2.38.

—A holding of the Nebraska Supreme Court that an insurance broker had no duty to advise the company for which it procured insurance that it should purchase workers' compensation insurance. See §§2.9, 2.30, 2.38, 3.30.

—The Kentucky Supreme Court's holding a health care provider's foreign captive insurer was not subject to

Kentucky's Unfair Claims Settlement Practices Act (UCSPA). See §§2.24, 3.29.

—The First Circuit's opinion affirming under Massachusetts law that a night club owner's liability insurer conducted an inadequate investigation of a claim against the owner by an underage exotic dancer who was severely injured in a car accident after becoming intoxicated at work, upholding a damages award of $1.8 million plus trebled damages for willful conduct under Mass. Gen. Laws §176D 3(9)(d), and stating that damages for emotional distress, mental anguish, and "fear of financial ruin" were recoverable. See §§2.31, 2.50, 2.69, 2.71–2.72.

—A decision of the California Court of Appeal that home services protection companies are not subject to tort liability for bad faith, as they are not insurance companies. See §3.29.

Other Developments

—A ruling of the California Court of Appeal approving punitive damages of 3 times compensatory damages and discussing constitutional factors. See §§1.17, 1.62, 1.66.

—The Washington Supreme Court's holding that the general duty of good faith set forth in the Washington insurance code does not create a private right of action against insurers or claim adjusters, and that claim adjusters are also not subject to suit under the state Consumer Protection Act. See §§1.19, 1.33.

—The Supreme Court of South Dakota's refusal to extend the doctrine of "equal consideration" to the first-party claims context. See §§1.20, 2.4.

—The Sixth Circuit's ruling that a statutory cap on punitive damages violated the right to a jury trial set forth in the Tennessee State Constitution. See §§1.33, 1.66.

—Decisions of the Eighth Circuit and a federal district court in New York holding attorney fee awards to be recoverable in bad faith cases. See §1.59.

—Opinions from federal district courts in Massachusetts, Nevada, and New York holding that insureds had not made a sufficient showing to support claims for punitive damages in bad faith cases. See §1.66.

—An opinion from the Supreme Court of Florida, reinstating a jury verdict against the insurer for $9.2 million and holding that the evidence supported the jury's finding of bad faith failure to settle where the insurer's claims adjuster failed to communicate with the claimant's attorney and the insured in critical ways. See §§2.7, 2.40.

—A holding from the Northern District of Georgia in which the court found no bad faith failure to settle where the insurer had complied with the *Wellstar* "safe harbor" rule in requiring a claimant to place funds in escrow to satisfy any potential lien. See §2.7.

—Three cases from federal and state courts discussing whether an insurer may attempt to justify the nonpayment of a claim based on after-acquired information not possessed at the time of the original denial. See §3.61.

—The Supreme Court of South Carolina's opinion analyzing when an insurer can be deemed to have waived the attorney-client privilege in bad faith litigation. See §3.70.

—A decision of the Kentucky Supreme Court affirming that in Kentucky bad faith claims can arise from both the Consumer Protection Act and the Unfair Claims Settlement Practices Act and reviewing Kentucky's bad faith law. See §§1.33, 2.2, 2.24.

—A Louisiana Court of Appeals review of the meaning of the two Louisiana bad faith statutes, La. Stat. Ann. §§22:1892 and 22:1973. See §1.33.

—A holding from the West Virginia Supreme Court that an insured had no standing to assert a private right of action against its liability insurer under the West Virginia Unfair Trade Practices Act. See §§1.33, 2.7, 2.24.

—The Supreme Court of Colorado's holding that the personal injury limitation in Colorado's survival statute did not bar an estate's recovery or limit its damages for bad faith, where the estate was substituted for a deceased insured. See §1.56.

—A federal district court ruling, affirmed by the Third Circuit, that a successful bad faith plaintiff was entitled to no attorney's fees under Pennsylvania's bad faith statute, where the court determined that only 13 percent of fees claimed by plaintiff's attorneys were reasonable, and plaintiffs requested fees of $1.12 million on claim with total award of $125,000. See §1.56.

—Under Texas law, the Fifth Circuit's affirmance that the insurer breached its duty to defend an additional insured general contractor, with damages of $655,500, applying the "8-corners rule" to determine whether the matter was covered by the policy. See §§1.56, 2.9, 2.24, 2.66.

—The Alaska Supreme Court's ruling upholding an award of nominal damages of $2, punitive damages of $450,000, and attorney's fees for an underinsured motorist (UIM) insurer's bad faith delay in paying the plaintiff's claim. See §§1.58, 1.59, 1.61, 1.62, 1.66, 4.28.

—Under Illinois law, a federal bankruptcy court awarding attorney's fees, costs, and a $60,000 penalty amount under 215 Ill. Comp. Stat. 5/155 because it found the insurer had committed "vexatious and unreasonable" delay in settling asbestos claims. See §§2.7, 2.70, 2.72.

—A California Court of Appeals opinion affirming holding of bad faith failure to defend against insurer, but reversing awards to plaintiff general contractor of *Brandt* attorney's fees and punitive damages and remanding for recalculation. See §§2.9, 2.38, 2.70, 2.74.

—A California Court of Appeal's order upholding certain California insurance regulations implementing the unfair claims settlement practices statute, Cal. Ins. Code §790.03, including regulations defining the terms "knowingly committed" and "willful" or "willfully." See §2.21.

—A Missouri appeals court upholding a jury verdict that the insurer's failure to pay the insured's third party asbestos claims was a vexatious refusal to pay and awarding attorney's fees under Mo. Rev. Stat. §375.420. See §§2.24, 2.70.

—The Fourth Circuit's discussion of the relationship between North Carolina's Unfair Claim Settlement Practices (UCSP) statute, N.C. Gen. Stat. Ann. §58-63-15, and its Unfair and Deceptive Trade Practices Act (UDTPA), N.C. Gen. Stat. Ann. §75-1.1. See §2.24.

—The Pennsylvania Supreme Court's holding that proof of ill will or self-interest is probative of whether an insurer knew or recklessly disregarded its lack of reasonable basis for denying a claim, but is not a prerequisite to prevail on a claim under Pennsylvania's "bad faith statute," Pa. Cons. Stat. §8371. See §1.33.

—The holding of the Supreme Judicial Court of Massachusetts that the amount of damages to be multiplied for a willful and knowing violation of the unfair claims practices statute (Mass. Gen. Laws Ann. ch. 176D) or the consumer protection statute (Mass. Gen. Laws Ann. ch. 93A) does not include postjudgment interest. See §§1.66, 2.71.

—A Texas appeals court's analysis of whether an insurer delayed payment under the Texas prompt payment statute (Tex. Ins. Code §§542.051–542.061) when it delivered a check to the insured's authorized counsel that was made jointly payable to both the insured and its counsel, and the counsel cashed the check without the insured's endorsement. See §1.11.

—The Texas Supreme Court's review and clarification of Texas precedent on whether an insured can recover policy benefits as actual damages for an insurer's unfair settlement practices under Tex. Ins. Code §541.060(a) absent a breach of contract. See §§1.33, 1.56.

—The Eleventh Circuit's holding that a damages determination in an underlying uninsured motorist case is not binding in a subsequent bad faith action where the insurer pursued its right to appeal but the appellate court did not review the errors alleged by the insurer in the jury's calculation of damages. See §§1.33, 1.56.

—The Ninth Circuit's discussion under California law of the options available to excess insurers when presented with a settlement offer that has been approved by the insured and the primary insurer. See §§1.59, 2.7, 2.9, 3.41.

—The consideration of proposed amendments to California Jury Instructions (CACI) pertaining to insurance bad faith by the Judicial Council of California, which accepted proposals to revise certain language in CACI No. 2332 defining bad faith failure to investigate, and to leave unchanged certain language in CACI No. 2334 on bad faith refusal to settle. See §4.28.

—A ruling from the U.S. District Court for the District of Connecticut, now on appeal to the Second Circuit, that an insurer's handling of claims from the Hartford Roman Catholic Diocesan Corp. related to liability under claims brought by persons abused by priests, although "certainly negligent, perhaps even reckless," did not rise to the level of bad faith; that the insurer's delay in claims handling did not constitute a "general business practice"; and that Connecticut does not recognize the affirmative defense of "reverse bad faith." See §§1.9, 1.11, 1.24, 2.24, 2.39.

— An appeals court holding, now on appeal to the Pennsylvania Supreme Court, interpreting Pennsylvania's "bad faith statute," Pa. Cons. Stat. §8371, and granting a new trial to the estate of a cancer victim whose insurer failed to pay claims under a cancer policy. See §§1.2, 1.9, 1.10.

—The Tenth Circuit's ruling under Colorado law upholding a jury verdict on the insured's claim of unreasonable delay and holding that the "fair debatability" of claim validity can be relevant but is not determinative. See §§1.11, 1.26.

—The Florida Supreme Court's holding that an insured is entitled to receive a determination of liability and damages in an uninsured motorist case before filing a first-party bad faith action under Fla. Stat. Ann. §624.155. See §1.33.

—Three decisions applying the Georgia "bad faith statute," Ga. Code §33–4-6. See §§1.19A, 1.33, 1.59.

—A ruling from the Supreme Court of Delaware confirming that the bad faith cause of action is grounded in contract law, and holding that punitive damages are available as a remedy for breach of the covenant of good faith where the plaintiff can show that the insurer acted with malice or reckless indifference. See §§1.34, 1.36.

—A decision of the U.S. District Court for the Northern District of Illinois denying an insured's claim for damages and attorney fees under 215 Ill. Comp. Stat. 5/115 where the insurer's denial of coverage was based on a reading of the policy that "was not completely out of bounds or foreclosed by prior authority," creating a bona fide dispute over the scope and application of coverage. See §§1.59, 1.66.

—A Third Circuit decision holding that under Pennsylvania law, a trial court erred in allowing evidence of a punitive damages award to be presented to the jury in the insured's bad faith case against his insurer, reasoning that the award was irrelevant because of the state's public policy against insuring for punitive damages. See §§2.73, 4.19A.

—The New Jersey Supreme Court's decision upholding an award of summary judgment for the insurer on a bad faith claim because the insurer acted in reliance on an unpublished opinion of the New Jersey Appellate Division when it rejected an arbitration award in favor of the insured and demanded a trial de novo. See §1.33.

—In California, a federal district court's denial of an insurer's motion for summary judgment on bad faith refusal to pay a claim, finding a triable issue of fact whether the insurer acted unreasonably, given available case law and issues of contract interpretation surrounding the meaning of "nursing home" in a long-term care policy. See §1.22.

—The Louisiana Supreme Court's responses to questions certified to it by the Fifth Circuit pertaining to the interpretation and reach of Louisiana's claims settlement practices statute. See §§1.26, 1.55, 2.7.

—The Fifth Circuit's affirmance of a $1,232,328.14 penalty interest award to an insured under the Texas Prompt Payment of Claims Statute, based on the insurer's failure to notify the insured of claim rejection upon receipt of information required "to secure final proof of loss." See §1.11.

—The Florida Supreme Court's resolution of a split among the appellate districts by holding that Citizens Property Insurance Corporation, a state-created property insurer, is immune from first-party bad faith claims brought under Fla. Stat. 624.155. See §3.29.

—A review of the "reverse bad faith" doctrine by the Sixth Circuit, which predicted that Kentucky law would not recognize such a tort. See §1.24.

—A Louisiana Court of Appeals decision upholding a jury award of $2,953,454 penalty under Louisiana's bad faith statute for failure to timely pay business interruption losses suffered by three radio stations during Hurricane Katrina. See §§1.27, 1.66.

—A landmark decision by a federal district court in California clearly holding that California's Elder Abuse Act, passed in 1991 and often ignored, provides a viable claim in first-party insurance bad faith cases involving the unreasonable withholding or denial of benefits owing to an elderly insured. The Elder Abuse Act was designed to protect elders by providing enhanced remedies that encourage private, civil enforcement of laws against elder abuse and neglect. See §1.55.

—An Illinois Appellate Court's dismissal of a complaint that, although it sufficiently alleged facts to establish a reasonable probability of recovery in excess of policy limits, failed to plead facts to establish a reasonable probability of a finding of liability against the insured. See §2.7.

—The Idaho Supreme Court's most recent clarification of the nature and elements of that state's tort of first-party bad faith. See §1.33.

—A number of significant decisions relating to the proportionality and constitutionality of punitive damages awards. See §§1.62, 1.66.

—A California Court of Appeal's clarification of the proposition that a breach of the implied covenant of good faith and fair dealing is itself a breach of contract, and it is therefore not necessary for an insured to allege that the insurer failed to comply with any specific provision of the policy. See §1.9.

—The South Dakota Supreme Court's explanation of the four circumstances under which punitive damages can be awarded against a principal because of the act of an agent. See §1.19.

—The Connecticut Supreme Court's detailed examination of an insurer's duty to defend, the consequences of a breach of that duty, and the standards for assessing the reasonableness of a settlement thereafter reached between the insured and the injured party. See §2.9.

—A Tenth Circuit decision emphasizing that the mere possibility of coverage creates a duty on the insurer's part to conduct a meaningful investigation of the underlying facts or risk a finding that coverage was denied without a reasonable basis. See §2.9.

—The Alaska Supreme Court's discussion of the two prevailing approaches to defining an insurer's duties in situations involving multiple insureds, and the Court's explanation of its reasons for adopting one of the two approaches, as a matter of first impression. See §2.50.

—The Washington Supreme Court's *en banc* decision explaining nine factors to be considered in determining the reasonableness of a settlement reached by the insured and an injured third party after a liability insurer has breached the implied covenant in denying coverage. See §2.65.

—The Alaska Supreme Court's conclusion that public policy was not violated by an award of attorney's fees to an automobile insurer that had brought a declaratory judgment action seeking a determination of its obligations. See §2.70.

—Several decisions discussing attorney-client privilege and the work product doctrine in connection with the discoverability of the insurer's claims files. See §3.70.

—The Florida Supreme Court's clarification that there is no common-law first-party cause of action, only the statutory cause of action codified at F.S.A. §§624.155. See §1.26.

—The Colorado Supreme Court's clarification of the relationship between that state's common-law and statutory causes of action for an insurer's denial of a claim or delay in payment. See §1.26.

—The Seventh Circuit's application of Wisconsin law in affirming a judgment for the insured, rejecting the insurer's defenses relating to the insured's justified and nonprejudicial delay in filing the claim. See §1.23.

—The West Virginia Supreme Court's clarification of that state's recognition of the right of a first-party insured to bring a bad faith cause of action under the common law and under the West Virginia Unfair Trade Practices Act. See §1.33.

—The holding of a federal district court that under Washington law a party prevailing on a first-party bad faith claim involving the insurer's bad faith in evaluating coverage may recover consequential damages even when that denial of coverage is ultimately determined to have been correct. See §1.56.

—The Hawaii Supreme Court's holding, as a matter of first impression, that if a first-party insurer commits bad faith, the insured need not prove economic or physical loss in order to recover damages for emotional distress. See §1.58.

—An Arizona Court of Appeals' reduction of a punitive damages award of $55 million to $155,000, a figure representing only a 1:1 ratio to compensatory damages. See §§1.66.

—A holding by the Massachusetts Supreme Judicial Court that due process was not violated by an award of damages against a tortfeasor's excess insurer in the amount of $22 million under the state's unfair business practices act. See §2.24.

—A Ninth Circuit decision noting splits of authority under California law, and declining to decide (1) whether a breach of the good faith duty to settle can be found in the absence of a settlement demand, and (2) whether the "genuine dispute doctrine" applies to the duty to settle third-party claims. See §§2.46, 2.48.

—The Colorado Supreme Court's holding, as a matter of first impression, that insurers have a good faith duty to promptly and effectively communicate with anyone they are reasonably aware legitimately needs information pertaining to the handling of a claim. See §1.19A.

—A Colorado Court of Appeals' rejection of the proposition that a showing of "fair debatability," without more, is necessarily sufficient to defeat a bad faith claim as a matter of law. See §1.33.

—The Eighth Circuit's explanation that under Iowa law, an insurer can defeat a bad faith claim by showing that it had at least one reasonable basis for denying a claim, and need not show that all of its positions were reasonable. See §1.33.

—The Louisiana Supreme Court's holding, as a matter of first impression, that the insureds in an action for failure to pay for wind damages following a hurricane were not required to show that the insurer had intended to "aggrieve" them in order to recover damages for emotional distress. See §1.58.

—The Mississippi Supreme Court's clarification that to prove a bad faith claim, an insured must show a level of negligence in conducting an investigation such that a proper investigation would have easily adduced evidence showing that the insurer's defenses were without merit. See §1.10.

—The Third Circuit's formulation of Pennsylvania law's heightened standard of proof as requiring an insured to provide evidence so "clear, direct, weighty, and convincing" as to enable the trier of fact to form a clear conviction, without hesitation, that the insurer acted in bad faith. See §1.33.

—The South Dakota Supreme Court's holding that an insurer's clear breach of contract, or denial of a claim that is not fairly debatable, may indicate the type of malice necessary to support an award of punitive damages. See §1.66.

—The Tenth Circuit's affirmance of summary judgment, under Utah law, on a claim for the intentional infliction of emotional distress on the grounds that the insurer's alleged conduct, although "unreasonable, unkind, and unfair, did not evoke outrage or revulsion." See §1.48.

—A federal district court's interpretation of Florida law as precluding an insurer's liability for bad faith in attempting to settle a claim against its insured where the evidence could not support a finding that the insurer had acted solely in furtherance of its own interests. See §2.4.

—The Seventh Circuit's explanation that, under Illinois law, an insurer's duty of good faith includes a duty to notify an insured of a potential conflict of interest, and to reimburse the reasonable expenses of a new attorney hired by the insured following such notification. See §2.9.

—The Rhode Island Supreme Court's clarification of an insurer's settlement duties in third-party cases, and, as a matter of first impression, its explanation of how that standard applies in a situation involving multiple claimants with claims exceeding policy limits. See §2.50.

—The Colorado Supreme Court's *en banc* holding that an insured driver suffered actual damages when he entered into a stipulated judgment in excess of policy limits, as required in order for a passenger, as the insured's assignee, to pursue a claim against the insurer for bad faith refusal to settle. See §2.60.

—The Florida Supreme Court's holding, in answering a certified question, that attorney-client privileged communications are not discoverable in an action for first-party bad faith. See §3.70.

—The Wisconsin Supreme Court's holding that the evidence supported a jury's finding that the insurer had acted in bad faith in agreeing to a settlement that, although within policy limits, had unnecessarily cost the insured all of its $500,000 deductible. See §2.2.

—A holding by the Washington Supreme Court that the insurer acted in bad faith as a matter of law by refusing to defend its insured based on a questionable interpretation of law, and by failing to avail itself of options such as proceeding under a reservation of rights or seeking declaratory relief. See §2.38.

—The California Supreme Court's clarification that the "genuine dispute" rule does not relieve an insurer of the obligation to thoroughly and fairly investigate a claim. See §1.10.

—The conclusion by a federal district court in South Dakota that the evidence had been sufficient to support a finding that the insurer's delay in paying a disability claim had been in bad faith, though an award of $6 million in punitive damages was excessive and would be reduced to $1.6 million. See §§1.11 and 1.66.

—A California Court of Appeal decision addressing a number of attorneys' fees issues, as well as holding that a liability insurer breached its duty to settle although there had never been a demand within policy limits, where a demand of $1.85 million had been well within the limits of the multiple insurers on the risk. An insured may recover despite the absence of an excess judgment, the court explained, if the insurer's misconduct went beyond a simple failure to settle, or if the insured suffered consequential damages apart from an excess judgment. See §§2.47, 2.52, and 2.70.

—A Pennsylvania court's acknowledgment of the potential applicability to first-party insurance cases of RESTATEMENT (SECOND) OF CONTRACTS, §367, according to which damages for emotional distress may be recovered for breach of contract where the breach was of a kind that serious emotional distress was a particularly likely result.

—The discussion by a U.S. District Court of the nature of the evidence required under California law to establish a cognizable claim of collusion in a settlement agreement between an insured and an injured third party. See §2.45.

—Relative to the *In re September 11 Litigation*, 723
F. Supp. 2d 534 (S.D.N.Y. 2010), a federal district court's
holding that, under New York law, an insurer has discretion
to settle, in good faith, one or more claims against it even if
doing so may jeopardize the ability of later recovering or
settling plaintiffs to collect on their claims: an insurer has
no duty to pay out claims ratably or to consolidate them.
See §2.50.

—Discussions by federal district courts in California of
the types of evidence a jury may consider in evaluating alleged bias in an insurer's investigation, including the "dishonest" selection of experts, and the unreasonableness of
the experts' conclusions. See §1.10.

—The Idaho Supreme Court's affirmance of an award of
punitive damages as remitted by the trial court to $1,890,000,
after the jury had awarded $6 million. The case involved
the insurer's delay in paying uninsured motorist benefits,
and successful claims for bad faith breach of contract and
the intentional infliction of emotional distress. See §1.66.

—The Washington Supreme Court's holding that a third
party may assert a cause of action for bad faith claims handling that is not dependent on the duty to indemnify, settle,
or defend. See §2.26.

—Decisions by two California Courts of Appeal and by a
federal district court in Pennsylvania concerning the effect
on summary judgment practice of evidence that an insurer
hired biased or "unreasonable" experts to evaluate claims.
See §§1.10 and 1.13.

—Clarification by the Eighth Circuit that under Iowa law
bad faith claims may be asserted only in connection with
denials of benefits or failures to settle, and that no claim
could therefore be asserted in connection with a health insurer's deceptive premium pricing policies and rate hikes.
See §1.19A.

—Decisions clarifying that District of Columbia law, previously conflicted, does not currently recognize a tort cause
of action for first-party bad faith. See §1.34.

—Florida decisions concerning the circumstances under which an insurer is bound by a negotiated final consent judgment entered against an insured who was not defended by the insurer. See §2.9.

—The Georgia Supreme Court's holding, in answer to a question certified by a federal district court, that an insurer may not be liable for bad faith failure to settle a third-party claim in the absence of a judgment against the insured in excess of policy limits. See §2.7.

—A holding by the Georgia Supreme Court that an automobile insurer that conditioned its acceptance of an assignee's offer to settle on the signing of a full release of the insured and the dismissal of the claim against the insured with prejudice, was not entitled to a safe harbor from bad faith liability. See §2.43.

—The Tenth Circuit's clarification of Kansas law as not requiring a judgment creditor to obtain an assignment of rights from the judgment debtor in order to bring a claim against the debtor's insurer for a negligent or bad faith failure to settle. See §2.54.

—The Ohio Supreme Court's holding that an insurer's alleged bad faith in denying a claim is not fraud, an illegal act, or a similarly unlawful act, as required to satisfy the second prong of the test for piercing the corporate veil and imposing liability on the insurer's parent corporation. See §3.30.

—A California Court of Appeal decision recognizing that bad faith liability, as well as liability for the intentional infliction of emotional distress, may be imposed on a health insurer who engages in "post-claims underwriting." See §§1.13 and 1.48.

—A $48.5 million dollar jury award against an insurance adviser who negligently bought an "off-the-shelf" insurance plan that failed to cover the insured's investment losses resulting from a change in a foreign government's economic policies. See §1.18.

—The Ninth Circuit's explanation and application of Arizona law concerning the showing of fraud in an insurance application that is necessary to entitle an insurer to deny coverage. See §§1.24 and 2.39.

—Discussions by California courts of the nature of a "genuine dispute" that entitles an insurer to summary judgment on a bad faith claim. See §1.33.

—The state of Washington's enactment of the Insurance Fair Conduct Act permitting the recovery of treble damages for an "unreasonable" denial of coverage or benefits. See §1.37.

—A decision by the Michigan Supreme Court accepting the argument that, by alleging that an insurer fraudulently induced the insured to accept an unreasonably low compensation rate for her in-home attendant care services, the insured asserted a common-law fraud claim that was distinct from a no-fault claim for benefits. See §1.55.

—Texas decisions upholding mental anguish awards in cases involving the bad faith handling of workers' compensation and homeowner's insurance claims. See §1.58.

—Decisions by the Idaho and Oregon Supreme Courts invoking due process concerns in radically reducing punitive damages awards in bad faith cases. See §§1.66 and 2.71.

—The clarification by a Minnesota Court of Appeals of the circumstances under which a fiduciary duty arises between insurer and insured, and the relation between a claim for breach of that duty and a claim for breach of the implied covenant of good faith and fair dealing. See §2.20.

—A further clarification by the Texas Supreme Court of the circumstances that trigger a liability insurer's "Stowers duty" to accept a reasonable settlement offer within policy limits. See §2.26.

—An *en banc* decision by the Colorado Supreme Court addressing the independence of a bad faith tort action against a workers' compensation insurer from remedies available under the workers' compensation statute. See §§1.25 and 1.28.

—A decision by the Connecticut Supreme Court holding that a judgment in favor of the insureds on a contract claim barred subsequent statutory and bad faith claims by operation of the doctrine of res judicata. See §§1.33 and 3.42.

—An opinion by the Pennsylvania Supreme Court addressing several issues concerning the relation of statutory and common-law bad faith claims. See §1.33.

—New York cases representing that jurisdiction's continued non-recognition of a first-party bad faith cause of action, but nonetheless holding that foreseeable damages may be recovered, beyond policy limits. See §1.34.

—The Florida Supreme Court's recognition that the obligee of a surety contract qualifies as "an insured" and is therefore entitled to sue a surety for bad faith refusal to settle claims. See §1.38.

—The affirmance of a number of large punitive damages awards in the first- and third-party contexts. See §§1.62 and 2.74.

—The Washington Supreme Court's clarification of a number of issues concerning an insurer's heightened obligation of fairness when it undertakes the defense of an insured under a reservation of rights. See §§2.10, 2.20, and 3.42.

—A decision by the Idaho Supreme Court clarifying and enumerating the factors to be considered in determining whether an insurer acted in bad faith in failing to settle a claim against its insured. See §2.29.

—The Washington Supreme Court's clarifying discussion of the evidentiary burdens relative to proof of a settlement's alleged collusiveness. See §2.45.

—The Kansas Supreme Court's elucidation of the requirements of a good faith investigation in the first-party context. See §1.10.

—Clarification by the Nebraska Supreme Court that unreasonable delay in paying a first-party claim may violate the implied covenant, even where the claim is ultimately paid. See §§1.11 and 1.33.

—A California Court of Appeal's holding that an insurer may be subject to vicarious liability for an agent's actionable negligence in failing to deliver agreed-upon coverage. See §1.18.

—The Vermont Supreme Court's clarification of that state's law concerning first-party bad faith, the availability of punitive damages, and the possibility of bad faith liability even in the absence of a breach of contract. See §1.33.

—The Tennessee Supreme Court's detailed explication of the elements of an insurer's duty of good faith in settling third-party claims. See §§2.4, 2.7, and 2.31.

—A decision by a California Court of Appeal rejecting the argument that a factual dispute regarding the existence of a duty to defend justifies an insurer's refusal to do so, and the court's affirmance of an award of punitive damages. See §§2.9, 2.38, and 2.74.

—Cases from Connecticut, Florida, and Illinois limiting in a number of ways the protections of the attorney-client privilege in connection with plaintiffs' discovery requests, and a case from Pennsylvania authorizing extremely broad discovery concerning an insurer's business practices as relevant to allegations of a "pattern and practice"of bad faith conduct. See §§3.69–3.70.

—The Tenth Circuit's holding under Colorado law that a jury had been entitled to assess $425,000 in damages in connection with its finding that the insurer acted in bad faith in conducting covert video surveillance without informing the insured that his disability insurance claim was under investigation. See §1.19A.

—Continuing major litigation and regulatory action against UnumProvident, described as an "outlaw company" by California's Insurance Commissioner. See §1.66.

—Publication by San Francisco plaintiff's attorney Ray Bourhis of an important muckraking book on bad faith in the insurance industry, including a call for legislation amending ERISA to permit bad faith claims. See §1.29.

—The Arizona Supreme Court's restrictive interpretation of the circumstances under which a *"Damron/Morris"* agreement may be held to constitute an improper attempt to "manufacture" a bad faith claim, and its dismissal of a liability insurer's claim for intentional interference with contractual relations against a plaintiff's attorney. See §2.45.

—Emphasis by a Pennsylvania Superior Court that Pennsylvania's bad faith statute permits an award of punitive damages upon a finding of bad faith alone without any other evidentiary prerequisite. See §§1.10, 1.33.

—A prediction by a federal district court that Hawaii law would permit the enforcement of stipulated judgments and the assignment of rights by insureds to third-party claimants where the insurer has failed to settle in good faith, even where the insurer has not refused to defend. See §2.63.

—A decision by the Supreme Court of Colorado rejecting the necessity of expert testimony to establish an insurer's standard of care where a statute provides evidence of that standard. See §4.16.

—The Ninth Circuit's conclusion, in affirming awards totaling $7.67 million, that because substantial evidence supported a jury's finding that the insurer had conducted a biased investigation, the insurer had been precluded from asserting a "genuine dispute" defense to bad faith liability. See §1.10.

—The Utah Supreme Court's holding that an accident victim had standing to assert a direct action against a liability insurer based on the victim's own contractual relationship with the insurer and the insurer's breach of settlement duties. See §1.10.

—A California court's holding that an insurer has a good faith duty to disclose to purchasers any planned and impending changes in premiums and benefits. See §1.14.

—The holding of a federal district court that under the Supreme Court's "dramatically changed analysis" of ERISA principles, a private cause of action under the Pennsylvania Unfair Practices Statute was saved from preemption. See §1.29.

—A California court's holding that an independent company hired to administer an insurer's polices was a "managing agent" whose tortious conduct could be imputed to the insurer for purposes of imposing punitive damages liability. See §1.19.

—The Colorado Supreme Court's holding that emotional distress is a foreseeable result of an insurer's bad faith delay in paying a claim, overruling prior authority for the proposition that emotional distress damages are recoverable only where the insured has suffered substantial property or economic loss. See §1.58.

—A Michigan court's holding that a bad faith failure-to-settle claim was not precluded by the fact that the insured and the claimant had agreed that the insured would be released from the excess judgment in the underlying action. See §2.43.

—Decisions from Arizona and New Jersey addressing the standards for evaluating the collusiveness and unenforceability against insurers of settlements reached between insureds and claimants. See §2.45.

—The South Dakota Supreme Court's reversal of summary judgment on a claim by an accident victim who had alleged that the defendant liability insurer had misrepresented the insured's policy limits during settlement negotiations. See §3.52.

Other important developments since 1990 covered in this cumulative supplement include:

—A number of decisions discussing the circumstances under which an agent, by virtue of a "special relationship" or otherwise, may be under a duty of good faith or due care with respect to advising an insured or conveying information. See §§1.14, 1.18.

—The Wisconsin Supreme Court's affirmance of $3.5 million in punitive damages against an insurer who had refused to reform a policy to correct a mutual mistake in the coverage applied for. See §1.19A.

—A number of developments concerning the scope of ERISA preemption, including the Supreme Court's grant of certiorari to resolve questions relating to ERISA preemption of claims relating to mixed eligibility and treatment decisions. See §§1.29-1.32.

—The Supreme Court's holding in a third-party bad faith case that due process is normally violated by an award of punitive damages in excess of a single-digit ratio to compensatory damages. See §§1.62, 2.71.

—A holding by the Ohio Supreme Court that the plaintiff in a bad faith action against a health insurer would be required to donate to charity two-thirds of a $30 million punitive damges award. See §1.66.

—The Pennsylvania Supreme Court's clarification that the cause of action created by the state's bad faith statute is not exclusive of a common law claim for bad faith breach of the duty to settle. See §2.24.

—A holding by the Illinois Supreme Court regarding the insurer's liability for the full amount of a settlement in excess of policy limits following the insurer's wrongful refusal to defend. See §2.63.

—A holding by the Idaho Supreme Court that an insured has the burden of proof on the "fairly debateable" issue, and that proof of coverage is an element of an insured's prima facie case. See §1.10.

—The rejection of the so-called directed verdict rule by the Rhode Island Supreme Court. See §1.10.

—The United States Supreme Court's reaffirmation of the broad principle of ERISA preemption represented by *Pilot Life Ins. Co. v. Dedeaux*. See §1.29.

—Clarifications by California and Massachusetts courts of the scope of an insurer's duty to provide an insured with independent counsel. See §2.9.

—The Alabama Supreme Court's rejection of all theories under which an excess insurer might sue a primary insurer for bad faith failure to settle. See §2.11.

—Clarification by the Texas Supreme Court of several aspects of the relation between an insurer's common law "Stowers" obligations and its duty to "attempt" settlement under Texas Insurance Code art. 21.21. See §2.24.

—A specification by the Illinois Supreme Court of the point at which an insurer's duty to settle arises. See §2.33.

—The resolution of a split of authority among the Illinois appellate courts concerning the validity of compelled assignments of bad faith failure-to-settle claims. See §2.60.

—An important decision by the California Supreme Court relating to assignments following stipulated judgments, holding that a defending insurer is not bound to a settlement that it did not participate in nor agree to. See §2.63.

—A number of large punitive damages verdicts in both first- and third-party bad faith cases. See §§1.66, 2.72.

—The Kentucky Supreme Court's holding that even if a claim is "fairly debatable," the insurer must still "debate fairly" by conducting an investigation that complies with the state's Unfair Claims Settlement Practices Act. See §1.10.

—The Alaska Supreme Court's elucidation of the circumstances that give rise to a "special relationship" and create a duty on the part of an insurance agent to advise an insured on the adequacy of coverage. See §1.14.

—Clarification by the California Supreme Court that the "genuine dispute doctrine" applies to factual as well as legal disputes. See §1.20.

—Two federal district court decisions holding that state law bad faith actions are "saved" from ERISA preemption. See §1.30.

—A federal district court decision discussing the circumstances under which Virginia law permits recovery of emotional distress damages for breach of an insurance contract. See §1.36.

—A California Supreme Court holding that the bad faith tort doctrine does not apply in the context of surety relationships. See §1.38.

—The Alabama Supreme Court's application of its "benchmark" for evaluating the possible excessiveness of punitive damages awards. See §1.62.

—The entry and affirmance around the country of a number of multi-million dollar punitive damages verdicts in first-party cases. See §1.66.

—Several cases addressing the issue of an insurer's right to reimbursement of defense costs following noncoverage determinations. See §2.9.

—The Ohio Supreme Court's abrogation of the attorney-client privilege in litigation alleging bad faith denials of coverage. See §3.70.

—The California Supreme Court's repudiation of the "comparative bad faith" defense in insurance litigation. See §1.24.

—The Arizona Supreme Court's holding that even when a claim is "fairly debatable," an insurer must still act reasonably in investigating, evaluating, and processing the claim. See §1.10.

—The Alabama Supreme Court's clarification that the "directed verdict rule" does not apply to cases involving an insurer's failure to investigate. See §1.20.

—Additional case law concerning the preemptive effect of the National Flood Insurance Act. See new §1.32A.

—The Missouri Supreme Court's recognition of an exception to the preemptive effect of the state's penalty statutes in a case allowing tort recovery on a defamation claim brought by an insured who had been compelled to "self-publish" defendant's arson accusation when applying for coverage with another insurer. See §1.27.

—Additional expressions of judicial dissatisfaction with the ERISA preemption doctrine as unfair to insureds. See §1.30.

—Clarification by the Texas Supreme Court that punitive damages are available for insurance bad faith only on a showing of malice, fraud, or grossly negligent conduct. See §1.66.

—The Alaska Supreme Court's holding that an insurer's salaried claims adjusters may be personally liable for failure to exercise reasonable care to avoid interfering with an insured's rights to defense and indemnity. See §3.30.

—The California Legislature's reinstatement of a private third-party right of action under the state's unfair claims settlement practices act. See §2.21.

—The Rhode Island Supreme Court's recognition of private claims under the state's unfair claims settlement practices act governed by what amounts to a strict liability standard. See §§2.19, 2.24.

—A holding by the Pennsylvania Supreme Court that an insurer's eventual payment of an excess verdict does not necessarily extinguish a bad faith claim, and that statutory damages are not exclusive in the third-party context. See §§2.7, 2.24.

—The Hawaii Supreme Court's rejection of the rule that an insurer has an obligation to pay for independent counsel for the insured if the insurer chooses to defend under a reservation of rights. See §2.9.

—The Maryland Supreme Court's holding that an insurer that refuses to perform its contractual duty to defend is subject to liability only for breach of contract, not for the tort of bad faith. See §2.9.

—The Hawaii courts' recognition that if an insurer assumes but mishandles the defense and through its mishandling causes actual harm to the insured, a bad faith claim is cognizable despite a later declaration that the insurer had no duty to defend in the first place. See §2.10.

—An anomalous decision by the Idaho Supreme Court declining to recognize any cause of action by an excess against a primary insurer for bad faith failure to settle. See §2.11.

—Additional authority for the proposition that the assignability of bad faith causes of action to judgment creditors includes claims for punitive damages. See §2.60.

—A holding by the Florida Supreme Court that emotional distress damages are recoverable under the state's bad faith statute for a health insurer's bad faith failure to pay a claim. See §1.58.

—The Washington Supreme Court's 1998 discussion of the remedy for an insurer's bad faith refusal to defend. See §2.9.

—The New York Court of Appeals' 1998 holding concerning the scope of an insurer's qualified duty to inform its insured of settlement offers. See §2.29.

—The 1998 holding by the Texas Supreme Court that insurance company employees are subject to individual liability under the state's unfair claims settlement practices statute. See §3.30.

—An important 1998 decision by a Georgia Court of Appeals concerning an insurer's problem in allocating insufficient policy limits to settle claims against multiple insureds. See §2.50.

—The Illinois Supreme Court's 1997 holding (resolving a long-standing split of authority) that Illinois law recognizes no common-law tort of first-party bad faith and that the statutory cause of action under §155 of the Illinois Insurance Code is exclusive. See §1.27.

—The Texas Supreme Court's 1997 modification of the standard for imposing liability for first-party bad faith. See §1.33.

—The Eighth Circuit's prediction that the Iowa Supreme Court would permit recovery of emotional distress damages for an insurer's failure to exercise good faith in representing an insured in a third-party action. See §2.69.

—The Massachusetts Supreme Judicial Court's replacement of the bad faith standard with a negligence standard in third-party cases. See §2.13.

—The Arizona Supreme Court's rejection of workers' compensation exclusivity with respect to common-law bad faith claims. See §1.28.

—The holding by the Mississippi Supreme Court that an inadequate investigation can be the basis for both first-party bad faith liability and punitive damages, despite the existence of an arguable basis for denial of the claim. See §1.10.

—First-time recognition of a bad faith cause of action in the first-party insurance context by the courts of Hawaii, Indiana, Kentucky, Nebraska, New Jersey, Puerto Rico, and Wyoming. See §1.33.

—The South Carolina Supreme Court's belated recognition, in 1996, of the tort of third-party bad faith. See §2.7.

—A 1996 holding by the Utah Supreme Court that a first-party bad faith cause of action sounds in contract, but that emotional distress damages are potentially available. See §1.34.

—The adoption by the West Virginia Supreme Court of what amounts to a standard of strict liability in third-party failure-to-settle cases. See §2.19.

—The Ohio Supreme Court's elimination of any intent element in Ohio's definition of first-party bad faith. See §1.9.

—The California Supreme Court's 1995 repudiation of the "stonewalling" tort it had first recognized in 1984. See §1.44.

—The Florida Supreme Court's recognition, in 1995, that third-party claimants have standing to sue under Florida's Unfair Claim Settlement Practices Statute and a similar 1996 holding by the Louisiana Supreme Court. See §2.24.

—The holding by the Arizona Supreme Court that an insurer can be liable in tort for a breach of the implied covenant of good faith and fair dealing even in the absence of proof that the insurer breached any express term of the insurance contract. See §1.33.

—Arizona's belated recognition of the doctrine of equitable subrogation affording an excess insurer a right of action against the primary insurer for bad faith failure to settle. (Arizona had been a minority holdout against the doctrine.) See §2.11.

—The holding by the Second Circuit that a private right of action may be pursued against insurers under New York's consumer protection statute (N.Y. Gen. Bus. Law §349). See §1.34.

—The appearance of the first decisions interpreting and applying new bad faith statutes in Louisiana and Pennsylvania. See §1.33.

—First-time recognition by the Delaware Supreme Court of the principle that every employment contract includes an implied covenant of good faith and fair dealing. See §1.42. And the Delaware Supreme Court's 1996 holdings that workers' compensation carriers owe a duty of good faith to claimants; that common-law bad faith actions by claimants are not barred by workers' compensation exclusivity; and that punitive damages may be available, though the bad faith cause of action sounds only in contract, if denial of coverage was willful or malicious. See §§1.28, 1.34.

—Montana's abandonment of its vanguard position with regard to application of the bad faith doctrine to commercial contracts. See §1.45.

—Important new law in some states on the authority of a soliciting agent to bind the insurer with respect to alleged misrepresentations by the insured in completing the application for coverage. See §1.18.

—Several cases holding that an insurer may not be entitled to resist payment of a claim on the basis of a novel or unresolved issue of law. See §§1.22, 1.66.

—Clarification and limitation by a California Court of Appeal of the principle that an insurer's litigation conduct can provide evidence of its breach of the duty of good faith. See §3.42.

—Recognition by a Florida appellate court that a primary insurer may be subject to bad faith liability to an excess insurer even in the absence of an underlying bad faith claim by the insured. See §2.11.

—Alabama, Arizona, California, and Wisconsin decisions recognizing that the third-party bad faith doctrine extends to refusals to defend the insured, as well as to failures to accept reasonable settlement offers. See §2.9.

—New authority for the majority view that an insurer is not insulated from excess liability for failure to settle by the fact that its mistaken belief in noncoverage may have been reasonable. See §§2.7 and 2.37.

—A useful and extended discussion by the Washington Supreme Court of the elements of a cause of action for the bad faith handling of a claim where the insurer has assumed an "enhanced" obligation by opting to defend under a reservation of rights. *Safeco Ins. Co. of Am. v. Butler*, 823 P.2d 499 (Wash. 1992). See §2.10.

—A holding by the Iowa Supreme Court in 1996 that negligent investigation cannot give rise to liability for negligence or for bad faith. See §1.10.

—A holding by a California Court of Appeal in 1996 that where an insurer tortiously breaches its duty to defend and the insured suffers a default judgment, the insurer is liable for that judgment even if it is later determined that the underlying claim was not covered. See §2.9.

—The Texas Supreme Court's 1996 announcement of rules designed to discourage collusive prejudgment assignments of third-party bad faith claims. See §2.63.

—Affirmances of a remarkable number of large punitive damages awards: *e.g.*, $12 million in *West Am. Ins. Co. v. Freeman*, 42 Cal. App. 4th 320, 44 Cal. Rptr. 2d 555 (1995) (see §2.2); $5 million in *Powers v. United Servs. Auto. Ass'n*, 114 Nev. 79, 962 P.2d 596 (1998) (see §1.66); $5 million (reduced from §22.5 million) in *Republic Ins. Co. v. Hires*, 810 P.2d 790 (Nev. 1991) (see §1.66); $4 million in *Americana Sav. Bank v. Aetna Casualty & Sur. Co.* (Orange County, Cal., Super. Ct. No. 651102, June 15, 1993) (see §2.74); $3.75 million in *Albert H. Wohlers & Co. v. Bartgis*, 114 Nev. 1249, 969 P.2d 949 (1998), *cert. denied*,

527 U.S. 1038 (1999) (see §§1.14, 1.20, 1.66); $3.2 million in *Walston v. Monumental Life Ins. Co.*, 923 P.2d 456 (Idaho 1996) (see §1.62); $2 million in *Farmland Mut. Ins. Co. v. Johnson*, 36 S.W.3d 368 (Ky. 2000) (see §1.66); $2 million in *State Farm Fire & Casualty Co. v. Simmons*, 857 S.W.2d 126 (Tex. Ct. App. 1993) (see §1.16); $2 million in *Commonwealth Lloyd's Ins. Co. v. Thomas*, 825 S.W.2d 135 (Tex. Ct. App. 1992) (see §1.16); $1.6 million in *Orangeburg Sausage Co. v. Cincinnati Ins. Co.*, 450 S.E.2d 66 (S.C. Ct. App. 1994) (see §1.66); $1.5 million in *Walker v. Farmers Ins. Exchange*, 153 Cal. App. 4th 965, 63 Cal. Rptr. 3d 507 (2007) (see §2.74); $1.5 million in *Texas Employers Ins. Ass'n v. Puckett*, 822 S.W.2d 133 (Tex. Ct. App. 1991) (see §1.66); $1.24 million in *State Farm Mut. Auto. Ins. Co. v. Grimes*, 722 So. 2d 637 (Miss. 1998) (see §§1.20, 1.66); $1 million in *Michigan Mut. Ins. Co. v. Sports, Inc.*, 698 N.E.2d 834 (Ind. Ct. App. 1998) (see §1.66); $1 million in *James v. Horace Mann Ins. Co.*, 371 S.C. 187, 638 S.E.2d 667 (2006) (see §1.62); $900,000 in *United Am. Ins. Co. v. Merrill*, 978 So. 2d 613 (Miss. 2007) (see §1.62).

—Jury verdicts involving some enormous punitive damages awards: *e.g.*, $120.5 million by a California jury in a non-ERISA action against an HMO that refused to authorize a cancer treatment recommended by its own doctors (see §1.32); $386 million by a Los Angeles jury in an action by Amoco Corporation against Lloyds (see §1.16); $145 million by a Utah jury in a third-party action, despite the fact that the insurer had ultimately paid the excess judgment (see §2.72); $86.7 million by a Los Angeles jury in an action brought by the government of American Samoa against its hurricane damage insurer (see §1.66); $77 million by a jury in Riverside County, California, in *Fox v. Health Net* (see §1.66); $57 million by an Orange County jury in *Surgin Surgical Instrumentation v. Farmers Group, Inc.* (see §2.74); $28 million by a Los Angeles jury in *Cates Constr., Inc. v. Talbot Partners* (see §1.38); $9 million by a Los Angeles jury in *Turner v. Equitable Life Assurance Soc'y* (see

§1.12); $6.5 million by a Los Angeles jury in *D.W. Stephan Enters., Inc. v. Gold Cities Ins. Agency* (see §1.12).

—The United States Supreme Court's ongoing examination of due process limitations on the size of punitive damages awards. See §1.62.

About the Supplement Editors

Sharon C. Rutberg is a legal writer, editor, and practicing attorney living in Seattle, Washington. She worked for the firm of Wilmer, Cutler & Pickering (now WilmerHale) in Washington, D.C., the Office of the White House Counsel, and the U.S. Department of State before moving to Seattle and starting her own law practice. Sharon holds a B.A. with honors from Swarthmore College; a J.D. *cum laude* from the Northwestern University Pritzker School of Law, where she served on the *Law Review;* and an LL.M. from the Seattle University School of Law.

Wendy Janis Malkin is a legal writer, editor, and practicing attorney and a member of the Washington State Bar Association. She received a B.A. from Sarah Lawrence College and a J.D. *magna cum laude* from Seattle University, where she was an associate editor of the *Law Review.* While in law school, Wendy served as a judicial extern in the U.S. District Court for the Western District of Washington. Before starting her own law practice, Wendy worked as nonpartisan counsel in the Washington state legislature.

Note: For the reader's convenience, the outline of each supplemented chapter has been reprinted, with each supplemented section indicated by an asterisk.

1

Direct Coverage Actions

I. CONTRACT LIABILITY

A. Availability of Extracontractual Remedies §1.1
B. Relationship Between Insurer and Insured §1.2*
C. Rule of Foreseeability: *Hadley v. Baxendale* §1.3
   1. Foreseeability in Insurance Cases §1.4
   2. Foreseeability of Mental Distress §1.5

II. TORT LIABILITY

A. Introduction §1.6*
B. Bad Faith
   1. Implied Covenant of Good Faith and Fair Dealing §1.7
   2. Development of the First-Party Bad Faith Doctrine—Landmark Cases §1.8
   3. Meaning of Term "Bad Faith" §1.9*
   4. Types of Bad Faith Conduct
      a. Inadequate Investigation §1.10*
      b. Delay §1.11*
      c. Deception §1.12*
      d. Wrongful Cancellation §1.13*
      e. Nondisclosure of Information §1.14*
      f. Interference With Recovery of Uninsured Losses §1.15*
      g. Conduct Specific to Fire Insurance Policies §1.16*
      h. Liability of Insurer for Conduct of Agents and Employees §1.17*

1

I. CONTRACT LIABILITY

§1.2   B. Relationship Between Insurer and Insured

Courts universally recognize certain "special" characteristics of the relationship between insurer and insured, and
impose upon insurers certain corresponding duties of care.
Recently, however, courts have tended to back off from
characterizing the relationship as truly "fiduciary" in nature. That tendency is particularly clear in California,
where the supreme court, having itself previously hinted at
an endorsement of the "fiduciary" label, decertified two intermediate appellate court opinions that had taken that
view: *Security Pac. Nat'l Bank v. Williams*, 213 Cal. App.
3d 927 (1989), and *Paul v. State Farm Fire & Casualty
Co.*, 193 Cal. App. 3d 223 (1987). At the same time, a number of decisions have expressly rejected the fiduciary characterization: *Vu v. Prudential Prop. & Casualty Ins. Co.*,
26 Cal. 4th 1142, 113 Cal. Rptr. 2d 70 (2001); *Progressive
West Ins. Co. v. Yolo County Superior Court*, 135 Cal. App.
4th 263, 37 Cal. Rptr. 3d 434 (2005); *Tran v. Farmers
Group, Inc.*, 104 Cal. App. 4th 1202, 128 Cal. Rptr. 2d 728

(2002); *Love v. Fire Ins. Exch.*, 221 Cal. App. 3d 1136, 271 Cal. Rptr. 246 (1990); *Henry v. Associated Indem. Co.*, 217 Cal. App. 3d 1405, 266 Cal. Rptr. 578 (1990); *Casey v. Metropolitan Life Ins. Co.*, 688 F. Supp. 2d 1086 (E.D. Cal. 2010) (California law); *Almon v. State Farm Fire & Casualty Co.*, 724 F. Supp. 765 (S.D. Cal. 1989); *Hassard, Bonnington, Roger & Huber v. Home Ins. Co.*, 740 F. Supp. 789 (S.D. Cal. 1990). Accord *Brodeur v. American Home Assurance Co.*, 169 P.3d 139 (Colo. banc 2007); *Bailey v. Allstate Ins. Co.*, 844 P.2d 1336 (Colo. Ct. App. 1992); *Corrado Bros. v. Twin City Fire Ins. Co.*, 562 A.2d 1188 (Del. 1989); *Hogan v. Provident Life & Accident Ins. Co.*, 665 F. Supp. 2d 1273 (M.D. Fla. 2009) (Florida law); *St. Paul Fire & Marine Ins. Co. v. A.P.I., Inc.*, 738 N.W.2d 401 (Minn. Ct. App. 2007); *Frye v. Southern Farm Bureau Casualty Ins. Co.*, 915 So. 2d 486 (Miss. Ct. App. 2005); *Martin v. State Farm Mut. Auto. Ins. Co.*, 960 F. Supp. 233 (D. Nev. 1997) (Nevada law); *Mirville v. Allstate Indem. Co.*, 71 F. Supp. 2d 1103 (D. Kan. 1999) (New York law); *Zochert v. Protective Life Ins. Co.*, 921 N.W.2d 479 (S.D. 2018); *Crim Truck & Tractor Co. v. Navistar Int'l Transp. Corp.*, 823 S.W.2d 591 (Tex. 1992); *Tectonic Realty Inv. Co. v. CNA Lloyd's Ins. Co.*, 812 S.W.2d 647 (Tex. Ct. App. 1991); *Van Noy v. State Farm Mut. Auto. Ins. Co.*, 16 P.3d 574 (Wash. 2001). See generally Douglas R. Richmond, "Trust Me: Insurers Are Not Fiduciaries to Their Insureds," 88 Ky. L.J. 1 (1999).

The remaining availability, in some jurisdictions, of a cause of action for an insurer's breach of fiduciary duty, is discussed in §§2.20, 3.49.

—For detailed discussions of the standards of good faith with respect to the "hybrid" relationship created by uninsured motorist coverage, see *LeFevre v. Westberry*, 590 So. 2d 154 (Ala. 1991); *Wineinger v. Ellis*, 855 N.E.2d 614 (Ind. Ct. App. 2006); *Fetch v. Quam*, 623 N.W.2d 357 (N.D. 2001); *Zappile v. Amex Assurance Co.*, 928 A.2d 251 (Pa. Super. Ct. 2007); *Ellwein v. Hartford Accident & Indem. Co.*, 142 Wash. 2d 766, 15 P.3d 640 (2001), *overruled on other grounds, Smith v. Safeco Ins. Co.*, 78 P.3d 1274 (Wash. 2003). But for a Nevada case holding that the duty of good faith is fully present in the context of uninsured motorist coverage, see *Pemberton v. Farmers Ins. Exch.*, 858 P.2d 380 (Nev. 1993). Accord *Voland v. Farmers Ins. Co.*, 189 Ariz. 448, 943 P.2d 808 (Ct. App. 1997); *Sullivan v. Allstate Ins. Co.*, 111 Idaho 304, 723 P.2d 848 (1986); *Brown v. Allstate Prop. & Casualty Ins Co.*, 184 F. Supp. 3d 1326 (M.D. Ala. 2016) (South Carolina law); *Leahy v. State Farm Mut. Auto. Ins. Co.*, 3 Wash. App. 2d 613, 418 P.3d 175 (2018); *Danner v. Auto-Owners Ins.*, 629 N.W.2d 159 (Wis. 2001); *State Farm Mut. Auto. Ins. Co. v. Shrader*, 882 P.2d 813 (Wyo. 1994). For a discussion of Virginia law concerning bad faith in an uninsured motorist case, see *Manu v. GEICO Casualty Co.*, 798 S.E.2d 598 (Va. 2017).

—In *Williams v. State Farm Mut. Auto. Ins. Co.*, 886 So. 2d 72 (Ala. 2003), the court granted summary judgment on an accident victim's action for bad faith failure to pay. The court cited *Howton v. State Farm Mut. Auto. Ins. Co.*, 507 So. 2d 448 (Ala. 1987), where it was held that a third-party accident victim may sue a tort-feasor's liability insurer directly only where "the insurer undertakes a new and independent obligation directly with a nonparty to the insurance contract in its efforts to negotiate a settlement of the third party's claim." 507 So. 2d at 450.

—In *Leal v. Allstate Ins. Co.*, 199 Ariz. 250, 17 P.3d 95 (Ct. App. 2000), the court refused to recognize a cause of action on behalf of a third party, who had been injured in an accident with defendant's insured, for breach of either an implied or an assumed duty of good faith. Plaintiff unsuccessfully argued that a duty of good faith existed by virtue of the insurer's letter stating that it considered anyone who had been in an accident with one of its policyholders a "customer" entitled to "quality customer service." The court reasoned that Allstate's "customer service pledge" did not amount to a promise to treat plaintiff as an insured. For similar facts and holding under Connecticut law, see *Hipsky v. Allstate Ins. Co.*, 304 F. Supp. 2d 284 (D. Conn. 2004).

—Because the implied covenant of good faith and fair dealing runs only between insurer and insured, the court in *Alex Robertson Co. v. Imperial Casualty & Indem. Co.*, 8 Cal. App. 4th 338, 10 Cal. Rptr. 2d 165 (1992), affirming summary judgment, held that standing to sue for a bad faith breach of the duty to defend did not extend to the other party to a contract that was referred to in an endorsement to the insured's liability policy. See also *Eastham v. Nationwide Mut. Ins. Co.*, 66 Ohio App. 3d 843, 586 N.E.2d 1131 (1990) (insured's mother lacked standing to sue for auto insurer's bad faith delay in paying her son's medical bills); *William Powell Co. v. Nat'l Indem. Co.*, 141 F. Supp. 3d 773 (S.D. Ohio. 2015) (Ohio law; dismissing insured's bad faith claim against 2 third-party claims administrators because insured lacked privity with defendants; noting Ohio does not provide bad faith claims where parties are not in privity with each other and declining to extend duty of good faith to third-party claims administrators). Compare *Diamond Woodworks, Inc. v. Argonaut Ins. Co.*, 109 Cal. App. 4th 1020, 135 Cal. Rptr. 2d 736 (2003) (client of employee leasing company had standing as third-party beneficiary to sue leasing company's workers' compensation insurer for bad faith). Concerning whether and under what circumstances the spouse of an insured may have standing to sue an insurer for bad faith, see §3.25.

—In *Rancosky v. Wash. Nat'l Ins. Co.*, 130 A.3d 79 (Pa. Super. 2015), *aff'd*, 170 A.3d 364 (Pa. 2017), the Pennsylvania Superior Court heard an appeal following a bench trial on an insured's bad faith claim. The insured, a deceased cancer patient, had sued the insurer for bad faith handling of her claims under a "cancer policy." The court noted that the insurer bore "a heightened duty of good faith . . . because of the special relationship between the insurer and its insured . . . ." *Id.* at 93.

II. TORT LIABILITY

§1.6   A. Introduction

For decisions declining to recognize a cause of action for negligent claims handling (as distinct from claims for breach of contract or breach of the implied covenant of good faith and fair dealing), see *Pate v. Rollison Logging Equipment, Inc.*, 628 So. 2d 337 (Ala. 1993); *French v. State Farm Ins. Co.*, 156 F.R.D. 159 (S.D. Tex. 1994) (Texas law). See also *Adelman v. Associated Int'l Ins. Co.*, 90 Cal. App. 4th 352, 108 Cal. Rptr. 2d 788 (2001) (declining to recognize claim by third parties foreseeably injured by insurer's negligent claims handling). Compare *Reynolds v. American Hardware Mut. Ins. Co.*, 115 Idaho 362, 766 P.2d 1243 (1988), and *Inland Group of Cos. v. Providence Washington Ins. Co.*, 985 P.2d 674 (Idaho 1999) (although a finding of bad faith may not be based on merely negligent conduct, Idaho law also recognizes negligence cause of action for unreasonable denial or delay in paying claim); *Essinger v. Liberty Mut. Fire Ins. Co.*, 534 F.3d 450 (5th Cir. 2008) (Mississippi law; lesser level of damages, including attorney's fees, may be appropriate where insurer lacked arguable basis for denying claim but conduct was not sufficiently egregious to justify punitive damages).

B. Bad Faith

§1.9   3. Meaning of Term "Bad Faith"

Cases representing the view that "bad faith" in the first-party insurance context means nothing more than unreasonableness have included *Thompson v. State Farm Mut. Auto. Ins. Co.*, 457 F. Supp. 3d 998 (D. Colo. 2020) (Colorado law; under Colo. Rev. Stat. §10–3-1115, only unreasonableness is required); *Adams v. Hawaii Med. Serv. Ass'n*, 145 Haw. 250, 450 P.3d 780 (2019) (bad faith claim can be grounded in alleged unreasonable handling of claim by insurer); *Wittig v. Allianz, A.G.*, 145 P.3d 738 (Haw. Ct. App. 2006); *Zoppo v. Homestead Ins. Co.*, 71 Ohio St. 3d 552, 644 N.E.2d 397 (1994) (eliminating intent element and overruling inconsistent Ohio authority); *Fifth Third Mortgage Co. v. Chicago Title Ins. Co.*, 692 F.3d 507, *reh'g & reh'g en banc denied* (6th Cir. 2012) (Ohio law); *Berkshire Life Ins. Co. of Am. v. Dorsky*, 178 F. Supp. 3d 625 (N.D. Ohio 2016) (Ohio law); *Bell v. Zurich Am. Ins. Co.*, 156 F. Supp. 3d 884 (N.D. Ohio 2015), *appeal dismissed* (6th Cir. 2016) (Ohio law); *Roach v. Atlas Life Ins. Co.*, 769 P.2d 158 (Okla. 1989); *Vickers v. Progressive N. Ins. Co.*, 353 F. Supp. 3d 1153 (N.D. Okla. 2018); *Weiser-Brown Operating Co. v. St. Paul Surplus Lines Ins. Co.*, 801 F.3d 512 (5th Cir. 2015) (Texas law); *Industrial Indem. Co. of the Northwest v. Kallevig*, 114 Wash. 2d 907, 792 P.2d 520 (1990); *Liberty Mut. Ins. Co. v. Tripp*, 95 Wash. App. 245, 974 P.2d 899 (1999), *review granted*, 139 Wash. 2d 1014 (2000); *Schreib v. American Family Mut. Ins. Co.*, 129 F. Supp. 3d 1129 (W.D. Wash. 2015).

The California standard is discussed at some length in *Twaite v. Allstate Ins. Co.*, 216 Cal. App. 3d 239, 264 Cal. Rptr. 598 (1989), where the court concludes that a "bad faith" refusal to pay benefits is simply a refusal "without proper cause." Compare *Aceves v. Allstate Ins. Co.*, 68 F.3d 1160 (9th Cir. 1995), insisting that under California law mere negligence is not the equivalent of bad faith. Accord, *Notrica v. State Compensation Ins. Fund*, 70 Cal. App. 4th 911, 83 Cal. Rptr. 2d 89 (1999). See also *Wilson v. 21st Century Ins. Co.*, 42 Cal. 4th 713, 68 Cal. Rptr. 3d 746, 171 P.3d 1082 (2007) (to fulfill obligation of good faith, insurer must give at least as much consideration to interests of insured as it gives to its own interests); *Ghazarian v. Magellan Health Inc.*, 53 Cal. App. 5th 171, 266 Cal. Rptr. 3d 841 (2020) (court must look past arguably reasonable denial to determine whether insurer fairly evaluated claim); *Mosley v. Pacific Specialty Ins. Co.*, 49 Cal. App. 5th 417, 436, 263

Cal. Rptr. 3d 28 (2020) (insured must show insurer acted unreasonably or without proper cause; affirming summary judgment for insurer where there was no clear controlling state law on coverage issue in question; noting insured must show insurer's denial of coverage was "prompted not by an honest mistake, bad judgment, or negligence, but rather by a conscious and deliberate act" (internal quotation marks omitted)); *Case v. State Farm Mut. Auto. Ins. Co.*, 30 Cal. App. 5th 397, 241 Cal. Rptr. 3d 458 (2018) (bad faith arises when insurer's denial of or delay in paying claim was unreasonable); *Carson v. Mercury Ins. Co.*, 210 Cal. App. 4th 409, 148 Cal. Rptr. 3d 518 (2012) (clarifying that breach of implied covenant of good faith and fair dealing is itself breach of contract, and it is not necessary to allege that any *specific provision* of contract was breached); *Major v. Western Home Ins. Co.*, 169 Cal. App. 4th 1197, 87 Cal. Rptr. 3d 556 (2009) (term "bad faith" does not connote positive misconduct of malicious or immoral nature; it simply means that insurer acted deliberately); *Bosetti v. The United States Life Ins. Co.*, 175 Cal. App. 4th 1208, 96 Cal. Rptr. 3d 744 (2009) (covenant of good faith can be breached by objectively unreasonable conduct, regardless of insurer's motives); *Gutowitz v. Transamerica Life Ins. Co.*, 126 F. Supp. 3d 1128 (C.D. Cal. 2015) (California law; test for bad faith in California turns on whether insurer's refusal or delay in paying benefits was unreasonable).

In the following cases, on the other hand, courts have taken the view that the term "bad faith" connotes some measure of deliberate malfeasance or subjective blameworthiness on an insurer's part: *Singleton v. State Farm Fire & Casualty Co.*, 928 So. 2d 280 (Ala. 2005); *Watson v. Life Ins. Co. of Ala.*, 74 So. 3d 470 (Ala. Civ. App. 2011); *Columbia Nat'l Ins. Co. v. Freeman*, 347 Ark. 423, 64 S.W.3d 720 (2002); *American Health Care Providers, Inc. v. O'Brien*, 318 Ark. 438, 886 S.W.2d 588 (1994); *First Marine Ins. Co. v. Booth*, 317 Ark. 91, 876 S.W.2d 255

(1994); *Reynolds v. Shelter Mut. Ins. Co.*, 313 Ark. 145, 852 S.W.2d 799 (1993); *Richison v. Boatmen's Ark., Inc.*, 64 Ark. App. 271, 981 S.W.2d 112 (1998); *Sims v. State Farm Mut. Auto. Ins. Co*, 894 F.3d 941 (8th Cir. 2018), reh'g & reh'g en banc denied (8th Cir. 2018), *reh'g & reh'g en banc denied* (8th Cir. 2018) (Arkansas law); *Metropolitan Prop. & Casualty Ins. Co. v. Calvin*, 802 F.3d 933, 940 (8th Cir. 2015) (Arkansas law; insurer misconduct must be "dishonest, malicious, or oppressive" (quoting *Aetna Cas. & Sur. Co. v. Broadway Arms Corp.*, 281 Ark. 128, 664 S.W.2d 463, 465 (1984) (cited in the main volume))); *Jackson v. Allstate Ins. Co.*, 785 F.3d 1193 (8th Cir. 2015) (same); *Allison v. Security Benefit Life Ins. Co.*, 980 F.2d 1213 (8th Cir. 1992) (Arkansas law); *Sullivan v. Allstate Ins. Co.*, 2006 WL 1000236 (Conn. Super. Ct. 2006); *Belz v. Peerless Ins. Co.*, 204 F. Supp. 3d 457 (D. Conn. 2016) (Connecticut law); *Hartford Roman Catholic Diocesan Corp. v. Interstate Fire & Casualty Co.*, 199 F. Supp. 3d 559, *aff'd*, 905 F.3d 84 (2d Cir. 2018) (Connecticut law); *Belz v. Peerless Ins. Co.*, 46 F. Supp. 3d 157 (D. Conn. 2014) (Connecticut law); *Exantus v. Metropolitan Prop. & Cas. Ins. Co.*, 582 F. Supp. 2d 239 (D. Conn. 2008) (Connecticut law); *Chester v. State Farm Ins. Co.*, 117 Idaho 538, 789 P.2d 534 (Ct. App. 1990); *Monroe Guar. Ins. v. Magwerks Corp.*, 829 N.E.2d 968 (Ind. 2005); *AG One Co-Op v. Scott*, 914 N.E.2d 860 (Ind. Ct. App. 2009); *Spencer v. Bridgewater*, 757 N.E.2d 208 (Ind. Ct. App. 2001); *Colley v. Indiana Farmers Mut. Ins. Group*, 691 N.E.2d 1259 (Ind. Ct. App. 1998); *Abstract & Title Guar. Co. v. Chicago Ins. Co.*, 489 F.3d 808 (7th Cir. 2007) (Indiana law); *Telamon Corp. v. Charter Oak Fire Ins. Co.*, 179 F. Supp. 3d 851(S.D. Ind. 2016), *appeal filed* (7th Cir. April 13, 2016) (Indiana law); *Jackson v. Allstate Ins. Co.*, 780 F. Supp. 2d 781 (S.D. Ind. 2011) (Indiana law); *Westfield v. Sheehan Ins. Co.*, 580 F. Supp. 2d 701 (S.D. Ind. 2008) (Indiana law); *Midamar v. National-Ben Franklin Ins. Co.*, 898 F.2d 1333 (8th Cir. 1990) (Iowa law); *Curry v. Fireman's Fund Ins. Co.*, 784 S.W.2d 176 (Ky. 1989); *Williams v. Ohio Nat'l Life Assurance Co.*, 364 F. Supp. 3d 605 (W.D.N.C. 2019) (North Carolina law); *Michael Borovsky Goldsmith LLC v. Jewelers Mut. Ins. Co.*, 359 F. Supp. 3d 306 (E.D.N.C. 2019); *Porter v. Oklahoma Farm Bur. Mut. Ins. Co.*, 330 P.3d 511 (Okla. 2014); *Isaac v. State Farm Mut. Auto. Ins. Co.*, 522 N.W.2d 752 (S.D. 1994); *Mitzel v. Employers' Ins.*, 878 F.2d 233 (8th Cir. 1989) (South Dakota law); *Amica Mut. Ins. Co. v. Schettler*, 768 P.2d 950 (Utah Ct. App. 1989); *McCullough v. Golden Rule Ins. Co.*, 789 P.2d 855 (Wyo. 1990).

The "intermediate view" referred to in the book, namely a requirement of unreasonableness coupled with either an awareness of that unreasonableness or a reckless disregard of the lack of a reasonable basis, has been endorsed by the Arizona Court of Appeals, in *Sobieski v. American Standard Ins. Co.*, 382 P.3d 89 (Ariz. Ct. App. 2016); by federal district courts applying Arizona law in *Montoya Lopez v. Allstate Ins. Co.*, 282 F. Supp. 2d 1095 (D. Ariz. 2003), *Young v. Allstate Ins. Co.*, 296 F. Supp. 2d 1111 (D. Ariz. 2003), and *Knoell v. Metropolitan Life Ins. Co.*, 163 F. Supp. 2d 1072 (D. Ariz. 2001); by the Colorado Supreme Court, in *Schultz v. Geico Casualty Co.*, 429 P.3d 844 (Colo. 2018), and *Dale v. Guaranty Nat'l Ins. Co.*, 948 P.2d 545 (Colo. 1997); by federal courts applying Colorado law in *Peterson v. USAA Life Ins. Co.*, 814 Fed. Appx. 408 (10th Cir. 2020), *Anderson v. State Farm Mut. Auto. Ins. Co.*, 416 F.3d 1143 (10th Cir. 2005), and *Thompson v. State Farm Mut. Auto. Ins. Co.*, *supra*; by the Iowa Supreme Court in *Wilson v. Farm Bureau Mut. Ins. Co.*, 714 N.W.2d 250 (Iowa 2006); by the Kentucky Supreme Court in *Travelers Indem. Co. v. Armstrong*, 565 S.W.3d 550 (Ky. 2018), *reh'g denied* (Ky. 2019); and by a federal district court applying Kentucky law in *Foster v. American Fire & Casualty Co.*, 219 F. Supp. 3d 590 (E.D. Ky. 2016); by the federal district court applying Minnesota law in *Selective Ins. Co. of S.C. v. Sela*, 353 F. Supp. 3d 847 (D. Minn. 2018); by the Fifth Circuit applying Mississippi law in *Mitchell v. State Farm*

Fire & Cas. Co., 954 F.3d 700 (5th Cir. 2020) (Mississippi law), and *Dey v. State Farm Mut. Auto. Ins. Co.*, 789 F.3d 629 (5th Cir. 2015) (Mississippi law); by the Nebraska Supreme Court, in *Williams v. Allstate Indem. Co.*, 669 N.W.2d 455 (Neb. 2003), *Radecki v. Mutual of Omaha Ins. Co.*, 255 Neb. 224, 583 N.W.2d 320 (1998), and *Braesch v. Union Ins. Co.*, 237 Neb. 44, 464 N.W.2d 769 (1991); by the Eighth Circuit applying Nebraska law in *McShane Constr. Co. v. Gotham Ins. Co.*, 867 F.3d 923 (8th Cir. 2017); by federal district courts applying Nevada law, in *Aiello v. Geico Gen. Ins. Co.*, 379 F. Supp. 3d 1123 (D. Nev. 2019), and *Fernandez v. State Farm Mut. Auto. Ins. Co.*, 338 F. Supp. 3d 1193 (D. Nev. 2018); by the New Jersey Supreme Court (limiting the cause of action to contract-measure damages), in *Pickett v. Lloyd's*, 131 N.J. 457, 621 A.2d 445 (1993), *cited with approval in Badiali v. New Jersey Mfrs. Ins. Grp.*, 220 N.J. 544 (2015); by a New York appellate court in *Jian Liang v. Progressive Cas. Ins. Co.*, 172 A.D.3d 696, 99 N.Y.S.3d 449 (2019); by Pennsylvania superior courts in *Rancosky v. Wash. Nat'l Ins. Co.*, 130 A.3d 79 (Pa. Super. 2015), *aff'd*, 170 A.3d 364 (Pa. 2017); *Mohney v. American Gen. Life Ins. Co.*, 116 A.3d 1123, 2015 PA Super 113, *appeal denied*, 130 A.3d 1291 (Pa. 2015), and *Condio v. Erie Ins. Exch.*, 899 A.2d 1136, 2006 PA Super 92 (2006); by courts in the Third Circuit applying Pennsylvania law, in *The Northwestern Mut. Life Ins. Co. v. Babayan*, 430 F.3d 121 (3d Cir. 2005), *Klinger v. State Farm Mut. Auto. Ins. Co.*, 115 F.3d 230 (3d Cir. 1997); by district courts in *Metropolitan Grp. Prop. & Casualty Ins. Co. v. Hack*, 312 F. Supp. 3d 439 (M.D. Pa. 2018) and *Whalen v. State Farm Fire & Casualty Co.*, 183 F. Supp. 3d 672 (E.D. Pa. 2016) (citing *Klinger, supra*); by the South Dakota Supreme Court, in *Johnson v. United Parcel Serv., Inc.*, 946 N.W.2d 1 (S.D. 2020), *Bertelsen v. Allstate Ins. Co.*, 833 N.W.2d 545 (S.D. 2013), and *Julson v. Federated Mut. Ins. Co.*, 562 N.W.2d 117 (S.D. 1997); by the Court of Appeals of Texas in *Garcia v. Lloyds*, 514 S.W.3d 257 (Tex. App. 2016); by the

Seventh Circuit applying Wisconsin law in *Blue v. Hartford Life & Accident Ins. Co.*, 698 F.3d 587 (7th Cir. 2012); by the Wyoming Supreme Court, in *Cathcart v. State Farm Mut. Auto. Ins. Co.*, 123 P.3d 579 (Wyo. 2005), and *State Farm Mut. Auto. Ins. Co. v. Shrader*, 882 P.2d 813 (Wyo. 1994).

See supplement §3.61 for discussion of the issue (covered in this section of the book) whether an insurer may attempt at trial to justify the nonpayment of a claim on the basis of after-acquired information not possessed at the time of the original denial.

4. Types of Bad Faith Conduct

This section contains discussion of types of bad faith conduct under both statutory and common-law bad faith claims.

§1.10 a. Inadequate Investigation

—In *Thomas v. Principal Fin. Group*, 566 So. 2d 735 (Ala. 1990), the Alabama Supreme Court reinstated a jury verdict for the insured on a bad faith claim against the issuer of a group life insurance policy. The insurer had denied a claim for the death of the insured's daughter on the ground that she was not a "dependent" within the meaning of the policy at the time of her death. The trial court had granted the insurer's motion for J.N.O.V. on the basis of the "directed verdict rule"—since there existed questions of fact on the coverage issue, the trial court believed that bad faith liability was precluded as a matter of law. (The "directed verdict rule" is discussed in the book and in §1.20 of this supplement.) The state supreme court rejected the application of the "directed verdict rule," holding that under the present circumstances it had not barred the jury's consideration of the bad faith claim. The court explained that this was not an "ordinary" bad faith case, since a question of fact on the coverage issue was raised only by virtue of the arguably negligent or reckless conduct and conclusions of claims examiners in failing to subject the results of their investigation to a "cognitive evaluation and review."

Other Alabama cases have involved the duty to investigate: *Alfa Mut. Fire Ins. Co.*, 738 So. 2d 815 (Ala. 1999) (reinstating judgment for insured; because of deficient nature of investigation, insurer would be charged with constructive knowledge that no reasonable basis existed for denial of claim); *Employees' Benefit Ass'n v. Grissett*, 732 So. 2d 968 (Ala. 1998) (explaining that bad faith may be proved either by satisfying "directed verdict rule" or by showing that insurer's failure to investigate was intentional or reckless); *Kervin v. Southern Guar. Ins. Co.*, 667 So. 2d 704 (Ala. 1995) (affirming summary judgment; insurer had no duty to investigate value of items as to which insurer disputed coverage); *Turner v. State Farm Fire & Casualty Co.*, 614 So. 2d 1029 (Ala. 1993) (invoking "directed verdict rule" (see §1.20) in affirming summary judgment for insurer on bad faith claim; before denying claim, insurer fulfilled its duty under *Jones v. Alabama Farm Bureau Mut. Casualty Co.*, 507 So. 2d 396 (Ala. 1986), to examine property to determine whether covered cause, or one of several other possible causes, was responsible for collapse of basement wall); *Standard Plan, Inc. v. Tucker*, 582 So. 2d 1024 (Ala. 1991) (affirming award of $500,000 in punitive damages: evidence supported finding that insurer intentionally or recklessly failed to investigate an auto insurance claim to determine whether any lawful basis for its denial existed); *Weaver v. Allstate Ins. Co.*, 574 So. 2d 771 (Ala. 1990) (recognizing rule that insurer incurs bad faith liability by intentionally failing to determine whether there is any lawful basis for its refusal to pay a claim, but affirming summary judgment in present case on ground that conflicting evidence had provided an arguable reason for nonpayment); *Georgia Pacific Consumer Prods. LP v. Zurich Am. Ins. Co.*, 184 F. Supp. 3d 1337 (S.D. Ala. 2016) (denying insurer's summary judgment motion where insured's complaint contains plausible allegations of insurer's failure to investigate).

For a comparable discussion of the "lying exception" to the directed verdict rule, see *Andrew Jackson Life Ins. Co. v. Williams*, 566 So. 2d 1172 (Miss. 1990). The Mississippi Supreme Court there points out that the directed verdict rule is inappropriate where it is the insured's contention that a "debatable" coverage issue has been raised only by virtue of the insurer's deliberate falsehoods. See also *Intercontinental Life Ins. Co. v. Lindblom*, 598 So. 2d 886 (Ala. 1992) (directed verdict rule held inapplicable where only evidence supporting insurer's noncoverage position was disputed testimony of insurer's own employees that lapse notices had been sent to the insured); *Ex parte Blue Cross & Blue Shield*, 590 So. 2d 270 (Ala. 1991) (directed verdict rule applied where insurer's refusal to pay gave rise to only "ordinary" bad faith claim).

—In *Sobieski v. American Standard Ins. Co.*, 382 P.3d 89 (Ariz. Ct. App. 2016), the court affirmed a judgment against the insurer for bad faith in handling a claim brought under an uninsured motorist policy. The court found that the insurer knew that even the slightest degree of fault on the part of the uninsured motorist could obligate it to pay benefits under the policy, but the insurer failed to interview all of the witnesses to the accident and failed to pursue inconsistencies in witness accounts. The court affirmed a jury award of $500,000 in compensatory damages, but reversed a punitive damages award of $1,000,000.

—In *Reynolds v. Shelter Mut. Ins. Co.*, 313 Ark. 145, 852 S.W.2d 799 (1993), the Arkansas Supreme Court held that a mere failure to investigate cannot give rise to a bad faith claim, since Arkansas law defines "bad faith" as involving dishonesty, malice, or oppression. See also *Sims v. State Farm Mut. Auto. Ins. Co*, 894 F.3d 941 (8th Cir. 2018), *reh'g & reh'g en banc denied* (8th Cir. 2018) (Arkansas law; insured's allegations that insurer should have conducted more thorough investigation and given more credence to her expert's evidence showed only negligence and fell short of dishonest, malicious, or oppressive conduct as matter of law). Compare *Metropolitan Prop. & Casualty Ins. Co. v. Calvin*, 802 F.3d 933 (8th Cir. 2015) (Arkansas law), in which the Eighth Circuit concluded that the insurer's investigation was at best aggressive, and that its length and scope did not support the insured's claim that the insurer's actions were malicious or oppressive.

—In *Phelps v. Provident Life & Accident Ins. Co.*, 60 F. Supp. 2d 1014 (C.D. Cal. 1999) (California law), a federal district court, granting the insurer's motion for summary adjudication, rejected the argument that the insurer had not investigated the claim adequately before concluding that the insured was no longer totally disabled and terminating payments under a disability policy. Addressing the insured's contention that the insurer had failed to conduct certain tests and had failed to repeat previous testing, the court wrote, "That Defendant did not exhaust all possible tests is not dispositive. Indeed, an insured would always be able to argue that something else should have been done." See also *Benavides v. State Farm Gen. Ins. Co.*, 136 Cal. App. 4th 1241, 39 Cal. Rptr. 3d 650 (2006) (insured cannot maintain claim for breach of implied covenant in absence of covered loss). Compare *Wilson v. 21st Century Ins. Co.*, 42 Cal. 4th 713, 68 Cal. Rptr. 3d 746, 171 P.3d 1082 (2007) ("genuine dispute" rule does not relieve insurer of obligation to thoroughly and fairly investigate, process, and evaluate claim; in present case, jury could find that insurer had no reasonable basis for conclusion that insured's injuries were minimal); *Ghazarian v. Magellan Health Inc.*, 53 Cal. App. 5th 171, 266 Cal. Rptr. 3d 841 (2020) (court must look past allegedly reasonable denial to determine whether insurer fairly evaluated claim; denying summary judgment to medical insurer that refused to authorize full amount of treatment for autistic child; insurer arguably did not fully investigate claim where physician acting on behalf of insurer admitted she had not read medical reports and 2 physicians who said full treatment was not warranted gave conflicting reasoning as to why); *Fadeeff v. State Farm Gen. Ins. Co.*, 50 Cal. App. 5th 94, 263 Cal. Rptr. 3d 453 (2020) (insureds brought claim for breach of covenant of good faith and fair dealing after insurer failed to fully pay insureds' claims for smoke damage to home from wildfire; denying summary judgment to insurer under genuine dispute doctrine where insurer partially relied on unlicensed adjuster, insurer's experts provided conflicting opinions, and unlicensed adjuster failed to adequately investigate insureds' supplemental claims); *Zubillaga v. Allstate Indem. Co.*, 12 Cal. App. 5th 1017, 219 Cal. Rptr. 3d 620 (2017) (under genuine dispute doctrine, testimony of expert does not automatically insulate insurer from bad faith claim; insured demonstrated issues of material fact where insured presented evidence that insurer continued to rely on expert opinion after insured subsequently presented insurer with facts about changing medical condition); *Chicago Title Ins. Co. v. AMZ Ins. Servs., Inc.*, 188 Cal. App. 4th 401, 115 Cal. Rptr. 3d 707 (2010) (substantial evidence supported jury's finding that property insurer acted in bad faith by failing to properly investigate claim where, without basis, insurer had summarily rejected validity and significance of binder that had been issued to insured); *Bosetti v. The United States Life Ins. Co.*, 175 Cal. App. 4th 1208, 96 Cal. Rptr. 3d 744 (2009) (when insurer is subjectively aware that it has hired biased expert, it is not objectively reasonable to rely on that expert as basis for invoking genuine dispute doctrine and seeking summary adjudication); *McCoy v. Progressive West Ins. Co.*, 171 Cal. App. 4th 785, 90 Cal. Rptr. 3d 74 (2009) (although insurer may rely on experts, summary judgment must be denied where evidence shows that insurer dishonestly selected its experts, that its experts were unreasonable, or that insurer failed to conduct thorough investigation); *Brehm IV v. 21st Century Ins. Co.*, 166 Cal. App. 4th 1225, 83 Cal. Rptr. 3d 410 (2008) (reversing dismissal of claim involving allegedly biased investigation; even insurer that pays full amounts of its policy may be liable for bad faith if improper claims handling caused detriment to insured); *Jordan v. Allstate Ins. Co.*, 148 Cal. App. 4th 1062, 56 Cal. Rptr. 3d 312 (2007) (reversing summary adjudication; home insurer's reasonable though erroneous interpretation of policy exclusion did not excuse failure to investigate other possible bases for insured's claim); *Shade Foods, Inc. v. Innovative Prods. Sales & Marketing, Inc.*, 78 Cal. App. 4th 847, 93 Cal. Rptr. 2d 364 (2000) (evidence supported finding of bad faith in failure to conduct adequate investigation); *Hangarter v. Provident Life & Accident Ins. Co.*, 373 F.3d 998 (9th Cir. 2004) (affirming judgment for insured and $7.67 million in damages; jury's finding that investigation had been biased was supported by sufficient evidence and precluded insurer's invocation of "genuine dispute" defense to bad faith liability); *Underwater Kinetics LLP v. Hanover Am. Ins. Co.*, ___ F. Supp. 3d ___, 2020 WL 6204628 (S.D. Cal. 2020) (denying summary judgment to insurer on bad faith claim where factual issues remained on whether insurer conducted adequate investigation; insured argued that claims related to computer hacking should not have been combined into one occurrence; insurer's reliance on expert was not enough to warrant summary judgment where insured argued that expert had no first-hand knowledge of circumstances of hacking, insurer did not conduct forensic analysis of insured's computer systems, and insurer allegedly created financial incentives to combine claims into 1 occurrence); *Vogt v. Minn. Life Ins. Co.*, 383 F. Supp. 3d 996 (E.D. Cal. 2019) (denying summary judgment for insurer under accidental death policy where jury could conclude that insurer failed to make adequate investigation of possibility that insured, who suffered from Parkinson's disease, died as result of head injury sustained in fall; insurer improperly disregarded California law that preexisting disease does not relieve insurer of liability for accidental death); *Kelly v.*

Provident Life & Accident Ins. Co., 734 F. Supp. 2d 1035 (S.D. Cal. 2010) (insurer's bias may be demonstrated by evidence that: (1) insurer misrepresented nature of investigatory proceedings; (2) insurer's employees lied in depositions or to insured; (3) insurer dishonestly selected its experts; (4) insurer's experts were unreasonable; or (5) insurer failed to conduct thorough investigation); *Keshish v. Allstate Ins. Co.*, 959 F. Supp. 2d 1226 (C.D. Cal. 2013) (under California law, even when insurer has relied on expert to determine insured's damages, court must deny summary judgment on bad faith claim if evidence shows that insurer dishonestly selected its expert, if expert was unreasonable, or if insurer otherwise failed to conduct thorough investigation); *Ayala v. Infinity Ins. Co.*, 713 F. Supp. 2d 984 (C.D. Cal. 2010) (California law; although independent expert's opinion will not automatically insulate insurer from bad faith claim if investigation itself was biased, in present case insurer's retention of independent expert demonstrated as matter of law that insurer conducted thorough and reasonable investigation before denying claim); *Bravo v. The United States Life Ins. Co.*, 701 F. Supp. 2d 1145 (E.C. Cal. 2010) (California law; denying motion for summary judgment; it is for jury to decide whether insurer's investigation was reasonable and fair if there is evidence that insurer dishonestly selected its experts or that experts were unreasonable).

In 2015, the Judicial Council of California approved a revision to the California Jury Instruction on bad faith failure to investigate, CACI No. 2332. See discussion in §4.28, *infra.*

—In *Wahlert v. Am. Standard Ins. Co. of Wis.*, 173 F. Supp. 3d 1187 (D. Colo. 2016), the court found that the plaintiff, who was injured in a car accident as a passenger in the insured's vehicle, failed to create a genuine issue of material fact as to the reasonableness of the insurer's investigation when the plaintiff presented evidence of physical impairment for the first time during litigation.

In *Thompson v. State Farm Mut. Auto. Ins. Co.*, 457 F.

Supp. 3d 998 (D. Colo. 2020) (Colorado law), the personal representative of the insured's estate brought a claim for bad faith after the insured passed away from an overdose of painkillers following a car accident and the insurer denied payment of underinsured motorist benefits after the insured's death. The insurer argued that its denial was fairly debatable because it was not clear that the death was a direct result of the car accident, and the death was not foreseeable. The court agreed that the insurer's denial of plaintiff's claim was fairly debatable, but held that the insurer was not entitled to summary judgment because genuine issues of material fact existed as to whether the insurer's investigation was reasonable. The insurer never obtained an independent medical evaluation, never reviewed the insured's medical records, and never corresponded with the coroner.

For another inadequate investigation case based on Colorado law see *Sandoval v. Unum Life Ins. Co. of Am.*, 952 F.3d 1233 (10th Cir. 2020) (Colorado law; granting summary judgment in favor of insurer on bad faith claim for benefits under disability insurance; insurer conducted reasonable investigation where insurer tried to contact insured's physician twice but was rebuffed, insurer interviewed insured, and insured hired 3 physicians, including specialists, to review insured's medical records).

—In *Sterling v. Provident Life & Accident Ins. Co.*, 619 F. Supp. 2d 1242 (M.D. Fla. 2009) (Connecticut law), a federal district court in Florida, while granting summary judgment, emphasized that a failure to conduct a reasonable investigation may be the basis of an actionable common-law bad faith claim under Connecticut law. But see *HDMG Entm't, LLC v. Certain Underwriters at Lloyd's of London Subscribing to Policy No. L009082*, 355 F. Supp. 3d 373 (D.S.C. 2018) (Connecticut law; Connecticut Supreme court has refused to extend bad faith actions to claims based solely on failure to investigate where investigation is not mandated in policy).

—A Florida statutory first-party bad faith claim was stated, the court held in *Hogan v. Provident Life & Accident Ins. Co.*, 665 F. Supp. 2d 1273 (M.D. Fla. 2009), by the allegation that the insurer set targets and goals for claims termination without regard to the merits of insureds' claims. See also *Fortune v. First Protective Ins. Co.*, 302 So. 3d 485 (Fla. Dist. Ct. App. 2020) (insureds brought claim for bad faith under Fla. Stat. Ann. §624.155 after insurer made lowball offer to cover hurricane damage to home; insureds argued that insurer failed to identify full scope of necessary repairs; court held that insurer's use of appraisal process and payment of appraisal award after cure period expired did not, as matter of law, cure alleged bad faith); *Kafie v. Northwestern Mut. Life Ins. Co.*, 834 F. Supp. 2d 1354 (S.D. Fla. 2011) (fact issues precluded summary judgment on statutory bad faith claim, particularly concerning manner in which insurer investigated and assessed insured's credibility in connection with claim under disability insurance policy).

—In *United Servs. Auto. Ass'n v. Carroll*, 486 S.E.2d 613 (Ga. Ct. App. 1997), a Georgia Court of Appeals affirmed a judgment for the insured on a statutory bad faith claim (Ga. Code Ann. §33-4-6), holding, *inter alia*, that the trial court did not err in denying a motion for a directed verdict in the face of evidence that no thorough investigation had been made before denial of the claim. The insurer did not have reasonable grounds to deny coverage in the absence of a complete investigation, the court held, notwithstanding the fact that a statement by the elderly insured herself had seemed to exclude coverage. The claims adjuster had made no attempt to clarify the insured's statement, the court emphasized, or to interview eyewitnesses. But see *Mock v. Cent. Mut. Ins. Co.*, 158 F. Supp. 3d 1332 (S.D. Ga. 2016) (Georgia law; granting summary judgment for insurer on statutory bad faith claims; it was reasonable for insurer to rely on investigators' findings at the time, although the court now finds that the investigator was not sufficiently qualified).

—In *Allstate Ins. Co. v. Fields*, 885 N.E.2d 728 (Ind. Ct. App. 2008), an Indiana Court of Appeals emphasized that the lack of a diligent investigation, without more, is not sufficient to support an award for breach of the insurer's duty to act in good faith. Accord *Villas at Winding Ridge v. State Farm Fire & Cas. Co.*, 942 F.3d 824 (7th Cir. 2019) (Indiana law; affirming summary judgment in favor of insurer where evidence at best showed initial inspection was inadequate, which alone did not constitute bad faith; insured failed to show any evidence insurer acted with culpable state of mind); *Jackson v. Allstate Ins. Co.*, 780 F. Supp. 2d 781 (S.D. Ind. 2011).

—In *Hollingsworth v. Schminkey*, 553 N.W.2d 591 (Iowa 1996), the Iowa Supreme Court, affirming summary judgment, held that under Iowa law, negligent investigation cannot support a negligence or bad faith claim, given the existence of a reasonable basis for denying coverage Accord, *Sampson v. American Standard Ins. Co.*, 582 N.W.2d 146 (Iowa 1998). Compare *The Weitz Co. v. Lloyd's of London*, 574 F.3d 885 (8th Cir. 2009) (Iowa law; summary judgment was precluded by fact issues as to whether insurer properly investigated claim and subjected results of investigation to reasonable evaluation and review).

—In *Conner v. Occidental Fire & Casualty Co. of N.C.*, 135 P.2d 1230 (Kan. 2006), the Kansas Supreme Court reinstated summary judgment for the insured, agreeing with the trial court that the insurer had failed to conduct a good faith investigation into the insured's property damage claim as shown by its violation of its own claims investigation procedures and its failure to interview two important witnesses.

—In *Morgan v. Golden Rule Ins. Co.*, 568 So. 2d 184 (La. Ct. App 1990), a Louisiana Court of Appeals held that a health insurer's duty to investigate a claim had included the duty to investigate the insured's medical condition before issuance of the policy, and affirmed awards of $15,000 in policy benefits, $15,000 in penalties, and $15,000 in attorney's fees. But see *Shreve v. State Farm Fire & Casualty Co.*, 247 So. 3d 1175 (La. Ct. App. 2018), *writ denied*, 255 So. 3d 574 (La. 2018) (affirming JNOV on bad faith claim under La. Stat. Ann. §22:1973 and dismissing $140,000 in noncontractual damages and $25,000 in attorney's fees; reasonable persons could not have found that insurer acted in bad faith toward insured when handling claim where insured did not discover crack in foundation of home until almost 3 years after alleged damaging act occurred, insurer hired engineer to evaluate crack within 2 weeks of claim, insurer's engineer found crack to be from source not covered under policy, and insurer hired second engineer who confirmed its first engineer's report when it was faced with conflicting report from insured's engineer).

　—In an action under the Massachusetts Unfair Claim Settlement Practices statute, the First Circuit, in *Pediatricians, Inc. v. Provident Life & Accident Ins. Co.*, 965 F.2d 1164 (1st Cir. 1992), rejected the argument that the insurer had violated Mass. Gen. L. ch. 176D, §3(9)(d) by refusing to pay a claim under a life insurance policy "without conducting a reasonable investigation based upon all available information." The court emphasized that §3(9)(d) requires only a *reasonable* investigation, and that a reasonable investigator "need not necessarily investigate that which it [reasonably] considers irrelevant." See also *River Farm Realty Trust v. Farm Fam. Casualty Ins. Co.*, 360 F. Supp. 3d 31 (D. Mass. 2019), aff'd, 943 F.3d 27 (1st Cir. 2019), *aff'd*, 943 F.3d 27 (1st Cir. 2019) (no evidence investigation was not reasonable where insurer conducted 2 investigations and provided 2 estimates and reference was conducted in light of continuing dispute between insured and insurer); *Gaffney v. AAA Life Ins. Co.*, 4 F. Supp. 2d 38 (D. Mass. 1998) (given existence of reasonable basis for denying coverage, deficient investigation is insufficient by itself to subject insurer to liability). Compare *Jucino v. Commerce Ins. Co.*, 2011 Mass. App. Div. 285, 2011 WL 6890187 (2011) (affirming judgment for insureds; auto insurer conducted unreasonable investigation where investigation had consisted solely of single phone call to one of insureds, which call was terminated when language barrier was encountered; insurer offered no rationale for fraud suspicion; and insurer did not contact police officer who had been at accident scene).

—In *Selective Ins. Co. of S.C. v. Sela*, 353 F. Supp. 3d 847 (D. Minn. 2018) (Minnesota law), the court held that Minn. Stat. Ann. §604.18 "requires courts to consider whether the claim was properly investigated and whether the results of the investigation were subjected to reasonable evaluation and review." 353 F. Supp. 3d at 864 (internal quotation marks omitted). The court held that the insurer did not act in bad faith when it refused to obtain an appraisal of property damage because its dispute with the insured related to whether coverage was required, and not to the amount of the claimed loss.

In *Peterson v. Western Nat'l Mut. Ins. Co.*, 946 N.W.2d 903 (Minn. 2020), the Supreme Court of Minnesota held that the trial court did not err in finding that the insurer did not act as a reasonable insurer would have in denying the plaintiff's claim for coverage, and that it knew or recklessly disregarded information that would have shown it had no objectively reasonable basis to deny benefits. Accordingly, the court upheld awards of $100,000 in taxable costs and $97,940.50 in attorney fees under Minn. Stat. §604.18. The court concluded that the insurer's failure to conduct an adequate investigation of the insured's claim under her underinsured motorist's policy, including disregarding a mountain of medical evidence that her accident caused severe headaches requiring Botox treatment, led it to unreasonably and recklessly deny her claim.

—Applying Mississippi law in a case involving an insurer's failure to conduct a reasonably thorough investigation of a claim for health insurance benefits under a major medical policy, the Fifth Circuit, in *Eichenseer v. Reserve Life Ins. Co.*, 881 F.2d 1355 (5th Cir. 1989), affirmed a judgment for the insured and awards of $1,000 in compensatory damages and $500,000 in punitives. The court explained that an insurance company must make reasonable efforts to obtain all available medical information relevant to a claim related to the health of an insured, and concluded that the trial court had not erred in finding that Reserve Life had acted with gross negligence and a reckless disregard for its insured's rights in denying Eichenseer's claim over a prolonged period of time without proper investigation. (The court noted that the trial court had been correct in concluding that Reserve Life had not possessed an arguable basis for denying Eichenseer's claim sufficient to preclude the imposition of punitive damages, where that "arguable basis" had been discovered by the insurer only after litigation began.) The United States Supreme Court accepted certiorari in *Eichenseer*, but subsequently remanded the case for reconsideration in light of *Pacific Mut. Life Ins. Co. v. Haslip*, 499 U.S. 1 (1991). The Fifth Circuit has now reaffirmed the judgment, engaging in a useful explication of the *Haslip* opinion. (See § 1.62 for discussion of the punitive damages aspect of *Eichenseer v. Reserve Life Ins. Co.*, 934 F.2d 1377 (5th Cir. 1991).) See also *United Servs. Auto. Ass'n v. Lisanby*, 47 So.2d 1172 (Miss. 2010) (to prove claim for bad faith refusal, insured must show level of negligence in conducting investigation such that proper investigation would have easily adduced evidence showing that insurer's defenses were without merit); *Windmon v. Marshall*, 926 So. 2d 867 (Miss. 2006) (given arguable reason to deny claim for underinsured motorist benefits, investigation that was at most negligent did not subject insurer to bad faith liability); *Murphree v. Federal Ins. Co.*, 707 So. 2d 523 (Miss. 1997) (deficient investigation does not by itself subject insurer to bad faith liability given existence of reasonable basis for denial of claim); *Dey v. State Farm Mut. Auto. Ins. Co.*, 789 F.3d 629 (5th Cir. 2015) (Mississippi law; any deficiencies in investigation were at worst negligence or bad judgment and therefore did not support bad faith claim; "[b]ad faith must be more than 'mere negligence, inadvertence, clerical errors, or honest mistakes'" (quoting Jeffrey Jackson, Miss. Ins. Law & Prac. §13:8 (2014))); *Broussard v. State Farm Fire & Casualty Co.*, 523 F.3d 618 (5th Cir. 2008) (Mississippi law; to qualify for punitive damages for negligent claim investigation, insurer's level of negligence must be such that proper investigation would easily have adduced evidence showing its defense to be without merit); *American States Ins. Co. v. Natchez Steam Laundry*, 131 F.3d 551 (5th Cir. 1998) (deficient investigation does not by itself subject insurer to bad faith liability given existence of reasonable basis for denial of claim).

—In *Minden v. Atain Specialty Ins. Co.*, 788 F.3d 750 (8th Cir. 2015), the Eighth Circuit applied Missouri law and affirmed a federal district court's holding that although the insurer had a duty to defend its insured, its conduct did not amount to a "vexatious" refusal to defend under Mo. Rev. Stat. §375.420 because the insurer had a reasonable cause to believe there was no coverage. The court held that the insurer was not required to look beyond an initial police report to decide to deny coverage, even though "further investigation might have unearthed the possibility of coverage."

—In *Salopek Trustee for Salopek Family Heritage Trust v. Zurich Am. Life Ins. Co.*, 446 F. Supp. 3d 886 (D.N.M. 2020) (New Mexico law), the insured's wife and trustee of a family trust alleged that the insurer failed to conduct an adequate investigation before accepting the risk of covering the insured through a life insurance policy. The court found that the insurer did not have such a pre-policy duty, so its failure to investigate when offering the policy could not be evidence of bad faith.

—In *Furr v. State Farm Mut. Auto. Ins. Co.*, 128 Ohio App. 3d 607, 716 N.E.2d 259 (1998), an Ohio Court of Appeals held that awards of compensatory and punitive damages were adequately supported by evidence that the insurer had breached its affirmative duty to conduct an adequate investigation of a one-car accident that had resulted in the insured's death. Compare *Retail Ventures, Inc. v. National Union Fire Ins. Co. of Pittsburgh, PA*, 691 F.3d 821 (6th Cir. 2012) (insurer did not engage in bad faith in course of investigating claim for coverage under computer fraud rider in commercial crime policy by requesting second legal opinion concerning meaning of policy term).

—Affirming awards of life insurance policy benefits and damages for bad faith, an Oklahoma Court of Appeals, in *Hall v. Globe Life & Accident Ins. Co.*, 968 P.2d 1263 (Okla. Civ. App. 1998), *cert. denied*, invoked the principle that "[a]n inadequte investigation by the insurance company may give rise to an inference of bad faith, requiring the question to be determined by the jury." See also *Sims v. Great Am. Life Ins. Co.*, 469 F.3d 870 (10th Cir. 2006) (explaining that under Oklahoma law, insurer fails to conduct reasonably appropriate investigation if (1) manner of investigation hints at sham defense or otherwise suggests that material facts were overlooked, or (2) insurer intentionally disregarded undisputed facts supporting insured's claim).

See §1.66 for discussion of *Harrell v. Old Am. Ins. Co.*, 829 P.2d 75 (Okla. Ct. App. 1991), *cert. denied*, in which an Oklahoma court affirmed awards of compensatory and punitive damages against a hospitalization insurer who had denied plaintiff's claims on the basis of the recommendation of a medical consultant who had failed to even contact plaintiff or her physicians. Compare *Shotts v. GEICO Gen. Ins. Co.*, 943 F.3d 1304 (10th Cir. 2019) (Oklahoma law; investigation of injuries incurred in automobile accident was reasonable where insurer began its investigation immediately after it learned of accident, reviewed all of insured's medical records, conducted additional review at insured's request, reevaluated claim and adjusted offer after insured objected to initial offer, and pursued peer review and additional medical documentation as needed).

—Reversing summary judgment in *Ivanov v. Farmers*

Ins. Co. of Or., 344 Or. 421, 185 P.3d 417 (2008), the Oregon Supreme Court held that, before it could prevail on summary judgment, an automobile insurer that denied insureds' personal injury protection (PIP) claims was required to establish that the denials were based on reasonable investigations. The insurer had a statutory obligation under Or. Rev. Stat. Ann. §§742.524(1)(a), 746.230(1), the court explained, to conduct a reasonable investigation sufficient to support a decision to deny a medical expense claim that is statutorily presumed to be reasonable and necessary.

—In *Zimmerman v. Harleysville Mut. Ins. Co.*, 860 A.2d 167 (Pa. Super. Ct. 2004), the Superior Court of Pennsylvania affirmed a judgment for the insured, and awards of compensatory and punitive damages, holding that the evidence supported the trial court's finding that the insurer had acted in bad faith in continuing to insist, in the absence of evidence or any reasonable basis, that the insured had known of and concealed the existence of a defect in the building's roof prior to the issuance of the policy. The court noted that the scope of the Pennsylvania Bad Faith statute now covers the investigatory conduct of an insurer during litigation. See also *Rancosky v. Wash. Nat'l Ins. Co.*, 130 A.3d 79 (Pa. Super. 2015), *aff'd*, 170 A.3d 364 (Pa. 2017) (implicit in Pa. Cons. Stat. §8371 is "requirement that the insurer properly investigate claims prior to refusing to pay"; in addition, bad faith conduct "includes evasion of the spirit of the bargain, lack of diligence and slacking off, willful rendering of imperfect performance, abuse of a power to specify terms, and interference with or failure to cooperate in the other party's performance"; granting estate of deceased a new trial on issue of bad faith where insurer failed to pay claims under cancer policy); *Mohney v. American Gen. Life Ins. Co.*, 116 A.3d 1123, 2015 PA Super 113, *appeal denied*, 130 A.3d 1291 (Pa. 2015) (vacating judgment for insurer and remanding for new trial for determination whether insurer acted with knowing or reckless misconduct in light of evidence that claim investigation was not "reasonably thorough and sufficient," and that misrepresentations of fact by claims investigator in communicating with insured rendered insurer's investigation "neither honest nor objective"); *Lincoln Benefit Life Co. v. Bowman*, 221 F. Supp. 3d 617 (E.D. Pa. 2016) (beneficiary of insured presented sufficient evidence in support of bad faith claim to survive summary judgment where insurer initially refused to accept accuracy of documents that showed decedent's body had been identified and cause of death had been determined; beneficiary alleged insurer failed to adequately investigate to determine accuracy of documents). Compare *Condio v. Erie Ins. Exch.*, 899 A.2d 1136, 2006 PA Super 92 (2006) (reversing judgment for insured; under circumstances, insurer did not act in bad faith when it denied claim for underinsured motorist benefits without undertaking more thorough investigation).

—The Supreme Court of South Dakota, reversing summary judgment in part, held in *Dakota, Minn. & Eastern R.R. Corp. v. Acuity*, 771 N.W.2d 623 (S. D. 2009), that genuine issues of material fact existed as to whether the insurer had failed to conduct a thorough investigation of a claim for uninsured motorist benefits, and whether the insurer had subjected the results of the investigation to reasonable evaluation and review. See also *Lead GHR Enters., Inc. v. Am. States Ins. Co.*, 369 F. Supp. 3d 909 (D.S.D. 2019) (South Dakota law; genuine issues of material fact existed as to whether insurer failed to conduct adequate investigation where insurer's own agent raised concerns about internal condition of fallen retaining wall but insurer's engineers did not examine wall's internal strength or otherwise evaluate it as possible cause of collapse); *Anderson v. Western Nat'l Mut. Ins. Co.*, 857 F. Supp. 2d 896 (D.S.D. 2012) (granting summary judgment on ground that value of insured's underinsured motorist claim was fairly debatable, but explaining circumstances under which evidence that insurer conducted inadequate investigation may preclude "fairly debatable" finding).

In *Sapienza v. Liberty Mut. Fire Ins. Co.*, 389 F. Supp. 3d 648 (D.S.D. 2019) (South Dakota law), insureds brought a bad faith claim against their insurer for refusing to indemnify them for the costs of demolishing their home after they lost a lawsuit with a neighbor and were forced by a court to demolish their newly constructed house. The court found that even if the insurer's investigation was inadequate, the insurer still had a reasonable basis for denying coverage for costs incurred in complying with the injunction because it was fairly debatable as to whether the injunctive relief constituted "damages" under the terms of the policy. See also §2.10.

—In *McKinnie v. State Farm Fire & Casualty Co.*, 298 F. Supp. 3d 1138 (M.D. Tenn. 2018), the court found that the insured's allegations were sufficient to state a claim for bad faith under Tennessee's bad faith statute (Tenn. Code Ann. §56-7-105) where the allegations included failing to pay the insured in full without conducting a reasonable investigation and refusing to adjust and investigate the insured's claim to obtain all available information before stating it had no further obligation. But see *Nylander v. Unum Life Ins. Co. of Am.*, 309 F. Supp. 3d 526 (M.D. Tenn. 2018) (granting summary judgment in favor of insurer on claim related to inadequate investigation).

—In *State Farm Mut. Auto Ins. Co. v. Zubiate*, 808 S.W.2d 590 (Tex. Ct. App. 1991), the court reduced a punitive damages award from $15 million to $660,000, but otherwise affirmed a judgment in favor of the policyholder, where the insurer had denied an accident claim for 15 months without taking the simple step of investigating the validity of its defense that the accident in question (in Mexico) had occurred more that 25 miles from the United States border. (Upon finally sending an investigator to measure the distance, the insurer had discoverd its "error," and had then attempted to change the basis for its denial.) For other Texas cases holding that the evidence of an inadequate investigation was sufficient to support a finding of a breach of the duty of good faith, see *State Farm Fire & Casualty Co. v. Simmons*, 963 S.W.2d 42 (Tex. 1998); *State Farm Lloyds v. Nicolau*, 951 S.W.2d 444 (Tex. 1997); *State Farm Lloyds v. Hamilton*, 265 S.W.3d 725 (Tex. App. 2008); *Pena v. State Farm Lloyds*, 980 S.W.2d 949 (Tex. Ct. App. 1998); *State Farm County Mut. Ins. Co. v. Moran*, 809 S.W.2d 613 (Tex. Ct. App. 1991). Compare *USAA Tex. Lloyds Co. v. Menchaca*, 545 S.W.3d 479 (Tex. 2018) (see discussion in §1.56); *United States Fire Ins. Co. v. Williams*, 955 S.W.2d 267 (Tex. 1997) (bad faith liability could not be premised on failure to investigate that was caused by insurer's reasonable, though erroneous, interpretation of workers' compensation commission rule); *Travelers Personal Security Ins. Co. v. McClelland*, 189 S.W.3d 846 (Tex. App. 2006) (homeowners' insurer did not engage in bad faith by hiring investigative engineer who worked almost exclusively for insurance companies); *Betco Scaffolds Co. v. Houston United Casualty Ins. Co.*, 29 S.W.3d 341 (Tex. Ct. App. 2000) (insurer had been under no duty to continue investigation beyond point where it had acquired sufficient evidence to establish reasonable basis for denial of claim); *Wells v. Minnesota Life Ins. Co.*, 885 F.3d 885 (5th Cir. 2018) (insurer may breach duty of good faith and fair dealing by failing to investigate claim, and cannot use investigation to create pretext for denial, or use failure to investigate to contend liability was not reasonably clear; however, insurer only breaches duty when it lacks reasonable basis for its denial or delay or should have known there was no such basis); *Thompson v. Zurich Am. Ins. Co.*, 664 F.3d 62 (5th Cir. 2011) (under Texas law, insurer's obligation to investigate claim is not unlimited, and scope of appropriate investigation will vary with claim's nature and complexity, but insurer cannot escape liability merely by failing to investigate so that it can contend that liability was never reasonably clear); *Greenville Townhome Owners Assoc., Inc. v. Philadelphia Indem. Ins. Co.*, 473 F. Supp. 3d 692 (N.D. Tex. 2020) (Texas law; granting insurer summary judgment on claims of common-law violations of duty of good faith and fair dealing and under Tex. Ins. Code §541.060 in connection with insurance claim for weather damage to condominium roof; insurer adequately and reasonably investigated claims and reasonably relied on report of engineer where insurer hired engineering firm to inspect roof and ordered reinspection after insured's public adjuster disagreed with engineer's report); *Ramirez v. Allstate Vehicle & Prop. Ins. Co.*, ___ F. Supp. 3d ___, 2020 WL 5806436 (S.D. Tex. 2020) (Texas law; holding insureds stated bad faith claims under Texas common law and unfair claims practices statutes by alleging misrepresentations by insurer concerning covered loss and failure to conduct reasonable investigation; insureds' complaint was sufficient under Fed. R. Civ. P. 9(b) standard for pleading fraud or misrepresentation; see also §1.26); *Douglas v. State Farm Lloyds*, 37 F. Supp. 2d 532 (S.D. Tex. 1999) (Texas law; granting insurer's motion for summary judgment; insured failed to raise fact issue as to adequacy of investigation of water damage claim under homeowners policy; insurer reasonably relied on report of engineering firm despite existence of countervailing evidence).

—In *Black v. Allstate Ins. Co.*, 100 P.3d 1163 (Utah 2004), the Utah Supreme Court, reversing summary judgment, held that an automobile accident victim had standing to assert a direct action against the liability insurer based on the victim's own contractual relationship with the insurer and the insurer's alleged breach of settlement duties in failing to diligently investigate and evaluate the tort-feasor's claim against the victim. The insurer's alleged breach did not give rise to a tort cause of action, the court held, and permitted recovery of only general and consequential damages for breach of contract.

—In an insurer's declaratory judgment action in which the insured counterclaimed for policy benefits and damages for bad faith denial of coverage based on inadequate investigation of a fire insurance claim (in violation of the state Consumer Protection Act), the Supreme Court of Washington affirmed jury awards of $128,000 for breach of contract, $20,000 for violation of the Consumer Protection Act, and attorney's fees in the sum of $64,422. *Industrial Indem. Co. of the Northwest v. Kallevig*, 114 Wash. 2d 907, 792 P.2d 520 (1990). The court held that the evidence supported a finding that the insurer denied coverage on the basis of "conjectural" arson suspicions without a reasonable investigation of evidence inconsistent with an arson theory.

—In *Schlussler v. American Family Mut. Ins. Co.*, 157 Wis. 2d 516, 460 N.W.2d 756 (Ct. App. 1990), a Wisconsin intermediate appellate court rejected an automobile insurer's argument that a finding of bad faith was precluded, in connection with its denial of a claim for medical treatment, because it had relied on the opinion of its independent medical examiner that the symptoms being treated were unrelated to the auto accident. Such reliance could not protect the insurer from liability, the court held, since the evidence had shown that the medical examiner had failed to review all the relevant medical records. The court affirmed awards of $14,000 for future chiropractic expenses, $10,000 for pain and suffering related to the insurer's bad faith, and $50,000 in punitive damages. See also *Lewis v. Paul Revere Life Ins. Co.*, 80 F. Supp. 2d 978 (E.D. Wis. 2000) (denying disability insurer's motion for summary judgment where reasonable juror could find that insurer's investigation and decision to cut off payments had not been "a product of a neutral, detached and diligent search for the facts").

—Reversing a grant of summary judgment, the Wyoming Supreme Court held, in *Hatch v. State Farm Fire & Casualty Co.*, 842 P.2d 1089 (Wyo. 1992), that a material issue of fact had been raised as to whether the insurer had committed bad faith by conducting its investigation of the insured's fire loss in a harassing, hostile, and unprofessional manner, even though the court agreed with the trial judge that the insurer had had a reasonable basis for denying the claim on the basis of its suspicion of arson.

—A number of cases have restated the principle that an inadequate investigation is not, in itself, a sufficient ground for recovery, where a reasonable basis for denying the claim did, in fact, exist, and where no harm therefore resulted from the insurer's lack of care: *State Farm Fire & Casualty Co. v. Brechbill*, 144 So. 3d 248 (Ala. 2013); *State Farm Fire & Casualty Co. v. Balmer*, 891 F.2d 874 (11th Cir. 1990) (Alabama law; affirming district court decision cited in the book); *Aetna Casualty & Sur. Co. v. Superior Court*, 161 Ariz. 437, 778 P.2d 1333 (Ct. App. 1989); *Prieto v. Paul Revere Life Ins. Co.*, 354 F.3d 1005 (9th Cir. 2004) (Arizona law); *McMillin Scripps N. Partnership v. Royal Ins. Co. of Am.*, 19 Cal. App. 4th 12, 23 Cal. Rptr. 2d 243 (1993); *Murray v. State Farm Fire & Casualty Co.*, 219 Cal. App. 3d 58, 268 Cal. Rptr. 33 (1990); *Brodkin v. State Farm Fire & Casualty Co.*, 217 Cal. App. 3d 210, 265 Cal. Rptr. 710 (1989); *Hydro Systems, Inc. v. Continental Ins. Co.*, 929 F.2d 472 (9th Cir. 1991) (California law); *Seastrom v. Farm Bureau Life Ins. Co.*, 601 N.W.2d 339 (Iowa 1999); *Morgan v. American Family Mut. Ins. Co.*, 534 N.W.2d 92 (Iowa 1995); *Clarendon Nat'l Ins. Co. v. Philadelphia Indem. Ins. Co.*, 954 F.3d 397 (1st Cir. 2020) (Massachusetts law); *Liberty Mut. Ins. Co. v. McKneely*, 862 So. 2d 530 (Miss. 2003); *Guy v. Commonwealth Life Ins. Co.*, 894 F.2d 1407 (5th Cir. 1990) (Mississippi law); *Williams v. Hartford Casualty Ins. Co.*, 83 F. Supp. 2d 567 (E.D. Pa. 2000) (Pennsylvania law); *Coventry Assocs., L.P. v. American States Ins. Co.*, 136 Wash. 2d 269, 961 P.2d 933 (1998) (assuming insured's ability to demonstrate harm); *Mills v. Regent Ins. Co.*, 152 Wis. 2d 294, 449 N.W.2d 294 (Wis. Ct. App. 1989). See also *Pacific Group v. First State Ins. Co.*, 70 F.3d 524 (9th Cir. 1995) (California law) (insurer has no duty to investigate where policy unambiguously excludes coverage); *Interiano v. Colonial Life & Accident Ins. Co.*, 460 F. Supp.

3d 945 (C.D. Cal. 2020) (California law; granting summary judgment for insurer on bad faith claim related to accidental death policy where insurer failed to investigate claim until after insured appealed initial denial; once insurer did investigate claim, it reasonably relied on case law for what qualified as accidental death); *Robinson v. State Farm Mut. Auto. Ins. Co.*, 137 Idaho 173, 45 P.3d 829 (2002) (insured has burden of proof on "fairly debatable" issue, and proof of coverage is element of prima facie case). But see *Ex parte Simmons*, 791 So. 2d 371 (Ala. 2000) (reversing summary judgment on bad faith claim where, although claim was fairly debatable, fact issue was raised as to fairness of reconsideration process followed by insurer); *Zilisch v. State Farm Mut. Auto. Ins. Co.*, 196 Ariz. 234, 995 P.2d 276 (2000) (even where claim is "fairly debatable," insurer must still act reasonably in investigating, evaluating, and processing claim, and whether insurer did so is jury question); *Amadeo v. Principal Mut. Life Ins. Co.*, 290 F.3d 1152 (9th Cir. 2002) (California law) (reversing summary judgment; insurer's failure to conduct reasonable investigation precluded summary judgment regardless of merits of contract claim); *Farmland Mut. Ins. Co. v. Johnson*, 36 S.W.2d 368 (Ky. 2000) (even if claim is "fairly debatable," insurer must still "debate fairly" by conducting investigation that complies with Kentucky Unfair Claim Settlement Practices Act); *Lewis v. Equity Nat'l Life Ins. Co.*, 637 So. 2d 183 (Miss. 1994) (rejecting holding of *Guy v. Commonwealth Life Ins. Co.*, *supra;* despite existence of arguable basis for denial of claim, inadequate investigation can be basis for both bad faith liability and punitive damages); *Powers v. United Servs. Auto. Ass'n*, 114 Nev. 79, 962 P.2d 596 (1998) (same); *Sobley v. Southern Natural Gas Co.*, 210 F.3d 561 (5th Cir. 2000) (Mississippi law) (reasonable basis to deny claim does not preclude bad faith liability if insurer failed to identify that basis before denial); *EOTT v. Certain Underwriters at Lloyd's*, 59 F. Supp. 2d 1072 (D. Mont. 1999) (Montana law) (to allow insurer to deny coverage first and then justify denial based on later-acquired information would subvert policy behind statute requiring insurer to conduct reasonable investigation based on all available information); *Skaling v. Aetna Ins. Co.*, 799 A.2d 997 (R.I. 2002) (reversing summary judgment; rejecting "directed verdict rule" and holding that failure to investigate and evaluate claim fairly may subject insurer to bad faith liability regardless of merits of insured's claim); *Wells v. Minnesota Life Ins. Co.*, *supra* (Texas law; although insurer may breach duty of good faith and fair dealing by failing to investigate claim, insurer only breaches duty when it lacks reasonable basis for its denial or delay or should have known there was no such basis); *Sonnett v. First Am. Title Ins. Co.*, 309 P.3d 799 (Wyo. 2013) (even if claim for benefits is fairly debatable, insurer may breach implied covenant by manner in which it investigates, handles, or denies claim).

§1.11 b. Delay

—On December 7, 1993, a Los Angeles jury awarded $39 million in compensatory damages and $386 million in punitives in a bad faith action by Amoco Corporation against Lloyd's of London in connection with Lloyd's "six-year stonewall" when Amoco sought reimbursement for judgments it suffered in actions by municipal customers who had purchased defective plastic pipe.

—For cases recognizing that unreasonable delay in the payment of a claim may subject an insurer to liability for bad faith, see *Neal v. State Farm Fire & Casualty Co.*, 908 F.2d 923 (11th Cir. 1990) (Alabama law; four-month delay was not unreasonable in light of insurer's reasonable suspicions of arson); *Livingston v. Auto Owners Ins. Co.*, 582 So. 2d 1038 (Ala. 1991) (prolonged delay can amount to wrongful denial of claim); *Government Employees Ins. Co. v. Gonzalez*, 403 P.3d 1153 (Alaska 2017) (upholding award of nominal damages of $2, punitive damages of $450,000, and attorney's fees for underinsured motorist (UIM) insurer's bad faith delay in paying claim); *Lockwood v. GEICO Gen. Ins. Co.*, 323 P.3d 691 (Alaska 2014) (reversing summary judgment denying plaintiff's bad faith claim because genuine issue of material fact existed as to whether insurer acted unreasonably in delaying payment on uninsured motorist benefits); *Columbia Nat'l Ins. Co. v. Freeman*, 347 Ark. 423, 64 S.W.3d 720 (2002) (sufficient evidence of oppressive conduct supported jury's bad faith finding relative to fire insurer's deliberate misplacement of documents, failure to pay insured's ongoing business expenses, and failure to comply with agreement concerning building repairs); *Truck Mortgage Group, Inc. v. Crusader Ins. Co.*, 98 Cal. App. 4th 857, 120 Cal. Rptr. 2d 228 (2002) (given overwhelming evidence of substantial covered damage, insurer acted in bad faith by insisting on inventory segregating covered from noncovered damage before paying undisputed portion of claim); *Carleton v. St. Paul Mercury Ins. Co.*, 30 Cal. App. 4th 1450, 36 Cal. Rptr. 2d 229 (1994) (delay was not unreasonable since broker's knowledge of loss could not be imputed to insurer); *Globe Indem. Co. v. Superior Court*, 6 Cal. App. 4th 725, 8 Cal. Rptr. 2d 251 (1992) (delay was not unreasonable where caused by insured's refusal to schedule examination under oath); *Gentry v. State Farm Mut. Auto. Ins. Co.*, 726 F. Supp. 2d 1160, 2010 WL 2903952 (E.D. Cal. 2010) (California law; summary judgment was precluded by fact issue as to whether it was reasonable for insurer to rely on advice of counsel in delaying handling of under-insured motorist claim); *Fisher v. State Farm Mut. Auto. Ins. Co.*, 419 P.3d 985 (Colo. Ct. App. 2015), *aff'd*, 418 P.3d 501 (Colo. 2018) (affirming judgment for insured on claim that insurer committed bad faith by unreasonably delaying payment of medical expenses that insurer had determined were owing under underinsured motorist's policy pending litigation of other damages); *Soicher v. State Farm Mut. Auto. Ins. Co.*, 351 P.3d 559 (Colo. Ct. App. 2015) (ordering judgment for insurer on bad faith claims due to lack of damages to insured that were caused by any unreasonable conduct of insurer; discussing contours of insurer's "unreasonable delay" as opposed to "unreasonable denial" of claim); *Etherton v. Owners Ins. Co.*, 829 F.3d 1209 (10th Cir. 2016) (Colorado law; "fair debatability" of claim validity can be relevant as to whether insurer acted reasonably in delaying payment of claim but is not determinative; upholding jury verdict for insured on claim of unreasonable delay); *Vaughn v. Producers Agriculture Ins. Co.*, 111 F. Supp. 3d 1251 (N.D. Fla. 2015) (Florida law; summary judgment granted to insurer on claim of bad faith failure to settle under F.S.A. §624.155; holding insured was not entitled to presumption that insurer acted in bad faith by failing to timely respond to insured's Civil Remedy Notice (CRN) because insurer's manner of responding was sufficient and timely); *Ticor Title Ins. Co. v. University Creek, Inc.*, 767 F. Supp. 1127 (M.D. Fla. 1991) (7½ months' delay in acting on claim violated Florida Unfair Insurance Trade Practices Act); *Wailua Assocs. v. Aetna Casualty & Sur. Co.*, 27 F. Supp. 2d 1211 (D. Haw. 1998) (Hawaii law; denying motion to dismiss); *Chester v. State Farm Ins. Co.*, 117 Idaho 538, 789 P.2d 534 (Idaho Ct. App. 1990); *Norman v. American Nat'l Fire Ins. Co.*, 198 Ill. App. 3d 269, 555 N.E.2d 1087 (1990); *Thornton v. Am. Interstate Ins. Co.*, 940 N.W.2d 1 (Iowa 2020) (delay of 1.5 years in determining that insured was permanently and totally disabled harmed insured by delaying his receipt of partial commutation, and such delay supported award of $58,452.42 in compensatory damages and $500,000 in punitive damages); *Foster v. American Fire & Casualty Co.*, 219 F. Supp. 3d 590 (E.D. Ky. 2016) (Kentucky law; 7-year delay between date of accident and settlement of claim and insurer's repeated requests for duplicate information and authorizations were sufficient evidence for bad faith claim to survive summary judgment); *Bell v. Steckler*, 285 So. 3d 561 (La. Ct. App. 2019) (affirming summary judgment for uninsured motorist insurer on issue of bad faith delay in tendering coverage where insured failed to overcome showing of reasonable disagreement as whether accident caused insured's injuries); *Daney v. Haynes*, 630 So. 2d 949 (La. Ct. App. 1993) (uncertainty as to total amount due under medical policy did not justify delay in payment of reasonable interim amount); *Benoit v. State Farm Auto. Ins. Co.*, 602 So. 2d 53 (La. Ct. App. 1992) (failure of insured to provide promised medical records did not excuse insurer's delay in paying undisputed amount); *Harvey-Latham Real Estate v. Underwriters at Lloyd's*, 574 So. 2d 13 (Miss. 1990); *James v. State Farm Mut. Auto. Ins. Co.*, 743 F.3d 65 (5th Cir. 2014) (Mississippi law; genuine issues of material fact existed as to whether insurer had arguable or legitimate basis for delaying payment of benefits); *Victor v. Manhattan Life Ins. Co.*, 772 S.W.2d 826 (Mo. Ct. App. 1989); *Hackler v. State Farm Mut. Auto. Ins. Co.*, 210 F. Supp. 3d 1250 (D. Nev. 2016) (Nevada law); *Jessen v. National Excess Ins. Co.*, 108 N.M. 625, 776 P.2d 1244 (1989); *Smith v. Nationwide Mut. Fire Ins. Co.*, 96 N.C. App. 215, 385 S.E.2d 152 (1989); *State Farm Fire & Casualty Co. v. Barton*, 897 F.2d 729 (4th Cir. 1990) (South Carolina law); *Palmetto Fed. Sav. Bank v. Industrial Title Ins. Co.*, 756 F. Supp. 925 (D. S.C. 1991) (South Carolina law; awarding $100,000 in punitive damages); *Universe Life Ins. Co. v. Giles*, 881 S.W.2d 44 (Tex. Ct. App. 1994) (unfounded delay in paying medical benefits supported award of $300,000 in punitive damages); *Fidelity & Casualty Co. v. Underwood*, 791 S.W.2d 635 (Tex. Ct. App. 1990).

And recognizing that even in the absence of coverage, unreasonable delay in the investigation of a claim may subject an insurer to bad faith liability (assuming the insured is able to prove consequential damage), see *Deese v. State Farm Mut. Auto. Ins. Co.*, 838 P.2d 1265 (Ariz. 1992); *Murray v. State Farm Fire & Casualty Co.*, 219 Cal. App. 3d 58, 268 Cal. Rptr. 33 (1990); *Mitchell v. State Farm Fire & Casualty Co.*, 15 F.3d 959 (10th Cir. 1994), *cert. denied*, Oct. 11, 1994

(Colorado law); *Schultz v. Allstate Ins. Co.*, 764 F. Supp. 1404 (D. Colo. 1991) (Colorado law); *Telamon Corp. v. Charter Oak Fire Ins. Co.*, 179 F. Supp. 3d 851, at 853 (S.D. Ind. 2016), *appeal filed* (7th Cir. Apr. 13, 2016) (Indiana law; dismissing claim based on insurer's manner of handling claim where insurer allegedly conducted an "exhaustive, expansive, and expensive" claims investigation for over a year that included requests for large amounts of documents, use of independent audit firm, and many examinations under oath; court dismissed claim because insured failed to show conscious wrongdoing); *Alan Corp. v. International Surplus Lines Inc. Co.*, 823 F. Supp. 33 (D. Mass. 1993) (action under Massachusetts consumer protection statute (Mass. Gen. L. ch. 93) based on violation of the state unfair claim settlement practices act (Mass. Gen. L. ch. 176D)); *Bertelsen v. Allstate Ins. Co.*, 833 N.W.2d 545 (S.D. 2013) (jury question was raised as to whether insurer consciously disregarded insured's rights by delaying process and payment of claim for approximately 1 year and therefore acted with presumed malice); *Snyder Gen. Corp. v. Great Am. Ins. Co.*, 928 F. Supp. 674 (N.D. Tex. 1996), *aff'd* (5th Cir. 1998) 133 F.3d 373 (Texas law). But see *Wells v. United States Life Ins. Co.*, 119 Idaho 160, 804 P.2d 333 (Ct. App. 1991), rejecting the notion of bad faith liability based on delay or denial in the absence of coverage; *Williams v. Ohio Nat'l Life Assurance Co.*, 364 F. Supp. 3d 605 (W.D.N.C. 2019) (North Carolina law; rejecting argument of delay as evidence of bad faith where plaintiff's claim under policy was reasonably in dispute). In a number of cases, courts have rejected bad faith claims where the delays in question had been at least in part attributable to the insured's own conduct. See also *Robinson v. State Farm Mut. Auto. Ins. Co.*, 137 Idaho 173, 45 P.3d 829 (2002) (insured has burden of proof on "fairly debatable" issue, and proof of coverage is element of prima facie case); *Block v. St. Paul Fire & Marine Ins. Co.*, 742 So. 2d 746 (La. Ct. App. 1999); *Lewis v. Nationwide Mut. Ins. Co.*, 742 A.2d 1207

(R.I. 2000) (affirming summary judgment where insured failed to prove breach of policy and where delays were largely attributable to conduct of insured himself); *Coventry Assocs. v. American States Ins. Co.*, 961 P.2d 933 (Wash. 1998); *Marathon Ashland Pipe Line LLC v. Maryland Casualty Co.*, 243 F.3d 1232 (10th Cir. 2001) (Wyoming law).

—The book discusses the tactic whereby an insurer attempts to condition payment of an undisputed portion of an insured's claim on the favorable settlement of a disputed portion. Cases recognizing that such a tactic constitutes insurer bad faith have included *Georgia Casualty & Sur. Co. v. White*, 582 So. 2d 487 (Ala. 1991); *Fisher v. State Farm Mut. Auto. Ins. Co.*, *supra*; *Wahlert v. Am. Standard Ins. Co. of Wis.*, 173 F. Supp. 3d 1187 (D. Colo. 2016) (Colorado law); *Chester v. State Farm Ins. Co.*, *supra*; *Cossitt v. Federated Guar. Mut. Ins. Co.*, 541 So. 2d 436 (Miss. 1989); *Thompson v. Shelter Mut. Ins. Co.*, 875 F.2d 1460 (10th Cir. 1989) (Oklahoma law); *Orangeburg Sausage Co. v. Cincinnati Ins. Co.*, 450 S.E.2d 66 (S.C. Ct. App. 1994). Compare *Voland v. Farmers Ins. Co.*, 943 P.2d 808 (Ariz. Ct. App. 1997) (no bad faith liability was incurred by insurer who insisted on arbitrating entire amount owed to insured under uninsured motorist policy, thereby delaying payment of amount indisputably owed); *Keefe v. Prudential Prop. & Casualty Ins. Co.*, 203 F.3d 218 (3d Cir. 2000) (Pennsylvania law) (insurer is not required to pay undisputed portion of uninsured motorist claim unless insured requests partial payment). See also *Cook v. Trinity Universal Corp.*, 584 So. 2d 813 (Ala. 1991), affirming summary judgment for the insurer, where the Alabama Supreme Court justified a related tactic in terms of the public policy that encourages the settlement of disputes through compromise.

—In *Hartford Roman Catholic Diocesan Corp. v. Interstate Fire & Casualty Co.*, 199 F. Supp. 3d 559, *aff'd*, 905 F.3d 84 (2d Cir. 2018), the federal district court applied Connecticut's heightened standard for insurer bad faith, holding that the insurer's dilatory conduct due to "failing to affirm or deny . . . claims on the basis of missing documentation while simultaneously failing to ask for documentation," while "certainly negligent, perhaps even reckless," did not arise from a dishonest purpose or sinister motive, and therefore did not constitute bad faith. *Id.* at 601.

—In *Garnett v. Transamerica Ins. Servs.*, 800 P.2d 656 (Idaho 1990), a case involving a fire insurer who repeatedly delayed and balked at paying claims for the costs of rebuilding a damaged commercial structure, the Idaho Supreme Court affirmed awards of $73,458 in policy benefits, $60,000 for bad faith, and $100,000 in punitive damages. The court quoted as follows from the testimony of a plaintiff's expert witness: "This has got to be about the most woeful, inadequate, screwed up file I ever saw in my life. . . . To have this kind of a file in this kind of a claim and to tell me that this is the claim file is ridiculous, it's outrageous, it's just unbelievable." 800 P.2d at 664. See also *Weinstein v. Prudential Prop. & Casualty Ins. Co.*, 149 Idaho 299, 233 P.3d 1221 (2010) (denying motion for new trial, though ordering reduction in punitive damages award, on claim involving insurer's intentional and unreasonable delay in paying uninsured motorist benefits).

—In *Bell v. Steckler, supra,* under Louisiana bad faith statutes La. Rev. Stat. §§22:1892 and 22:1973, the Louisiana appeals court affirmed summary judgment for an insurer under an uninsured motorist policy on the issue of bad faith delay in tendering coverage where the insured failed to overcome a showing of reasonable disagreement as to whether the accident caused the insured's injuries.

—In *River Farm Realty Trust v. Farm Fam. Casualty Ins. Co.*, 360 F. Supp. 3d 31 (D. Mass. 2019), *aff'd*, 943 F.3d 27 (1st Cir. 2019), the court held that delays in handling the insured's claims resulted from the insurer's record-keeping errors and other carelessness, and did not constitute the type of "extreme or egregious business wrongs" needed to give rise to liability under Mass. Gen. Laws chs. 93A and 176D. See also §1.37.

—Concerning delay in paying a legitimate claim as grounds for a finding of statutory liability under Missouri law for "vexatious refusal to pay," (V.A.M.S. §375.420), see *Dhyne v. State Farm Fire & Casualty Co.*, 188 S.W.3d 454 (Mo. banc 2006).

—Reversing summary judgment in *Shelton v. State Farm Mut. Auto. Ins. Co.*, 337 Mont. 378, 160 P.3d 531 (2007), the Montana Supreme Court held that genuine issues of material fact were raised by evidence of the insurer's failure to settle the claim in question for 3 years. The plaintiff showed a failure by the insurer to collect records and reports and to share important information among experts, the court explained, and the insurer had refused to pay benefits less than or equal to the minimum shown by internal evaluations.

—In *LeRette v. American Med. Security, Inc.*, 270 Neb. 545, 705 N.W.2d 41 (2005), the Supreme Court of Nebraska emphasized that even if an insurer ultimately pays a claim, its initial denial of the claim may provide the basis for a viable cause of action for breach of the implied covenant. The Eighth Circuit in *Hayes v. Met. Prop. & Casualty Ins. Co.*, 908 F.3d 370 (8th Cir. 2018), upheld an award of bad faith damages to an insured where the insurer had waited 18 months before asserting that the insured's policy was rescinded *ab initio* based on information it had 5 days after learning of the insured's claim.

—In *Lola Roberts Beauty Salon, Inc. v. Leading Ins. Grp. Ins. Co.*, 160 A.D.3d 824, 76 N.Y.S.3d 79 (2018), the court affirmed summary judgment in favor of insurer on insured's claim for consequential damages in an action for breach of contract and breach of the implied convent of good faith and fair dealing. The court held that the insurer made a prima facie showing that the alleged delay was not the proximate cause of the insurer's loss of its business, where it was undisputed that a stop work order issued by a government agency prevented the insured from securing the necessary work permits to repair water damage prior to the time the insured permanently ceased operations.

In *D.K. Prop., Inc. v. Nat'l Union Fire Ins. Co.*, 168 A.D.3d 505, 92 N.Y.S.3d 231 (2019), the court allowed the insured's claim for breach of the implied covenant of good faith and fair dealing to proceed where some of the allegations indicated that damages could have been foreseeable at the time the contract was made. The insured made an insurance claim after construction on an adjoining building damaged its building, and the insured alleged that the insurer engaged in delays during the claims process, including making unreasonable and burdensome demands for information over a 3-year period. The court stated that foreseeability should be decided on a fully developed record, not on a motion to dismiss, and the insured did not need to present a pleading that explained or described how each category of consequential damages was foreseeable at the time of the contract.

Answering questions certified by the Second Circuit, the New York Court of Appeals, in *First Fin. Ins. Co. v. Jetco Contracting Group*, 1 N.Y.3d 64, 769 N.Y.S.2d 459, 801 N.E.2d 835 (N.Y. 2003), and disagreeing with the trial court, which had held that 48-day delay in denying coverage had been reasonable because it was occasioned by the insurer's investigation into other possible sources of coverage, the Court of Appeals held (1) the insurer could not justify the delay on that basis where the denial had, in fact, been based on other grounds, (a purported late notice of occurrence); and (2) given the absence of a proper basis for the delayed notification, 48 days was unreasonable as a matter of law.

—In *Government Employees Ins. Co. v. Quine*, 264 P.3d 1245 (Okla. 2011), the Oklahoma Supreme Court answered in the negative the following question certified by a federal district court:

Does an insurer's refusal to unconditionally tender partial payment of UIM benefits amount to a breach of the obligation to act in good faith and deal fairly when (1) the insured's economic/special damages have been fully recovered through the tortfeasor's liability insurance; (2) the insurer promptly investigates and places a value on the claim; (3) there is a legitimate dispute regarding the insured's noneconomic/general damages; and (4) benefits due have not been firmly established?

—In *Kilmer v. Connecticut Indem. Co.*, 189 F. Supp. 2d 237 (M.D. Pa. 2002) (Pennsylvania law), a federal district court denied summary judgment on the basis of the two-part test for evaluating a bad faith claim under Pennsylvania law: clear and convincing evidence (1) that the insurer lacked a reasonable basis for denying benefits and (2) that the insurer knew or recklessly disregarded its lack of a reasonable basis. While not disputing that a delay had occurred, the insurer argued that its actions had fallen within the limits of permissible insurer activity. The court conceded that the case was not egregious but emphasized that the insurer had never developed any evidence to support its fraud suspicions, nor taken any of the normal actions in pursuit of a fraud claim contention. Moreover, there was expert testimony that the six-month delay in conducting an examination under oath had been unreasonable.

—In *McElgunn v. Cuna Mut. Ins. Soc'y*, 700 F. Supp. 2d 1141 (D. S.D. 2010), a federal district court applying South Dakota law held that the evidence was sufficient to support a finding that the insurer's delay in paying a disability claim had been in bad faith, but a punitive damages award of $6 million, which stood in a ratio of 30-to-1 to compensatory damages, exceeded due process limits and would be reduced to a ratio of 8-to-1, or $1.6 million. The court also held, *inter alia*: (1) an insurance expert's testimony was not prohibited medical testimony where it was offered for the purpose of explaining the significance of certain information found in a medical report in the context of claims determination; (2) evidence related to other claims in other states was relevant to issues of the insurer's intent; (3) jury had been properly allowed to consider awarding punitive damages where there was evidence that the insurer's delay had been part of a scheme that relied on an interpretation of the time-filing provision that was known by the insurer to be incorrect. In *Zochert v. Protective Life Ins. Co.*, 921 N.W.2d 479 (S.D. 2018), the court held that the insured did not demonstrate any lack of reasonable basis for the insurer's delay in making payments, stating that "waiting for an insured to furnish sufficient proof of loss pursuant to the requirements of the policy is a reasonable basis for not paying benefits." *Id.* at 491.

—In 1997, in *Universe Life Ins. Co. v. Giles*, 950 S.W.2d 48 (Tex. 1997), the Texas Supreme Court slightly altered the standard for first-party bad faith liability by specifying that such liability is incurred only where an insurer denies or delays payment after its liability has become "reasonably clear." The previous formulation—delay or denial "with no reasonable basis"—had become "too oppressive" on the insurance industry, the court explained. See also *Minnesota Life Ins. Co. v. Vasquez*, 192 S.W.3d 774 (Tex. 2006); *Allison v. Fire Ins. Exch.*, 98 S.W.3d 277 (Tex. App. 2003).

In *Weiser-Brown Operating Co. v. St. Paul Surplus Lines Ins. Co.*, 801 F.3d 512 (5th Cir. 2015) (Texas law), the Fifth Circuit upheld a federal district court's award of $1,232,328.14 in penalty interest to an insured based on the conclusion that the insurer violated §542.056 of the Texas Prompt Payment of Claims Statute. The Fifth Circuit affirmed that the insurer failed to notify the insured of its rejection of a claim under a policy covering "loss of control" of an oil well within the 15-day period required by the Prompt Payment Statute because the insurer had received "information required by the insurer to secure final proof of loss." 801 F.3d at 519–20. The court rejected the insurer's argument that it had no duty to notify the insured because the insured had not provided every piece of information requested by the insurer. The court concluded that the question triggering the notification requirement was whether the insured had suffered a loss, not the extent of such loss. It ruled that whether information required "to secure final proof of loss" under §542.056 "will depend on the facts and circumstances involved in a given case." *Id.* at 522. The Fifth Circuit in *Agredano v. State Farm Lloyds*, 975 F.3d 504, 507 (5th Cir. 2020), cited *Weiser-Brown Operating Co. v. St. Paul Surplus Lines Ins. Co.*, *supra*, and cases from the Texas Supreme Court in support of the rule that "it is not necessary for a plaintiff to prove that the insurer acted wrongfully or in bad faith" in order to recover statutory interest of 18 percent and attorney fees for violation of the Texas Prompt Payment Statute, Tex. Ins. Code ch. 542.

In *Gusma Props., L.P. v. Travelers Lloyds Ins. Co.*, 514 S.W.3d 319 (Tex. App. 2016), the court analyzed whether an insurer delayed payment under the Texas Prompt Payment statutory provisions (Tex. Ins. Code §§542.051–.061) when it delivered a check to the insured's authorized counsel that was made jointly payable to both the insured and its counsel, and when the counsel cashed the check without the insured's indorsement and retained the full check amount of $1.85 million. The court found that the insured constructively received the check when it was delivered to its attorney under Texas Uniform Commercial Code (U.C.C.) law, and that the insured was bound to its agent under common-law principles. In upholding summary judgment in favor of the insurer, the court commented that creating strict liability penalties for failure to pay would create uncertainty and hesitation for insurers, which would not promote the prompt payment of claims. In *Garcia v. Lloyds*, 514 S.W.3d 257 (Tex. App. 2016), the court held that the insured's late payment claim failed as a matter of law under the Texas Prompt Payment provisions (Texas Ins. Code Chapter 542) because the insurer paid the insured a full and timely appraisal award. For another case on the Texas Prompt Payment statute, see *Hinojos v. State Farm Lloyds*, 569 S.W.3d 304 (Tex. App. 2019) (affirming summary judgment in favor of insurer on claim for violation of Texas Prompt Payment statute where insurer made reasonable payment to insurer within statutory period and subsequent payment outside statutory period was due to delay on part of insured in initiating appraisal process).

In *Lakeside FBBC, LP v. Everest Indem. Ins. Co.*, ___ F. Supp. 3d ___, 2020 WL 1814405 (W.D. Tex. 2020) (Texas law), the plaintiff brought claims under the Texas Prompt Payment of Claims Act (Tex. Ins. Code §542.051–.061) over the insurer's payments for storm damage to the insured's apartment complex. The court held that claims under the statute were precluded where the insured delayed providing reasonably requested documentation to the insurer on one claim and never provided reasonably requested documents for a second claim. The court rejected the argument that the statutory deadlines for payment are triggered when the insurer receives notice of the claim; it stated that the deadlines are triggered when the insurer receives the necessary documentation to process the claim.

—In *Tang v. C.A.R.S. Protection Plus, Inc.*, 734 N.W.2d 169 (Wis. Ct. App. 2007), a Wisconsin Court of Appeals affirmed a judgment in favor of a car owner against the issuer of a service contract. The court held that the evidence supported findings that the defendant's behavior exhibited an unwillingness to be straightforward, and that its long delays appeared to be attempts to induce the plaintiff to act in ways that the company could argue breached the contract and relieved it of any responsibility.

—In *Farmers Ins. Exch. v. Shirley*, 958 P.2d 1040 (Wyo. 1998), the Wyoming Supreme Court held that in a first-party bad faith case involving a delay of payment as distinguished from a denial of payment, the jury must be instructed that liability depends on a finding that the insurer "not only acted without justification, but acted intentionally and used deceit, nondisclosure, reneging on promises, violation of industry custom and deliberate attempts to obfuscate" (958 P.2d at 1050).

§1.12 c. Deception

—In March 1993, a Los Angeles County Superior Court jury, in *Turner v. Equitable Life Assurance Soc'y*, No. BC-013960, awarded the insured $208,000 in compensatory damages and $9 million in punitives for conduct that it said had been part of an egregious pattern of "predatory buy-outs," wherein the insurer delayed payments on lifetime disability policy claims, and then, exploiting the insureds' economic desparation, offered to buy out their policies for a fraction of the policies' lifetime value. The pattern of conduct is thought to have victimized hundreds of Equitable policyholders, and was the subject of a string of suits, nationwide, similar to Shirley Turner's.

And on February 24, 1994, a Los Angeles County Superior Court, in *D.W. Stephan Enters., Inc. v. Gold Cities Ins. Agency*, No. BC-067855, assessed $249,416 in compensatory damages and $6.5 million in punitives against an insurer who had deceptively delivered a policy with an altered policy number and coverage limit in an attempt to avoid paying a claim for the destruction of the insured's business in a fire in the aftermath of the Rodney King verdict.

In *Helus v. Equitable Life Assurance Soc'y of the United States*, 309 F. Supp. 2d 1170 (N.D. Cal. 2004), the court granted summary judgment on a bad faith claim brought by the insured under a disability income insurance policy. Because there was a genuine issue of fact as to whether the insured was totally disabled within the meaning of the policy, the court held that bad faith liability could not be predicated on the allegation that the insurer had misrepresented the content of two medical evaluations.

—In *Rentrite, Inc. v. Sentry Select Ins. Co.*, 293 Ga. App. 643, 667 S.E.2d 888 (2008), a Georgia Court of Appeals reversed summary judgment, holding that the insured could sustain a bad faith cause of action based on the allegation that the insurer had misrepresented the policy's requirements and misled the insured into believing that his failure to provide certain information had voided the policy's coverage.

—In *Adams v. Hawaii Med. Serv. Ass'n*, 145 Haw. 250, 450 P.3d 780 (2019), the Hawaii Supreme Court vacated the court of appeals' award of summary judgment for a health insurer on a bad faith claim where a material question of fact existed as to whether the insurer's handling of a cancer patient's claim for coverage of his treatment was unreasonable. Evidence showed that the insurer may have misled the patient, his wife, and his doctor to believe that an allogenic stem cell transplant to treat his multiple myeloma was covered under his policy before denying his claim.

— In *Salopek Trustee for Salopek Family Heritage Trust v. Zurich Am. Life Ins. Co.*, 446 F. Supp. 3d 886 (D.N.M. 2020) (New Mexico law), the insured's wife and the trustee of the family trust alleged that the insurer misrepresented pertinent facts or policy issues related to the insured's life insurance policy. The court found that the insured failed to present specific evidence to support the allegation. The court also found that the insured's arguments related to not understanding the incontestability clause were unpersuasive where the wording of the clause in the policy closely tracked the wording in the statute, and where a signed delivery receipt showed that the insured received a copy of the policy before its effective date.

—In *Berg v. Nationwide Mut. Ins. Co.*, 189 A.3d 1030, 2018 Pa. Super. 153 (2018), the court vacated the judgment against the insurer on a bad faith claim under 42 Pa. C.S.A. §8371. The court found that the insurer did not act in bad faith where it sent the insured's car to several body shops to assess the damage sustained in a car accident, determined that the car could be repaired and paid for the repair, did not have actual or constructive knowledge that the repairs done were faulty, and purchased the car from the insured when it realized the repairs were faulty. Over the dissent of one justice, the court found no evidence on the record to support bad faith and noted that the trial judge included large volumes of irrelevant information in his opinion.

—Reversing a judgment N.O.V., a Texas Court of Appeals, in *Hampton v. State Farm Mut. Auto. Ins. Co.*, 778 S.W.2d 476 (Tex. Ct. App. 1989), reinstated a jury verdict for the insureds in an action involving the insurer's denial of a claim for underinsured motorist benefits. The jury had awarded $25,000 for mental anguish, in addition to another $25,000 in punitive damages for the insurer's breach of the implied covenant of good faith and fair dealing. The court of appeals explained that the evidence supported the insureds' claim that they had been led by the insurer to believe that a settlement with the tort-feasor was a necessary step toward recovery under the underinsurance provisions. After the insureds had reached such a settlement for the tortfeasor's low liability policy limits, however, State Farm had changed its story, and tried to insist that the settlement with the tort-feasor was res judicata as to any claim by the insureds for benefits under the State Farm policy.

§1.13 d. Wrongful Cancellation

—Discussing and applying the Alabama rule that the wrongful cancellation of an insurance policy, unrelated to any refusal to pay an actual claim, cannot give rise to a bad faith cause of action, see *Baker v. State Farm Gen. Ins. Co.*, 585 So. 2d 804 (Ala. 1991).

And in three Alabama cases, debatable reasons for the denial of claims, sufficient to preclude bad faith liability, were found by virtue of the insureds' arguably untimely payment of premiums: *Aplin v. American Sec. Ins. Co.*, 568 So. 2d 757 (Ala. 1990); *Badners v. Prudential Life Ins. Co.*

of Am., 567 So. 2d 1242 (Ala. 1990); *Scott v. United of Omaha Life Ins. Co.*, 749 F. Supp. 1089 (M.D. Ala. 1990). —See *Williams v. State Farm Fire & Casualty Co.*, 216 Cal. App. 3d 1540, 265 Cal. Rptr. 644 (1990), holding, *inter alia*, that the insurer could not be found liable for bad faith in connection with the cancellation of a policy that did not meet its underwriting guidelines. See also *Schimmel v. Norcal Mut. Ins. Co.*, 39 Cal. App. 4th 1282, 46 Cal. Rptr. 2d 401 (1995) (holding that no cause of action was stated by allegation that insurer's decision not to renew professional liability policy had been based on reasons that violated public policy). Compare *Hailey v. California Physicians' Serv.*, 158 Cal. App. 4th 452, 69 Cal. Rptr. 3d 789 (2008) (purpose of statutory prohibition on post-claims underwriting is to prevent unexpected cancellation of health care coverage at time it is needed most; summary judgment on bad faith claim was precluded by fact issue as to whether health care service plan had delayed decision to rescind policy because of omission of medical history on application until claims submitted exceeded monthly premiums); *Helfand v. National Union Fire Ins. Co.*, 10 Cal. App. 4th 869, 13 Cal. Rptr. 2d 295 (1992) (affirming bad faith judgment on basis of finding that insurer's attempted cancellation had been arbitrary and without legal justification); *Mackey v. Bristol West Ins. Servs. of Cal.*, 105 Cal. App. 4th 1247, 130 Cal. Rptr. 2d 536 (2003) (statutory requirement of 10-day notice of cancellation of automobile liability policy for nonpayment of premium is not satisfied by notice sent prior to date on which premium is due).

—In *State Farm Mut. Auto. Ins. Co. v. Drury*, 222 Ga. App. 196, 474 S.E.2d 64 (1996), a Georgia Court of Appeals held that a grant of summary judgment in favor of the insured was warranted where the insurer, lacking any evidence that the policy had been cancelled, nonetheless denied a claim on that basis.

—In *Peerless Enter., Inc. v. Kruse*, 317 Ill. App. 3d 133, 738 N.E.2d 988 (2000), the court affirmed judgment for the insured in connection with the insurer's unreasonable interpretation of a cancellation request. Following a covered accident, the insurer had interpreted the insured's unambiguous request for a "pro rata" cancellation (to be effective after the accident) as a request for a cancellation retroactive to the date of inception of coverage. The court held applicable §155 of the Illinois Insurance Code, which provides an extracontractual remedy for an insurer's refusal to recognize liability in a vexatious and unreasonable manner.

—Representing the consensus view that an insurer's duty of good faith does not come into play in connection with the decision whether or not to renew a policy, see *Ansalve v. State Farm Mut. Auto. Ins. Co.*, 737 So. 2d 948 (La. Ct. App. 1999).

—It was held in *Guy v. Commonwealth Life Ins. Co.*, 894 F.2d 1407 (5th Cir. 1990) (Mississippi law), that rescission of a health insurance policy had not been justified on the basis of errors and omissions on the application relating to the applicant's medical history, where the insurer's agent had filled in the incorrect answers without asking the applicant the questions.

—The Eighth Circuit in *Hayes v. Met. Prop. & Casualty Ins. Co.*, 908 F.3d 370 (8th Cir. 2018) (Nebraska law), upheld an award of damages to an insured for the insurer's bad faith and rejected the insurer's argument that it had rescinded the insurance policy *ab initio* due to alleged misrepresentations on the application. The court upheld the federal district court's conclusion that the insurer did not prove that the insured made misrepresentations to the insurer's detriment. In any event, the courts concluded, the insurer was estopped from claiming policy rescission because it had waited 18 months before asserting that the insured's policy was rescinded based on information it had 5 days after learning of the insured's claim.

— In *Salopek Trustee for Salopek Family Heritage Trust v. Zurich Am. Life Ins. Co.*, 446 F. Supp. 3d 886 (D.N.M. 2020) (New Mexico law), the insured's wife and the trustee of the family trust alleged bad faith after the insurer rescinded the life insurance policy following the insured's death. The policy contained an incontestability clause, which allowed the insurer to rescind the policy within 2 years of issuance if it found the insured made a misrepresentation on the application. The court granted summary judgment in favor of the insurer where the insurer had a reasonable basis for the denial of benefits based on evidence that the insured made misrepresentations about his tobacco and alcohol use.

—In *Berkshire Life Ins. Co. of Am. v. Dorsky*, 178 F. Supp. 3d 625 (N.D. Ohio 2016) (Ohio law), the court granted summary judgment in favor of the insurer on the insured's breach of the covenant of good faith and fair dealing counterclaim because the insurer was reasonably justified when it denied a claim that was fairly debatable, and the insurer acted within the terms of the policy when it rescinded the policy two days before the end of the incontestability period. In *Farmers Ins. of Columbus, Inc. v. Lister*, 2006-Ohio-142, 2006 WL 92946 (Ct. App. 2006), an Ohio Court of Appeals, affirming a judgment on a jury verdict in favor of the insurer, held that evidence of the cancellation of the insured's policy in retaliation for his filing of a claim was not relevant to the issue of the insurer's bad faith handling of the claim itself.

—Applying Oklahoma law in *Vining v. Enterprise Fin. Group, Inc.*, 148 F.3d 1206 (10th Cir. 1998), the Tenth Circuit affirmed a bad faith judgment, including $400,000 in punitive damages, against an insurer who was proved to have engaged in a systematic scheme of cancelling or rescinding policies (on the ground of purportedly "material" misrepresentations) as soon as a claim was made, without determining whether it had good cause to do so. That conduct constituted bad faith, the court held, whether or not a legitimate coverage dispute was ultimately found to exist in the case of the present plaintiff. Compare *Edens v. Netherlands Inc. Co.*, 834 F.3d 1116 (10th Cir. 2016), *cert.*

denied, ___ U.S. ___, 137 S. Ct. 1375 (2017) (Oklahoma law; distinguishing *Vining, supra,* and holding that under Oklahoma law insured must be entitled to coverage to prevail on claim of bad faith).

—Under Pennsylvania law, it was held in *Perkins v. State Farm Ins. Co.,* 589 F. Supp. 2d 559 (M.D. Pa. 2008), that a statutory bad faith claim was stated by the allegation that, in wrongfully terminating the insured's first-party medical coverage, the insurer had abused the peer review organization process by engaging a PRO that did substantial work for the insurer and thus had a financial interest in providing a biased determination.

In *Power v. Erie Family Life Ins. Co.,* 813 Fed. Appx. 751 (3d Cir. 2020) (Pennsylvania law), the court upheld summary judgment for the insurer on the claim by the owner of a life insurance policy owner that the insurer acted in bad faith by failing to notify the owner that the policy was about to lapse due to nonpayment of the premium. The insurer sent notices, although it had no contractual duty to provide them; its business practice to send such notices did not establish such a duty; and in any event the owner failed to receive the notices because he did not provide correct address information to the insurer.

—In *Mitchell v. Fortis Ins. Co.,* 686 S.E.2d 176 (S.C. 2009), the Supreme Court of South Carolina, while reducing an award of punitive damages from $15 million to $10 million (see §1.66, *infra*), affirmed a judgment for an insured who proved to a jury's satisfaction that the insurer had rescinded the insured's health insurance policy even after it had learned that its basis for rescission was erroneous. The court noted that evidence that the insurer had engaged in "post-claim underwriting" was probative of the insurer's bad faith.

—In *Johnson v. United Parcel Serv., Inc.,* 946 N.W.2d 1 (S.D. 2020), a workers' compensation insurer terminated medical payments paid to an employee despite a Department of Labor order stating that the employee was entitled to medical expenses related to her workplace injury. The insurer terminated its payments after consulting with an attorney who told the insurer it could terminate the payments after a neurologist determined that the employee's former employment no longer contributed to her condition. The court found the termination of benefits to be unreasonable because the insurer was required to use the statutory procedure to modify the Department order before terminating payments. However, the court remanded the case for a new trial, finding that the lower court erred by preventing the insurer from presenting evidence to support its advice-of-counsel defense. Such evidence was critical for the jury's determination of whether the insurer knew there was no reasonable basis for terminating payments.

—A Texas Court of Appeals, in *Koral Indus., Inc. v. Security-Conn. Life Ins. Co.*, 788 S.W.2d 136 (Tex. Ct. App. 1990), reversed a judgment for the insured on several extra-contractual causes of action arising from the insurer's handling of a claim on a life insurance policy. The court reasoned that the insurer's right to rescind the policy was established by a jury finding that the insured had intentionally misrepresented his medical history, and that given the insurer's right to rescind, and the consequent failure of the insured's contract cause of action, it would be inconsistent to impose extra-contractual liability on the insurer in connection with its handling of the (invalid) claim. Other Texas courts, however, have recognized that the unreasonable cancellation of a policy may support a bad faith claim: *Union Bankers Ins. Co. v. Shelton*, 889 S.W.2d 278 (Tex. 1994); *Hopkins v. Highlands Ins. Co.*, 838 S.W.2d 819 (Tex. Ct. App. 1992) (reversing summary judgment); *Parsaie v. United Olympia Life Ins. Co.*, 29 F.3d 219 (5th Cir. 1994) (Texas law).

§1.14 e. Nondisclosure of Information

—In *Pitts v. Boody*, 688 So. 2d 832 (Ala. Civ. App. 1996), an

Alabama Court of Appeals, reversing summary judgment, held that assuming the existence of a confidential relationship, the covenant of good faith had required an automobile insurer to disclose to its insured the existence of uninsured motorist coverage. (Whether a confidential relationship existed, the court held, was a question of fact.) Compare *Hanks v. Alfa Mut. Ins. Co.*, 753 So. 2d 1161 (Ala. Civ. App. 1999) (affirming summary judgment; when insured bought limited endorsement to homeowner's policy adding coverage for jewelry and silver, no duty was breached by agent's failure to inform insured of availability of alternative endorsement not subject to policy's dollar limitations).

—In *Peter ex rel. Peter v. Schumacher Enters., Inc.*, 22 P.3d 481 (Alaska 2001), the court reversed summary judgment because of factual questions concerning existence of a "special relationship" that may have created a duty on an insurance agent's part to recommend to plaintiff that she increase her uninsured motorist coverage. A special relationship may arise, the court explained, when the agent misrepresents the nature of the coverage, or when the agent voluntarily assumes responsibility for selecting an appropriate policy. Here, plaintiff said that she had requested "full coverage," and the agent had failed to clarify that request or to inform plaintiff that she had options other than the 50/100 coverage he provided.

—Applying the California rule (discussed in this section of the book), that the duty of good faith requires an insurer to disclose policy terms to its insured, see *Ramirez v. USAA Casualty Ins. Co.*, 234 Cal. App. 3d 391, 285 Cal. Rptr. 757 (1991) (extending the duty to unnamed insureds such as the insured's motorcycle passenger). See also *Pastoria v. Nationwide Ins. Co.*, 112 Cal. App. 4th 1490, 6 Cal. Rptr. 3d 148 (2003) (insurer has duty to disclose to purchasers planned and impending changes in premiums and benefits).

However, a California Court of Appeal, in *Twaite v. Allstate Ins. Co.*, 216 Cal. App. 3d 239, 264 Cal. Rptr. 598

(1989), affirming summary judgment for the insurer, held that bad faith liability could not be based on the insurer's failure to inform the insured of his right to obtain an independent appraisal of his loss, where the insured had never disputed the insurer's valuation.

—In *Adams v. Hawaii Med. Serv. Ass'n*, 145 Haw. 250, 450 P.3d 780 (2019), the Hawaii Supreme Court vacated the court of appeals' award of summary judgment for a health insurer on a bad faith claim where a material question of fact existed as to whether the insurer's handling of a cancer patient's claim for coverage of his treatment was unreasonable. Evidence showed that the insurer may have failed to inform the patient, his wife, and his doctor that an allogenic stem cell transplant to treat his multiple myeloma was not covered under his policy despite knowing that he intended to seek coverage.

—In *Earl v. State Farm Mut. Auto. Ins. Co.*, 91 N.E.3d 1066 (Ind. Ct. App. 2018), the court reversed an award of summary judgment for the insurer, holding that the insured had raised a question of material fact as to whether the insurer acted in bad faith when it failed to disclose the existence of a $2 million personal liability umbrella policy ("PLUP") in response to the insured's interrogatories regarding its policy coverage.

—In *Nielsen v. United Servs. Auto. Ass'n*, 244 Ill. App. 3d 658, 612 N.E.2d 526 (1993), it was held that an insurer's duty of good faith does not require the insurer to review the adequacy of an insured's policy when the policy is renewed. See also *Moore ex rel. Moore v. Johnson County Farm Bureau*, 343 Ill. App. 3d 581, 798 N.E.2d 790 (2003) (unlike insurance brokers, neither insurers nor their agents owe duty to insureds to determine "adequate" coverage even when specifically requested).

—A Maryland appellate court, in *Sadler v. Loomis Co.*, 776 A.2d 25 (Md. Ct. App. 2001), affirmed summary judgment on a claim by a policyholder who alleged that her insurance agency had been negligent in failing to provide her with sufficient information to enable her to make an informed decision concerning the amount of liability coverage she should carry. The court emphasized that plaintiff had adduced no circumstances giving rise to any "special relationship," and that her allegations amounted to only a failure to give unsolicited advice.

In *International Bhd. of Teamsters v. Willis Corroon Corp. of Maryland*, 369 Md. 724, 802 A.2d 1050 (2002), the Maryland Supreme Court reversed summary judgment that had been granted in favor of the insurer in an action against a broker for negligent failure to obtain requested coverage. The court held that whether an insured is contributorily negligent in failing to read a policy and discover an error is a jury question that must be answered in light of the particular circumstances.

—In *Clarendon Nat'l Ins. Co. v. Philadelphia Indem. Ins. Co.*, 954 F.3d 397 (1st Cir. 2020) (Massachusetts law), the First Circuit upheld the trial court's denial of a claim that an insurer violated Mass. Gen. Laws chs. 93A and 176B by failing to adequately inform its insured, the property manager, of the basis of its coverage denial for alleged water damage to property, where the property owner's underlying complaint failed to plausibly allege coverage.

—Reversing summary judgment, the Montana Supreme Court, in *Thomas v. Northwestern Nat'l Ins. Co.*, 973 P.2d 804 (Mont. 1998), held that an insurer has an affirmative duty to provide adequate notice of changes in coverage when a previously issued policy is renewed. Whether an insured has an obligation to read the policy depends on the particular facts and circumstances, the court explained, and here reasonable minds could differ as to the existence of such an obligation. The facts of the case involved the insurer's insertion of an expanded pollution exclusion in a commercial general liability policy.

—In *Albert H. Wohlers & Co. v. Bartgis*, 114 Nev. 1249, 969 P.2d 949 (1998), *cert. denied*, 527 U.S. 1038 (1999), the Nevada Supreme Court held that a finding of bad faith and awards of compensatory and punitive damages were supported by evidence that the insurer had failed to inform the insured of the insertion into a medical insurance policy of a new ancillary-charges-limitation provision that represented a significant change in benefits.

—In *Sintros v. Hamon*, 148 N.H. 478, 810 A.2d 553 (2002), affirming summary judgment, the New Hampshire Supreme Court held that, in the absence of a special relationship, the defendant insurance agent had been under no duty to recommend adequate liability and underinsured motorist coverage. Factors indicating the existence of a special relationship, the court explained, include "an express agreement, long established relationships of entrustment in which the agent clearly appreciates the duty of giving advice, additional compensation apart from premium payments, and the agent holding out as a highly-skilled expert coupled with reliance by the insured." 810 A.2d at 556. *Sintros* was subsequently discussed and applied in *DeWyngaerdt v. Bean Ins. Agency, Inc.*, 855 A.2d 1267 (N.H. 2004).

—In *Aden v. Fortsch*, 776 A.2d 792 (N.J. 2001), the New Jersey Supreme Court held that in an action against an agent for negligent failure to procure adequate coverage, the agent was not entitled to present a comparative negligence defense based on the insured's failure to read the policy. And in *Edwards v. Prudential Prop. & Casualty Co.*, 357 N.J. Super. 196, 814 A.2d 1115 (Ct. App. Div. 2003), it was held that the defendant automobile liability insurers who had defended the plaintiff class of insureds in personal injury actions had been under no duty to inform the insureds of their rights under their policies' "Compensation Provision." Those provisions would have entitled the insureds, had they made claims, to reimbursement for expenses and lost earnings caused by attendance at hearings or trials. The court rejected the contention that the implied covenant of good faith requires insurers to advise insureds of their policy rights or to explain express and unambiguous policy language. See also *President v. Jenkins*, 853

A.2d 247 (N.J. 2004) (agents and brokers must exercise reasonable skill in advising customers when placing coverage but need not conduct empirical investigation of customers' insurance situations).

—In *Salas v. Mountain States Mut. Casualty Co.*, 145 N.M. 542, 202 P.3d 801 (2009), the New Mexico Supreme Court concluded (145 N.M. at 551, 202 P.3d at 810):

> Because Defendant had actual knowledge of Plaintiff's status as a class-two insured . . . while a passenger in the insured motor vehicle, we conclude that Defendant had an affirmative duty to disclose to Plaintiff the availability of insurance coverage. . . . Defendant . . . breached its duty of disclosure. Thus, Defendant is equitably estopped from enforcing the consent-to-settle exclusionary provision to limit or deny Plaintiff's entitlement to UIM benefits. We remand the present case to the Court of Appeals for consideration of Plaintiff's claim for bad faith and unfair claims practices.

—Reversing the denial of a property insurer's motion for summary judgment, a New York court held in *Schunk v. New York Cent. Mut. Fire Ins. Co.*, 237 A.D.2d 913, 655 N.Y.S.2d 210 (1997), that the insurer had been under no duty to call to the insured's attention the policy's two-year limitations period.

—It has been held under Ohio law that although an agent has a duty of reasonable care to advise insureds of their needs, there can be no liability for breach of that duty where a commercial insured has breached its corresponding duty to examine the coverage provided and know the contents of its policies. *Island House Inn, Inc. v. State Auto Ins. Cos.*, 150 Ohio App. 3d 522, 782 N.E.2d 156 (2002); *Fry v. Walters & Peck Agency*, 141 Ohio App. 3d 303, 750 N.E.2d 1194 (2001).

—A Pennsylvania court, in *Banker v. Valley Forge Ins. Co.*, 401 Pa. Super. 367, 585 A.2d 504 (1991), reversed the dismissal of a complaint alleging that an insurance broker breached the duty of full disclosure that is included within the duty of good faith and fair dealing. The broker had agreed to change the insured's coverage to make no-fault medical coverage under her auto insurance policy excess to the coverage under her medical insurance policy, without correcting her misconception that the two types of medical coverages were redundant without this change.

Reciting the principle that an insurer's duty of good faith includes the duty to inform the insured of his or her rights under a policy, another Pennsylvania court, in *Goll v. Insurance Co. of N. Am.*, 611 A.2d 1255 (Pa. Super. Ct. 1992), reversed summary judgment in favor of the insurer, holding that the statute of limitations had been tolled by the insurer's failure to inform the insured of pending appellate litigation that later established the insured's right to additional benefits. Compare *Treski v. Kemper Nat'l Ins. Co.*, 449 Pa. Super. 620, 674 A.2d 1106 (1996) (insurer's duty of good faith did not require explanation to insured of collateral consequences of coverage choices).

In *Power v. Erie Family Life Ins. Co.*, 813 Fed. Appx. 751 (3d Cir. 2020) (Pennsylvania law), the court upheld summary judgment for the insurer on the claim by the owner of a life insurance policy that the insurer acted in bad faith by failing to notify the owner that the policy was about to lapse due to nonpayment of the premium. The insurer sent notices, although it had no contractual duty to provide them; its business practice to send such notices did not establish such a duty; and in any event the owner failed to receive the notices because he did not provide correct address information to the insurer.

—In *Pickens v. Texas Farm Bureau Ins. Co.*, 836 S.W.2d 803 (Tex. Ct. App. 1992), the court affirmed summary judgment for the insurer, rejecting, *inter alia*, the argument that the insurer had breached any duty to advise the insured that its liability coverage was inadequate. Accord *Commonwealth Lloyds Ins. Co. v. Downs*, 853 S.W.2d 104 (Tex. Ct. App. 1993).

In *Ramirez v. Allstate Vehicle & Prop. Ins. Co.*, ___ F. Supp. 3d ___, 2020 WL 5806436 (S.D. Tex. 2020) (Texas law), the federal district court held that the insured stated bad faith claims under Texas common law and unfair claims practices statutes by alleging misrepresentations by the insurer concerning covered loss and its failure to conduct a reasonable investigation. The insureds' complaint was sufficient under the Fed. R. Civ. P. 9(b) standard for pleading fraud or misrepresentation. See also §1.26.

—In *Booska v. Hubbard Ins. Agency, Inc.*, 627 A.2d 333 (Vt. 1993), the Vermont Supreme Court, affirming summary judgment for the insurer, stressed that the task of reading and understanding a policy's text is that of the insured, and that an agent is not required to warn the insured about the impact of necessarily complex contract language on every eventuality.

—In *Anderson v. State Farm Mut. Ins. Co.*, 2 P.3d 1029 (Wash. Ct. App. 2000), a Washington court of appeals, reversing in part a grant of summary judgment, held that the insurer's failure to mention to its insured the availability of uninsured motorist benefits was, as a matter of law, a breach of the insurer's duty of good faith. Compare *AAS-DMP Mgmt., L.P. Liquidating Trust v. Acordia Northwest, Inc.*, 63 P.3d 860 (Wash. Ct. App. 2003) (although special relationship created affirmative duty on part of broker to competently advise insured, fact issue existed as to whether insured had reasonably relied to his detriment on broker's failure to advise him of 2-year suit limitation in policy broker obtained for insured).

§1.15 f. Interference With Recovery of Uninsured Losses

—In *Bennett v. ITT Hartford Group, Inc.*, 846 A.2d 560 (N.H. 2004), the New Hampshire Supreme Court reversed summary judgment on a bad faith claim predicated on the allegation that the plaintiff's property insurer had falsely assured the insured that it was pursuing a subrogation action against the manufacturer of a defective clothes dryer which had caused a fire in the insured's home. By making that false assurance and threatening to cancel the policy if the insured conducted his own investigation, the insurer had deprived the insured of the opportunity to gather evidence and pursue his claim against the manufacturer.

—It was held by the South Dakota Supreme Court, in *Julson v. Federated Mut. Ins. Co.*, 562 N.W.2d 117 (S.D. 1997), that a property insurer that had paid its policy limits did not act in bad faith by pursuing and settling a subrogation action against third-party tortfeasors, even though the insurer settled that action before the insured had been made whole. The property insurer, as an equitable subrogee, was not required to delay recovery from the tortfeasors until the insured had exhausted his own efforts to collect from them.

§1.16 g. Conduct Specific to Fire Insurance Policies

Courts in the following cases affirmed bad faith judgments for insureds where insurers were found to have denied fire insurance claims on the basis of inadequate arson investigations or unsubstantiated or insincere arson suspicions: *Livingston v. Auto Owners Ins. Co.*, 582 So. 2d 1038 (Ala. 1991) (prolonged delay based on unsupported arson suspicions raised factual issue as to insurer's bad faith); *Georgia Farm Bureau Mut. Ins. Co. v. Richardson*, 217 Ga. App. 201, 457 S.E.2d 181 (1995); *Norman v. American Nat'l Fire Ins. Co.*, 198 Ill. App. 3d 269, 555 N.E.2d 1087 (1990) (insurer had evidence of fire's incendiary origin and of insured's opportunity, but no evidence of financial motive or of spouse's complicity); *McLaughlin v. State Farm Mut. Auto. Ins. Co.*, 30 F.3d 861 (7th Cir. 1994) (Indiana law; though reversing award of punitive damages); *Wagner v. Midwestern Indem. Co.*, 83 Ohio St. 3d 287, 699 N.E.2d 507

(1998); *LeForge v. Nationwide Mut. Fire Ins.* Co., 82 Ohio App. 3d 692, 612 N.E.2d 1318 (1992) (affirming judgment for insured and award of extracontractual damages, but not punitives, where jury found insurer's arson suspicion to have been without reasonable basis); *Asmaro v. Jefferson Ins. Co.*, 62 Ohio App. 3d 110, 574 N.E.2d 1118 (1989) (reversing award of extracontractual damages because of failure to prove amounts, but affirming bad faith judgment where insurer continued to resist claim on arson grounds even after its own investigation tended to exonerate the insured); *Rose v. Hartford Underwriters Ins. Co.*, 203 F.3d 417 (6th Cir. 2000) (Ohio law; indictment of insured for arson did not conclusively establish reasonable basis for denial of claim; on summary judgment motion, indictment should be considered along with other evidence); *Kilmer v. Connecticut Indem. Co.*, 189 F. Supp. 2d 237 (M.D. Pa. 2002) (Pennsylvania law; denying insurer's motion for summary judgment in case involving evidence that insurer had never developed any evidence to support arson suspicions nor taken any normal investigative actions); *State Farm Fire & Casualty Co. v. Barton*, 897 F.2d 729 (4th Cir. 1990) (South Carolina law; evidence supported finding that State Farm intentionally ignored significant evidence that fire was set by intruders, and used its resources to "pin" arson on insured); *Brooks v. Milbank Ins. Co.*, 605 N.W.2d 173 (S.D. 2000) (insurer knew or should have known that arson admission of insured's friend had been coerced by threats of criminal prosecution if he failed to "cooperate"); *Aetna Casualty & Sur. Co. v. Garza*, 906 S.W.2d 543 (Tex. Ct. App. 1995); *State Farm Fire & Casualty Co. v. Simmons*, 857 S.W.2d 126 (Tex. Ct. App. 1993) (affirming awards of $75,000 in policy benefits, $200,000 for emotional distress, and $2 million in punitives, where evidence supported finding that insurer had begun investigation with intent to deny claim but had failed to discover substantial evidence of arson); *Commonwealth Lloyd's Ins. Co. v. Thomas*, 825 S.W.2d 135 (Tex. Ct. App. 1992) (affirming awards of

$708,000 in actual damages, including emotional distress, and $2 million in punitive damages for the insurer's bad faith in denying a claim on the basis of an incomplete and biased arson investigation); *Automobile Ins. Co. v. Davila*, 805 S.W.2d 897 (Tex. Ct. App. 1991) (reversing punitives, but affirming compensatory and emotional distress damages, where the insurer had denied the claim without investigating implausible aspects of an unsupported arson accusation by the insured's estranged spouse); *Industrial Indem. Co. of the Northwest v. Kallevig*, 114 Wash. 2d 907, 792 P.2d 520 (1990) (insurer ignored and failed to investigate report by own claims examiner that fire's cause may have been faulty wiring; insurer was not entitled to rely exclusively on disputed conclusion of fire department that cause was incendiary). See also *Carrol v. Allstate Ins. Co.*, 262 Conn. 433, 815 A.2d 119 (2003) (affirming award of $500,000 in general damages for negligent infliction of emotional distress in connection with arson accusation, but vacating award of $60,000 in punitive damages); *Hatch v. State Farm Fire & Casualty Co.*, 842 P.2d 1089 (Wyo. 1992) (even apart from reasonableness or unreasonableness of arson suspicions, insurer incurred bad faith liability by virtue of hostile, harassing, and unprofessional nature of investigation).

In the following cases, on the other hand, it was held that the insurers' suspicions of arson had sufficient basis to preclude bad faith liability in connection with the denial of fire insurance claims: *S & W Properties, Inc. v. American Motorists Ins. Co.*, 668 So. 2d 529 (Ala. 1995); *Bush v. Alabama Farm Bureau Mut. Casualty Ins. Co.*, 576 So. 2d 175 (Ala. 1991); *Jackson v. Allstate Ins. Co.*, 785 F.3d 1193 (8th Cir. 2015) (Arkansas law); *Gregg v. Allstate Ins. Co.*, 126 F.3d 1080 (8th Cir. 1997) (Arkansas law); *Kyu Shup Lee v. Crusader Ins. Co.*, 49 Cal. App. 4th 1750, 57 Cal. Rptr. 2d 550 (1996); *Allstate Ins. Co. v. Madan*, 889 F. Supp. 374 (C.D. Cal. 1995) (California law); *Grange Mut. Casualty Co. v. Law*, 223 Ga. App. 748, 479 S.E.2d 357 (1996); *Southern*

Fire & Casualty Inc. Co. v. Northwest Ga. Bank, 209 Ga. App. 867, 434 S.E.2d 729 (1993); *Sheffield v. State Farm Fire & Casualty Co.*, 165 F. Supp. 3d 1375 (S.D. Ga. 2016) (Georgia law); *Indiana Ins. Co. v. Plummer Power Mower & Tool Rental, Inc.*, 590 N.E.2d 1085 (Ind. Ct. App. 1992); *Foster v. State Farm Fire & Casualty Co.*, 674 F.3d 663 (7th Cir. 2012) (Indiana law); *Lummis v. State Farm Fire & Casualty Co.*, 469 F.3d 1098 (7th Cir. 2006) (Indiana law); *Allstate Ins. Co. v. Coffey*, 796 F. Supp. 1017 (E.D. Ky. 1992) (Kentucky law); *Polk v. Dixie Ins. Co.*, 897 F.2d 1346 (5th Cir. 1990) (Mississippi law); *United States Fidelity & Guar. Co. v. King Enters., Inc.*, 982 F. Supp. 415 (N.D. Miss. 1997) (Mississippi law); *Polizzi Meats, Inc. v. Aetna Life & Casualty Co.*, 931 F. Supp. 328 (D.N.J. 1996) (New Jersey law); *Farmers Ins. of Columbus, Inc. v. Lister*, 2006-Ohio-142, 2006 WL 92946 (Ct. App. 2006); *Thomas v. Allstate Ins. Co.*, 974 F.2d 706 (6th Cir. 1992) (Ohio law); *Corbo Props., Ltd. v. Seneca Ins. Co.*, 771 F. Supp. 2d 877 (N.D. Ohio 2011) (Ohio law); *Hale v. A.G. Ins. Co.*, 138 P.3d 567 (Okla. Civ. App. 2006); *Trahan v. Fire Ins. Exch.*, 179 S.W.3d 669 (Tex. App. 2005); *State Farm Fire & Casualty Co. v. Vandiver*, 970 S.W.2d 109 (Tex. Ct. App. 1998); *State Farm Lloyds, Inc. v. Polasek*, 847 S.W.2d 279 (Tex. Ct. App. 1992); *St. Paul Lloyd's Ins. Co. v. Fong Chun Huang*, 808 S.W.2d 524 (Tex. Ct. App. 1991); *St. Paul Guardian Ins. Co. v. Luker*, 801 S.W.2d 614 (Tex. Ct. App. 1990); *Thrash v. State Farm Fire & Casualty Co.*, 992 F.2d 1354 (5th Cir. 1993) (Texas law); *Tucker v. State Farm Fire & Casualty Co.*, 981 F. Supp. 461 (S.D. Tex. 1997) (Texas law); *State Farm Fire & Casualty Co. v. Woods*, 925 F. Supp. 1174 (E.D. Tex. 1996) (Texas law); *Standard Fire Ins. Co. v. Rominger*, 827 F. Supp. 1277 (S.D. Tex. 1993) (Texas law); *Dixon v. State Farm Fire & Casualty Co.*, 799 F. Supp. 691 (S.D. Tex. 1992) (Texas law); *Young v. Fire Ins. Exch.*, 182 P.3d 911 (Utah Ct. App. 2008); *State Farm Fire & Casualty Co. v. Walker*, 157 Wis. 2d 459, 459 N.W.2d 605 (Ct. App. 1990). See also *Munoz v. State Farm Lloyds of Tex.*, 522 F.3d 568

(5th Cir. 2008) (Texas law; federal trial court commits reversible error when it permits plaintiff in suit for fire insurance proceeds to present evidence of his non-prosecution or acquittal on related criminal arson charges).

§1.17 h. Liability of Insurer for Conduct of Agents and Employees

—In *McCann v. Gulf Nat'l Life Ins. Co.*, 574 So. 2d 654 (Miss. 1990), the Mississippi Supreme Court, reversing a directed verdict for the insurer, applied the minority Mississippi rule according to which an insurer can be held fully liable for both actual and punitive damages, for the misconduct of its agents, without any requirement of authorization or ratification. The case involved allegations of fraud on the part of an agent in "assisting" the insureds in filling out applications for burial insurance policies. The court cited the following Mississippi cases as standing for insurer's liability for punitive damages in connection with agent fraud or misrepresentation in the application process: *Andrew Jackson Life Ins. Co. v. Williams*, 566 So. 2d 1172 (Miss. 1990); *National Life & Accident Ins. Co. v. Miller*, 484 So. 2d 329 (Miss. 1985); and *Southern United Life Ins. Co. v. Caves*, 481 So. 2d 764 (Miss. 1985). For a Fifth Circuit decision applying the same Mississippi rule, see *Nichols v. Shelter Life Ins. Co.*, 923 F.2d 1158 (5th Cir. 1991).

—The following additional cases contain discussions and holdings relative to the question of an insurer's liability for the acts of agents and employees: *Walter v. Simmons*, 169 Ariz. 229, 818 P.2d 214 (Ct. App. 1991) (affirming judgment for the insured: dismissal of independent adjuster from case for lack of contractual duty did not require dismissal of action against insurer because insurer's duty of good faith was nondelegable); *Fireman's Fund Ins. Co. v. Haslam*, 29 Cal. App. 4th 1347, 35 Cal. Rptr. 2d 135 (1994) (affirming judgment for insurer against broker: insurer was entitled to indemnity from agent whose negligence had caused insurer to incur bad faith liability); *Vigilante v. Phoenix Mut. Life Ins. Co.*, 755 F. Supp. 25 (D. Mass. 1991) (granting summary judgment; insurer had no duty to investigate criminal records of its agents and was not liable for agent's misappropriation of funds where it was unclear which of several companies agent was representing in the transaction); *Barhonovich v. American Nat'l Ins. Co.*, 947 F.2d 775 (5th Cir. 1991) (Mississippi law; affirming summary judgment: insurer's local agent had neither express nor apparent authority to defraud insured, and insurer therefore was not bound by agent's actions with respect either to simple breach of contract claim, or to claim for punitive damages for willful and malicious breach of contract). But see, *contra*, *McCann v. Gulf Nat'l Life Ins. Co.*, *supra*.

—A Texas Court of Appeals, in *William H. McGee & Co. v. Schick*, 792 S.W.2d 513 (Tex. Ct. App. 1990), upheld the bad faith liability of an insurance company's managing agent, who issued policies on behalf of the company, collected premiums, and paid claims. The court rejected the argument that the agent, as a nonparty to the insurance contract, was not bound by any duty of good faith and fair dealing. The court reasoned that under Texas law, the duty of good faith arises from the special insurance relationship, not exclusively from the insurance contract itself. For similar holdings, see *Mazik v. GEICO Gen. Ins. Co.*, 35 Cal. App. 5th 455, 247 Cal. Rptr. 3d 450 (2019) (evidence was sufficient to show that employee of insurer was managing agent where employee had substantial independent authority and judgment to handle claims exceeding $35,000 and broad regional powers over adjusters and managers in cases up to $100,000; conduct of employee was sufficient to support punitive damages award against insurer for $1 million where employee intentionally omitted important facts about insured's medical condition in reports and in information given to insurer's experts and grossly trivialized insured's diagnoses and treatments); *Williams v. Farmers*

Ins. Group, Inc., 781 P.2d 156 (Colo. Ct. App. 1989) (insurer's "attorney-in-fact" and management company for claims handling purposes was subject to bad faith liability despite lack of direct contractual relationship with insured: to hold otherwise would deny insureds recovery from claims-handling entity primarily responsible for their damages); *Londo v. McLaughlin*, 402 Pa. Super. 527, 587 A.2d 744 (1991) (reversing dismissal: duty of good faith applies to insurance brokers as well as to insurers themselves); *Banker v. Valley Forge Ins. Co.*, 401 Pa. Super. 367, 585 A.2d 504 (1991) (same). Compare *HB Dev., LLC v. Western Pac. Mut. Ins.*, 86 F. Supp. 3d 1164 (E.D. Wash. 2015) (Washington law; insurance agent could not be liable for bad faith failure to defend or indemnify an insured); *Tenner v. Prudential Ins. Co. of Am.*, 872 F. Supp. 1571 (E.D. Tex. 1994) (insurance agents cannot be held individually liable for breach of employer's duty of good faith).

§1.18 i. Liability of Insurer for Conduct of Soliciting Agents

—A soliciting agent had apparent authority to bind the insurer so that his misrepresentations as to coverage were attributable to the insurer, a Texas Court of Appeals held in *Paramount Nat'l Life Ins. Co. v. Williams*, 772 S.W.2d 255 (Tex. Ct. App. 1989), affirming a judgment for the insured on causes of action for breach of contract, bad faith, fraud, and violations of both the Texas Insurance Code and the Texas Deceptive Trade Practices Act, in connection with denial of health insurance claims and cancellation of the policy for nondisclosure of the insured's full medical history. The soliciting agent had informed the insured that the company needed to know an applicant's medical history for the past five years, and had recorded only that limited information. The court rejected the insurer's argument that the soliciting agent could not bind the insurer on a theory of either actual or apparent authority.

Compare *Nationwide Mut. Fire Ins. Co. v. Pabon*, 903
So. 2d 759 (Ala. 2004) (where insured signed application,
insurer could lawfully deny payment under homeowner's
policy on grounds of material misrepresentations regardless of agent's role in inserting false information); *Sherrin
v. Northwestern Nat'l Life Ins. Co.*, 2 F.3d 373 (11th Cir.
1993) (Alabama law; where agent was responsible for misrepresentation concerning insured's nonsmoker status, insurer was liable for breach of contract when it refused to
pay claim, but was not liable for bad faith in absence of
evidence that insurer had reason to have known that agent,
not the insured, was source of misrepresentation); *Neil v.
Nationwide Mut. Fire Ins. Co.*, 81 Ark. App. 67, 98 S.W.3d
448 (2003) (insurer cannot avoid liability on basis of facts
misstated in application as result of fraud, negligence, or
mistake on part of agent acting within real or apparent
scope of authority); *Hall v. Modern Woodmen of Am.*, 882
F. Supp. 830 (E.D. Ark. 1994), *aff'd*, 68 F.3d 1120 (8th Cir.
1995) (Arkansas law; soliciting agent's knowledge of false
information on application for life insurance could not be
imputed to insurer where agent was not shown to have apparent authority to bind insurer); *R & B Auto Ctr., Inc. v.
Farmers Group, Inc.*, 140 Cal. App. 4th 327, 44 Cal. Rptr. 3d
426 (2006) (agent's failure to deliver agreed-upon coverage
may constitute actionable negligence, and insurer may be
held vicariously liable for agent's negligence); *Tran v.
Farmers Group, Inc.*, 104 Cal. App. 4th 1202, 128 Cal. Rptr.
2d 728 (2002) (attorney-in-fact for interinsurance exchange
may be sued for breach of fiduciary duty and bad faith);
Butcher v. Truck Ins. Exch., 77 Cal. App. 4th 1442, 92
Cal. Rptr. 2d 521 (2000) (reversing summary judgment; insurer and soliciting agent could be held to coverage that
insured had requested and been promised); *Macey v. Allstate Prop. & Casualty Ins. Co.*, 220 F. Supp. 2d 1116 (N.D.
Cal. 2002) (California law; recognizing that "special duty"
arises, *inter alia*, where agent misrepresents nature, extent, or scope of coverage being offered); *J. Smith Lanier*

& *Co. v. Southeastern Forge, Inc.*, 280 Ga. 508, 630 S.E.2d 404 (2006) (brokers are not subject to bad faith liability under Georgia Insurance Code, and potential liability is limited to terms of policy that broker negligently failed to procure); *Moore ex rel. Moore v. Johnson County Farm Bureau*, 343 Ill. App. 3d 581, 798 N.E.2d 790 (2003) (unlike insurance brokers, neither insurers nor their agents owe duty to insureds to determine "adequate" coverage even when specifically requested); *Golden Rule Ins. Co. v. Tomlinson*, 335 P.3d 1178 (Kan. 2014) (insurance intermediary constituted "soliciting agent," rather than broker of health insurer, and therefore insurer was liable for agent's actions in submitting application for health insurance that failed to disclose proposed insured's preexisting condition); *Holton v. Ak Ins. Assoc., Inc.*, 255 Mich. App. 318, 661 N.W.2d 248 (2003) (Michigan's tort reform legislation does not permit insurance agent sued for negligent failure to provide adequate coverage to allocate fault to entity responsible for insured's underlying damages); *Mladineo v. Schmidt*, 53 So. 3d 1154 (Miss. 2010) (fact issues precluded summary judgment on negligence claim against agency in connection with its coverage advice; but summary judgment was correctly granted on claim for negligent misrepresentation in light of "duty to read" and "imputed knowledge" doctrines; overruling in part *American Income Life Ins. Co. v. Hollins*, 830 So. 2d 1230 (Miss. 2002)); *Owens v. Mississippi Farm Bureau Casualty Ins. Co.*, 910 So. 2d 1065 (Miss. 2005) (agent has no absolute, court-created duty to explain insured's right to purchase additional uninsured motorist coverage over and above amount required by statute; overruling *Aetna Casualty & Sur. Co. v. Berry*, 669 So. 2d 56 (Miss. 1996)); *American Income Life Ins. Co. v. Hollins*, 830 So. 2d 1230 (Miss. 2002), *overruled in part by Mladineo v. Schmidt, supra* (affirming judgment for insured and awards of actual and punitive damages; evidence supported finding that agent had apparent authority to bind insurer when he filled out application for insured but omitted significant facts that insured had fully disclosed, and insurer's rescission of policy after claims were made constituted bad faith); *Salopek Trustee for Salopek Family Heritage Trust v. Zurich Am. Life Ins. Co.*, 446 F. Supp. 3d 886 (D.N.M. 2020) (New Mexico law; even if insurer's agent had knowledge of misrepresentation on life insurance application and that knowledge could be imputed to insurer, that imputed knowledge did not void contract provisions, although it might estop insurer from asserting them); *Luther v. Seawell*, 662 S.E.2d 1 (N.C. Ct. App. 2008) (by signing application, insured adopted representations as his own, and fact that agent physically filled out form did not support claims against insurer and agent for failure to procure insurance and fraud); *Greenburg v. Life Ins. Co.*, 177 F.3d 507 (6th Cir. 1999) (reversing dismissal; predicting that, under circumstances, Ohio law would recognize claim that insurer had breached duty of good faith based on agent's dishonest sales tactics); *City Nat'l Bank & Trust Co. v. Jackson Nat'l Life Ins. Co.*, 804 P.2d 463 (Okla. Ct. App. 1990) (Oklahoma law does not impute agent's knowledge to insurer for purposes of imposing bad faith liability); *Oulds v. Principal Mut. Life Ins. Co.*, 6 F.3d 1431 (10th Cir. 1993) (Oklahoma law; same); *Willis v. Midland Risk Ins. Co.*, 42 F.3d 607 (10th Cir. 1994) (Oklahoma law; soliciting agent may bind insurer by acts, agreements, and representations properly made in connection with application, and misunderstanding between soliciting agent and underwriting agent may not be basis of defense to liability for bad faith); *Miller v. Miller Creek Homes, Inc.*, 195 Or. App. 310, 97 P.3d 687 (2004) (where evidence showed that company, its agent, and customer all understood that agent owed primary allegiance to company, agent could not be sued for economic damages resulting from alleged negligence in arranging for effective date of homeowner's policy); *Toy v. Metropolitan Life Ins. Co.*, 593 Pa. 20, 928 A.2d 186 (2007) (statute authorizing award of punitive damages for insurer's bad faith does not extend to allegations that insurer engaged in deceptive or unfair conduct in soliciting insured to purchase policy); *Al's Café, Inc. v. Sanders Ins. Agency*, 2003 PA Super. 110, 820 A.2d 745 (2003) (recognizing that agent/broker's duty of reasonable care includes duty to ascertain whether selected insurer is reputable and financially sound); *Pressley v. The Travelers Prop. Casualty Corp.*, 2003 PA Super. 58, 817 A.2d 1131 (2003) (automobile liability insurer and its agent were jointly and severally liable for agent's misrepresentations concerning coverage); *The Northwestern Mut. Life Ins. Co. v. Babayan*, 430 F.3d 121 (3d Cir. 2005) (Pennsylvania law; agent was not liable for negligence even if insured had relied on his advice when answering certain questions on disability income application; policy rescission had been based on insured's bad faith response to another question and there was therefore no causal relation between agent's conduct and injury to insured); *Maryland Ins. Co. v. Head Indus. Coatings & Servs., Inc.*, 906 S.W.2d 218 (Tex. Ct. App. 1995) (agent's knowledge that clerical error had deprived insured of intended coverage could be imputed to insurer for bad faith purposes); *Parsaie v. United Olympia Life Ins. Co.*, 29 F.3d 219 (5th Cir. 1994) (Texas law; reversing summary judgment; actions of soliciting agent could be imputed to insurer for purposes of recovering against insurer for deceptive practices and negligence). *AAS-DMP Mgmt., L.P. Liquidating Trust v. Acordia Northwest, Inc.*, 63 P.3d 860 (Wash. Ct. App. 2003) (identifying factors that may create "special relationship" between broker and insured); *Trinity Evangelical Lutheran Church & School-Friestadt v. Tower Ins. Co.*, 661 N.W.2d 789 (Wis. 2003) (affirming award of $3.5 million in punitive damages where insurer had refused to reform policy to correct mutual mistake arising from agent's error in filling out application; following *Trible v. Tower Ins. Co.*, 168 N.W.2d 148 (Wis. 1969)). See also *Century Sur. Co. v. Crosby Ins., Inc.*, 124 Cal. App. 4th 116, 21 Cal. Rptr. 3d 115 (2004) (reversing dismissal of fraud and negligence causes of action; insurance company could sue insured's broker where application contained information broker knew or should have known to be false).

—On October 26, 2008, a federal district court jury in Los Angeles awarded a San Diego natural gas supplier $48.5 million, finding that a Delaware-based risk insurance adviser negligently bought a policy that had failed to cover the company's foreign investment losses. The award matched the value of the company's failed investments in Argentinean natural gas companies. The company proved that the defendant had bought an "off-the-shelf" insurance plan from AIG that was not geared to the vagaries of foreign economies. (The plaintiff's losses resulted from a 2002 change in Argentinean economic policy that eliminated a promise that returns on foreign investments would be paid in dollars rather than pesos.) *Sempra Energy v. Marsh USA, Inc.*, CV075431SJO.

§1.19 j.　Liability of Insurer for Conduct of Claims Agents

—Also holding that independent claims adjusters owe no duty of good faith to insureds: *Sanchez v. Lindsey Morden Claims Servs., Inc.*, 72 Cal. App. 4th 249, 84 Cal. Rptr. 2d 799 (1999); *Scribner v. A.I.U. Ins. Co.*, 43 Conn. Supp. 147, 647 A.2d 48 (Super. Ct. 1994); *King v. National Sec. Fire & Casualty Co.*, 656 So. 2d 1338 (Fla. Dist. Ct. App. 1995); *Schwartz v. State Farm Mut. Auto. Ins. Co.*, 174 F.3d 875 (7th Cir. 1999) (Indiana law); *Wolverton v. Bullock*, 35 F. Supp. 2d 1278 (D. Kan. 1998) (Kansas law); *Eubanks v. GAB Business Servs., Inc.*, 909 S.W.2d 212 (Tex. Ct. App. 1995); *Coffman v. Scott Wetzel Servs., Inc.*, 908 S.W.2d 516 (Tex. Ct. App. 1995); *Natividad v. Alexsis, Inc.*, 875 S.W.2d 695 (Tex. 1994); *Hung Duc Bui v. St. Paul Mercury Ins. Co.*, 981 F.2d 209 (5th Cir. 1993) (Texas law).

—In *Textron Financial Corp. v. National Union Fire Ins. Co.*, 118 Cal. App. 4th 1061, 13 Cal. Rptr. 3d 586 (2004), *disapproved on other grounds by Zhang v. Superior Court (Cal. Cap. Ins. Co.)*, 57 Cal. 4th 364, 304 P.3d 163 (2013), it was held by a California Court of Appeal that an independent company hired to administer an insurer's policies was a "managing agent" whose tortious attempts to mislead an insured concerning the insurer's potential liability could be imputed to the insurer for purposes of imposing punitive damages liability.

—According to the holding of the Colorado Supreme Court in *Scott Wetzel Servs., Inc. v. Johnson*, 821 P.2d 804 (Colo. 1991), an independent adjuster owes a duty of good faith to an insured despite the absence of a direct contractual relationship. See also *Jordan v. City of Aurora*, 876 P.2d 38 (Colo. Ct. App. 1993) (applying *Scott Wetzel* holding retroactively).

—Under Mississippi law, an independent adjuster can only incur independent liability when its conduct constitutes gross negligence, malice, or reckless disregard for the rights of the insured. *Gallagher Bassett Servs., Inc. v. Jeffcoat*, 887 So. 2d 777 (Miss. 2004); *Bass v. California Life Ins. Co.*, 581 So. 2d 1087 (Miss. 1991).

—In *Power v. Erie Family Life Ins. Co.*, 813 Fed. Appx. 751 (3d Cir. 2020) (Pennsylvania law), the court upheld summary judgment for the insurer on the claim by the owner of a life insurance policy owner that the insurer acted in bad faith by failing to notify the owner that the policy was about to lapse due to nonpayment of the premium. The insurer sent notices, although it had no contractual duty to provide them; its business practice to send such notices did not establish such a duty; and in any event the owner failed to receive the notices because he did not provide correct address information to the insurer. The court noted that the fact one of the insurer's agents might have told the policy owner that "nothing would happen to the policy without [him] being notified" did not affect the finding of no bad faith because the agent had no power to alter the policy verbally.

—In *Charleston Dry Cleaners & Laundry v. Zurich American Ins. Co.*, 355 S.C. 614, 586 S.E.2d 586 (2003), the South Carolina Supreme Court declined to recognize a negligence cause of action against an independent adjuster or adjusting company.

— In *Bertelsen v. Allstate Ins. Co.*, 833 N.W.2d 545 (S. D. 2013), the South Dakota Supreme Court explained the four circumstances under which punitive damages can be awarded against a principal because of an act by an agent: (1) the principal or a managerial agent authorized the act; (2) the agent was unfit and the principal was reckless in employing or retaining him; (3) the agent was employed in a managerial capacity; or (4) the principal or a managerial agent ratified or approved the act.

—In *Keodalah v. Allstate Ins. Co.*, 194 Wash. 2d 339, 449 P.3d 1040 (2019), the Washington Supreme Court reversed the court of appeals to hold that Wash. Rev. Code §48.01.030, a provision of the Washington Insurance Code imposing a general duty of "all persons" to act in good faith in the insurance context, did not create a private right of action for insurance bad faith against insurance claim adjusters or anyone else. The court also held that the state Consumer Protection Act did not create a private right of action against insurance claim adjusters, and that actions under the CPA are limited to those by insureds against their insurers.

§1.19A k. Other Types of Bad Faith Conduct [NEW]

—In *Mitchell v. State Farm Fire & Casualty Co.*, 642 So. 2d 462 (Ala. 1994), the Alabama Supreme Court, affirming summary judgment, held that the insurer's duty of good faith did not require it to supervise the contractor it had hired to repair the insured's fire-damaged house, or to expressly inform the insured that it did not intend to do so.

—In *Tanadgusix Corp. v. ARM Ltd.*, 429 F. Supp. 3d 677 (D. Alaska 2019) (Alaska law), a health and welfare trust (insured) brought breach of contract and bad faith claims against a stop-loss insurer after the insurer denied hospital claims and adjusted the terms of a policy by increasing a patient's laser (*i.e.*, deductible). The court held that summary judgment was precluded where the insured argued that the insurer did more than adjust the policy terms in what was arguably reasonable reliance on a misrepresentation clause in the contract; the insured alleged that the insurer delayed resetting the laser until after the patient died, which effectively prevented the insured from switching to another stop-loss carrier.

—In *Cachet v. Gemini Ins. Co.*, 2009 WL 692324 (D. Ariz. 2009), a federal district court held that under Arizona law no bad faith cause of action could be stated by an insured in connection with a dispute over the amount of a refund owed to him following the cancellation of a policy. "No claim was being paid on the policy," the court emphasized, "or defense of Plaintiffs being undertaken by the insurance company. Accordingly, they are looking merely at a pecuniary issue rather than one involving their protection or security." 2009 WL at *2. See also *Beaudry v. Insurance Co. of the West*, 203 Ariz. 86, 50 P.3d 836 (Ct. App. 2002) (no bad faith cause of action could be based on insurer's decision whether to pay dividends on workers' compensation policy, or how much to pay).

—In *Security Officers Serv., Inc. v. State Compensation Ins. Fund*, 17 Cal. App. 4th 887, 21 Cal. Rptr. 2d 653 (1993), a California Court of Appeal, reversing dismissal, held that the implied covenant of good faith and fair dealing requires a workers' compensation insurer to conduct its functions of defending, investigating, reserving, and settling claims with good faith regard for their impact on the premiums the insured will be assessed and on policy dividends it may receive. In accord with its conclusion, the court cited *Corrado Bros. v. Twin City Fire Ins. Co.*, 562 A.2d 1188 (Del. 1989); *National Sur. Corp. v. Fast Motor Serv.*, 213 Ill. App. 3d 500, 572 N.E.2d 1083 (1991); *Transit Casualty*

Co. v. Topeka Transp. Co., 8 Kan. App. 2d 597, 663 P.2d 308 (1983); *Deerfield Plastics v. Hartford Ins.*, 404 Mass. 484, 536 N.E.2d 322 (1989); and *Transport Indemnity Co. v. Dahlen Transport, Inc.*, 281 Minn. 253, 161 N.W.2d 546 (1968). See also *Notrica v. State Compensation Ins. Fund*, 70 Cal. App. 4th 911, 83 Cal. Rptr. 2d 89 (1999); *MacGregor Yacht Corp. v. State Compensation Ins. Fund*, 63 Cal. App. 4th 448, 74 Cal. Rptr. 2d 473 (1998); *Northwinds Abatement, Inc. v. Employers' Ins.*, 258 F.3d 345 (5th Cir. 2001) (Texas law). See also *Beaudry v. Insurance Co. of the West, supra* (reversing summary judgment; insured could sue for breach of contract and bad faith relative to insurer's decision to reduce dividends payable under workers' compensation policy). Compare *Tilbury Constructors, Inc. v. State Compensation Ins. Fund*, 137 Cal. App. 4th 466, 137 Cal. Rptr. 3d 392 (2006) (workers' compensation insurer's performance in handling subrogation, which allegedly led to settlement of third-party claim for unreasonably small amount and significant increase in insured's premiums, did not give rise to cause of action for breach of contract or for breach of implied covenant of good faith and fair dealing); *Blanchard v. Mid-Century Ins. Co.*, 933 N.W.2d 631, 2019 S.D. 54 (S.D. 2019) (insurer's decision to appeal award of workers' compensation insurance to injured claimant was not made in bad faith where claimant failed to prove absence of reasonable basis for appeal; insurer may challenge workers' compensation claims that are "fairly debatable"; post-litigation conduct of insurer's attorney was not relevant; see also §1.20).

In *Ghazarian v. Magellan Health Inc.*, 53 Cal. App. 5th 171, 266 Cal. Rptr. 3d 841 (2020), the court denied summary judgment to a medical insurer who refused to cover the requested amount of service hours for a certain treatment for an autistic child. The court stated that the insurer needed to show not only that a reasonable dispute existed, but also that its medical necessity guidelines were consistent with community medical standards. The court concluded that the insurer arguably did not fully investigate the claim, and that the insurer had a pattern of reducing covered service hours for this treatment when children reached age 7, despite having no medical evidence that supported reduction at that age.

In *Underwater Kinetics LLP v. Hanover Am. Ins. Co.*, ___ F. Supp. 3d ___, 2020 WL 6204628 (S.D. Cal. 2020) (California law), the court denied summary judgment to an insurer on a bad faith claim. The court held that factual issues remained as to whether the insurer conducted an adequate investigation, and whether claims related to computer hacking should have been combined into one occurrence. The insured alleged that a consultant hired by the insurer offered financial renumeration to the insured's consultant in exchange for an opinion that the claims should be combined into one occurrence.

In *Sheahan v. State Farm Gen. Ins. Co.*, 394 F. Supp. 3d 997 (N.D. Cal. 2019), a class action brought by homeowners who alleged that State Farm undervalued their homes when issuing home protection policies and then undercalculated their damages after the 2017 California wildfires, the federal district court agreed that there can be no claim for bad faith where benefits due under the policy were paid, unless "improper claims handling causes detriment to the insured." *Id.* at 1003–04 (internal quotation marks omitted). The court gave plaintiffs leave to amend their complaint with allegations of specific examples of underpayment consistent with the contract terms.

—In *Royal Macabees Life Ins. Co. v. Choren*, 393 F.3d 1175 (10th Cir. 2005) (Colorado law), the Tenth Circuit concluded that the jury had been entitled, under Colorado law, to assess $425,000 in economic and noneconomic damages in connection with its finding that the insurer had acted in bad faith in conducting covert video surveillance of the insured without informing him that his claim under a policy of disability insurance was under investigation.

In *Dunn v. American Family Ins.*, 251 P.3d 1232 (Colo.

Ct. App. 2010), a Colorado court held as a matter of first impression that the insurer has a good faith duty to promptly and effectively communicate with anyone it is reasonably aware legitimately needs information pertaining to the handling of a claim. The court therefore reversed summary judgment and returned the case to trial on the question whether defendant had breached this good faith duty to communicate where, according to the plaintiffs, a contractor hired by the defendant had been unable to obtain the insurer's confirmation that certain repairs would be covered under the policy, causing delay and the worsening and spread of mold contamination in the plaintiffs' home.

In *Zolman v. Pinnacol Assurance*, 261 P.3d 490 (Colo. Ct. App. 2011), a Colorado court affirmed summary judgment, finding no evidence that the insurer had acted improperly in establishing its incentive compensation plan for employees in such a way as to cause adjusters to focus solely on profit in evaluating claims.

—In *Belz v. Peerless Ins. Co.*, 204 F. Supp. 3d 457 (D. Conn. 2016), the court held that a genuine factual dispute remained as to whether an insurer denied a claim with the knowledge that the claim was covered under the policy where the insurer had a practice of not applying the "collapse provision" of a homeowner's policy to a structure that was standing, despite a long-standing principle under Connecticut case law that a collapse may be found if a structure is standing but its structural integrity is compromised.

—In *Bryant v. GeoVera Specialty Ins. Co.*, 271 So. 3d 1013 (Fla. Dist. Ct. App. 2019), the court permitted a bad faith claim against a homeowner's insurance company to proceed under Florida's Unfair Claim Settlement Practices Act (Fla. Stat. Ann. §624.155). The insured had tried to recover compensation for water damage under a homeowner's insurance policy. The insured alleged that the insurer incorrectly denied benefits by invoking a $1,000 water leakage sublimit in its initial formal response to the claim. The court noted that Florida case law does not require a breach of contract as a prerequisite to a bad faith claim, but Florida law does require a court to determine liability for coverage and the extent of damages before a bad faith claim is ripe. The court determined the essential factors to make the bad faith claim ripe through application of the confession-judgment doctrine in the contract phase of the case. The court found that under the doctrine, the insurer admitted to the judgment where it limited its initial payment to the leakage sublimit but then paid the appraisal award of $37,663.62 after the initiation of the lawsuit but before the final judgment.

—In *Ussery v. Allstate Fire & Casualty Ins. Co.*, 150 F. Supp. 3d 1329 (M.D. Ga. 2015) (Georgia law), the court granted summary judgment to the insured on its claim under O.C.G.A. §33–4-6 for bad faith refusal to pay a claim. The court applied *Transp. Ins. Co. v. Piedmont Constr. Grp., LLC*, 301 Ga. App. 17, 686 S.E.2d 824 (2009), to hold that because the insurer had both relied on a doubtful interpretation of the law to deny coverage and failed to raise any defense to the plantiff's claim of bad faith, the plaintiff was entitled to summary judgment. The insurer had "stubbornly rel[ied]" on its position that the insurer was judicially estopped from submitting a reliable valuation of its personal property losses due to an earlier, lower valuable in a bankruptcy proceeding, but its position had no reasonable basis in Georgia law. See discussion in §1.24, *infra*.

—In *Wittig v. Allianz, A.G.*, 145 P.3d 738 (Haw. Ct. App. 2006), a Hawaii Court of Appeals held that a workers' compensation insurance carrier's settlement offer, which included terms requiring the employee's resignation from employment and release of the carrier from liability, did not constitute a refusal to settle for purposes of asserting a claim for breach of the implied covenant. The offer was not nonnegotiable and did not preclude the employee from making a counteroffer.

—In *Cedillo v. Farmers Ins. Co.*, 163 Idaho 131, 408 P.3d 886 (2017), the court noted that a dispute over the amount of claimed damages could form the basis of a bad faith claim if the amount of damages to which the insured was entitled was not fairly debatable. The court affirmed summary judgment for the insurer, however, because the insured failed to show that a genuine issue of material fact existed on the "fairly debatable" element.

—In *Gore v. Indiana Ins. Co.*, 376 Ill. App. 3d 282, 876 N.E.2d 156 (2007), an Illinois Appellate Court, affirming the dismissal of claims by a class of property owners, held that out-of-state insurers subject to a privilege tax did not violate their duty of good faith and fair dealing by allegedly passing the tax on to insureds in the form of higher premiums.

—In an action for bad faith failure to pay underinsured motorist benefits, it was held in *Brady v. Allstate Indem. Co.*, 788 N.E.2d 916 (Ind. Ct. App. 2003) that the insurer who insured both the tortfeasor and the victim did not commit bad faith by allowing its two adjusters to share information.

In *Kimmel v. Western Reserve Life Assurance Co. of Ohio*, 627 F.3d 607 (7th Cir. 2010) (Indiana law), the Seventh Circuit held that no bad faith claim could be based on the insurer's failure to either accept or deny an application for life insurance before the applicant's death, even though the insurer had inexplicably closed the application before receiving requested medical records, and had not sent any notification that the application had been rejected.

—In *Rakes v. Life Investors Ins. Co.*, 582 F.3d 886 (8th Cir. 2009), the Eighth Circuit held that under Iowa law no bad faith claim could be asserted against an insurer in connection with the allegation that the insurer had purposefully underpriced long-term care policies without disclosing planned future premium increases, and had then lied about the reasons for the rate hikes. The tort of bad faith arises, the court explained, only in situations where the insurer has denied benefits or has refused to settle a third-party claim within policy limits.

—In *Mitchell v. State Farm Fire & Cas. Co.*, 954 F.3d 700

(5th Cir. 2020) (Mississippi law), the Fifth Circuit dismissed the insured's claim for bad faith under the handling of a homeowner's insurance policy. The insurer denied a portion of coverage based on an element of depreciation in determining the home's "actual cash value." There was no bad faith because the relevant law was unsettled and therefore the insurer had an arguable basis for coverage denial.

—Applying Missouri law, the Eighth Circuit, in *BJC Health Sys. v. Columbia Casualty Co.*, 478 F.3d 908 (8th Cir. 2007), held that a jury question had been raised as to whether an insurer acted in bad faith in making an actuarial determination that allegedly breached the premium guarantee contract between insurer and hospital network.

—In *Williams v. Union Fid. Life Ins. Co.*, 329 Mont. 158, 123 P.3d 213 (2005), the Supreme Court of Montana held that summary judgment was precluded by the existence of genuine issues of material fact as to whether insurer's failure to include fact-specific health questions on its application for credit life insurance constituted fraud and bad faith. The action arose from the denial of a claim for benefits following the death of the insured, whose application had allegedly misrepresented the condition of his health.

—In *Fernandez v. State Farm Mut. Auto. Ins. Co.*, 338 F. Supp. 3d 1193 (D. Nev. 2018) (Nevada law), the federal district court found that whether the insurer had a reasonable basis to deny the insured's claim was an issue of genuine dispute where the insurer had no evidence to support its position that the insured would have recovered all of her medical expenses from workers' compensation had she filed such a claim. The district court found that a clause in the insurance policy that reduced the insurer's liability by any amount that could have been paid by workers' compensation was a violation of Nevada public policy.

—In *Crespi v. NJ Cure*, 2006 WL 771137 (N.J. Super. Ct. App. Div. 2006), it was held that the insurer breached its duty of good faith and fair dealing by failing to place the insured on notice that uninsured motorist coverage was contingent upon the filing of a lawsuit against the alleged tortfeasors, and the insurer was therefore estopped from asserting the statutory limitations period as a basis for denying the insured's claim.

—In *Aurelius Capital Master, Inc. v. MBIA Ins. Corp.*, 695 F. Supp. 2d 68 (S.D.N.Y. 2010) (New York law) it was held that policyholders stated a bad faith claim against an insurer whose business was to provide "credit enhancement insurance," guaranteeing payments of principal and interest in securities and other financial instruments against issuer defaults. Any issuer selling securities backed by MBIA possessed MBIA's credit rating, but, it was alleged, the companies had undertaken a reorganization knowing the negative effect that it would have on their credit rating.

—Under Ohio law, it was held in *Wilson v. Ohio Casualty Ins. Co.*, 185 Ohio App. 3d 276, 923 N.E.2d 1187 (2009), an insurer violates its duty of good faith if it remains silent about a limitations period in the face of a potential claim.

—In *Berry v. Banner Life Ins. Co.*, 718 Fed. Appx. 259 (5th Cir. 2018), the Fifth Circuit held that Oklahoma law does not recognize a third-party beneficiary's claim against an insurer for negligence. A claim for failure to deal fairly with an insured requires the plaintiff to establish willful, malicious, or oppressive conduct by the insurer. Where the insured mistakenly allowed the plaintiff's name to be removed as a beneficiary of her ex-husband's life insurance policy, contrary to the requirement of their divorce decree, the plaintiff could not show that the insurer acted intentionally and therefore had no cognizable claim for tort damages.

In *Shotts v. GEICO Gen. Ins. Co.*, 943 F.3d 1304 (10th Cir. 2019) (Oklahoma law), the court held that an insurer did not act in bad faith when it failed to pay the full amount of a claim under an uninsured motorist policy because the insurer had waived its right of subrogation to allow the insured to recover the policy limits of the underinsured driver's policy. The court found that the requirement for uninsured motorist insurers to make prompt payment of the full amount of the claim does not apply if the insurer has waived its right to subrogation.

—Reversing summary judgment, an Oregon appellate court, in *Morrow v. Red Shield Ins. Co.*, 212 Or. App. 653, 159 P.3d 384 (2007), held that an obligation by an insurer to process insureds' requests for address changes is encompassed within the duty of good faith and fair dealing. The defendant had failed to record the plaintiff's request for an address change and had sent a renewal quote to the wrong address.

—In *Zimmerman v. Harleysville Mut. Ins. Co.*, 860 A.2d 167 (Pa. Super. Ct. 2004), the Superior Court of Pennsylvania affirmed a judgment for the insured and awards of compensatory and punitive damages, holding that the evidence supported the trial court's finding that the insurer had acted in bad faith, *inter alia*, in refusing to make a "joint loss" payment during the litigation process.

In *Condio v. Erie Ins. Exch.*, 899 A.2d 1136, 2006 PA Super 92 (2006), a Pennsylvania Superior Court reversed a judgment for the insured, holding that under the circumstances the insurer had not acted in bad faith when it selected an arbitrator in a UIM proceeding based on his relationship to the firm of the attorney representing the insurer. See also *Hampton v. Geico Ins. Co.*, 759 F. Supp. 2d 632 (W.D. Pa. 2010) (allegation that insurer repeatedly selected peer review organization with financial interest in providing biased reviews of insureds' medical treatment would, if proven, subject insurer to bad faith remedies under 42 Pa. C.S.A. §8371).

In *Kunji Harrisburg, LLC v. Axis Surplus Ins. Co.*, 447 F. Supp. 3d 303 (E.D. Pa. 2020) (Pennsylvania law), the insured brought a bad faith claim under 42 Pa. Cons. Stat. §8371 related to an insurance claim for wind damage to roof shingles. The court denied summary judgment to the insurer where a genuine issue of material fact existed as to whether the insurer was notified of the claim and ignored it or whether the insurer addressed the claim through a denial letter on a related claim.

—In *Blanchard v. Mid-Century Ins. Co.*, *supra*, the Supreme Court of South Dakota held that an insurer's decision to appeal an award of workers' compensation insurance to an injured claimant was not made in bad faith where the claimant failed to prove absence of reasonable basis for appeal. See also discussion *supra* in this section.

—In *Courchaine v. Commonwealth Land Title Ins. Co.*, 174 Wash. App. 27, 296 P.3d 913 (2012), a Washington Court of Appeals explained that the fact that an insurer reexamines its coverage position and rejects a claim after first accepting it does not, standing alone, establish bad faith. But in the present case, the court emphasized, the trial court's finding that the defendant title insurer acted in bad faith when it failed to abide by its initial assessment was supported by the testimony of the former employee who had made the initial assessment: he testified that the reason advanced for the subsequent denial was "horrible."

In *Leahy v. State Farm Mut. Auto. Ins. Co.*, 3 Wash. App. 2d 613, 418 P.3d 175 (2018), the court held that whether the plaintiff's underinsured motorist (UIM) coverage insurer acted in bad faith when it denied coverage for plaintiff's medical expenses based solely on conclusions of the insurer's expert, disregarding conflicting evidence from plaintiff's expert, was a question of material fact and remanded for trial. The court rejected as "a remarkable position" the insurer's statement that it need only have a reasonable basis for its coverage decision, and emphasized that the duty of good faith and fair dealing applies to UIM insurers.

—In *Trinity Evangelical Lutheran Church & School-Friestadt v. Tower Ins. Co.*, 661 N.W.2d 789 (Wis. 2003), the Wisconsin Supreme Court affirmed an award of $3.5 million in punitive damages against an insurer who had refused to reform the plaintiff's policy to correct a mutual mistake that had arisen from an agent's error in filling out the application for coverage. The court cited and followed

Trible v. Tower Ins. Co., 168 N.W.2d 148 (Wis. 1969). More recently, the Wisconsin Supreme Court held that an insurer did not act in bad faith when it retained funds it received in subrogation when such action was permitted by the insurance policy. *Dufour v. Progressive Classic Ins. Co.*, 370 Wis. 2d 313, 881 N.W.2d 678 (2016).

A number of decisions have held that the duty of good faith does not extend to conduct prior to formation of the contract (for example, to the purchase transaction). See, *e.g., Jonathan Neil & Assoc. v. Jones*, 33 Cal. 4th 917, 16 Cal. Rptr. 3d 849 (2004) (except relative to certain situations involving workers' compensation policies, bad faith claims may not be based on disputes concerning premiums, only on insurers' performance of claims handling functions); *Macomber v. Travelers Prop. & Casualty*, 261 Conn. 620, 804 A.2d 180 (2002); *Simper v. Farm Bureau Mut. Ins. Co.*, 974 P.2d 1100 (Idaho 1999) (limiting tort of bad faith to misconduct in claims handling); *Toy v. Metropolitan Life Ins. Co.*, 593 Pa. 20, 928 A.2d 186 (2007) (statute authorizing award of punitive damages for insurer's bad faith does not extend to allegations that insurer engaged in deceptive or unfair conduct in soliciting insured to purchase policy); *Weisblatt v. Minnesota Mut. Life Ins. Co.*, 4 F. Supp. 2d 371 (E.D. Pa. 1998) (relative to Pennsylvania's bad faith statute); *Frith v. Guardian Life Ins. Co.*, 9 F. Supp. 2d 734 (S.D. Tex. 1998) (Texas law); *Aul v. Golden Rule Ins. Co.*, 737 N.W.2d 24 (Wis. Ct. App. 2007) (Court of Appeals was not appropriate body to set policy that would extend implied covenant of good faith and fair dealing to underwriting process concerning health insurance policies).

See §3.42 concerning an insurer's litigation conduct as the possible basis of a bad faith claim.

5. Defenses in Bad Faith Cases

This section contains discussion of defenses to both statutory and common-law bad faith claims.

§1.20 a. Insurer's Privilege To Consider Own Interests

In the following cases, courts have endorsed the "directed verdict rule," according to which an insured must be entitled to a directed verdict on his or her policy claim to avoid a directed verdict for the insurer on a bad faith cause of action: *Shelter Mut. Ins. Co. v. Barton*, 822 So. 2d 1149 (Ala. 2001); *Burkett v. Burkett*, 542 So. 2d 1215 (Ala. 1989); *State Farm Fire & Casualty Co. v. Balmer*, 891 F.2d 874 (11th Cir. 1990) (Alabama law); *Curry v. Fireman's Fund Ins. Co.*, 784 S.W.2d 176 (Ky. 1989). See supplement §1.10 for a discussion of cases recognizing a "lying exception" to the directed verdict rule, applicable to situations where it is the insured's contention that the insurer's "reasonable" or "arguable" basis for denying the claim is based on intentional falsehoods. A related exception to the directed verdict rule was identified by the Alabama Supreme Court in *Intercontinental Life Ins. Co. v. Lindblom*, 598 So. 2d 886 (Ala. 1992), where the only evidence favorable to the insurer on the coverage claim was the disputed testimony of the insurer's own employees that the insured had been sent notices stating that the policy had lapsed. Accord *Loyal Am. Life Ins. Co. v. Mattiace*, 679 So. 2d 229 (Ala. 1996), *cert. denied*, 519 U.S. 949 (1996). And in *State Farm Fire & Casualty Co. v. Slade*, 747 So. 2d 293 (Ala. 1999), it was held that Alabama's directed verdict rule does not apply in cases involving an insurer's failure to investigate. Compare *Ex parte Alfa Mut. Ins. Co.*, 799 So. 2d 957 (Ala. 2001) (new trial was required on both claims where jury had inconsistently found that insurer acted in bad faith but did not breach insurance contract).

Decisions rejecting the directed verdict rule have included *Linthicum v. Nationwide Life Ins. Co.*, 150 Ariz. 354, 723 P.2d 703 (Ct. App. 1985); *Brewer v. American & Foreign Ins. Co.*, 837 P.2d 236 (Colo. Ct. App. 1992); *Hendley v. American Nat'l Fire Ins. Co.*, 842 F.2d 267 (11th Cir. 1988) (Georgia law); *Reuter v. State Farm Mut. Auto. Ins.*

Co., 469 N.W.2d 250 (Iowa 1991); *Farmland Mut. Ins. Co.*
v. Johnson, 36 S.W.2d 368 (Ky. 2000); *State Farm Mut.*
Auto. Ins. Co. v. Grimes, 722 So. 2d 637 (Miss. 1998); *Al-*
bert H. Wohlers & Co. v. Bartgis, 114 Nev. 1249, 969 P.2d
949 (1998), *cert. denied*, 527 U.S. 1038 (1999); *Bilden v.*
United Equitable Ins. Co., 921 F.2d 822 (8th Cir. 1990)
(North Dakota law); *Skaling v. Aetna Ins. Co.*, 799 A.2d
997 (R.I. 2002); *State Farm Fire & Casualty Co. v. Barton*,
897 F.2d 729 (4th Cir. 1990) (South Carolina law); *State*
Farm Mut. Auto. Ins. Co. v. Zubiate, 808 S.W.2d 590 (Tex.
Ct. App. 1991).

The principle that an insurer does not commit bad faith
by compelling the insured to seek legal redress, as long as
the case involves a substantial legal or factual disagreement, has been recognized in the following cases: *Peek v.*
Reserve Nat'l Life Ins. Co., 585 So. 2d 1303 (Ala. 1991);
Butler v. Hartford Accident & Indem. Co., 585 So. 2d 1309
(Ala. 1991); *McGuire v. State Farm Mut. Auto. Ins. Co.*,
582 So. 2d 1077 (Ala. 1991); *Thompson v. National Health*
Ins. Co., 549 So. 2d 12 (Ala. 1989); *Aurafin-Oro Am., LLC*
v. Federal Ins. Co.,188 Fed. Appx. 565 (9th Cir. 2006) (Cali-
fornia law); *Anderson v. State Farm Mut. Auto. Ins. Co.*,
416 F.3d 1143 (10th Cir. 2005) (Colorado law); *Vulcan Life*
Ins. Co. v. Davenport, 191 Ga. App. 79, 380 S.E.2d 751
(1989); *Fittje v. Calhoun County Mut. County Fire Ins.*
Co., 195 Ill. App. 3d 340, 552 N.E.2d 353 (1990); *Backwater,*
Inc. v. Penn-American Ins. Co., 448 F.3d 962 (7th Cir. 2006)
(Indiana law); *Central Life Ins. Co. v. Aetna Casualty &*
Sur. Co., 466 N.W.2d 257 (Iowa 1991); *Dirks v. Farm Bu-*
reau Mut. Ins. Co., 465 N.W.2d 857 (Iowa 1991); *Johnson v.*
American Family Mut. Ins. Co., 674 N.W.2d 88 (Iowa
2004); *Cornell v. Grinnell Mut. Reinsurance*, 2006 WL
2419134 (Iowa Ct. App. 2006); *Bellville v. Farm Bureau*
Mut. Ins. Co., 680 N.W.2d 378 (Table), 2004 WL 356056
(Iowa Ct. App. 2004) (unpublished); *Bentley v. Bentley*, 172
S.W.3d 375 (Ky. 2005); *Sculimbrene v. Paul Revere Ins. Co.*,
925 F. Supp. 505 (E.D. Ky. 1996) (Kentucky law); *Polk v.*
Dixie Ins. Co., 897 F.2d 1346 (5th Cir. 1990) (Mississippi

law); *Marshall v. Universal Life Ins. Co.*, 831 P.2d 651 (Okla. Ct. App. 1991); *City Nat'l Bank & Trust Co. v. Jackson Nat'l Life Ins. Co.*, 804 P.2d 463 (Okla. Ct. App. 1990); *Bostick v. ITT Hartford Group, Inc.*, 56 F. Supp. 2d 580 (E.D. Pa. 1999) (Pennsylvania law); *Jordan v. Union Ins. Co.*, 771 F. Supp. 1031 (D.S.D. 1991) (South Dakota law); *Provident Am. Ins. Co. v. Castaneda*, 988 S.W.2d 189 (Tex. 1998); *Lyons v. Millers Casualty Ins. Co.*, 866 S.W.2d 597 (Tex. 1993); *Chicago Title Ins. Co. v. Alford*, 3 S.W.3d 164 (Tex. Ct. App. 1999); *State Farm Lloyds, Inc. v. Polasek*, 847 S.W.2d 279 (Tex. Ct. App. 1992); *General Mfg. Co. v. CNA Lloyd's*, 806 S.W.2d 297 (Tex. Ct. App. 1991); *National Union Fire Ins. Co. v. Hudson Eng'g Co.*, 780 S.W.2d 417 (Tex. Ct. App 1989); *Henry v. Mutual of Omaha Ins. Co.*, 503 F.3d 425 (5th Cir. 2007) (Texas law).

In *Tobel v. Travelers Ins. Co.*, 968 P.2d 148 (Ariz. Ct. App. 1999), an Arizona Court of Appeals, while reversing summary judgment, held that the fact the trial judge had (mistakenly) agreed with the insurer on the coverage issue meant that the coverage issue must have been "fairly debatable" and that bad faith liability was therefore precluded. And in *Robinson v. State Farm Mut. Auto Ins. Co.*, 137 Idaho 173, 45 P.3d 829 (2002), the Idaho Supreme Court clarified that the insured, not the insurer, bears the burden of proof on the "fairly debatable" issue. Accord *Engineered Structures, Inc. v. Travelers Prop. Casualty Co. of Am.*, 822 Fed. Appx. 606 (9th Cir. 2020) (Idaho law); *Shelter Mut. Ins. Co. v. Barton, supra.*

In the absence of a bona fide issue, of course, forcing the insured to litigate may subject the insurer to liability: *Norman v. American Nat'l Fire Ins. Co.*, 198 Ill. App. 3d 269, 555 N.E.2d 1087 (1990); *United Farm Bureau Mut. Ins. Co. v. Ira*, 577 N.E.2d 588 (Ind. Ct. App. 1991). (Though it was held in *Republic Ins. Co. v. Stoker*, 903 S.W.2d 338 (Tex. Ct. App. 1995), that an insurer incurs no liability for denying a claim for an invalid reason if a valid reason actually existed.) Courts have disagreed as to whether the existence of a "reasonable basis" is a question of law or a question of fact.

See, *e.g.*, *Filippo Indus., Inc. v. Sun Ins. Co.*, 74 Cal. App. 4th 1429, 88 Cal. Rptr. 2d 881 (1999) (question of fact); *State Farm Mut. Auto. Ins. Co. v. LaForet*, 658 So. 2d 55 (Fla. 1995) (question of fact); *John J. Jerue Truck Broker, Inc. v. Insurance Co. of N. Am.*, 646 So. 2d 780 (Fla. Dist. Ct. App. 1994) (question of fact; emphasizing that "fairly debatable" nature of coverage issue does not preclude recovery for violation of unfair insurance trade practices statute); *DeBruycker v. Guaranty Nat'l Ins. Co.*, 880 P.2d 819 (Mont. 1994) (same); *Wetherbee v. Economy Fire & Casualty Co.*, 508 N.W.2d 657 (Iowa 1993) (question of law); *Dean v. Austin Mut. Ins. Co.*, 869 P.2d 256 (Mont. 1994) (question of fact); *Lewis v. Nationwide Mut. Ins. Co.*, 742 A.2d 1207 (R.I. 2000) (question of law); *United States Fire Ins. Co. v. Williams*, 955 S.W.2d 267 (Tex. 1997) (question of law).

Courts generally hold the foregoing principle to be true even if the insurer is resisting payment of a claim pending judicial resolution of an *unsettled* issue of law: *Attorneys Ins. Mut. Inc. v. Smith, Blocker & Lowther*, 703 So. 2d 866 (Ala. 1996); *Morris v. Paul Revere Life Ins. Co.*, 109 Cal. App. 4th 966, 135 Cal. Rptr. 2d 718 (2003); *Opsal v. United Servs. Auto. Ass'n*, 2 Cal. App. 4th 1197, 10 Cal. Rptr. 2d 352 (1991); *Maddux v. Philadelphia Life Ins. Co.*, 77 F. Supp. 2d 1123 (S.D. Cal. 1999) (California law); *Aceves v. Allstate Ins. Co.*, 827 F. Supp. 1473 (S.D. Cal. 1993), *aff'd in relevant part*, 68 F.3d 1160 (9th Cir. 1995) (California law); *Fireman's Fund Ins. Co. v. Dean*, 212 Ga. App. 262, 441 S.E.2d 436 (1994); *Shipes v. Hanover Ins. Co.*, 884 F.2d 1357 (11th Cir. 1989) (Georgia law); *Enoka v. AIG Haw. Ins. Co.*, 109 Haw. 537, 128 P.3d 850 (2006); *Colonial Penn Ins. Co. v. First Ins. Co.*, 71 Haw. 42, 780 P.2d 1112 (1989); *Masonic Temple Ass'n of Crawfordsville v. Indiana Farmers Mut. Ins. Co.*, 779 N.E.2d 21 (Ind. Ct. App. 2002); *Empire Fire & Marine Ins. Co. v. Simpsonville Wrecker Serv., Inc.*, 880 S.W.2d 886 (Ky. Ct. App. 1994); *Boston Symphony Orchestra v. Commercial Union Ins. Co.*, 406 Mass. 7, 545 N.E.2d 1156 (1989); *Cossitt v. Nationwide Mut. Ins. Co.*, 551 So. 2d 879 (Miss.

1989); *McFarland v. Utica Fire Ins. Co.*, 814 F. Supp. 518 (S.D. Miss. 1992), *aff'd without op.* (5th Cir. Jan. 6, 1994) (Mississippi law); *Dunn v. State Farm Fire & Casualty Co.*, 927 F.2d 869 (5th Cir. 1991) (Mississippi law); *Mastellone v. Lightning Rod Mut. Ins. Co.*, 175 Ohio App. 3d 23, 884 N.E.2d 1130 (2008) (insurer's denial of coverage for loss caused by mold was justified by Supreme Court's subsequently issued decision); *Skinner v. John Deere Ins. Co.*, 998 P.2d 1219 (Okla. 2000); *Bailey v. Farmers Ins. Co.*, 137 P.3d 1260 (Okla. Civ. App. 2006); *Coblentz v. Oklahoma Farm Bureau Mut. Ins. Co.*, 915 P.2d 938 (Okla. Ct. App. 1995); *Devich v. Commercial Union Ins. Co.*, 867 F. Supp. 1230 (W.D. Pa. 1994) (Pennsylvania law); *Shumbert v. Time Ins. Co.*, 329 S.C. 605, 496 S.E.2d 653 (Ct. App. 1998); *McCracken v. United States Fire Ins. Co.*, 802 F. Supp. 30 (W.D. Tex. 1992) (Texas law); *Mencel v. Farmers Ins. Co.*, 86 Wash. App. 480, 937 P.2d 627 (1997); *Samuels Recycling Co. v. CNA Ins. Cos.*, 223 Wis. 2d 233, 588 N.W.2d 385 (Ct. App. 1998); *Madsen v. Threshermen's Mut. Ins. Co.*, 149 Wis. 2d 594, 439 N.W.2d 607 (Ct. App. 1989); *Gainsco Ins. Co. v. Amoco Prod. Co.*, 53 P.3d 1051 (Wyo. 2002). See also *Harrington v. Guaranty Nat'l Ins. Co.*, 628 So. 2d 323 (Ala. 1993) (finding of bad faith was precluded where insurer had honestly though mistakenly acted in ignorance of recent case law); *Tomaselli v. Transamerica Ins. Co.*, 25 Cal. App. 4th 1766, 31 Cal. Rptr. 2d 224 (1994) (insurer could not be subject to "secondary" bad faith liability for choosing to appeal rather than pay "primary" bad faith judgment); *Interiano v. Colonial Life & Accident Ins. Co.*, 460 F. Supp. 3d 945 (C.D. Cal. 2020) (California law; bad faith claim was precluded where insurer reasonably relied on case law for what qualified as accidental death even though court found case law unpersuasive and found for insured on contract claim); *Tozer v. Scott Wetzel Servs., Inc.*, 883 P.2d 496 (Colo. Ct. App. 1994) (employer could not incur bad faith liability by appealing workers' compensation award); *Allstate Ins. Co. v. Jacobs*, 208 A.D.2d 578, 617 N.Y.S.2d 360 (1994) (insurer did not commit bad faith by exercising contractual right to demand trial de novo); *Kunji Harrisburg, LLC v. Axis Surplus Ins. Co.*, 447 F. Supp. 3d 303 (E.D. Pa. 2020) (Pennsylvania law; insurer did not act in bad faith where insurer made reasonable legal conclusion based on uncertain area of law on whether tarp used on roof qualified as roof); *Blanchard v. Mid-Century Ins. Co.*, 933 N.W.2d 631, 2019 S.D. 54 (S.D. 2019) (insurer did not commit bad faith by appealing award of workers' compensation insurance to injured claimant where claimant failed to prove absence of reasonable basis for appeal); *Mid-Century Ins. Co. of Texas v. Boyte*, 80 S.W.3d 546 (Tex. 2002) (insurer's duty of good faith ends when insured obtains judgment against insurer, and no bad faith claim may be based on insurer's appeal of judgment in breach of contract action); *Oram v. State Farm Lloyds*, 997 S.W.2d 163 (Tex. Ct. App. 1998) (insurer's position could not be deemed "unreasonable" where recent Texas Supreme Court decision rejecting that same position had described contrary Fifth Circuit holding as "reasonable" though mistaken). However, in *First Fin. Ins. Co. v. Rainey*, 195 Ga. App. 655, 394 S.E.2d 774 (1990), *cert. granted*, a Georgia Court of Appeals recognized an exception to the general principle. The court affirmed a bad faith judgment for the insured, and awards of compensatory and punitive damages, holding that the evidence supported a finding that the insurer's insistence on litigating an unresolved legal issue was, in reality, merely a tactic in a bad faith war of attrition. The decision to file a declaratory judgment action had made no economic sense, the court pointed out, and since the claim involved a freak accident, there had been no rational need for guidance in dealing with future similar claims. "Surely," the court remarked, "the requirement of good faith demands some sense of proportionality in these matters" (394 S.E.2d at 778). See also *Georgia Farm Bureau Mut. Ins. Co. v. Jackson*, 522 S.E.2d 716 (Ga. Ct. App. 1999) (14 months after notice of claim, insurer was not entitled to invoke "doubtful question of law" that arose only from "implications" of policy, not from actual policy language); *Mixson, Inc. v. American Loyalty Ins. Co.*, 349 S.C. 394, 562 S.E.2d 659 (Ct. App. 2002) (affirming summary judgment for insured on coverage issue but reversing summary judgment for insurer on bad faith claim; jury issue was raised as to whether insurer acted in bad faith in raising argument, never previously addressed by courts, that ATM machine was not a "safe" within meaning of policy).

—In *Guebara v. Allstate Ins. Co.*, 237 F.3d 987 (9th Cir. 2001), the Ninth Circuit clarified that under California law the "genuine dispute doctrine" applies to factual as well as legal disputes, so that existence of a genuine factual dispute permits entry of summary judgment in favor of an insurer on a bad faith claim. Accord *Benavides v. State Farm Gen. Ins. Co.*, 136 Cal. App. 4th 1241, 39 Cal. Rptr. 3d 650 (2006); *Chateau Chamberay Homeowners Ass'n v. Associated Int'l Ins. Co.*, 90 Cal. App. 4th 335, 108 Cal. Rptr. 2d 776 (2001); *Fraley v. Allstate Ins. Co.*, 81 Cal. App. 4th 1282, 97 Cal. Rptr. 2d 386 (2000); *Arness v. Allstate Ins. Co.*, 150 Fed. Appx. 649 (9th Cir. 2005) (California law); *Feldman v. Allstate Ins. Co.*, 322 F.3d 660 (9th Cir. 2003) (California law); *Chierfue Her v. State Farm Ins. Co.*, 92 F. Supp. 3d 957 (E.D. Cal. 2015) (California law); *Adams v. Allstate Ins. Co.*, 187 F. Supp. 2d 1207 (C.D. Cal. 2002); *Cardiner v. Provident Life & Accident Ins. Co.*, 158 F. Supp. 2d 1088 (C.D. Cal. 2001); *Benton v. Allstate Ins. Co.*, 2001 WL 210685 (C.D. Cal. 2001). See also *Fadeeff v. State Farm Gen. Ins. Co.*, 50 Cal. App. 5th 94, 263 Cal. Rptr. 3d 453 (2020) (issue of reasonableness based on genuine dispute could not be decided on summary judgment on facts of case).

A number of California decisions have recognized that an insurer may defend itself against allegations of bad faith and malice in claims handling with evidence that the insurer relied on the advice of competent counsel. This defense was discussed in *State Farm Mut. Auto. Ins. Co. v. Superior Court (Johnson Kinsey, Inc.)*, 228 Cal. App. 3d

721, 279 Cal. Rptr. 116 (1991), where the court held that advice of counsel is not an affirmative defense that must be specifically pleaded. Accord *Vickers v. Progressive N. Ins. Co.*, 353 F. Supp. 3d 1153 (N.D. Okla. 2018); *Larsen v. Allstate Ins. Co.*, 857 P.2d 263 (Utah Ct. App. 1993). See also *Johnson v. United Parcel Serv., Inc.*, 946 N.W.2d 1 (S.D. 2020) (workers' compensation insurer should have been permitted to present evidence of its reliance on advice of counsel in its determination that it was reasonable to terminate medical payments to employee; such evidence was critical piece in jury's determination of whether insurer knew there was no reasonable basis for terminating benefits; such evidence was also critical for jury to determine award of punitive damages). Compare *Giampapa v. American Family Mut. Ins. Co.*, 919 P.2d 838 (Colo. Ct. App. 1995), stating that reliance on the advice of counsel does not preclude an insurer's liability for bad faith; *Peterson v. Western Nat'l Mut. Ins. Co.*, 946 N.W.2d 903 (Minn. 2020) (discussed in this section); Also compare *Blanchard v. Mid-Century Ins. Co.*, *supra* (bad litigation conduct of insurer's attorney was not relevant to determination of whether insurer committed bad faith by appealing award of workers' compensation insurance to injured claimant, and there was no bad faith because claimant failed to prove absence of reasonable basis for appeal).

—In *Peterson v. Western Nat'l Mut. Ins. Co.*, *supra*, the Supreme Court of Minnesota held that the trial court did not err in finding that the insurer did not act as a reasonable insurer would have in denying the plaintiff's claim for coverage, and that it knew or recklessly disregarded information that would have let it know it had no objectively reasonable basis to deny benefits. Accordingly, the court upheld awards to the insured of $100,000 in taxable costs and $97,940.50 in attorney fees under Minn. Stat. §604.18, Minnesota's Insurance Standard of Conduct statute. The court concluded that the insurer's failure to conduct an adequate investigation of the insured's claim under her underinsured motorist's policy, including disregarding a mountain of medical evidence that her automobile accident caused severe headaches requiring Botox treatment, led it to unreasonably and recklessly deny her claim. The court rejected the insurer's defense that it had relied on the opinion of its outside litigation counsel that the insurer could prevail in a jury trial. The court stated (946 N.W.2d at 915):

> Whether an insurer may possibly convince a jury at trial . . . is not the inquiry under section 604.18, subdivision 2. The inquiry is whether a reasonable insurer, having conducted a full investigation and a fair evaluation that considers and weighs all of the facts before it, would have denied the insured the benefits of the insurance policy in the first place.

—In *Zochert v. Protective Life Ins. Co.*, 921 N.W.2d 479 (S.D. 2018), the Supreme Court of South Dakota refused to extend the tort doctrine of "equal consideration," applicable to the third-party claims process, to the first-party claims context. The court explained that an "insurer determining a first-party claim does not act like a fiduciary with respect to its insured as it does for a claim by a third-party against the insured." *Id.* at 489 (internal quotation marks omitted). The court concluded that reading into a first-party contract an implied duty of the insurer to give equal consideration to the interests of the insured as to its own interests would fundamentally alter first-party insurance policies, in which insurer and insured have "distinct and even conflicting interests." *Id.*

In *Lead GHR Enters., Inc. v. Am. States Ins. Co.*, 369 F. Supp. 3d 909 (D.S.D. 2019) (South Dakota law), the federal district court refused to extend the equal consideration duty to the first-party context, holding that there is no duty for an insurer to give the interests of its insured equal consideration to its own in the first-party context, citing *Zochert v. Protective Life Ins. Co., supra.*

—The somewhat unclear position of the Washington

courts concerning summary judgment standards on bad faith claims has been clarified in *Smith v. Safeco Ins. Co.*, 78 P.3d 1274 (Wash. 2003), and *American States Ins. Co. v. Symes of Silverdale, Inc.*, 78 P.3d 1266 (Wash. 2003). Those two companion decisions overruled *Ellwein v. Hartford Accident & Indem. Co.*, 142 Wash. 2d 766, 15 P.3d 640 (2001), to the extent that it purported to introduce a new summary judgment standard by placing the burden on the insured to prove entitlement to coverage as a matter of law. An insurer does *not* demonstrate entitlement to summary judgment merely by introducing evidence of a reasonable basis for denying coverage, the Washington Supreme Court held in *Smith* and *Symes*.

§1.21 b. Custom in the Industry

—In *Texas Employers Ins. Ass'n v. Puckett*, 822 S.W.2d 133 (Tex. Ct. App. 1991), the court affirmed a judgment for the insured and awards of $150,000 for emotional distress and $1.5 million in punitive damages (see §1.66) holding, *inter alia*, that an insured is not required to show the insurer's noncompliance with industry standards and practices in order to prove that the insurer acted unreasonably.

§1.22 c. Ambiguity of Policy

In several cases, courts have held that an insurer's reasonable, even if mistaken, interpretation of an ambiguous policy provision or exclusion cannot be the basis of bad faith liability in connection with the denial of a claim: *H & H Brokerage, Inc. v. Vanliner Ins. Co.*, 168 F.3d 1124 (8th Cir. 1999) (Arkansas law); *Karen Kane, Inc. v. Reliance Ins. Co.*, 202 F.3d 1180 (9th Cir. 2000) (California law); *Franceschi v. American Motorists Ins. Co.*, 852 F.2d 1217 (9th Cir. 1988) (California law); *Freidline v. Shelby Ins. Co.*, 774 N.E.2d 37 (Ind. 2002); *USA Life One Ins. Co. v. Nuckolls*, 682 N.E.2d 534 (Ind. 1997); *Hancock v. Safeway*

Ins. Co., 741 So. 2d 155 (La. Ct. App. 1999); *Williams v. Ohio Nat'l Life Assurance Co.*, 364 F. Supp. 3d 605 (W.D.N.C. 2019) (North Carolina law); *Berkshire Life Ins. Co. of Am. v. Dorsky*, 178 F. Supp. 3d 625 (N.D. Ohio 2016) (Ohio law); *Wolf v. Prudential Ins. Co. of Am.*, 50 F.3d 793 (10th Cir. 1995) (Oklahoma law); *Pressman v. Aetna Casualty & Sur. Co.*, 574 A.2d 757 (R.I. 1990). Compare *Amadeo v. Principal Mut. Life Ins. Co.*, 290 F.3d 1152 (9th Cir. 2002) (California law; reversing summary judgment; insurer's interpretation of policy was sufficiently arbitrary or unreasonable to entitle jury to find that it was adopted in bad faith); *Gutowitz v. Transamerica Life Ins. Co.*, 126 F. Supp. 3d 1128 (C.D. Cal. 2015) (California law; denying summary judgment to insurer on bad faith claim because triable issue of fact existed whether its policy interpretation was reasonable, given available case law and issues of contract interpretation regarding meaning of "nursing home" in long-term care policy; citing and quoting *Amadeo, supra*).

§1.23 d. Failure of Insured To Cooperate

—An insurer's requirement that the insured submit to an examination under oath as a condition precedent to the payment of a claim for residential theft loss was reasonable as a matter of law, the Ninth Circuit held in *West v. State Farm Fire & Casualty Co.*, 868 F.2d 348 (9th Cir. 1989). (Accord *Brizuela v. Calfarm Ins. Co.*, 116 Cal. App. 4th 578, 10 Cal. Rptr. 3d 661 (2004); *California Fair Plan Ass'n v. Superior Court*, 115 Cal. App. 4th 158, 8 Cal. Rptr. 3d 746 (2004); *Globe Indem. Co. v. Superior Court*, 6 Cal. App. 4th 725, 8 Cal. Rptr. 2d 251 (1992).) The court in *West* accordingly affirmed summary judgment in favor of the insurer on causes of action for breach of contract, violation of Cal. Ins. Code §790.03, bad faith, and intentional infliction of emotional distress. (The action, originally filed in California state court, had been removed by the insurer on the basis of diversity of citizenship.) The insured's only contention on appeal to the Ninth Circuit had been that "reasonableness" is always a question of fact not subject to summary judgment. The court noted that both California and federal courts have held that reasonableness becomes a question of law when only one conclusion about the conduct's reasonableness is possible (citing *Terry v. Atlantic Richfield Co.*, 72 Cal. App. 3d 962, 140 Cal. Rptr. 510 (1977), and *McKenzie v. Lamb*, 738 F.2d 1005 (9th Cir. 1984)). For somewhat similar facts and holding, see *Turner v. Liberty Nat'l Fire Ins. Co.*, 681 So. 2d 589 (Ala. Civ. App. 1996) (affirming directed verdict on bad faith claim because of insured's failure to answer adjustors' questions and to be examined under oath); *Knowledge A-Z, Inc. v. Sentry Ins.*, 857 N.E.2d 411 (Ind. Ct. App. 2007) (affirming summary judgment; provision in insurance policy that required insured to submit to examination under oath was not "cooperation" clause but rather requirement that insured perform specific duties; compliance with provision was therefore not optional nor subject to trial court determination of reasonableness and prejudice); *National Athletic Sportswear, Inc. v. Westfield Ins. Co.*, 528 F.3d 508 (7th Cir. 2008) (Indiana law; showing of prejudice is not necessary and insurance company need only show material breach to prevail on claim that insured breached policy provision requiring insured to submit to examination under oath); *Employers Mut. Casualty Co. v. Skoutaris*, 453 F.3d 915 (7th Cir. 2006) (same); *Brown v. Danish Mut. Ins. Co.*, 550 N.W.2d 171 (Iowa Ct. App. 1996) (insured's refusal to be examined under oath was fatal to bad faith claim); *Phillips v. Allstate Indem. Co.*, 848 A.2d 681 (Md. Ct. Spec. App. 2004) (invocation of Fifth Amendment constitutes breach of insurance contract if it leads to failure to answer material questions during examination under oath); *Metlife Auto & Home v. Cunningham*, 797 N.E.2d 18 (Mass. App. Ct. 2003) (insured breached duty to cooperate by invoking Fifth Amendment during examination under oath relative to coverage for fatal stabbing he allegedly committed); *United*

States Fidelity & Guar. Co. v. Wigginton, 964 F.2d 487 (5th Cir. 1992) (Mississippi law; despite pendency of criminal arson charges against insured, fire policy was rendered void by insured's three-month refusal to submit to examination under oath); *Gates v. State Farm Gen. Ins. Co.,* 740 F. Supp. 1237 (S.D. Miss. 1990), *aff'd without op.,* 928 F.2d 401 (5th Cir. 1991) (Mississippi law; fire insurer's requirement of examinations under oath was reasonable and did not unreasonably delay payment, where insureds themselves had twice requested postponements of examinations); *Wright v. Farmers Mut. of Neb.,* 669 N.W.2d 462 (Neb. 2003) (insured's refusal during examination under oath to answer questions about finances and other insurance was material breach that prejudiced insurer as matter of law); *Krigsman v. Progressive N. Ins. Co.,* 864 A.2d 330 (N.H. 2005) (affirming judgment for insurer; insured's failure to cooperate in scheduling contractually required examination under oath justified denial of coverage even in absence of showing of prejudice); *Lester v. Allstate Prop. & Cas. Ins. Co.,* 743 F.3d 469 (6th Cir. 2014) (Tennessee law; insurer's duty of good faith did not require it to show insured its investigative files before requiring her to submit to examination under oath). Compare *Ahmadi v. Allstate Ins. Co.,* 22 P.3d 576 (Colo. Ct. App. 2001) (in refusing to submit to examinations under oath outside each other's presence, co-insureds did not breach cooperation clause of auto insurance policy).

In the following cases, courts have evaluated the consequences of various types of noncooperation by insureds, often reiterating the principle that an insured's own breach of contract is a defense to a bad faith claim against the insurer only if the insured's breach was so serious as to have justified cancellation of the policy: *Cigna Property & Casualty Ins. Co. v. Polaris Pictures Corp.,* 159 F.3d 412 (9th Cir. 1998) (federal law; affirming summary judgment on contract and bad faith claims and granting rescission of policy of maritime insurance on grounds of insured's concealment of loss history); *Bush v. Ford Life Ins. Co.*, 682 So. 2d 46 (Ala. 1996) (insured's misrepresentation of medical history provided reasonable basis for denial of health insurance claim); *Truck Mortgage Group, Inc. v. Crusader Ins. Co.*, 98 Cal. App. 4th 857, 120 Cal. Rptr. 2d 228 (2002) (affirming judgment for insured; evidence supported finding that insurer's demand for unavailable information had been a ploy for avoiding payment of legitimate claim); *Kardly v. State Farm Mut. Auto. Ins. Co.*, 207 Cal. App. 3d 479, 255 Cal. Rptr. 40 (1989), *op. after further proceedings*, 31 Cal. App. 4th 1746, 37 Cal. Rptr. 2d 612 (1995) (right to sue for bad faith was not forfeited when insured settled with tort-feasor and destroyed insurer's contractual right to subrogation); *Milhouse v. Travelers Commercial Ins. Co.*, 982 F. Supp. 2d 1088 (C.D. Cal. 2013) (California law; whether homeowner's failure to provide sworn proof of loss from fire within 60 days after demand meant they did not fulfill their obligation to cooperate such that insurer was not obligated to pay for any personal property coverage was for jury); *Summit Bank & Trust v. Am. Modern Home Ins. Co.*, 71 F. Supp. 3d 1168 (D. Colo. 2014) (Colorado law; denying insurer's motion for summary judgment; "no action" clause of policy that allegedly precluded insured from filing suit due to failure to produce documentation did not apply to bad faith claim; conduct of insurer is at issue in first-party bad faith actions, not conduct of insured (quoting *Emenyonu v. State Farm Fire & Casualty Co.*, 885 P.2d 320 (1994), *reh'g denied* (Colo. Ct. App. 1994))); *Ussery v. Allstate Fire & Casualty Ins. Co.*, 150 F. Supp. 3d 1329 (M.D. Ga. 2015) (Georgia law; granting summary judgment for insured on bad faith denial of coverage claim where insurer failed to establish that insured was judicially estopped from claiming true value of its personal property lost in fire; insured had submitted lower valuation in prior bankruptcy claim but then amended valuation prior to discharge in bankruptcy; insurer submitted no evidence that insured acted with intent to defraud insurer); *Wittig v.*

Allianz, A.G., 145 P.3d 738 (Haw. Ct. App. 2006) (employee could not establish that workers' compensation insurance carrier acted in bad faith in refusing to settle claim where employee failed to respond to insurer's settlement offer and failed to make counteroffer or engage in meaningful negotiations); *Tran v. State Farm Mut. Auto. Ins. Co.*, 999 F. Supp. 1369 (D. Haw. 1998) (Hawaii law; emphasizing that covenant of good faith is not waived merely because claimant fails to abide by terms of policy); *Jacobson v. State Farm Mut. Auto. Ins. Co.*, 30 P.3d 949 (Idaho 2001) (summary judgment was properly granted on bad faith claim where delay in payment had been result of insured's refusal to undergo medical exam and to provide medical releases); *Allstate Ins. Co. v. Fields*, 885 N.E.2d 728 (Ind. Ct. App. 2008) (insurer did not act in bad faith as matter of law in failing to pay benefits where insured had failed to provide completed proof of loss form required by policy); *Jackson v. Allstate Ins. Co.*, 780 F. Supp. 2d 781 (S.D. Ind. 2011) (Indiana law) (1-year delay in denying claim was due not to insurer's bad faith inaction but rather to insured's failure to provide medical documentation of injuries); *Blue Diamond, Inc. v. Liberty Mut. Ins. Co.*, 21 F. Supp. 2d 631 (S.D. Miss. 1998) (Mississippi law; insured's failure to cooperate with insurer's efforts to conduct an audit precluded insurer's liability for bad faith in connection with cancellation of policy of workers' compensation insurance); *Cooper v. New York Cent. Mut. Fire Ins. Co.*, 72 A.D.3d 1556, 900 N.Y.S.2d 545 (2010) (denying motion to dismiss: fact issues existed as to whether insured had valid reasons for failing to provide insurer with requested documents, or whether insured willfully failed to cooperate with insurer's investigation of claim for property damage); *Viles v. Security Nat'l Ins. Co.*, 788 S.W.2d 566 (Tex. 1990) (insured's right to sue for bad faith was not eradicated by his failure to submit sworn proof of loss as required by policy, where claim was denied prior to date proof of loss form was due); *Columbia Universal Life Ins. Co. v. Miles*, 923 S.W.2d 803 (Tex. Ct.

App. 1996) (insured's concealment of medical history was reasonable basis for rescission of policy, even though insurer conducted flawed investigation); *Lakeside FBBC, LP v. Everest Indem. Ins. Co.*, ___ F. Supp. 3d ___, 2020 WL 1814405 (W.D. Tex. 2020) (Texas law; granting summary judgment in favor of insurer for claim under Texas Prompt Payment of Claims Act (Tex. Ins. Code §§542.051–.061) where insured delayed providing reasonably requested documentation to insurer on one claim and never provided reasonably requested documents for second claim; statutory deadlines are triggered when insurer receives necessary documentation to process claim); *Alhamzawi v. GEICO Casualty Co.*, 216 F. Supp. 3d 764 (N.D. Tex. 2016) (Texas law; granting summary judgment in favor of insurer in common-law bad faith claim where insured failed to follow insurer's procedure for requesting supplemental payment for repair of damaged vehicle); *Wickswat v. Safeco Ins. Co.*, 78 Wash. App. 958, 904 P.2d 767 (1995) (insured's misrepresentations were sufficiently material to bar bad faith claim against insurer); *Miller v. Safeco Ins. Co. of Am.*, 683 F.3d 805 (7th Cir. 2012) (Wisconsin law; affirming judgment for insured; insurer had no reasonable basis to deny claim for homeowner's policy benefits based on insured's four-month delay in reporting claim, where delay had been caused by need to contact attorney and to schedule appropriate inspections, and where there had been no resulting prejudice to insurer); *Harper v. Fidelity & Guar. Life Ins. Co.*, 234 P.3d 1211, 2010 WY 89 (2010) (life insurer did not breach duty of good faith by rescinding insurance policy after determining that there were material misrepresentations in insured's application). Compare *Soicher v. State Farm Mut. Auto. Ins. Co.*, 351 P.3d 559 (Colo. Ct. App. 2015) (discussing insured's duty of good faith and fair dealing, which in Colorado is broader than insured's duty to cooperate; breach of duty to cooperate generally bars a claim for benefits, while breach of duty of good faith will not necessarily bar such a claim).

—In a case involving facts similar to those of *Gruenberg v. Aetna Ins. Co.*, 9 Cal. 3d 566, 108 Cal. Rptr. 480 (1973) (discussed in the book), a Wisconsin Court of Appeals affirmed summary judgment in favor of the insurer, holding, *inter alia*, that the Fifth Amendment had not protected the insured from answering the insurer's arson-related questions under oath, and that the insured's claim had been properly denied on the basis of circumstantial evidence of arson. *State Farm Fire & Casualty Co. v. Walker*, 157 Wis. 2d 459, 459 N.W.2d 605 (Ct. App. 1990). (Unlike the situation in *Gruenberg*, it appears that no criminal charges were pending against the insured at the time of the insurer's examination.)

§1.24 e. Insured's Own Bad Faith Conduct

—In *James River Ins. Co. v. Hebert Schenk, P.C.*, 523 F.3d 915 (9th Cir. 2008), the Ninth Circuit discussed Arizona law concerning the showing of fraud in an insurance application that is necessary to allow an insurer to deny coverage. Reversing summary judgment on the insured's claims for breach of contract and bad faith, the Ninth Circuit explained it is normally for the trier of fact to determine whether an insurer's application question elicited an insured's false factual response, constituting actual fraud.

—On June 22, 2000, the California Supreme Court, in *Kransco v. American Empire Surplus Lines Ins. Co.*, 23 Cal. 4th 390, 97 Cal. Rptr. 2d 151 (2000), issued an opinion essentially rejecting the "comparative bad faith" defense in insurance litigation. Although *Kransco* was a third-party case, the California Supreme Court expressly overruled *California Casualty Gen. Ins. Co. v. Superior Court (Gorgei)*, 173 Cal. App. 3d 274, 218 Cal. Rptr. 817 (1985), the first-party case that had been the leading authority supporting availability of a comparative bad faith defense. (*Gorgei* is discussed in the book.) The court emphasized that while an insurer's breach of the duty of good faith is governed by tort principles, an insured's breach of the covenant is not a tort, and the scope of the insured's duty is confined by the express contractual provisions of the policy. The court also held that neither could the comparative *negligence* of an insured (here involving discovery misconduct) operate to shield the insurer from full responsibility for its bad faith failure to settle. (The court distinguished and did not address the correctness of *Patrick v. Maryland Casualty Co.*, 217 Cal. App. 3d 1566, 267 Cal. Rptr. 24 (1990), a case involving a first-party insured's negligent acts, outside the contractual relationship between the parties, following an insurer's bad faith failure to pay a claim under a homeowner's policy.)

The court added that an insured's fraudulent conduct may be separately actionable, and that evidence of the insured's misconduct or breach of its express obligations may support a number of contract defenses to a bad faith action, by voiding coverage, factually disproving the insurer's bad faith by showing that the insurer acted reasonably under the circumstances, or forming the basis of a separate contract claim. See also *California Fair Plan Ass'n v. Politi*, 220 Cal. App. 3d 1612, 270 Cal. Rptr. 2d 243 (1990), and *Agricultural Ins. Co. v. Superior Court*, 70 Cal. App. 4th 385, 82 Cal. Rptr. 2d 594 (1999) (two Court of Appeal decisions anticipating and apparently consistent with the California Supreme Court's holding in *Kransco*); *Castro v. State Farm Gen. Ins. Co.*, 256 F. Supp. 1048 (N.D. Cal. 2017) (granting summary judgment on bad faith claim where insurer was justified in voiding policy due to insured's fraudulent actions).

—In *Hartford Roman Catholic Diocesan Corp. v. Interstate Fire & Casualty Co.*, 199 F. Supp. 3d 559, *aff'd*, 905 F.3d 84 (2d Cir. 2018) (Connecticut law), the federal district court found no guidance in Connecticut law concerning the availability of a "reverse bad faith" affirmative defense for an insurer. The court applied the law ar-ticulated by the California Supreme Court in *Kransco v. American Empire*, *supra,* and concluded that "Connecticut does not, and is not likely to, permit an affirmative defense of bad faith by insurers." *Hartford,* 199 F. Supp. 3d at 600.

—A Florida Court of Appeal, in *Nationwide Property & Casualty Ins. Co. v. King,* 568 So. 2d 990 (Fla. Dist. Ct. App. 1990), affirming a judgment for the insured in a third-party case, held that the trial judge had not erred in striking the insurer's comparative bad faith defense. Without discussion or citation of authority, the court stated simply: "We decline to create a new affirmative defense of comparative bad faith." 568 So. 2d at 990–91. In *Cousin v. GEICO Gen. Ins. Co.,* 719 Fed. Appx. 954 (11th Cir. 2018), the U.S. Court of Appeals for the Eleventh Circuit held that under Florida law, courts review the "totality of the circumstances" applicable to an insured's bad faith claim, including the conduct of the insured and the insured's attorney, "especially to the extent that they impede the insurer's good faith duty to investigate facts and give fair consideration to settlement." *Id.* at 960. The court held that the trial court did not err in considering the insured's counsel's delays in providing information that the insurer needed to evaluate the insured's claim when the trial court granted summary judgment to the insurer. See also §1.33.

—In *Ussery v. Allstate Fire & Casualty Ins. Co.,* 150 F. Supp. 3d 1329 (M.D. Ga. 2015) (Georgia law), the court granted summary judgment to the insured on its claim that the insurer denied its coverage claim in bad faith. The insurer asserted the affirmative defense that the insured was not entitled to coverage because it breached the policy's "Misrepresentation Clause" by submitting a valuation of personal property lost in a fire that destroyed the plaintiff's residence. The plaintiff had previously submitted a much lower personal property valuation in a bankruptcy proceeding, but the insurer's own adjuster testified that the valuation submitted to the insurer appeared accurate. When the insurer discovered the discrepancy, the insured amended its bankruptcy valuation, effective back to the filing of the bankruptcy petition. The court held that in Georgia, "misrepresentations on a proof of loss must be material and made with the intent to defraud the insurer." *Id.* at 1343 (citations and internal quotation marks omitted). Because the insurer offered no evidence of intent to defraud, the court granted summary judgment on the plaintiff's claim for loss of personal property.

—Holding that Hawaii law does not recognize a partial defense of comparative bad faith, see *Wailua Assocs. v. Aetna Casualty & Sur. Co.*, 27 F. Supp. 2d 1211 (D. Haw. 1998).

—In *Kelly v. State Farm Mut. Auto. Ins. Co.*, 764 F. Supp. 1337 (S.D. Iowa 1991), a federal district court held that the Iowa comparative fault statute does not apply to causes of action where the common law does not recognize negligence as a defense, and hence does not apply to first-party bad faith cases. The court explained an insured's breach of obligations under an insurance contract does not excuse an insurer from its duty of good faith, and contributory fault is not a defense to bad faith failure to pay a claim. See also *Johnson v. Farm Bureau Mut. Ins. Co.*, 533 N.W.2d 203 (Iowa 1995), holding that there exists no reverse bad faith cause of action for the submission of a frivolous claim.

—In *State Auto Prop. & Casualty Ins. Co. v. Hargis*, 785 F.3d 189 (6th Cir. 2015), the Sixth Circuit predicted that Kentucky law would not recognize a tort claim of "reverse bad faith" against an insured, and affirmed the federal district court's rejection of the insurer's claim. The court noted that the tort of reverse bad faith has not been recognized by "any other jurisdiction." *Id.* at 192. The Sixth Circuit surveyed the law of various other jurisdictions and applied the reasoning in *Agricultural Ins. Co.*, *Kransco*, and *Johnson, supra*, and *Tokles* and *First Bank, infra*.

—In *Schulz v. Liberty Mut. Ins. Co.*, 940 F. Supp. 27 (D. Mass. 1996), a federal district court concluded that Massachusetts law does not recognize "reverse" bad faith claims by insurers against insureds.

—In *Stephens v. Safeco Ins. Co. of Am.*, 258 Mont. 142,

852 P.2d 565 (1993), the Montana Supreme Court held that because the special relationship between insurer and insured is not symmetrical, a "reverse" bad faith claim sounds only in contract, not in tort, and an insurer's tort cannot be offset comparatively by an insured's contract breach.

— In *Salopek Trustee for Salopek Family Heritage Trust v. Zurich Am. Life Ins. Co.*, 446 F. Supp. 3d 886 (D.N.M. 2020) (New Mexico law), the insured's wife and the trustee of the family trust alleged bad faith after the insurer rescinded the life insurance policy following insured's death. The policy contained an incontestability clause, which allowed the insurer to rescind the policy within 2 years of issuance if it found the insured made misrepresentations on the application. The court granted summary judgment in favor of the insurer where the insurer had a reasonable basis for the denial of benefits based on evidence that the insured misrepresented his tobacco and alcohol use.

—In *Tokles & Son v. Midwestern Indem. Co.*, 65 Ohio St. 3d 621, 605 N.E.2d 936 (1992), the Ohio Supreme Court declined to recognize the tort of "reverse" bad faith, reasoning that the inequality of bargaining power makes the insured/insurer relationship unsymmetrical, and that there are other avenues for an insurer to pursue in the event that an insured submits a fraudulent claim.

—Representing the rejection of a comparative bad faith defense by the courts of Oklahoma, see *First Bank v. Fidelity & Deposit Ins. Co.*, 928 P.2d 298 (Okla. 1996).

—An Oregon court of appeals, in *Stumpf v. Continental Casualty Co.*, 102 Or. App. 302, 794 P.2d 1228 (1990), declined to recognize a defense of comparative bad faith.

—In *Isaac v. State Farm Mut. Auto. Ins. Co.*, 522 N.W.2d 752 (S.D. 1994), the South Dakota Supreme Court explained that because the tort of bad faith is an intentional tort, no defense was available to the insurer based on asserted contributory negligence on the part of counsel for the insured.

—In *Southland Lloyd's Ins. Co. v. Tomberlain*, 919 S.W.2d 822 (Tex. Ct. App. 1996), *writ denied*, a Texas court of appeals declined to recognize a defense of comparative bad faith.

§1.25 f. Limitations Period

—In *Jones v. Alfa Mut. Ins. Co.*, 1 So. 3d 23 (Ala. 2008), the Alabama Supreme Court held that summary judgment on statute of limitations grounds was precluded by genuine issues of material fact as to when the insurer actually denied the insureds' claim under a farm owner's policy, and as to when the insureds would have or should have known of facts that would reasonably have led them to discover that their claim had been denied.

—A number of additional California cases have held that bad faith claims are not ordinarily "actions on the policy" within the meaning of the standard policy's 1-year limitations period, and that the applicable limitations period is the 4-year period for claims based on written contracts: *Love v. Fire Ins. Exch.*, 221 Cal. App. 3d 1136, 271 Cal. Rptr. 246 (1990) (noting that to extent insureds sought tort remedies on claim for breach of implied covenant, claim was governed instead by 2-year statute of limitations under Cal. Code Civ. Proc. §339(1)); *Weiner v. Allstate Ins. Co.*, 223 Cal. App. 3d 1201, 273 Cal. Rptr. 66 (1990); *Associates Nat'l Mortgage Corp. v. Farmers Ins. Exch.*, 217 Cal. App. 3d 562, 266 Cal. Rptr. 56 (1990). See also *Blue Shield of Cal. Life & Health Ins. Co. v. Superior Court*, 192 Cal. App. 4th 727, 120 Cal. Rptr. 3d 713 (2011) (policy language stating that suit concerning any "matter arising out of" policy must be commenced "no later than three years" after denial set 3-year time limit for insured's tortious bad faith cause of action, lengthening statutory 2-year limitations period).

A number of other California cases have apparently recognized the general rule, but have nonetheless held that a policy's own time-to-sue provision may apply to a bad faith claim that is "fundamentally" a claim on the policy, or that is a "transparent" attempt to avoid the 1-year time bar: *Jang v. State Farm Fire & Casualty Co.*, 50 Cal. App. 4th 1291, 95 Cal. Rptr. 2d 917 (2000); *CBS Broadcasting, Inc. v. Fireman's Fund Ins. Co.*, 70 Cal. App. 4th 1075, 83 Cal. Rptr. 2d 197 (1999); *Prieto v. State Farm Fire & Casualty Co.*, 225 Cal. App. 3d 1188, 275 Cal. Rptr. 362 (1990); *Magnolia Square Homeowners Ass'n v. Safeco Ins. Co. of Am.*, 221 Cal. App. 3d 1049, 271 Cal. Rptr. 1 (1990); *State Farm Fire & Casualty Co. v. Superior Court*, 210 Cal. App. 3d 604, 258 Cal. Rptr. 413 (1989); *Abari v. State Farm Fire & Casualty Co.*, 205 Cal. App. 3d 530, 252 Cal. Rptr. 565 (1988); *Lawrence v. Western Mut. Ins. Co.*, 204 Cal. App. 3d 565, 251 Cal. Rptr. 319 (1988); *Campanelli v. Allstate Ins. Co.*, 85 F. Supp. 2d 980 (C.D. Cal. 2000) (California law); *Sullivan v. Allstate Ins. Co.*, 964 F. Supp. 1407 (C.D. Cal. 1997) (California law). (*Abari v. State Farm Fire & Casualty Co.*, *supra*, was cited with apparent approval by the state supreme court in *Prudential-LMI Commercial Ins. Co. v. Superior Court*, 51 Cal. 3d 674, 274 Cal. Rptr. 387 (1990).) The court of appeal in *Weiner v. Allstate Ins. Co.*, *supra*, in insisting on the nonapplicability of the policy's time-to-sue provision, pointed out that the contrary cases can all be distinguished: they all involved situations where the insured was seeking bad faith damages in connection with the insurer's handling of a claim that had, *itself*, not been presented within the policy's 1-year period.

Concerning the "delayed discovery" rule, and the standard for establishing when a 1-year limitations period in an insurance policy begins to run, see *Prudential-LMI Commercial Ins. Co. v. Superior Court*, *supra; Ward v. Allstate Ins. Co.*, 964 F. Supp. 307 (C.D. Cal. 1997). It was held in *Kapimallis v. Allstate Ins. Co.*, 104 Cal. App. 4th 667, 128 Cal. Rptr. 2d 358 (2002) that the defendant insurer could be liable for bad faith and for violation of California's Unfair Competition Law for treating the date of the Northridge earthquake as the date of "loss" for every insured and failing to make the individual determinations mandated by the delayed discovery rule.

Concerning equitable tolling of the 1-year limitations period, see *Prudential-LMI Commercial Ins. Co. v. Superior Court, supra* (1-year period is tolled between time of notification and time of denial); *Singh v. Allstate Ins. Co.,* 63 Cal. App. 4th 135, 73 Cal. Rptr. 2d 546 (1998) (1-year period is not further tolled even where insured requests reconsideration of denial); *Gaylord v. Nationwide Mut. Ins. Co.,* 776 F. Supp. 2d 1101 (E.D. Cal. 2011) (unlike insurer's agreement to reopen and reinvestigate, limitations period is tolled neither by invitation to provide further information, nor by statement of willingness to reconsider upon receipt of further pertinent information).

And for a holding that an insurer was equitably estopped from invoking a policy's 1-year limitations period because the insurer had failed to warn the insured of the period's imminent expiration, see *Spray, Gould & Bowers, v. Associated Int'l Ins. Co.,* 71 Cal. App. 4th 1260, 84 Cal. Rptr. 2d 552 (1999). The court cited a provision of the California Insurance Department's "Fair Claims Settlement Practices Regulations" that requires an insurer to disclose to an insured all time limits that may be applicable to the insured's claim. For a related holding, see *Superior Dispatch, Inc. v. Insurance Corp. of N.Y.,* 181 Cal. App. 4th 175, 104 Cal. Rptr. 3d 508 (2010) (summary judgment was precluded by fact issue as to whether insured reasonably relied on nondisclosure of 1-year limitations period; insured's retention of counsel did not establish as matter of law that reliance had been unreasonable). Compare *Love v. Fire Ins. Exch., supra* (insurer was not estopped to plead statute of limitations merely because when it denied claim it failed to inform insured of pertinent laws or legal theories upon which insured could rely in later lawsuit challenging denial of claim).

In *21st Century Ins. Co. v. Superior Court,* 127 Cal. App. 4th 1351, 26 Cal. Rptr. 3d 476 (2005), and *20th Century Ins. Co. v. Superior Court (Ahles),* 90 Cal. App. 4th 1247, 109 Cal. Rptr. 2d 611 (2001), a California Court of Appeal rejected constitutional challenges to a statute that revives for

1 year otherwise time-barred contract and bad faith claims arising out of the 1994 Northridge earthquake.

—In *Brodeur v. American Home Assurance Co.*, 169 P.3d 139 (Colo. 2007), an *en banc* decision filed in October of 2007, the Colorado Supreme Court held, *inter alia*, that the 2-year limitations period on the claimant's bad faith tort claims against her employer's workers' compensation insurer and claims adjuster was not equitably tolled by the pendency of the workers' compensation proceeding.

According to the Colorado Court of Appeals in *Harmon v. Fred S. James & Co.*, 899 P.2d 258 (Colo. Ct. App. 1994), the "continuing violation" doctrine has no application to bad faith claims.

In *Olson v. State Farm Mut. Auto. Ins. Co.*, 174 P.3d 849 (Colo. Ct. App. 2007), it was held: (1) the implied covenant of good faith and fair dealing does not impose upon an automobile insurer a legal duty to inform the insured of when the statute of limitations would run on a claim for uninsured motorist coverage; and (2) as a matter of first impression, the time for accrual of a claim is not tolled pending the insured's consultation with an attorney.

In *Thompson v. State Farm Mut. Auto. Ins. Co.*, 457 F. Supp. 3d 998 (D. Colo. 2020) (Colorado law), the court held that a 2-year statute of limitations applies to claims under Colo. Rev. Stat. § 10-3-1115.

—The Connecticut Supreme Court, in *Lees v. Middlesex Ins. Co.*, 219 Conn. 644, 594 A.2d 952 (1991), expressed disagreement with the California approach represented by *Abari v. State Farm, supra,* and *Lawrence v. Western Mut. Ins. Co., supra,* and held that neither a claim under the Unfair Insurance Practices Act, nor a claim under the Unfair Trade Practices Act is an "action on the policy" subject to the policy's 1-year limit in its time-to-sue provision.

Under Connecticut law, according to the Second Circuit, bad faith claims are governed by the 3-year general tort statute of limitations (Conn. Gen. Stat. § 52-577). *City of West Haven v. Commercial Union Ins. Co.*, 894 F.2d 540

(2d Cir. 1990). See also *Independence Ins. Serv. Corp. v. Hartford Life Ins. Co.*, 472 F. Supp. 2d 183 (D. Conn. 2007); *Guillory v. Allstate Ins. Co.*, 476 F. Supp. 2d 171 (D. Conn. 2007).

—In *Cagle v. State Farm Fire & Casualty Co.*, 236 Ga. App. 726, 512 S.E.2d 717 (1999), it was held that recovery was barred under Georgia's bad faith statute (Ga. Code. Ann. §33-4-6), because of the insured's failure to wait the prescribed 60 days to file suit after demanding payment of benefits. This was true, the court held, even though compliance with the 60-day requirement would have caused the policy's limitations period to elapse.

In *Auto-Owners Ins. Co. v. Ogden*, 569 S.E.2d 833 (Ga. 2002), the Georgia Supreme Court, reversing summary judgment, held that fact issues had been raised concerning the applicability of the rule that an insurer waives a policy's 1-year limitations period if, by its actions, it leads the insured to believe that such a waiver has occurred and that the claim will be paid.

—Federal district courts in Hawaii have reached conflicting conclusions concerning the limitations period for bad faith claims. See *Guillermo v. Hartford Life & Accident Ins. Co.*, 986 F. Supp. 1334 (D. Haw. 1997) (predicting that state supreme court would hold that bad faith claims are subject to Hawaii's 6-year "catch-all" statute of limitations); *Baird v. State Farm Mut. Auto. Ins. Co.*, 11 F. Supp. 2d 1204 (D. Haw. 1998) (predicting that state supreme court would apply 2-year limitations period applicable to tort claims), *aff'd without op.*, (9th Cir. 1999).

—Under Indiana law, since an insurer's breach of the duty of good faith sounds only in contract, a cause of action for breach of that duty is an action "on the policy" that is governed by the policy's time-to-sue provision. *Troxell v. American States Ins. Co.*, 596 N.E.2d 921 (Ind. Ct. App. 1992); *Trzeciak v. State Farm Fire & Casualty Co.*, 809 F. Supp. 2d 900 (N.D. Ind. 2011). In *Union Auto. Indem. Ass'n v. Shields*, 79 F.3d 39 (7th Cir. 1996) (Indiana law), the Seventh Circuit held that an uninsured motorist carrier had no duty to warn its insured concerning expiration of the policy's time-to-sue provision.

—Holding that under Iowa law bad faith claims are ordinarily "claims on the policy" subject to the policy's time-to-sue provision, see *Stahl v. Preston Mut. Ins. Ass'n*, 517 N.W.2d 201 (Iowa 1994); *Ingrim v. State Farm Fire & Casualty Co.*, 249 F.3d 743 (8th Cir. 2001) (Iowa law). To avoid a policy's limitations provision, the *Stahl* court held, an insured must allege "conduct on the part of the insurer giving rise to an independent or collateral cause of action." 517 N.W.2d at 203.

—In *Smith v. Citadel Ins. Co.*, 285 So. 3d 1062 (La. 2019), the Supreme Court of Louisiana held that first-party bad faith claims against an insurer, which fall under La. Stat. Ann. §22:1973, arise out of an insurer's contractual obligations, and therefore are governed by the 10-year prescriptive period under La. C.C. art. 3499, not the 1-year prescriptive period for delictual actions.

—In *Nunheimer v. Continental Ins. Co.*, 68 F. Supp. 2d 75 (D. Mass. 1999), a federal district court held that claims under the Massachusetts consumer protection and unfair claims settlement practices statutes arising from non-payment of benefits under a property insurance policy were governed by the policy's 2-year limitations provision that, in turn, was specified by Mass. Gen. L. ch. 175, §99. The claims were time-barred, the court held, since the "loss" commencing the limitations period was contamination from underground storage tanks, not the insurer's denial of benefits. See also *Schwartz v. Travelers Indem. Co.*, 50 Mass. App. Ct. 672, 740 N.E.2d 1039 (2001) (limitations period on statutory bad faith claim began to run when insured knew or should have known of inadequate investigation, not at later time claim was formally denied).

—In *Frye v. Southern Farm Bureau Casualty Ins. Co.*, 915 So. 2d 486 (Miss. Ct. App. 2005), a Mississippi Court of Appeals rejected the insured's attempted invocation of the doctrine of fraudulent concealment to toll the statute of limitations in a suit alleging fraud in connection with the sale of disability income coverage. Knowledge of the terms of the automobile insurance policy was imputed to the insureds, the court explained, emphasizing that the insurer had sent copies of the policy, declarations page, and renewal notices to the insureds throughout the life of the policy.

—In *Goldstein v. Massachusetts Mut. Life Ins. Co.*, 32 A.D.3d 821, 820 N.Y.S.2d 852 (2006), the New York Supreme Court, Appellate Division, held that the insured's causes of action alleging intentional and negligent infliction of emotional distress, breach of duty, and bad faith were governed by the 1-year statute of limitations for intentional torts to the extent that they alleged intentional conduct, and by the 3-year statute of limitations governing personal injury claims insofar as they alleged negligent conduct. Compare *Blanar v. State Farm Ins. Cos.*, 34 A.D.3d 1333, 824 N.Y.S.2d 702 (2006) (insured's action seeking first-party coverage under homeowners policy was governed by 2-year limitations period provided by policy, rather than 6-year limitations period for breach of contract actions). See also *Cooper v. New York Cent. Mut. Fire Ins. Co.*, 72 A.D.3d 1556, 900 N.Y.S.2d 545 (2010) (dismissal on grounds of untimeliness was precluded by fact issue raised by allegation that insurer had engaged in course of conduct that had lulled insured into inactivity in belief that her claim would ultimately be processed); *Endemann v. Liberty Ins. Corp.*, 390 F. Supp. 3d 362 (N.D.N.Y. 2019), *partial reconsideration*, 2020 WL 5027421 (N.D.N.Y. 2020) (allowing claim for breach of implied covenant of good faith and fair dealing to proceed even though contract claim was barred under contract's limitations period; conduct alleged was different from conduct alleged under contract claim, and therefore good faith and fair dealing claim was not duplicative of contract claim).

—In *Bullet Trucking, Inc. v. Glen Falls Ins. Co.*, 84 Ohio

App. 3d 327, 616 N.E.2d 1123 (1992), an Ohio Court of Appeals held that a motor truck cargo insurance policy's "time-to-sue" provision had no application to the insured's bad faith claim, which was governed by the 4-year limitations period contained in Ohio Rev. Code Ann. §2305.09(D).

—In October of 2007, the Pennsylvania Supreme Court, in *Ash v. Continental Ins. Co.*, 932 A.2d 877 (Pa. 2007), clarified that a claim under the state's bad faith statute, (42 Pa. C.S.A. §8371), is a statutorily created tort action and is therefore subject to a 2-year statute of limitations, rather than the catch-all 6-year limitations period. (The court also addressed a number of issues concerning the relation between statutory and common-law bad faith claims.)

Under Pennsylvania law, it was held in *CRS Auto Parts, Inc. v. National Grange Mut. Ins. Co.*, 645 F. Supp. 2d 354 (E.D. Pa. 2009), a common-law bad faith claim sounds in contract and is thus subject to the four-year statute of limitations for contract actions (42 Pa. C.S.A. §5525). See also *Cozzone v. AXA Equitable Life Ins. Soc'y*, 858 F. Supp. 2d 452, 2012 WL 871201 (M.D. Pa. 2012) (reiterating that 4-year limitations period applies to common-law bad faith claims, and 2-year period applies to claims under 42 Pa. C.S.A. §8371).

—In *Murray v. San Jacinto Agency, Inc.*, 800 S.W.2d 826 (Tex. 1990), the Texas Supreme Court held that a first-party bad faith cause of action accrues for limitations purposes on the date coverage is denied. The court thus overruled that portion of its own decision in *Arnold v. National County Mut. Fire Ins. Co.*, 725 S.W.2d 165 (Tex. 1987), which had held that the bad faith cause of action accrues on the date a separate coverage suit is resolved unfavorably to the insurer. The *Murray* holding was held to apply retroactively in *Liberty Mut. Fire Ins. Co. v. Richards*, 810 S.W.2d 232 (Tex. Ct. App. 1991), and was subsequently followed in *Abe's Colony Club, Inc. v. C & W Underwriters, Inc.*, 852 S.W.2d 86 (Tex. Ct. App. 1993). In *Long v.*

State Farm Fire & Casualty Co., 828 S.W.2d 125 (Tex. Ct. App. 1992), it was held that although a belatedly added bad faith claim had accrued at the time the insured's claim was denied and was subject to a two-year statute of limitations, the claim was timely because it related back to the time of the insured's filing of a claim for breach of contract.

—In *Greene v. Stevens Gas Serv.*, 858 A.2d 238 (Vt. 2004), the Vermont Supreme Court held that a property insurance policy's two-year limitations period governed a bad faith claim that was based on the insurer's denial of coverage. (The court declined, however, to adopt a general rule that *all* bad faith claims, regardless of the nature of the allegations, are similarly claims "on the policy" for limitations purposes.)

—Answering a federal district court's certified question, the West Virginia Supreme Court, in *Wilt v. State Auto. Mut. Ins. Co.*, 506 S.E.2d 608 (W. Va. 1998), held that bad faith claims are subject to the 1-year limitations period for tort actions set forth in W. Va. Code §55-2-12.

And in *Sizemore v. State Farm Gen. Ins. Co.*, 202 W. Va. 591, 505 S.E.2d 654 (1998), the West Virginia Supreme Court held (1) that the 1-year limitations period prescribed by the legislature for standard fire insurance policies (W. Va. Code §33-17-2) applies to claims for fire losses under multiline policies; and (2) that because the policy claim in the present case was time-barred, the insured could not "substantially prevail" on the policy claim and therefore could not recover compensatory or punitive damages for bad faith. (See book §1.36 for a discussion of *Hayseeds, Inc. v. State Farm Fire & Casualty Co.*, 352 S.E.2d 73 (W. Va. 1986), and the West Virginia doctrine that permits awards of extracontractual damages in cases where an insured "substantially prevails" on a policy claim without regard to the insurer's good or bad faith.)

§1.25A g. Lack of Coverage [NEW]

—In *Peterson v. USAA Life Ins. Co.*, 814 Fed. Appx. 408 (10th Cir. 2020) (Colorado law), the Tenth Circuit held that the insurer was entitled to summary judgment on the plaintiff's bad faith claim because the insurer had properly denied coverage where the insured misrepresented material aspects of his medical history upon applying for the policy.

—In *ABK, LLC v. Mid-Century Ins. Co.*, 166 Idaho 92, 454 P.3d 1175 (2019), the Idaho Supreme Court granted the defendant insurer summary judgment on the insured's bad faith claim where the insurer was also entitled to summary judgment on the issue of whether coverage existed. "Fundamental to the claim of bad faith is the idea that there must be coverage of the claim under the policy." 454 P.3d at 1186 (internal quotation marks omitted).

—In *Pogue v. Principal Life Ins. Co.*, 979 F.3d 534 (6th Cir. 2020) (Kentucky law), the Sixth Circuit held that an insurer cannot act in bad faith if the insurer was not obligated to pay the claim.

—In *GeoVera Specialty Ins. Co. v. Joachin*, 964 F.3d 390 (5th Cir. 2020) (Louisiana law), the insurer brought an action seeking a declaratory judgment that it did not have any duty to indemnify the insureds under a homeowner's insurance policy after a fire destroyed the insureds' home. The insureds brought counterclaims, seeking contractual and bad faith damages. The court agreed with the insurer that the insureds were not covered under the policy because the insurance policy had a clear residency requirement, and the insureds had never resided in their newly purchased home. The district court dismissed the insureds' counterclaim for bad faith, stating that the insureds could not assert bad faith claims without first establishing coverage, and the Fifth Circuit affirmed.

6. Exclusiveness of Statutory Remedies

§1.26 a. Unfair Claim Settlement Practices Statutes

—In *Kisselman v. American Family Mut. Ins. Co.*, 292 P.3d 964, 2011 WL 6091708 (Colo. Ct. App. 2011), *cert. denied*, 2012 WL 4482571 (Colo. 2012), it was held that C.R.S.A. §§10-3-1115 and 10-3-1116 created an express private right of action in favor of an insured when an insurer unreasonably denies or delays payment of a claim, in addition to and different from a common-law bad faith claim. The court also held that the General Assembly intended those statutes to apply prospectively to an insurer's acts occurring after August 5, 2008, regardless of when the original claim for benefits was made. Accord, *Vaccaro v. American Family Ins. Group*, 275 P.3d 750 (2012), *as modified on denial of rehearing* (Colo. Ct. App. 2012). See *Fisher v. State Farm Mut. Auto. Ins. Co.*, 419 P.3d 985 (Colo. Ct. App. 2015), *aff'd*, 418 P.3d 501 (Colo. 2018) (affirming jury award of bad faith damages to insured for insurer's delay in paying undisputed medical costs due to litigation of other damages; contrasting C.R.S.A. §10–3-1115 with common-law insurance bad faith claim, noting that there is no recklessness component to the statutory claim, and "only element at issue" in statutory claim is "whether an insurer denied benefits without a reasonable basis" (quoting *Vaccaro v. American Family Ins. Group, supra*, at 760)); accord *Schultz v. Geico Casualty Co.*, 429 P.3d 844 (Colo. 2018); *Sandoval v. Unum Life Ins. Co. of Am.*, 952 F.3d 1233 (10th Cir. 2020) (Colorado law); *Thompson v. State Farm Mut. Auto. Ins. Co.*, 457 F. Supp. 3d 998 (D. Colo. 2020) (Colorado law); *Wahlert v. Am. Standard Ins. Co. of Wis.*, 173 F. Supp. 3d 1187 (D. Colo. 2016). See also *American Family Mut. Ins. Co. v. Barriga*, 2018 CO 42, 418 P.3d 1181 (Colo. 2018) (under Colo. Rev. Stat. §10-3-116 (1), insured may recover 2 times covered benefit upon proving benefits were unreasonably delayed or denied; lower court erred by doubling damages awarded by jury, then reducing award by amount unreasonably delayed but ultimately paid by insurer to insured; plain language of statute allows insured to recover double damages for delay even though insured ultimately received delayed amount from insurer, just as statute allows insured to recover double damages for denial of benefits and recover those benefits from insurer in separate contract claim); *Guarantee Trust Life Ins. Co. v. Estate of Casper*, 2018 CO 43, 418 P.3d 1163 (Colo. 2018) (insured's estate was substituted for insured when insured died after jury reached its verdict but before final order was entered; survival statute, Colo. Rev. Stat. §13-20-101(1), did not bar estate's recovery or limit its damages under Colo. Rev. Stat. §10-3-116); *Etherton v. Owners Ins. Co.*, 829 F.3d 1209 (10th Cir. 2016) (Colorado law; claimant successfully asserting unreasonable delay or denial by insurer under C.S.R.A. §§10–3-1115 or 10–3-1116 can receive covered benefit plus two times benefit amount). The *Etherton* court relied on *Hansen v. Am. Fam. Mut. Ins. Co.*, 2013 WL 6673066 (Colo. App. 2013), *rev'd on other grounds sub nom. Am. Family Mut. Ins. Co.*, 375 P.3d 115 (Colo. 2016).

In *TBL Collectibles, Inc. v. Owners Ins. Co.*, 285 F. Supp. 3d 1170 (D. Colo. 2018), the federal district court applying Colorado law denied the insurer's motion for summary judgment because the insurer had failed to show as a matter of law that its denial of the insured's claim was reasonable. The court rejected the insurer's argument that it had shown that the plaintiff's claim was "fairly debatable" and therefore was entitled to summary judgment. The court held that "the 'fair debatability' of an insurance claim does not, under Colorado law, preclude a finding that an insurer unreasonably delayed or denied payment of benefits under Colo. Rev. Stat. §10-3-1115." 285 F. Supp. 3d at 1202 (citing cases) (distinguishing rule in California). Accord *Schultz v.*

Geico Casualty Co., supra; Thompson v. State Farm Mut. Auto. Ins. Co., supra.

—In *Belz v. Peerless Ins. Co.*, 204 F. Supp. 3d 457 (D. Conn. 2016), the court denied the insurer's motion for summary judgment on a claim for violations of the Connecticut Unfair Insurance Practices Act and the Connecticut Unfair Trade Practices Act where the insured presented evidence that the insurer refused to cover similar claims in three separate matters. Under the statutes, a plaintiff must show that the alleged act was done with enough frequency to indicate that it was a general business practice. Connecticut allows a separate claim for breach of covenant of good faith and fair dealing. See also *Courteau v. Teachers Ins. Co.*, 243 F. Supp. 3d 215 (D. Conn. 2017).

—In 2012, the Florida Supreme Court clarified that there is no common-law first-party insurance bad faith cause of action under Florida law, only the statutory cause of action codified at F.S.A. §624.155. *QBE Ins. Corp. v. Chalfonte Condo. Apartment Ass'n*, 94 So. 3d 541 (Fla. 2012). See also *United Prop. & Casualty Ins. Co. v. Chernick*, 94 So. 3d 646 (Fla. Dist. Ct. App. 2012); *Chalfonte Condo. Apartment Ass'n v. QBE Ins. Corp.*, 695 F.3d 1215, 2012 WL 4120395 (11th Cir. 2012). But see *Citizens Prop. Ins. Co. v. Perdido Sun Condo. Ass'n*, 164 So. 3d 663 (Fla. 2015) (Florida Supreme Court noted in dicta that although statutory first-party bad faith claims are not "willful torts" in Florida, bad faith claim could be elevated to willful tort, depending on facts of case).

—In *Collins v. Life Ins. Co.*, 228 Ga. App. 301, 491 So. 2d 514 (1997), a Georgia court restated the principle that Georgia's bad faith statute (Ga. Code Ann. §33-4-6) provides the exclusive remedy for a bad faith denial of benefits. Accord *Phila. Indem. Ins. Co. v. First Multiple Listing Servs., Inc.*, 173 F. Supp. 3d 1314 (N.D. Ga. 2016) (listing elements to prevail on bad faith claims under Georgia's bad faith statute and discussing summary judgment standard for bad faith claims under statute). See also *Thompson v. Homesite Ins. Co. of Ga.*, 345 Ga. App. 183, 812 S.E.2d 541 (2018), *cert. denied* (Ga. 2018) (insured failed to state claim under Ga. Code Ann. §33-4-6 where insured's demand for payment failed to give notice to insurer that it would face bad faith claim if it did not pay; lower court erred by failing to dismiss insured's claim for attorney's fees after lower court correctly dismissed insured's bad faith claim under statute; even where insured brings additional claims that are distinct from bad faith claim under statute, if additional claims are based on failure to pay claim, Ga. Code Ann. §33-4-6 is exclusive vehicle through which insured may claim attorney's fees).

—In *Aquilina v. Certain Underwriters at Lloyd's Syndicate #2003*, 407 F. Supp. 3d 1016 (D. Haw. 2019) (Hawaii law), in which insureds brought claims of fraudulent and misleading conduct against insurers and agents/brokers, the court noted that there is no private right of action for violations of the Insurance Code at Haw. Stat. §431:13–102. However, the court held that the Insurance Code did not preempt actions under the Unfair and Deceptive Acts or Trade Practices Act (UDAP) §480–2. The court also acknowledged the availability of a first-party bad faith action under common law. See §§1.33, 1.37.

—Kentucky recognizes several categories of bad faith claims against insurance companies, including first-party bad faith under common-law, first-party and third-party bad faith under the Kentucky Unfair Claims Settlement Practices Act, and first-party bad faith under the Kentucky Consumer Protection Act. See *Foster v. American Fire & Casualty Co.*, 219 F. Supp. 3d 590 (E.D. Ky. 2016).

—In *Kelly v. State Farm Fire & Casualty Co.*, 169 So. 3d 328 (La. 2015), the Louisiana Supreme Court affirmed the holding of the Fifth Circuit in *Stanley v. Trinchard*, 500 F.3d 411 (5th Cir. 2007), that Louisiana's claim settlement practices statute, La. Rev. Stat. Ann. §22:1973(A), is a codification of a "jurisprudentially-recognized cause of action in favor of insureds for an insurer's bad faith failure to settle." 169 So. 3d at 336. See discussion in §2.7, *infra*. For application of the bad faith statute, see *Shreve v. State Farm Fire & Casualty Co.*, 247 So. 3d 1175 (La. Ct. App. 2018), *writ denied*, 255 So. 3d 574 (La. 2018) (affirming JNOV on bad faith claim under La. Stat. Ann. §22:1973 and dismissing $140,000 in noncontractual damages and $25,000 in attorney's fees; reasonable persons could not have found that insurer acted in bad faith toward insured when handling claim where insured did not discover crack in foundation of home until almost 3 years after alleged damaging act occurred, insurer hired engineer to evaluate crack within 2 weeks of claim, insurer's engineer found crack to be from source not covered under policy, and insurer hired second engineer who confirmed its first engineer's report when it was faced with conflicting report from insured's engineer).

In *Smith v. Citadel Ins. Co.*, 285 So. 3d 1062 (La. 2019), the Supreme Court of Louisiana held that first-party bad faith claims against an insurer, which fall under La. Stat. Ann. §22:1973, arise out of an insurer's contractual obligations, and therefore are governed by the 10-year prescriptive period under La. C.C. art. 3499, not the 1-year prescriptive period for delictual actions.

—In *Peterson v. Western Nat'l Mut. Ins. Co.*, 946 N.W.2d 903 (Minn. 2020), the Supreme Court of Minnesota stated in a footnote that Minn. Stat. §§72A.01-.52, the Unfair Claims Practices Act, is not an exclusive remedy, and permitted the insured to recover taxable costs and attorney fees under Minn. Stat. §604.18 as a result of the insurer's failure to conduct a reasonable investigation and to pay the insured's claim for coverage. See §1.10.

—Montana's Unfair Trade Practices Act (Mont. Code Ann. §33-18-242(3)) did not preempt a common-law bad faith claim concerning the insurer's renewal practices, the Montana Supreme Court held in *Thomas v. Northwestern Nat'l Ins. Co.*, 973 P.2d 804 (Mont. 1998). The court distinguished the present case from ones involving the mishandling of claims, where statutory preemption does apply. See also *Williams v. Union Fid. Life Ins. Co.*, 329 Mont. 158, 123 P.3d 213 (2005) (bad faith claim could be asserted in connection with conduct that occurred prior to application process, namely insurer's failure to include fact-specific health questions on its application form for credit life insurance policy).

—In *Pioneer Chlor Alkali Co. v. National Union Fire Ins. Co.*, 863 F. Supp. 1237 (D. Nev. 1994), it was emphasized that the remedy for violation of the Nevada Unfair Claim Settlement Practices statute is not exclusive of the common-law remedy for bad faith. Whereas a statutory violation may be established without proof of any particular mental element, the court explained, a common-law violation requires proof that a claim was knowingly denied without any reasonable basis. See also *Allstate Ins. Co. v. Thorpe*, 170 P.3d 989 (Nev. 2007) (medical providers who brought declaratory judgment action against automobile insurers to recover for violation of prompt payment statute (West's NRSA 690B.012) had no private right of action; they were required to seek administrative remedies and could not file suit in district court after those remedies were exhausted); *Hackler v. State Farm Mut. Auto. Ins. Co.*, 210 F. Supp. 3d 1250 (D. Nev. 2016) (under Nevada unfair trade practices statute, §686A.310, plaintiff must prove that officer, director, or department head of insurer knowingly permitted violations; under Nevada's prompt payment statute, §690B.012, there is no private right of action).

—In *In re Bernstein*, 156 A.D.2d 683, 549 N.Y.S.2d 446 (1989), a New York court affirmed the dismissal of cross-complaints by a life insurance policy beneficiary, with the following explanation (156 A.D.2d at 684, 549 N.Y.S.2d at 447):

> To the extent that the . . . cross claims sought punitive damages for failure to pay over the proceeds of a life insurance policy . . . they are clearly insufficient.

Even if we were to read the allegations in the light most favorable to [the respondent], they fail to set forth "sufficient evidentiary allegations of ultimate facts of a fraudulent and deceitful scheme in dealing with the general public as to imply a criminal indifference to civil obligations." [Citations omitted.] To the extent that the cross claims can be read to allege that [the insurer] failed to promptly investigate the competing claims to the policy proceeds and failed to make a good faith effort to effectuate a prompt and fair settlement of the claims, they are preempted by Insurance Law §2601 [citations omitted].

—Under Pennsylvania law, it was reiterated by the court in *Kramer v. State Farm Fire & Casualty Ins. Co.* 603 A.2d 192 (Pa. Super. Ct. 1992), no direct tort cause of action for bad faith exists in addition to the statutory remedy of the Unfair Insurance Practices Act (though common-law causes of action for fraud and deceit are permitted). See also *Whalen v. State Farm Fire & Casualty Co.*, 183 F. Supp. 3d 672 (E.D. Pa. 2016) (Pennsylvania law; in Pennsylvania, insurer bad faith claim provided by statute at Pa. Cons. Stat. §8371). A common-law bad faith claim sounds only in contract, it was held in *CRS Auto Parts, Inc. v. National Grange Mut. Ins. Co.*, 645 F. Supp. 2d 354 (E.D. Pa. 2009). Holding that there is no right to jury trial on statutory bad faith claims, see *Mishoe v. Erie Ins. Co.*, 762 A.2d 369 (Pa. Super. Ct. 2000).

In *Metropolitan Grp. Prop. & Casualty Ins. Co. v. Hack*, 312 F. Supp. 3d 439 (M.D. Pa. 2018), an insurer brought an action for declaratory judgment and punitive damages for common-law fraud against an insured for making a fraudulent medical claim, and the insured made a counterclaim for bad faith under 42 Pa. Cons. Stat. §8371. The insurer sought to dismiss the counterclaim by arguing that the Pennsylvania Motor Vehicle Financial Responsibility Law (75 Pa. Cons. Stat. §1797) preempted §8371 claims when an insurer denied its insured first-party medical benefits. The court stated that §8371 provided a private cause of action and damages for bad faith denials of insurance claims, while §1797 provided a claim and damages for first-party disputes over the reasonableness or necessity of medical treatment. The court held that alleged misconduct in the counterclaim that was within the scope of §1797 was preempted and dismissed those portions of the counterclaim. However, allegations that did not fall under its scope, such as determinations of causation of injury and issues of contract interpretation, were permitted to survive as cognizable claims under §8371.

In *Clapps v. State Farm Ins. Cos.*, 447 F. Supp. 3d 293 (E.D. Pa. 2020) (Pennsylvania law), the federal district court held that the insured's claim under the Unfair Trade Practices and Consumer Protection Law (UTPCPL) was barred by the economic loss doctrine, following *Werwinski v. Ford Motor Co.*, 286 F.3d 661 (3d Cir. 2002). The court confirmed that no private cause of action exists under Pennsylvania's Unfair Insurance Practices Act (UIPA) or Unfair Claims Settlement Practices (UCSP) regulations. The court dismissed the insured's complaint under the Pennsylvania bad faith statute, Pa. Cons. Stat. §8371, for failure to plead bad faith with more than conclusory allegations, but granted leave to amend the complaint.

—Since Tennessee law does not recognize a common-law tort for an insurer's bad faith conduct toward an insured, the court emphasized in *Wynne v. Stonebridge Life Ins. Co.*, 694 F. Supp. 2d 871 (W.D. Tenn. 2010), any claims of bad faith must be brought under Tennessee's bad faith statute, West's T.C.A. § 56-7-105. See also *American Nat'l Prop. & Casualty Co. v. Stutte*, 105 F. Supp. 3d 849 (E.D. Tenn. 2015). For a case that grants summary judgment in favor of insurer on a claim related to inadequate investigation under the bad faith statute, see *Nylander v. Unum Life Ins. Co. of Am.*, 309 F. Supp. 3d 526 (M.D. Tenn. 2018). In *Lindenberg v. Jackson Nat'l Life Ins. Co.*, 912 F.3d 348 (6th Cir. 2019), *cert. denied*, ___ U.S. ___, 140 S. Ct.

635 (2019), the Sixth Circuit held that the bad faith statute was not the sole remedy, and that insureds could also seek damages for common-law bad faith breach of contract.

—In *USAA Tex. Lloyds Co. v. Menchaca*, 545 S.W.3d 479 (Tex. 2018), the Texas Supreme Court stated that Tex. Ins. Code §541.060(a) grants insureds a private right of action against insurers that engage in certain bad faith practices. The court also reviewed and clarified Texas precedent on whether an insured can recover policy benefits as actual damages for an insurer's statutory violation absent a finding that the insured had a contractual right to the benefits under the insurance policy. In the case under review, a jury answered "no" when asked whether the insurer failed to comply with the terms of the insurance policy in denying to pay damages to the insured after her home was damaged by a hurricane. However, the jury answered "yes" when asked whether the insurer engaged in unfair or deceptive practices in violation of the Texas Insurance Code, including whether the insurer refused to pay the claim for damages without conducting a reasonable investigation. The jury awarded the insured $11,350 as actual damages, which the jury calculated by using the difference between what the insurer should have paid under the policy and the amount actually paid. The Texas Supreme Court ultimately remanded the case for a new trial based on the irreconcilable and fatal conflict in the jury's answers, but it sought to clarify its precedent before it reached its decision. The court stated the general rule that an insured cannot recover policy benefits as actual damages for an insurer's violation of the Texas Insurance Code if the insured does not have a right to the benefits under the policy. The court went on to provide four more rules that add nuance and exceptions to the general rule. See discussion in §1.56. See also *State Farm Lloyds v. Fuentes*, 597 S.W.3d 925 (Tex. App. 2020) (reconsidering on remand in light of *Menchaca*; affirming trial court after applying 5 rules of *Menchaca* to facts of case); *Hinojos v. State Farm Lloyds*, 569 S.W.3d 304 (Tex. App. 2019) (refusing to distinguish case from *Menchaca* to allow extra-contractual claims where insurer did not breach contract but insured was entitled to coverage under policy; court affirmed summary judgment in favor of insurer where insured received full appraisal award and failed to show independent injury). Under Texas law, insureds may bring a claim for violation of the duty of good faith and fair dealing as well as a claim under Tex. Ins. Code §541.060. See *Greenville Townhome Owners Assoc., Inc. v. Philadelphia Indem. Ins. Co.*, 473 F. Supp. 3d 692 (N.D. Tex. 2020).

In *Ramirez v. Allstate Vehicle & Prop. Ins. Co.*, ___ F. Supp. 3d ___, 2020 WL 5806436 (S.D. Tex. 2020) (Texas law), the federal district court held that the insured stated bad faith claims under Texas unfair claims practices statutes, Tex. Ins. Code §§541.060(a)(1) and 542.003(b)(1), prohibiting misrepresentations by insurers, where the insurer misrepresented the coverage available under the insureds' homeowner's policy. The insureds' complaint was sufficient under the Fed. R. Civ. P. 9(b) standard for pleading fraud or misrepresentation.

For cases addressing recovery for improper delay in payment of claims under the Texas Prompt Payment Statute, Tex. Ins. Code ch. 542, see §1.11.

—The court in *Workland & Witherspoon, PLLC v. Evanston Ins. Co.*, 141 F. Supp. 3d 1148 (E.D. Wash. 2015) stated that under Washington law, a bad faith cause of action is distinct from a cause of action under Washington's Insurance Fair Conduct Act. The court in *Perez-Crisantos v. State Farm Fire & Casualty Co.*, 187 Wash. 2d 669, 389 P.3d 476 (2017), held that first-party insureds do not have a private right of action for regulatory violations under Washington's Insurance Fair Conduct Act.

—Concerning the private right of action under W. Va. Code §33-11-4(9), see *Dodrill v. Nationwide Mut. Ins. Co.*, 491 S.E.2d 1 (W. Va. 1997), where the court wrote: "[W]e hold that to maintain a private action based on alleged violations of W. Va. Code §33-11-4(9) in the settlement of a single insurance claim, the evidence should establish that the conduct in question constitutes more than a single violation of [the statute], that the violations arise from separate, discrete acts or omissions in the claim settlement, and that they arise from a habit, custom, usage, or business policy of the insurer, so that. . . . the conduct can be considered a 'general business practice.' . . ." 491 S.E.2d at 13. See also *Wetzel v. Employers Serv. Corp. of W. Va.*, 221 W. Va. 610, 656 S.E.2d 55 (2007) (administrator of self-insured employer's workers' compensation program was not engaged in business of insurance and therefore could not be liable for alleged bad faith refusal to pay claims under Unfair Trade Practices Act).

§1.27 b. Penalty Statutes

—In *American Family Mut. Ins. Co. v. Barriga*, 2018 CO 42, 418 P.3d 1181 (Colo. 2018), the Supreme Court of Colorado considered whether damages awarded under Colo. Rev. Stat. §10-3-116 must be reduced by the amount of damages delayed but ultimately received by the insured. Under the statute, an insured may recover 2 times the covered benefit upon proving the benefits were unreasonably delayed or denied. The court determined that the lower court erred by doubling the damages awarded by a jury under Colo. Rev. Stat. §10-3-116 and then reducing the award by the amount unreasonably delayed but ultimately paid by the insurer to the insured. The court found that the plain language of the statute allows an insured to recover double damages for delay even though the insured ultimately received the delayed amount from the insurer, just as the statute allows an insured to recover double damages for the denial of benefits and recover those benefits from insurer in a separate contract claim.

It was held in *Williams v. Farmers Ins. Group, Inc.*, 781

P.2d 156 (Colo. Ct. App. 1989), that the statutory remedy for wrongful termination of PIP (personal injury protection) benefits created by enactment of the Colorado Auto Accident Reparations Act, Colo. Rev. Stat. §§10-4-701 et. seq. (1987 Repl. Vol. 4A), did not preempt the existing common-law tort action for bad faith breach of an insurance contract. Accord *Sanderson v. Allstate Ins. Co.*, 738 F. Supp. 432 (D. Colo. 1990). (The *Williams* court also held that entitlement to treble damages under the act requires proof that the insurer acted "willfully and wantonly" only by a preponderance of the evidence.)

—Under Georgia law, it was emphasized in *Great Sw. Express Co. v. Great Am. Ins. Co. of N.Y.*, 292 Ga. App. 757, 665 S.E.2d 878 (2008), absent some special relationship beyond that between insurer and insured, an insured's exclusive remedy for a bad faith refusal to pay is the remedy provided by Ga. Code Ann. §33-4-6 for a penalty and attorneys' fees.

—Concerning the Illinois Supreme Court's belated clarification of Illinois law—no common-law tort of first-party bad faith is recognized, and the penalty statute (Ill. Ins. Code §155) provides the exclusive remedy—see *Cramer v. Insurance Exch. Agency*, 174 Ill. 2d 513, 675 N.E.2d 897 (1996). Holding that $25,000 is the maximum penalty that may be awarded under Ill. Ins. Code §155, see *Nelles v. State Farm Fire & Casualty Co.*, 318 Ill. App. 3d 399, 742 N.E.2d 420 (2000). As of January 1, 2004, the maximum penalty available under §155 is $60,000. See *In re CFB Liquidating Corp.*, 581 B.R. 317 (Bkrtcy. N.D. Cal. 2017), *aff'd*, 591 B.R. 396 (N.D. Cal. 2018) (Illinois law; discussed in §§2.7, 2.70, 2.72).

—In *Durio v. Horace Mann Ins. Co.*, 74 So. 3d 1159 (La. 2011), the Louisiana Supreme Court held that contractual amounts due pursuant to the terms of an insurance contract may not be included as damages in calculating penalties against the insurer for violating the duty of good faith and fair dealing. The court thus abrogated *Neal Auction*

Co. v. Lafayette Ins. Co., 13 So. 3d 1135 (La. Ct. App. 2009); *Wegener v. Lafayette Ins. Co.*, 34 So. 3d 932 (La. Ct. App. 2009); and *Buffman v. Lafayette Ins. Co.*, 36 So. 3d 1004 (La. Ct. App. 2010). See also *Citadel Broad. Corp. v. Axis U.S. Ins. Co.*, 162 So. 3d 470 (La. Ct. App.), *writ denied*, 170 So. 3d 969 (La. 2015) (upholding jury award of $2,953,454 in penalties under Louisiana bad faith statute in business interruption case stemming from Hurricane Katrina; see discussion in §1.66, *infra*); *Anco Insulations, Inc. v. Nat'l Union Fire Ins. Co. of Pittsburgh, Pa.*, 787 F.3d 276 (5th Cir. 2015) (discussed in §1.61, *infra*).

—In *Peterson v. Western Nat'l Mut. Ins. Co.*, 946 N.W.2d 903 (Minn. 2020), the Supreme Court of Minnesota held that the trial court did not err in finding that the insurer did not act as a reasonable insurer would have in denying the plaintiff's claim for coverage, and that it knew or recklessly disregarded information that showed it had no objectively reasonable basis to deny benefits. Accordingly, the court upheld awards of $100,000 in taxable costs and $97,940.50 in attorney fees under Minn. Stat. §604.18. The court concluded that the insurer's failure to conduct an adequate investigation of the insured's claim under her underinsured motorist's policy, including disregarding a mountain of medical evidence that her accident caused severe headaches requiring Botox treatment, led it to unreasonably and recklessly deny her claim.

—In *Overcast v. Billings Mut. Ins. Co.*, 11 S.W.3d 62 (Mo. banc 2000), the Missouri Supreme Court recognized an exception to the preemptive effect of the state's penalty statutes, allowing a tort recovery on a defamation claim brought by an insured who had been compelled to "self-publish" defendant's arson accusation when attempting to secure a new policy from another insurer. The nonpreemption principle announced by the court in *Overcast* appears to be a narrow one, limited in application to torts independent of any contractual breach. (The generally preemptive effect of the penalty statutes was discussed and upheld in *Catron v. Columbia Mut. Ins. Co.*, 723 S.W.2d 5 (Mo. 1987).) For cases applying Missouri's statutes providing statutory penalties and attorney's fees for vexatious refusal to pay, Mo. Rev. Stat. §§375.420 and 375.296, see *Dhyne v. State Farm Fire & Casualty Co.*, 188 S.W.3d 454 (Mo. banc 2006) (affirming judgment for insured in action to recover uninsured motorist benefits and damages for vexatious refusal to pay); *Merseal v. Farm Bureau Town & Country Ins. Co. of Mo.*, 396 S.W.3d 467 (Mo. App. 2013) (upholding jury award of statutory damages and attorney's fees under §375.420 for insurer's refusal to pay homeowners insurance claim without reasonable cause).

—In *McKinnie v. State Farm Fire & Casualty Co.*, 298 F. Supp. 3d 1138 (M.D. Tenn. 2018), the court found that the Tennessee Unfair Trade Practices and Unfair Claims Settlement Act (Titles 50 and 56 of the Tennessee Code) did not eliminate the common-law claim for punitive damages in breach of insurance contract cases. The insured was permitted to proceed on both a common-law claim for punitive damages for breach of insurance contract and a claim for a statutory penalty under the bad faith statute. Accord *Lindenberg v. Jackson Nat'l Life Ins. Co.*, 912 F.3d 348 (6th Cir. 2019), *cert. denied*, ___ U.S. ___, 140 S. Ct. 635 (2019).

§1.28 c. Workers' Compensation Statutes

—Four decisions of the Alabama Supreme Court have reiterated the rule that workers' compensation exclusivity precludes a carrier's liability for bad faith: *Stewart v. Mathews Indus., Inc.*, 644 So. 2d 915 (Ala. 1994); *Gibson v. Southern Guar. Ins. Co.*, 623 So. 2d 1065 (Ala. 1993); *Farley v. CNA Ins. Co.*, 576 So. 2d 158 (Ala. 1991); *Wooley v. Shewbart*, 569 So. 2d 712 (Ala. 1990).

—Reversing the Arizona Court of Appeals decision that was summarized in this section of the 1994 supplement, the Arizona Supreme Court, in *Hayes v. Continental Ins. Co.*,

178 Ariz. 264, 872 P.2d 668 (1994), held that the relevant provision of the state workers' compensation statute (Ariz. Rev. Stat. §23-930) was *not* intended by the legislature to preempt common-law bad faith claims.

—Under California law, jurisdiction rests with the courts, not with the Workers' Compensation Appeals Board, when an employer asserts bad faith and breach of contract claims against its workers' compensation carrier: *Salimi v. State Compensation Ins. Fund*, 54 Cal. App. 4th 216, 62 Cal. Rptr. 2d 640 (1997); *Lance Camper Mfg. Corp. v. Republic Indem. Co.*, 44 Cal. App. 4th 194, 51 Cal. Rptr. 2d 622 (1996); *Tricor Cal., Inc. v. State Compensation Ins. Fund*, 30 Cal. App. 4th 230, 35 Cal. Rptr. 2d 550 (1994). See also *Vacanti v. State Compensation Ins. Fund*, 24 Cal. 4th 800, 102 Cal. Rptr. 2d 562 (2001) (reversing dismissal of claims for antitrust and RICO violations, interference with contractual relations, and statutory unfair competition by medical providers against workers' compensation insurers, because such claims were based on wrongful acts outside scope of workers' compensation bargain). After further proceedings in *Lance Camper Mfg. Corp.*, *supra*, the Court of Appeal affirmed judgment for the insured and awards of compensatory and punitive damages totaling $6.3 million. *Lance Camper Mfg. Corp. v. Republic Indem. Co.*, 90 Cal. App. 4th 1151, 109 Cal. Rptr. 2d 515 (2001).

In *Rangel v. Interinsurance Exch. of the Auto. Club*, 4 Cal. 4th 1, 14 Cal. Rptr. 2d 783 (1992), the state supreme court reinstated a judgment on the pleadings in favor of the insurer, holding that the insurer had been under no duty to pay benefits to the insured during the pendency of workers' compensation proceedings. According to the language of the policy, the court explained, the amount owed the insured, including the amount of loss-reduction attributable to a workers' compensation award, was to be settled by arbitration, and that amount could not be determined until the workers' compensation claim was resolved. See also *Case v. State Farm Mut. Auto. Ins. Co.*, 30 Cal. App. 5th

397, 241 Cal. Rptr. 3d 458 (2018) (insurer did not act in bad faith when it declined to pay benefits or arbitrate until workers' compensation claim had been resolved, including determination of amounts paid *or payable* by workers' compensation).

—In *Brodeur v. American Home Assurance Co.*, 169 P.3d 139 (Colo. 2007), an *en banc* decision filed in October of 2007, the Colorado Supreme Court held: (1) bad faith tort remedies are distinct and separate from remedies under the Workers' Compensation Act, and the two types of claims are resolved independently; (2) the claimant's bad faith tort claim against the workers' compensation insurer accrued on the date the claimant's attorney stated in a letter that the insurer was handling the claim in bad faith, and the statute of limitations began to run on that date and was not equitably tolled, even though the claimant had a pending administrative workers' compensation proceeding; and (3) rulings made by an administrative law judge or the Industrial Claims Appeals Board are not binding on a court's determination of a bad faith tort claim.

As noted in the book, the Colorado Supreme Court has held that a workers' compensation claimant may sue a workers' compensation carrier for bad faith despite the lack of a direct contractual relationship. (A claimant's common-law cause of action for bad faith was not abrogated by an amendment increasing statutory penalties for mishandling claims, the state supreme court held in *Vaughan v. McMinn*, 945 P.2d 404 (Colo. 1997).) And a Colorado Court of Appeals, in *Johnson v. Scott Wetzel, Inc.*, 779 P.2d 786 (Colo. Ct. App. 1990), *aff'd*, 821 P.2d 804 (Colo. 1991), has extended that reasoning to allow a claimant to sue the independent adjuster hired by a self-insured employer. And concerning the Colorado statutory requirement that an insured must seek workers' compensation benefits before suing for no-fault personal injury protection benefits, see *Schultz v. Allstate Ins. Co.*, 764 F. Supp 1404 (D. Colo. 1991) (denying summary judgment because the conclusion that the insured should have applied first for workers' compensation benefits did not preclude findings that some of the insurer's alternate grounds for delaying payment had been asserted in bad faith).

—In *DeOliveira v. Liberty Mut. Ins. Co.*, 273 Conn. 487, 870 A.2d 1066 (2005), the Connecticut Supreme Court acknowledged a possible exception in cases involving particularly egregious claims-handling conduct, but held that, in general, workers' compensation statutory remedies are exclusive of common-law bad faith claims.

—Under Delaware law, the state supreme court held in *Pierce v. International Ins. Co.*, 671 A.2d 1361 (Del. 1996), workers' compensation carriers owe a duty of good faith to claimants as third-party beneficiaries to the contract between insurer and employer, and common-law bad faith actions by claimants against insurers are not precluded by the exclusivity provision of the workers' compensation statute. (See also *Thurston v. Liberty Mut. Ins. Co.*, 16 F. Supp. 2d 441 (D. Del. 1998).) The court noted that the bad faith cause of action sounds only in contract, however, and damages for emotional distress are not available, though punitive damages may be available if denial of coverage was willful or malicious.

—Under Hawaii law, an employee must first exhaust administrative remedies, but may then bring a bad faith action against a workers' compensation carrier. *Taylor v. Standard Ins. Co.*, 28 F. Supp. 2d 588 (D. Haw. 1997).

—Under Idaho law, it was held in *Van Tine v Idaho State Ins. Fund*, 889 P.2d 717 (Idaho 1994), *op. after further proc.*, 880 P.2d 566 (Idaho 1999), a bad faith claim for the fund's failure to pay benefits comes within the exclusive jurisdiction of the Idaho Industrial Commission.

—Holding that the Indiana Workers' Compensation Board has exclusive jurisdiction over claims of employer or insurer bad faith in adjusting a workers' compensation claim, see *Borgman v. State Farm Ins. Co.*, 713 N.E.2d 851 (Ind. Ct. App. 1999). See also *Sims v. United States Fidelity &*

Guar. Co., 782 N.E.2d 345 (Ind. 2003) (rejecting constitutional challenges to Ind. Code section 22-3-4-12.1, which gives workers' compensation board exclusive jurisdiction in determining whether employer or insurer acted in bad faith in adjusting or settling claims).

—Answering questions certified from a federal district court, the Iowa Supreme Court, in *Reedy v. White Consol. Indus., Inc.*, 503 N.W.2d 601 (Iowa 1993), held: (1) Iowa law recognizes an action against a self-insured employer for bad faith failure to pay a workers' compensation claim for medical benefits; and (2) exhaustion of remedy and primary jurisdiction doctrines do not apply to such independent tort actions, but courts should adopt a discretionary abstention policy pending administrative determination. The court noted that it had previously rejected application of the exclusive remedy provision in the context of bad faith tort actions against workers' compensation carriers, in *Boylan v. American Motorists Ins. Co.*, 489 N.W.2d 742 (Iowa 1992). See also *Wilson v. Liberty Mut. Group*, 666 N.W.2d 163 (Iowa 2003); *Brown v. Liberty Mut. Ins. Co.*, 513 N.W.2d 762 (Iowa 1994); *Jackson v. Travelers Ins. Co.*, 26 F. Supp. 2d 1153 (S.D. Iowa 1998).

For a case that discusses a bad faith claim against an employer's workers' compensation carrier, see *Thornton v. Am. Interstate Ins. Co.*, 940 N.W.2d 1 (Iowa 2020) (delay of 1.5 years in determining that insured was permanently and totally disabled harmed insured by delaying his receipt of partial commutation, and such delay supported award of $58,452.42 in compensatory damages and $500,000 in punitive damages).

In *De Dios v. Indem. Ins. Co. of N. Am.*, 927 N.W.2d 611 (Iowa 2019), the Supreme Court of Iowa answered a certified question from a federal district court, holding that a common-law cause of action for bad faith failure to pay a workers' compensation claim is not available against a third-party claims administrator of a workers' compensation insurance company.

—Also holding that under Kentucky law, common-law bad faith claims are preempted by the workers' compensation scheme: *General Accident Ins. Co. v. Blank*, 873 S.W.2d 580 (Ky. Ct. App. 1993).

—Applying Mississippi law, a federal district court held, in *Billingsley v. United Technologies Motor Sys.*, 895 F. Supp. 119 (S.D. Miss. 1995), that an employee may not bring a bad faith action based on the denial of workers' compensation benefits before exhausting administrative remedies. See also *Walls v. Franklin Corp. and Employers Ins. of Wausau*, 797 So. 2d 73 (Miss. 2001) (employee may not pursue bad faith action for refusal to pay benefits until Workers' Compensation Commission has determined that requested benefits are "reasonable and necessary").

—In *Brewington v. Employers Fire Ins. Co.*, 992 P.2d 237 (Mont. 1999), the Montana Supreme Court held that an injured worker who had received workers' compensation benefits could pursue statutory and common-law bad faith claims in connection with the insurer's refusal to pay attorneys' fees incurred in the workers' compensation proceedings. (Significantly, the court also held that the Montana Unfair Claim Practices Act does not preempt common bad faith claims by third-party claimants.)

—In *Ihm v. Crawford & Co.*, 254 Neb. 818, 580 N.W.2d 115 (1998), the Nebraska Supreme Court held that the doctrine of workers' compensation exclusivity precludes maintenance of common-law bad faith actions.

—In *Falline v. GNLV Corp.*, 823 P.2d 888 (Nev. 1991), the Nevada Supreme Court held that the penalty provisions of the state workers' compensation statute do not preempt a tort action against a self-insured employer or its administrator/agent for negligent or bad faith failure or refusal to process and pay a workers' compensation claim. The court added, however, that any such action was subject to a $50,000 total recovery limit, and that punitive damages, but not emotional distress damages, are precluded.

In *Fernandez v. State Farm Mut. Auto. Ins. Co.*, 338

F. Supp. 3d 1193 (D. Nev. 2018) (Nevada law), the federal district court found that whether the insurer had a reasonable basis to deny the insured's claim was an issue of genuine dispute where the insurer had no evidence to support its position that the insured would have recovered all of her medical expenses from workers' compensation had she filed such a claim. The court found that a clause in the insurance policy that reduced the insurer's liability by any amount that could have been paid by workers' compensation was a violation of Nevada public policy. The court noted that the insured should not be allowed double recovery, but concluded that reducing recovery by theoretical benefits, not actual benefits, leaves the insured less than whole.

—In *Cruz v. Liberty Mut. Ins. Co.*, 119 N.M. 301, 889 P.2d 1223 (1995), the New Mexico Supreme Court discussed the retroactive effect of a 1991 amendment to the workers' compensation statute that abrogated the civil right of action for insurance bad faith in the workers' compensation context, and placed all such claims under the exclusive jurisdiction of the Workers' Compensation Administration. See also *Kitchell v. Public Serv. Co.*, 972 P.2d 344 (N.M. 1998).

—Upholding the exclusive jurisdiction of the North Carolina Industrial Commission over bad faith claims in workers' compensation cases, see *Johnson v. First Union Corp.*, 504 S.E.2d 808 (N.C. Ct. App. 1998), *review granted*, Dec. 30, 1998.

—In *Sizemore v. Continental Casualty Co.*, 142 P.3d 47 (Okla. 2006), the Supreme Court of Oklahoma held that nothing in the Workers' Compensation Act's exclusive remedy provision extends common-law immunity to an insurance carrier for its failure to act in good faith and to deal fairly in payment of an award. A common-law tort action therefore exists, the court emphasized, for an insurance carrier's bad faith in refusing to pay a workers' compensation award. The court rejected the holdings of *Kuykendall v. Gulfstream Aerospace Technologies*, 2002 OK 96, 66 P.3d 374 (Okla. 2002), and *DeAnda v. AIU Ins.*, 2004 OK 54, 98 P.3d 1080 (Okla. 2004).

In *Meeks v. Guarantee Ins. Co.*, 392 P.3d 278 (Okla. 2017), the Supreme Court of Oklahoma emphasized the proper application of *Summers v. Zurich Am. Ins. Co.*, 213 P.3d 565 (Okla. 2009). The court in *Summers* explained the certification procedures and requirements required under the Oklahoma Worker's Compensation Act before an employee can bring a bad faith tort claim in a district court. Under *Summers*, the employee must obtain an order from a Worker's Compensation Court "indicating that benefits '(1) have been ordered in a final order of the Workers' Compensation Court[,] . . . (2) have been certified as having not been provided as ordered,' and (3) that the insurer failed to demonstrate good cause for its failure to obey the WCC orders." 392 P.3d at 285 (quoting *Summers*, 213 P.3d at 568). The certification procedures and requirements were initially stated by the court in *Sizemore, supra*. In *Meeks*, the court held that the employee could commence a bad faith cause of action in district court because the Worker's Compensation Court order obtained by the employee satisfied the second recognized certification category under *Summers* where the insurer ultimately paid the benefits but did not do so "as ordered."

—Under Pennsylvania law, it was held in *Santiago v. Pennsylvania Nat'l Mut. Casualty Ins. Co.*, 613 A.2d 1235 (Pa. Super. Ct. 1992), the exclusivity provision of the state workers' compensation act precludes the maintenance of bad faith tort actions relating to improper claims handling. Accord *Fry v. Atlantic States Ins. Co.*, 700 A.2d 974 (Pa. Super. Ct. 1997); *Winterberg v. Transportation Ins. Co.*, 72 F.3d 318 (3d Cir. 1995). Compare *Martin v. Lancaster Battery Co.*, 530 Pa. 11, 606 A.2d 444 (1992), in which the state supreme court declined to apply the exclusive remedy provision in a case involving allegations of fraudulent misrepresentation by the employer.

—Under Rhode Island law, it was held in *Cianci v. Nationwide Ins. Co.*, 659 A.2d 662 (R.I. 1995), injured workers lack standing to bring bad faith claims against workers' compensation carriers.

—Under South Dakota law, only after a workers' compensation claimant has exhausted his or her remedies under the state workers' compensation statutes may a trial court hear a bad faith claim for denial of workers' compensation benefits. *Zuke v. Presentation Sisters, Inc.*, 589 N.W.2d 925 (S.D. 1999). See also *Hein v. Acuity*, 731 N.W.2d 231 (S.D. 2007) (workers' compensation claimant's bad faith claim against insurer, alleging that insurer filed counterclaim against claimant in bad faith in separate action in which claimant sought rehabilitation benefits, was premature, where claimant's request for such benefits was pending before Department of Labor, and because central element of bad faith cause of action is whether there has been wrongful denial of benefits). In *Lagler v. Menard, Inc.*, 2018 S.D. 53, 915 N.W.2d 707 (2018), an appeal under South Dakota's worker's compensation statute, the Supreme Court of South Dakota awarded attorney's fees under S.D. Codified Laws §58-12-3 (Insurance Claims and Benefits statute) for vexatious denial of a worker's compensation claim. The insurer refused to pay for a second surgery for the claimant against the advice of the claimant's treating physician. The insurer based its refusal on a purported telephone conversation with a nurse in the treating physician's office who told the insurer that the claimant's symptoms were unrelated to the workplace injury. However, the insurer was unable to identify the nurse, nobody in the physician's office said they had such a conversation with the insurer, and the claimant's medical file contained no record of such a conversation. The insurer did not obtain an independent medical examination of the claimant, so the treating physician's advice was the only opinion available.

In *Johnson v. United Parcel Serv., Inc.*, 946 N.W.2d 1 (S.D. 2020), a workers' compensation insurer terminated medical payments paid to an employee despite a Department of Labor order stating that the employee was entitled to medical expenses related to her workplace injury. The insurer terminated its payments after consulting with an attorney who told the insurer it could terminate the payments after a neurologist determined that the employee's former employment no longer contributed to her condition. The court found the termination of benefits to be unreasonable because the insurer was required to use the statutory procedure to modify the Department order before terminating payments. However, the court remanded the case for a new trial, finding that the lower court erred by preventing the insurer from presenting evidence to support its advice-of-counsel defense. Such evidence was critical for the jury's determination of whether the insurer knew there was no reasonable basis for terminating payments.

—Under Texas law, it is now clearly established that a workers' compensation claimant may sue the carrier for common-law bad faith. See, *e.g.*, *Natividad v. Alexsis, Inc.*, 875 S.W.2d 695 (Tex. 1994) (but declining to recognize claim against independent adjusting firm); *Texas Mut. Ins. Co. v. Ruttiger*, 265 S.W.3d 651 (Tex. App. 2008) (affirming judgment for claimant including award of $100,000 for mental anguish); *Wolford v. American Home Assurance Co.*, 263 S.W.3d 12 (Tex. App. 2006) (affirming summary judgment for insurer on present facts); *Ramirez v. Transcontinental Ins. Co.*, 881 S.W.2d 818 (Tex. Ct. App. 1994); *Rogers v. CIGNA Ins. Co.*, 881 S.W.2d 177 (Tex. Ct. App. 1994); *Packer v. Travelers Indem. Co.*, 881 S.W.2d 172 (Tex. Ct. App. 1994); *GAB Business Servs., Inc. v. Moore*, 829 S.W.2d 345 (Tex. Ct. App. 1992); *Seale v. American Motorist Ins. Co.*, 798 S.W.2d 382 (Tex. Ct. App. 1990); *Rodriguez v. American Gen. Fire & Casualty Co.*, 788 S.W.2d 583 (Tex. Ct. App. 1990); *Bastian v. Travelers Ins. Co.*, 784 F. Supp. 1253 (N.D. Tex. 1992) (Texas law). But the question sometimes arises whether the terms of the settlement of the injury claim preclude a bad faith cause of action because the settlement acknowledged the existence of a bona fide dispute over coverage. Cases involving this issue, and turning on the specific language of the settlement agreement, have included *Rangel v. Hartford Accident & Indem. Co.*, 821 S.W.2d 196 (Tex. Ct. App. 1991) (claimant was collaterally estopped by compromise judgment in workers' compensation proceeding to relitigate findings that liability and extent of injury were uncertain); *Torchia v. Aetna Casualty & Sur. Co.*, 804 S.W.2d 219 (Tex. Ct. App. 1991) (claimant's settlement of workers' compensation claim precluded insurer's liability for bad faith); *Coleman v. Lumbermens Mut. Casualty Co.*, 786 S.W.2d 445 (Tex. Ct. App. 1990) (terms of settlement acknowledged only existence of dispute, not of reasonable basis for insurer's position); and *Price v. Texas Employers' Ins. Ass'n*, 782 S.W.2d 938 (Tex. Ct. App. 1989) (terms of settlement established that insurer had reasonable basis for disputing coverage). And see *American Motorists Ins. Co. v. Fodge*, 63 S.W.3d 801 (Tex. 2001), for a holding that an employee could not pursue a claim for extra-contractual damages for workers' compensation insurer's denial of medical benefits where no claim for such benefits had been presented at a contested hearing before the Workers' Compensation Commission. (The Commission had ordered payment of temporary income benefits that the carrier had denied.) Concerning the circumstances under which administrative remedies must be exhausted, see *Schwartz v. The Ins. Co. of the State of Penn.*, 274 S.W.3d 270 (Tex. App. 2008); *Texas Mut. Ins. Co. v. Ruttiger, supra.*

—Under Utah law, it was held in *Savage v. Educators Ins. Co.*, 908 P.2d 862 (Utah 1995), an employee, being merely a third-party claimant and lacking privity of contract, may not bring a bad faith claim against his or her employer's workers' compensation carrier. See also *Gunderson v. May Dep't Stores Co.*, 955 P.2d 346 (Utah Ct. App. 1998).

—For a holding, under Vermont law, that injured workers

have the right to proceed directly against their employers' workers' compensation carriers, and concerning the insurer's duty of good faith in fulfilling obligations under a settlement agreement, see *Racine v. American Int'l Adjustment Co.*, 980 F. Supp. 745 (D. Vt. 1997).

§1.29 d. ERISA

The case for amending ERISA to permit bad faith claims against insurers has been forcefully argued in a book by San Francisco attorney Ray Bourhis entitled *Insult to Injury: Insurance, Fraud and the Big Business of Bad Faith* (Berrett-Koehler, 2005). Bourhis, who has represented plaintiffs in a number of landmark actions against UnumProvident and other insurers, (see, e.g., *Hangarter v. Provident Life & Accident Ins. Co.*, 373 F.3d 998 (9th Cir. 2004), discussed in §1.66, *infra*), has obtained the support of Ted Kennedy in promoting the idea of statutory reform, and, as of late 2005, was negotiating with John McCain in pursuit of a bipartisan approach to the issue. And on October 26, 2005, Bourhis and law partner Alice J. Wolfson filed a class action complaint in San Francisco County Superior Court seeking billions of dollars in premium refunds and damages for claims fraudulently denied by UnumProvident to California policyholders. (*Hangarter v. The Paul Revere Life Ins. Co.*, 05-446073). (On October 3, 2005, California Insurance Commissioner John Garamendi announced a settlement that requires UnumProvident to pay the state $8 million in fines, reconsider thousands of claim denials, and change the way it processes claims. In a press conference announcing the settlement, Garamendi called UnumProvident "an outlaw company" that "has a corporate policy established at the highest level to systematically deny legitimate claims.")

But courts presented with the question for the first time have generally continued to hold that ERISA preemption extends not only to common-law bad faith causes of action against group insurers, but also to statutory causes of action under unfair claim settlement practices statutes, and under penalty statutes. See, *e.g.*, *Gilbert v. Alta Health & Life Ins. Co.*, 276 F.3d 1292 (11th Cir. 2001) (Alabama law; Alabama bad faith cause of action codified at Ala. Code §27-12-24 (2001)); *Kidneigh v. UNUM Life Ins. Co. of Am.*, 345 F.3d 1182 (10th Cir. 2003) (Colorado statutory causes of action); *Kelly v. Sears, Roebuck & Co.*, 882 F.2d 453 (10th Cir. 1989) (Colorado statutory causes of action); *Glynn v. Bankers Life & Casualty Co.*, 297 F. Supp. 2d 424 (D. Conn. 2003) (Connecticut Unfair Trade Practice Act); *Fischman v. Blue Cross & Blue Shield*, 775 F. Supp. 528 (D. Conn. 1990) (Connecticut Unfair Insurance Practices Act); *Altieri v. Cigna Dental Health, Inc.*, 753 F. Supp. 61 (D. Conn. 1990) (same); *Yardley v. U.S. Healthcare, Inc.*, 698 A.2d 979 (Del. Super. Ct. 1996), *aff'd without op.*, 693 A.2d 1083 (Del. 1997) (Delaware Unfair Claim Settlement Practices Act, assuming existence of private right of action thereunder); *Swerhun v. Guardian Life Ins. Co. of Am.*, 979 F.2d 195 (11th Cir. 1992) (Florida's bad faith statute); *Cockey v. Life Ins. Co. of N. Am.*, 804 F. Supp. 1571 (S.D. Ga. 1992) (Georgia's bad faith statute); *Summers v. United States Tobacco Co.*, 214 Ill. App. 3d 878, 574 N.E.2d 206 (1991) (Illinois penalty statute); *Pane v. Dandan*, 763 F. Supp. 281 (N.D. Ill. 1991) (same); *Curry v. Cincinnati Equitable Ins. Co.*, 834 S.W.2d 701 (Ky. Ct. App. 1992) (claims under Kentucky unfair claims settlement practices act and Kentucky consumer protection act); *Cramer v. Association of Life Ins. Co.*, 569 So. 2d 533 (La. 1990), *cert. denied*, 499 U.S. 938 (1991) (Louisiana penalty statute); *Provident Life & Accident Ins. Co. v. Sharpless*, 364 F.3d 634 (5th Cir. 2004) (Louisiana statute that bars cancellation of policies because of insureds' innocent or nonmaterial misrepresentations); *Ryan v. Fallon Community Health Plan*, 921 F. Supp. 34 (D. Mass. 1996) (Massachusetts law); *Kelly v. Pan-American Life Ins. Co.*, 767 F. Supp. 1406 (W.D. Mo. 1991) (Missouri penalty statute); *Elliot v. Fortis*

Benefits Ins. Co., 337 F.3d 1138 (9th Cir. 2003) (Montana Unfair Trade Practice Act); *Greany v. Western Farm Bureau Life Ins. Co.*, 973 F.2d 812 (9th Cir. 1992) (claims under Montana's unfair claims settlement practices statute); *Hollaway v. UNUM Life Ins. Co. of Am.*, 89 P.3d 1022 (Okla. 2003) (Oklahoma's common law of bad faith); *Allison v. UNUM Life Ins. Co. of Am.*, 381 F.3d 1015 (10th Cir. 2004) (Oklahoma's bad faith law); *Conover v. Aetna US Healthcare*, 320 F.3d 1076 (10th Cir. 2003) (same); *Barber v. UNUM Life Ins. Co. of Am.*, 383 F.3d 134 (3d Cir. 2004) (Pennsylvania's bad faith statute); *Nguyen v. Healthguard of Lancaster, Inc.*, 282 F. Supp. 2d 296 (E.D. Pa. 2003) (Pennsylvania Bad Faith statute); *McGuigan v. Reliance Standard Life Ins. Co.*, 256 F. Supp. 2d 345 (E.D. Pa. 2003) (Pennsylvania's bad faith statute); *Snook v. Penn State Geisinger Health Plan*, 241 F. Supp. 2d 485 (M.D. Pa. 2003) (Pennsylvania's bad faith statute); *Boudra v. Humana Health Ins. Co.*, 730 F. Supp. 1432 (W.D. Tenn. 1990) (Tennessee penalty statute); *Bishop v. Provident Life & Casualty Co.*, 749 F. Supp. 176 (E.D. Tenn. 1990) (same); *Silva v. Aetna Life Ins. Co.*, 805 S.W.2d 820 (Tex. Ct. App. 1991) (claims under Tex. Ins. Code art. 21.21, §16); *Ramirez v. Inter Continental Hotels*, 890 F.2d 760 (5th Cir. 1989) (same); *Hogan v. Kraft Foods*, 969 F.2d 142 (5th Cir. 1992) (claims under Tex. Ins. Code art. 21.21 and Texas Deceptive Trade Practices Act, Tex. Bus. & Com. Code Ann. §§17.41 et seq.); *Optimal Health Care Servs., Inc. v. Travelers Ins. Co.*, 791 F. Supp. 163 (E.D. Tex. 1992) (same); *Ball v. Life Planning Servs., Inc.*, 421 S.E.2d 223 (W. Va. 1992) (claims under West Virginia unfair claims settlement practices act).

Although the reasoning and language of *Pilot Life Ins. Co. v. Dedeaux*, 481 U.S. 41 (1987) (discussed in book §1.30), is, unfortunately, broad enough to support the view that statutory causes of action, like common-law claims, are preempted, a few courts have held otherwise. See, *e.g.*, *Stone v. Disability Mgmt. Servs.*, 288 F. Supp. 2d 684 (M.D.

Pa. 2003) (applying "dramatically changed" analysis of *Kentucky Ass'n of Health Plans, Inc. v. Miller*, 538 U.S. 329 (2003) in holding that Pennsylvania unfair practices statute permitting award of punitive damages for bad faith conduct was saved from preemption); *Rosenbaum v. UNUM Life Ins. Co. of Am.*, 2002 WL 1769899 (E.D. Pa. 2002) (cause of action under Pennsylvania's bad faith statute); *Mayfield v. Hartford Ins. Co.*, 699 F. Supp 605 (W.D. Tex. 1988) (cause of action under Texas unfair insurance practices statute). And in *Memorial Hosp. Sys. v. Northbrook Life Ins. Co.*, 904 F.2d 236 (5th Cir. 1990), the Fifth Circuit made a distinction between causes of action brought by plan members, and causes of action brought against group insurers by third parties, holding that ERISA preemption does *not* extend to the latter. (The case involved an action by a hospital against the insurer under Tex. Ins. Code art. 21.21 in connection with the insurer's misrepresentation to the hospital that a patient was covered under a group plan.)

With respect to another ERISA-related issue, a number of courts have held that insurers waived their preemption defense to common-law or statutory bad faith causes of action by failing to raise the defense in a timely fashion in the trial court: *Hughes v. Blue Cross*, 215 Cal. App. 3d 832, 263 Cal. Rptr. 850 (1989); *Rehabilitation Inst. v. Equitable Life Assurance Soc'y of the U.S.*, 131 F.R.D. 99 (W.D. Pa. 1990); *Pan Am. Life Ins. Co. v. Erbauer Constr. Corp.*, 791 S.W.2d 146 (Tex. Ct. App. 1990). And in *Hermann Hosp. v. Aetna Life Ins. Co.*, 803 S.W.2d 351 (Tex. Ct. App. 1990), it was held that ERISA did not preempt a hospital's claims against an insurer for misrepresenting that a patient had coverage.

In *UNUM Life Ins. Co. of Am. v. Ward*, 526 U.S. 358 (1999), the United States Supreme Court, affirming a 1998 Ninth Circuit decision, held that the district court had erred in granting summary judgment for an insurer on the ground that the insured had submitted his claim for disability benefits under an ERISA-governed policy outside the policy's time limit. The Supreme Court agreed with the Ninth Circuit that California's "notice-prejudice rule" is saved from

ERISA preemption because it is a "law which regulates insurance" within the meaning of ERISA's "saving" clause (29 U.S.C. §1144(b)(2)(A)). According to California's "notice-prejudice rule," an insurer cannot avoid liability because of an untimely proof of claim unless the insurer shows that it was prejudiced by the delay. A few courts construed the *Ward* decision as casting doubt on the continued vitality of the holding of *Pilot Life Ins. Co. v. Dedeaux, supra,* that ERISA preempts any state law that conflicts with the statute's enforcement provisions. See *Colligan v. UNUM Life Ins. Co., supra; Hall v. UNUM Life Assurance Co.,* No. 97-M-1828 (D. Colo. 1999) (unpublished). However, the *Pilot Life* decision was subsequently reaffirmed by the Supreme Court in *Rush Prudential HMO, Inc. v. Moran,* 536 U.S. 355 (2002), thus ratifying the view taken by a number of other courts that *Ward* did not overrule *Pilot Life sub silentio.* See, *e.g., Conover v. Aetna US Healthcare, supra; Hotz v. Blue Cross/Blue Shield,* 292 F.3d 57 (1st Cir. 2002); *Howard v. Coventry Health Care,* 293 F.3d 442 (8th Cir. 2002); *Walker v. Southern Co. Servs., Inc.,* 279 F.3d 1289 (11th Cir. 2002); *Adams v. UNUM Life Ins. Co.,* 200 F. Supp. 2d 796 (N.D. Ohio 2002); *Little v. UNUMProvident,* 196 F. Supp. 2d 659 (S.D. Ohio 2002). (In *Rush Prudential* the Supreme Court held that ERISA does not preempt an Illinois statute requiring independent review of HMOs' determinations as to whether treatment is medically necessary.)

The test for ERISA preemption was further amplified in *Aetna Health Inc. v. Davila,* 542 U.S. 200 (2004), involving allegations of negligence in the handling of coverage decisions in violation of the Texas Health Care Liability Act.

§1.30 (1) The Reasoning of *Pilot Life Ins. Co. v. Dedeaux*

Several courts have considered issues relating to the removal to federal court of causes of action against group insurers (see discussion in book of *Metropolitan Life Ins.*

Co. v. Taylor, 481 U.S. 58 (1987)). In *Davis v. American Gen. Group Ins. Co.,* 732 F. Supp. 1132 (N.D. Ala. 1990), a federal district court ordered that the insured's bad faith cause of action be remanded to state court when the insurer made a motion to dismiss on the ground that no ERISA claim could be stated. The court held that where a complaint does not present a federal claim on its face, removal is not justified by the mere possibility of an ERISA-preemption defense. See also *Hensley v. Philadelphia Life Ins. Co.,* 878 F. Supp. 1465 (N.D. Ala. 1995) (granting motion to remand where insurer had failed to allege, much less prove, requisites of ERISA plan); *Wright v. Sterling Investors Life Ins. Co.,* 747 F. Supp. 653 (N.D. Ala. 1990) (removal is not justified by insurer's conclusory allegation that dispute implicates ERISA). A remand was also ordered in *McDonough v. Blue Cross,* 131 F.R.D. 467 (W.D. Pa. 1990), on the ground that plaintiffs were seeking types of consequential damages, including damages for fraud and wrongful death of the insured, that are not recoverable under ERISA. And in *Davis v. John Alden Life Ins. Co.,* 746 F. Supp. 44 (D. Kan. 1990), the court held that where a group insurer has successfully removed a case to federal court on the ground of ERISA preemption, the insured's complaint should be liberally construed as stating cognizable ERISA claims. Similarly, in *HCA Health Servs., Inc. v. Rosner,* 207 Ill. App. 3d 829, 566 N.E.2d 397 (1990), it was held that the trial court had abused its discretion in denying the insured leave to amend his complaint to state an ERISA claim to substitute for his preempted state law claims. (In *Total Plan Servs., Inc. v. Texas Retailers Ass'n,* 925 F.2d 142 (5th Cir. 1991), the Fifth Circuit held that the Anti-Injunction Act (28 U.S.C. §2283) prevents the federal courts from enjoining state court litigation of state law claims preempted by ERISA.)

Concerning ERISA's preemptive effect with respect to causes of action other than bad faith, it was held in *Miller v. Aetna Life & Casualty Co.,* 162 Ariz. 588, 785 P.2d 108

(Ct. App. 1989), that ERISA preempted claims for negligent misrepresentation, and for the intentional infliction of emotional distress. *Foster v. Blue Cross & Blue Shield*, 969 F. Supp. 1020 (E.D. Mich. 1997).

And it was similarly held by a United States District Court, in *Johnson v. Reserve Life Ins. Co.*, 765 F. Supp. 1478 (C.D. Cal. 1991), that ERISA remedies preempted a claim against the insurer for negligent failure to assist a plan member in obtaining her benefits under the plan. See also *Eid v. Duke*, 816 A.2d 844 (Md. 2003) (ERISA preempted malpractice claim against physician hired by health plan not for treatment purposes but solely to make "pure eligibility" decision); *Cleghorn v. Blue Shield of Calif.*, 408 F.3d 1222 (9th Cir. 2005) (ERISA preempted state law claims relating to benefits denial despite allegation that plan's emergency care policy violated state statute requiring coverage of emergency treatment); *Marks v. Watters*, 322 F.3d 316 (4th Cir. 2003) (ERISA preempted malpractice and related claims against health insurer and claims management company relating to purely administrative decisions). Compare *Cicio v. Vytra Healthcare*, 321 F.3d 83 (2d Cir. 2003) (ERISA did not preempt malpractice claim against HMO for refusal to authorize treatment); *Villazon v. Prudential Health Care Plan, Inc.*, 843 So. 2d 842 (Fla. 2003) (ERISA does not preempt malpractice claims against HMOs); *Finderne Mgmt. Co., Inc. v. Barrett*, 355 N.J. Super. 170, 809 A.2d 842 (2002) (ERISA did not preempt claims against agents who misrepresented tax consequences of life insurance policies included in employee benefit plan); *Holroyd v. Requa*, 361 S.C. 43, 603 S.E.2d 417 (Ct. App. 2004) (ERISA did not preempt fraud and professional negligence claims against agents in connection with misrepresentations made in touting ERISA-governed health insurance plan and in failing to inform insured of plan's financial difficulties).

Although the reasoning of *Pilot Life Ins. Co. v. Dedeaux*, 481 U.S. 41 (1987), has been sharply criticized, (see, *e.g.*,

Suggs v. Pan Am. Life Ins. Co., 847 F. Supp. 1324 (S.D. Miss. 1994)), its holding was reaffirmed in *Rush Prudential HMO, Inc. v. Moran*, 536 U.S. 355 (2002), which held that ERISA does not preempt an Illinois statute requiring independent review of HMOs' determinations as to whether treatment is medically necessary. The *Rush* opinion put to rest the argument that *Pilot Life* was overruled *sub silentio* by *UNUM Life Ins. Co. of Am. v. Ward*, 526 U.S. 358 (1999) (see discussion in §1.29, *supra*).

Emphasizing that ERISA preempts state-law claims arising from the wrongful withholding of benefits under a health insurance plan, even though ERISA does not provide a damages remedy in connection with such claims, see *Turner v. Fallon Community Health Plan, Inc.*, 127 F.3d 196 (1st Cir. 1997).

Note that the meaning of the phrase "relate to" as used in ERISA's preemption provision was addressed in *New York Conference of Blue Cross v. Travelers Ins. Co.*, 514 U.S. 645 (1995). The Supreme Court held that a New York state surcharge on hospital bills paid by commercial insurers and HMOs did not "relate to" employee benefit plans in the relevant sense and was therefore not preempted.

In *Kentucky Ass'n of Health Plans, Inc. v. Miller*, 538 U.S. 329 (2003), the Supreme Court, in holding that ERISA does not preempt Kentucky's "any willing provider" statute, clarified that a state law "regulates insurance" for purposes of ERISA non-preemption if it (1) is specifically directed toward the insurance industry and (2) substantially affects the risk pooling arrangement between insurer and insured. In *Anderson v. Continental Casualty Co.*, 258 F. Supp. 2d 1127 (E.D. Cal. 2003), the court applied this two-part test in holding that ERISA does not preempt California's "process of nature" rule according to which a disability insurer must cover disabilities that follow an accident in the time required by the "process of nature," irrespective of policy language setting a 1-year limit. And in *Stone v. Disability Mgmt. Servs.*, 288 F. Supp. 2d 684 (M.D. Pa. 2003), the court held that the "dramatically changed" analysis of *Kentucky Ass'n of Health Plans, Inc. v. Miller, supra,* required the conclusion that the Pennsylvania unfair practices statute, permitting award of punitive damages for bad faith conduct, was saved from preemption. Compare *Hollaway v. UNUM Life Ins. Co. of Am.*, 89 P.3d 1022 (Okla. 2003) (Oklahoma's common law of bad faith does not substantially affect risk-pooling arrangement between insurers and insureds within meaning of *Miller*).

The test for ERISA preemption was further amplified in *Aetna Health Inc. v. Davila*, 542 U.S. 200 (2004), involving allegations of negligence in the handling of coverage decisions in violation of the Texas Health Care Liability Act. See also *Connecticut General Life Ins. Co. v. Insurance Comm'r for State of Md.*, 810 A.2d 425 (Md. 2002) (ERISA does not preempt Maryland statute providing method for insureds to grieve benefits denials by health insurers); *Popoola v. MD-Individual Practice Ass'n*, 244 F. Supp. 2d 577 (D. Md. 2003) (ERISA did not preempt antisubrogation provisions of Maryland's HMO statute relative to class action challenging HMO's practice of asserting subrogation interest in recoveries obtained by insureds from tortfeasors); *McKandes v. Blue Cross & Blue Shield Assoc.*, 243 F. Supp. 2d 380 (D. Md. 2003) (same). Compare *Levine v. United Healthcare Corp.*, 402 F.3d 156 (3d Cir. 2005) (New Jersey's anti-subrogation statute, NJ SA 2A-15-97, does not fall within scope of savings clause in ERISA's preemption provision).

§1.31 (2)　Identifying ERISA Plans for Preemption Purposes

In the following cases, courts have considered issues relating to the definition of an "ERISA plan" for purposes of applying the statutory preemption rule of *Pilot Life Ins. Co. v. Dedeaux*, 481 U.S. 41 (1987): *Marshall v. Bankers Life & Casualty Co.*, 2 Cal. 4th 1045, 10 Cal. Rptr. 2d 72

(1992) (group health policy was ERISA plan despite employer's lack of administrative responsibility where employer paid premiums); *Dearth v. Great Republic Life Ins. Co.*, 9 Cal. App. 4th 1256, 12 Cal. Rptr. 2d 78 (1992) (ERISA preempted D. nclaims against both insurer and agent where plan failed to meet criteria for nonpreemption listed in 29 C.F.R. §2510.3-1(j))); *Rogers v. Prudential Ins. Co.*, 218 Cal. App. 3d 1132, 267 Cal. Rptr. 499 (1990) (trial court erred in granting summary judgment for employer on common-law claims where it was unclear whether employer contributed to payment of premiums); *Lambert v. Pacific Mut. Life Ins. Co.*, 211 Cal. App. 3d 456, 259 Cal. Rptr. 398 (1989) (ERISA preemption was not negated or waived by failure of plan administrator to comply with ERISA reporting requirements); *Peters v. Boulder Ins. Agency, Inc.*, 829 P.2d 429 (Colo. Ct. App. 1991) (ERISA plan was not created where employer's only role was as purchaser); *Sindelar v. Canada Transp., Inc.*, 520 N.W.2d 203 (Neb. 1994) (preemption rule applies only if employer actively participates in design and day-to-day operation of plan); *Tierney v. UNUM Life Ins. Co. of Am.*, 97 S.W.3d 842 (Tex. App. 2003) (stating that employer has burden of proving existence of ERISA plan and discussing factors relevant to determination; summary judgment was precluded by existence of questions of fact); *Universe Life Ins. Co. v. Giles*, 881 S.W.2d 44 (Tex. Ct. App. 1994) (employer's mere purchase of insurance did not create ERISA plan where employer neither directly nor indirectly owned, controlled, administered, or assumed responsibility for policy or benefits); *Robertson v. GEM Ins. Co.*, 828 P.2d 496 (Utah Ct. App. 1992) (reversing dismissal of common-law claims: sole fact that employer had helped make arrangements for insurance for employees was insufficient to support conclusion, as matter of law, that ERISA plan existed); *Anderson v. UNUM Provident Corp.*, 369 F.3d 1257 (11th Cir. 2004) (disability policy was governed by ERISA by virtue of employer's involvement in administration despite fact that employer had asked insurer to remove ERISA language from policy documents); *Waks v. Empire Blue Cross/Blue Shield*, 263 F.3d 872 (9th Cir. 2001) (conversion policies issued to former employees are not ERISA plans); *LaVenture v. Prudential Ins. Co. of Am.*, 237 F.3d 1042 (9th Cir. 2001) (non-ERISA disability plan covering only company's owners was not converted into ERISA plan merely because employer subsequently sponsored separate ERISA plan covering employees); *Demars v. CIGNA Corp.*, 173 F.3d 443 (1st Cir. 1999) (conversion policies issued to former employees are not ERISA plans); *Painter v. Golden Rule Ins. Co.*, 121 F.3d 436 (8th Cir. 1997) (conversion policies issued to former employees qualify as ERISA plans); *Zavora v. Paul Revere Life Ins. Co.*, 145 F.3d 1118 (9th Cir. 1998) (reversing summary judgment; notwithstanding proof that employer made no contributions, that participation was voluntary, and that employer received no consideration for administrative services, fact issues were raised in light of evidence that employer had apparently "endorsed" plan); *Johnson v. Watts Regulator Co.*, 63 F.3d 1129 (1st Cir. 1995) (for preemption rule to apply, employer must actively participate in design and day-to-day operation of plan); *Crull v. Gem Ins. Co.*, 58 F.3d 1386 (9th Cir. 1995) (employer's payment of 25% of premiums and role as administrator were sufficient factors to show establishment of ERISA plan); *Fugarino v. Hartford Life & Accident Ins. Co.*, 969 F.2d 178 (6th Cir. 1992) (ERISA plan is present if employer does more than purchase group insurance and advise employees of its availability, or if plan fails to meet each of exclusionary criterion listed in Department of Labor regulations, 29 C.F.R. §2510.3-1(j)); *Kanne v. Connecticut Gen. Life Ins. Co.*, 867 F.2d 489 (9th Cir. 1988) (preemption rule applies only if employer *intended to create* ERISA plan); *Hansen v. Continental Ins. Co.*, 940 F.2d 971 (5th Cir. 1991) ("ERISA plan" was created where employer endorsed group accidental death policy and employed administrator to receive claims and forward them to insurer); *Barrientos v. Reliance Standard Life Ins. Co.*, 911 F.2d 1115 (5th Cir. 1990) (common-law claims relating to death benefit plan did not escape preemption by virtue of fact that plan was not covered by ERISA's "deemer" clause (explained in book §1.30)); *Harper v. American Chambers Life Ins. Co.*, 898 F.2d 1432 (9th Cir. 1990) (whether plan is "ERISA plan" is question of fact, and district court erred in deciding question as matter of law, and also in dismissing complaint without permitting insureds to amend to state ERISA claims); *Insco v. Aetna Health & Life Ins. Co.*, 673 F. Supp. 2d 1180 (D.Nev. 2009) (ERISA did not preempt Nevada administrative code provisions on which employee based her negligence claims relating to administrator's selection and retention of in-network health care providers); *Gregory v. Metropolitan Life Ins. Co.*, 648 F. Supp. 2d 591 (D. Vt. 2009) (ERISA preempted bad faith claim brought by participant in self-funded ERISA disability plan against insurance company that was plan's claim administrator); *Pearl v. Monarch Life Ins. Co.*, 289 F. Supp. 2d 324 (E.D.N.Y. 2003) (disability policy was not governed by ERISA where insured, owner and shareholder of three-person medical practice, was not properly characterized as "employee"); *Stanton v. Paul Revere Life Ins. Co.*, 37 F. Supp. 2d 1159 (S.D. Cal. 1999) (disability insurance policy bought to compensate professional corporation for loss of its principal employee's services was not "employee benefit plan" for ERISA preemption purposes); *Gray v. New York Life Ins. Co.*, 879 F. Supp. 99 (N.D. Ala. 1995) (no ERISA plan was created where employer did not make contributions, endorse policy, collect premiums, or receive consideration for services, and where participation was voluntary); *Hubbard v. State Mut. Life Assurance Cos. of Am.*, 832 F. Supp. 1079 (E.D. Tex. 1993) (discussing diagnostic characteristics of ERISA plans, and holding that plaintiff failed to raise fact issue as to source of funding); *Elco Mechanical Contractors, Inc. v. Builders Supply Ass'n*, 832 F. Supp. 1054 (S.D. W. Va. 1993) (for preemption rule to apply, employer must actively participate in design and day-to-day operation of plan); *Du Mortier v. Massachusetts Gen. Life Ins. Co.*, 805 F. Supp. 816 (C.D. Cal. 1992) (cancer insurance policy established and administered by insurance company was not ERISA plan where employer was involved only to permit marketing of policy, to distribute forms, and to make payroll deductions); *Miller v. National Brokerage Servs., Inc.*, 782 F. Supp. 1440 (D. Nev. 1991) (life insurance plan was ERISA plan even if employer had not committed itself to plan's continuation); *Holcomb v. Pilot Life Ins. Co.*, 754 F. Supp. 524 (N.D. Miss. 1991) (preemption was not defeated by failure of plan to comply with ERISA regulatory requirements); *Cote v. Durham Life Ins. Co.*, 754 F. Supp. 18 (D. Conn. 1991) (group health policy was an "ERISA plan" where employer made contributions and payroll deductions and was responsible for plan's administration); *Foxworth v. Durham Life Ins. Co.*, 745 F. Supp. 1227 (S.D. Miss. 1990) ("ERISA plan" is one created by employer with intent to benefit employees as employees through organized program with reasonably ascertainable system of financing, benefits, beneficiaries, and claims procedures); *Hollister v. Molander*, 744 F. Supp. 846 (N.D. Ill. 1990) (group insurance policy was "ERISA plan" where employer had contractual relationship with insurer and contributed part of premiums); *Brady v. Empire Blue Cross/ Blue Shield*, 732 F. Supp. 678 (W.D. La. 1990) (group policy was not "ERISA plan" where employer did not own, control, administer, or assume responsibility for policy).

§1.32 (3)   ERISA Procedures and Remedies

For extended discussions of the standards by which courts review denials of ERISA plan benefits under the principles of *Firestone Tire & Rubber Co. v. Bruch*, 489 U.S. 101 (1989) (discussed in the book), see *Gurnack v. John Hancock Mut. Life Ins. Co.*, 406 Mass. 748, 550 N.E.2d 391 (1990); *Newell v. Prudential Ins. Co. of Am.*, 904 F.2d

644 (11th Cir. 1990); *Brown v. Blue Cross & Blue Shield, Inc.*, 898 F.2d 1556 (11th Cir. 1990).

Concerning the principle that an ERISA administrator's conflict of interest permits a court to consider evidence outside the administrative record on *de novo* review of a benefits denial, see *Wright v. R.R. Donnelley & Sons Co. Group Benefits Plan*, 402 F.3d 67 (1st Cir. 2005); *Locher v. UNUM Life Ins. Co. of Am.*, 389 F.3d 288 (2d Cir. 2004); *DeFelice v. American Int'l Life Assurance Co. of N.Y.*, 112 F.3d 61 (2d Cir. 1997); *Allison v. UNUM Life Ins. Co. of Am.*, 381 F.3d 1015 (10th Cir. 2004).

In *Black & Decker Disability Plan v. Nord*, 538 U.S. 822, (2003), the Supreme Court rejected the "treating physician rule" that had been endorsed by the Ninth Circuit below, as well as by the Sixth Circuit in *Darland v. Fortis Benefits Ins. Co.*, 317 F.3d 516 (6th Cir. 2003). According to the rejected rule, ERISA plan administrators were required to defer to the opinion of the treating physician. According to the Supreme Court, ERISA requires only a "full and fair" assessment and a clear statement of reasons for a denial of benefits and does not require an administrator to give the treating physician's opinion more weight than other relevant information.

Also holding that punitive damages are not recoverable by an insured in a statutory ERISA action, see *Yardley v. U.S. Healthcare, Inc.*, 698 A.2d 979 (Del. Super. Ct. 1996), *aff'd without op.*, 693 A.2d 1083 (Del. 1997); *Harris v. Blue Cross & Blue Shield*, 729 F. Supp. 49 (N.D. Tex. 1990). A few decisions (a small minority), however, have concluded that ERISA *does* permit recovery of consequential and punitive damages. See, *e.g., Lawrence v. Jackson Mack Sales, Inc.*, 837 F. Supp. 771 (S.D. Miss. 1992); *East v. Long*, 785 F. Supp. 941 (N.D. Ala. 1992); *Weems v. Jefferson-Pilot Life Ins. Co.*, 663 So. 2d 905 (Ala. 1995). Concerning the recoverability of prejudgment interest, see *Rivera v. Benefit Trust Life Ins. Co.*, 921 F.2d 692 (7th Cir. 1991).

The significance of the protection that HMOs receive from ERISA with respect to private-sector health plans, and the inadequacy of ERISA remedies, was highlighted in January 1999 when a jury in San Bernardino County, California, awarded a record $120.5 million to the widow of a former government employee who had been refused cancer treatment despite the recommendation of the HMO's own doctors. (Claims by government employees are not subject to ERISA preemption.) The award included $116 million in punitive damages. *Goodrich v. Aetna U.S. Health Care*, No. RCV20499. (The jury verdict was discussed by HMO critic Jamie Court in an op-ed piece titled "Jury's Verdict Is a Loud and Clear Message to HMOs," in the *Los Angeles Times*, Jan. 27, 1999, at A15.)

Concerning exhaustion of administrative remedies, it was held in *Gallegos v. Mt. Sinai Medical Ctr.*, 210 F.3d 803 (7th Cir. 2000), that if the insured had been able to prove reliance on the insurer's misleading deadline information, the insurer would have been estopped from asserting the insured's failure to file for a review of her plan within the 60-day period specified in the summary plan description. (ERISA regulations expressly permit such 60-day time limits, the court noted.)

§1.32A e.   National Flood Insurance Act [NEW]

A number of decisions have considered the preemptive effect of the National Flood Insurance Act (42 U.S.C. §4001 et seq.) on state-law bad faith and other tort claims by insureds against private insurers. Specifically, the preemption question relates to the "Write Your Own" program authorized by Congress in 1983, under which private insurance companies write their own policies, remit the premiums to the flood insurance administration, and draw money from FEMA to pay claims. Representing the nonpreemption position and holding that private insurers under the program are responsible for their own tortious conduct, see *Spence v. Omaha Indem. Ins. Co.*, 996 F.2d 793 (5th Cir. 1993); *Zumbrun v. United Servs. Auto. Ass'n*, 719 F. Supp. 890 (N.D. Cal. 1989); *Cohen v. State Farm Fire &*

Casualty Ins. Co., 68 F. Supp. 2d 1151 (C.D. Cal. 1999); *Davis v. Travelers Property & Casualty Co.*, 96 F. Supp. 2d 995 (N.D. Cal. 2000); *Stanton v. State Farm Fire & Casualty Co.*, 78 F. Supp. 2d 1029 (D.S.D. 1999); *Moore v. Allstate Ins. Co.*, 995 P.2d 231 (Alaska 2000).

Taking the propreemption position, see *C.E.R. 1988, Inc. v. The Aetna Casualty & Sur. Co.*, 386 F.3d 263 (3d Cir. 2004); *Van Holt v. Liberty Mutual Fire Ins. Co.*, 143 F.3d 783 (3d Cir. 1998); *Gibson v. American Bankers Ins. Co.*, 289 F.3d 943 (6th Cir. 2002); *Peal v. North Carolina Farm Bureau Mut. Ins. Co.*, 212 F. Supp. 2d 508 (E.D.N.C. 2002); *Mason v. Witt*, 74 F. Supp. 2d 955 (N.D. Cal. 1999); *Stapelton v. State Farm Fire & Casualty Co.*, 11 F. Supp. 2d 1344 (M.D. Fla. 1998); *McCormick v. Travelers Ins. Co.*, 86 Cal. App. 4th 404, 103 Cal. Rptr. 2d 258 (2001).

§1.32B f. Private Medicare Program [NEW]

—In *Hofler v. Aetna US Healthcare of Cal.*, 296 F.3d 764 (9th Cir. 2002), the Ninth Circuit held that federal law did not completely preempt state law causes of action, including bad faith claims, brought against a Medicare HMO. Pursuant to the provisions of the "Medicare+Choice" program enacted in 1997, a Medicare beneficiary may contract to receive benefits through private managed health care programs. The plaintiff alleged that her late husband's cancer condition had been belatedly diagnosed because of his Medicare HMO's failure to provide medically necessary exams, tests, and treatment.

7. Status of First-Party Bad Faith Tort Doctrine by Jurisdiction

§1.33 a. Jurisdictions Recognizing Doctrine

Alabama: See *Employees' Benefit Ass'n v. Grissett*, 732 So. 2d 968 (Ala. 1998), for an explanation of the two ways in which first-party bad faith may be proved under Alabama law: (1) by showing that the insured was entitled to a directed verdict on a contract claim, and (2) by showing that the insurer's failure to investigate was intentional or reckless. See also *State Farm Fire & Casualty Co. v. Brechbill*, 144 So. 3d 348 (Ala. 2013); *Jones v. Alfa Mut. Ins. Co.*, 1 So. 3d 23 (Ala. 2008); *National Ins. Ass'n v. Sockwell*, 829 So. 2d 11 (Ala. 2002); *Acceptance Ins. Co. v. Brown*, 832 So. 2d 1, 2001 WL 729283 (Ala. 2001); *Ex parte Alfa Mut. Ins. Co.*, 799 So. 2d 957 (Ala. 2001); *Shelter Mut. Ins. Co. v. Barton*, 822 So. 2d 1149 (Ala. 2001); *Ex parte Simmons*, 791 So. 2d 371 (Ala. 2000); *Watson v. Life Ins. Co. of Ala.*, 74 So. 3d 470 (Ala. Civ. App. 2011).

Alaska: In *Harmon v. State Farm Mut. Auto. Ins. Co.*, 394 P.3d 796 (Idaho 2017), the Idaho Supreme Court applied Alaska law to a dispute regarding damage to a motor home. The court noted that Alaska has adopted the independent tort of bad faith in first-party cases. The tort may be alleged if the insured can show the absence of a reasonable basis for denying the claim under the facts and circumstances. The court required a finding that a duty under the contract had been breached before it allowed the bad faith claim to proceed. See also *Government Employees Ins. Co. v. Gonzalez*, 403 P.3d 1153 (Alaska 2017) (upholding award of nominal damages of $2, punitive damages of $450,000, and attorney's fees for underinsured motorist (UIM) insurer's tortious bad faith delay in paying claim).

Arizona: In *Deese v. State Farm Mut. Auto. Ins. Co.*, 838 P.2d 1265 (Ariz. 1992), the Arizona Supreme Court held that an insurer may be held liable in tort for breach of the implied covenant of good faith and fair dealing even in the absence of proof of the insurer's breach of any expressed term of the insurance contract. In so holding, the court reversed the court of appeals decision discussed in this section of the 1992 supplement, *Deese v. State Farm Mut. Auto. Ins. Co.*, 168 Ariz. 337, 813 P.2d 318 (Ct. App. 1991), and overruled *Nationwide Ins. Co. v. Stevens*, 166 Ariz. 372, 802 P.2d 1071 (Ct. App. 1990). Also concerning the situations under which tort damages are available in first-party insurance bad faith cases, see *Zilisch v. State Farm Mut. Auto. Ins. Co.*, 196 Ariz. 234, 995 P.2d 276 (2000); *Taylor v. State Farm Mut. Auto. Ins. Co.*, 185 Ariz. 174, 913 P.2d 1092 (1996); *Dodge v. Fidelity & Deposit Co. of Maryland*, 161 Ariz. 344, 778 P.2d 1240 (1998); *Beaudry v. Insurance Co. of the West*, 203 Ariz. 86, 50 P.3d 836 (Ct. App. 2002); *James River Ins. Co. v. Hebert Schenk, P.C.*, 523 F.3d 915 (9th Cir. 2008) (Arizona law).

Arkansas: For additional Arkansas cases continuing to include an element of affirmative dishonest or malicious conduct in the definition of the term "bad faith," see *Columbia Nat'l Ins. Co. v. Freeman*, 347 Ark. 423, 64 S.W.3d 720 (2002); *American Health Care Providers, Inc. v. O'Brien*, 318 Ark. 438, 886 S.W.2d 588 (1994); *First Marine Ins. Co. v. Booth*, 317 Ark. 91, 876 S.W.2d 255 (1994); *Reynolds v. Shelter Mut. Ins. Co.*, 313 Ark. 145, 852 S.W.2d 799 (1993); *Metropolitan Prop. & Casualty Ins. Co. v. Calvin*, 802 F.3d 933(8th Cir. 2015); *Jackson v. Allstate Ins. Co.*, 785 F.3d 1193 (8th Cir. 2015); *Hortica-Florists' Mut. Ins. Co. v. Pittman Nursery Corp.*, 729 F.3d 846 (8th Cir. 2013) (Arkansas law); *Baker v. Safeco Ins. Co. of Am.*, 175 F.3d 618 (8th Cir. 1999).

California: See cases cited throughout this chapter relative to California's application of the tort cause of action for first-party bad faith (defined as "unreasonablness"), as first recognized by the state supreme court in its pioneering decision in *Gruenberg v. Aetna Ins. Co.*, 9 Cal. 3d 566, 108 Cal. Rptr. 480 (1973) (discussed at length in book §1.8). For discussions of the nature of a "genuine dispute" that will entitle an insurer to summary judgment on a bad faith claim, see *Wilson v. 21st Century Ins. Co.*, 42 Cal. 4th 713, 68 Cal. Rptr. 3d 746, 171 P.3d 1082 (2007); *Ghazarian v. Magellan Health Inc.*, 53 Cal. App. 5th 171, 266 Cal. Rptr. 3d 841 (2020); *Fadeeff v. State Farm Gen. Ins. Co.*, 50 Cal. App. 5th 94, 263 Cal. Rptr. 3d 453 (2020); *Zubillaga v. Allstate Indem. Co.*, 12 Cal. App. 5th 1017, 219 Cal. Rptr. 3d 620 (2017); *Bosetti v. The United States Life Ins. Co.*, 175 Cal. App. 4th 1208, 96 Cal. Rptr. 3d 744 (2009); *McCoy v. Progressive West Ins. Co.*, 171 Cal. App. 4th 785, 90 Cal. Rptr. 3d 74 (2009); *Brehm VI v. 21st Century Ins. Co.*, 166 Cal. App. 4th 1225, 83 Cal. Rptr. 3d 410 (2008); *Interiano v. Colonial Life & Accident Ins. Co.*, 460 F. Supp. 3d 945 (C.D. Cal. 2020) (California law); *Chierfue Her v. State Farm Ins. Co.*, 92 F. Supp. 3d 957 (E.D. Cal. 2015) (California law). And see *Carson v. Mercury Ins. Co.*, 210 Cal. App. 4th 409, 148 Cal. Rptr. 3d 518 (2012), clarifying that a breach of the implied covenant is *itself* a breach of an insurance contract, and that alleging a breach of a *specific provision* of the contract is not a prerequisite to such a claim.

Colorado: For discussions of the doctrine, see *Schultz v. Geico Casualty Co.*, 429 P.3d 844 (Colo. 2018) (discussed below); *Brodeur v. American Home Assurance Co.*, 169 P.3d 139 (Colo. banc 2007) (addressing independence of bad faith tort cause of action against workers' compensation insurer from remedies available under workers' compensation statute); *American Family Mut. Ins. Co. v. Allen*, 102 P.3d 333 (Colo. banc 2004) (holding that Unfair Claims Practices Act may be used as valid evidence of industry standards and expert testimony is not required); *Goodson v. American Standard Ins. Co. of Wis.*, 89 P.3d 409 (Colo. 2004) (discussing requirements for asserting claim and measures of damages); *Fisher v. State Farm Mut. Auto. Ins. Co.*, 419 P.3d 985 (Colo. Ct. App. 2015), *aff'd*, 418 P.3d 501

(Colo. 2018) (contrasting standard under common-law bad faith claim with standard under C.R.S.A. §10–3-1115); *Soicher v. State Farm Mut. Auto. Ins. Co.*, 351 P.3d 559 (Colo. Ct. App. 2015); *Vaccaro v. American Family Ins. Group*, 275 P.3d 750 (2012) *as modified on denial of rehearing* (Colo. Ct. App. 2012); *Kisselman v. American Family Mut. Ins. Co.*, 292 P.3d 964, 2011 WL 6091708 (Colo. Ct. App. 2011), *cert. denied*, 2012 WL 4482571 (Colo. 2012) (C.R.S.A. §§10-3-1115 and 10-3-1116 created express private right of action for insured when insurer unreasonably denies or delays payment of claim, in addition to and different from common-law bad faith claim; General Assembly intended those statutes to apply prospectively to insurer's acts occurring after August 5, 2008, regardless of when original claim for benefits was made); *Dunn v. American Family Ins.*, 251 P.3d 1232 (Colo. Ct. App. 2010) (insurers have good faith duty to promptly and effectively communicate with anyone they are reasonably aware legitimately needs information pertaining to handling of claim); *Sanderson v. American Family Mut. Ins. Co.*, 251 P.3d 1213 (Colo. Ct. App. 2010) (rejecting proposition that "fair debatability," without more, is necessarily sufficient to defeat bad faith claim as matter of law); *Breaux v. American Family Mut. Ins. Co.*, 554 F.3d 854 (10th Cir. 2009) (emphasizing need for plaintiff to prove either that insurer knew that its conduct was unreasonable or recklessly disregarded that unreasonableness); *TBL Collectibles, Inc. v. Owners Ins. Co.*, 285 F. Supp. 3d 1170 (D. Colo. 2018) (see discussion in §1.26). The Colorado Supreme Court, in *Farmers Group, Inc. v. Williams*, 805 P.2d 419 (Colo. 1991), has held that common-law bad faith claims in auto insurance cases are not preempted by the treble damages provision of the no-fault statute.

In *Schultz v. Geico Casualty Co.*, *supra*, the Colorado Supreme Court reviewed the standards for common-law bad faith (insurer acted unreasonably and with knowledge of or reckless disregard for lack of reasonable basis for denying a claim) and the statutory remedy under Colo. Rev. Stat. Ann. §10-3-1115 (denial of claim without reasonable basis). Concerning the insurer's argument that it acted reasonably because coverage was "fairly debatable," the court quoted *Sanderson v. Am. Family Mut. Ins. Co.*, *supra*, for the rule that fair debatability "is not a threshold inquiry that is outcome determinative as a matter of law, nor is it both the beginning and the end of the analysis in a bad faith case." 429 P.3d at 848. The court went on to reaffirm the "well-established principle" that an insurer cannot not rely on information it did not have at the time it made its coverage decision to show that its decision was reasonable. *Id.* at 848–49.

Connecticut: See *Powell v. Infinity Ins. Co.*, 282 Conn. 594, 922 A.2d 1073 (2007) (affirming summary judgment; judgment in favor of insureds on contract claim for uninsured motorist benefits was res judicata barring claims of bad faith and violation of Unfair Trade Practices Act and Unfair Insurance Practices Act); *Sullivan v. Allstate Ins. Co.*, 2006 WL 1000236 (Conn. Super. Ct. 2006) (affirming summary judgment; emphasizing that claim for breach of implied covenant of good faith and fair dealing is not legally sufficient unless "dishonest purpose or sinister motive" is alleged); *Sterling v. Provident Life & Accident Ins. Co.*, 619 F. Supp. 2d 1242 (M.D. Fla. 2009) (Connecticut law; granting summary judgment, but emphasizing that failure to conduct reasonable investigation may be basis of actionable common-law bad faith claim); *Exantus v. Metropolitan Prop. & Cas. Ins. Co.*, 582 F. Supp. 2d 239 (D Conn. 2008) (affirming summary judgment; no evidence would support finding that insurer had engaged in conduct evidencing "some interested or sinister motive" or "dishonest purpose").

District of Columbia: See §1.34 of this supplement. (Classified in the main volume as a jurisdiction that recognizes a tort cause of action for first-party bad faith, the District of Columbia has been moved in this supplement to the "expressly rejecting" category, in light of more recent case law.)

Florida: In 2012, the Florida Supreme Court clarified that there is no common-law first-party insurance bad faith cause of action under Florida law, only the statutory cause of action codified at F.S.A. §624.155. *QBE Ins. Corp. v. Chalfonte Condo. Apartment Ass'n*, 94 So. 3d 541 (Fla. 2012). See also *United Prop. & Casualty Ins. Co. v. Chernick*, 94 So. 3d 646 (Fla. Dist. Ct. App. 2012); *Chalfonte Condo. Apartment Ass'n v. QBE Ins. Corp.*, 695 F.3d 1215, 2012 WL 4120395 (11th Cir. 2012). But see *Citizens Prop. Ins. Co. v. Perdido Sun Condo. Ass'n*, 164 So. 3d 663 (Fla. 2015) (Florida Supreme Court noted in dicta that although statutory first-party bad faith claims are not "willful torts" in Florida, bad faith claim could be elevated to willful tort, depending on facts of case). Responding to a question certified by the Eleventh Circuit concerning the measure of damages in a first-party action for bad faith failure to settle an uninsured motorist claim under Fla. Stat. §624.155, the Florida Supreme Court, in *Continental Ins. Co. v. Jones*, 592 So. 2d 240, 241 (Fla. 1992), wrote: "We recently addressed this issue in *McLeod v. Continental Ins. Co.*, 591 So. 2d 621 (Fla. 1992), and held that the damages recoverable . . . are those damages which are the natural, proximate, probable, or direct consequences of the insurer's bad faith. We further held that such damages may include, but are not limited to, interest, court costs, and reasonable attorney's fees incurred by the plaintiff." In *McLeod*, the court had amplified this holding by emphasizing that in an uninsured motorist case, an excess judgment does not qualify as damages resulting from a violation of the statute. (That latter portion of the *McLeod* holding was subsequently over-ruled legislatively: see Fla. Stat. §627.727(10), enacted June 25, 1992; *Adams v. Fidelity & Casualty Co.*, 147 F.R.D. 265 (S.D. Fla. 1993).) No private cause of action is provided by Fla. Stat. ch. 641 (the Health Mainte-nance Organization Act), it was held in *Greene v. Well Care HMO, Inc.*, 778 So. 2d 1037 (Fla. Dist. Ct. App. 2001). See also *Cammarata v. State Farm Fla. Ins. Co.*, 152 So. 3d 606 (Fla. Dist. Ct. App. 2014), *review denied*, 171 So. 3d 120 (Fla. 2015) (no cause of action for bad faith exists under F.S.A. §624.155 until the insur-er's liability for coverage has been established); *Scott v. Progressive Express Ins. Co.*, 932 So. 2d 475 (Fla. Dist. Ct. App. 2006); *The Florida Physicians Union, Inc. v. United Healthcare of Fla.*, 837 So. 2d 1133 (Fla. Dist. Ct. App. 2003).

In *Fridman v. Safeco Ins. Co. of Ill.*, 185 So. 3d 1214 (Fla. 2016), the Florida Supreme Court held that an in-sured is entitled to receive a determination of liability and damages in an uninsured motorist case before the insured files a first-party bad faith action under F.S.A. §624.155. The court referred to "a long line of cases from this Court that hold that a determination of liabil-ity and the full extent of damages is a prerequisite to a bad faith cause of action." 185 So. 3d at 1216 (citing *Vest v. Travelers Ins. Co.*, 753 So. 2d 1270 (Fla. 2000) and other cases). The *Fridman* court further held that such determination of damages is binding on the par-ties to the subsequent bad faith litigation, and that the trial court did not err when it retained jurisdiction to let the insured file a bad faith cause of action. See also *Bryant v. GeoVera Specialty Ins. Co.*, 271 So. 3d 1013 (Fla. Dist. Ct. App. 2019) (bad faith claim is not ripe until insurer's liability for coverage and extent of dam-ages has been determined). Compare *Bottini v. GEICO*, 859 F.3d 987 (11th Cir. 2017) (Florida law; damages de-termination in underlying uninsured motorist case is not binding in subsequent bad faith action where insurer did pursue its right to appeal but appellate court did not review errors alleged by insurer in jury's calculation of damages; insurer is not obligated to pursue further discretionary review; citing *Fridman, supra*).

In *Fortune v. First Protective Ins. Co.*, 302 So. 3d 485 (Fla. Dist. Ct. App. 2020), insureds brought a claim for bad faith under Fla. Stat. Ann. §624.155 after their insurer made a lowball offer to cover hurricane damage to their home. The insureds argued that the insurer failed to identify the full scope of necessary repairs. The lower court determined as a matter of law that the insurer cured a Civil Remedy Notice of Insurer's Violations (CRN) by invoking the appraisal process before the CRN was filed and paying the appraisal award more than 60 days after the CRN was filed. However, the appellate court held that insurer's use of the appraisal process and payment of the appraisal award after the cure period expired did not, as a matter of law, cure the alleged bad faith, and it reversed and remanded for further proceedings to allow the bad faith claim to go forward.

In *Cadle v. GEICO Gen. Ins. Co.*, 838 F.3d 1113 (11th Cir. 2016) (Florida law), an uninsured motorist case, the court upheld a federal district court order granting judgment as a matter of law to the insurer, reducing a jury award of $900,000 in noneconomic damages for injuries the insured sustained in an automobile accident to the policy limit of $75,000. The court concluded that the insured had failed to provide the insurer timely evidence that she had been *permanently injured*, thus rendering her ineligible for noneconomic damages under Fla. Stat. Ann. §627.737(2).

In *Cousin v. GEICO Gen. Ins. Co.*, 719 Fed. Appx. 954 (11th Cir. 2018), the U.S. Court of Appeals for the Eleventh Circuit stated that under Florida law, the "totality of the circumstances" approach applied to the insured's bad faith claim, brought under Fla. Stat. Ann. §624.155. The court declined to reverse summary judgment for the underinsured motorist (UIM) insurer because the trial court had taken into account the insured's counsel's delays in providing information that the insurer needed to evaluate the insured's claim. However, the court remanded the bad faith claims so that the jury could consider the reasonableness and accuracy of the insurer's settlement offer, and noted "the general rule that the issue of bad faith is a question for the jury." *Id.* at 960. See also §1.24.

Georgia: For cases construing and applying Georgia's bad faith statute, see *Lee v. Mercury Ins. Co. of Ga.*, 343 Ga. App. 729, 748, 808 S.E.2d 116, 133 (2017), *cert. denied* (Ga. 2018) (affirming summary judgment for insurer on bad faith claim; penalties for bad faith are not authorized where insurer had "any reasonable ground to contest the claim," even if genuine issue of fact exists as to whether insurer's conduct in denying claim was based in part on bad faith); *Old Republic Nat'l Title Ins. Co. v. RM Kids, LLC*, 337 Ga. App. 638, 788 S.E.2d 542 (2016) (affirming summary judgment for insurer on claim of bad faith refusal to pay under Ga. Code Ann. §33–4-6, where material issues of fact existed whether claim was excluded under policy, making insurer's refusal to pay reasonable under the circumstances); *Great Sw. Express Co. v. Great Am. Ins. Co. of N.Y.*, 292 Ga. App. 757, 665 S.E.2d 878 (2008) (absent some special relationship beyond that between insurer and insured, insured's exclusive remedy for bad faith refusal to pay is remedy under Ga. Code Ann. §33-4-6 for penalty and attorneys' fees); *Atlantic Title Ins. Co. v. Aegis Funding Corp.*, 287 Ga. App. 392, 651 S.E.2d 507 (2007) (lender's title insurer acted in bad faith by failing to pay lenders' claims or cure defects caused by nonpayment of prior mortgagees); *King v. Atlanta Casualty Ins. Co.*, 279 Ga. App. 554, 631 S.E.2d 786 (2006) (affirming summary judgment for insurer on claim under Georgia Code Ann. § 33-4-7, which imposes affirmative duties of good faith on insurer of property covered by motor vehicle liability insurance policy); *Brown v. Ohio Casualty Ins. Co.*, 239 Ga. App. 251, 519 S.E.2d 726 (1999) (recovery under bad faith statute requires proof that insured made demand for payment of claim at least 60 days before filing suit); *Collins v. Life Ins. Co.*, 228 Ga. App. 301, 491 So. 2d 514 (1997) (restating principle that bad faith statute is exclusive remedy for bad faith denial of benefits); *State Farm Mut. Auto. Ins. Co. v. Ainsworth*, 198 Ga. App. 740, 402 S.E.2d 759 (1991) (affirming denial of summary judgment in action alleging that insurer failed to allow insured to determine priority of optional no-fault benefits payments); *Collins v. State Farm Mut. Auto. Ins. Co.*, 197 Ga. App. 309, 398 S.E.2d 207 (1990) (insurer has burden of proof on issue of good faith). (Georgia Code Ann. §33-34-6(c) allows punitive damages to be assessed for bad faith refusals to pay benefits within 60 days of proper proof of loss.)

Hawaii: In 1996, the Hawaii Supreme Court accorded belated first-time recognition to the tort of first-party bad faith, in *Best Place Ins. Co. v. Penn Am. Ins. Co.*, 82 Haw. 120, 920 P.2d 334 (1996). Upholding the retroactive applicability of the *Best Place* decision, see *Catron v. Tokio Marine Mgmt., Inc.*, 90 Haw. 407, 978 P.2d 845 (1999). See also *Adams v. Hawaii Med. Serv. Ass'n*, 145 Haw. 250, 450 P.3d 780 (2019) (vacating summary judgment for health insurer on bad faith claim; question existed whether insurer's handling of cancer patient's claim for coverage of treatment was unreasonable; see also §§1.9, 1.12, 1.14); *Guajardo v. AIG Haw. Ins. Co.*, 187 P.3d 580 (Haw. 2008) (issues of fact precluded summary judgment on claim that insurer breached duty of good faith, and whether insured suffered damages as result of any misrepresentation by insurer of terms of underinsured motorist policy); *Aquilina v. Certain Underwriters at Lloyd's Syndicate #2003*, 407 F. Supp. 3d 1016 (D. Haw. 2019) (Hawaii law; dismissing complaint of insureds alleging fraudulent and misleading conduct by insurers and agents/brokers, with leave to amend; acknowledging first-party bad faith tort right of action under *Best Place, supra*, but holding plaintiffs failed to satisfy Fed. R. Civ. P. 9(b) requirement to plead fraud with particularity); *State Farm Fire & Casualty Co. v. GP West, Inc.*, 190 F. Supp. 3d 1003 (D. Haw. 2016) (granting summary judgment for insurer on claim of breach of covenant of good faith and fair dealing where insurer relied on governing law and reasonable interpretation of policy provisions in refusing to defend; citing *Best Place, supra*).

Idaho: For additional statements of Idaho law's inclusion of an element of intentional misconduct in the definition of first-party bad faith, see *ABK, LLC v. Mid-Century Ins. Co.*, 166 Idaho 92, 454 P.3d 1175 (2019); *Seiniger Law Office, P.A. v. North Pac. Ins. Co.*, 145 Idaho 241, 178 P.3d 606 (2008); *Simper v. Farm Bureau Mut. Ins. Co.*, 974 P.2d 1100 (Idaho 1999); *Chester v. State Farm Ins. Co.*, 117 Idaho 538, 789 P.2d 534 (Ct. App. 1990). See also *Cedillo v. Farmers Ins. Co.*, 163 Idaho 131, 408 P.3d 886 (2017); *Lakeland True Value Hardware, LLC v. The Hartford Fire Ins. Co.*, 153 Idaho 716, 291 P.3d 399 (2012) (whether claim was fairly debatable is question of law); *Weinstein v. Prudential Prop. & Casualty Ins. Co.*, 149 Idaho 299, 233 P.3d 1221 (2010) (denying motion for new trial, though ordering reduction in punitive damages award, on claim involving insurer's intentional and unreasonable delay in paying uninsured motorist benefits); *Robinson v. State Farm Mut. Auto. Ins. Co.*, 137 Idaho 173, 45 P.3d 829 (2002) (insured has burden of proof on "fairly debatable" issue, and proof of coverage is element of prima facie case); *McGilvray v. Farmers New World Life Ins. Co.*, 28 P.3d 380 (Idaho

2001) (emphasizing principle that insurer does not commit bad faith by denying claim that is "fairly debatable"); *Engineered Structures, Inc. v. Travelers Prop. Casualty Co. of Am.*, 822 Fed. Appx. 606 (9th Cir. 2020) (Idaho law; insured failed to present evidence that its claim for coverage was not fairly debatable; once insurer submits evidence to support reasonable dispute about coverage, burden shifts to insured to show clear entitlement to coverage).

In *Cummings v. Stephens*, 157 Idaho 348, 359 (2014), *reh'g denied* (Idaho 2014), the Idaho Supreme Court included this summary of the nature of that state's doctrine of first-party bad faith:

> This Court has created a tort of bad faith applicable to insurance companies. That tort is not a tortious breach of contract, but a breach of a duty imposed as a consequence of a contractual relationship. *White v. Unigard Mut. Ins. Co.*, 112 Idaho 94, 97, 730 P.2d 1014, 1017 (1986). To recover against an insurance company on the tort of bad faith, the insured must show: (1) the insurer intentionally and unreasonably denied or delayed payment; (2) the insured's claim was not fairly debatable; (3) the insurer's denial or delay was not the result of good faith mistake; and (4) the resulting harm was not fully compensable by contract damages. *Lovey v. Regence BlueShield of Idaho*, 139 Idaho 37, 48, 72 P.3d 877, 888 (2003).

See also *Cedillo v. Farmers Ins. Co.*, *supra*; *Harmon v. State Farm Mut. Auto. Ins. Co.*, 394 P.3d 796 (Idaho 2017), discussed in the Alaska section, *supra*.

Indiana: Indiana, formerly listed in §1.36 in the book as a jurisdiction permitting the recovery of punitive damages in contract actions, has now belatedly joined those jurisdictions recognizing a bad faith tort cause of action in the first-party insurance context. *Erie Ins. Co. v. Hickman by Smith*, 622 N.E.2d 515 (Ind. 1993). Citing this book in noting the lack of a uniform approach among the individual states, and the variety of ways in which bad faith claims may arise, the court stated: "We need not determine the precise extent of that duty today. However, we make these general observations. The obligation of good faith and fair dealing with respect to the discharge of the insurer's contractual obligation includes the obligation to refrain from (1) making an unfounded refusal to pay policy proceeds; (2) causing an unfounded delay in making payment; (3) deceiving the insured; and (4) exercising any unfair advantage to pressure an insured into a settlement of his claim." 622 N.E.2d at 519 n.2 and accompanying text. See also *Earl v. State Farm Mut. Auto. Ins. Co.*, 91 N.E.3d 1066 (Ind. Ct. App. 2018) (quoting *Erie Ins. Co. v. Hickman by Smith, supra*). Some subsequent decisions have emphasized that an element of conscious wrongdoing must be present to support a finding of bad faith. See, e.g., *Allstate Ins. Co. v. Fields*, 885 N.E.2d 728 (Ind. Ct. App. 2008); *Spencer v. Bridgewater*, 757 N.E.2d 208 (Ind. Ct. App. 2001); *Abstract & Title Guar. Co. v. Chicago Ins. Co.*, 489 F.3d 808 (7th Cir. 2007) (Indiana law); *Telamon Corp. v. Charter Oak Fire Ins. Co.*, 179 F. Supp. 3d 851(S.D. Ind. 2016), *appeal filed* (7th Cir. April 13, 2016) (Indiana law); *Jackson v. Allstate Ins. Co.*, 780 F. Supp. 2d 781 (S.D. Ind. 2011) (Indiana law); *Westfield v. Sheehan Ins. Co.*, 580 F. Supp. 2d 701 (S.D. Ind. 2008) (Indiana law).

Iowa: In *Wilson v. Farm Bureau Mut. Ins. Co.*, 714 N.W.2d 250 (Iowa 2006), the Iowa Supreme Court, affirming summary judgment for the insurer, explained that to establish a bad faith claim, the insured had been required to prove: (1) that the insurer had no reasonable basis for denying its demand to pay the amount of an amended judgment in excess of underinsured motorist's policy limits; and (2) that the insurer knew or had reason to know that its denial lacked a reasonable basis. See also *Rodda v. Vermeer Manuf. & EMC Risk Servs., Inc.*, 734 N.W.2d 480 (Iowa 2007) (whether claim is open to dispute on any logical basis, and is thus "fairly debatable," can generally be determined by court as matter of law; in present case, question whether employee could receive both unemployment benefits and workers' compensation benefits was fairly debatable, and employer did not act in bad faith when it denied employee healing-period benefits while employee was receiving unemployment benefits); *Penford Corp. v. National Union Fire Ins. Co. of Pittsburgh*, 662 F.3d 497 (8th Cir. 2011) (when bad faith claim is fairly debatable, insurer is entitled to debate it whether debate concerns matter of fact or of law, and whether claim is fairly debatable can generally be decided as matter of law by court); *Liberty Mut. Ins. Co. v. Pella Corp.*, 650 F.3d 1161 (8th Cir. 2011) (Iowa law) (insurer can defeat bad faith claim by showing that it had at least one reasonable basis for denying claim, and need not show that all of its positions were reasonable); *Adam v. Stonebridge Life Ins. Co.*, 612 F.3d 967 (8th Cir. 2010) (life insurer had reasonable basis for denying benefits, and had no duty to investigate further, where insured had misrepresented his medical history); *The Weitz Co. v. Lloyd's of London*, 574 F.3d 885 (8th Cir. 2009) (summary judgment was precluded by fact issues as to whether insurer properly investigated claim and subjected results of investigation to reasonable evaluation and review); *Merriam v. National Union Fire Ins. Co. of Pittsburgh*, 572 F.3d 579 (8th Cir. 2009) (affirming summary judgment; emphasizing existence of debatable issue and noting that improper investigation cannot alone sustain bad faith tort claim if insurer had objectively reasonable basis for denial); *Spencer v. Annett Holdings, Inc.*, 905 F. Supp. 2d 953 (S.D. Iowa 2012) (under Iowa law, first-party bad faith is an intentional tort involving insurer's knowing failure to exercise honest and informed judgment when insured seeks compensation for injury; it applies to all insurers, including self-insured employers); *Morse v. State Farm Fire & Casualty Co.*, 733 F. Supp. 2d 1065 (S.D. Iowa 2010) (granting motion for summary judgment; fact that insurer's position is ultimately found to lack merit is not sufficient by itself to establish lack of reasonable basis for denying claim, nor is imperfect investigation sufficient cause for recovery if insurer had objectively reasonable basis).

Kentucky: The Kentucky Supreme Court, in *Curry v. Fireman's Fund Ins. Co.*, 784 S.W.2d 176 (Ky. 1989), has done an about-face, and has now recognized the doctrine of first-party bad faith that it expressly rejected in *Federal Kemper Ins. Co. v. Hornbeck*, 711 S.W.2d 844 (Ky. 1986) (see book §1.34). The court in *Curry* endorsed a dissenting opinion in *Federal Kemper*, where Justice Leibson argued that an insurer should be liable for bad faith if it knowingly or recklessly denies a claim without a reasonable basis. In *Curry* itself, the court reinstated a judgment for the insured based on a jury verdict awarding $50,000 in consequential damages and $15,000 in punitives. The case involved the insurer's denial of a claim for theft loss under a standard business policy. It was the insured's contention that he had expressly requested an "all risks" policy, and that theft coverage had been omitted from the policy due to an error on the part of the insurer's local agent. See also *Knotts v. Zurich Ins. Co.*, 197 S.W.3d 512 (Ky. 2006), addressing a claim under the state's Unfair Claims Settlement Practices Act, (K.R.S. 304.12-230), and holding that evidence of insurer's settlement behavior that occurs after underlying suit has been filed may be introduced in a subsequent bad faith action, but that introduction in the subsequent bad faith action of evidence of insurer's litigation conduct and strategies in the underlying suit is prohibited; *Philadelphia Indem.*

Ins. Co. v. Youth Alive, Inc., 732 F.3d 645 (6th Cir. 2013) (Kentucky law; insurer's interpretation of policies was not so obviously implausible as to give rise to bad claim, nor did bad claim arise from insurer's conduct in refusing to settle claims pending outcome of its declaratory judgment action); *Foster v. American Fire & Casualty Co.*, 219 F. Supp. 3d 590 (E.D. Ky. 2016) (insured's claims for bad faith under common law and Kentucky Unfair Claims Settlement Practices Act survived summary judgment where insured sought compensatory damages, including damages for emotional distress, for alleged delay in paying benefits for uninsured motorist coverage); *Lee v. Medical Protective Co.*, 904 F. Supp. 2d 648 (E.D. Ky. 2012) (Kentucky law; insurer did not act in bad faith in appealing or seeking discretionary review of jury's medical malpractice verdict, nor in failing to make offer to settle until after appellate review was completed). In *Pedicini v. Life Ins. Co. of Ala.*, 682 F.3d 522 (6th Cir. 2012), the Sixth Circuit, reversing summary judgment in a case involving the insurer's failure to pay the full amount of benefits under a supplemental cancer insurance policy, summarized the three elements that a plaintiff must establish under Kentucky law to succeed on such a claim.

In *Indiana Ins. Co. v. Demetre*, 527 S.W.3d 12 (Ky. 2017), the Kentucky Supreme Court summarized Kentucky law of bad faith applicable to both first- and third-party claims. Common-law bad faith claims "flow from the insurer's breach of the covenant to good faith and fair dealing." *Id.* at 26 (citing *Davidson v. American Freightways, Inc.* 25 S.W.3d 94 (Ky. 2000)). Bad faith claims can also arise from the Kentucky Consumer Protection Act and the Unfair Claims Settlement Practices Act. See §§1.37, 2.24. The court then quoted the test applicable to all insurance bad faith actions in Kentucky, from *Wittmer v. Jones*, 864 S.W.2d 885 (Ky. 1993), in which the court "'gathered all of the bad faith liability theories under one roof and established a test applicable to all bad faith actions,' whether first-party or third-party claims and whether based on common law or statute." 527 S.W.3d at 26 (quoting *Davidson*, 25 S.W.3d at 100). The *Wittmer* test contains three required elements: "(1) the insurer must be obligated to pay the claim under the terms of the policy; (2) the insurer must lack a reasonable basis in law or fact for denying the claim; and (3) it must be shown that the insurer either knew there was no reasonable basis for denying the claim or acted with reckless disregard for whether such a basis existed." *Indiana Ins. Co.*, 527 S.W.3d at 26 (quoting *Davidson*, 25 S.W.3d at 100 (quoting *Wittmer*, 864 S.W.2d at 890)). See also *Travelers Indem. Co. v. Armstrong*, 565 S.W.3d 550 (Ky. 2018), *reh'g denied* (Ky. 2019) (stating test, and holding that where coverage was "fairly debatable," insurer did not lack reasonable basis for denying claim). See also §2.2.

Louisiana: Louisiana's bad faith statute (La. Rev. Stat. Ann. §22:1220, effective July 6, 1990, and renumbered as §22:1973) provides: "An insurer . . . owes to his insured a duty of good faith and fair dealing. The insurer has an affirmative duty to adjust claims fairly and promptly and to make a reasonable effort to settle claims with the insured or the claimant, or both. Any insurer who breaches these duties shall be liable for any damages sustained by the breach." The largely identical provisions of La. Rev. Stat. Ann. §22:1892 (formerly §22:658) were construed and applied by the Louisiana Supreme Court in *Guillory v. Lee*, 16 So. 3d 1104 (La. 2009). It was held in *Premium Fin. Co. v. Employers' Reinsurance Corp.*, 761 F. Supp. 450 (W.D. La. 1991), that the statute is not retrospective in application, and does not apply to an insurer's conduct after the initiation of litigation. But concerning that second holding, see *contra*, *Harris v. Fontenot*, 606 So. 2d 72 (La. App. 1992). Concerning the non-retroactivity of 2006 amendments to

La. Rev. Stat. Ann. §22:1892 (formerly §22:658), see *Thompson v. State Farm Fire & Casualty Co.*, 2009 WL 537149 (E.D. La. 2009). Concerning the interpretation of the Louisiana statute, see also *Kelly v. State Farm Fire & Casualty Co.*, 169 So. 3d 328 (La. 2015) (discussed in §2.7, *infra*); *Shreve v. State Farm Fire & Casualty Co.*, 247 So. 3d 1175 (La. Ct. App. 2018) , *writ denied*, 255 So. 3d 574 (La. 2018); *Anco Insulations, Inc. v. Nat'l Union Fire Ins. Co. of Pittsburgh, Pa.*, 787 F.3d 276 (5th Cir. 2015) (discussed in §1.61, *infra*).

In 2018, the Louisiana Court of Appeals in *Lind v. United Servs. Auto. Ass'n*, 242 So. 3d 576 (La. Ct. App. 2018), reviewed the meaning of the two Louisiana bad faith statutes, La. Stat. Ann. §§22:1892 and 22:1973. Both statutes provide for penalties, including attorney's fees, to be assessed against an insurer for failure to pay a claim where the insurer's actions were "arbitrary, capricious, or without probable cause." 242 So. 3d at 585. This term is synonymous with the term "vexatious," meaning "unjustified, without reasonable cause or excuse." *Id.* "Both phrases describe an insurer whose willful refusal of a claim is not based on a good faith defense. Thus, an insurer who does not tender unconditionally a reasonable payment, a figure over which reasonable minds could not differ, will be subject to penalties and attorney fees." *Id.* at 585–86. The court in *Lind* concluded that the insurer acted arbitrarily and capriciously and awarded the insured a penalty of 50 percent of the damages to which the insured was entitled for its loss.

In *Smith v. Citadel Ins. Co.*, 285 So. 3d 1062 (La. 2019), the Supreme Court of Louisiana held that first-party bad faith claims against an insurer, which fall under La. Stat. Ann. §22:1973, arise out of an insurer's contractual obligations, and therefore are governed by the 10-year prescriptive period under La. C.C. art. 3499, not the 1-year prescriptive period for delictual actions.

Maryland: Discussing Maryland's first-party bad faith statute (Md. Code Ann., Cts. & Jud. Proc. §3-1701, effective October 1, 2007), and rejecting a challenge to its retroactive application, see *Cecilia Schwaber Trust Two v. Hartford Accident & Indem. Co.*, 636 F. Supp. 2d 481 (D. Md. 2009).

Massachusetts: In *NextSun Energy Littleton, LLC v. Acadia Ins. Co.*, ___ F. Supp. 3d ___, 2020 WL 5821630 (D. Mass. 2020), the federal district court addressed the claim of breach of the implied covenant of good faith and fair dealing in the insurance context. The court held that an insurer does not breach the duty merely by contesting coverage. The court stated that "[t]ypically, a breach of the implied covenant involves 'bad faith' conduct 'implicating a dishonest purpose, consciousness of wrong, or ill will in the nature of the fraud.'" 2020 WL 5821630, at *16 (internal quotation marks omitted). The court found no evidence that the insurer "took any dishonest or deceitful actions to deprive plaintiff of the benefit of the policy." *Id.*

Mississippi: Concerning Mississippi's unusually narrow doctrine of first-party bad faith, requiring a showing of egregious insurer misconduct involving malice or gross negligence, see *United Am. Ins. Co. v. Merrill*, 978 So. 2d 613 (Miss. 2007); *Baker Donelson Bearman & Caldwell, P.C. v. Muirhead*, 920 So. 2d 440 (Miss. 2006); *Liberty Mut. Ins. Co. v. McKneely*, 862 So. 2d 530 (Miss. 2003); *Gordon v. National States Ins. Co.*, 851 So. 2d 363 (Miss. 2003); *Caldwell v. Alfa Ins. Co.*, 686 So. 2d 1092 (Miss. 1996); *King v. Progressive Gulf Ins. Co.*, 913 So. 2d 1065 (Miss. Ct. App. 2005); *MIC Life Ins. Co. v. Hicks*, 2000 WL 804657 (Miss. Ct. App. 2000); *Mitchell v. State Farm Fire & Cas. Co.*, 954 F.3d 700 (5th Cir. 2020) (Mississippi law); *Cox v. Provident Life & Acc. Ins. Co.*, 878 F.3d 504 (5th Cir. 2017); *James v. State Farm Mut. Auto. Ins. Co.*, 743 F.3d 65 (5th Cir.

2014); *Essinger v. Liberty Mut. Fire Ins. Co.*, 534 F.3d
450 (5th Cir. 2008); *Spansel v. State Farm Fire & Casualty Co.*, 683 F. Supp. 2d 444 (S.D. Miss. 2010); *WMS
Indus., Inc. v. Federal Ins. Co.*, 588 F. Supp. 2d 727
(S.D. Miss. 2008).

Montana: Concerning Montana's Unfair Trade Practices Act
(MCA 33-18-201), and the scope of its preemptive effect, see *Draggin' Y Cattle Co. v. Junkermier, Clark,
Campanella, Stevens, P.C.*, 395 Mont. 316 (2019); *White
v. State*, 371 Mont. 1, 305 P.3d 795 (2013); *Williams v.
Union Fid. Life Ins. Co.*, 329 Mont. 158, 123 P.3d 213
(2005); *High Country Paving, Inc. v. United Fire &
Casualty Co.*, 365 F. Supp. 3d 1093 (D. Mont. 2019); *Ray
v. Washington Nat'l Ins. Co.*, 190 F.R.D. 658 (D. Mont.
1999).

Nebraska: In January of 1991, the Nebraska Supreme Court
extended first-time recognition to a tort cause of action
for first-party bad faith. *Braesch v. Union Ins. Co.*, 237
Neb. 44, 464 N.W.2d 769 (1991). And in *LeRette v. American Med. Security, Inc.*, 270 Neb. 545, 705 N.W.2d 41
(2005), the Nebraska Supreme Court held: (1) the insureds had not been required to prevail on their breach
of contract cause of action as a prerequisite to prevailing on their bad faith cause of action; (2) the insurer's
ultimate decision to certify coverage for a medical procedure did not preclude a bad faith claim; but (3) the
insurer's refusal to pre-certify coverage for the procedure was fairly debatable—a question appropriately decided by the court as a matter of law—and the insurer
had therefore not acted in bad faith in initially refusing
to certify coverage. See also *Hayes v. Met. Prop. & Casualty Ins. Co.*, 908 F.3d 370 (8th Cir. 2018) (upholding
bad faith damages award in absence of breach of contract claim, which had been time barred; see also
§§1.11, 1.13). For a case holding that no private right
of action is provided by the Nebraska Unfair Insurance

Trade Practices Act, see *McShane Constr. Co. v. Gotham Ins. Co.*, 867 F.3d 923 (8th Cir. 2017).

Nevada: The viability of a common-law remedy for first-party insurance bad faith under Nevada law was recognized in *Allstate Ins. Co. v. Thorpe*, 170 P.3d 989 (Nev. 2007), and in *Pioneer Chlor Alkali Co. v. National Union Fire Ins. Co.*, 863 F. Supp. 1237 (D. Nev. 1994). See also *Estate of LoMastro v. American Family Ins. Group*, 195 P.3d 339 (Nev. 2008); *Wallace v. U.S.A.A. Life Gen. Agency, Inc.*, 862 F. Supp. 2d 1062, 2012 WL 1068313 (D. Nev. 2012); *Turk v. TIG Ins. Co.*, 616 F. Supp. 2d 1044 (D. Nev. 2009)

New Hampshire: Although the New Hampshire Supreme Court has generally declined to extend tort remedies to the first party context (see *Lawton v. Great Southwest Fire Ins. Co.*, 118 N.H. 607, 392 A.2d 576 (1978)), summary judgment was reversed in *Bennett v. ITT Hartford Group, Inc.*, 846 A.2d 560 (N.H. 2004), a first-party case involving the allegation that the plaintiff's property insurer had falsely assured the insured that it was pursuing a subrogation action against the manufacturer of a defective clothes dryer, and had deprived the insured of the opportunity to gather evidence and pursue his claim against the manufacturer. The issue was similar to those that normally arise in third-party cases, the court reasoned, and recognition of a first-party bad faith tort claim was therefore appropriate under these "unusual and narrow circumstances."

New Jersey: Listed in §1.35 in the book and previous editions of this supplement as an undecided jurisdiction, New Jersey has now taken the step of recognizing a first-party bad faith cause of action, but one limited to contract-measure damages. *Pickett v. Lloyd's*, 131 N.J. 457, 621 A.2d 445 (1993). The court defined "bad faith" as the denial of a claim without a reasonable basis, together with the insurer's awareness or reckless disregard of the lack thereof. See also *Badiali v. New Jersey Mfrs. Ins. Grp.*, 220 N.J. 544 (2015); *Universal-Rundle Corp. v. Commercial Union Ins. Co.*, 319 N.J. Super. 223, 725 A.2d 76 (1999); *Kolbe v. BAC Home Loans Servicing, LP*, 695 F.3d 1118 (1st Cir. 2012), *aff'd on reh'g en banc*, 738 F.3d 432 (1st Cir. 2013) (New Jersey law).

In *Badiali v. New Jersey Mfrs. Ins. Grp.*, *supra*, the New Jersey Supreme Court reviewed and upheld the "salutary" rule in *Pickett v. Lloyds*, *supra*, that "mere failure to settle a debatable claim does not constitute bad faith." *Badiali*, 220 N.J. at 554–55. The court upheld an award of summary judgment to the insurer on the insured's bad faith claim because the insurer acted in reliance on an unpublished opinion of the New Jersey Appellate Division when it rejected an arbitration award in favor of the insured and demanded a trial de novo.

New Mexico: See *Jackson Nat'l Life Ins. Co. v. Receconi*, 827 P.2d 118 (N.M. 1992), for an elucidation of New Mexico's unusual approach to first-party insurance bad faith, which combines into one inquiry the insurer's liability for bad faith and its liability for punitive damages. "[T]he assessment of punitive damages for breach of an insurance policy requires evidence of bad faith or malice in the insurer's refusal to pay a claim. 'Bad faith' has been defined as 'any frivolous or unfounded refusal to pay.' [Citations omitted.]" 827 P.2d at 134. Also discussing the nature of an insurer's good faith obligations, see *American Nat'l Prop. & Casualty Co. v. Cleveland*, 293 P.3d 954 (N.M. Ct. App. 2012); *U.S. ex rel. Custom Grading Inc. v. Great Am. Ins. Co.*, 952 F. Supp. 2d 1259 (D.N.M. 2013); *Anderson Living Trust v. Conoco-Phillips Co.*, 952 F. Supp. 2d 979 (D.N.M. 2013); *Hauff v. Petterson*, 755 F. Supp. 2d 1138 (D.N.M. 2010).

North Carolina: Applying the North Carolina doctrine of common-law first-party bad faith in the context of business liability insurance, see *Williams v. Ohio Nat'l Life Assurance Co.*, 364 F. Supp. 3d 605 (W.D.N.C. 2019) (finding of bad faith requires aggravated or outrageous conduct, and does not arise from honest disagreement about validity of claim).

North Dakota: Concerning North Dakota's recognition of a common-law bad faith cause of action in the first-party insurance context, see *Seifert v. Farmers Union Mut. Ins. Co.*, 497 N.W.2d 694 (N.D. 1993); *Moore v. American Family Mut. Ins. Co.*, 576 F.3d 781 (8th Cir. 2009).

Ohio: In *Motorists Mut. Ins. Co. v. Said*, 63 Ohio St. 3d 690, 590 N.E.2d 1228 (1992), the Ohio Supreme Court clarified the nature of the conduct sufficient to subject an insurer to liability for first-party bad faith, and for punitive damages. Bad faith liability arises, the court explained, where the insurer refuses to satisfy an insured's claim with no lawful basis for such refusal, coupled with actual knowledge of that fact, or where the insurer intentionally refuses to determine whether any lawful basis exists. Entitlement to punitive damages requires an additional showing of a dishonest purpose, an intent to mislead or deceive, or a calculated scheme to defeat the insured's claim. See also *Mundy v. Roy*, 2006 WL 522380 (Ohio Ct. App. 2006) (reversing summary judgment for insurer; bad faith claim can arise from dispute over value of pain and suffering or amount of insured's damages, and claim was not precluded by fact that insurer relied on expert's opinion); *Fifth Third Mortgage Co. v. Chicago Title Ins. Co.*, 692 F.3d 507, *reh'g & reh'g en banc denied* (6th Cir. 2012) (title insurer acted in bad faith when it refused coverage based on condition that was nowhere found or even intimated in policy itself, and where policy terms otherwise plainly required insurer to cover loss); *Toledo-Lucas*

County Port Auth. v. Axa Marine & Aviation Ins. (UK), Ltd., 220 F. Supp. 2d 868 (N.D. Ohio 2002) (predicting that Ohio Supreme Court would hold that there can be no bad faith liability in absence of coverage).

Oklahoma: For discussions of first-party bad faith claims under Oklahoma law, see *Newport v. USAA*, 11 P.3d 190 (Okla. 2000); *Barnes v. Oklahoma Farm Bureau Mut. Ins. Co.*, 11 P.3d 162 (Okla. 2000); *Pitts v. West Am. Ins. Co.*, 212 P.3d 1237 (Okla. Civ. App. 2009); *Bannister v. State Farm Mut. Auto. Ins. Co.*, 692 F.3d 1117 (10th Cir. 2012) (Oklahoma law); *Flores v. Monumental Life Ins. Co.*, 620 F.3d 1248 (10th Cir. 2010); *Sims v. Great Am. Life Ins. Co.*, 469 F.3d 870 (10th Cir. 2006); *Willis v. Midland Risk Ins. Co.*, 42 F.3d 607 (10th Cir. 1994). See also *Edens v. Netherlands Inc. Co.*, 834 F.3d 1116 (10th Cir. 2016), *cert. denied*, ___ U.S. ___, 137 S. Ct. 1375 (2017) (Oklahoma law; reviewing Oklahoma law of insurance bad faith and confirming that insured must be entitled to coverage to prevail on claim of bad faith (citing *Badillo v. Mid Century Ins. Co.*, 121 P.3d 1080 (Okla. 2005); *Bannister, supra*)).

Pennsylvania: In *CRS Auto Parts, Inc. v. National Grange Mut. Ins. Co.*, 645 F. Supp. 2d 354 (E.D. Pa. 2009), a federal district court made clear that a common-law bad faith claim under Pennsylvania law sounds only in contract. Accord, *Zaloga v. Provident Life & Accident Ins. Co. of Am.*, 671 F. Supp. 2d 623 (M.D. Penn. 2009). See also *McDonough v. State Farm Fire & Casualty Co.*, 365 F. Supp. 3d 552 (E.D. Pa. 2019) (Pennsylvania recognizes no common-law bad faith claim separate from breach of contract claim); *Papurello v. State Farm Fire & Casualty Co.*, 144 F. Supp. 3d 746 (W.D. Pa. 2015) (Pennsylvania law; recognizing implied contractual duty of good faith and fair dealing in Pennsylvania, but dismissing insured's class-action claim for breach of that duty where challenged policy provision was clear and unambiguous). Pennsylvania's bad faith statute (42 Pa. Cons. Stat. §8371, effective July 1, 1990), provides:

> In an action arising under an insurance contract, if the court finds that the insurer has acted in bad faith towards the insured, the court may take all of the following actions:
> (1) Award interest on the amount of the claim from the date the claim was made by the insured in an amount equal to the prime rate of interest plus 3%.
> (2) Award punitive damages against the insurer.
> (3) Assess court costs and attorney's fees against the insurer.

Cases interpreting and applying the statute have included: *Rancosky v. Washington Nat'l Ins. Co*, 170 A.3d 364 (Pa. 2017) (to prevail on bad faith claim under §8371, plaintiff must show (1) insurer did not have reasonable basis to deny benefits under policy and (2) insurer knew or recklessly disregarded its lack of reasonable basis for denying claim; proof of ill-will or self-interest is probative of second prong, but is not prerequisite for succeeding on bad faith claim); *Ash v. Continental Ins. Co.*, 932 A.2d 877 (Pa. 2007) (addressing several issues concerning relation between statutory and common-law bad faith claims, and holding that claim under bad faith statute is subject to 2-year statute of limitations); *Berg v. Nationwide Mut. Ins. Co.*, 189 A.3d 1030, 2018 Pa. Super. 153 (2018) (see discussion in §1.12); *Greene v. United Servs. Auto. Ass'n*, 2007 Pa. Super. 344, 936 A.2d 1178 (2007) (holding (1) action for bad faith may extend to insurer's investigative practices; and (2) insurer's motive of self-interest or ill will is not required element, but proof of such motive is probative of element that insurer knew or recklessly disregarded its lack of reasonable basis for denying claim); *Zimmerman v. Harleysville Mut.*

Ins. Co., 860 A.2d 167 (Pa. Super. Ct. 2004) (Pennsylvania statute permits award of punitive damages upon finding of bad faith without any other evidentiary prerequisite); *Ridgeway v. U.S. Life Credit Life Ins. Co.*, 2002 Pa. Super. 54, 793 A.2d 972 (2002) (statute did not apply to insurer's postjudgment and postsettlement conduct in delaying payment); *Adamski v. Allstate Ins. Co.*, 738 A.2d 1033 (Pa. Super. Ct. 1999) (statute did not apply to denial of coverage that took place before July 1, 1990, statute's effective date); *Nealy v. State Farm Mut. Auto. Ins. Co.*, 695 A.2d 790 (Pa. Super. Ct. 1997) (underinsured motorist arbitration panels lack jurisdiction to address statutory bad faith claims); *Boring v. Erie Ins. Group*, 641 A.2d 1189 (Pa. Super. Ct. 1994) (statute does not apply only to actions involving automobile insurance); *Amica Mut. Ins. Co. v. Fogel*, 656 F.3d 167 (3d Cir. 2011) (Pennsylvania law; heightened standard of proof requires insured to provide evidence so clear, direct, weighty, and convincing as to enable clear conviction, without hesitation, that insurer acted in bad faith); *Colantuno v. Aetna Ins. Co.*, 980 F.2d 908 (3d Cir. 1992) (statute applies to all insurance contracts, regardless of contract date: relevant inquiry is date of alleged bad faith conduct); *Kunji Harrisburg, LLC v. Axis Surplus Ins. Co.*, 447 F. Supp. 3d 303 (E.D. Pa. 2020) (Pennsylvania law; summary judgment denied on bad faith claim related to coverage for wind damage to roof where genuine issue of material fact existed as to whether insurer was notified of claim and ignored it or whether insurer addressed claim through denial letter on related claim; summary judgment granted on bad faith claim related to coverage for water damage to roof where insurer made reasonable legal conclusion based on uncertain area of law on whether tarp used on roof qualified as roof); *Clapps v. State Farm Ins. Cos.*, 447 F. Supp. 3d 293 (E.D. Pa. 2020) (Pennsylvania law; dismissing bad faith claim under Pa.

Cons. Stat. §8371, with leave to amend, where complaint stated mere conclusory allegations with no factual detail); *Ironshore Specialty Ins. Co. v. Conemaugh Health Sys., Inc.*, 423 F. Supp. 3d 139 (W.D. Pa. 2019) (Pennsylvania law; denial of payment of claim not required to state claim for bad faith under Pa. Cons. Stat. §8371); *Metropolitan Grp. Prop. & Casualty Ins. Co. v. Hack*, 312 F. Supp. 3d 439 (M.D. Pa. 2018) (portions of counterclaim for bad faith brought under 42 Pa. Cons. Stat. §8371 were preempted by Pennsylvania Motor Vehicle Financial Responsibility Law, 75 Pa. Cons. Stat. §1797; see discussion in §1.26); *Whalen v. State Farm Fire & Casualty Co.*, 183 F. Supp. 3d 672 (E.D. Pa. 2016) (Pennsylvania law; denying insured's motion for summary judgment on bad faith claim under Pa. Cons. Stat. §8371 where record did not show "clear and convincing evidence" of bad faith failure to provide information, conduct investigation, or explain coverage decisions); *Papurello v. State Farm Fire & Casualty Co.*, *supra* (upholding individual plaintiff's claim under Pa. Cons. Stat. §8371 for bad faith denial of coverage, and dismissing class action claims where class plaintiffs failed to adequately allege bad faith breach of contract); *Simmons v. Nationwide Mut. Fire Ins. Co.*, 788 F. Supp. 2d 404 (W.D. Pa. 2011) (emphasizing that common-law claims for insurance bad faith are not cognizable under Pennsylvania law); *Johnson v. State Farm Life Ins. Co.*, 695 F. Supp. 2d 201 (W.D. Pa. 2010) (Pennsylvania law recognizes no common-law tort action for bad faith in insurance cases, and there is no private cause of action for violations of Unfair Insurance Practices Act, 40 P.S. § 1171.1 et seq.); *Anderson v. Nationwide Ins. Enter.*, 187 F. Supp. 2d 447 (W.D. Pa. 2002) (insurer's refusal to arbitrate uninsured motorist carrier claim constituted bad faith as matter of law, though appropriateness of punitive damages was jury question); *Younis Bros. v. CIGNA Worldwide Ins. Co.*, 882

F. Supp. 1468 (E.D. Pa. 1994), *aff'd*, 91 F.3d 13 (3d Cir. 1996) (rejecting constitutional challenge to bad faith statute); *Strange v. Nationwide Mut. Ins. Co.*, 867 F. Supp. 1209 (E.D. Pa. 1994) (Pennsylvania law recognizes no common-law bad faith cause of action); *Eastern Stainless Corp. v. American Protection Ins. Co.*, 829 F. Supp. 797 (D. Md. 1993) (Pennsylvania law; statute does not apply only to actions involving automobile insurance); *Turner Constr. Co. v. First Indem. of Am. Ins. Co.*, 829 F. Supp. 752 (E.D. Pa. 1993) (to prove violation of statute, insured must prove "general business practice"); *Margolies v. State Farm Fire & Casualty Co.*, 810 F. Supp. 637 (E.D. Pa. 1992) (statutory bad faith claims are not governed by policies' time-to-sue provisions); *Henry v. State Farm Ins. Co.*, 788 F. Supp. 241 (E.D. Pa. 1992) (statute applies to post–effective date conduct even if policy was issued before effective date); *Singer v. State Farm Mut. Auto. Ins. Co.*, 785 F. Supp. 510 (E.D. Pa. 1992) (bad faith statute cannot be applied to claims alleging denial of first-party benefits in violation of §1797 of Pennsylvania's Motor Vehicle Financial Responsibility Law, 75 Pa. Cons. Stat. Ann. §§1701 et seq.); *American Franklin Life Ins. Co. v. Galatti*, 776 F. Supp. 1054 (E.D. Pa. 1991) (same); *Seeger v. Allstate Ins. Co.*, 776 F. Supp. 986 (M.D. Pa. 1991) (same; statute applies to auto insurance cases notwithstanding arguably "more specific" provisions of Pennsylvania Motor Vehicle Financial Responsibility Law); *Barbaro v. Old Line Life Ins. Co. of Am.*, 785 F. Supp. 70 (E.D. Pa. 1992) (statute does not apply to claims denied before statute's effective date); *American Int'l Underwriters Corp. v. Zurn Indus., Inc.*, 771 F. Supp. 690 (W.D. Pa. 1991) (same); *Liberty Mut. Ins. Co. v. Paper Mfg. Co.*, 753 F. Supp. 156 (E.D. Pa. 1990) (same); *Coyne v. Allstate Ins. Co.*, 771 F. Supp. 673 (E.D. Pa. 1991) (same; statute is applicable to policies issued before state's effective date); *W.W. Management & Dev. Co. v. Scottsdale Ins. Co.*, 769 F. Supp.

178 (E.D. Pa. 1991) (statute is not unconstitutionally vague nor violative of due process).

Puerto Rico: In November 1993, a federal district court wrote, in *Event Producers, Inc. v. Tyser & Co.*, 854 F. Supp. 35, 39 (D. P.R. 1993): "[G]iven the trend in other states and the general tendency in Puerto Rico to protect consumers, we find that there can be a bad faith action against an insurer, and that Puerto Rico's Supreme Court would so declare. The standard would be either conscious wrongdoing,-reckless indifference or the lack of a reasonable basis for-denying a claim."

Rhode Island: In *Borden v. Paul Revere Life Ins. Co.*, 935 F.2d 370 (1st Cir. 1991), the First Circuit held, inter alia, that the trial judge did not err in omitting to direct the jury to make separate findings on the two separate theories of statutory and common-law bad faith. The court explained that the Rhode Island bad faith statute has, in fact, supplanted any common-law cause of action. (R.I. Gen. Laws §9-1-33 is discussed in this section of the book.) In *Skaling v. Aetna Ins. Co.*, 799 A.2d 997 (R.I. 2002), the Rhode Island Supreme Court discussed summary judgment standards and burdens in first-party bad faith cases, rejecting, *inter alia*, the automatic application of the "directed verdict rule." (See §1.20, supra.)

South Carolina: Concerning the elements of a claim for bad faith refusal to pay first-party benefits, see *The City of Myrtle Beach v. United National Ins. Co.*, 739 F. Supp. 2d 876 (D.S.C. 2010) (citing *Howard v. State Farm Mut. Auto. Ins. Co.*, 316 S.C. 445, 450 S.E.2d 582 (1994); *Crossley v. State Farm Mut. Auto. Ins. Co.*, 307 S.C. 354, 415 S.E.2d 393 (1992)); *Collins v. Auto-Owners Ins. Co.*, 759 F. Supp. 2d 728 (D.S.C. 2010) (South Carolina law). See also *In re Mt. Hawley Ins. Co.*, 427 S.C. 159, 829 S.E.2d 707 (2019) (affirming tort action for bad faith refusal to pay benefits under insurance policy, both in first-party and third-party context).

South Dakota: *Bertelsen v. Allstate Ins. Co.*, 833 N.W.2d
545 (S.D. 2013) (reversing for evidentiary and instruc-
tional errors jury's awards of $150,000 in compensatory
damages and $1.5 million in punitive damages; earlier
state Supreme Court opinions in same case had established only that insurer's *legal duty* was not fairly debatable, but bad faith is *intentional* tort, and trial court
in recent retrial had erroneously foreclosed insurer
from asserting factual matters such as *negligence* in
processing claim); *Bertelsen v. Allstate Ins. Co.*, 796
N.W.2d 685 (S.D. 2011) (because clear breach of contract is strong evidence of bad faith and summary judgment should have been granted in insured's favor on
breach of contract claim, trial court's error in submitting issue of breach of contract to jury prejudiced insureds' substantial rights on bad faith claim); *Bertelsen
v. Allstate Ins. Co.*, 764 N.W.2d 495 (S.D. 2009) (reversing summary judgment; insurer breached contractual
duty to immediately pay medical benefits for bodily injury after insured's workers' compensation claim was
denied, and factual dispute existed as to insurer's intent
in denying coverage); *Dakota, Minn. & Eastern R.R.
Corp. v. Acuity*, 771 N.W.2d 623 (S.D. 2009) (genuine
issues of material fact existed as to whether insurer
had failed to conduct thorough investigation of claim
for uninsured motorist benefits, and whether insurer
had subjected results of investigation to reasonable
evaluation and review); *Hein v. Acuity*, 731 N.W.2d 231
(S.D. 2007) (workers' compensation claimant's bad
faith claim against insurer, alleging that insurer filed
counterclaim against claimant in bad faith in separate
action in which claimant sought rehabilitation benefits,
was premature, where claimant's request for such benefits was pending before Department of Labor, and because central element of bad faith cause of action is
whether there has been wrongful denial of benefits);
Hammonds v. Hartford Fire Ins. Co., 501 F.3d 991 (8th

Cir. 2007) (insurer's delay of benefits payments, under workers' compensation policy, for attendant care for insured following his serious injury was not bad faith denial of benefits under South Dakota law absent evidence that insured suffered compensable loss of services or attendant care as result of payment delays); *Arp v. AON/Combined Ins. Co.*, 300 F.3d 913 (8th Cir. 2002) (reversing summary judgment on workers' compensation claim by claimant who presented evidence that insurer had unreasonably refused to agree that he was permanently disabled; discussing and applying South Dakota bad faith standard); *Landon v. American Family Mut. Ins. Co.*, 293 F. Supp. 3d 879 (D.S.D. 2017) (denying insurer's motion to dismiss insured's bad faith claim; reviewing test for first-party bad faith claims in South Dakota); *Anderson v. Western Nat'l Mut. Ins. Co.*, 857 F. Supp. 2d 896 (D.S.D. 2012) (insurer may be liable for bad faith if it conducts inadequate investigation and fails to locate information indicating insured's entitlement to benefits); *Berry v. Time Ins. Co.*, 798 F. Supp. 2d 1015 (D.S.D. 2011) (South Dakota law) (punitive damages would be supported by allegations that policy administrator willfully failed to provide correct information, placed unreasonable limitations on home healthcare providers, and refused to negotiate home healthcare arrangements); *McElgunn v. Cuna Mut. Ins. Soc'y*, 700 F. Supp. 2d 1141 (D.S.D. 2010) (evidence was sufficient to support finding that insurer's delay in paying disability claim had been in bad faith, but punitive damages award of $6 million would be reduced to $1.6 million). For a case reviewing the tort of first-party insurance bad faith, based on the "special relationship" between insurer and insured, see *Zochert v. Protective Life Ins. Co.*, 921 N.W.2d 479 (S.D. 2018).

Tennessee: Addressing issues relative to the construction and application of Tennessee's bad faith statute (Tenn. Code Ann. §56-7-105), see *Lindenberg v. Jackson Nat'l*

Life Ins. Co., 912 F.3d 348 (6th Cir. 2019), *cert. denied*, ___ U.S. ___, 140 S. Ct. 635 (2019) (Tennessee law; discussed in this section); *Heil Co. v. Evanston Ins. Co.*, 690 F.3d 722 (6th Cir. 2012), *abrogation recognized by Lindenberg v. Jackson Nat'l Life Ins. Co., supra* (Tennessee law); *Nylander v. Unum Life Ins. Co. of Am.*, 309 F. Supp. 3d 526 (M.D. Tenn. 2018); *American Nat'l Prop. & Casualty Co. v. Stutte*, 105 F. Supp. 3d 849 (E.D. Tenn. 2015); *Wynne v. Stonebridge Life Ins. Co.*, 694 F. Supp. 2d 871 (W.D. Tenn. 2010); *Hampton v. Allstate Ins. Co.*, 48 F. Supp. 2d 739 (M.D. Tenn. 1999). In *Lindenberg v. Jackson Nat'l Life Ins. Co., supra*, the Sixth Circuit held that the bad faith statute was not the exclusive remedy for insurer bad faith, and affirmed an award of statutory and common-law punitive damages to an insured under a bad faith breach of contract claim. The court reviewed the standard for imposition of a bad faith penalty under Tenn. Code Ann. §56-7-105, stating that a bad faith penalty was barred where there were "legitimate grounds for disagreement about the coverage of the insurance policy." 912 F.3d at 361 (internal quotation marks omitted).

Texas: As reflected in the book, the Texas Supreme Court initially recognized the doctrine of first-party bad faith in 1987, in *Arnold v. National County Mut. Fire Ins. Co.*, 725 S.W.2d 165 (Tex. 1987). In 1997, in *Universe Life Ins. Co. v. Giles*, 950 S.W.2d 48 (Tex. 1997), the court altered the standard for first-party bad faith liability by specifying that such liability is incurred only where an insurer denies or delays payment after its liability has become "reasonably clear." The previous formulation—delay or denial "with no reasonable basis" —had become "too oppressive" on the insurance industry, the court explained. See also *State Farm Lloyds v. Hamilton*, 265 S.W.3d 725 (Tex. App. 2008); *Allison v. Fire Ins. Exch.*, 98 S.W.3d 277 (Tex. App. 2003). Compare *Ramirez v. Allstate Vehicle & Prop. Ins. Co.*, ___

F. Supp. 3d ___, 2020 WL 5806436 (S.D. Tex. 2020) (Texas law; stating insurer must have "reasonable basis" to delay or deny coverage under Texas common law, but also stating it must have been "reasonably clear" to insurer there must be no coverage; also stating delay or denial must be proximate cause of plaintiff's injury).

In *Marino v. State Farm Fire & Casualty Co.*, 787 S.W.2d 948 (Tex. 1990), reversing summary judgment on an insured's bad faith claim, the court held that a judg-ment in the insured's favor on a contract cause of action, entered three weeks before issuance of the *Arnold* decision, was not res judicata as to the insured's subsequently filed bad faith claim, given the substantial intervening change in decisional law. Compare *United Neurology, P.A. v. Hartford Lloyd's Ins. Co.*, 101 F. Supp. 3d 584 (S.D. Tex. 2015), *aff'd mem.*, 624 Fed. Appx. 225 (5th Cir. 2015), in which a federal district court applying Texas law granted the insurer's motion for summary judgment on bad faith claims based on common law and on the Texas Insurance Code and Deceptive Trade Practices Act because the insured's underlying breach of contract claims had failed.

In *USAA Tex. Lloyds Co. v. Menchaca*, 545 S.W.3d 479 (Tex. 2018), the Texas Supreme Court stated that the Tex. Ins. Code §541.060(a) grants insureds a private right of action against insurers that engage in certain bad faith practices. The court also reviewed and clarified Texas precedent on whether an insured can recover policy benefits as actual damages for an insurer's statutory violation absent a finding that the insured had a contractual right to the benefits under the insurance policy. See discussion in §1.56. See also *State Farm Lloyds v. Fuentes*, 597 S.W.3d 925 (Tex. App. 2020) (reconsidering on remand in light of *Menchaca*; affirming trial court after applying 5 rules of *Menchaca* to facts of case); *Hinojos v. State Farm Lloyds*, 569 S.W.3d 304

(Tex. App. 2019) (refusing to distinguish case from *Menchaca* to allow extra-contractual claims where insurer did not breach contract but insured was entitled to coverage under policy; court affirmed summary judgment in favor of insurer where insured received full appraisal award and failed to show independent injury); *Thomas v. State Farm Lloyds*, 218 F. Supp. 3d 506 (N.D. Tex. 2016) (dismissing bad faith claims under insurance code and common law where court found no breach of contract and insured failed to show injury independent of policy claim or extreme act on part of insurer).

In *Murray v. San Jacinto Agency*, 800 S.W.2d 826 (Tex. 1990), the Texas Supreme Court overruled one of the ancillary holdings of *Arnold v. National County Mut. Fire Ins. Co., supra.* In *Murray*, the court held that the limitations period on a bad faith claim begins to run on the date the claim is denied, rather than, as *Arnold* had held, on the date a coverage suit is resolved unfavorably to the insurer. (Holding the *Arnold* decision to be fully retroactive, see *Commonwealth Lloyd's Ins. Co. v. Thomas*, 825 S.W.2d 135 (Tex. Ct. App. 1992).)

And see supplement §1.17 for discussion of *William H. McGee & Co. v. Schick*, 792 S.W.2d 513 (Tex. Ct. App. 1990), holding that an insurer's managing agent could be subject to liability for bad faith notwithstanding the absence of a direct contractual relationship to the insured.

For discussions of the interaction between the common-law cause of action for bad faith and statutory causes of action under the Unfair Claims Settlement Practices Act and the Deceptive Trade Practices Act, see *Minnesota Life Ins. Co. v. Vasquez*, 192 S.W.3d 774 (Tex. 2006); *Rocor Int'l, Inc. v. National Union Fire Ins. Co.*, 77 S.W.3d 253 (Tex. 2002); *Maryland Ins. Co. v. Head Industrial Coatings & Servs., Inc.*, 938 S.W.2d 27 (Tex. 1996); *GuideOne Lloyds Ins. Co. v. First Baptist Church of Bedford*, 268 S.W.3d 822 (Tex. App. 2008); *Texas Mut. Ins. Co. v. Ruttiger*, 265 S.W.3d 651 (Tex. App. 2008); *Lundstrom v. United Servs. Auto. Ass'n*,

192 S.W.3d 78 (Tex. App. 2006); *Allstate Indem. Co. v. Hyman*, 2006 WL 694014 (Tex. App. 2006); *Allison v. Fire Ins. Exch.*, *supra*; *Progressive County Mut. Ins. Co. v. Boman*, 780 S.W.2d 436 (Tex. App. 1989); *Lawyers Title Ins. Corp. v. Doubletree Partners, L.P.*, 739 F.3d 848 (5th Cir. 2014); *Luna v. Nationwide Prop. & Casualty Ins. Co.*, 798 F. Supp. 2d 821 (S.D. Tex. 2011); *SHS Investment v. Nationwide Mut. Ins. Co.*, 798 F. Supp. 2d 811 (S.D. Tex. 2011); *Lee v. Catlin Specialty Ins. Co.*, 766 F. Supp. 2d 812 (S.D. Tex. 2011); *Vought Aircraft Indus., Inc. v. Falvey Cargo Underwriting, Ltd.*, 729 F. Supp. 2d 814 (N.D. Tex. 2010). For a discussion of Texas Insurance Code §541.003, prohibiting unfair or deceptive acts or practices in the insurance industry, see *Weiser-Brown Operating Co. v. St. Paul Surplus Lines Ins. Co.*, 801 F.3d 512 (5th Cir. 2015) (applying "reasonable basis" test to affirm federal district court's judgment as a matter of law in favor of insurer on first-party bad faith claim based on insurer's alleged conduct during litigation where evidence at trial established bona fide coverage dispute).

In *Garcia v. Lloyds*, 514 S.W.3d 257 (Tex. App. 2016), the court granted summary judgment in favor of the insurer on a common-law bad faith claim and statutory bad faith claims. The court commented that in most circumstances, a bad faith claim is successful when a plaintiff shows a breach of contract accompanied by an independent tort. It is possible to succeed on a bad faith claim without a breach of contract, but the insured would have to show conduct so extreme that it would cause injury independent of the policy claim. See also *National Security Fire & Casualty Co. v. Hurst*, 523 S.W.3d 840 (Tex. App. 2017), *reh'g denied*, *petition for review filed* (Tex. App. 2017).

Vermont: In *Monahan v. GMAC Mortgage Corp.*, 2005 VT 110, 893 A.2d 298 (2005), the Vermont Supreme Court confirmed that a cause of action for breach of the implied covenant of good faith and fair dealing against an insurer sounds in tort, and that such a cause of action may arise even absent a breach of contract, but that punitive damages are available only if the insured can demonstrate that the insurer's conduct demonstrated actual malice. A sufficient showing of fraudulent conduct can satisfy the actual malice requirement, the court noted, even where some of the elements of the tort of fraud are not proven.

Washington: Concerning claims for first-party bad faith and for violations of the Washington Consumer Protection Act, see *Smith v. Safeco Ins. Co.*, 78 P.3d 1274 (Wash. 2003); *American States Ins. Co. v. Symes of Silverdale, Inc.*, 78 P.3d 1266 (Wash. 2003); *Van Noy v. State Farm Mut. Auto. Ins. Co.*, 16 P.3d 574 (Wash. 2001); *Coventry Assocs. v. American States Ins. Co.*, 961 P.2d 933 (Wash. 1998); *Leahy v. State Farm Mut. Auto. Ins. Co.*, 3 Wash. App. 2d 613, 418 P.3d 175 (2018); *Keodalah v. Allstate Ins. Co.*, 3 Wash. App. 2d 31, 413 P.3d 1059 (2018), *rev'd in part*, 194 Wash. 2d 339, 449 P.3d 1040 (2019); *Berkshire Hathaway Homestate Ins. Co. v. SQI, Inc.*, 132 F. Supp. 3d 1275 (W.D. Wash. 2015), *appeal dismissed* (9th Cir. 2017); *HB Dev., LLC v. Western Pac. Mut. Ins.*, 86 F. Supp. 3d 1164 (E.D. Wash. 2015); *Graham-Bingham Irrevocable Trust v. John Hancock Life Ins. Co. USA*, 827 F. Supp. 2d 1275 (W.D. Wash. 2011); *Lakehurst Condo. Owners Ass'n v. State Farm Fire & Casualty Co.*, 486 F. Supp. 2d 1205 (W.D. Wash. 2007).

On May 15, 2007, Washington Governor Christine Gregoire signed into law the Insurance Fair Conduct Act (Wash. Rev. Code §48.30.015), which became effective on July 22, 2007. The major feature of this act is the availability of treble damages for an "unreasonable" denial of coverage or benefits, or for a violation of a Washington Administrative Code provision regulating insurance trade practices. (Previously, the Washington Consumer Protection Act permitted the trebling of actual damages only up to a limit of $10,000 per claim.)

For a discussion of first-party bad faith tort claims and claims under the Washington IFCA and CPA, see *Wall v. Country Mut. Ins. Co.*, 319 F. Supp. 3d 1227 (W.D. Wash. 2018) (insured brought bad faith claim and claim under IFCA on mistaken belief diamond in her ring had been stolen and replaced with fake diamond and all parties believed diamond was fake until expert was hired; amount expended to hire jewelry expert could be characterized as damages/harm under IFCA); *Schreib v. American Family Mut. Ins. Co.*, 129 F. Supp. 3d 1129 (W.D. Wash. 2015) (discussing requirement of pleading and proving "actual damages" and proximate cause requirement). In a case of first impression in Washington, the federal district court in *Schreib, supra,* concluded that emotional distress damages do not constitute "actual damages" under the IFCA. For a case that considers enhanced damages under IFCA, see *MKB Constructors v. American Zurich Ins. Co.*, 711 Fed. Appx. 834 (9th Cir. 2017) (unpublished) (Washington law; enhanced damages not excessive where enhanced damages awarded were less than actual damages awarded; lower court did not err in sending question of enhanced damages to jury despite statutory provision related to court assessing enhanced damages).

In *Perez-Crisantos v. State Farm Fire & Casualty Co.*, 187 Wash. 2d 669, 389 P.3d 476 (2017), the Washington Supreme Court held that first-party insureds do not have a private right of action for regulatory violations under Washington's Insurance Fair Conduct Act.

In 2018 in *Keodalah v. Allstate Ins. Co., supra,* a Washington intermediate appellate court held that an insured stated a claim against an individual insurance adjuster for bad faith conduct under the Washington CPA and concluded that the insured did not have to show a contractual relationship to establish such claim. The court held that an individual or corporate insurance adjuster may be liable for bad faith, based on a breach of duty imposed by the Washington insurance code, Wash. Rev. Code §48.01.030, noting the statute applies to "all persons."

In 2019, however, the Washington Supreme Court partially reversed the court of appeals in *Keodalah v. Allstate Ins. Co., supra.* The court held that the Washington Insurance Code provision at issue did not create a private right of action against *anyone*, whether insurers or their agents. (Indeed, the court noted that if read to create a private right of action against "all persons," the provision could permit insurers to sue their insureds for bad faith.) The court also held that the private right of action available under the Consumer Protection Act for bad faith conduct applied only to insurers, not to claims adjusters. The court left undisturbed the court of appeals' holding that the Insurance Fair Conduct Act did not create a private right of action, based on *Perez-Cristanos v. State Farm Fire & Casualty Co., supra.*

West Virginia: In *Loudin v. National Liability & Fire Ins. Co.*, 716 S.E.2d 696 (W. Va. 2011), the West Virginia Supreme Court, collecting authorities, noted that the parties in the present proceeding did not dispute the fact that West Virginia recognizes the right of an insured first party to bring a bad faith cause of action against his or her insurer under the common law and under the West Virginia Unfair Trade Practices Act. See also *State ex rel. State Auto Prop. Ins. Cos. v. Stucky*, 239 W. Va. 729, 806 S.E.2d 160 (2017); *Kenney v. Independent Order of Foresters*, 744 F.3d 901 (4th Cir. 2014).

Wisconsin: Applying the Wisconsin doctrine of first-party bad faith in the context of underinsured motorist coverage, see *Danner v. Auto-Owners Ins.*, 629 N.W.2d 159

(Wis. 2001). And affirming an award of $3.5 million in punitive damages against an insurer that had refused to reform a policy to correct a mutual mistake arising from its agent's error in filling out an application for coverage, see *Trinity Evangelical Lutheran Church & School-Friestadt v. Tower Ins. Co.*, 661 N.W.2d 789 (Wis. 2003). See also *Dufour v. Progressive Classic Ins. Co.*, 370 Wis. 2d 313, 881 N.W.2d 678 (2016) (noting that bad faith sounds in tort, not contract; no bad faith where insured did not breach any duty under the policy by retaining funds it received in subrogation); *Brethorst v. Allstate Prop. & Casualty Ins. Co.*, 798 N.W.2d 467 (Wis. 2011) (insured provided sufficient evidence of breach of contract to entitle her to proceed with discovery on bad faith claim); *Blue v. Hartford Life & Accident Ins. Co.*, 698 F.3d 587 (7th Cir. 2012) (Wisconsin law; affirming summary judgment; insurer acted reasonably in terminating long-term disability benefits under "any occupation" standard after doctors indicated that insured had improved to point of being able to perform light or sedentary work); *Miller v. Safeco Ins. Co. of Am.*, 683 F.3d 805 (7th Cir. 2012) (affirming judgment for homeowners where insurer had acted in bad faith by denying coverage based on preexisting conditions; by denying coverage based on insured's delay in filing claim; and by denying coverage based on insured's failure to mitigate damages).

Wyoming: Answering questions certified from the Tenth Circuit, the Wyoming Supreme Court has now accorded first-time recognition to the tort doctrine of first-party bad faith, in *McCullough v. Golden Rule Ins. Co.*, 789 P.2d 855 (Wyo. 1990). The court endorsed the "fairly debatable" standard for assessing the insurer's privilege to resist a claim, and rejected the argument that the remedies available under the state unfair claim settlement practices statute were intended by the legislature to be exclusive of any common-law tort remedy. For discussions and applications of Wyoming's first-party bad faith tort doctrine, see *Sonnett v. First Am. Title Ins. Co.*, 309 P.3d 799 (Wyo. 2013) (even if claim for benefits is fairly debatable, insurer may breach implied covenant by manner in which it investigates, handles, or denies claim); *Harper v. Fidelity & Guar. Life Ins. Co.*, 234 P.3d 1211, 2010 WY 89 (2010) (life insurer did not breach duty of good faith by rescinding insurance policy after determining that there were material misrepresentations in insured's application; distinguishing cases involving prohibited practice of "post-claim underwriting"); *Cathcart v. State Farm Mut. Auto. Ins. Co.*, 123 P.3d 579 (Wyo. 2005) (to establish breach of implied covenant, insured must show: (1) absence of any reasonable basis for denial of claim; and (2) insurer's knowledge or reckless disregard of absence of reasonable basis); *Gainsco Ins. Co. v. Amoco Prod. Co.*, 53 P.3d 1051 (Wyo. 2002) (absence of controlling authority on interpretation of pollution exclusion gave insurer reasonable basis for denying coverage); *Ahrenholtz v. Time Ins. Co.*, 968 P.2d 946 (Wyo. 1998) (insured must prove absence of reasonable basis for denial of claim and insurer's knowledge or reckless disregard of absence of reasonable basis); *State Farm Mut. Auto. Ins. Co. v. Shrader*, 882 P.2d 813 (Wyo. 1994) (manner of handling even fairly debatable claim can constitute bad faith); *Marathon Ashland Pipe Line LLC v. Maryland Casualty Co.*, 243 F.3d 1232 (10th Cir. 2001) (oppressive or intimidating claims practices may subject insurer to bad faith liability even in absence of coverage); *White v. Continental Gen. Ins. Co.*, 831 F. Supp. 1545 (D. Wyo. 1993) (denying motion for summary judgment: fact issue was raised as to existence and bad faith nature of insurer's practice of "post-claim underwriting").

§1.34 b. Jurisdictions Expressly Rejecting Doctrine

Delaware: Representing Delaware's position that a cause of action for an insurer's breach of the duty of good faith and fair dealing sounds only in contract, see *Enrique v. State Farm Mut. Auto. Ins.*, 142 A.3d 506 (Del. 2016); *Pierce v. International Ins. Co.*, 671 A.2d 1361 (Del. 1996); *Tackett v. State Farm Fire & Casualty Ins. Co.*, 653 A.2d 254 (Del. 1995); *Travelers Indem. Co. v. Lake*, 594 A.2d 38 (Del. 1991). (The court in *Pierce v. International Ins. Co.*, *supra*, noted, however, that punitive damages may be available if the insurer's conduct was willful or malicious.)

District of Columbia: Although an isolated federal district court decision in 1984 analyzed District of Columbia law as recognizing a tort cause of action for first-party bad faith (see *Washington v. Group Hosp., Inc.*, 585 F. Supp. 517 (D. D.C. 1984)), the clear weight of authority now holds otherwise. See *Choharis v. State Farm Fire & Casualty Co.*, 961 A.2d 1080 (D.C. Ct. App. 2008); *Capitol Specialty Ins. Corp. v. Sanford Wittels & Heisler, LLP*, 793 F. Supp. 2d 399 (D. D.C. 2011); *Nugent v. UNUM Life Ins. Co. of Am.*, 752 F. Supp. 2d 46 (D. D.C. 2010); *Fireman's Fund Ins. Co. v. CTIA-The Wireless Ass'n*, 480 F. Supp. 2d 7 (D. D.C. 2007); *American Registry of Pathology v. Ohio Casualty Ins. Co.*, 401 F. Supp. 2d 75 (D. D.C. 2005); *Washington v. Government Employees Ins. Co.*, 769 F. Supp. 383 (D.D.C. 1991).

Illinois: Concerning the state supreme court's belated clarification of Illinois law—no common-law tort of first-party bad faith is recognized, and Ill. Ins. Code §155 provides the exclusive remedy—see *Cramer v. Insurance Exch. Agency*, 174 Ill. 2d 513, 675 N.E.2d 897

(1996). See also *The Weitz Co. v. Lloyd's of London*, 574 F.3d 885 (8th Cir. 2009) (Illinois law does not recognize non-statutory tort cause of action for first-party bad faith); *Hill v. State Farm Mut. Auto. Ins. Co.*, 166 Cal. App. 4th 1438, 83 Cal. Rptr. 3d 651 (2008) (stating that under Illinois law implied covenant of good faith provides tort cause of action only where insurer breaches duty to settle third-party claim).

Kansas: Reasserting Kansas' nonrecognition of a cause of action for first-party bad faith, see *Chance v. Farm Bureau Mut. Ins. Co.*, 756 F. Supp. 1440 (D. Kan. 1991). Concerning K.S.A. 40-256, and an insured's entitlement to recover attorneys' fees upon proof of an insurer's "vexatious" refusal to pay the full amount of a covered loss without just cause or excuse, see *Conner v. Occidental Fire & Casualty Co. of N.C.*, 135 P.3d 1230 (Kan. 2006).

Louisiana: Reasserting Louisiana's position that common-law bad faith causes of action in the first-party context are preempted by the state's penalty statute, see *Defelice Indus., Inc. v. Harris*, 573 So. 2d 463 (La. Ct. App. 1991).

Maine: Representing Maine's refusal to recognize a common-law bad faith cause of action in the first-party insurance context, see *Stull v. First Am. Title Ins. Co.*, 745 A.2d 975 (Me. 2000); *Greenwall v. Maine Mut. Fire Ins. Co.*, 715 A.2d 949 (Me. 1998); *Colford v. Chubb Life Ins. Co.*, 687 A.2d 609 (Me. 1996); *Marquis v. Farm Family Mut. Ins. Co.*, 628 A.2d 644 (Me. 1993).

Maryland: Reiterating Maryland's nonrecognition of a common-law cause of action for first-party bad faith, see *McCauley v. Suls*, 123 Md. App. 179, 716 A.2d 1129 (1998); *Reicher v. Berkshire Life Ins. Co. of Am.*, 360 F.3d 1 (1st Cir. 2004); *King v. GEICO*, 843 F. Supp. 56 (D. Md. 1994); *Stephens v. Liberty Mut. Fire Ins. Co.*,

821 F. Supp. 1119 (D. Md. 1993); *Yuen v. American Republic Ins. Co.*, 786 F. Supp. 531 (D. Md. 1992). Discussing Maryland's first-party bad faith statute (Md. Code Ann., Cts. & Jud. Proc. §3-1701, effective October 1, 2007) and rejecting a challenge to its retroactive application, see *Cecilia Schwaber Trust Two v. Hartford Accident & Indem. Co.*, 636 F. Supp. 2d 481 (D. Md. 2009).

Michigan: Reiterating Michigan's nonrecognition of a cause of action for first-party bad faith, see *Isagholian v. Transamerica Ins. Corp.*, 208 Mich. App. 9, 527 N.W.2d 13 (1994); *Axis Ins. Co. v. Innovation Ventures, LLC*, 737 F. Supp. 2d 685 (E.D. Mich. 2010); *Resolution Trust Corp. v. Fidelity & Deposit Co.*, 885 F. Supp. 228 (D. Kan. 1995) (Michigan law); *Aetna Casualty & Sur. Co. v. Dow Chem. Co.*, 883 F. Supp. 1101 (E.D. Mich. 1995); *LLMD, Inc. v. Marine Midland Realty Credit Corp.*, 789 F. Supp. 657 (E.D. Pa. 1992) (Michigan law).

Minnesota: Reiterating Minnesota's nonrecognition of a tort cause of action for first-party bad faith, see *St. Paul Fire & Marine Ins. Co. v. A.P.I., Inc.*, 738 N.W.2d 401 (Minn. Ct. App. 2007); *Cherne Contracting Corp. v. Wassau Ins. Co.*, 572 N.W.2d 339 (Minn. Ct. App. 1997). For a discussion of several issues concerning M.S.A. §604.18, which creates a statutory private cause of action for first-party bad faith, see *Friedberg v. Chubb & Son, Inc.*, 800 F. Supp. 2d 1020 (D. Minn. 2011). See also *Peterson v. Western Nat'l Mut. Ins. Co.*, 946 N.W.2d 903 (Minn. 2020) (upholding award of costs and attorney fees under Minn. Stat. §604.18 and discussing applicable standards); *Selective Ins. Co. of S.C. v. Sela*, 353 F. Supp. 3d 847 (D. Minn. 2018) (discussing standards for bad faith claim under Minn. Stat. Ann. §604.18).

Missouri: Reiterating Missouri's nonrecognition of the doctrine of first-party bad faith, see *Shafer v. Automobile Club Inter-Ins. Exch.*, 778 S.W.2d 395 (Mo. Ct. App.

1989). In *Overcast v. Billings Mut. Ins. Co.*, 11 S.W.3d 62 (Mo. banc 2000), the Missouri Supreme Court recognized an exception to the preemptive effect of the state's penalty statutes, allowing a tort recovery on a defamation claim brought by an insured who had been compelled to "self-publish" defendant's arson accusation when attempting to secure a new policy from another insurer. The nonpreemption principle announced by the court in *Overcast* appears to be a narrow one, limited in application to torts independent of any contractual breach. (The generally preemptive effect of the penalty statutes was discussed and upheld in *Catron v. Columbia Mut. Ins. Co.*, 723 S.W.2d 5 (Mo. 1987).)

Although no first-party bad faith right of action is available in Missouri, insureds may seek recovery for vexatious refusal to pay under Mo. Rev. Stat. §§375.420 and 375.296, which provide for statutory penalties and attorney's fees. See *Dhyne v. State Farm Fire & Casualty Co.*, 188 S.W.3d 454 (Mo. banc 2006) (affirming judgment for insured in action to recover uninsured motorist benefits and damages for vexatious refusal to pay); *Merseal v. Farm Bureau Town & Country Ins. Co. of Mo.*, 396 S.W.3d 467 (Mo. App. 2013) (upholding jury award of statutory damages and attorney's fees under §375.420 for insurer's refusal to pay homeowners insurance claim without reasonable cause).

New Hampshire: Declining to reexamine *Lawton v. Great Southwest Fire Ins. Co.*, 118 N.H. 607, 392 A.2d 576 (1978), and reiterating New Hampshire's nonrecognition of a cause of action for first-party bad faith, see *Bell v. Liberty Mut. Ins. Co.*, 776 A.2d 1260 (N.H. 2001).

New York: Although there is some lack of consistency in the formulation of the New York rule, courts generally continue to hold that extracontractual damages are unavailable in the absence of proof of an insurer's fraudulent scheme aimed at the general public: *Rocanova v. Equitable Life Assurance Soc'y of U.S.*, 83 N.Y.2d 603, 634 N.E.2d 940, 612 N.Y.S.2d 339 (1994); *Grazioli v. Encompass Ins. Co.*, 40 A.D.3d 696, 835 N.Y.S.2d 682 (2007); *Paterra v. Nationwide Mut. Fire Ins. Co.*, 38 A.D.3d 511, 831 N.Y.S.2d 468 (2007); *Alexander v. Geico Ins. Co.*, 35 A.D.3d 989, 826 N.Y.S.2d 777 (2006); *Vaveris v. Hermitage Ins. Co.*, 24 A.D.3d 537, 806 N.Y.S.2d 688 (2005); *Zawahir v. Berkshire Life Ins. Co.*, 22 A.D.3d 841, 804 N.Y.S.2d 405 (2005); *Batas v. Prudential Ins. Co. of Am.*, 724 N.Y.S.2d 3 (App. Div. 2001); *American Transit Ins. Co. v. Associated Int'l Ins. Co.*, 690 N.Y.S.2d 237 (App. Div. 1999); *Cunningham v. Security Mut. Ins. Co.*, 689 N.Y.S.2d 290 (App. Div. 1999); *Scavo v. Allstate Ins. Co.*, 238 A.D.2d 571, 657 N.Y.S.2d 193 (1997); *Ahmadi v. GEICO*, 204 A.D.2d 374, 612 N.Y.S.2d 50 (1994); *McLaughlin v. American Int'l Assurance Co.*, 580 N.Y.S.2d 763 (App. Div. 1992); *Belco Petroleum Corp. v. AIG Oil Rig, Inc.*, 164 A.D.2d 583, 565 N.Y.S.2d 776 (1991); *Kinnarney v. Natale Auto Body*, 157 A.D.2d 938, 550 N.Y.S.2d 194 (1990); *Telemaque v. New York Property Ins. Underwriting Ass'n*, 556 N.Y.S.2d 391 (App. Div. 1990); *In re Bernstein*, 156 A.D.2d 683, 549 N.Y.S.2d 446 (1989); *Silverman v. State Farm Fire & Casualty Co.*, 22 Misc. 3d 591, 867 N.Y.S.2d 881 (Supr. Ct. 2008); *Monga v. Security Mut. Life Ins. Co. of N.Y.*, 2002 WL 31777872 (Supr. Ct., Monroe Co., N.Y. 2002). But see *Panasia Estates, Inc. v. Hudson Ins. Co.*, 10 N.Y.3d 200, 856 N.Y.S.2d 513, 886 N.E.2d 135 (2008) (insured may recover foreseeable damages, beyond limits of policy, for breach of duty to investigate and settle claims in good faith); *Acquista v. New York Life Ins. Co.*, 285 A.D.2d 73, 730 N.Y.S.2d 272 (2001) (reluctantly noting that to recognize doctrine of first-party bad faith would represent "extreme change" in New York law, and therefore adopting "more conservative approach" according to which damages for breach of duty to investigate and settle first-party claims in bad faith are not limited to amount specified in policy); *Jolicoeur v. American Transit Ins. Co.*, 159 A.D.2d 236, 552 N.Y.S.2d 215 (1990) (affirming denial of summary judgment on bad faith claim involving insurer's alleged misrepresentations concerning amount of coverage); *United States Fidelity & Guar. Co. v. Pressler*, 158 A.D.2d 419, 551 N.Y.S.2d 921 (1990) (stating that compensatory damages may be recovered in connection with insurer's mishandling of claim); *Egan Marine Corp. v. Great Am. Ins. Co. of N.Y.*, 665 F.3d 800 (7th Cir. 2011) (New York law precluded claim that insurer had breached its duty of good faith where conduct underlying that claim was same conduct that generated breach of contract claim); *Dickler v. CIGNA Property & Casualty Co.*, 957 F.2d 1088 (3d Cir. 1992); *Endemann v. Liberty Ins. Corp.*, 390 F. Supp. 3d 362 (N.D.N.Y. 2019), *partial reconsideration*, 2020 WL 5027421 (N.D.N.Y. 2020) (claim for breach of implied covenant of good faith and fair dealing allowed to proceed even though contract claim was barred under contract's limitations period; conduct alleged was different from conduct alleged under contract claim, and therefore good faith and fair dealing claim was not duplicative of contract claim); *Sunrise One, LLC v. Harleysville Ins. Co. of N.Y.*, 293 F. Supp. 3d 317 (E.D.N.Y. 2018) (insured may recover consequential damages for insurer's bad faith refusal to pay claim and parties reasonably contemplated such damages upon executing insurance contract; to show bad faith insured must demonstrate that no reasonable carrier would have denied coverage; affirming summary judgment for insurer); *K. Bell & Assocs., Inc. v. Lloyd's Underwriters*, 827 F. Supp. 985 (S.D.N.Y. 1993). For a discussion of the uncertainty, see *In re Eurospark Indus., Inc. v. Massachusetts Bay Ins. Co.*, 288 B.R. 177, 2003 WL 215383 (Bankr. E.D.N.Y. 2003).

In October 1992, the Second Circuit, in *Riordan v. Nationwide Mut. Fire Ins. Co.*, 977 F.2d 47 (2d Cir. 1992), held that a private right of action may be pursued against insurers under the state's consumer protection statute (N.Y. Gen. Bus. Law §349), which permits recovery of actual damages and attorney's fees. At the same time the Second Circuit issued its opinion in *Riordan*, it certified to the New York Court of Appeals two questions the answers to which might have dramatically altered the status of first-party bad faith actions in New York. (On January 21, 1993, however, after the insurer satisfied the judgment in full, the Second Circuit dismissed the certification of the questions as moot.) Historically, New York courts have held that the pallid administrative remedies of the unfair claims settlement practices statute preempt any common-law cause of action unless the plaintiff can allege a fraudulent scheme aimed at the general public, and even under those circumstances the lower appellate courts have split on the availability of punitive damages.

Oregon: Although Oregon should probably still be listed among those states that refuse to recognize a bad faith tort cause of action in the first-party context (see cases cited in book, *Strader v. Grange Mut. Ins. Co.*, 179 Or. App. 329, 39 P.3d 903 (2002), and *Richardson v. Guardian Life Ins. Co. of Am.*, 161 Or. App. 615, 984 P.2d 917 (1999)), it should be noted that one anomalous case has appeared to cast doubt on the continued vitality of the nonrecognition decisions: *McKenzie v. Pacific Health & Life Ins. Co.*, 118 Or. App. 377, 847 P.2d 879 (1993). See also *Morrow v. Red Shield Ins. Co.*, 212 Or. App. 653, 159 P.3d 384 (2007) (summary judgment was precluded on claim that insurer breached duty of good faith and fair dealing by issues of fact as to whether property insurer had received insured's notice of address change in acceptable form). Concerning Oregon's personal injury protection (PIP) statutes and the requirement that an automobile insurer is required to establish that its denials were based on reasonable investigations before it can prevail on summary judgment, see *Ivanov v. Farmers Ins. Co. of Or.*, 344 Or. 421, 185 P.3d 417 (2008). See also *Scott v. State Farm Mut. Auto. Ins. Co.*, 345 Or. 146, 190 P.3d 372 (banc 2008) (application that insured submitted for PIP benefits constituted "proof of loss" for UM benefits, and thus insured was entitled to attorneys' fees per Or. Rev. Stat. Ann. §742.061; abrogating *Mosley v. Allstate Ins. Co.*, 165 Or. App. 304, 996 P.2d 513 (2000)).

Utah: The position of the Utah courts was clarified in *Billings v. Union Bankers Ins. Co.*, 918 P.2d 461 (Utah 1996), where the state supreme court stated that a first-party bad faith cause of action sounds in contract only, but emotional distress damages are potentially available in accordance with the ordinary contract-law rule of foreseeability. See also *Jones v. Farmers Ins. Exch.*, 286 P.3d 301, 2012 WL 3677052 (Utah 2012); *United States Fidelity & Guar. Co. v. United States Sports Specialty Ass'n*, 270 P.3d 464 (Utah 2012); *Black v. Allstate Ins. Co.*, 100 P.3d 1163 (Utah 2004); *Blakely v. USAA Casualty Ins. Co.*, 633 F.3d 944 (10th Cir. 2011). In *Machan v. UNUM Life Ins. Co. of Am.*, 116 P.3d 342 (Utah 2005), the court held that there is no private cause of action under Utah Code §31A-26-301, which requires timely payment of insurance claims.

Virginia: Reiterating Virginia's nonrecognition of a bad faith cause of action in the first-party context, see *L & E Group v. Days Inns of Am., Inc.*, 992 F.2d 55 (4th Cir. 1993); *Joyce v. Lincoln Nat'l Life Ins. Co.*, 845 F. Supp. 353 (E.D. Va. 1993). (Though see *Levine v. Selective Ins. Co. of Am.*, 250 Va. 282, 462 S.E.2d 81 (1995), apparently recognizing a first-party bad faith cause of action sounding in contract.) In *Manu v. GEICO Casualty Co.*, 798 S.E.2d 598 (Va. 2017), the court held that

Virginia Code §8.01-66.1(D)(1) does not create a duty on an insurer to pay an uninsured motorist claim before insured has obtained a judgment against the uninsured tortfeasor. The statute does allow the insured to recover the amount due in contract damages plus double interest and attorney's fees and costs in an uninsured motorist bad faith action. Concerning Va. Code Ann. §8.01-66.1(A), the Virginia statute that provides for attorney's fees and the doubling of awards against auto insurers who, in bad faith, fail to pay claims of $2,500 or less, see *Nationwide Mut. Ins. Co. v. St. John*, 524 S.E.2d 649 (Va. 2000).

§1.35 c. Undecided and Conflicted Jurisdictions

District of Columbia: Although there remains some room for argument, the weight of recent District of Columbia authority clearly represents a refusal to recognize a tort cause of action for first-party bad faith. See §1.34, *supra*.

Illinois: Concerning the state supreme court's belated clarification of Illinois law—no common-law tort of first-party bad faith is recognized, and Ill. Ins. Code §155 provides the exclusive remedy—see *Cramer v. Insurance Exch. Agency*, 174 Ill. 2d 513, 675 N.E.2d 897 (1996).

Maine: The uncertain nature of Maine law concerning the availability of extracontractual damages for nonpayment of an insurance claim was recognized and discussed by a federal district court in *Seabury Housing Assocs. v. Home Ins. Co.*, 695 F. Supp. 1244 (D. Me. 1988). The court noted that by way of dictum in one third-party case (*Linscott v. State Farm Mut. Auto. Ins. Co.*, 368 A.2d 1161 (Me. 1977)), the state supreme court had indicated that a duty of good faith is implied in insurance contracts. And the court also discussed the enactment by the Maine legislature of a statute creating a civil remedy for policyholders aggrieved by an insurer's unreasonable denial of a claim (24-A Me. Rev. Stat. Ann. §2436-A, effective Sept. 29, 1987). It remains unclear, the *Seabury* court concluded, whether Maine courts recognize a common-law cause of action independent of the statute, or whether they view the new statutory remedy as exclusive. In light of that uncertainty, the court denied summary judgment on the insured's claim that the insurer had acted in bad faith in denying "soft costs" coverage under a builder's risk policy. (See book App. pt. III for summary of the 1987 statutory provisions referred to in *Seabury*.)

New Jersey: See §1.33.

New York: See §1.34.

Vermont: Reiterating the indeterminacy of Vermont law concerning recognition or nonrecognition of the bad faith tort doctrine in the first-party context, see *Booska v. Hubbard Ins. Agency, Inc.*, 627 A.2d 333 (Vt. 1993).

§1.36 d. Jurisdictions Allowing Punitive Damages in Contract Actions

Alabama: In *Independent Fire Ins. Co. v. Lunsford*, 621 So. 2d 977 (Ala. 1993), the Alabama Supreme Court reversed a bad faith judgment against an insurer, finding a reasonable though mistaken basis for denial of the claim, but nonetheless affirmed an award of damages for emotional distress for breach of the insurance policy. Such damages are available for breach of contract, the court explained, if the jury finds that "'the contractual duties imposed by this contract are so coupled with matters of mental solicitude as to the duty that is owed, that a breach of that duty will necessarily or reasonably result in mental anguish.'" 621 So. 2d at 979, quoting from *Orkin Exterminating Co. v. Donavan*, 519 So. 2d 1330 (Ala. 1988).

Delaware: In *Enrique v. State Farm Mut. Auto. Ins.*, 142 A.3d 506 (Del. 2016), the Supreme Court of Delaware confirmed that the bad faith cause of action is grounded in contract law, but due to the special nature of the insurance relationship, punitive damages are available as a remedy for breach of the covenant of good faith where the plaintiff can show that the insurer acted with malice or reckless indifference. See *Pierce v. International Ins. Co.*, 671 A.2d 1361 (Del. 1996), for discussion of the Delaware principle that punitive damages may be available in the context of a contract action if the insurer's conduct was willful or malicious. Delaware cases on the issue were surveyed by the court in *Reiver v. Murdoch & Walsh, P.A.*, 625 F. Supp. 998 (D. Del. 1985).

Indiana: Indiana law has now recognized the bad faith tort doctrine in the first-party context (see §1.33), and no longer recognizes the availability of punitive damages in actions for breach of contract (see *Miller Brewing Co. v. Best Beers, Inc.*, 608 N.E.2d 975 (Ind. 1993)).

Massachusetts: Under Massachusetts law, the state Supreme Judicial Court held in *John Hancock Mut. Life Ins. Co. v. Banerji*, 858 N.E.2d 277 (Mass. 2006), damages for emotional distress as a result of a breach of contract may be recovered if they result from physical harm or are the result of intentional or reckless conduct of an extreme and outrageous nature.

New York: A party can recover punitive damages for breach of contract, it was held in *Aragona v. Allstate Ins. Co.*, 969 N.Y.S.2d 863 (Dist. Ct. 2013), only where the breach of contract also involves a fraud evincing a high degree of moral turpitude, and demonstrating such wanton dishonesty as to imply a criminal indifference to civil obligations if the conduct was aimed at the public generally.

Pennsylvania: The Pennsylvania Supreme Court has endorsed §367 of the RESTATEMENT (SECOND) OF CONTRACTS, according to which damages for emotional distress may be recoverable on a contract where the breach is of a kind that serious emotional distress was a particularly likely result. *Birth Center v. St. Paul Cos., Inc.*, 567 Pa. 386, 787 A.2d 376 (2001). The possible applicability of §367 to first-party insurance cases was again noted in *Johnson v. State Farm Life Ins. Co.*, 695 F. Supp. 2d 201 (W.D. Pa. 2010).

Tennessee: *Lindenberg v. Jackson Nat'l Life Ins. Co.*, 912 F.3d 348 (6th Cir. 2019), *cert. denied*, ___ U.S. ___, 140 S. Ct. 635 (2019) (holding that statutory damages were not exclusive for bad faith breach of contract claim against insurer and upholding award of $3 million in punitive damages).

Virginia: In *Moorhead v. State Farm Fire & Casualty Co.*, 123 F. Supp. 2d 1004 (W.D. Va. 2000), the court denied summary judgment on the basis of the principle of Restatement (Second) of Contracts, §353, that emotional distress damages may be available for breach of contract where the nature of the breach is such that serious emotional disturbance was a "particularly likely result." The present case, involving the assertedly unjustified denial of a fire insurance claim, presented an issue of fact for the jury, the court held. (The court noted that the Restatement's test is disjunctive, permitting recovery based either upon the nature of the contract or upon the nature of the breach.)

§1.37 e. Jurisdictions Recognizing Private Right of Action Under Consumer Protection Acts

Colorado: In *Anderson v. State Farm Mut. Auto. Ins. Co.*, 416 F.3d 1143 (10th Cir. 2005) (Colorado law), the Tenth Circuit affirmed the dismissal of claims for common-law bad faith and for violation of the Colorado Consumer

Protection Act. With respect to the latter claim, the court held that the insurer did not engage in a deceptive trade practice in enforcing certain exclusions in contracts providing underinsured and uninsured motorist coverage. The insurer's position reflected a reasonable interpretation of existing case law, the court explained, and the insurer did not make any representations it should have known to be false or act with reckless disregard. See also *Brodeur v. American Home Assurance Co.*, 169 P.3d 139 (Colo. banc 2007) (emphasizing "private" wrongs are not actionable under Colorado Consumer Protection Act and holding that public nature of workers' compensation program did not automatically satisfy necessary public impact element of CCPA claim); *Mullen v. Allstate Ins. Co.*, 232 P.3d 168 (Colo. App. 2009) (insurer did not violate CPA by failing to advise policyholders that they had received no benefit from premiums paid for UM/UIM coverage on more than 1 vehicle); *Peterson v. USAA Life Ins. Co.*, 353 F. Supp. 3d 1099 (D. Colo. 2018), *aff'd*, 814 Fed. Appx. 408 (10th Cir. 2020) (plaintiff failed to show significant impact on public of challenged trade practice allegedly resulting in denial of life insurance claims, as required to sustain CPA claim, where insurer denied fewer than 1 percent of claims, resulting in at most de minimis impact).

Hawaii: In *Aquilina v. Certain Underwriters at Lloyd's Syndicate #2003*, 407 F. Supp. 3d 1016 (D. Haw. 2019) (Hawaii law), where insureds brought claims of fraudulent and misleading conduct against insurers and agents/brokers, the court acknowledged private rights of action under the Unfair and Deceptive Acts or Trade Practices Act (UDAP), Haw. Stat. §480–2 (which it held was not preempted by the Insurance Code, Haw. Stat. §431:13–102) and the Uniform Deceptive Trade Practices Act (UDTPA), Haw. Stat. §481A-3. The court also acknowledged the availability of a first-party bad faith action under common law. The court dismissed the complaint with leave to amend for, *inter alia*, failure to satisfy the Fed. R. Civ. P. 9(b) requirement to plead fraud with particularity. See §§1.26, 1.33.

Kentucky: In *Indiana Ins. Co. v. Demetre*, 527 S.W.3d 12 (Ky. 2017), the Kentucky Supreme Court affirmed that in Kentucky bad faith claims can arise from the Kentucky Consumer Protection Act. See also §2.24. The court quoted the test applicable to all insurance bad faith actions in Kentucky, from *Wittmer v. Jones*, 864 S.W.2d 885 (Ky. 1993), in which the court "'gathered all of the bad faith liability theories under one roof and established a test applicable to all bad faith actions,' whether first-party or third-party claims and whether based on common law or statute." 527 S.W.3d at 26 (quoting *Davidson*, 25 S.W.3d at 100). The *Wittmer* test contains three required elements:

> (1) the insurer must be obligated to pay the claim under the terms of the policy; (2) the insurer must lack a reasonable basis in law or fact for denying the claim; and (3) it must be shown that the insurer either knew there was no reasonable basis for denying the claim or acted with reckless disregard for whether such a basis existed.

Indiana Ins. Co., 527 S.W.3d at 26 (quoting *Davidson*, 25 S.W.3d at 100 (quoting *Wittmer*, 864 S.W.2d at 890)).

Massachusetts: It was held in *Sidney Binder, Inc. v. Jewelers Mut. Ins. Co.*, 28 Mass. App. Ct. 459, 552 N.E.2d 568 (1990), that an insurer may sue an insured under the state consumer protection statute (Mass. Gen. Laws Ann. ch. 93A) for filing a fraudulent claim. The consumer protection statute may not, however, serve as the vehicle for a suit by one insurer against another insurer. *Transamerica Ins. Group v. Turner Constr. Co.*, 33 Mass. App. Ct. 446, 601 N.E.2d 473 (1992). Conduct that violates the Massachusetts Unfair Claims Practices statute (Mass. Gen. L. ch. 176D) is evidence of unfairness in an action under the consumer protection statute. *Pacific Indem. Co. v. Lampro*, 86 Mass. App. Ct. 60, 12 N.E.3d 1037 (2014); *Chery v. Metropolitan Prop. & Casualty Ins. Co.*, 79 Mass. App. Ct. 697, 948 N.E.2d 1278 (2011); *Hartunian v. Pilgrim Ins. Co.*, 2012 WL 5877477 (Mass. App. Div. 2012); *Clarendon Nat'l Ins. Co. v. Philadelphia Indem. Ins. Co.*, 954 F.3d 397 (1st Cir. 2020) (Massachusetts law); *River Farm Realty Trust v. Farm Fam. Casualty Ins. Co.*, 360 F. Supp. 3d 31 (D. Mass. 2019), *aff'd*, 943 F.3d 27 (1st Cir. 2019); *Brown Daltas & Assoc., Inc. v. General Accident Ins. Co. of Am.*, 844 F. Supp. 58 (D. Mass. 1994).

In *Aquino v. United Prop. & Cas. Co.*, 483 Mass. 820, 143 N.E.3d 379 (2020), the court held that denial of coverage did not breach the insurer's duty of good faith and fair dealing under Mass. Gen. Laws §93A where the coverage decision was supported by a "plausible, reasoned legal position" in case law, although the case was very old and the insurer's position turned out to be wrong. The court also held that the insurer's faulty drafting of its policy language did not result in a violation of Mass. Gen. Laws §93A where the insured failed to show that the improper drafting caused harm. *See also NextSun Energy Littleton, LLC v. Acadia Ins. Co.*, ___ F. Supp. 3d ___, 2020 WL 5821630 (D. Mass. 2020) (Massachusetts law; no violation of consumer protection statutes in case of good faith dispute over insurance coverage, based on plausible policy interpretation).

Michigan: The Michigan Consumer Protection Act (Mich. Comp. Laws §445.901 et seq.) allows actions by private individuals against insurers for deceptive practices. *Nesbitt v. American Community Mut. Ins. Co.*, 236 Mich. App. 215, 600 N.W.2d 427 (1999); *Smith v. Globe Life Ins. Co.*, 223 Mich. App. 264, 565 N.W.2d 877

(1997), *aff'd in part and rev'd in part*, 597 N.W.2d 28 (Mich. 1999).

Minnesota: Concerning an insured's private right of action under Minn. Stat. §§325F.68-325F.70, see *Parkhill v. Minnesota Mut. Life Ins. Co.*, 995 F. Supp. 983 (D. Minn. 1998).

New York: In October 1992, the Second Circuit, in *Riordan v. Nationwide Mut. Fire Ins. Co.*, 977 F.2d 47 (2d Cir. 1992), held that a private right of action may be pursued against insurers under the state's consumer protection statute (N.Y. Gen. Bus. Law §349), which permits recovery of actual damages and attorney's fees. See also *Brown v. Government Employees Ins. Co.*, 156 A.D.3d 1087, 66 N.Y.S.3d 733 (2017) (trial court erred in granting insurer's motion to dismiss where insured alleged that she was harmed by insurer who engaged in consumer-oriented pattern and practice aimed at public at large in wrongfully denying no-fault claims by pressuring physicians it hired to perform independent medical evaluations that supported denial of benefits; allegations were sufficient to state cognizable claim under General Business Law §349 at prediscovery stage); *Page One Auto Sales v. Commercial Union Ins. Cos.*, 176 Misc. 2d 820, 674 N.Y.S.2d 577 (1998), emphasizing that the statute requires a showing of a broad impact on consumers at large; *Endemann v. Liberty Ins. Corp.*, 390 F. Supp. 3d 362 (N.D.N.Y. 2019), *partial reconsideration*, 2020 WL 5027421 (N.D.N.Y. 2020) (allowing claim brought under N.Y. Gen. Bus. Law §349 to proceed at pre-discovery phase to allow insured to show broader impact on consumers at large).

North Carolina: See *High Country Arts & Crafts Guild v. Hartford Fire Ins. Co.*, 126 F.3d 629 (4th Cir. 1997), for a discussion of the relation between a claim under the North Carolina Unfair Claims Settlement Practices Act (N.C. Gen. Stat. §58-63-15(11)) and a claim under the

North Carolina Unfair Trade Practices Act (N.C. Gen. Stat. §75-16.1). See also *Page v. Lexington Ins. Co.*, 628 S.E.2d 427 (N.C. Ct. App. 2006); *Elliott v. American States Ins. Co.*, 883 F.3d 384 (4th Cir. 2018); *Williams v. Ohio Nat'l Life Assurance Co.*, 364 F. Supp. 3d 605 (W.D.N.C. 2019). See also §2.24.

Pennsylvania: A federal district court, in *Williams v. State Farm Mut. Auto. Ins. Co.*, 763 F. Supp. 121 (E.D. Pa. 1991), has taken the position that the Pennsylvania unfair claim settlement practices statute preempts *all* private actions against insurers, including claims under the Unfair Trade Practices and Consumer Protection Act. In so holding, the court expressly disagreed with *Hardy v. Pennock Ins. Agency, Inc.*, 529 A.2d 471 (Pa. Super. Ct. 1987) (cited in this section of the book). Another federal district court decision has, however, continued to adhere to the more limited preemption position represented by *Hardy*, and *Pekular v. Eich*, 355 Pa. Super. 276, 513 A.2d 427 (1986). See *Brownell v. State Farm Mut. Ins. Co.*, 757 F. Supp. 526 (E.D. Pa. 1991). See also *Smith v. Nationwide Mut. Fire Ins. Co.*, 935 F. Supp. 616 (W.D. Pa. 1996); *Parasco v. Pacific Indem. Co.*, 870 F. Supp. 644 (E.D. Pa. 1994); *Boyce v. Nationwide Mut. Ins. Co.*, 842 F. Supp. 822 (E.D. Pa. 1994).

An insured must exhaust administrative remedies before bringing an action under the state consumer protection statute (73 Pa. Cons. Stat. §§201-1 et seq.) based on an insurer's violation of the Pennsylvania Title Insurance Companies Act: *Moy v. Schreiber Deed Sec. Co.*, 572 A.2d 758 (Pa. Super. Ct. 1990).

Texas: Concerning the interaction of the common-law bad faith cause of action with a cause of action under §17.46 of the Texas Deceptive Trade Practices Act (Tex. Bus. & Com. Code §§17.41 et seq.), and a cause of action under article 21.21 of the Texas Insurance Code, see

Allstate Indem. Co. v. Hyman, 2006 WL 694014 (Tex. App. 2006); *Allied Gen. Agency, Inc. v. Moody*, 788 S.W.2d 601 (Tex. App. 1990); *William H. McGee & Co. v. Schick*, 792 S.W.2d 513 (Tex. App. 1990).

Washington: Concerning the private right of action against an insurer under the Washington Consumer Protection Act (Wash. Rev. Code §§19.86.020 et seq.) based on an an unreasonable denial of coverage, see *Van Noy v. State Farm Mut. Auto. Ins. Co.*, 16 P.3d 574 (Wash. 2001); *Seattle Pump Co. v. Traders & General Ins. Co.*, 970 P.2d 361 (Wash. 1999); *Leingang v. Pierce County Medical Bureau, Inc.*, 131 Wash. 2d 133, 930 P.2d 288 (1997); *Industrial Indem. Co. of the Southwest v. Kallevig*, 114 Wash. 2d 907, 792 P.2d 520 (1990); *Leahy v. State Farm Mut. Auto. Ins. Co.*, 3 Wash. App. 2d 613, 418 P.3d 175 (2018); *Keodalah v. Allstate Ins. Co.*, 3 Wash. App. 2d 31, 413 P.3d 1059 (2018), *rev'd in part*, 194 Wash. 2d 339, 449 P.3d 1040 (2019); *James E. Torina Fine Homes, Inc. v. Mutual of Enumclaw Ins. Co.*, 74 P.3d 648 (Wash. App. 2003); *Pain Diagnostics & Rehabilitation Assocs. v. Brockman*, 988 P.2d 972 (Wash. Ct. App. 1999); *Wolf v. League Gen. Ins. Co.*, 85 Wash. App. 113, 931 P.2d 184 (1997); *Starczewski v. Unigard Ins. Group*, 61 Wash. App. 267, 810 P.2d 58 (1991); *Insurance Co. v. Highlands Ins. Co.*, 59 Wash. App. 782, 801 P.2d 284 (1990); *Berkshire Hathaway Homestate Ins. Co. v. SQI, Inc.*, 132 F. Supp. 3d 1275 (W.D. Wash. 2015), *appeal dismissed* (9th Cir. 2017); *HB Dev., LLC v. Western Pac. Mut. Ins.*, 86 F. Supp. 3d 1164 (E.D. Wash. 2015); *Scanlon v. Life Ins. Co. of N. Am.*, 670 F. Supp. 2d 1181 (W.D. Wash. 2009). The federal district court in *HB Dev.*, *supra*, granted summary judgment to the insurer on the insured's CPA claim, finding no material dispute whether the insurer committed a deceptive act or practice when it sent notification to the insured that its policy had changed from an "occurrence based" to a "claims made" policy.

On May 15, 2007, Washington Governor Christine Gregoire signed into law the Insurance Fair Conduct Act (RCW 48.30.015), which became effective on July 22, 2007. The major feature of this act is the availability of treble damages for an "unreasonable" denial of coverage or benefits, or for a violation of a Washington Administrative Code provision regulating insurance trade practices. (Previously, the Washington Consumer Protection Act permitted the trebling of actual damages only up to a limit of $10,000 per claim.) See *Wall v. Country Mut. Ins. Co.*, 319 F. Supp. 3d 1227 (W.D. Wash. 2018) (insured brought bad faith claim and claim under IFCA on mistaken belief diamond in her ring had been stolen and replaced with fake diamond and all parties believed diamond was fake until expert was hired; amount expended to hire jewelry expert could be characterized as damages/harm under IFCA); *Schreib v. American Family Mut. Ins. Co.*, 129 F. Supp. 3d 1129 (W.D. Wash. 2015) (concluding in a case of first impression in Washington that emotional distress damages do not constitute "actual damages" under the IFCA); see also *Berkshire Hathaway Homestate Ins. Co.*, *supra*, (granting summary judgment for insurer on IFCA bad faith claim). For a case that considers enhanced damages under IFCA, see *MKB Constructors v. American Zurich Ins. Co.*, 711 Fed. Appx. 834 (9th Cir. 2017) (unpublished) (enhanced damages not excessive where enhanced damages awarded were less than actual damages awarded; lower court did not err in sending question of enhanced damages to jury despite statutory provision related to court assessing enhanced damages). The court in *Perez-Crisantos v. State Farm Fire & Casualty Co.*, 187 Wash. 2d 669, 389 P.3d 476 (2017), held that first-party insureds do not have a private right of action for regulatory violations under Washington's Insurance Fair Conduct Act. Accord *Keodalah v. Allstate Ins. Co.*, *supra*.

8. Extensions of Bad Faith Tort Liability Beyond Insurance Context

§1.38 a. Surety Relationships

—In *O'Connor v. Star Ins. Co.*, 83 P.3d 1 (Alaska 2003), the Alaska Supreme Court held that a licensing bond surety owed no implied duty of good faith to a client of the bonded contractor and therefore had no duty to investigate the client's claim against the contractor.

—In *Dodge v. Fidelity & Deposit Co.*, 161 Ariz. 344, 778 P.2d 1240 (1998), the Arizona Supreme Court held that a homeowner could assert a bad faith claim against a contractor's surety.

—In *Cates Constr., Inc. v. Talbot Partners*, 21 Cal. 4th 28, 86 Cal. Rptr. 2d 855 (1999), the California Supreme Court held that tort recovery is not permitted for a breach of the implied covenant of good faith and fair dealing in the context of a construction performance bond. "A construction performance bond is not an insurance policy," the court wrote. "Nor is it a contract otherwise marked by elements of adhesion, public interest or fiduciary responsibility, such that an extracontractual remedy is necessitated in the interests of social policy." 21 Cal. 4th at 60, 86 Cal. Rptr. 2d at 885.

—In *Transamerica Premier Ins. Co. v. Brighton Sch. Dist.*, 940 P.2d 348 (Colo. 1997), the Colorado Supreme Court recognized a common-law cause of action in tort for a commercial surety's failure to act in good faith when processing claims made by an obligee under the terms of a performance bond.

Concerning the recognition by Colorado law that a first-party bad faith cause of action may be asserted against sureties, see *Brighton Sch. Dist. 27J v. Transamerica Premier Ins. Co.*, 923 P.2d 328 (Colo. Ct. App. 1996).

—In *PSE Consulting, Inc. v. Frank Mercede & Sons, Inc.*, 267 Conn. 279, 838 A.2d 135 (2004), the Connecticut

Supreme Court held that a surety is not entitled to indemnification from its principal for payments made to the claimant in bad faith. The court further held that the improper motive that must be shown to establish bad faith in this context means only "for a dishonest purpose," not actual fraud.

—Delaware law recognizes a bad faith cause of action by the obligee under a performance bond against a breaching surety. *International Fidelity Ins. Co. v. Delmarva Sys. Corp.*, 2001 WL 541469 (Del. Super. Ct. 2001).

—In *Dadeland Depot, Inc. v. St. Paul Fire & Marine Ins. Co.*, 945 So. 2d 1216 (Fla. 2006), the Florida Supreme Court, answering certified questions, held that the obligee of a surety contract qualified as "an insured" and was therefore entitled to sue surety for bad faith refusal to settle claims pursuant to F.S.A. §624.155 (1)(b)(1). See also *Dadeland Depot, Inc. v. St. Paul Fire & Marine Ins. Co.*, 483 F.3d 1265 (11th Cir. 2007) (holding, after Florida Supreme Court answered certified questions, *supra*, that summary judgment on bad faith claim was precluded by existence of fact questions as to whether surety adequately investigated project owner's complaints of contractor default, and as to whether surety performed obligations under performance bond).

—In *First Nat'l Bank v. Lustig*, 96 F.3d 1554 (5th Cir. 1996) (Kentucky law), the Fifth Circuit recognized the potential liability for bad faith of the issuer of a "Banker's Blanket Bond," but reversed a judgment for the bank and an award of bad faith damages on the ground that in the present case the surety had a reasonable basis for the denial of coverage.

—In *K-W Indus. v. National Sur. Corp.*, 231 Mont. 461, 754 P.2d 502 (1988), the Montana Supreme Court held that a subcontractor may sue a surety in tort on a payment bond.

—In *Great Am. Ins. Co. v. General Builders*, 934 P.2d 257 (Nev. 1997), the Nevada Supreme Court declined to recognize a tortious bad faith claim by a principal against a surety for cancellation of performance and payment bonds. The court reasoned that there was no "special relationship" between the parties, since both were commercial entities represented by professional agents and were never in inherently unequal bargaining positions.

—Denying a motion for summary judgment, a federal district court, in New Jersey, in *United States ex rel. Don Siegel Constr. Co. v. Atul Constr. Co.*, 85 F. Supp. 2d 414 (D.N.J. 2000), held that the beneficiary on a Miller Act bond may maintain a bad faith claim against the surety for delayed payment. The court emphasized that a breach of the duty of good faith will be found only if no valid reason existed to delay payment and the surety knew or recklessly disregarded that fact.

—The Tenth Circuit, in *Adair State Bank v. American Casualty Co.*, 949 F.2d 1067 (10th Cir. 1991), applied the Oklahoma first-party bad faith doctrine in the context of a dispute concerning a "Banker's Blanket Bond" that included fidelity coverage for fraudulent or dishonest acts of officers and employees.

—Pennsylvania's bad faith statute (42 Pa. Cons. Stat. §8371) does not apply to sureties, because a surety bond is not included in the statute's definition of "insurance policy." *Superior Precast, Inc. v. Safeco Ins. Co. of Am.*, 71 F. Supp. 2d 438 (E.D. Pa. 1999). The court reasoned that fundamental differences between insurance and surety agreements militate against recovery of the special statutory measures of damages in surety bond cases. See also *Reginella Construction Co. v. Travelers Casualty & Sur. Co. of Am.*, 949 F. Supp. 2d 599 (W.D. Penn. 2013).

—Authority from the Texas Supreme Court makes clear that there is no common-law duty of good faith and fair dealing between a surety and a bond obligee, and further that a surety has no liability to an obligee under Tex. Ins. Code art. 21.21: *Dallas Fire Ins. Co. v. Texas Contractors Sur. & Casualty Agency*, 159 S.W.3d 895 (Tex. 2004); *Insurance Co. of N. Am. v. Morris*, 981 S.W.2d 667 (Tex.

1998); *Associated Indem. Corp. v. CAT Contracting, Inc.*, 964 S.W.2d 276 (Tex. 1998); *Great Am. Ins. Co. v. North Austin Municipal Utility Dist. No. 1*, 908 S.W.2d 415 (Tex. 1995). See also *Tacon Mechanical Contractors v. Aetna Casualty & Sur. Co.*, 65 F.3d 486 (5th Cir. 1995).

b. Wrongful Discharge From Employment

§1.40 (1)   California Law: *Foley v. Interactive Data Corp.*

As discussed in the book, the California Supreme Court, in eliminating the tort remedy for breach of the implied covenant of good faith and fair dealing, seemed to hint that it might be receptive to the argument that emotional distress damages are recoverable for breach of the implied covenant even under a breach of contract theory. *Foley v. Interactive Data Corp.*, 47 Cal. 3d 654, 254 Cal. Rptr. 211 (1988). Although the supreme court has subsequently declined opportunities to resolve the question, plaintiffs attorneys have been pressing the argument at the trial court and intermediate appellate court levels—successfully, in some instances. (The question of the availability of emotional distress damages for breach of an employment contract is analytically the same whether plaintiff is claiming a breach of express or implied-in-fact contract terms, or a breach of the implied-in-law covenant of good faith and fair dealing.)

On August 1, 1990, a unanimous superior court jury in Southern California deliberated for only an hour and a half before awarding a wrongfully discharged administrator $1.23 million on causes of action for breach of implied contract, bad faith, and discharge in violation of public policy. *Hughes v. Guadalupe Homes* (Rancho Cucamonga, Cal., Super. Ct.). Noteworthy was the fact that the jury was instructed that foreseeable damages for breach of an employment contract may include damages for emotional distress, and the total award in fact included $107,550 for emotional distress on the contract cause of action. Plaintiff Hughes (represented by James Stoneman, then of the author's Claremont, California, office) was the former director of a publicly funded home for disturbed children. His primary contention during the four-week trial was that he had been terminated in retaliation for his objections to the improper use of AFDC funds by his employer. The instruction on emotional distress damages for breach of contract given to the jury by Judge Phil Schaeffer was derived from *Westervelt v. McCullough,* 68 Cal. App. 198, 228 P. 734 (1924), and read as follows:

> Where it is foreseeable at the time the implied or express contract arises that a discharge in breach of the contract will create mental and emotional distress, the plaintiff employee is entitled to recover, in addition to economic losses, for all emotional distress proximately caused by the discharge, if you find that the contract relates to matters which directly concern the comfort, happiness or personal welfare of the plaintiff.

Pursuant to this instruction, the jury returned an express finding that it had been foreseeable at the time the contract arose that emotional distress would result from its breach.

Eight months earlier, in November 1989, a United States District Court Judge in San Francisco issued an order permitting plaintiff to offer proof that emotional distress had been a foreseeable consequence of plaintiff's discharge from employment. *Mosely v. Metropolitan Life Ins. Co.* (N.D. Cal. No. C-88-0905 RFP). District Judge Robert Peckham noted in his order that a second factual inquiry would involve the foreseeability of emotional distress due to plaintiff's inability to find an appropriate managerial position after his termination. Judge Peckham wrote as follows:

> Plaintiff provides a litany of cases showing that California courts recognize that emotional distress may by recovered for breaches of contract that "so affect

the vital concerns of the individual that severe mental distress is a foreseeable result of the breach." *Allen v. Jones* (1980) 104 Cal App 3d 207 (breach of contract with mortuary regarding shipment of cremation ashes). See, *e.g.*, *Windeler v. Scheers Jewelers* (1970) 8 Cal App 3d 844 (breach of contract with jeweler regarding loss of plaintiff's jewelry); *Wynn v. Monterey Club* (1980) 111 Cal App 3d 789 (breach of contract with casino owner that barred spouse, a compulsive gambler, from using casino).

Whether this reasoning should be extended to the employment context appears to be an unsettled area of California law. The California Supreme Court in *Foley* and *Newman v. Emerson Radio Corp.*, 48 Cal. 3d 973, 258 Cal. Rptr. 592 (1989)] intended to preclude tort damages, such as emotional distress, in connection with wrongful termination claims. However, the exception for foreseeable contract damages retains relevance to the present case . . . . The issue thus reduces to whether the plaintiff's emotional distress caused by termination was foreseeable by both parties. This is an issue of fact which must be resolved at trial after both parties present their respective evidence.

In two 1990 decisions, California Courts of Appeal affirmed jury awards based in part on findings that the implied covenant of good faith and fair dealing had been breached. In *Luck v. Southern Pac.*, 218 Cal. App. 3d 1, 267 Cal. Rptr. 618 (1990), the court affirmed awards for lost compensation, emotional distress, and punitive damages on causes of action for breach of the implied covenant and intentional infliction of emotional distress. Plaintiff in *Luck* had been discharged for refusing to comply with the employer's unconstitutional drug-testing requirement.

And in *Seubert v. McKesson Corp.*, 223 Cal. App. 3d 1514, 273 Cal. Rptr. 296 (1990), the court affirmed a San Francisco Superior Court jury award of $240,000 on a discharged computer salesman's causes of action for bad faith and misrepresentation. The court rejected, *inter alia*, the employer's argument that at-will language in Seubert's job application constituted an "integrated" agreement that had precluded a finding of implied contract rights and hence any successful claim for breach of the implied covenant.

In *Sheppard v. Morgan Keegan & Co.*, 218 Cal. App. 3d 61, 266 Cal. Rptr. 784 (1990), another California Court of Appeal reversed summary judgment that had been granted in favor of a Tennessee stock brokerage firm, in an action by a California broker lured to Memphis only to be fired before commencing work. The court held that although plaintiff had failed to establish the existence of a requirement of good cause for discharge, the facts implicated the implied covenant of good faith. The court reasoned that implicit in the implied covenant is the understanding that an employer "cannot expect a new employee to sever his former employment and move across the country only to be terminated before the ink dries on his new lease, or before he has had a chance to demonstrate his ability to satisfy the requirements of the job." 218 Cal. App. 3d at 67, 266 Cal. Rptr. at 787. Concerning the nature of the obligation of good faith, the court explained that it depends upon the contract and the parties' justified expectations. The court quoted from *Kendall v. Ernest Pestana, Inc.*, 40 Cal. 3d 488, 500, 220 Cal. Rptr. 818, 826 (1985): "Where a contract confers on one party a discretionary power affecting the rights of the other, a duty is imposed to exercise that discretion in good faith and in accordance with fair dealing."

In two decisions issued in 2002, federal courts applying California law held that fact issues were raised on claims for breach of the implied covenant of good faith and fair dealing in connection with the nonpayment of promised commissions. *Kelly v. SkyTel Communications*, 32 Fed. Appx. 283, 2002 WL 461363 (9th Cir. 2002); *McCollum v. Xcare.Net, Inc.*, 212 F. Supp. 2d 1142 (N.D. Cal. 2002).

§1.42 (3)   Other Jurisdictions

—See *ARCO Alaska, Inc. v. Akers*, 753 P.2d 1150 (Alaska 1988), affirming compensatory damages but reversing an award of punitives, holding that under Alaska law a breach of the implied covenant of good faith and fair dealing in the employment context is a tort only if a violation of public policy is involved. The state supreme court's most recent discussions of the duty of good faith and fair dealing in the employment context are contained in *Witt v. State Dept. of Corr.*, 75 P.3d 1030 (Alaska 2003); *Charles v. Interior Reg'l Housing Auth.*, 55 P.3d 57 (Alaska 2002); *Pitka v. Interior Reg'l Housing Auth.*, 54 P.3d 785 (Alaska 2002); *Holland v. Union Oil Co. of Cal., Inc.*, 993 P.2d 1026 (Alaska 1999); *French v. Jadon, Inc.*, 911 P.2d 20 (Alaska 1996). See also *Derendinger v. Kiewit Constr. Co.*, 272 F. Supp. 2d 850 (D. Alaska 2003).

—Under Colorado law, the bad faith tort doctrine does not extend to the at-will employment context. *Decker v. Browning-Ferris Indus.*, 931 P.2d 436 (Colo. 1997); *Hoyt v. Target Stores*, 981 P.2d 188 (Colo. Ct. App. 1998); *Donohue v. Unipac Serv. Corp.*, 847 F. Supp. 1530 (D. Colo. 1994). See also *Fuhlrodt v. Rela, Inc.*, 71 Fed. Appx. 615 (9th Cir. 2003) (referring to Colorado's position as "unresolved").

—Representing Connecticut's rejection of the tort of bad faith in the at-will employment context, see *Barry v. Posi-Seal Int'l, Inc.*, 40 Conn. App. 577, 672 A.2d 514 (1996); *Cowen v. Federal Express Corp.*, 25 F. Supp. 2d 33 (D. Conn. 1998).

—Addressing a question of first impression under Delaware law, the state supreme court, in *Merrill v. Crothall-American, Inc.*, 606 A.2d 96 (Del. 1992), reversing summary judgment, held that every employment contract includes an implied covenant of good faith that is breached by conduct containing "an aspect of fraud, deceit, or misrepresentation," as where an employer "induces another to enter into an employment contract through action, words, or the withholding of information, which is intentionally deceptive in some way material to the contract." 606 A.2d at 101. In the present case, it was alleged that the employer had knowingly allowed plaintiff to assume that the duration of his employment would be indefinite, when in fact the employer had intended it to be of strictly limited duration. For subsequent discussions and application of the Delaware version of the bad faith doctrine in the employment termination context, see *E.I. Dupont de Nemours & Co. v. Pressman*, 679 A.2d 96 (Del. 1992); *Schuster v. Derocili*, 775 A.2d 1029 (Del. 2001); *Conneen v. MBNA Am. Bank, N.A.*, 334 F.3d 318 (3d Cir. 2003); *Toner v. Allstate Ins. Co.*, 821 F. Supp. 256 (D. Del. 1993).

—Under Florida law, there can be no liability for violation of the implied covenant of good faith and fair dealing absent a breach of a contract's express terms. *Burger King Corp. v. Holder*, 844 F. Supp. 1528 (S.D. Fla. 1993).

—Idaho has recognized a contract cause of action for breach of the implied covenant of good faith and fair dealing in the employment context. *Metcalf v. Intermountain Gas Co.*, 778 P.2d 744 (Idaho 1989). Reversing summary judgment for the employer, the Idaho Supreme Court endorsed the reasoning of the Arizona Supreme Court in *Wagenseller v. Scottsdale Memorial Hosp.*, 147 Ariz. 370, 710 P.2d 1025 (1985), and concluded that "any action by either party which violates, nullifies or significantly impairs any benefit of the employment contract is a violation of the implied-in-law covenant of good faith and fair dealing which we adopt today." 778 P.2d at 750. The court took pains to distinguish the foregoing formulation from the "amorphous concept of bad faith," and also specifically declined to recognize a tort cause of action for breach of the implied covenant. See also *Crea v. FMC Corp.*, 16 P.3d 272 (Idaho 2000); *Burton v. Atomic Workers Fed. Credit Union*, 119 Idaho 17, 803 P.2d 518 (1990); *Stefano v. Micron Technology, Inc.*, 65 Fed. Appx. 139 (9th Cir. 2003).

The court in *Metcalf* specified that the newly recognized doctrine would be of prospective application only, and would be applied only to breaches that occurred after *Metcalf*'s effective date. That holding was subsequently modified, however, in *Sorensen v. Comm Tek, Inc.*, 799 P.2d 70 (Idaho 1990), where a majority of the court concluded that the *Metcalf* holding should be applied to all cases that had been *filed* at the time the decision was issued on August 8, 1989. For an application of the Idaho version of the doctrine, see *Jones v. Micron Technology, Inc.*, 923 P.2d 486 (Idaho Ct. App. 1996), holding that evidence that the employer had recorded false reasons for plaintiff's discharge did not support a bad faith cause of action.

—There continues to be some ambiguity in Illinois concerning recognition or nonrecognition of a bad faith contract cause of action. Representing the dominant view that Illinois law recognizes no cause of action for breach of the implied covenant of good faith and fair dealing in the at-will employment context, see *Spann v. Springfield Clinic*, 217 Ill. App. 3d 419, 577 N.E.2d 488 (1991); *Foy v. City of Chicago*, 194 Ill. App. 3d 611, 551 N.E.2d 310 (1990); *Harrison v. Sears, Roebuck & Co.*, 189 Ill. App. 3d 980, 546 N.E.2d 248 (1989); *Corrigan v. Cactus Int'l Trading Co.*, 771 F. Supp. 262 (N.D. Ill. 1991); *LaScola v. US Sprint Communications*, 739 F. Supp. 431 (N.D. Ill. 1990); *MacDonald-Smith v. FMC Corp.*, 713 F. Supp. 264 (N.D. Ill. 1989). For a continuing hint of contrary authority, however, see *Patton v. University of Chicago Hosps.*, 706 F. Supp. 627 (N.D. Ill. 1989) (recognizing existence of implied covenant of good faith in connection with implied-in-fact contract terms).

—According to the First Circuit, Indiana law recognizes no implied duty of good faith and fair dealing with respect to at-will employment contracts. *Dykes v. DePuy, Inc.*, 140 F.3d 31 (1st Cir. 1998).

—Kansas law declines to recognize any bad faith cause of action in connection with at-will employment contracts. *Dickens v. Snodgrass, Dunlop & Co.*, 255 Kan. 164, 872

P.2d 252 (1994); *Claytor v. Computer Assocs. Int'l, Inc.*, 262 F. Supp. 2d 1188 (D. Kan. 2003).

—In *Norris v. Lumbermen's Mut. Cas. Co.*, 881 F.2d 1144 (1st Cir. 1989), the First Circuit discussed the Massachusetts version of the employer bad faith doctrine, and rejected the argument that it is applicable only to nonsalaried employees and to situations involving discharge to avoid payment of already-earned commissions. The court accordingly reversed dismissal of an insurance company employee's complaint alleging he had been fired for voicing concerns about safety standards at an insured's nuclear power plant. To the extent that he claimed he was entitled to additional benefits related to past services, the court reasoned, plaintiff stated a cause of action under Massachusetts bad faith law. See also *Whelan v. Intergraph Corp.*, 889 F. Supp. 15 (D. Mass. 1995); *Masso v. U.P.S. of Am., Inc.*, 884 F. Supp. 15 (D. Mass. 1995).

—Concerning Minnesota law, see *Holman v. CPT Corp.*, 457 N.W.2d 740 (Minn. Ct. App. 1990), for a discussion and application of the principle that a discharge designed to avoid payment of commissions to an employee will constitute bad faith entitling the employee to relief. (The court relied on *Buysse v. Paine, Webber, Jackson & Curtis, Inc.*, 623 F.2d 1244 (8th Cir. 1980).) Representing Minnesota's nonrecognition of the cause of action in other factual contexts, see *Singleton v. Christ the Servant Evangelical Lutheran Church*, 541 N.W.2d 606 (Minn. Ct. App. 1996), *cert. denied*, 519 U.S. 870 (1996); *Brozo v. Oracle Corp.*, 324 F.3d 661 (8th Cir. 2003); *Johnson v. Minnesota Historical Soc.*, 931 F.2d 1239 (8th Cir. 1991).

—See *Dandridge v. Chromcraft Corp.*, 914 F. Supp. 1396 (N.D. Miss. 1996), concerning Mississippi's nonrecognition of any implied covenant of good faith and fair dealing in the context of at-will employment.

—Although the Montana courts were among the pioneers in developing the bad faith tort cause of action in the employment context, that cause of action has now been eliminated in favor of the exclusive (and limited) remedies of the Montana Wrongful Discharge From Employment Act, Mont. Code Ann. §§39-2-901-39-2-914, enacted in 1987. The constitutionality of the act has now been upheld by the Montana Supreme Court, in *Meech v. Hillhaven West, Inc.*, 776 P.2d 488 (Mont. 1989), where the court rejected the argument that in eradicating the common-law bad faith cause of action, and limiting the measures of damages for wrongful discharge, the act abridged constitutional rights to equal protection and "full legal redress." A strong dissent in *Meech* by Justice Sheehy includes the following remarks concerning the erstwhile Montana bad faith cause of action: "[T]o make certain that a wronged employee would have to take his or her lumps without a legal basis for proper recovery, the legislature adopted Section 8. . . . The purpose of Section 8 is to negate by elimination any possible employee claim of tort based upon an implied covenant of good faith and fair dealing in the employment contract. This provision takes Montana out of the mainstream of American legal thought." 776 P.2d at 508. "This is the blackest judicial day in the eleven years that I have sat on this court," Justice Sheehy wrote in the opening paragraph of his dissent. "Indeed it may be the blackest judicial day in the history of the state." 776 P.2d at 507. Also upholding the constitutionality of the Wrongful Discharge From Employment Act, see *Johnson v. State*, 776 P.2d 1221 (Mont. 1989).

—Analyzing New Jersey law as still unresolved, see *Schlichtig v. Inacom Corp.*, 272 F. Supp. 2d 597 (D.N.J. 2003).

—For a case concerning the Nevada bad faith discharge cause of action (discussed in this section of the book), see *D'Angelo v. Gardner*, 819 P.2d 206 (Nev. 1991).

—The New Mexico Supreme Court, while recognizing that at-will employment contracts do contain an implied covenant of good faith and fair dealing, has declined to recognize a tort remedy for its breach. *Bourgeous v. Horizon Healthcare Corp.*, 872 P.2d 852 (N.M. 1994). See also

Clayton v. Vanguard Car Rental U.S.A., Inc., 761 F. Supp. 2d 1210 (D. N. Mex. 2010) (fact issue existed as to whether employer breached implied covenant of good faith when it terminated manager for signing letter drafted by employees requesting higher pay).

—Oregon, previously an "unsettled" jurisdiction, has clarified its position on the implied covenant of good faith and fair dealing. The state supreme court explained in *Sheets v. Knight*, 308 Or. 220, 223, 779 P.2d 1000, 1008 (1989): "This court has never held that a duty of good faith and fair dealing applies to at-will employment contracts, insofar as the right to discharge is concerned. For a number of reasons, we decline to do so now." The court did add, however, that "a duty of good faith and fair dealing is appropriate in matters pertaining to ongoing performance of at-will employment agreements." 308 Or. at 233, 779 P.2d at 1008. Accord *Elliott v. Tektronix, Inc*, 102 Or. App. 388, 796 P.2d 361 (1990), where the court wrote: "We conclude that the parties to an employment at will contract are not subject to the implied duty of good faith and fair dealing insofar as the right to terminate is involved. However, if the parties agree to restrict the right to terminate at will, the duty of good faith applies to the restrictive terms, as it does to the performance of all of the contractual terms except the right to terminate itself." 102 Or. App. at 396, 796 P.2d at 365. See also *Downs v. Waremart, Inc.*, 137 Or. App. 119, 903 P.2d 888 (1995), *rev'd in part on other grounds*, 324 Or. 307, 926 P.2d 314 (1996)

—Utah, formerly a strict at-will state, has now apparently recognized a cause of action for breach of the implied covenant of good faith and fair dealing in the at-will employment context (at least by way of state supreme court dictum), in *Berube v. Fashion Centre, Ltd.*, 771 P.2d 1033 (Utah 1989). See also *Brehany v. Nordstrom, Inc.*, 812 P.2d 49 (Utah 1991) (emphasizing that implied covenant does not create substantive rights and cannot turn at-will relationship into one requiring good cause for discharge).

—For a discussion of the circumstances that may create a "special relationship," under Wyoming law, and subject an employer to tort liability for the bad faith discharge of an employee, see *Life Care Ctrs. of Am., Inc. v. Dexter*, 65 P.3d 385 (Wyo. 2003); *VanLente v. University of Wyo. Research Corp.*, 975 P.2d 594 (Wyo. 1999); *Andrews v. Southwest Wyo. Rehab. Ctr.*, 974 P.2d 948 (Wyo. 1999); *Anderson v. South Lincoln Special Cemetery Dist.*, 972 P.2d 136 (Wyo. 1999); *Jewell v. North Big Horn Hosp. Dist.*, 953 P.2d 135 (Wyo. 1998); *Terry v. Pioneer Press, Inc.*, 947 P.2d 273 (Wyo. 1997); *Wilder v. Cody Country Chamber of Commerce*, 868 P.2d 211 (Wyo. 1994); *McIlravy v. Kerr-McGee Corp.*, 119 F.3d 876 (10th Cir. 1997); *Worman v. Farmers Coop. Ass'n*, 4 F. Supp. 2d 1052 (D. Wyo. 1998).

—In the following cases, courts have reaffirmed their jurisdictions' refusal to recognize any cause of action in the at-will employment context for breach of an implied covenant of good faith and fair dealing: *Nelson v. Phoenix Resort Corp.*, 888 P.2d 1375 (Ariz. Ct. App. 1994); *Hew-Len v. F.W. Woolworth*, 737 F. Supp. 1104 (D. Haw. 1990) (Hawaii law); *Wade v. Kessler Institute*, 172 N.J. 327, 798 A.2d 1251 (2002); *Noye v. Hoffman-LaRoche, Inc.*, 238 N.J. Super. 430, 570 A.2d 12 (1990) (recognizing, however, that if implied-in-fact contract has arisen, breach of implied covenant of good faith may be basis for award of contract-measure damages); *Labus v. Navistar Int'l Transp. Corp.*, 740 F. Supp. 1053 (D.N.J. 1990) (New Jersey law); *Sheth v. New York Life Ins. Co.*, 273 A.D.2d 72, 709 N.Y.S.2d 74 (2000); *Naylor v. CEAG Elec. Corp.*, 158 A.D.2d 760, 551 N.Y.S.2d 349 (1990); *Liu v. Beth Israel Medical Ctr.*, 2003 WL 21488081 (S.D.N.Y. 2003) (recognizing cause of action only in limited context of discharge to deprive employee of earned commission); *Mirabella v. Turner Broadcasting Sys., Inc.*, 2003 WL 21146657 (N.D.N.Y. 2003) (same); *Wait v. Beck's N. Am., Inc.*, 241 F. Supp. 2d 172 (N.D.N.Y. 2003); *Lorenz v. CSX Corp.*, 736 F. Supp. 650 (W.D. Pa. 1990) (New York law); *Lawford v. New York Life Ins. Co.*, 739 F. Supp.

906 (S.D.N.Y. 1990) (New York law); *Collins & Aikman Floor Coverings Corp. v. Froehlich*, 736 F. Supp. 480 (S.D.N.Y 1990) (New York law); *Hapner v. Tuesday Morning, Inc.*, 2003 Ohio 781, 92 FEP 213 (Ct. App. 2003); *Hundley v. Dayton Power & Light Co.*, 148 Ohio App. 3d 556, 774 N.E.2d 330 (2002); *Brandenburger v. Hilti, Inc.*, 52 Ohio App. 3d 21, 556 N.E.2d 212 (1989); *Kuhn v. St. John & Western Shore Hosp.*, 50 Ohio App. 3d 23, 552 N.E.2d 240 (1989); *Pyle v. Ledex, Inc.*, 49 Ohio App. 3d 139, 551 N.E.2d 205 (1988); *Hawley v. Dresser Indus., Inc.*, 737 F. Supp. 445 (S.D. Ohio 1990) (Ohio law); *Greinader v. Diebold, Inc.*, 747 F. Supp. 417 (S.D. Ohio 1990) (Ohio law); *Williams v. Reidman*, 339 S.C. 251, 529 S.E.2d 28 (Ct. App. 2000); *Osborn v. University Medical Assoc. of Med. Univ. of S.C.*, 278 F. Supp. 2d 720 (D.S.C. 2003); *Peterson v. Glory House*, 433 N.W.2d 653 (S.D. 1989); *McClendon v. Ingersoll-Rand Co.*, 779 S.W.2d 69 (Tex. 1989), *rev'd on other grounds*, 498 U.S. 133 (1990); *Oliver v. Rogers*, 976 S.W.2d 792 (Tex. Ct. App. 1998); *Caton v. Leach Corp.*, 896 F.2d 939 (5th Cir. 1990) (Texas law); *Derthick v. Bassett-Walker, Inc.*, 904 F. Supp. 510 (W.D. Va. 1995), *aff'd without op.*, 106 F.3d 390 (4th Cir. 1997) (Virginia law); *Shell v. Metropolitan Life Ins. Co.*, 396 S.E.2d 174 (W. Va. 1990); *McMahon v. Pennsylvania Life Ins. Co.*, 891 F.2d 1251 (7th Cir. 1989) (Wisconsin law); *Leonard v. Converse County School Dist. No. 2*, 788 P.2d 119 (Wyo. 1990); *Horne v J.W. Gibson Well Serv. Co.*, 894 F.2d 1194 (10th Cir. 1990) (Wyoming law).

c. Commercial Contracts

§1.43 (1) California Law

It was held in *Trustees of the Capital Wholesale Elec. Co. Profit Sharing & Trust Fund v. Shearson Lehman Bros.*, 221 Cal. App. 3d 617, 270 Cal. Rptr. 566 (1990), that the relationship between investor and stock broker does not have the necessary special characteristics to warrant recognition of a tort cause of action for the broker's breach of the implied covenant of good faith and fair dealing. The court relied on the reasoning of *Foley v. Interactive Data Corp.*, 47 Cal. 3d 654, 254 Cal. Rptr. 211 (1988), which held that the relationship between employer and employee lacks the special characteristics of trust and adhesion; *Bionghi v. Metropolitan Water Dist.*, 70 Cal. App. 4th 1358, 83 Cal. Rptr. 2d 388 (1999) (same holding re relationship between contractor and client); and *Wallis v. Superior Court*, 160 Cal. App. 3d 1109, 207 Cal. Rptr. 123 (1984) (see book §1.43), which laid out five criteria for deciding whether the breach of a particular type of contract can give rise to a bad faith tort cause of action. For similar analyses and holdings with respect to other types of commercial relationships, see *Copesky v. Superior Court*, 229 Cal. App. 3d 525, 280 Cal. Rptr. 338 (1991) (bank and commercial depositor: overruling *Commercial Cotton Co. v. United Cal. Bank*, 163 Cal. App. 3d 511, 209 Cal. Rptr. 551 (1985), discussed in this section of the book); *Careau & Co. v. Security Pac. Business Credit, Inc.*, 222 Cal. App. 3d 1371, 272 Cal. Rptr. 387 (1990) (borrower and lender); *Harrell v. 20th Century Ins. Co.*, 934 F.2d 203 (9th Cir. 1991) (California law; buyer and seller of a business); *Denholm v. Houghton Mifflin & Co.*, 912 F.2d 357 (9th Cir. 1990) (California law; publisher and author); *General Sec. Servs. Corp. v. County of Fresno*, 815 F. Supp. 2d 1123 (E.D. Cal. 2011) (provider of electronic monitoring services and county government). In *Krieger v. Nick Alexander Imports, Inc.*, 234 Cal. App. 3d 205, 285 Cal. Rptr. 717 (1991), the court did not reach the issue (affirming summary judgment instead on statute of limitations grounds), but seemed to imply that no special relationship could be found in a "traditional" buyer-seller relationship.

As discussed in the book, California Court of Appeal decisions have held that the relationship between a bank and its depositors, like the lender-borrower relationship, is not sufficiently "special" to implicate the bad faith tort doctrine. See *Lee v. Bank of Am.*, 218 Cal. App. 3d 914, 267 Cal. Rptr. 387 (1990). The state supreme court has decertified an isolated court of appeal decision holding otherwise: *Security Pac. Nat'l Bank v. Williams*, 213 Cal. App. 3d 927 (1989), *ordered not to be published in official reports.*

§1.44 (2) The California "Stonewalling" Tort

In August 1995, the California Supreme Court, in *Freeman & Mills, Inc. v. Belcher Oil Co.*, 11 Cal. 4th 85, 44 Cal. Rptr. 2d 420 (1995), overruled the 1984 decision that had recognized the "*Seaman's* tort" cause of action for bad faith denial of contract (*Seaman's Direct Buying Serv., Inc. v Standard Oil Co.*, 36 Cal. 3d 752, 206 Cal. Rptr. 354 (1984)). The court wrote: "we have concluded that the *Seaman's* court incorrectly recognized a tort cause of action based on the defendant's bad faith denial of the existence of a contract between the parties. That holding has been widely criticized by legal scholars, has caused considerable confusion among lower courts, and has been rejected by the courts of several other jurisdictions. These critics convincingly argue that the *Seaman's* decision is confusing and ambiguous, analytically flawed, and promotes questionable policy. After careful review of all the foregoing considerations, we conclude that our *Seaman's* holding should be overruled." 11 Cal. 4th at 88, 44 Cal. Rptr. 2d at 421. For a decision giving retroactive application to the *Freeman & Mills* holding, see *Norager v. Nakamura*, 42 Cal. App. 4th 1817, 50 Cal. Rptr. 2d 481 (1996).

§1.45 (3) Other Jurisdictions

—When the book was published in 1990, it was accurate to characterize the courts of Montana as having gone the furthest in extending the bad faith tort doctrine to ordinary commercial contracts. Subsequently, however, the state supreme court has done a sharp about-face. In *Story v. City of Bozeman*, 791 P.2d 767 (Mont. 1990), the court described as "excessive" the tort remedy recognized in such cases as *Nicholson v. United Pac. Ins. Co.*, 710 P.2d 1342 (Mont. 1985) (discussed in the book). The court in *Story* held that henceforth the remedy would apply only under "exceptional circumstances," involving a "special relationship" between the parties. To identify such special relationships, the court adopted the five criteria set forth by a California Court of Appeal, in *Wallis v. Superior Court*, 160 Cal. App. 3d 1109, 207 Cal. Rptr. 123 (1984) (see book §1.43). Other Montana holdings on the issue have included the following: *Cate v. First Bank (N.A.)—Billings*, 865 P.2d 277 (Mont. 1993) (affirming summary judgment: absent express or implied contract, borrower could not base claim for breach of implied covenant on his disappointed "justifiable expectations" of continued credit from bank); *Citizens First Nat'l Bank v. Moe Motor Co.*, 813 P.2d 400 (Mont. 1991) (no special relationship existed between lender and borrower); *First Sec. Bank & Trust Co. v. VZ Ranch*, 807 P.2d 1341 (Mont. 1991) (same); *Beaverhead Bar Supply, Inc. v. Harrington*, 805 P.2d 560 (Mont. 1991) (no special relationship existed between parties to soft-drink distributorship); *Trad Indus., Ltd. v. Brogan*, 805 P.2d 54 (Mont. 1991) (no special relationship existed between parties to common commercial contract for sale of goods); *Montana Bank v. Ralph Meyers & Son*, 769 P.2d 1208 (Mont. 1989) (implied covenant cannot be breached unless one or more of contract's express terms are also breached); *O'Bagy v. First Interstate Bank*, 785 P.2d 190 (Mont. 1990) (no implied covenant arises from relationship between real property seller and closing agent); *Kinniburgh v. Garrity*, 798 P.2d 102 (Mont. 1990) (no "special relationship" existed between landowner and logging contractor).

—Cases from jurisdictions other than California and Montana involving the applicability of the bad faith tort doctrine to commercial contracts of various kinds have included the following: *Burkons v. Ticor Title Ins. Co.*, 813 P.2d 710 (Ariz. 1991) (allegations failed to state claim for tort damages for bad faith breach of escrow contract); *McAllister v. Citibank*, 829 P.2d 1253 (Ariz. Ct. App. 1992) (affirming summary judgment on bad faith claim against lender: borrower failed to prove existence of special relationship involving elements of trust, public interest, or adhesion); *Firstar Metro. Bank & Trust v. Federal Deposit Ins. Corp.*, 964 F. Supp. 1353 (D. Ariz. 1997) (Arizona law; where plaintiff sought only contract measure damages for loan participant's breach of implied covenant of good faith, it was not necessary for plaintiff to plead or prove existence of "special relationship"); *Country Corner Food & Drug, Inc. v. First State Bank & Trust Co.*, 332 Ark. 645, 966 S.W.2d 894 (1998) (tort of bad faith applies only in context of insurance contracts); *Duffield v. First Interstate Bank, N.A.*, 13 F.3d 1403 (10th Cir. 1994) (Colorado law; affirming award of $6 million in contract-measure consequential damages for bank's bad faith invocation of mortgage assignment provision); *Beco Constr. Co. v. City of Idaho Falls*, 124 Idaho 859, 865 P.2d 950 (1993) (affirming summary judgment in action involving public competitive bidding; court declined to address applicability of tort of bad faith, as opposed to claim for breach of implied covenant of good faith and fair dealing); *Idaho First Nat'l Bank v. Bliss Valley Foods, Inc.*, 824 P.2d 841 (Idaho 1991) (declining to extend bad faith doctrine to lender/borrower relationship); *Koehler v. First Nat'l Bank*, 232 Ill. App. 3d 679, 597 N.E.2d 1261 (1992) (declining to extend bad faith doctrine to lender/borrower relationship); *Kham & Nate's Shoes, Inc. v. First Bank*, 97 B.R. 420 (N.D. Ill. 1989) (Illinois law; bank held liable for bad faith for reneging on refinancing agreement); *State Nat'l Bank v. Academia, Inc.*, 802 S.W.2d 282 (Tex. Ct. App. 1990) (Illinois law; reversing multimillion-dollar verdict in favor of defaulting commercial borrower, on ground that under Illinois law the covenant of good faith does not create an independent cause of action); *Home Sav. Ass'n v. State Bank*, 763 F. Supp. 292 (N.D. Ill. 1991) (same); *Baker v. Sun Co.*, 985 F. Supp. 609 (D. Md. 1997)

(Maryland law; bad faith cause of action does not extend to relationship between franchisee and franchisor); *Quality Auto. Co. v. Signet Bank/Maryland*, 775 F. Supp. 849 (D. Md. 1991) (Maryland law; holding, in action relating to commercial loan and security agreement, that Maryland law recognizes a tort cause of action for violation of the U.C.C.'s good faith requirement); *Simmons Oil Corp. v. Holly Corp.*, 852 P.2d 523 (Mont. 1993) (declining to extend bad faith tort doctrine to commercial lending relationship); *Hilton Hotels Corp. v. Butch Lewis Prods., Inc.*, 107 Nev. 226, 808 P.2d 919 (1991), *after remand*, 109 Nev. 1043, 862 P.2d 1207 (1993) (although contract damages were potentially available for breach of the covenant of good faith, tort damages were not, given absence of "special element of reliance or fiduciary duty" in relationship between hotel and boxing promoter); *MBIA Ins. Corp. v. Countrywide Home Loans, Inc.*, 87 A.D.3d 287, 928 N.Y.S.2d 229 (2011) (financial guarantee insurance provider's cause of action for breach of implied covenant against mortgage loan originator alleging bad faith exercise of discretion was not viable because it was duplicative of breach of contract claim alleging that originator had not abided by industry standards); *Telephone Management Corp. v. Goodyear Tire & Rubber Co.*, 32 F. Supp. 2d 960 (N.D. Ohio 1998), *aff'd without op.*, (6th Cir. 2000) (Ohio law; bad faith cause of action is limited to insurance context and would not be extended to situation involving breach of consulting contract); *Phoenix Technologies, Inc. v. TRW, Inc.*, 840 F. Supp. 1055 (E.D. Pa. 1994) (Ohio law; bad faith tort doctrine has no extension beyond insurance context); *Embry v. Innovative Aftermarket Sys. L.P*, 247 P.3d 1158, 2010 OK 82 (Okla. 2010) (addendum to financing contract purchased for consumer to cover gap between debt and car's value in event of total loss involved "special relationship" necessary to support tort recovery for bad faith on part of addendum's marketer); *Roberts v. Wells Fargo AG Credit Corp.*, 990 F.2d 1169 (10th Cir. 1993) (Oklahoma law; declining to extend bad faith tort doctrine to commercial lending context); *United States Nat'l Bank v. Boge*, 311 Or. 550, 814 P.2d 1082 (1991) (good faith requirement of U.C.C. preempts any similar common-law requirement); *Norwood v Atlantic Richfield Co.*, 814 F. Supp. 1459 (D. Or. 1991) (Oregon law; declining to extend bad faith tort doctrine to franchise relationship); *Commonwealth v. E-Z Parks, Inc.*, 620 A.2d 712 (Pa. Commw. Ct. 1993) (relationship between commercial landlord and tenant gives rise to no special duty of good faith); *Bohm v. Commerce Union Bank*, 794 F. Supp. 158 (W.D. Pa. 1992) (Pennsylvania law does not extend bad faith doctrine to lender/borrower relationship); *Garrett v. BankWest, Inc.*, 459 N.W.2d 833 (S.D. 1990) (South Dakota Supreme Court declined to extend bad faith tort doctrine to dispute between farmer and lender); *Formosa Plastics Corp. USA v. Presidio Eng'rs & Contractors Corp.*, 960 S.W.2d 41 (Tex. 1998) (there exists no general duty of good faith and fair dealing in connection with arms' length commercial transactions); *Federal Deposit Ins. Corp. v. Coleman*, 795 S.W.2d 706 (Tex. 1990) (no special relationship existed between insured creditor and F.D.I.C.); *Vogel v. Travelers Indem. Co*, 966 S.W.2d 748 (Tex. Ct. App. 1998) (bad faith tort cause of action may not be asserted in connection with borrower-lender relationship); *Oliver v. Rogers*, 976 S.W.2d 792 (Tex. Ct. App. 1998) ("special relationship" necessary to provide basis for bad faith claim did not exist merely because buyer and seller of business had previously been employee and employer); *Eller v. NationsBank, N.A.*, 975 S.W.2d 803 (Tex. Ct. App. 1998) (bad faith claim could not be asserted against bank by lessor of safe-deposit box); *Electro Assocs., Inc. v. Harrop Constr. Co.*, 908 S.W.2d 21 (Tex. Ct. App. 1995) (no special relationship exists between general contractor and subcontractor); *Hallmark v. Hand*, 885 S.W.2d 471 (Tex. Ct. App. 1994) (stock purchase agreements involve no special relationship sufficient to support bad faith tort actions); *Wheeler v. Yettie Kersting Memorial Hosp.*, 866 S.W.2d 32 (Tex. Ct. App.

1993) (declining to extend bad faith tort doctrine to hospital/patient relationship that was already subject to extensive regulation); *Central Sav. & Loan Ass'n v. Stemmons N.W. Bank*, 848 S.W.2d 232 (Tex. Ct. App. 1992) (declining to extend bad faith tort doctrine to relationship between issuer of letter of credit and beneficiary); *McDonald v. Foster Mortgage Corp.*, 834 S.W.2d 573 (Tex. Ct. App. 1992) (neither lender/borrower nor mortgagor/mortgagee relationship gives rise to special duty of good faith); *Hurd Enters., Ltd. v. Bruni*, 828 S.W.2d 101 (Tex. Ct. App. 1992) (lessor/ lessee relationship will not support bad faith cause of action); *Crowder v. Tri-C Resources, Inc.*, 821 S.W.2d 393 (Tex. Ct. App. 1991) (no special relationship exists between parties to joint operating agreement); *Texstar N. Am., Inc. v. Ladd Petroleum Corp.*, 809 S.W.2d 672 (Tex. Ct. App. 1991) (no special relationship exists between lender and borrower; stating that bad faith tort doctrine applies only in insurance context); *Security Bank v. Dalton*, 803 S.W.2d 443 (Tex. Ct. App. 1991) (same); *Nance v. Resolution Trust Corp.*, 803 S.W.2d 323 (Tex. Ct. App. 1990) (same); *Herndon v. First Nat'l Bank*, 802 S.W.2d 396 (Tex. Ct. App. 1991) (same); *Georgetown Assocs., Ltd. v. Home Fed. Sav. & Loan Ass'n*, 795 S.W.2d 252 (Tex. Ct. App. 1990) (same); *Schmueser v. Burkburnett Bank*, 937 F.2d 1025 (5th Cir. 1991) (same); *Adolph Coors Co. v. Rodriguez*, 780 S.W.2d 477 (Tex. Ct. App. 1989) (no special relationship existed between supplier and distributor; reversing awards of $1.5 million in compensatory damages and $10 million in punitives); *Childers v. Pumping Sys., Inc.*, 968 F.2d 565 (5th Cir. 1992) (Texas law; relationship between corporation and shareholders does not give rise to special duty of good faith); *Roberts v. Dayton Hudson Corp.*, 914 F. Supp. 1421 (N.D. Tex. 1996) (Texas law) (self-insured department store owed no good faith duty concerning settlement of claim by injured shopper); *Coca-Cola Bottling Co. v. Coca-Cola Co.*, 769 F. Supp 599 (D. Del. 1991) (Texas law; no special relationship exists between manufacturer and bottler); *Federal*

Sav. & Loan Ins. Corp. v. Wilson, 722 F. Supp. 306 (N.D. Tex. 1989) (same); *Federal Sav. & Loan Ins. Corp. v. Atkinson-Smith Univ. Park Joint Venture*, 729 F. Supp. 1130 (N.D. Tex. 1989) (no special relationship exists between lender and borrower; predicting that Texas Supreme Court will disagree with contrary holding in *Coleman v. Federal Sav. & Loan Ins. Corp.*, 762 S.W.2d 243 (Tex. Ct. App. 1988)); *Monahan v. GMAC Mortgage Corp.*, 2005 VT 110, 893 A.2d 298 (2005) (negligent indifference may be below standard demanded by implied covenant without rising to level of malice necessary for punitive damages, and in present case mortgagee was not liable to mortgagors for punitive damages in connection with breach of implied covenant by failing to pay mortgagor's flood insurance premiums); *JoAnn's Launder Ctr., Inc. v. Chase Manhattan Bank, N.A.*, 854 F. Supp. 387 (D. V.I. 1994) (Virgin Islands law; bad faith tort doctrine does not extend to borrower-lender relationship); *Cenex, Inc. v. Arrow Gas Serv.*, 896 F. Supp. 1574 (D. Wyo. 1995) (Wyoming law; no special relationship exists between buyer and seller of business).

§1.46 C. Intentional Interference With a Protected Property Interest

See *Niemeyer v. United States Fidelity & Guar. Co.*, 789 P.2d 1318 (Okla. 1990), for a case recognizing the availability of a cause of action for tortious interference with contract in the insurance context. The Oklahoma Supreme Court reversed the dismissal of a claim brought by an insured against the tortfeasor's liability insurer who had allegedly provided false information to the insured's uninsured motorist coverage carrier, thus interfering with the insured's efforts to negotiate a fair settlement. In permitting maintenance of the interference cause of action, the court emphasized that no bad faith claim could have been asserted, because of the lack of any contractual relationship between Niemeyer and United States Fidelity, or between the two insurance companies.

D. Intentional Infliction of Emotional Distress

§1.48 2. Necessary Allegations and Proof

—Reinstating summary judgment in *Ex parte Mutual Sav. Life Ins. Co.*, 698 So. 2d 772 (Ala. 1997), the Supreme Court of Alabama held that a life insurer did not engage in "atrocious and utterly intolerable conduct" by allowing a policy on the insured's life to remain in effect and continuing to collect premiums for nine months after learning that the insured's sister had forged the insured's name on the policy application and that she had obtained another policy on the insured's son by similar means before he was killed by the insured's brother. The court also found a lack of substantial evidence that the insured had suffered extreme emotional distress.

—An insured stated a facially plausible claim for intentional infliction of emotional distress under California law, the court held in *Jones v. AIG Risk Mgmt., Inc.*, 726 F. Supp. 2d 1049 (N.D. Cal. 2010), by alleging that repeated and lengthy delays by the insurer and its agents in the handling of an underinsured motorist claim had been the result of an established policy and concerted course of conduct designed to inflict delay on a person whom defendants knew to be vulnerable. The court distinguished *Coleman v. Republic Ins. Co. of Calif.*, 132 Cal. App. 4th 403, 33 Cal. Rptr. 3d 744 (2005), where it was held that delay or denial of an insurance claim is not sufficiently outrageous to support a cause of action for IIED. Here, the court held, the alleged facts went beyond mere delay, and the court refused to strike a claim for punitive damages. Supporting its conclusion that a purposeful policy of delay or a concerted course of conduct *can* provide a basis for an IIED claim, the court cited *Fletcher v. Western Nat'l Life Ins. Co.*, 10 Cal. App. 3d 376, 89 Cal. Rptr. 78 (1970), and *Hernandez v. General Adjustment Bureau*, 199 Cal. App. 3d 999, 245 Cal. Rptr. 288 (1988).

In *Hailey v. California Physicians' Serv.*, 158 Cal. App. 4th 452, 69 Cal. Rptr. 3d 789 (2007), it was held that extreme and outrageous conduct was alleged by allegation that health care service plan delayed asserting perceived legal right to rescind subscriber's contract due to omissions in application until after subscriber suffered serious injury.

In *Barbour v. UNUM Life Ins. Co. of Am.*, 803 F. Supp. 2d 1135 (S.D. Cal. 2011), the court denied a motion for summary judgment, holding that an issue of fact existed as to whether outrageous conduct by the insurer in connection with the termination of the insured's long-term disability benefits had caused the insured to suffer severe or extreme emotional distress.

—In *Carrol v. Allstate Ins. Co.*, 262 Conn. 433, 815 A.2d 119 (2003), the Connecticut Supreme Court vacated an award of $60,000 in punitive damages against an insurer that had conducted a biased investigation (with possible racist overtones) of its arson suspicions in connection with a fire insurance claim. Holding that the evidence failed to support the required finding of outrageousness, the court nonetheless affirmed an award of $500,000 in general damages for the negligent infliction of emotional distress. Citing *Carroll, supra*, and granting a motion to strike, see *Sullivan v. Allstate Ins. Co.*, 2006 WL 1000236 (Conn. Super. Ct. 2006).

—In *Sterling v. Provident Life & Accident Ins. Co.*, 619 F. Supp. 2d 1242 (M.D. Fla. 2009), a federal district court denied the insurer's motion for summary judgment, holding that a genuine issue of material fact existed as to whether the insured suffered severe emotional distress due to the insurer's termination of his $9,000 per month disability payments, precluding summary judgment on the insured's claim for negligent infliction of emotional distress.

—In *Enoka v. AIG Haw. Ins. Co.*, 109 Haw. 537, 128 P.3d 850 (2006), the Hawaii Supreme Court, affirming summary judgment, held that an automobile insurer's denial, based on an invalid statute of limitations defense, of a claim for no-fault benefits was not outrageous conduct that would support a claim for the intentional infliction of emotional distress.

—In *Weinstein v. Prudential Prop. & Casualty Ins. Co.*, 149 Idaho 299, 233 P.3d 1221 (2010), the Idaho Supreme Court held that the evidence had supported an award of $210,000 for the intentional infliction of emotional distress, based on the insurer's refusal to pay uninsured motorist benefits on the insureds' minor daughter's undisputed medical bills before settlement of the entire UM claim. The insureds suffered depression resulting from embarrassment and harassment by bill collectors, were threatened that their child would not be able to receive further medical treatment, and had liens placed on their house by medical providers.

—In *Hackler v. State Farm Mut. Auto. Ins. Co.*, 210 F. Supp. 3d 1250 (D. Nev. 2016), the court allowed a claim for intentional infliction of emotional distress to survive summary judgment based on the bad faith action of the insurer. The case provides the elements for the claim in Nevada.

—In *Setzer v. Farmers Ins. Co.*, 185 Fed. Appx. 748 (10th Cir. 2006) (Oklahoma law), the Tenth Circuit, affirming the dismissal of a claim by an automobile accident victim, held that the insurer's obtaining of medical records beyond the scope of the victim's authorization was not "outrageous" or "highly offensive to a reasonable person."

—In *Blakely v. USAA Casualty Ins. Co.*, 633 F.3d 944 (10th Cir. 2011) (Utah law), the Tenth Circuit, affirming summary judgment, held that the insurer's alleged conduct in handling insureds' claim for fire damage under a homeowner's policy "did not evoke outrage or revulsion, even if it was unreasonable, unkind, and unfair." The insureds alleged that the insurer had acted unreasonably in taking its initial position regarding the loss amount; that the adjuster had refused to communicate with them and had denied the existence of an obvious smell of smoke; that the insurer had delegated the adjustment of a contents claim to a nonadjuster; and that the insurer had refused to pay for any repairs other than structural ones.

E. Fraud

§1.52 1. Elements of the Cause of Action

—In *Landon v. American Family Mut. Ins. Co.*, 293 F. Supp. 3d 879 (D.S.D. 2017), the court denied the insurer's motion to dismiss the insured's claim for first-party bad faith, rejecting the insurer's argument that the plaintiff had to comply with the requirements of Fed. R. Civ. P. 9(b) for pleading fraud. The court applied the holding of another 2017 case, *Haney v. American Family Mut. Ins. Co.*, 223 F. Supp. 3d 921 (D.S.D. 2017), that Rule 9(b) heightened pleading standards "do not apply to first-party bad faith claims under South Dakota law." 293 F. Supp. 3d at 884 (internal quotation marks omitted). See also §3.52.

2. Types of Insurer Misrepresentations

§1.53 a. Misrepresentation of Scope of Coverage

—In *Liberty Nat'l Life Ins. Co. v. Sanders*, 792 So. 2d 1069 (Ala. 2000), the Alabama Supreme Court affirmed judgment for the insured (but reduced the award of punitive damages) on a fraud claim alleging that the insurer and an agent had failed to disclose that the policy plaintiff had purchased paid only a limited benefit if the insured died within three years.

—In *R & B Auto Ctr., Inc. v. Farmers Group, Inc.*, 140 Cal. App. 4th 327, 44 Cal. Rptr. 3d 426 (2006), a California Court of Appeal held that fact issues were raised on insured's misrepresentation claim concerning whether insurer was liable for agents' inaccurate representations that used car dealership's lemon law policy would cover used cars. Compare *The Mega Life & Health Ins. Co. v. Superior*

Court, 172 Cal. App. 4th 1522, 92 Cal. Rptr. 3d 399 (2009) (health insurer owed no duty to be truthful to husband of prospective insured about scope of coverage where insurance was being offered only to his wife and there was no possibility that husband would detrimentally change his position based on any misrepresentations).

—In *Mullen v. Allstate Ins. Co.*, 232 P.3d 168 (Colo. App. 2009), a Colorado Court of Appeals held that an insurer did not conceal a material fact nor commit negligent misrepresentation by failing to disclose to insured that the purchase of UM/UIM coverage on additional vehicles provided little or no additional benefit.

—In *Mladineo v. Schmidt*, 53 So. 3d 1154 (Miss. 2010), the Mississippi Supreme Court, invoking the "duty to read" and "imputed knowledge" doctrines, held that the insureds failed to establish that they had reasonably relied on alleged assurances by the defendant insurance agency that their homeowner's policy contained flood coverage.

—In *Guthrie Clinic, Ltd. v. Travelers Indem. Co.*, 2000 WL 1853044 (M.D. Pa. 2000) (Pennsylvania law), the court denied a motion to dismiss a fraud claim based on the allegation that, at renewal, the insurer had substantially changed certain provisions in an umbrella liability policy without notifying the insured. See also *Toy v. Metropolitan Life Ins. Co.*, 593 Pa. 20, 928 A.2d 186 (2007) (genuine issue of material fact as to whether insured justifiably relied on alleged fraudulent misrepresentations regarding content of policy precluded summary judgment in insured's action under Unfair Trade Practices and Consumer Protection Law).

—In *Thomas v. State Farm Lloyds*, 218 F. Supp. 3d 506 (N.D. Tex. 2016), the court dismissed a claim for misrepresentation of scope of coverage and provided the elements necessary to prevail on a fraud claim. See also *Ramirez v. Allstate Vehicle & Prop. Ins. Co.*, ___ F. Supp. 3d ___, 2020 WL 5806436 (S.D. Tex. 2020) (Texas law; holding insureds stated bad faith claims under Texas common law and unfair claims practices statutes by alleging misrepresentations by insurer concerning covered loss and failure to conduct reasonable investigation; insureds' complaint was sufficient under Fed. R. Civ. P. 9(b) standard for pleading fraud or misrepresentation; see also §1.26).

—In *Berkshire Hathaway Homestate Ins. Co. v. SQI, Inc.*, 132 F. Supp. 3d 1275 (W.D. Wash. 2015), *appeal dismissed* (9th Cir. 2017) (Washington law), the federal district court stated that in Washington, "an insurer that omits pertinent information about the policy is guilty of bad faith only if that omission was unreasonable in light of the circumstances existing at the time." *Id.* at 1289. The court denied the insured's bad faith claim based on misrepresentation where the insurer's reservation of rights letter included a reference to the policy provision in question, and where in any event there was no evidence that the insurer's failure to mention the provision was unreasonable at the time the letter was sent.

§1.55 c. Other Types of Misrepresentations

—Concerning the Alabama Supreme Court's replacement of a "justifiable reliance" standard with a "reasonable reliance" standard relative to misrepresentation claims against insurers and agents, see *Baker v. Metropolitan Life Ins. Co.*, 907 So. 2d 419 (Ala. 2005); *Liberty Nat'l v. Ingram*, 887 So. 2d 222 (Ala. 2004); and *Alfa Life Ins. Corp. v. Green*, 881 So. 2d 987 (Ala. 2003).

—The California Elder Abuse Act (Cal. Welf. & Inst. Code §15600 et seq.) was signed into law in 1991 "to protect elders by providing enhanced remedies which encourage private, civil enforcement of laws against elder abuse and neglect." *Negrete v. Fidelity & Guar. Life Ins. Co.*, 444 F. Supp. 2d 998, 1001 (C.D. Cal. 2006). Although both plaintiffs' and defense attorneys have tended to overlook it, elder abuse is often a viable claim in a first-party insurance bad faith case involving the unreasonable withholding or denial of benefits owing to an elderly insured. For the clearest and most recent articulation of this view, see *Rosove v. Continental Cas. Co.*, 2014 WL 2766161 (C.D. Cal. 2014). See also *Johnston v. Allstate Ins. Co.*, 2013 WL 2285361 (S.D. Cal. 2013); *Keshish v. Allstate Ins. Co.*, 959 F. Supp. 2d 1226 (C.D. Cal. 2013).

—In *Brodeur v. American Home Assurance Co.*, 169 P.3d 139 (Colo. banc 2007), the Colorado Supreme Court affirmed summary judgment on a fraud cause of action against a workers' compensation insurer and claim adjuster. A misrepresentation in a letter stating that treatment for the claimant's back injury had not been authorized was an incorrect legal opinion concerning the meaning and effect of administrative regulations, the court explained, and since the denial of treatment was based on a misrepresentation of law rather than a misrepresentation of fact, there was no actionable fraud.

—Under District of Columbia law, it was held in *Choharis v. State Farm Fire & Casualty Co.*, 961 A.2d 1080 (D.C. Ct. App. 2008), conduct occurring during the course of a contract dispute may be the subject of a fraudulent or negligent misrepresentation claim only when that conduct implicates a duty independent of that arising out of the contract itself so that an action for breach of contract would not reach the damages sustained as a result of the tort. In the present case, the court explained, affirming summary judgment, the insurer's alleged acts during disputes about claims had not caused any expenses that were not recoverable under contract principles.

—In *Hogan v. Provident Life & Accident Ins. Co.*, 665 F. Supp. 2d 1273 (M.D. Fla. 2009), the court held that an insured had to satisfy the heightened pleading requirements for fraud claims in asserting a claim under West's F.S.A. §626.9541, which creates a cause of action against an insurer for making a material misrepresentation to effect settlement of an insured's claim on less favorable terms than contractually required.

—In *Cramer v. Insurance Exch. Agency*, 174 Ill. 2d 513, 675 N.E.2d 897 (1997), the Illinois Supreme Court (although acknowledging that Ill. Ins. Code §155 does not preempt a common-law fraud cause of action) held that a fraud claim was not stated by the allegation that the insurer had fabricated a prior notice of cancellation solely to deny the insured's claim under a homeowner's policy. That allegation sounded only in contract, the court held, because it was barren of any element of reliance.

—In *Kelly v. State Farm Fire & Casualty Co.*, 169 So. 3d 328 (La. 2015), the Louisiana Supreme Court answered questions certified to it by the Fifth Circuit. State Farm had failed to notify its insured under an automobile liability policy of a letter from a third-party claimant submitting medical bills and proposing payment of policy limits. At trial, the insured was found liable for an amount far in excess of the policy limits. The Louisiana court considered the question: Can "an insurer . . . be found liable under [La. Rev. Stat. Ann. §22:1973(B)(1)] for misrepresenting or failing to disclose facts that are not related to the insurance policy's coverage"? The court held in the affirmative, stating that under the statute a misrepresentation or failure to disclose "pertinent facts" could be bad faith conduct, whether or not the facts were "related to the insurance policy's coverage." In light of this and other holdings, the Fifth Circuit vacated its opinion affirming summary judgment for State Farm and remanded to the federal district court for further proceedings. *Kelly v. State Farm Fire & Casualty Co.*, 605 Fed. Appx. 420 (5th Cir. 2015) (unpublished). See also discussion Section 2.7, *infra*.

—In *Cooper v. Berkshire Life Ins. Co.*, 148 Md. App. 41, 810 A.2d 1045, *cert. denied*, 373 Md. 407, 818 A.2d 1105 (Md. 2003), a Maryland appellate court reversed summary judgment on fraud and negligent misrepresentation claims brought by an insured against the issuer of a life insurance policy and the insurer's agents, holding that the insurer could be liable for misrepresenting the financial assumptions underlying an "illustration" of a "disappearing premium" that was attached to the policy. On this theory, the insured could seek to prove that the "illustration" did not correctly reflect financial information known to the insurer at the time it was written. However, the court held, the insurer could not be found liable on the theory that its agents had misrepresented to the insured that the premium—as "illustrated"—was guaranteed to disappear within 10 years, because such an oral representation was contrary to the policy's written explanation that the 10-year payment term was only contingent. The agents themselves, however, might be subject to liability for such misrepresentations— even though they were contrary to the policy's terms—if the insured were able to show that his reliance had been reasonable because it was based on a relationship of trust and confidence.

—In *Cooper v. Auto Club Ins. Ass'n*, 481 Mich. 399, 751 N.W.2d 443 (2008), the Michigan Supreme Court accepted the argument that, by alleging that an insurer fraudulently induced the insured to accept an unreasonably low compensation rate for her in-home attendant care services, the insured asserted a common-law fraud claim that was distinct from a no-fault claim for benefits, and that such claim was therefore not subject to the 1-year-back rule of MCL 500.3145(1).

—In *Perkins v. State Farm Ins. Co.*, 589 F. Supp. 2d 559 (M.D. Pa. 2008), a federal district court held that the "gist of the action" doctrine required dismissal of a Pennsylvania common-law fraud claim alleging the wrongful termination of first-party medical coverage. The court emphasized that the alleged fraud concerned only the insurer's performance of its contractual duties, and that the fraud claim was collateral to and dependent upon a breach of contract claim.

—In *Dziadek v. Charter Oak Fire Ins. Co.*, 867 F.3d 1003 (8th Cir. 2017) (South Dakota law), the Eight Circuit affirmed a district court ruling in which a jury found in favor of an insured on a claim for deceit related to benefits due under an uninsured motorist policy. The insurer's deceitful actions included telling the insured orally and in writing that there was no coverage under the policy when there was coverage, withholding the uninsured motorist provision when sending a portion of the policy with an indication that the insured was not covered, and attempting to withhold a full copy of the policy by inaccurately describing the length of the policy when the insured attempted to get a full copy 2 years after the first request.

　—In *Harvey v. Centene Mgmt. Co., LLC*, 357 F. Supp. 3d 1073 (E.D. Wash. 2018), plaintiff (individually and on behalf of all others similarly situated) brought an adequate class action claim for violation of Washington's Consumer Protection Act, Wash. Rev. Code ch. 19.86, against a health insurer's management company where the defendants engaged in unfair or deceptive practices by failing to provide sufficient providers within network, failing to pay legitimate claims, and failing to provide the benefits and coverage as represented.

III.　DAMAGES IN FIRST-PARTY BAD FAITH CASES

A. Compensatory Damages

§1.56　1. General Principles

　—In *Guarantee Trust Life Ins. Co. v. Estate of Casper*, 2018 CO 43, 418 P.3d 1163 (Colo. 2018), the Supreme Court of Colorado considered the operation of the survival statute, Colo. Rev. Stat. §13-20-101(1), with regard to bad faith claims. The insured died after the jury reached its verdict but before the final order was entered, and the insured's estate was substituted for insured. The court specifically analyzed whether the personal injury limitation of the survival statute would limit the insured's damages for bad faith breach of the insurance contract. The court held that the survival statute did not bar the estate's recovery or limit its damages for a claim for bad faith breach of insurance contract or for a claim under the bad faith statute (Colo. Rev. Stat. §10-3-116).

—In *McLeod v. Continental Ins. Co.*, 573 So. 2d 864 (Fla. Dist. Ct. App. 1990), *aff'd*, 591 So. 2d 621 (Fla. 1992), the court rejected the insured's argument that, having unsuccessfully sought uninsured motorist benefits from his insurer, and having been obliged to sue the tortfeasor to prove his entitlement to those benefits, the measure of damages in a subsequent bad faith action against the insurer was the full amount of the verdict obtained against the tortfeasor, even though that amount exceeded policy limits. The court explained that the concept of the recoverability of an excess verdict could not be imported here from the third-party context. The court wrote (573 So. 2d at 867):

> In the case of a first-party bad faith claim, the first element of damages is the value of the insured's claim, as determined by the underlying tort verdict, up to the insured's policy limits. The second element . . . is those damages proximately caused by the insurer's bad faith. . . . Thus, the insured obtains the full benefit of his insurance contract, and is compensated for the egregious conduct of the insurer. In cases where the underlying tort verdict exceeds his uninsured motorist coverage, the insured is disadvantaged because he cannot collect the full value of his claim; however, that disadvantage results from the tortfeasor's insolvency and not from the chance occurrence of his insurance company's bad faith.

Following the state supreme court's affirmance in *McLeod*, see *Continental Ins. Co. v. Jones*, 592 So. 2d 240 (Fla. 1992). Similar reasoning was endorsed by a California Court of Appeal in *State Farm Mut. Auto Ins. Co. v. Superior Court (Balen)*, 123 Cal. App. 4th 1424, 20 Cal. Rptr. 3d 850 (2004).

However, the portion of the *McLeod* holding that prohibited an insured from recovering an amount in excess of the policy limits in a first-party bad faith claim was overturned by the Florida legislature. Fla. Stat. §627.727(10), enacted June 25, 1992. See *Fridman v. Safeco Ins. Co. of Ill.*, 185 So. 3d 1214 (Fla. 2016) (court notes that subsequent to legislature's response to *McLeod*, damages includes any amount in excess of policy limits in both first-party and third-party bad faith claims). Accord *Bottini v. GEICO*, 859 F.3d 987 (11th Cir. 2017). See also *Fridman v. Safeco Ins. Co. of Ill.*, 185 So. 3d 1214 (Fla. 2016) (jury determination of liability and damages in underlying uninsured motorist case is binding in subsequent bad faith action if parties have had opportunity for appellate review of trial errors). Compare *Bottini v. GEICO*, 859 F.3d 987 (11th Cir. 2017) (Florida law; damages determination in underlying uninsured motorist case is not binding in subsequent bad faith action where insurer did pursue its right to appeal but appellate court did not review errors alleged by insurer in jury's calculation of damages; insurer is not obligated to pursue further discretionary review); *Cadle v. GEICO Gen. Ins. Co.*, 838 F.3d 1113 (11th Cir. 2016) (Florida law; granting judgment as matter of law to insurer where insured failed to provide insurer with evidence of permanent injury from auto accident within cure period; evidence of permanent injury is required by statute to recover noneconomic damages for injury from auto accident).

—Under Mississippi law, it was explained in *Broussard v. State Farm Fire & Casualty Co.*, 523 F.3d 618 (5th Cir. 2008), that an insurer who is not liable for punitive damages because its decision to deny a claim, although without a reasonably arguable basis, did not rise to level of an independent tort may nonetheless be liable for consequential or extra-contractual damages, such as attorneys' fees, costs, and other economic losses. Neither extra-contractual damages, such as awards for attorney's fees and emotional distress, nor punitive damages are available when the insurer can demonstrate an arguable or legitimate basis for denial of the claim; see *McGlothin v. State Farm Mut. Ins. Co.*, 297 F. Supp. 3d 635 (S.D. Miss. 2018), *vacated on other grounds*, 925 F.3d 741 (5th Cir. 2019) (granting summary judgment on extra-contractual and punitive damages in favor of insurer; insurer had legitimate basis to deny uninsured motorist benefits to insured after she was rear-ended by fireman who was immune from tort claims, where court was presented with issue of first impression and had to use principles of statutory construction to interpret two conflicting statutes before it held that insured was entitled to benefits).

—In *Lola Roberts Beauty Salon, Inc. v. Leading Ins. Grp. Ins. Co.*, 160 A.D.3d 824, 76 N.Y.S.3d 79 (2018), the court affirmed summary judgment in favor of insurer on insured's claim for consequential damages in an action for breach of contract and breach of the implied convent of good faith and fair dealing. The court held that the insurer made a prima facie showing that the alleged delay was not the proximate cause of the insurer's loss of its business, where it was undisputed that a stop work order issued by a government agency prevented the insured from securing the necessary work permits to repair water damage prior to the time the insured permanently ceased operations.

—In *USAA Tex. Lloyds Co. v. Menchaca*, 545 S.W.3d 479 (Tex. 2018), the Texas Supreme Court stated that the Tex. Ins. Code §541.060(a) grants insureds a private right of action against insurers that engage in certain bad faith practices. The court also reviewed and clarified Texas precedent on whether an insured can recover policy benefits as actual damages for an insurer's statutory violation absent a finding that the insured had a contractual right to the benefits under the insurance policy. In the case under review, a jury answered "no" when asked whether the insurer failed to comply with the terms of the insurance policy in denying to pay damages to the insured after her home was damaged by a hurricane. However, the jury answered "yes" when asked whether the insurer engaged in unfair or deceptive practices in violation of the Texas Insurance Code, including whether the insurer refused to pay the claim for damages without conducting a reasonable investigation. The jury awarded the insured $11,350 as actual damages, which the jury calculated by using the difference between what the insurer should have paid under the policy and the amount actually paid. The Texas Supreme Court ultimately remanded the case for a new trial based on the irreconcilable and fatal conflict in the jury's answers, but it sought to clarify its precedent before it reached its decision.

The court began by stating the general rule that an insured cannot recover policy benefits as actual damages for an insurer's violation of the Texas Insurance Code if the insured does not have a right to the benefits under the policy. The court went on to provide four more rules that add nuance and exceptions to the general rule. The second rule is the entitled-to-benefits rule, which allows an insured who establishes the right to benefits under the policy to recover the benefits as actual damages under the insurance code if the statutory violation of the insurer caused the loss of benefits. The third rule is the benefits-lost rule, which allows the insured to recover benefits as actual damages under the Texas Insurance Code even if the insured has no rights to the benefits, but the violation of the insurer must have caused the insured to lose its contractual right to the benefits. The fourth rule is the independent-injury rule, which allows the insured to recover benefits as actual damages even without a contractual right to the benefits if the insured's conduct was so extreme that it caused an injury independent of the loss of policy benefits. The fifth rule stated by the court is the no-recovery rule, which the court called a corollary of the first four rules. Under the no-recovery rule, the insured cannot recover any damages based on the insurer's violation of the Texas Insurance Code if the insured had no right to receive benefits under the policy and the insured sustained no injury independent of a right to benefits. For cases that apply *Menchaca*, see *State Farm Lloyds v. Fuentes*, 597 S.W.3d 925 (Tex. App. 2020) (reconsidering on remand in light of *Menchaca*; affirming trial court after applying 5 rules of *Menchaca* to facts of case); *Hinojos v. State Farm Lloyds*, 569 S.W.3d 304 (Tex. App. 2019) (refusing to distinguish case from *Menchaca* to allow extra-contractual claims where insurer did not breach contract but insured was entitled to coverage under policy; court affirmed summary judgment in favor of insurer where insured received full appraisal award and failed to show independent injury).

The *Menchaca* decision caused the Fifth Circuit to reconsider its position on the independent-injury rule. See *Aldous v. Darwin Nat'l Assurance Co.*, 889 F.3d 798 (5th Cir. 2018); *Lyda Swinerton Builders, Inc. v. Oklahoma Sur. Co.*, 903 F.3d 435 (5th Cir. 2018) (reversing and remanding ruling related to claim under Chapter 541 of the Texas Insurance Code in light of *Menchaca, supra*; if insured can establish that insurer's misrepresentations caused it to be deprived of benefit under insurance contract, insured can recover defense costs it incurred as actual damages under Chapter 541 without limitation from independent-injury rule; insured could recover treble damages under Chapter 541 if insurer knowingly committed alleged acts).

In *Laird v. CMI Lloyds*, 261 S.W.3d 322 (Tex. App. 2008), it was emphasized that an insured is not entitled to recover extra-contractual damages unless the insurer's acts or omissions caused injury independent of the injury resulting from a wrongful denial of policy benefits.

—Under Washington law, it was held in *Graham-Bingham Irrevocable Trust v. John Hancock Life Ins. Co. USA*, 872 F. Supp. 2d 1275 (W.D. Wash. 2011), a plaintiff prevailing on a first-party claim that an insurer acted in bad faith in evaluating coverage may recover consequential damages even when the denial of coverage is ultimately determined to be correct. Such damages may include the expense of hiring an expert to investigate whether coverage was due.

See also *Wall v. Country Mut. Ins. Co.*, 319 F. Supp. 3d 1227 (W.D. Wash. 2018) (insured brought bad faith claim and claim under Insurance Fair Conduct Act (Wash. Rev. Code §48.30.015) on mistaken belief diamond in her ring had been stolen and replaced with fake diamond and all parties believed diamond was fake until expert was hired; insurer may be liable for bad faith and unreasonable conduct even where there is ultimately no coverage; even de minimus harm of amount expended to hire jewelry expert is sufficient to support claim).

—In *Jones v. Secura Ins. Co.*, 638 N.W.2d 575 (Wis. 2002), the Wisconsin Supreme Court held that contractual damages proximately caused by an insurer's bad faith were recoverable in a bad faith action, even though those same measures of damages would also have been recoverable in an action for breach of contract that was now time-barred. (The contract claim was subject to a 1-year limitations period, while Wisconsin has a 2-year limitations statute for bad faith claims.)

§1.57 2. Economic Loss

—In a case decided on March 28, 1991, involving a California statute (Civ. Code §3291) requiring payment of prejudgment interest on awards of compensatory and punitive damages for personal injuries where a settlement offer was rejected and plaintiff has won a larger amount at trial, the California Supreme Court held that the statute does not apply to awards in insurance bad faith actions, and vacated an interest award of $300,000. *Gourley v. State Farm Mut. Auto. Ins. Co.*, 53 Cal. 3d 121, 279 Cal. Rptr. 307 (1991). The court reasoned that bad faith actions primarily seek damages for economic losses, not for "personal injuries" within the meaning of the statute. An outraged dissent by Justices Mosk and Broussard accuses the majority of creating a special exemption for insurers, and argues that the decision will simply encourage insurers' stalling tactics. (The supreme court decision in *Gourley* left intact a $1.5 million punitive damages award. See supplement §1.66.) See also *George F. Hillenbrand, Inc. v. Insurance Co. of N. Am.*, 20 Cal. Rptr. 3d 380 (2004) (unpublished) (applying *Gourley* to preclude recovery of prejudgment interest in malicious prosecution action based on insurer's assertion of disingenuous declaratory judgment claim); *Durment v. Burlington Ins. Co.*, 820 Fed. Appx. 561 (9th Cir. 2020) (California law; claimant failed to demonstrate economic loss where insureds assigned settlement costs and attorneys' fees to claimant through settlement agreement but insureds did not actually incur such losses; citing *Gourley* in stating that settlement agreement did not involve sort of concrete interference with property rights that California courts require to show economic loss).

In February 1998, a federal court jury in San Diego awarded $27 million in compensatory damages to three developers and a homeowners' association in connection with the insurer's bad faith withdrawal of a defense in a construction defect action. The verdict is said to represent the largest award of compensatory damages for bad faith in California history: *Pershing Park Villas H.O.A. v. Reliance Ins. Co.*, No. 95-1918. See Los Angeles Daily Journal, Mar. 4, 1998, at 2. (On the insurers' motion for new trial, plaintiffs agreed to remit all but approximately $5 million of the jury's award. The judgment was affirmed: *Pershing Park Villas Homeowners Ass'n v. United Pac. Ins. Co.*, 219 F.3d 895 (9th Cir. 2000).)

Concerning the recoverability and measure of damages for lost profits in a first-party bad faith action, see *Shade Foods, Inc. v. Innovative Prods. Sales & Marketing, Inc.*, 78 Cal. App. 4th 847, 93 Cal. Rptr. 2d 364 (2000).

—In *Greenough v. Farm Bureau Mut. Ins. Co. of Idaho*, 142 Idaho 589, 130 P.3d 1127 (2006), an action by the personal representative of an insured's estate to recover underinsured motorist benefits, the Idaho Supreme Court held that prejudgment interest began to accrue 60 days after submission of sufficient proof of loss, not on the date of the accident. The court thus overruled *Schilling v. Allstate Ins. Co.*, 980 P.2d 1014 (Idaho 1999); *Walton v. Hartford Ins. Co.*, 818 P.2d 320 (Idaho 1991); *Emery v. United P. Ins. Co.*, 815 P.2d 442 (Idaho 1991); and *Brinkman v. Aid Ins. Co.*, 766 P.2d 1227 (Idaho 1988).

—In *Thornton v. Am. Interstate Ins. Co.*, 940 N.W.2d 1 (Iowa 2020), the insured brought a bad faith claim against his former employer's workers' compensation carrier after the carrier took 1.5 years to determine that he was permanently and totally disabled, which delayed the insured's receipt of partial commutation. The court held that the insured was not entitled to damages for loss of use of money where the insured failed to show that he would have invested the money in such a way that the delay resulted in economic loss. The court also held that he was not entitled to recover for loss of real estate opportunity where he failed to show that he would have been better off paying a mortgage on a large home than paying rent on his small apartment.

—In *Lawrence v. Will Darrah & Assocs.*, 445 Mich. 1, 516 N.W.2d 43 (1994), the Michigan Supreme Court affirmed an award of damages for lost profits that had foreseeably resulted from the insurer's delay in paying a claim.

—Reversing the denial of the insured's motion to assert a claim for consequential damages, a New York court held, in *Sabbeth Indus., Inc. v. Pennsylvania Lumbermen's Mut. Ins. Co.*, 656 N.Y.S.2d 475 (App. Div. 1997), that since the fire policy at issue provided business interruption coverage, consequential damages were reasonably foreseeable and within the parties' contemplation at the time of contracting. See also *D.K. Prop., Inc. v. Nat'l Union Fire Ins. Co.*, 168 A.D.3d 505, 92 N.Y.S.3d 231 (2019) (insured's allegations met pleading requirements with respect to consequential damages; to recover consequential damages, such damages must be foreseen or should have been foreseen when contract was made; foreseeability should be decided on fully developed record, not on motion to dismiss; in pleadings, insured does not need to explain or describe how each category of consequential damages was foreseeable at time of contract). Also concerning an insured's right to recover consequential damages resulting from a failure to provide coverage, see *Silverman v. State Farm Fire & Casualty Co.*, 22 Misc. 3d 591, 867 N.Y.S.2d 881 (Supr. Ct. 2008).

—In *Paramount Nat'l Life Ins. Co. v. Williams*, 772 S.W.2d 255 (Tex. Ct. App. 1989), an action involving non-payment of health insurance claims, the court affirmed awards, *inter alia*, of $40,281 in past medical expenses and $4,000 for damage to credit. Compare *Allstate Indem. Co. v. Forth*, 204 S.W.3d 795 (Tex. 2006) (former insured lacked standing to sue insurer in absence of any injury where medical providers had apparently accepted insurer's payment of PIP benefits at discounted rate).

—In *Black v. Allstate Ins. Co.*, 100 P.3d 1163 (Utah 2004), the Utah Supreme Court, reversing summary judgment, held that an automobile accident victim had standing to assert a direct action against the liability insurer based on the victim's own contractual relationship with the insurer and the insurer's alleged breach of settlement duties in failing to diligently investigate and evaluate the tort-feasor's claim against the victim. The insurer's alleged breach did not give rise to a tort cause of action, the court held, and permitted recovery of only general and consequential damages for breach of contract.

§1.58 3. Emotional Distress

—In *Independent Fire Ins. Co. v. Lunsford*, 621 So. 2d 977 (Ala. 1993), the Alabama Supreme Court reversed a bad faith judgment against an insurer, finding a reasonable though mistaken basis for the denial of the claim, but nonetheless affirmed an award of damages for emotional distress for breach of the insurance policy. Such damages are available for breach of contract, the court explained, if the jury finds that "'the contractual duties imposed by this contract are so coupled with matters of mental solicitude as to the duty that is owed, that a breach of that duty will necessarily or reasonably result in mental anguish.'" 621 So. 2d at 979, quoting from *Orkin Exterminating Co. v. Donavan*, 519 So. 2d 1330 (Ala. 1988). Also concerning the evidence necessary to support an award for mental anguish, see *National Ins. Ass'n v. Sockwell*, 829 So. 2d 111 (Ala. 2002).

—In *Government Employees Ins. Co. v. Gonzalez*, 403 P.3d 1153 (Alaska 2017), the Supreme Court of Alaska upheld a jury award of $1 in nominal damages for "[m]ental suffering, anxiety, humiliation, and emotional distress," *id.* at 1159, as well as $1 for financial hardship, for a underinsured motorist (UIM) insurer's bad faith delay in paying the plaintiff's claim. The trial court had concluded that the jury found the plaintiff was harmed but failed to prove the amount of injury with the requisite degree of certainty. The high court also upheld a punitive damages award of $450,000. See §1.66.

—In *Clayton v. United Servs. Auto. Ass'n*, 54 Cal. App. 4th 1158, 63 Cal. Rptr. 2d 419 (1997), a California Court of Appeal affirmed a judgment on a jury verdict awarding damages for emotional distress, holding that such damages could be awarded even in the absence of a showing that the insured's emotional distress flowed from substantial economic loss caused by the defendant automobile insurer's bad faith attempt to settle an underinsured motorist claim for a fraction of the policy limits. The court disagreed with the reasoning of *Blake v. Aetna Life Ins. Co.*, 99 Cal. App. 3d 901, 160 Cal. Rptr. 528 (1979), according to which emotional distress, to be compensable, must flow from financial hardship attributable to nonpayment. In accord with *Blake v. Aetna Life Ins. Co.*, *supra*, see *Major v. Western Home Ins. Co.*, 169 Cal. App. 4th 1197, 87 Cal. Rptr. 3d 556 (2009); *Maxwell v. Fire Ins. Exch.*, 60 Cal. App. 4th 1446,

70 Cal. Rptr. 2d 866 (1998). Compare *Jordan v. Allstate Ins. Co.*, 148 Cal. App. 4th 1062, 56 Cal. Rptr. 3d 312 (2007) (in first-party insurance bad faith cases, insured may seek damages for emotional distress resulting from the insurance company's unreasonable withholding of policy benefits and any abusive or coercive conduct in so doing).

—In *Goodsen v. American Standard Ins. Co. of Wisc.*, 89 P.3d 409 (Colo. 2004), the Colorado Supreme Court overruled *Farmers Group v. Trimble*, 768 P.2d 1243 (Colo. Ct. App. 1988) (a third-party case), to the extent that *Trimble* held that emotional distress damages may be recovered for the bad faith breach of an insurance contract only where the emotional distress has resulted from substantial property or economic loss. Emotional distress is a foreseeable result of an insurer's bad faith delay in paying a claim, the Colorado Supreme Court held, even where the claim is ultimately paid in full.

Concerning the calculation, under Colorado law, of an award of damages for emotional distress in an action for bad faith and for willful and wanton breach of an insurance contract, see *Giampapa v. American Family Mut. Ins. Co.*, 12 P.3d 839 (Colo. Ct. App. 2000). The court held that the trial judge had erred in ignoring the "thin skull doctrine" and in taking into account, in limiting the award, the insured's preexisting psychological condition. Compare *Schuessler v. Wolter*, 310 P.3d 151, 2012 WL 1881002 (Colo. Ct. App. 2012) (noneconomic damages award of $325,000 against workers' compensation insurer for unreasonably refusing to pay claim was supported by evidence and was not excessive).

—In *Cadle v. GEICO Gen. Ins. Co.*, 838 F.3d 1113 (11th Cir. 2016), the court addressed the interrelationship of Florida's bad faith statute and a Florida statute that requires certain medical proof to recover noneconomic damages for injuries that arise from an automobile accident. The court held that an insured must present timely and sufficient evidence that its injury is a permanent injury before the insured can proceed on a bad faith claim for non-economic damages.

Under Florida's bad faith statute (Fla. Stat. §624.155), emotional distress damages are recoverable for a health insurer's bad faith failure to pay a claim. *Time Ins. Co. v. Burger*, 712 So. 2d 389 (Fla. 1998). Distinguishing *Time Ins. Co*, the court in *Midland Life Ins. Co. v. Otero*, 1999 WL 1143732 (Fla. Dist. Ct. App. 1999), held that emotional distress damages were not recoverable in a case involving a discriminatory refusal to insure on the basis of national origin. (Under Fla. Stat. §624.155, a civil remedy is available against an insurer who refuses to insure on the basis of race, color, creed, marital status, sex, or national origin.)

—Under Hawaii law, a federal district court held, in *Tran v. State Farm Mut. Auto. Ins. Co.*, 999 F. Supp. 1369 (D. Haw. 1998), emotional distress damages are among the full range of tort remedies available for insurance bad faith. And in *Miller v. Hartford Life Ins. Co.*, 268 P.3d 418 (Haw. 2011), the state supreme court held, as a matter of first impression, that if a first-party insurer commits bad faith, an insured need not prove economic or physical loss in order to recover damages for emotional distress.

—Damages for emotional distress are recoverable in bad faith actions under Indiana law, a federal district court recognized in *Schimizzi v. Illinois Farmers Ins. Co.*, 928 F. Supp. 760 (N.D. Ind. 1996), but the court held excessive the amount of such damages awarded in the present case, involving bad faith handling and nonpayment of medical bills, and ordered reduction of emotional distress damages from $100,000 to $25,000. Also emphasizing the availability of damages for emotional distress in bad faith actions, see *Patel v. United Fire & Casualty Co.*, 80 F. Supp. 2d 948 (N.D. Ind. 2000).

—Standing for the recoverability, under Kansas law, of consequential damages for breach of an insurance contract, see *Royal College Shop, Inc. v. Northern Ins. Co.*,

895 F.2d 670 (10th Cir. 1990) (Kansas law; affirming award of $175,000 for loss of a business as an ongoing concern in action relating to claims under policy of fire insurance). (Note that Kansas courts recognize a rule of statutory preemption with respect to the common-law bad faith doctrine: see *Spencer v. Aetna Life & Casualty Ins. Co.*, 227 Kan. 914, 611 P.2d 149 (1980).)

—Standing for the recoverability of damages for emotional distress under Kentucky's Unfair Claims Settlement Practices Statute (Ky. Rev. Stat. Ann. §304.12-230), see *FB Ins. Co. v. Jones*, 864 S.W.2d 926 (Ky. Ct. App. 1993). For a discussion of what constitutes sufficient evidence to survive summary judgment when seeking recovery for emotional distress under the Kentucky Unfair Claims Settlement Practices Act and a common-law bad faith claim, see *Foster v. American Fire & Casualty Co.*, 219 F. Supp. 3d 590 (E.D. Ky. 2016).

—In *Wegener v. Lafayette Ins. Co.*, 60 So. 3d 1220 (La. 2011), the Louisiana Supreme Court held, as a matter of first impression, that the plaintiff homeowners, in an action for failure to pay for wind damage following a hurricane, were not required to show that the insurer had intended to "aggrieve" them in order to recover damages for mental distress.

—Also following *Kewin v. Massachusetts Mut. Life Ins. Co.*, 409 Mich. 401, 295 N.W.2d 50 (1980) (see book), in holding that emotional distress damages may not be recovered for breach of a health insurance policy, see *Taylor v. Blue Cross/Blue Shield*, 517 N.W.2d 864 (Mich. Ct. App. 1994).

—In *Stewart v. Gulf Guaranty Life Ins. Co.*, 846 So. 2d 192 (Miss. 2002), the Mississippi Supreme Court affirmed a jury award of $500,000 for emotional distress in a case involving various types of egregious misconduct by the insurer in connection with a credit disability claim. Two dissenting justices objected to the fact that the award for emotional distress was 142 times larger than the amount of actual damages and argued that the insurer's conduct had been merely negligent. The Court also affirmed an award of $500,000 in punitive damages despite the fact that the insurer had had an arguable basis for contesting the claim. See also *Hoover v. United Servs. Auto. Ass'n*, 125 So. 3d 636 (Miss. 2013) (where insurer had an "arguable" basis for denying insureds' property damages claims, insurer could not be liable for emotional distress and mental anguish); *United Am. Ins. Co. v. Merrill*, 978 So. 2d 613 (Miss. 2007) (beneficiary under life insurance policy was entitled to damages for emotional distress and mental anguish based on insurer's breach of contract in denying claim).

—In *Brown v. Government Employees Ins. Co.*, 156 A.D.3d 1087, 66 N.Y.S.3d 733 (2017), the insured alleged she was harmed by an insurance company's refusal to pay no-fault insurance benefits after the insured was injured in a car accident. The insured alleged that the insurer routinely denied no-fault claims by pressuring physicians hired by the insurance company to find facts that supported denial of benefits when the physicians performed independent medical evaluations. The appellate court held that the trial court properly dismissed the insured's claim for emotional distress damages in the breach of contract claim because the insured failed to allege a duty upon which liability was based that was separate from the duty under the contract. However, a dissenting justice wrote that the insured should be entitled to seek damages for emotional distress in the breach of contract claim because the insured bargained for the intangible benefit of peace of mind given the nature of no-fault benefits, so damages for emotional distress that resulted from the wrongful denial were within the contemplation of the parties as a probable result of a breach at the time of contracting.

—Under Ohio law, in *Bell v. Zurich Am. Ins. Co.*, 156 F. Supp. 3d 884 (N.D. Ohio 2015), *appeal dismissed* (6th Cir. 2016), the federal district court awarded the insured $100,000 in compensatory damages for emotional distress in a default judgment on a claim for breach of duty to act in good faith where the insurer engaged in delay and made substantial errors in the investigation, including using medical records of another individual with the same name as decedent and disregarding a coroner's findings. The insurance claim was under an accidental death and dismemberment policy, and the widow of the deceased had limited resources to pay the decedent's debts.

—The Fourth Circuit, applying South Carolina law, in *State Farm Fire & Casualty Co. v. Barton*, 897 F.2d 729 (4th Cir. 1990), affirmed actual and punitive damages in connection with an insurer's bad faith denial of a fire insurance claim (see supplement §1.16), but the court reversed an award of $120,000 in consequential damages for emotional distress. The court held that none of the evidence established that plaintiff's emotional distress had been proximately caused by the insurer's failure to pay the claim, rather than by the fact that the insured's home had been destroyed by fire.

—Under Texas law, an ordinary claim for emotional distress in connection with a bad faith claim does not require plaintiffs to expose the records of their entire medical history to discovery by the insurer, it was held in *Midkiff v. Shaver*, 788 S.W.2d 399 (Tex. Ct. App. 1990). The court accordingly vacated a trial court order compelling discovery, reasoning that plaintiffs needed to supply only those medical records that pertained to the specific symptoms allegedly attributable to the insurer's conduct. For affirmances of awards for emotional distress, see *State Farm Lloyds v. Fuentes*, 597 S.W.3d 925 (Tex. App. 2020) (reconsidering on remand in light of *USAA Tex. Lloyds Co. v. Menchaca*, 545 S.W.3d 479 (Tex. 2018); affirming trial court's award of $27,000 in past and future mental anguish damages after applying fourth rule of *Menchaca* to facts of case and finding that independent injury existed); *State Farm Lloyds v. Hamilton*, 265 S.W.3d 725 (Tex. App. 2008) (insureds' testimony adequately described nature, duration, and severity of mental anguish resulting from homeowner insurer's bad faith denial of claim for foundation damage caused by plumbing leak); *Texas Mut. Ins. Co. v. Ruttiger*, 265 S.W.3d 651 (Tex. App. 2008) (there was some evidence to establish that workers' compensation claimant whose claim was denied without reasonable investigation suffered high degree of mental pain that substantially disrupted his daily life such that $100,000 mental anguish award was justified); *Standard Fire Ins. Co. v. Stephenson*, 955 S.W.2d 665 (Tex. Ct. App. 1997) (insurer's bad faith failure to conduct reasonable investigation of claim for death benefits under Workers' Compensation Act); *Beaston v. State Farm Life Ins. Co.*, 861 S.W.2d 268 (Tex. Ct. App. 1993) (proof of Insurance Code violation supported award for mental anguish despite absence of jury finding that insurer had acted "knowingly"); *Commonwealth Lloyd's Ins. Co. v. Thomas*, 825 S.W.2d 135 (Tex. Ct. App. 1992) (fire insurer's delay in payment and unsupported accusations of arson); *State Farm Mut. Auto. Ins. Co. v. Zubiate*, 808 S.W.2d 590 (Tex. Ct. App. 1991) (auto insurer's delay and failure to investigate). Compare *American Nat'l Ins. Co. v. Paul*, 927 S.W.2d 239 (Tex. Ct. App. 1996), holding emotional distress damages unavailable where the insurer had not engaged in knowing misconduct.

—The position of the Utah courts was clarified in *Billings v. Union Bankers Ins. Co.*, 918 P.2d 461 (Utah 1996), where the state supreme court explained that a first-party bad faith cause of action sounds in contract only, but emotional distress damages are potentially available in accordance with the ordinary contract-law rule of foreseeability.

—The Washington Supreme Court sitting *en banc* noted in dicta that it has never addressed whether emotional distress damages are available for insurance bad faith claims. *Schmidt v. Coogan*, 181 Wash. 2d 661, 676 (banc 2014). The court reviewed decisions in which the Washington Court of Appeals had stated that such damages were available and observed that in those cases the appellate court had not analyzed the question. The Washington high court did not reach the issue because the case before it was a legal malpractice case, not a bad faith case, although a dissenting justice had argued that the present case should be analogized to a bad faith case for purposes of ruling on the availability of emotional distress damages. *Id.* at 685–90 (Stephens, J., dissenting).

—Concerning the requirement, under Wyoming law, that an insured must prove economic loss to be entitled to an award of emotional distress damages in a first-party bad faith action, see *Farmers Ins. Exch. v. Shirley,* 958 P.2d 1040 (Wyo. 1998); *State Farm Mut. Auto. Ins. Co. v. Shrader,* 882 P.2d 813 (Wyo. 1994).

§1.59 4. Attorney's Fees

—In *Government Employees Ins. Co. v. Gonzalez,* 403 P.3d 1153 (Alaska 2017), the Supreme Court of Alaska upheld an award of attorney's fees and costs totaling $164,019.69 to a underinsured motorist (UIM) plaintiff who was injured due to the insurer's bad faith delay in paying her claim. The court rejected the defendant's argument that the plaintiff could not be considered the prevailing party because she did not win all of her claims. The court noted that she succeeded on her bad faith claim and recovered a sizable punitive damages award.

—In *Chavarria v. State Farm Mut. Auto. Ins. Co.,* 165 Ariz. 334, 798 P.2d 1343 (Ct. App. 1990), *review denied,* an Arizona Court of Appeals held attorney's fees to be nonrecoverable by the prevailing plaintiff on an insurance bad faith claim, declining to apply the "private attorney general exception" to the "American rule." According to Arizona law, attorney's fees may be recovered in a bad faith action only insofar as they relate to the insured's attempt to secure payment of policy benefits: amounts expended in an effort to obtain extracontractual damages for bad faith are not recoverable. *Schwartz v. Farmers Ins. Co.*, 166 Ariz. 33, 800 P.2d 20 (Ct. App. 1990).

—Under California law, it was held in *California Fair Plan Ass'n v. Politi*, 220 Cal. App. 3d 1612, 270 Cal. Rptr. 243 (1990), a "reverse bad faith" claim by an insurer against its insured sounds only in contract, not in tort, and attorney's fees are not recoverable by the insurer. The court accordingly reversed an award of $75,000 in attorney's fees awarded by a jury in connection with the insurer's theory that the insured's fraudulent concealment of encumbrances on their title to the insured property had constituted a breach of the implied convenant of good faith and fair dealing.

For a decision relying on *Brandt v. Superior Court*, 37 Cal. 3d 813, 210 Cal. Rptr. 211 (1985) (see book), for the proposition that an insured may not recover attorney's fees expended in obtaining amounts in excess of the policy, see *Slottow v. American Casualty Co.*, 10 F.3d 1355 (9th Cir. 1993) (California law). Accord *Teleflex Med. Inc. v. National Union Fire Ins. Co.*, 851 F.3d 976 (9th Cir. 2017) (California law). See also *Cassim v. Allstate Ins. Co.*, 33 Cal. 4th 780, 16 Cal. Rptr. 3d 374 (2004) (*Brandt* fee award must be based on percentage of hours worked on contract claim regardless of proportion of compensatory damages attributable to contract as opposed to tort claim); *Jordan v. Allstate Ins. Co.*, 148 Cal. App. 4th 1062, 56 Cal. Rptr. 3d 312 (2007) (legal fees reasonably incurred by insured to compel payment of benefits due, as distinguished from fees attributable to prove insurer's bad faith, are recoverable as damages in bad faith action); *Textron Financial Corp. v. National Union Fire Ins. Co.*, 118 Cal. App. 4th 1061, 13 Cal. Rptr. 3d 586 (2004), *disapproved on other grounds by Zhang v. Superior Court (Cal. Cap. Ins. Co.)*, 57 Cal. 4th 364, 304 P.3d 163 (2013) (*Brandt* permitted recovery of only those fees actually incurred by insured by virtue of 40% contingency fee agreement, not reasonable value of counsel's services); *Burnaby v. Standard Fire Ins. Co.*, 40

Cal. App. 4th 787, 47 Cal. Rptr. 2d 326 (1995) (insured may not recover fees expended in connection with insurer's appeal from judgment awarding damages for bad faith); *Truck Mortgage Group, Inc. v. Crusader Ins. Co.*, 98 Cal. App. 4th 857, 120 Cal. Rptr. 2d 228 (2002) (recognizing "near impossibility" of accurately segregating fees incurred in proving bad faith from those incurred in obtaining policy benefits and holding that trial court did not abuse discretion in making estimate based on result achieved, complexity of case, and experience of counsel); *McGregor v. Paul Revere Life Ins. Co.*, 369 F.3d 1099 (9th Cir. 2004) (disagreeing with *Burnaby v. Standard Fire Ins. Co.*, *supra*, and predicting that California Supreme Court will hold that *Brandt* permits recovery of fees incurred in defending against insurer's appeal).

In *Essex Insurance Co. v. Five Star Dye House, Inc.*, 38 Cal.4th 1252, 45 Cal. Rptr. 3d 362 (2006), the California Supreme Court held that an injured third party to whom the insured had assigned his claims against his liability insurer was entitled to recover attorneys' fees incurred in recovering policy benefits wrongfully withheld. The court disapproved *Xebec Development Partners, Ltd. v. National Union Fire Ins. Co.*, 12 Cal. App. 4th 501, 15 Cal. Rptr. 2d 726 (1993). But see *Durment v. Burlington Ins. Co.*, 820 Fed. Appx. 561 (9th Cir. 2020) (California law; claimant not entitled to recover attorneys' fees where insureds assigned attorneys' fees to claimant through settlement agreement but insureds did not actually incur such fees; citing *Essex Insurance Co. v. Five Star Dye House, Inc.*, *supra*, in stating that assignee can show economic loss based on costs incurred by assignor, but assignor must actually incur such costs).

—In *Guarantee Trust Life Ins. Co. v. Estate of Casper*, 2018 CO 43, 418 P.3d 1163 (Colo. 2018), the Supreme Court of Colorado stated that the award of attorney's fees and court costs under the bad faith statute, Colo. Rev. Stat. §10-3-116 (1), was not discretionary, and it was appropriate to consider such damages as actual damages.

—In *Mock v. Cent. Mut. Ins. Co.*, 158 F. Supp. 3d 1332 (S.D. Ga. 2016) (Georgia law), the federal district court denied the insured's motion for attorney's fees under O.C.G.A. §§33-4-6(a) and 13-6-11 on grounds that insurer had reasonable cause for refusing the insured's claim. See also *Thompson v. Homesite Ins. Co. of Ga.*, 345 Ga. App. 183, 812 S.E.2d 541 (2018), *cert. denied* (Ga. 2018) (lower court erred by failing to dismiss insured's claim for attorney's fees after lower court correctly dismissed insured's bad faith claim under statute; even where insured brings additional claims that are distinct from bad faith claim under statute, if additional claims are based on failure to pay claim, Ga. Code Ann. §33-4-6 is exclusive vehicle through which insured may claim attorney's fees).

—In *Enoka v. AIG Haw. Ins. Co.*, 109 Haw. 537, 128 P.3d 850 (2006), the Hawaii Supreme Court held that in light of a specific statute that precluded automobile insurers from being awarded attorney's fees in absence of a finding that the claimant's action was fraudulent or frivolous, the insurer that had prevailed in the present action for non-fault benefits was not entitled to costs and fees under the general statute that allows costs and fees to prevailing parties.

—Concerning Idaho law, see *Garnett v. Transamerica Ins. Servs.*, 800 P.2d 656 (Idaho 1990) (in action to recover wrongly withheld policy benefits, attorney's fees may be awarded under Idaho Code §41-1839(1), unless punitive damages are so disproportionate as to have apparently also encompassed attorney's fees). See also *Parsons v. Mutual of Enumclaw Ins. Co.*, 143 Idaho 743, 152 P.3d 614 (2007) (requiring underinsured motorist carrier to pay attorneys' fees based on one-third contingency fee agreement, rather than hourly fee, was not abuse of discretion in action alleging failure to timely pay claim).

—For a case awarding attorney's fees to an insured as a component of sanctions against an insurer for the frivolous appeal of a judgment awarding the insured benefits under a policy of life insurance, see *Rosenburg v. Lincoln*

Am. Life Ins. Co., 883 F.2d 1328 (7th Cir. 1989) (Illinois and federal law). See also *Verbaere v. Life Investors Ins. Co.*, 226 Ill. App. 3d 289, 589 N.E.2d 753 (1992) (affirming award of attorney's fees as sanction for insurer's unreasonable refusal to pay benefits under credit-disability policy); *Cooke v. Jackson Nat'l Life Ins. Co.*, 243 F. Supp. 3d 987 (N.D. Ill. 2017), *appeal dismi*ssed, 882 F.3d 630 (7th Cir. 2018) (awarding attorney's fees to insured under §155 of the Illinois Insurance Code where insurer's denial of coverage was based on good faith dispute but insurer unreasonably and unnecessarily extended litigation by 1 year). But see *Lakeshore Sail Charters LLC v. Acadia Ins. Co.*, 168 F. Supp. 3d 1048, 1058 (N.D. Ill. 2016), *appeal dismissed* (7th Cir. 2016) (denying insured's claim for attorney fees under 215 Ill. Comp. Stat. 5/115 because, *inter alia*, insurer's denial of coverage, while incorrect, was based on reading of policy that "was not completely out of bounds or foreclosed by prior authority"; noting that "no recovery is permitted under § 5/155 if there was a bona fide dispute concerning the scope and application of insurance coverage" (internal quotation marks omitted)).

—In *Thornton v. Am. Interstate Ins. Co.*, 940 N.W.2d 1 (Iowa 2020), the insured brought a bad faith claim against his former employer's workers' compensation carrier after the carrier took 1.5 years to determine that he was permanently and totally disabled, which delayed the insured's receipt of partial commutation. The court reduced the jury's award of $52,000 in attorneys' fees to $18,452.42 where the insured was not entitled to attorneys' fees outside the dates the insurer began to engage in bad faith.

—In *Conner v. Occidental Fire & Casualty Co. of N.C.*, 135 P.3d 1230 (Kan. 2006), the Kansas Supreme Court held that whether an insurer has refused without just cause or excuse to pay the full amount of an insured's loss, for purposes of the insured's entitlement to recover attorney's fees, is a question for the trier of fact, subject to limited appellate review.

—In *Lind v. United Servs. Auto. Ass'n*, 242 So. 3d 576 (La. Ct. App. 2018), under two Louisiana bad faith statutes, La. Stat. Ann. §§22:1892 and 22:1973, the court awarded a penalty, including attorney's fees, in the amount of 50 percent of the damages to which the insured was entitled for its loss where the insurer acted arbitrarily and capriciously in refusing to pay a claim to the insured.

—In *Jucino v. Commerce Ins. Co.*, 2011 Mass. App. Div. 285, 2011 WL 6890187 (2011), it was held that awards of attorneys' fees in the amounts of $2,500 were reasonable in an action for failure to pay PIP benefits for chiropractic services stemming from an auto accident. An hourly rate of $200 was reasonable, the court held, and the fact that the insureds recovered only nominal damages did not warrant vacating the fee awards.

—Representing the Michigan rule that attorney's fees are not recoverable in bad faith actions, see *Burnside v. State Farm Fire & Casualty Co.*, 208 Mich. App. 422, 528 N.W.2d 749 (1995). Attorney's fees may be recovered under the No-Fault Act (Mich. Comp. Laws §500.3142) when an insurer unreasonably withholds benefits due under a no-fault insurance policy. See *Nahshal v. Fremont Ins. Co.* 324 Mich. App. 696, 922 N.W.2d 662 (2018) (judgment that insurer owed personal injury protection (PIP) benefits that had not been paid created rebuttable presumption that refusal or delay was unreasonable; insurer failed to overcome statutory presumption).

—In *Peterson v. Western Nat'l Mut. Ins. Co.*, 946 N.W.2d 903 (Minn. 2020), the Supreme Court of Minnesota held that the trial court did not err in finding that the insurer did not act as a reasonable insurer would have in denying the plaintiff's claim for coverage, and that it knew or recklessly disregarded information that showed it had no objectively reasonable basis to deny benefits. Accordingly, the court upheld awards of $100,000 in taxable costs and $97,940.50 in attorney fees under Minn. Stat. §604.18. The court concluded that the insurer's failure to conduct an adequate investigation of the insured's claim under her underinsured motorist's policy, including disregarding a mountain of medical evidence that her accident caused severe headaches requiring Botox treatment, led it to unreasonably and recklessly deny her claim.

—See *Windmon v. Marshall*, 926 So. 2d 867 (Miss. 2006), for the proposition that under Mississippi law, "extracontractual damages" recoverable on a bad faith claim against an insurer include reasonable attorney's fees and costs, as well as other economic losses. But see *Mitchell v. State Farm Fire & Cas. Co.*, 954 F.3d 700, 708 (5th Cir. 2020) (Mississippi law; no punitive or extracontractual damages, including attorneys' fees, were available where the insurer had arguable basis for denying claim).

—In *Hayes v. Met. Prop. & Casualty Ins. Co.*, 908 F.3d 370 (8th Cir. 2018), the Eighth Circuit upheld an award to a policyholder of attorneys' fees as insurer bad faith damages under Nebraska's attorneys' fee statute, Neb. Rev. Stat. §44-359.

—Under Nevada law, the Ninth Circuit held in *Merrick v. Paul Revere Life Ins. Co.*, 500 F.3d 1007 (9th Cir. 2007), there is no categorical rule that a finding of bad faith against an insurer entitles the insured to an award of attorneys' fees under West's N.R.S.A. 18.010(2)(b).

—In *Shore Orthopaedic Group v. The Equitable Life Assurance Soc'y*, 397 N.J. Super. 614, 938 A.2d 962 (2008), after the insured under a disability overhead expense policy was granted summary judgment in an action seeking benefits, the court held (1) the action was a first-party action, and thus the insured could not recover attorneys' fees under the rule that allows such recovery in third-party actions; and (2) the insurer's defense could not be deemed "frivolous," so as to allow insured to recover attorneys' fees under the frivolous litigation statute.

—Under New Mexico law (N.M. Stat. Ann. §39-2-1 (1978)), attorney's fees may be awarded to an insured where the trier of fact determines that the insurer acted unreasonably in failing to pay a claim. *Jessen v. National Excess Ins. Co.*, 108 N.M. 625, 776 P.2d 1244 (1989). In *Jessen*, the court held that the necessary finding of unreasonableness was impliedly present by virtue of the jury's decision to award punitive damages.

—In *Stein v. Lawyers Title Ins. Co.*, 100 A.D.3d 622, 953 N.Y.S.2d 303 (2012), it was held that consequential damages resulting from a breach of the covenant of good faith and fair dealing may be recoverable in the insurance contract context if they were within the contemplation of the parties as a probable result of a breach at the time of or prior to contracting. In the present case, the court held, the insured could not seek attorney's fees because the policy contained no provision permitting such recovery. See also *Endemann v. Liberty Ins. Corp.*, 390 F. Supp. 3d 362 (N.D.N.Y. 2019), *partial reconsideration*, 2020 WL 5027421 (N.D.N.Y. 2020) (attorney's fees are recoverable as component of consequential damages in breach of covenant of good faith and fair dealing if such damages were reasonably contemplated). But *cf. D.K. Prop., Inc. v. National Union Fire Ins. Co. of Pittsburgh, PA*, 59 Misc. 3d 714, 74 N.Y.S.3d 469 (2018), *rev'd on other grounds*, 168 A.D.3d 305 (2019) (legal fees incurred from insured's separate suit to recover directly from tortfeasor recoverable as reasonably foreseeable damages resulting from insurer's bad faith; legal fees incurred in insured's action against insurer to settle rights under policy are not recoverable except under narrow exception where insured can prove that no reasonable insurer would have challenged claim under facts of case and insurer had no arguable basis to challenge claim; insured may proceed with claim for attorney's fees under narrow exception where insured alleged that insurer's own engineer agreed to key fact in favor of insured).

—Under Ohio law, in *Bell v. Zurich Am. Ins. Co.*, 156 F. Supp. 3d 884 (N.D. Ohio 2015), *appeal dismissed* (6th Cir. 2016), the court awarded the insured $33,240 in compensatory damages for legal fees in a default judgment on a claim for breach of duty to act in good faith.

—An award of $32,250 in attorney's fees in a bad faith action was affirmed by the Tenth Circuit, applying Oklahoma law, in *Thompson v. Shelter Mutual Ins. Co.*, 875 F.2d 1460 (10th Cir 1989). "In Oklahoma," the court explained, "an insured may recover costs and attorney's fees incurred in suing the insurer if the judgment recovered exceeds all written settlement offers made by the insurer. Okla. Stat. tit. 36, § 3629(B)." 875 F.2d at 1463. The court rejected the insurer's argument that the trial court should have separated fees expended on the contract claim from those expended seeking extracontractual tort damages for bad faith. "We have noted that Oklahoma's courts have read this statute broadly, . . . and find no indication in the statute that an insured who otherwise qualifies as a 'prevailing party' should not be allowed fees for attorney time spent successfully prosecuting a claim of bad faith." 875 F.2d at 1164. See also *Barnes v. Oklahoma Farm Bureau Mut. Ins. Co.*, 11 P.3d 162 (Okla. 2000) (attorneys' fees are not ordinarily recoverable as element of damages for bad faith refusal to pay uninsured or underinsured motorist claims; overruling *Brashier v. Farmers Ins. Co.*, 925 P.2d 20 (Okla. 1996)); *Taylor v. State Farm Fire & Casualty Co.*, 981 P.2d 1253 (Okla. 1999) (recoverable damages for first-party bad faith include attorney's fees and prejudgment interest); *Regional Air, Inc. v. Canal Ins. Co.*, 639 F.3d 1229 (10th Cir. 2011) (Oklahoma law) (once litigant establishes itself as prevailing party, award of attorneys' fees and costs under 36 Okl. Stat. Ann. §3629(B) must follow).

—In *Scott v. State Farm Mut. Auto. Ins. Co.*, 345 Or. 146, 190 P.3d 372 (banc 2008), the Oregon Supreme Court, *en banc*, held that the application that the insured had submitted for PIP benefits constituted a "proof of loss" for UM benefits, and thus the insured was entitled to attorneys' fees *per* Or. Rev. Stat. Ann. §742.061. The decision abrogated *Mosley v. Allstate Ins. Co.*, 165 Or. App. 304, 996 P.2d 513 (2000).

—Applying Pennsylvania law, the Third Circuit held in *Polselli v. Nationwide Mut. Fire Ins. Co.*, 126 F.3d 524 (3d Cir. 1997), that an insured who prevails on a claim under Pennsylvania's bad faith statute (42 Pa. Cons. Stat. Ann. §8371) may recover attorney's fees for time spent prosecuting the bad faith claim itself, in addition to fees attributable to prosecuting the underlying contract claim. Accord *Bonenberger v. Nationwide Mut. Ins. Co.*, 2002 Pa. Super. 14, 791 A.2d 378 (2002). Compare *Clemens v. New York Central Mut. Fire Ins. Co.*, 264 F. Supp. 3d 618 (M.D. Pa. 2017), *aff'd*, 903 F.3d 396 (3d Cir. 2018) (after determining under lodestar method that reasonable attorney's fees would be 13% of fees billed by plaintiff's attorneys, court denied petition for attorney's fees in entirety except to award interest to plaintiff; court used its discretion under Pennsylvania's bad faith statute to deny attorney's fees where attorneys presented court with reconstructed time records rather than contemporaneous time records and time records contained excessive time entries, duplicative entries, vague entries such as phone calls with no further information, generic categorical entries such as "file maintenance" with no further information, and entries for professional time that should have been billed as nonprofessional time; attorneys requested fees of $1.12 million on claim that had total award of $125,000).

—In *Lagler v. Menard, Inc.*, 2018 S.D. 53, 915 N.W.2d 707 (S.D. 2018), an appeal under South Dakota's worker's compensation statute, the Supreme Court of South Dakota awarded attorney's fees under S.D. Codified Laws §58-12-3 (Insurance Claims and Benefits statute) for vexatious denial of a worker's compensation claim. The insurer refused to pay for a second surgery for the claimant against the advice of the claimant's treating physician. The insurer based its refusal on a purported telephone conversation with a nurse in the treating physician's office who told the insurer that the claimant's symptoms were unrelated to the workplace injury. However, the insurer was unable to identify the nurse, nobody in the physician's office said they had such a conversation with the insurer, and the claimant's medical file contained no record of such a conversation. The insurer did not obtain an independent medical examination of the claimant, so the treating physician's advice was the only opinion available.

Under South Dakota law, the portion of attorney's fees related to a bad faith claim, as opposed to a claim for the breach of an insurance contract, are not recoverable by an insured. *Isaac v. State Farm Mut. Auto. Ins. Co.*, 522 N.W.2d 752 (S.D. 1994); *Crabb v. National Indem. Co.*, 205 N.W.2d 633 (S.D. 1973); *Kirchoff v. American Casualty Co.*, 997 F.2d 401 (8th Cir. 1993). Compare, holding that a jury's rejection of a bad faith claim did not preclude an attorneys' fees award under South Dakota law: *Tripp v. Western Nat'l Mut. Ins. Co.*, 664 F.3d 1200 (8th Cir. 2011); *Bjornestad v. Progressive N. Ins. Co.*, 664 F.3d 1195 (8th Cir. 2011). See also *Bertelsen v. Allstate Ins. Co.*, 833 N.W.2d 545 (S.D. 2013) (insurer's failure to immediately pay insured's claim for medical expenses was without reasonable cause and was grounds for statutory award of attorneys' fees; award in amount of $180,561.51 was reasonable).

—Attorney's fees are recoverable under the Texas Deceptive Practices Act, a Texas Court of Appeals noted in *Fidelity & Casualty Co. v. Underwood*, 791 S.W.2d 635 (Tex. Ct. App. 1990), affirming a judgment for the insured in an action brought under that statute as well as under article 21.21 of the Texas Insurance Code. See also *Standard Fire Ins. Co. v. Stephenson*, 955 S.W.2d 665 (Tex. Ct. App. 1997) (emphasizing that juries should be instructed to award attorney's fees in specific dollar amounts, not as percentage of judgment). See §1.11 for discussion of recovery of attorneys' fees under the Texas Prompt Payment Statute, Tex. Ins. Code ch. 542.

—In *Monahan v. GMAC Mortgage Corp.*, 2005 VT 110, 893 A.2d 298 (2005), the Vermont Supreme Court held that the trial court abused its discretion in awarding attorney's fees to the plaintiff mortgagors based solely on the same bad faith conduct for which the jury had awarded compensatory and consequential damages, in the absence of any litigation-related bad faith or delay sufficient to justify an award under an exception to the "American Rule."

—See *Lemasters v. Nationwide Mut. Ins. Co.*, 232 W. Va. 215, 751 S.E.2d 735 (2013); *Richardson v. Kentucky Nat'l Ins. Co.*, 216 W.Va. 464, 607 S.E.2d 793 (2004); *McCormick v. Allstate Ins. Co.*, 505 S.E.2d 454 (W. Va. 1998); *Paxton v. Municipal Mut. Ins. Co.*, 503 S.E.2d 537 (W. Va. 1998); *Jones v. Wesbanco Bank Parkersburg*, 460 S.E.2d 627 (W. Va. 1995); and *Hadorn v. Shea*, 456 S.E.2d 194 (W. Va. 1995); for decisions by the West Virginia Supreme Court discussing and applying *Hayseeds, Inc. v. State Farm Fire & Casualty Co.*, 352 S.E.2d 73 (W. Va. 1986) (discussed in book). In *Richardson v. Kentucky Nat'l Ins. Co.*, *supra*, the Supreme Court of Appeals of West Virginia held as a matter of first impression that when a policyholder substantially prevails on a first party insurance claim against an insurer and becomes entitled to a reasonable attorney's fee under *Hayseeds, Inc. v. State Farm Fire & Casualty Co.*, *supra*, and its progeny, the amount of the attorney's fee is to be determined by the circuit judge and not by a jury. Having so held, the *Richardson* court proceeded to provide guidance on the factors to be considered and weighed in calculating a "reasonable" fee.

—Holding that under Wisconsin law, attorney's fees are a recoverable item of damages in first-party bad faith actions, see *DeChant v. Monarch Life Ins. Co.*, 547 N.W.2d 592 (Wis. 1996). Compare *Stewart v. Farmers Ins. Group*, 321 Wis. 2d 391, 773 N.W.2d 513 (Wis. App. 2009) (insureds' attorneys' fees were compensatory damages, not taxable costs, and were thus encompassed in stipulated judgment so as to preclude insureds from recovering fees under W.S.A. 814.04(2)).

—The Wyoming Supreme Court, in *Stewart Title Guaranty Co. v Tilden*, 181 P.3d 94 (Wyo. 2008), held (1) the insured's claim for attorneys' fees under the statute (Wyo.

Stat. Ann. §26-15-124) that allows fees to be awarded in cases where an insurer unreasonably or without cause refuses coverage was not subject to the 14-day filing deadline in the rule governing attorneys' fee motions; and (2) an arbitrator's award in which arbitrator determined that an award of fees was outside the scope of his powers did not bar an award of fees in a later action by the insured claiming fees under §26-15-124. For another case applying §26-15-124, see *Lexington Ins. Co. v. Precision Drilling Co., L.P.*, 951 F.3d 1185 (10th Cir. 2020) (Wyoming law; denying attorney's fees and prejudgment interest to additional insured; additional insured failed to establish bad faith where insurer had cogent argument as to why additional insured should not be covered).

B. Punitive Damages

§1.61 2. Requirement of Actual Damages

—In *Government Employees Ins. Co. v. Gonzalez*, 403 P.3d 1153 (Alaska 2017), the Supreme Court of Alaska upheld an award of nominal damages of $2, punitive damages of $450,000, and attorney's fees for an underinsured motorist (UIM) insurer's bad faith delay in paying the plaintiff's claim. The court explained that nominal damages may be awarded where a plaintiff showed she suffered actual harm but the pecuniary amount was undetermined. The court went on to conclude that the actual harm suffered by plaintiff included her post-lawsuit recovery of a claim award of $83,487.50 in UIM benefits plus interest, and that such actual amount justified the punitive damages award of $450,000.

—In *Anco Insulations, Inc. v. Nat'l Union Fire Ins. Co. of Pittsburgh, Pa.*, 787 F.3d 276 (5th Cir. 2015), the Fifth Circuit applied Louisiana law to hold that an insured must prove actual damages in order to recover a statutory bad faith penalty award under La. Rev. Stat. Ann. §22:1892(B)(1).

The statute provided for a mandatory penalty award "in addition" to the amount of "the actual loss." The court distinguished *Oubre v. Louisiana Citizens Fair Plan*, 79 So. 3d 987 (2011), *reh'g denied* (La. 2012), *cert. denied*, 567 U.S. 935 (2012), in which the Louisiana Supreme Court held that discretionary penalties under La. Rev. Stat. Ann. §22:1973(C) could be awarded even when the insured had not suffered any actual damages.

—In *Lead GHR Enters., Inc. v. Am. States Ins. Co.*, 369 F. Supp. 3d 909 (D.S.D. 2019) (South Dakota law) the court stated that punitive damages are not permitted without an award of compensatory damages.

—In *Lindenberg v. Jackson Nat'l Life Ins. Co.*, 147 F. Supp. 3d 694 (W.D. Tenn. 2015), *aff'd in part, rev'd in part on other grounds & vacated in part on other grounds*, 912 F.3d 348 (6th Cir. 2019), *cert. denied*, ___ U.S. ___, 140 S. Ct 635 (2019) (Tennessee law), the federal district court stated that "[i]t is undisputed that actual damages must first be established before punitive damages can be awarded." *Id.* at 704.

§1.62 3. Ratio Between Compensatory and Punitive Damages

In *State Farm Mut. Auto. Ins. Co. v. Campbell*, 538 U.S. 408 (2003), a decision issued on April 7, 2003, the Supreme Court held that ". . . few awards exceeding a single-digit ratio between punitive and compensatory damages, to a significant degree, will satisfy due process." 538 U.S. at 425. The court reversed a decision of the Utah Supreme Court that had reinstated a $145 million punitive damages award, in addition to $1 million in compensatory damages, in a case involving an insurer's bad faith refusal to accept a policy limits settlement offer on a claim against its insured. The majority opinion stated that the present case was "neither close nor difficult" under the three "guideposts" for excessiveness as set forth in *BMW of N. Am., Inc. v. Gore*,

517 U.S. 559 (1996). (In that earlier decision, the court had not mentioned any specific ratio as a constitutional limit.) On remand, the Utah Supreme Court reduced the punitive damages award from $145 million to $9 million, (ignoring the Supreme Court's suggestion by way of dictum that $1 million would probably be the appropriate amount in the present case). *Campbell v. State Farm Mut. Auto. Ins. Co.*, 98 P.3d 409 (Utah 2004). For a case where the court found a punitive damages award unconstitutionally excessive under the three guideposts for excessiveness as set forth in *BMW of N. Am., Inc. v. Gore, supra,* see *King v. GEICO Indem. Co.*, 712 Fed. Appx. 649 (9th Cir. 2017) (unpublished) (Montana law).

Prior to issuing the decision in *BMW of N. Am., Inc. v Gore, supra,* the Supreme Court had examined the same issue in *Pacific Mut. Life Ins. Co. v. Haslip,* 499 U.S. 1 (1991), and *TXO Prod. Corp. v. Alliance Resources Corp.*, 509 U.S. 443 (1993), declining in both cases to hold that the large awards in question were constitutionally excessive.

Among the cases cleared from the United States Supreme Court docket in the wake of *Pacific Mutual,* and remanded to state courts for reconsideration in light of the *Pacific Mutual* decision, was at least one other insurance bad faith case: *Eichenseer v. Reserve Life Ins. Co.*, 881 F.2d 1355 (5th Cir. 1989) (Mississippi law; see §1.10), involving a $500,000 award to a Mississippi woman who had been forced to wait more than three years for her insurer to pay a $6,658 health insurance claim. After remand, the Fifth Circuit again affirmed the judgment: *Eichenseer v. Reserve Life Ins. Co.*, 934 F.2d 1377 (5th Cir. 1991). The Fifth Circuit interpreted the *Haslip* decision as requiring that two questions be answered in evaluating the constitutionality of a punitive damages award: "(1) whether the circumstances of the case indicate that the award is reasonable, and (2) whether the procedure used in assessing and reviewing the award imposes a sufficiently definite and meaningful constraint on the discretion of the factfinder." The first test is satisfied "if there are any circumstances of probative force that support the amount of the award," the court reasoned: the size of the award and the compensatory/punitive ratio are relevant but not dispositive factors.

—In *Prudential Ballard Realty Co. v. Weatherly*, 792 So. 2d 1045 (Ala. 2000), not an insurance case, the Alabama Supreme Court established a 3:1 ratio as the "benchmark" for evaluating punitive damages awards, with the burden on plaintiff to justify a higher ratio and the burden on defendant to justify a lower one. A 13:1 ratio was subsequently held excessive and a 6:1 ratio appropriate in *Liberty Nat'l Life Ins. Co. v. Sanders*, 792 So. 2d 1069 (Ala. 2000), an action against an insurer and agent for sales fraud.

—In *Government Employees Ins. Co. v. Gonzalez*, 403 P.3d 1153 (Alaska 2017), the Supreme Court of Alaska upheld an award of nominal damages of $2, punitive damages of $450,000, and attorney's fees for an underinsured motorist (UIM) insurer's bad faith delay in paying the plaintiff's claim. The court held that the actual harm suffered by plaintiff included her post-lawsuit recovery of a claim award of $83,487.50 in UIM benefits plus interest, and that such actual amount resulted in a "reasonable single-digit ratio" of actual to punitive damages under *State Farm Mut. Auto. Ins. Co. v. Campbell, supra*. 493 P.3d at 1165. The court also noted the punitive damages award was not much greater than a comparable civil penalty of $250,000 under Alaska Stat. §21.36.910, and was less than the maximum allowed punitive damages award of $500,000 under Alaska Stat. §09.17.020(f).

—In *Arellano v. Primerica Life Ins. Co.*, 332 P.3d 597 (Ariz. Ct. App. 2014), the court held that the jury's findings that the insurer made promises of coverage through an agent, forged signatures, cancelled the application without notifying the insured or returning the insured's payment, and later denied a claim weighed in favor of affirming a punitive damages award. But a 13:1 ratio between punitive and compensatory damages was "unconstitutionally improper" under the Due Process Clause and mandated reduction to an "appropriate and warranted" 4:1 ratio, resulting in a punitive damages award of $328,000.

—In *Diamond Woodworks, Inc. v. Argonaut Ins. Co.*, 109 Cal. App. 4th 1020, 135 Cal. Rptr. 2d 736 (2003), the court applied the principle of *State Farm Mut. Auto. Ins. Co. v. Campbell, supra,* in holding that a punitive damages award of $5.5 million was constitutionally excessive relative to the $258,570 in compensatory damages that had been awarded on a fraud cause of action against a workers' compensation insurer. Compare *Mazik v. GEICO Gen. Ins. Co.,* 35 Cal. App. 5th 455, 247 Cal. Rptr. 3d 450 (2019) (affirming lower court's reduction of punitive damages award from $4 million to $1 million; punitive damages award of 3 times compensatory damages was within range permitted by due process clause; factors to consider in determining whether amount of punitive damages is constitutionally permissible are degree of reprehensibility of conduct, disparity between actual or potential harm suffered and punitive damages awarded, and difference between punitive damages award and civil penalties authorized in comparable cases); *Textron Financial Corp. v. National Union Fire Ins. Co.,* 118 Cal. App. 4th 1061, 13 Cal. Rptr. 3d 586 (2004), *disapproved on other grounds by Zhang v. Superior Court (Cal. Cap. Ins. Co.),* 57 Cal. 4th 364, 304 P.3d 163 (2013) (holding that ratio of 4 to 1 was appropriate in action involving managing agent's use of deceit in attempt to conceal insurer's potential liability, and reducing punitive damages from $10 million to $360,000 after trial court had already reduced award to $1.7 million); *Hangarter v. Provident Life & Accident Ins. Co.,* 373 F.3d 998 (9th Cir. 2004) (award of $5 million in punitives, representing ratio of 2.6:1, was not excessive in action for bad faith denial of disability claim).

—In *Walston v. Monumental Life Ins. Co.,* 923 P.2d 456 (Idaho 1996), the Idaho Supreme Court affirmed an award of $3.2 million in punitive damages, rejecting the argument that the award was excessive either because it stood in a ratio of 26:1 to compensatory damages, or because it represented 5 percent of the insurer's annual profits. The facts involved fraud in the marketing of a life insurance policy, and bad faith denial of benefits. Compare *Hall v. Farmers Alliance Mut. Ins. Co.*, 145 Idaho 313, 179 P.3d 276 (2008) (due process would be violated by punitive damages award of $660,000 for delaying payment of property damage claim, but reduction to $74,600 in 4:1 ratio to compensatory damages was permissible).

—In *Lind v. United Servs. Auto. Ass'n*, 242 So. 3d 576 (La. Ct. App. 2018), under two Louisiana bad faith statutes, La. Stat. Ann. §§22:1892 and 22:1973, the court awarded penalties and attorney's fees in the amount of 50 percent of the damages to which the insured was entitled for its loss where the insurer acted arbitrarily and capriciously in refusing to pay a claim to the insured.

—In *United Am. Ins. Co. v. Merrill*, 978 So. 2d 613 (Miss. 2007), the Mississippi Supreme Court held that a punitive damages award of $900,000 in a beneficiary's action against a life insurer for the wrongful denial of a claim was not excessive. The court noted that the award was less than five times the amount of compensatory damages and less than one-half of 1% of the insurer's net worth.

—Under Ohio law, in *Bell v. Zurich Am. Ins. Co.*, 156 F. Supp. 3d 884 (N.D. Ohio 2015), *appeal dismissed* (6th Cir. 2016), the court applied Ohio's cap on punitive damages to a default judgment on a claim for breach of duty to act in good faith when it limited the punitive damages award to two times the amount of compensatory damages.

—In *Hollock v. Erie Ins. Exch.*, 2004 Pa. Super. 13, 842 A.2d 409 (2004), it was held that an award of $2.8 million in punitives, representing a 10:1 ratio of punitive to compensatory damages, was both warranted and constitutionally acceptable in an action against an underinsured motorist carrier under Pennsylvania's bad faith statute. See also *Grossi v. Travelers Personal Ins. Co.*, 79 A.3d 1141

(Pa. Super. Ct. 2013), *appeal denied* (Pa. 2014) (in action for bad faith based on insurer's evaluation and processing of underinsured motorist claim, punitive damages award of $1,252,325 was not disproportionate where ratio of punitive damages to compensatory damages was either 4:1 or 5:1, depending on measure of compensatory damages; punitive damages award did not violate due process).

—In *James v. Horace Mann Ins. Co.*, 371 S.C. 187, 638 S.E.2d 667 (2006), the Supreme Court of South Carolina held that $1 million punitive damages award that was 6.82 times the actual damages award was "reasonably related" to the actual harm suffered. The case involved a homeowners insurer's bad faith denial of coverage for a dog bite.

—In *Dziadek v. Charter Oak Fire Ins. Co.*, 867 F.3d 1003 (8th Cir. 2017) (South Dakota law), the Eighth Circuit held that a punitive damages award of $2.75 million that was 4.3 times the compensatory damages award was not excessive and was likely to survive any due process challenges. The case was a deceit claim against an insurer related to delay in paying benefits under an uninsured motorist policy.

—The Utah Supreme Court in *Crookston v. Fire Ins. Exch.*, 817 P.2d 789 (Utah 1991) remanded a $4 million punitive damages award for reconsideration of its possible excessiveness. In the course of a lengthy and detailed discussion, the court proposed, *inter alia*, the following evaluative rule:

> The general rule to be drawn from our past cases appears to be that where the punitives are well below $100,000, punitive damage awards beyond a 3 to 1 ratio to actual damages have seldom been upheld and that where the award is in excess of $100,000, we have indicated some inclination to overturn awards having ratios of less than 3 to 1. . . . If the ratio . . . falls within the range that this court has consistently upheld, then the trial court may assume that the award is not excessive. . . . If the award exceeds [that ratio] the trial judge is

not bound to reduce it. However, if such an award is upheld, the trial judge must make a detailed and reasoned articulation of the grounds for concluding that the award is not excessive in light of the law and the facts.

—In *Trinity Evangelical Lutheran Church v. Tower Ins. Co.*, 251 Wis. 2d 212, 641 N.W.2d 504 (Ct. App. 2002), *aff'd*, 661 N.W.2d 789 (Wis. 2003) a Wisconsin appellate court applied the three-part test set forth in *BMW of N. Am., Inc. v. Gore*, 517 U.S. 559 (1996), in holding nonexcessive a $3.5 million award that was at a 7:1 ratio to compensatory damages. See also *Kimble v. Land Concepts, Inc.*, 353 Wis. 2d 377, 845 N.W.2d 395 (2014), *cert. denied*, ___ U.S. ___, 135 S. Ct. 359 (2014) (jury award of $1 million in punitive damages for breach of contract and bad faith in refusing to defend bore no reasonable relationship to compensatory damages award or potential harm faced by insureds, and thus was excessive and violated due process; ratio of punitive damages to the sum of jury's compensatory damages award of $29,738.49 plus $40,000 that insureds spent to gain access to their property was approximately 14:1, and there were no special circumstances calling for such a high ratio).

§1.63 4. Significance of Insurer's Financial Worth

—In *Andrew Jackson Life Ins. Co. v. Williams*, 566 So. 2d 1172 (Miss. 1990) (see supplement §1.10), the Mississippi Supreme Court affirmed, *inter alia*, an award of $200,000 in punitive damages. The court rejected the argument that the amount was excessive because it represented 5.25 percent of the insurer's net worth. While the court acknowledged that a 1987 decision (*Mutual Life Ins. Co. v. Estate of Wesson*, 517 So.2d 521 (Miss. 1987)) had referred to .1 percent of net worth as a standard, the court explained that there had been no intent when that opinion was written to establish any hard and fast rule.

Other holdings relating the permissible size of an award of punitive damages to the insurer's net worth have included the following: *Adams v. Murakami*, 54 Cal. 3d 105, 284 Cal. Rptr. 318 (1991) (to permit meaningful review of punitive damages awards, plaintiff seeking punitive damages must introduce evidence of defendant's financial condition at trial); *Tomaselli v. Transamerica Ins. Co.*, 25 Cal. App. 4th 1269, 31 Cal. Rptr. 2d 433 (1994) (reversing punitive damages award for lack of sufficient supporting evidence of insurer's financial worth); *Lenz v. CNA Assurance Co.*, 42 Conn. Supp. 514, 630 A.2d 1082 (Super. Ct. 1993) (since purpose of punitive damages is deterrence under Connecticut Unfair Trade Practices Act, defendant insurer was obliged to disclose records of financial condition at time of trial, as well as during period between injury and trial); *United Am. Ins. Co. v. Merrill*, 978 So. 2d 613 (Miss. 2007) (punitive damages award of $900,000 in beneficiary's action against life insurer for wrongful denial of claim was not excessive where it was less than one-half of 1% of the insurer's net worth and less than five times the amount of compensatory damages); *Republic Ins. Co. v. Hires*, 810 P.2d 790 (Nev. 1991) (in light of insurer's net worth of $172 million, $22.5 million award was larger than necessary to operate as a deterrent and would be reduced to $5 million); *Dardinger v. Anthem Blue Cross & Blue Shield*, 98 Ohio St. 3d 77, 781 N.E.2d 121 (2002) (punitive damages award representing 28% of health insurer's annual net profits was excessive and would be reduced from $49 million to $30 million); *State Farm Mut. Auto. Ins. Co. v. Zubiate*, 808 S.W.2d 590 (Tex. Ct. App. 1991) (introduction of evidence of defendant's net worth is necessary to enable jury to calculate award's deterrent effect, and does not violate defendant's constitutional rights); *Eichenseer v. Reserve Life Ins. Co.*, 934 F.2d 1377 (5th Cir. 1991) (reasonableness of $500,000 award was supported by fact that award represented only one-third of 1% of insurer's net worth of $157 million).

§1.65 6. Effect of Statute on Availability of Punitive Damages

Rulings concerning the exclusivity or nonexclusivity of various statutory remedies are discussed generally in §§1.26–1.28. The following cases discuss how a specific statutory remedy affects the availability of punitive damages.

—In *McKinnie v. State Farm Fire & Casualty Co.*, 298 F. Supp. 3d 1138 (M.D. Tenn. 2018), the court found that the Tennessee Unfair Trade Practices and Unfair Claims Settlement Act (Titles 50 and 56 of the Tennessee Code) does not eliminate the common-law claim for punitive damages in breach of insurance contract cases. The insured was permitted to proceed on both a common-law claim for punitive damages for breach of insurance contract and a claim for a statutory penalty under the bad faith statute. Accord *Lindenberg v. Jackson Nat'l Life Ins. Co.*, 912 F.3d 348 (6th Cir. 2019), *cert. denied*, ___ U.S. ___, 140 S. Ct. 635 (2019).

§1.66 7. Particular Cases by Jurisdiction

Alabama

National Ins. Ass'n v. Sockwell, 829 So. 2d 111 (Ala. 2002) (discussing and applying Alabama punitive damages factors and standards in affirming award of $600,000); *Liberty Nat'l Life Ins. Co. v. Sanders*, 792 So. 2d 1069 (Ala. 2000) (reducing punitive damages award from $135,000 to $60,000 in action against insurer and agent for sales fraud); *Alfa Mut. Fire Ins. Co. v. Thomas*, 738 So. 2d 815 (Ala. 1999) (reducing punitive damages from $325,000 to $40,000 on claim for insurance sales fraud); *Employees' Benefit Ass'n v. Grissett*, 732 So. 2d 968 (Ala. 1998) (reducing award of $150,000 to $15,000 where insurer had acted arbitrarily but not maliciously, and where original award had stood in ratio of 170 to 1 to compensatory damages); *Affiliated FM*

Ins. Co. v. Stephens Enters., 641 So. 2d 780 (Ala. 1994) (award of $250,000 in punitives was adequately supported by evidence suggesting that insurer had been aware of lack of reasonable basis for denial of claim and had attempted to manufacture defense through creation of "cover-up"); *Principal Fin. Group v. Thomas*, 585 So. 2d 816 (Ala. 1991) (in action involving group life insurer's refusal to pay benefits in connection with death of participant's child, award of $750,000 in punitives was not excessive taking into account grievous nature of harm, highly reprehensible nature of insurer's conduct, and fact that insurer's assets were measured in billions of dollars); *Standard Plan, Inc. v. Tucker*, 582 So. 2d 1024 (Ala. 1991) (affirming award of $500,000 in punitive damages against insurer who rescinded insured's policy without appropriate investigation); *Atchafalaya Marine, LLC v. National Union Fire Ins. Co. of Pittsburgh, Pa.*, 959 F. Supp. 2d 1313 (S.D. Ala. 2013) (after discussing and applying factors to be considered under Alabama law in determining reasonableness of punitive damages award, holding that award of $350,000 in punitive damages in addition to $100,000 in compensatory damages was in ratio that comported with due process and was not excessive; under Alabama law, punitive damages award should "sting" but not "destroy" defendant); *Youngblood v. Lawyers Title Ins. Corp.*, 746 F. Supp 71 (S.D. Ala. 1989) (punitive damages award of $500,000 was justified by insurer's testimony that it would act in same way again if same situation arose, and that verdict would not affect way it did business).

Note that in *Prudential Ballard Realty Co. v. Weatherly*, 792 So. 2d 1045 (Ala. 2000), not an insurance case, the Alabama Supreme Court established a 3-to-1 ratio as the "benchmark" for evaluating punitive damages awards, with the burden on plaintiff to justify a higher ratio of punitive damages to compensatory damages, and the burden on defendant to justify a lower one.

Alaska

Government Employees Ins. Co. v. Gonzalez, 403 P.3d 1153, 1165 (Alaska 2017) (upholding award of nominal damages of $2 and punitive damages of $450,000 for underinsured motorist (UIM) insurer's bad faith delay in paying plaintiff's claim; holding actual harm suffered by plaintiff included her post-lawsuit recovery of claim award of $83,487.50 in UIM benefits plus interest, and that such actual amount resulted in a "reasonable single-digit ratio" of actual to punitive damages); *Nelson v. Progressive Corp.*, 976 P.2d 859 (Alaska 1999) (affirming denial of insured's motion for new trial; although jury found that insurer had misrepresented certain facts, misrepresentations could have been deemed insufficiently outrageous to warrant award of punitive damages); *State Farm Mut. Auto. Ins. Co. v. Weiford*, 831 P.2d 1264 (Alaska 1992) (reversing award of $1.2 million in punitive damages where, despite some evidence of bad motive, insurer had increased settlement offers as information accumulated about seriousness of plaintiff's injuries, and where final offer was reasonable and only $2,000 less than amount awarded by arbitrator); *Ace v. Aetna Life Ins. Co.*, 139 F.3d 1241 (9th Cir. 1998) (reinstating award of punitive damages in action for mishandling of disability insurance claim, but reducing award as excessive from $16.5 million to $381,000, reasoning that Alaska courts would not approve award exceeding three times amount of compensatory damages awarded); *Tanadgusix Corp. v. ARM Ltd.*, 429 F. Supp. 3d 677 (D. Alaska 2019) (Alaska law; actions of stop-loss insurer in adjusting terms of policy by resetting patient's laser (*i.e.*, deductible) and denying hospital claims could be found sufficiently reckless to support punitive damages); *Ace v. Aetna Life Ins. Co.*, 40 F. Supp. 2d 1125 (D. Alaska 1999) (various breaches of duty by insurer that caused insured to become destitute and homeless warranted award of $950,000 in punitive damages).

Arizona

In *Nardelli v. Metropolitan Group Prop. & Casualty Ins. Co.*, 277 P.3d 789 (Ariz. Ct. App. 2012), a case where there was sufficient evidence to support a finding that the insurer's decision to repair the insured's vehicle rather than to "total" it had been unreasonable, the court reduced the jury's award of $55 million in punitive damages to $155,000, holding that the record did not justify awarding punitive damages at a ratio above 1:1 to compensatory damages. (The Superior Court had already reduced the award to $620,000, a reduction the Court of Appeals deemed insufficient to comply with the Supreme Court's due process standards.) In *Sobieski v. American Standard Ins. Co.*, 382 P.3d 89 (Ariz. Ct. App. 2016), the court reversed a punitive damages award of $1,000,000 to an insured who likened the conduct of its insurer to the conduct of the insurer in the *Nardelli* case, *supra*. In *Sobieski*, the insured argued that the insurer had business policies and programs in place that compelled claims adjusters to value company profits over the rights of its insureds, but the insured failed to show a profit-driven atmosphere resembling the one in the *Nardelli* case.

Arkansas

In *Columbia Nat'l Ins. Co. v. Freeman*, 347 Ark. 423, 64 S.W.3d 720 (2002), the Arkansas Supreme Court held that sufficient evidence of oppressive conduct supported a jury's finding of bad faith relative to a fire insurer's deliberate misplacement of documents, its failure to pay the insured's ongoing business expenses, and its failure to comply with an agreement concerning building repairs. The verdict consisted of $170,000 in compensatory damages and $200,000 in punitive damages.

California

Fadeeff v. State Farm Gen. Ins. Co., 50 Cal. App. 5th 94, 263 Cal. Rptr. 3d 453 (2020) (insureds brought claim for breach of covenant of good faith and fair dealing after insurer failed to fully pay insureds' claims for smoke damage to their home from wildfire; denying summary judgment to insurer on punitive damages despite deposition of 1 insured in which she stated she did not believe insurer acted with intent to harm her and despite insureds' reliance on public adjuster to submit documents to insurance without their review); *Mazik v. GEICO Gen. Ins. Co.*, 35 Cal. App. 5th 455, 247 Cal. Rptr. 3d 450 (2019) (evidence was sufficient to show that employee of insurer was managing agent; conduct of employee was sufficient to support punitive damages award against insurer for $1 million where employee intentionally omitted important facts about insured's medical condition in reports and in information given to insurer's experts and grossly trivialized insured's diagnoses and treatments); *Major v. Western Home Ins. Co.*, 169 Cal. App. 4th 1197, 87 Cal. Rptr. 3d 556 (2009) (evidence was sufficient to support finding that claims adjuster was "managing agent" for insurer and that insurer was liable for punitive damages; award of over $646,000 was not constitutionally excessive); *Jordan v. Allstate Ins. Co.*, 148 Cal. App. 4th 1062, 56 Cal. Rptr. 3d 312 (2007) (explaining that insured may be entitled to recover punitive damages for first-party bad faith if insured can prove by clear and convincing evidence that insurer not only denied or delayed payment of benefits unreasonably, but, in doing so, was guilty of malice, oppression, or fraud); *Textron Financial Corp. v. National Union Fire Ins. Co.*, 118 Cal. App. 4th 1061, 13 Cal. Rptr. 3d 586 (2004), *disapproved on other grounds by Zhang v. Superior Court (Cal. Cap. Ins. Co.)*, 57 Cal. 4th 364, 304 P.3d 163 (2013) (holding that ratio of 4 to 1 was appropriate in action involving managing agent's use of deceit in attempt to conceal insurer's potential liability, and reducing punitive damages from $10 million to $360,000 after trial court had already reduced award to $1.7 million);

Diamond Woodworks, Inc. v. Argonaut Ins. Co., 109 Cal. App. 4th 1020, 135 Cal. Rptr. 2d 736 (2003) (applying principle of *State Farm Mut. Auto. Ins. Co. v. Campbell*, 538 U.S. 408 (2003), in holding that punitive damages award of $5.5 million was constitutionally excessive relative to the $258,570 in compensatory damages awarded on fraud cause of action against workers' compensation insurer); *Lance Camper Mfg. Corp. v. Republic Indem. Co.*, 90 Cal. App. 4th 1151, 109 Cal. Rptr. 2d 515 (2001) (affirming awards of compensatory and punitive damages totaling $6.3 million against workers' compensation insurer that set reserves unreasonably high); *Basich v. Allstate Ins. Co.*, 87 Cal. App. 4th 1112, 105 Cal. Rptr. 2d 153 (2001) (affirming summary judgment on punitive damages claim where insured's evidence failed to satisfy California's heightened "clear and convincing" standard for evidence establishing "oppression, fraud, or malice"); *Shade Foods, Inc. v. Innovative Prods. Sales & Marketing, Inc.*, 78 Cal. App. 4th 847, 93 Cal. Rptr. 2d 364 (2000) (reversing awards of punitive damages totaling $13 million because of insufficient evidence of "despicable" conduct); *Mock v. Michigan Millers Mut. Ins. Co.*, 4 Cal. App. 4th 306, 5 Cal. Rptr. 2d 594 (1992) (reversing award of punitive damages because of trial judge's omission of phrase "despicable conduct" from explanation to jury of proof necessary to justify award of punitive damages, per 1987 amendment to Cal. Civ. Code §3294); *Patrick v. Maryland Casualty Co.*, 217 Cal. App. 3d 1566, 267 Cal. Rptr. 24 (1990) (punitive damages issue should not have been submitted to jury where evidence showed conduct that was not "malicious, fraudulent, or oppressive," but only "witless and infected with symptoms of bureaucratic inertia and inefficiency"; reversing award of $250,000); *Gourley v. State Farm Mut. Auto. Ins. Co.*, 217 Cal. App. 3d 1111, 265 Cal. Rptr. 634 (1990) (affirming $1.5 million in punitive damages in favor of insured under uninsured motorist policy; insurer was not entitled to resist claim on basis of novel legal argument (insured's nonuse of seat belt at time her car was hit by drunk driver); reliance on patently untenable defense in denying its insured a reasonable settlement amounted to bad faith). *Gourley* was reversed in part on March 28, 1991, with directions to vacate an award of prejudgment interest: *Gourley v. State Farm Mut. Auto. Ins. Co.*, 53 Cal. 3d 121, 279 Cal. Rptr. 307 (1991). See also *Underwater Kinetics LLP v. Hanover Am. Ins. Co.*, ___ F. Supp. 3d ___, 2020 WL 6204628 (S.D. Cal. 2020) (California law; denying summary judgment on request for punitive damages where factual disputes remained on insurer's handling of claim; stating that some courts have found failure to conduct adequate investigation to be sufficient to support punitive damages); *Gutowitz v. Transamerica Life Ins. Co.*, 126 F. Supp. 3d 1128, 1153 (C.D. Cal. 2015) (granting insurer summary judgment on punitive damages claim where insured cited no evidence that insurer acted "maliciously, oppressively or fraudulently" in denying claim); *Chierfue Her v. State Farm Ins. Co.*, 92 F. Supp. 3d 957 (E.D. Cal. 2015) (granting insurer summary judgment on claims for bad faith and punitive damages; noting that while punitive damages are available for breach of covenant of good faith and fair dealing due to "special relationship" between insurer and insured, there can be no punitive damages without a finding of bad faith).

In December 1993, a Superior Court jury in Riverside County, California, awarded a total of $89.1 million, including $77 million in punitive damages, to the survivors of a woman whose health maintenance organization denied coverage for a bone marrow transplant (called HDCT/ABMT), to treat her advanced breast cancer. *Fox v. Health Net*, No. 219692 (attorney Mark Hiepler for plaintiff). When Health Net first denied coverage on the ground that the procedure is "experimental" or "investigational" (under research), plaintiff's family launched a relentless publicity campaign against Health Net, and a fund-raising campaign that eventually allowed plaintiff to undergo the bone marrow procedure in April 1992.

In September 1995, a Los Angeles County Superior Court jury awarded a total of $86.7 million to the government of American Samoa in connection with the bad faith refusal of its insurer to pay more than a small portion of a claim for the catastrophic damage inflicted by hurricane Val in 1991. *American Samoa Gov't v. Affiliated FM Ins.*, No. BC 069439. The award was the largest in the California courts in 1995. At issue was the validity of a belatedly added exclusion, never approved by the insured, purporting to exclude hurricane damage caused by waves and wind-driven water. The award included $57.8 million in punitive damages, an amount that may be reduced as excessive in light of the insurer's relatively modest assets of approximately $70 million. (Plaintiffs' attorneys unsuccessfully sought to have the insurer's parent company added to the judgment.)

Other notable punitive damages awards in California first-party cases have included *Hangarter v. UNUMProvident*, No. C99-5286 (N.D. Cal. Feb. 2002) ($5 million for bad faith cut-off of disability benefits); *Flight Research, Inc. v. Ranger Ins. Co.*, No. LC042481 (Los Angeles County Super. Ct. Feb. 9, 2001) ($7,222,500 against insurer that had refused in bad faith to cover necessary costs of repairing rare airplane). (Note in connection with *Hangarter*, *supra*, that the television newsmagazine *Dateline NBC* aired a segment in October 2002, examining an apparent pattern of similar behavior on the part of UNUM-Provident. The $5 million award was affirmed in *Hangarter v. Provident Life & Accident Ins. Co.*, 373 F.3d 998 (9th Cir. 2004).) On October 3, 2005, California Insurance Commissioner John Garamendi announced a settlement that requires UnumProvident to pay the state $8 million in fines, reconsider thousands of claim denials, and change the way it processes claims. In a press conference announcing the settlement, Garamendi called UnumProvident "an outlaw company" that "has a corporate policy established at the highest level to systematically deny legitimate claims."

San Francisco attorney Ray Bourhis, who represented the plaintiff in *Hangarter*, has published a book highlighting fraudulent insurance practices such as those routinely engaged in by UnumProvident: *Insult to Injury: Insurance, Fraud and the Big Business of Bad Faith* (Berrett-Koehler, 2005). And, on October 26, 2005, Bourhis and law partner Alice J. Wolfson filed a class action complaint in San Francisco County Superior Court seeking billions of dollars in premium refunds and damages for claims fraudulently denied by UnumProvident to California policyholders. (*Hangarter v. The Paul Revere Life Insuance Co.*, 05-446073).

In *Anderson v. Allstate Ins. Co.*, 45 Fed. Appx. 754 (9th Cir. 2002), the Ninth Circuit reversed an award of punitive damages in an action relating to the bad faith handling of a toxic mold claim. The trial court had already reduced an $18 million jury award to $2.5 million, but the Ninth Circuit held that no award of punitive damages was warranted given the absence of evidence of "malice, oppression, or fraud."

Colorado

Guarantee Trust Life Ins. Co. v. Estate of Casper, 2018 CO 43, 418 P.3d 1163 (Colo. 2018) (insured's estate was substituted for insured when insured died after jury reached its verdict but before final order was entered; punitive damages award survived insured's death and no part of survival statute (Colo. Rev. Stat. §13-20-101(1)), including personal injury limitation or penalty limitation, limited insured's punitive damages award in bad faith claim; attorney's fees and court costs were actual damages under bad faith statute (Colo. Rev. Stat. §10-3-116(1)) for the purpose of calculating punitive damages).

South Park Aggregates, Inc. v. Northwestern Nat'l Ins. Co., 847 P.2d 218 (Colo. Ct. App. 1992) (affirming award of $457,000 in punitive damages in addition to $915,000 on bad faith claim relating to "all risk" insurer's conduct in ignoring evidence pointing to vandalism, a covered risk, and denying claim on basis of policy exclusions for mechanical breakdowns and employee infidelity).

Florida

In *Hogan v. Provident Life & Accident Ins. Co.*, 665 F. Supp. 2d 1273 (M.D. Fla. 2009), denying a motion for judgment on the pleadings, the court held that the insured adequately pleaded a claim for punitive damages under the Florida statute (West's F.S.A. §624.155(5)) that authorizes punitive damages for insurance law violations occurring with such frequency as to indicate a general business practice. The insured alleged, *inter alia*, that the insurer had engaged in a scheme to deny claims, setting targets and goals for claims termination without regard to their merits.

Georgia

Old Republic Nat'l Title Ins. Co. v. RM Kids, LLC, 337 Ga. App. 638, 651–52, 788 S.E.2d 542 (2016) (trial court did not err in directing verdict denying insured's claim for prejudgment interest under Ga. Code Ann. §7-4-15 where the parties disputed the amount of damages at trial; therefore, damages were not liquidated (*i.e.*, "the sum owed is fixed and certain, with no bona fide controversy over the amount,"), making prejudgment interest inappropriate (internal quotation marks omitted)).

Hawaii

Tran v. State Farm Mut. Auto. Ins. Co., 999 F. Supp. 1369 (D. Haw. 1998) (granting summary judgment on punitive damages claim in absence of evidence of required degree of malice or criminal indifference).

Idaho

In *Weinstein v. Prudential Prop. & Casualty Ins. Co.*, 149 Idaho 299, 233 P.3d 1221 (2010), the Idaho Supreme Court affirmed an award of punitive damages as remitted by the trial court to $1,890,000, after the jury had awarded $6 million. The remitted amount was in a ratio of 9:1 to compensatory damages, near but not exceeding, the court held, the due process limits established by U.S. Supreme Court decisions. The case involved the insurer's intentional and unreasonable delay in paying uninsured motorist benefits, and successful claims for bad faith breach of contract and the intentional infliction of emotional distress.

Hall v. Farmers Alliance Mut. Ins. Co., 145 Idaho 313, 179 P.3d 276 (2008) (due process would be violated by punitive damages award of $660,000 for delaying payment of property damage claim, but reduction to $74,600 in 4:1 ratio to compensatory damages was permissible); *Garnett v. Transamerica Ins. Servs.*, 800 P.2d 656 (Idaho 1990) (affirming $100,000 in punitive damages for unreasonable nonpayment of replacement costs claims under policy of fire insurance; award of punitive damages was supported by expert that handling of claim had been "ridiculous," "outrageous," and "an extreme deviation from the standard of care in claims handling in this part of the country at the time").

Illinois

In *Lakeshore Sail Charters LLC v. Acadia Ins. Co.*, 168 F. Supp. 3d 1048 (N.D. Ill. 2016), *appeal dismissed* (7th Cir. 2016), the court granted the insurer summary judgment on the insured's claim for statutory damages under 215 Ill. Comp. Stat. 5/115 because, *inter alia*, the insurer's denial of coverage, while incorrect, was based on a reading of the policy that "was not completely out of bounds or foreclosed by prior authority." 168 F. Supp. 3d at 1058. The court noted that "no recovery is permitted under § 5/155 if there was a bona fide dispute concerning the scope and application of insurance coverage." *Id.* (internal quotation marks omitted). The court also found no evidence that the insurer committed bad faith delay in paying the insured's claim.

Indiana

Monroe Guar. Ins. v. Magwerks Corp., 829 N.E.2d 968 (Ind. 2005) (holding that good faith dispute over insurance coverage does not preclude claim for punitive damages for bad faith when coverage is denied); *USA Life One Ins. Co. v. Nuckolls*, 682 N.E.2d 534 (Ind. 1997) (explaining that punitive damages may be awarded only on clear and convincing evidence that insurer acted with malice, fraud, gross negligence, or oppressiveness, and that duty of good faith may be violated without necessarily subjecting insurer to punitive damages); *Sullivan v. American Casualty Co.*, 605 N.E.2d 134 (Ind. 1992) (reinstating summary judgment on claim for punitive damages where summary judgment had been properly entered on claim for compensatory damages); *Erie Ins. Co. v. Hickman*, 605 N.E.2d 161 (Ind. 1992) (vacating reversal of award of punitive damages: to be sufficient, proof of entitlement to punitive damages needs only to support reasonable inference of malice, fraud, gross negligence, or oppressiveness, and does not need to exclude every reasonable hypothesis of innocent conduct); *Michigan Mut. Ins. Co. v. Sports, Inc.*, 698 N.E.2d 834 (Ind. Ct. App. 1998) (punitive damages award of $1 million for bad faith handling of fire insurance claim did not violate due process despite 14:1 ratio between punitive and compensatory damages); *United Farm Bureau Mut. Ins. Co. v. Ira*, 577 N.E.2d 588 (Ind. Ct. App. 1991) (affirming $105,000 in punitive damages against insurer who stonewalled on claim in reliance on deficient investigation and in face of substantial evidence indicating coverage); *Miller v. Farmers Ins. Group*, 560 N.E.2d 1261 (Ind. Ct. App. 1990) (punitive damages issue properly withheld from jury where evidence showed at most negligence, mistake, or over-zealousness on insurer's part in denying uninsured motorist claim on erroneous ground that insured had caused accident); *Schimizzi v. Illinois Farmers Ins. Co.*, 928 F. Supp. 760 (N.D. Ind. 1996) (reducing award of punitive damages from $600,000 to $135,000 for auto insurer's bad faith failure to pay medical expenses; insurer's conduct was not especially egregious, and 13-to-1 ratio of punitive to compensatory damages was excessive).

Iowa

In *Thornton v. Am. Interstate Ins. Co.*, 940 N.W.2d 1 (Iowa 2020), the insured brought a bad faith claim against his former employer's workers' compensation carrier after the carrier took 1.5 years to determine that he was permanently and totally disabled, which delayed the insured's receipt of partial commutation. The court reduced the jury's award of $6.75 million in punitive damages to $500,000 where there was no evidence of a pattern of bad faith conduct on part of insurer. A ratio of less than 10:1 is generally appropriate; a ratio of 18:1, which is what the jury awarded, would not be out of bounds in the most egregious cases.

Kentucky

Farmland Mut. Ins. Co. v. Johnson, 36 S.W.3d 368 (Ky. 2000) (affirming award of $2 million in punitive damages in action involving insurer's misrepresentation of provisions of fire insurance policy and inadequate investigation of claim). Concerning the standards for an insured's entitlement to a punitive damages instruction on a first-party bad faith claim, see also *Riddle v. Southern Farm Bureau Life Ins. Co.*, 421 F.3d 400 (6th Cir. 2005) (Kentucky law).

Louisiana

Lind v. United Servs. Auto. Ass'n, 242 So. 3d 576 (La. Ct. App. 2018) (under two Louisiana bad faith statutes, La. Stat. Ann. §§22:1892 and 22:1973, insured entitled to penalties and attorney's fees in amount of 50 percent of damages to which insured was entitled for its loss where insurer acted arbitrarily and capriciously in refusing to pay claim to insured); *Citadel Broad. Corp. v. Axis U.S. Ins. Co.*, 162 So. 3d 470 (La. Ct. App.), *writ denied*, 2015 WL 3477492 (La. 2015) (in case arising from business interruption losses to three radio stations during Hurricane Katrina, upholding jury award of $2,953,454 penalty under Louisiana's bad faith statute, La. Rev. Stat. Ann. §22:1892, for insurer's failure to pay within statutory time period that portion of claim insurer had agreed was covered).

Massachusetts

In *Anderson v. National Union Fire Ins. Co.*, 476 Mass. 377, 67 N.E.3d 1232 (2017), the plaintiffs brought actions under the consumer protection statute (Mass. Gen. Laws Ann. ch. 93A) and the unfair claims practices statute (Mass. Gen. Laws Ann. ch. 176D) alleging that the defendants' primary and excess insurers engaged in egregious and deliberate behavior to deprive them of fair compensation for injuries sustained when the plaintiffs were struck by a bus while crossing a street. The Superior Court had held that the insurers' behavior was willful and egregious and required the maximum penalty permitted under Mass. Gen. Laws Ann. ch. 93A. The Superior Court included postjudgment interest in the "amount of judgment" to be multiplied under Section 93A, and the appeals court affirmed. The Supreme Judicial Court held that postjudgment interest is not an element of compensatory damages. The court vacated the judgment and held that the amount of damages to be multiplied for a willful and knowing violation of Section 176D or Section 93A does not include postjudgment interest. Compare *River Farm Realty Trust v. Farm Fam. Casualty Ins. Co.*, 360 F. Supp. 3d 31 (D. Mass. 2019), *aff'd*, 943 F.3d 27 (1st Cir. 2019) (no punitive damages would be available for violation of ch. 93A because alleged bad practices were not "willful or knowing," such as coercion, extortion, fraud, or some similar type of misrepresentation or abusive litigation).

Mississippi

United Am. Ins. Co. v. Merrill, 978 So. 2d 613 (Miss. 2007) (punitive damages award of $900,000 in beneficiary's action against life insurer that wrongfully denied claim was not excessive; award was less than five times amount of compensatory damages and less than one-half of 1% of insurer's net worth); *Gordon v. National States Ins. Co.*, 851 So. 2d 363 (Miss. 2003) (affirming summary judgment in light of evidence that life insurer had arguable basis for denying claim; entitlement to punitive damages requires evidence of malice, gross negligence, or reckless disregard of insured's rights); *Stewart v. Gulf Guaranty Life Ins. Co.*, 846 So. 2d 192 (Miss. 2002) (affirming award of $500,000 even though insurer had arguable basis for contesting claim); *Jenkins v. Ohio Casualty Ins. Co.*, 794 So. 2d 228 (Miss. *en banc* 2001) (pendency of declaratory relief action between tortfeasor and liability insurer was legitimate reason for provisional denial of uninsured motorist benefits and barred claim for punitive damages); *State Farm Mut. Auto. Ins. Co. v. Grimes*, 722 So. 2d 637 (Miss. 1998) (affirming award of $1.24 million in punitive damages despite trial court's refusal to grant insured a directed verdict on breach of contract claim and despite some evidence of fraud on insured's part); *American Funeral Assurance Co. v. Hubbs*, 700 So. 2d 283 (Miss. 1997) (reversing $200,000 punitive damages award; punitive damages statute does not apply to contract actions, and evidence, showing nothing more than negligence, did not meet common-law punitive damages standard); *Harvey-Latham Real Estate v. Underwriters at Lloyd's*, 574 So. 2d 13 (Miss. 1990) (reversing summary judgment for fire insurer; court held that case may go to jury, but engaged in unusual extended advisory discussion of jury instructions and need to constrain jury's discretion relative to assessment of punitive damages); *Vaughn v. Monticello Ins. Co.*, 838 So. 2d 983, 2001 WL 1264429 (Miss. Ct. App. 2001) (citing *State Farm Mut. Auto. Ins. Co. v. Grimes*, *supra*, for proposition that punitive damages claim may go to jury only if insurer had no "legitimate or arguable reason" to deny claim and if insured makes showing of "malice, gross negligence, or wanton disregard" of his or her rights, and discussing factors relevant to determining whether delay or denial was "unreasonable"); *Mitchell v. State Farm Fire & Cas. Co.*, 954 F.3d 700, 708 (5th Cir. 2020) (Mississippi law; no punitive damages were available where insurer had arguable basis for claim denial; punitive damages are only available with showing that insurer both lacked "arguable or legitimate basis for denying the claim" and acted willfully, maliciously, or "with gross and reckless disregard" of insured's rights); *Broussard v. State Farm Fire & Casualty Co.*, 523 F.3d 618 (5th Cir. 2008) (Mississippi law; punitive damages instruction was not warranted where insurer had arguable basis for denying claim under homeowners policy for destruction of home during hurricane on grounds that home was destroyed by water, not wind, and was thus excluded from coverage); *Guaranty Serv. Corp. v. American Employers' Ins. Co.*, 893 F.2d 725 (5th Cir. 1990) (legitimate "pocketbook" dispute could not support award of punitive damages under Mississippi standard requiring "intentional wrong, insult, abuse or such gross negligence as to consist of an independent tort"; affirming dismissal of claim); see also *Dey v. State Farm Mut. Auto. Ins. Co.*, 789 F.3d 629 (5th Cir. 2015) (Mississippi law; parties' "pocketbook dispute" over value of claim did not support insured's claim for bad faith).

Missouri

In *Minden v. Atain Specialty Ins. Co.*, 788 F.3d 750 (8th Cir. 2015), the Eighth Circuit applied Missouri law and affirmed a federal district court's holding that although the insurer had a duty to defend its insured, its conduct did not amount to a "vexatious" refusal to defend under Mo. Rev. Stat. §375.420 because the insurer had a reasonable cause to believe there was no coverage. The court held that the insurer was not required to look beyond an initial police report to decide to deny coverage, even though "further investigation might have unearthed the possibility of coverage." See also *Dhyne v. State Farm Fire & Casualty Co.*, 188 S.W.3d 454 (Mo. banc 2006) (affirming judgment for insured in action to recover uninsured motorist benefits and statutory penalty for vexatious refusal to pay); *Merseal v. Farm Bureau Town & Country Ins. Co. of Mo.*, 396 S.W.3d 467 (Mo. Ct. App. 2013) (upholding jury award of statutory penalty and attorney's fees under §375.420 for insurer's refusal to pay homeowners insurance claim without reasonable cause).

Montana

Shelton v. State Farm Mut. Auto. Ins. Co., 337 Mont. 378, 160 P.3d 531 (2007) (reversing summary judgment; insured's admission that she had honest disagreement with underinsured motorist carrier over value of personal injury case did not establish that insurer acted without malice and was not liable for punitive damages; even given honest disagreement over total value, insurer could have acted with malice by failing to pay minimum amount); *Sandman v. Farmers Ins. Exch.*, 969 P.2d 277 (Mont. 1998) (in light of requirement of "clear and convincing evidence," record supported jury's decision not to award punitive damages notwithstanding findings, measured against lesser standard, that insurer had engaged in unfair claim settlement practices and fraudulent conduct); *Dees v. American Nat'l Fire Ins. Co.*, 861 P.2d 141 (Mont. 1993) (affirming $300,000 in punitive damages, reduced from $575,000, in action pursuant to Montana's bad faith statute (Mont. Code Ann. §33-18-242), which creates a private right of action under Montana's unfair claims settlement practices statute (Mont. Code Ann. §33-18-101), in connection with hail insurer's denial of claim for crop damage on basis of inadequate investigation).

Nevada

Albert H. Wohlers & Co. v. Bartgis, 969 P.2d 949 (Nev. 1998) (affirming award of $3.75 million as reduced from $7.5 million on evidence that insurer had failed to inform insured of insertion into medical insurance policy of new ancillary-charges-limitation provision that represented significant change in benefits); *Powers v. United Servs. Auto. Ass'n*, 114 Nev. 79, 962 P.2d 596 (1998) (affirming award of $5 million in punitive damages in action involving insurer's deficient and self-serving investigation of maritime accident); *Guaranty Nat'l Ins. Co. v. Potter*, 912 P.2d 267 (Nev. 1996) (reducing from $1 million to $250,000 award of punitive damages in action involving underinsured motorist carrier's delay in paying for independent medical examinations; even though award amounted to only 1 percent of insurer's net worth, award was excessive because of nonegregiousness of insurer's overall conduct); *Republic Ins. Co. v. Hires*, 810 P.2d 790 (Nev. 1991) (holding that in view of insurer's net worth of $172 million, award of $22.5 million in punitive damages was excessive and would be reduced to $5 million); *United Fire Ins. Co. v. McClelland*, 780 P.2d 193 (Nev. 1989) (affirming award of $500,000 in punitive damages against group accident and health insurer; "oppression, fraud, or malice" standard satisfied by evidence that insurer consciously withheld from insured information concerning company's financial difficulties until after onset of illness had rendered insured uninsurable by any solvent carrier); *Merrick v. Paul Revere Life Ins. Co.*, 500 F.3d 1007 (9th Cir. 2007) (Nevada law) (vacating award of $10 million in punitive damages in action against disability insurer and remanding for new trial; district court erred in failing to instruct jury that it could not punish defendants for conduct that harmed only non-parties); *Fernandez v. State Farm Mut. Auto. Ins. Co.*, 338 F. Supp. 3d 1193 (D. Nev. 2018) (Nevada law; request for punitive damages dismissed on motion for summary judgment where insured failed to meet threshold needed to prove oppression, fraud, or malice on insurer's part).

New Mexico

Teague-Strebeck Motors, Inc. v. Chrysler Ins. Co., 985 P.2d 1183 (N.M. Ct. App. 1999) (holding that trial court properly declined to award punitive damages in absence of evidence of conduct more egregious than that sufficient to support finding of bad faith); *Paiz v. State Farm Fire & Casualty Co.*, 880 P.2d 300 (N.M. 1994) (reversing award of punitive damages where evidence showed at most gross negligence, not required element of reckless disregard or "evil motive"); *Jackson Nat'l Life Ins. Co. v. Receconi*, 827 P.2d 118 (N.M. 1992) (striking award of $50,000 in punitive damages on basis that insurer's rejection of claim had been neither frivolous nor unfounded: see §1.33).

New York

Flores-King v. Encompass Ins. Co., 29 A.D.3d 627, 818 N.Y.S.2d 221 (2006) (insureds were not entitled to recover punitive damages where complaint failed to assert facts to support contention that insurer's conduct was egregious or fraudulent, or that it evidenced wanton dishonesty so as to imply criminal indifference to civil obligations to public generally); *Bread Chalet, Inc. v. Royal Ins. Co.*, 224 A.D.2d 650, 639 N.Y.S.2d 73 (1996) (denial of coverage under binder did not entitle insured to punitive damages where insured failed to present sufficient evidence of fraudulent or deceitful scheme in dealing with general public or of criminal indifference to civil obligations); *Jolicoeur v. American Transit Ins. Co.*, 159 A.D.2d 236, 552 N.Y.S.2d 215 (1990) (affirming denial of summary judgment; questions of fact existed whether insurer's misrepresentations as to amount of coverage constituted bad faith, and, if so, whether conduct evidenced "criminal indifference to civil obligations" warranting imposition of punitive damages). Compare *Brown v. Government Employees Ins. Co.*, 156 A.D.3d 1087, 66 N.Y.S.3d 733 (2017) (trial court properly dismissed insured's claim for punitive damages where insured failed to allege tort independent of parties' duties under contract); *Dinstber III v. Allstate Ins. Co.*, 110 A.D.3d 1410, 974 N.Y.S.2d 171 (2013) (insured failed to allege a breach of duty distinct from contractual obligations of insurer when he alleged bad faith by automobile insurer based on failure to promptly investigate no-fault claim and to renew his policy; thus, insured's allegations did not support a claim for punitive damages); *Endemann v. Liberty Ins. Corp.*, 390 F. Supp. 3d 362 (N.D.N.Y. 2019), *partial reconsideration*, 2020 WL 5027421 (N.D.N.Y. 2020) (insured failed to allege independent tort for fraud or any other independent tort on which insured could recover punitive damages).

Ohio

Dardinger v. Anthem Blue Cross & Blue Shield, 98 Ohio St. 3d 77, 781 N.E.2d 121 (2002) (remitting punitive damages award against health insurer from $49 million to $30 million and requiring that estate of deceased insured donate two-thirds of that amount to charity); *Bell v. Zurich Am. Ins. Co.*, 156 F. Supp. 3d 884 (N.D. Ohio 2015), *appeal dismissed* (6th Cir. 2016) (granting insured $293,959 in punitive damages in a default judgment on a claim for breach of duty to act in good faith where insurer's conduct demonstrated conscious disregard for insured's rights and established great probability of causing substantial harm where insurer engaged in delay and made substantial errors in the investigation, including using medical records of another individual with same name as decedent and disregarding coroner's findings; insurance claim was under accidental death and dismemberment policy and widow of deceased had limited resources to pay decedent's debts).

Oklahoma

Newport v. USAA, 11 P.3d 190 (Okla. 2000) (award of $1.5 million in punitive damages was neither unjustified nor excessive in action involving low-ball offers on claim for uninsured motorist benefits); *Barnes v. Oklahoma Farm*

Bureau Mut. Ins. Co., 11 P.3d 162 (Okla. 2000) (award of $1.5 million in punitive damages was not excessive in action involving unreasonable failure to pay uninsured motorist benefits); *Cooper v. National Union Fire Ins. Co.*, 921 P.2d 1297 (Okla. Ct. App. 1996) (in action involving failure to timely pay workers' compensation benefits, trial court did not err in refusing to submit punitive damages issue to jury in absence of clear and convincing evidence of evil intent); *Alsobrook v. National Travelers Life Ins. Co.*, 852 P.2d 768 (Okla. Ct. App. 1992) (affirming $100,000 in punitive damages for health insurer's denial of claims without adequate investigation); *Harrell v. Old Am. Ins. Co.*, 829 P.2d 75 (Okla. Ct. App. 1991), *cert. denied* (affirming punitive damages award of $250,000 for insurer's denial without investigation of claim under hospitalization policy: punitive damages instruction satisfied due process, and amount was not excessive relative to insurer's net worth); *Haberman v. The Hartford Ins. Group*, 443 F.3d 1257 (10th Cir. 2006) (Oklahoma law; given evidence from which jury could find that insurer's bad faith conduct in denying $548,000 in uninsured motorist coverage was particularly egregious, punitive damages award of $100,000 was not grossly excessive notwithstanding 20:1 ratio between punitive and compensatory damages); *Willis v. Midland Risk Ins. Co.*, 42 F.3d 607 (10th Cir. 1994) (whether insurer acted in bad faith in denying claim based on location endorsement not mentioned in binder was for jury, but insured was correctly barred from seeking punitive damages in absence of evidence of intentionally wrongful acts); *Capstick v. Allstate Ins. Co.*, 998 F.2d 810 (10th Cir. 1993) (Oklahoma law; affirming $2 million in punitive damages for auto insurer's denial of claim without adequate investigation).

Oregon

In *Strawn v. Farmers Ins. Co. of Or.*, 350 Or. 336, 258 P.3d 1199 (2011), involving class allegations that the insurer had instituted a claims handling process that arbitrarily reduced payments on coverage for medical benefits, the Oregon Supreme Court held that the issue of the alleged excessiveness of the jury's $8 million punitive damages award had not been properly before the Court of Appeals and therefore should not have been vacated. The Supreme Court explained that waiver had been one of the trial court's two alternative reasons for rejecting the insurer's claim of constitutional excessiveness, and the waiver finding had not been challenged on appeal.

Pennsylvania

Punitive damages were properly awarded on a claim under Pennsylvania's bad faith statute (42 Pa. Cons. Stat. Ann. §8371) relating to the insurer's delay in paying a claim for underinsured motiorist benefits, the Third Circuit held in *Klinger v. State Farm Mut. Auto. Ins. Co.*, 115 F.3d 230 (3d Cir. 1997). Both intent and reckless indifference will constitute sufficient mental states to support punitive damages awards under Pennsylvania law, the court explained. See also *Zimmerman v. Harleysville Mut. Ins. Co.*, 860 A.2d 167 (Pa. Super. Ct. 2004) (affirming award of punitive damages based on finding that insurer acted in bad faith, *inter alia*, in refusing to make a "joint loss" payment during the litigation process); *Willow Inn, Inc. v. Public Serv. Mut. Ins. Co.*, 399 F.3d 224 (3d Cir. 2005) (in case involving delay in paying fire insurance benefits, award of $150,000 in punitive damages was not disproportionate to reprehensibility of conduct but was close to constitutionally permitted maximum); *Fahy v. Nationwide Mut. Fire Ins. Co.*, 885 F. Supp. 678 (M.D. Pa. 1995) (emphasizing insurer's statutory entitlement to jury trial where punitive damages are sought).

South Carolina

Mitchell v. Fortis Ins. Co., 686 S.E.2d 176 (S.C. 2009) (ratio of 13.9 to one in computing punitive damages award in connection with insurer's reprehensible rescission of health insurance policy was grossly excessive and violative of due process, and remittitur from $15 million to $10 million would therefore be ordered); *James v. Horace Mann Ins. Co.*, 371 S.C. 187, 638 S.E.2d 667 (2006) (punitive damages award against homeowners' insurer in amount of $1 million in insured's bad faith action regarding coverage for dog bite was not excessive and comported with due process); *Orangeburg Sausage Co. v. Cincinnati Ins. Co.*, 450 S.E.2d 66 (S.C. Ct. App. 1994) (award of over $1.6 million in punitive damages was reasonable considering nature of misconduct, actual damage award of $800,000, and insurer's net worth); *Palmetto Fed. Sav. Bank v. Industrial Valley Title Ins. Co.*, 756 F. Supp. 925 (D.S.C. 1991) (awarding $100,000 in punitive damages for delay in payment of title insurance benefits in reckless disregard of insured's rights).

South Dakota

Bertelsen v. Allstate Ins. Co., 833 N.W.2d 545 (S.D. 2013) (punitive damages can be awarded against principal because of act by agent only if: (1) principal or managerial agent authorized the act; (2) agent was unfit and principal was reckless in employing him; (3) agent was employed in managerial capacity; or (4) principal or managerial agent ratified or approved the act); *Bertelsen v. Allstate Ins. Co.*, 796 N.W.2d 685 (S.D. 2011) (insurer's clear breach of contract or denial of claim that is not fairly debatable may indicate malice, supporting award of punitive damages); *Isaac v. State Farm Mut. Auto. Ins. Co.*, 522 N.W.2d 752 (S.D. 1994) (whether insurer acted in reckless disregard of insured's rights so as to justify award of punitive damages was jury question, given that when insurer finally offered policy limits, offer was conditioned on release of bad faith claim); *Bierle v. Liberty Mut. Ins. Co.*, 992 F.2d 873 (8th Cir. 1993) (South Dakota law; affirming granting of insurer's motion for summary judgment as to punitive damages: South Dakota law requires showing of malice, and evidence relative to underinsured motorist insurer's handling of personal injury claim failed to satisfy that demanding standard as matter of law); *McElgunn v. Cuna Mut. Ins. Soc'y*, 700 F. Supp. 2d 1141 (D.S.D. 2010) (evidence was sufficient to support finding that insurer's delay in paying disability claim was in bad faith, but punitive damages award of $6 million, which stood in ratio of 30-to-1 to compensatory damages, exceeded due process limits and would be reduced to ratio of 8-to-1, or $1.6 million).

Tennessee

In *Lindenberg v. Jackson Nat'l Life Ins. Co.*, 147 F. Supp. 3d 694 (W.D. Tenn. 2015), *aff'd in part, rev'd in part & vacated in part*, 912 F.3d 348 (6th Cir. 2019), *cert. denied*, ___ U.S. ___, 140 S. Ct. 635 (2019) (Tennessee law), the federal district court held that where the plaintiff established at trial that the insurer acted in bad faith and recklessly, and where the plaintiff established actual damages, the plaintiff was entitled to punitive damages. The jury awarded the plaintiff $3 million in punitive damages, but the insurer argued that Tennessee's statutory cap on punitive damages awards in civil cases, Tenn. Code Ann. §29–39–104, would limit the award to $500,000. The federal district court certified to the Tennessee Supreme Court the question of whether the statutory punitive damages cap violates the Tennessee Constitution, but the Tennessee Supreme Court declined to consider the question. The Sixth Circuit held that the statutory cap violated the right to a jury trial set forth in the Tennessee State Constitution and upheld the full punitive damages award. *Lindenberg v. Jackson Nat'l Life Ins. Co.*, 912 F.3d 348 (6th Cir. 2019), *cert. denied*, ___ U.S. ___, 140 S. Ct. 635 (2019).

Texas

State Farm Lloyds v. Nicolau, 951 S.W.2d 444 (Tex. 1997) (reversing award of punitive damages for failure of evidence to support finding that insurer's conduct had created reasonable probability of serious harm to insured); *Universe Life Ins. Co. v. Giles*, 950 S.W.2d 48 (Tex. 1997) (reversing award of punitive damages in absence of showing that insurer's conduct had exposed insured to required type of serious risk); *Twin City Fire Ins. Co. v. Davis*, 904 S.W.2d 663 (Tex. 1995) (trial court correctly struck award of punitive damages where jury had awarded no damages apart from policy benefits); *Transportation Ins. Co. v. Moriel*, 879 S.W.2d 10 (Tex. 1994) (reversing award of $1 million in punitive damages where evidence failed to show necessary malicious, fraudulent, or grossly negligent conduct in addition to bad faith; punitive damages may be awarded only on showing that insurer was aware its actions would probably result in extraordinary harm of type not ordinarily associated with breach of contract or bad faith); *Allison v. Fire Ins. Exch.*, 98 S.W.3d 277 (Tex. App. 2003) (reversing $17 million punitive damages award for insurer's handling of mold claim in absence of evidence that insurer "knowingly" breached duty of good faith); *Standard Fire Ins. Co. v. Stephenson*, 955 S.W.2d 665 (Tex. Ct. App. 1997) (explaining that showing of malice is insufficient to support award of exemplary damages for bad faith; insured must show that insurer was actually aware that its actions involved "extreme risk," *i.e.*, high probability of serious harm such as death, grievous physical injury, or financial ruin); *Commonwealth Lloyd's Ins. Co. v. Thomas*, 825 S.W.2d 135 (Tex. Ct. App. 1992) (award of $2 million in 3 to 1 ratio to actual damages was not disproportionate; jury instructions adequately constrained juy's discretion per *Pacific Mutual Life Ins. Co. v. Haslip*, 499 U.S. 1 (1991) (see §1.62)); *Texas Employers Ins. Ass'n v. Puckett*, 822 S.W.2d 133 (Tex. Ct. App. 1991) (affirming $1.5 million punitive damages award holding that Texas' jury instructions and review procedures satisfy *Pacific Mutual Life Ins. Co. v. Haslip, supra*); *State Farm Mut. Auto. Ins. Co. v. Zubiate*, 808 S.W.2d 590 (Tex. Ct. App. 1991) (reducing without explanation $15 million punitive damages award to $660,000 in action involving auto insurer's failure to investigate its faulty grounds for denying claim); *Munoz v. State Farm Lloyds of Tex.*, 522 F.3d 568 (5th Cir. 2008) (Texas law; insured homeowners were not entitled to punitive damages where there was no showing that insurer's actions had been grossly negligent or had resulted in extraordinary harm; to recover punitive damages, insured must demonstrate that insurer was actually aware that its actions would probably result in harm not ordinarily associated with breach of contract or with bad faith denial of claim, such as death, grievous physical injury, or financial ruin).

On June 1, 2001, a Texas jury awarded a homeowner $32 million in punitive damages for the insurer's bad faith conduct in connection with a property damage claim involving toxic mold. *Ballard v. Fire Ins. Exch.* (Tex. Dist. Ct., Travis Co., June 1, 2001, No. 99-05252). See *Lawyers Weekly USA*, June 11, 2001 (2001 LWUSA 458).

See §1.11 for discussion of recovery of statutory penalties under the Texas Prompt Payment Statute, Tex. Ins. Code ch. 542.

Utah

Crookston v. Fire Ins. Exch., 817 P.2d 789 (Utah 1991) (remanding $4 million punitive damages award for reconsideration and to require trial judge to place in record his reasons for concluding that award was not disproportionate; see discussion of *Crookston* in supplement §1.62).

Vermont

In *Monahan v. GMAC Mortgage Corp.*, 2005 VT 110, 893 A.2d 298 (2005), the Vermont Supreme Court confirmed that a cause of action for breach of the implied covenant sounds in tort, but explained that, as in the present case, "negligent indifference," though below the standard demanded by the implied covenant, does not rise to the level of malice necessary for an award of punitive damages.

West Virginia

McCormick v. Allstate Ins. Co., 505 S.E.2d 454 (W. Va. 1998) (affirming summary judgment on punitive damages claim in absence of evidence suggesting "actual malice" as required under standard set forth in *Hayseeds, Inc. v. State Farm Fire & Casualty Ins. Co.*, 352 S.E.2d 73 (W. Va. 1989)); *Berry v. Nationwide Mut. Fire Ins. Co.*, 381 S.E.2d 367 (W. Va. 1989) (affirming award of $500,000 in punitive damages; evidence that insurer knew claim was valid but denied it "willfully, maliciously and intentionally" supported punitive damages instruction).

Wisconsin

Trinity Evangelical Lutheran Church & School-Friestadt v. Tower Ins. Co., 661 N.W.2d 789 (Wis. 2003) (affirming award of $3.5 million in punitive damages where insurer had refused to reform policy to correct mutual mistake arising from agent's error in filling out application; following *Trible v. Tower Ins. Co.*, 168 N.W.2d 148 (Wis. 1969)). See also *Kimble v. Land Concepts, Inc.*, 353 Wis. 2d 377, 845 N.W.2d 395 (2014), *cert. denied*, ___ U.S. ___, 135 S. Ct. 359 (2014) (jury award of $1 million in punitive damages for breach of contract and bad faith in refusing to defend bore no reasonable relationship to compensatory damages award or potential harm faced by insureds, and thus was excessive and violated due process; ratio of punitive damages to the sum of jury's compensatory damages award of $29,738.49 plus $40,000 that insureds spent to gain access to their property was approximately 14 to 1, and there were no special circumstances calling for such a high ratio).

Wyoming

Farmers Ins. Exch. v. Shirley, 958 P.2d 1040 (Wyo. 1998) (mandating revised jury instructions on punitive damges while reversing judgment for insured, including award of $1.5 million in punitive damages, because of insured's failure to prove substantial economic loss as required in actions for first-party bad faith).

2

Excess Liability Actions

I. THEORIES OF EXCESS LIABILITY

III. INSURER'S DEFENSES TO LIABILITY FOR EXCESS JUDGMENT

IV. THIRD-PARTY JUDGMENT CREDITOR'S RIGHT OF ACTION

I. THEORIES OF EXCESS LIABILITY

A. Introduction

§2.1 1. In General

In this supplement, Chapter 2 deals with cases in the third-party context, including both excess liability and other third-party cases. In contrast, Chapter 1 deals with cases in the first-party, or direct coverage, context.

§2.2 2. Insurer's Right To Control Settlement

Several cases have held that malpractice insurers cannot be subject to bad faith liability for settling claims within policy limits against the wishes of the insureds: *New Plumbing Contractors, Inc. v. Edwards, Sooy & Byron*, 99 Cal. App. 4th 799, 121 Cal. Rptr. 2d 472 (2002); *Shuster v. South Broward Hosp. Dist. Physicians' Professional Liab. Ins. Trust*, 590 So. 2d 174 (Fla. 1992) (affirming dismissal); *Freeman v. Cohen*, 969 So. 2d 1150 (Fla. Dist. Ct. App. 2007); *Sharpe v. Physicians Protective Trust Fund*, 578 So. 2d 806 (Fla. Dist. Ct. App. 1991) (affirming dismissal); *Bleday v. OUM Group*, 645 A.2d 1358 (Pa. Super. Ct. 1994); *Papudesu v. Medical Malpractice Joint Underwriting Ass'n of R.I.*, 18 A.3d 495 (R.I. 2011); *Dear v. Scottsdale Ins. Co.*, 947 S.W.2d 908 (Tex. Ct. App. 1997); *United Capital Ins. Co. v. Bartolotta's Fireworks Co.*, 200 Wis. 2d 284, 546 N.W.2d 198 (Ct. App.1996). See also *Western Polymer Technology, Inc. v. Reliance Ins. Co.*, 32 Cal. App. 4th 14, 38 Cal. Rptr. 2d 78 (1995) (bad faith claim could not be based on policy limits settlement that harmed insured's reputation); *Miller v. Sloan, Listrom, Eisenbarth, Sloan & Glassman*, 267 Kan. 245, 978 P.2d 922 (1999) (Kansas Health Care Provider Insurance Act did not require Health Care Stabilization Fund to obtain defendant doctor's consent before settling malpractice claim); *Cash v. State Farm Mut. Auto.*

Ins. Co., 528 S.E.2d 372 (N.C. Ct. App.), *review granted,*
2000 WL 1007053 (N.C. 2000) (insurer has right to settle
even fraudulent claims for reasons of cost); *Caplan v. Fell-
heimer Eichen Braverman & Kaskey*, 68 F.3d 828 (3d Cir.
1995) (Pennsylvania law; policy language giving insurer control over settlement permitted insurer to settle suit that presented no valid claim despite fact that settlement precluded
insured from bringing malicious prosecution claim). Compare *West Am. Ins. Co. v. Freeman*, 42 Cal. App. 4th 320, 44
Cal. Rptr. 2d 555 (1995) (afffirming award of $12 million in
punitive damages based on insurer's settlement of meritless claim to avoid defense costs); *Saucedo v. Winger*, 22
Kan. App. 259, 915 P.2d 129 (1996) (holding that insurer
may not settle without insured's consent unless policy specifically so provides). See also *Hurvitz v. St. Paul Fire &
Marine Ins. Co.*, 109 Cal. App. 4th 918, 135 Cal. Rptr. 2d 703
(2003) (involving settlement of defamation claims).

—In *Global Hawk Ins. Co. (RRG) v. Wesco Ins. Co.*, 424
F. Supp. 3d 848 (C.D. Cal. 2019) (California law), the court
held that the insurer's denial of coverage for the insured
did not amount to breach of the implied covenant of good
faith and fair dealing where the insurer, under a mistaken
belief that Texas law applied, believed that *G.A. Stowers
Furniture Co. v. Am. Indem. Co.*, 15 S.W.2d 544 (Tex. Civ.
App. 1929) gave it the right and obligation to settle a third-
party claim for the policy limits even though it did not get a
release of claims against the insured. The court held that
while the denial of coverage would have likely been unlawful in California, breach of the implied covenant of good
faith and fair dealing was precluded because the denial was
based on a genuine dispute as to whether Texas law required it to accept the settlement offer.

—Although in general, under Illinois law, no true fiduciary relationship exists between an insurer and its insured, an exception is created "when a liability insurance
company employs policy terms that obtain the irrevocable
power to determine whether an offer to compromise a

personal-injury claim will be accepted or rejected." *O'Neil v. Gallant Ins. Co.*, 769 N.E.2d 100, 110 (Ill. Ct. App. 2002). See also *Western States Ins. Co. v. O'Hara*, 357 Ill. App. 3d 509, 828 N.E.2d 842 (2005) (under common interest exception to attorney-client privilege, insured may discover communications between insurer and attorney retained by insurer in connection with claim against insured where insured challenges good faith nature of settlement with third-party claimant).

—In *Indiana Ins. Co. v. Demetre*, 527 S.W.3d 12 (Ky. 2017), the Kentucky Supreme Court summarized Kentucky law of bad faith. Common-law bad faith claims "flow from the insurer's breach of the covenant to good faith and fair dealing." *Id.* at 26 (citing *Davidson v. American Freightways, Inc.* 25 S.W.3d 94 (Ky. 2000)). Bad faith claims can also arise from the Kentucky Consumer Protection Act and the Unfair Claims Settlement Practices Act. See §§1.37, 2.24. The court then quoted the test applicable to all insurance bad faith actions in Kentucky, from *Wittmer v. Jones*, 864 S.W.2d 885 (Ky. 1993), in which the court "'gathered all of the bad faith liability theories under one roof and established a test applicable to all bad faith actions,' whether first-party or third-party claims and whether based on common law or statute." 527 S.W.3d at 26 (quoting *Davidson*, 25 S.W.3d at 100). The *Wittmer* test contains three required elements:

> (1) the insurer must be obligated to pay the claim under the terms of the policy; (2) the insurer must lack a reasonable basis in law or fact for denying the claim; and (3) it must be shown that the insurer either knew there was no reasonable basis for denying the claim or acted with reckless disregard for whether such a basis existed.

Indiana Ins. Co., 527 S.W.3d at 26 (quoting *Davidson*, 25 S.W.3d at 100 (quoting *Wittmer*, 864 S.W.2d at 890)).

—In *Nationwide Mut. Ins. Co. v. Public Serv. Co.*, 112

N.C. 345, 435 S.E.2d 561 (Ct. App. 1993), the North Carolina Court of Appeals, affirming summary judgment for the insurer, acknowledged that an insurer must act in good faith in reaching any settlement agreement, including one, as here, that was within policy limits but that placed the financial burden predominately upon the insured because of a high deductible. To raise an issue of bad faith with respect to such a settlement, however, there must be some allegation beyond the mere fact that, because of the deductible, the insured was liable for the larger share of the settlement. In the present case, not only was there no such additional allegation, but the insured had actually conceded that the settlement was reasonable. See also *Hartford Accident & Indem. Co. v. U.S. Natural Resources, Inc.*, 897 F. Supp. 466 (D. Or. 1995) (Oregon law); *Roehl Transp., Inc. v. Liberty Mut. Ins. Co.*, 784 N.W.2d 542 (Wis. 2010) (evidence supported jury's finding that insurer acted in bad faith in reaching settlement within policy limits but that cost insured all of its $500,000 deductible; insurer's investigation and handling of claim were deficient in several respects, and expert witness testified that claim could have been settled for around $100,000). Compare *New Hampshire Ins. Co. v. Ridout Roofing Co.*, 68 Cal. App. 4th 495, 69 Cal. Rptr. 2d 286 (1998) (despite insured's after-the-fact contention that claims were not covered, implied covenant of good faith could not limit express grant to insurer of right to settle claims and to thereafter seek reimbursement of deductible from insured); *Commerce & Indus. Ins. Co. v. North Shore Towers Management, Inc.*, 162 Misc. 2d 778, 617 N.Y.S.2d 632 (1994) (acknowledging that bad faith claim may be based on insurer's settlement that makes insured liable for deductible, but holding that here insured failed to carry burden of proving that claims in question had not merited settlement in amounts agreed to).

—For discussions by the Rhode Island Supreme Court of the principle that an insurer breaches its duty of good faith if it denies its insured permission to settle within a tort-feasor's policy limits when it has no obvious and reasonable basis to withhold permission, see *Fraioli v. Metropolitan Property & Casualty Ins. Co.*, 748 A.2d 273 (R.I. 2000); *Bolton v. Quincy Mut. Fire Ins. Co.*, 730 A.2d 1079 (R.I. 1989).

—In *Elworthy v. Hawkeye-Security Ins. Co.*, 166 Fed. Appx. 353 (10th Cir. 2006), the Tenth Circuit, affirming summary judgment, held that under Wyoming law, a homeowner's insurer did not breach the implied covenant by settling a contractor's claim against the homeowner, despite the insured's contention that the settlement damaged his ability to recover on his counterclaims against the contractor. The Tenth Circuit emphasized that the policy did not place an affirmative duty on the insurer to represent the homeowner in his affirmative claims against the contractor, or place an affirmative duty on the insurer to seek the insured's consent before settling claims against him.

B. Insurer's Liability for Bad Faith

2. Formulation of Standard for Insurer's Conduct

§2.4   a. Weighing of Insurer's and Insured's Interests

—In *Clearwater v. State Farm Mut. Auto. Ins. Co.*, 164 Ariz. 256, 792 P.2d 719 (1990), the Arizona Supreme Court explained that, while in first-party cases an insurer is entitled to resist claims that are "fairly debatable," a different standard applies in the third-party context: an insurer must give "equal consideration" to the insured's interests. The court accordingly reinstated a judgment for a third-party claimant-assignee, holding that the court of appeals had been wrong in finding error in the trial court's refusal lto instruct on the "fairly debatable" standard. (The insurer had rejected three policy limits offers of $50,000, and the jury had then awarded $125,000 to the parents of a motorcyclist killed in a traffic accident.) See also *Acosta v. Phoenix Indem. Ins. Co.*, 153 P.3d 401 (Ariz. Ct. App. 2007) (reversing summary judgment; insurer must evaluate claim objectively and as though it alone would be responsible for payment of any judgment rendered).

— In *Harvey v. GEICO Gen. Ins. Co.*, 259 So. 3d 1 (Fla. 2018), *cert. denied*, 2018 WL 6681741 (Fla. 2018), the Supreme Court of Florida emphasized that the insurer must act in good faith and with due regard for the interests of the insured. The court further stated that in avoiding excess judgment, the insurer must act with the same haste and precision as if it were in the insured's shoes. Under Florida law, it was held in *Cardenas v. Geico Casualty Co.*, 760 F. Supp. 2d 1305 (M.D. Fla. 2011), granting summary judgment, that the insurer under an automobile policy had not acted *solely* based on its own interest in attempting to settle a claim against its insured, as would have been required to establish the insurer's liability for bad faith.

—In *Hughes v. First Acceptance Ins. Co. of Ga.*, 343 Ga. App. 693, 808 S.E.2d 103 (2017), *rev'd on other grounds*, 305 Ga. 489, 826 S.E.2d 71 (2019), the Court of Appeals of Georgia stated that in deciding whether to settle a claim within the policy limits, the insurer must give equal consideration to the interests of the insured.

—In *Anastasi v. Fidelity Nat'l Title Ins. Co.*, 137 Haw. 104, 366 P.3d 160 (2016), the Supreme Court of Hawaii upheld the intermediate appellate court's denial of a title insurer's motion for summary judgment on its insured's bad faith claim. The court held that there was a genuine issue of material fact whether the insurer "demonstrated a greater concern for its own monetary interest than for the insured's financial risk" when it continued litigating a claim involving an allegedly forged warranty deed, rather than paying its insured's claim, in light of evidence that it knew for months that the deed had been forged. *Id.* at 115. The court remanded for determination of whether the insurer had violated the enhanced good-faith standard applicable to an insurer defending an insured under a reservation of rights.

—In *Truck Ins. Exch. v. Bishara*, 916 P.2d 1275 (Idaho 1996), the Idaho Supreme Court announced its adoption of the "equal consideration" standard for evaluating an insurer's good faith duty to settle within policy limits.

—For discussion and application of the Illinois rule that in negotiating settlements in which recovery may exceed policy limits, the insurer must give the interest of the insured consideration at least equal to its own, see *Rogers Cartage Co. v. Travelers Indem. Co.*, 2018 IL App. (5th) 160098, 103 N.E.3d 504 (2018), *appeal denied*, 108 N.W.3d 885 (Ill. 2018) (see discussions in §§2.38, 2.45); *Mid-America Bank v. Commercial Union Ins. Co.*, 224 Ill. App. 3d 1083, 587 N.E.2d 81 (1992); *O'Neill v. Gallant Ins. Co.*, 769 N.E.2d 100 (Ill. Ct. App. 2002).

—In *Johnson v. American Family Mut. Ins. Co.*, 674 N.W.2d 88 (Iowa 2004), the Iowa Supreme Court adhered to the rule that, in both first- and third-party cases, an insurer needs only to show the existence of a reasonable basis for its actions in order to defeat a bad faith claim. As controlling on this issue, the court cited *Henke v. Iowa Home Mut. Casualty Co.*, 250 Iowa 1123, 97 N.W.2d 168 (1959), and *Ferris v. Employers Mut. Casualty Co.*, 255 Iowa 511, 122 N.W.2d 263 (1963). Compare *Wierck v. Grinnell Mut. Reinsurance Co.*, 456 N.W.2d 191 (Iowa 1990), and *Berglund v. State Farm Mut. Auto. Ins. Co.*, 121 F.3d 1225 (8th Cir. 1997), (Iowa law; recommending that insurers apply the "disregard the limits" approach in making settlement decisions).

—In *Smith v. Audubon Ins. Co.*, 679 So. 2d 372 (La. 1996), the Louisiana Supreme Court stated that an insurer is protected from liability for a bad faith failure to settle if the situation was such that reasonable minds could have differed concerning the insured's liability in the underlying case.

—In *O'Leary-Alison v. Metropolitan Property & Casualty Ins. Co.*, 752 N.E.2d 795 (Mass. App. Ct. 2001), the court recited the principle of Massachusetts law that an insurer's good faith (though mistaken) evaluation of a claim cannot subject it to bad faith liability. Accordingly, the court affirmed a judgment for the insurer despite the fact that the company had refused to offer more than $20,000 to pay a claim that later resulted in a jury verdict of $125,000. The insurer's doubts about the value of the claim had been rational, the court held.

—Under New York law, it was held in *Greenidge v. Allstate Ins. Co.*, 446 F.3d 356 (2d Cir. 2006), an insurer does not breach its duty of good faith when it makes a mistake in judgment or even when it behaves negligently, only when it demonstrates a gross disregard for its insured's interests and deliberately or recklessly fails to place on equal footing the interests of its insured with its own interests when considering a settlement offer.

—In *Zochert v. Protective Life Ins. Co.*, 921 N.W.2d 479 (S.D. 2018), the Supreme Court of South Dakota refused to extend the tort doctrine of "equal consideration," applicable to the third-party claims process, to the first-party claims context. The court explained that an "insurer determining a first-party claim does not act like a fiduciary with respect to its insured as it does for a claim by a third-party against the insured." *Id.* at 489 (internal quotation marks omitted). The court concluded that reading into a first-party contract an implied duty of the insurer to give equal consideration to the interests of the insured as to its own interests would fundamentally alter first-party insurance policies, in which insurer and insured have "distinct and even conflicting interests." *Id.*

In *Sapienza v. Liberty Mut. Fire Ins. Co.*, 389 F. Supp. 648 (D.S.D. 2019) (South Dakota law), the court stated that in third-party cases the insurer must give equal consideration to its own interests and the interests of the insured, citing *Zochert v. Protective Life Ins. Co., supra.*

—In *Johnson v. Tennessee Farmers Mut. Ins. Co.*, 205 S.W.3d 365 (Tenn. 2006), the Tennessee Supreme Court, reinstating a judgment on a jury verdict in favor of the insured, wrote in part as follows: "Bad faith refusal to settle is defined, in part, as an insurer's disregard or demonstrable indifference toward the interests of its insured. [Citation omitted.] This indifference may be proved circumstantially. [Citation omitted.] Bad faith on the part of the insurer can be proved by facts that tend to show 'a willingness on the part of the insurer to gamble with the insured's money in an attempt to save its own money or any intentional regard of the financial interests of the plaintiff in the hope of escaping full liability imposed upon it by its policy.' [Citation omitted.] If the claim exceeds the policy limits, then the insurer's conduct is subject to close scrutiny because there is a potential conflict of interest between the insurer and the insured.' [Citation omitted.]" 205 S.W.3d at 370.

—Under Washington law, in *Schreib v. American Family Mut. Ins. Co.*, 129 F. Supp. 3d 1129, 1135 (W.D. Wash. 2015), the federal district court noted that although an insurer "typically owes a heightened duty to 'give equal consideration to the insured's interests and its own interests,'" *id.* (citing cases), this enhanced duty does not apply in an uninsured motorist's (UIM) case.

§2.5   b. "No Policy Limits" Approach

—Courts in the following cases endorsed the "disregard the limits" formula for describing the approach an insurer must take to settlement offers, to give the required "equal consideration" to the interests of its insured: *Clearwater v. State Farm Mut. Auto. Ins. Co.*, 164 Ariz. 256, 792 P.2d 719 (1990) (see supplement §2.4); *McKinley v. Guaranty Nat'l Ins. Co.*, 144 Idaho 247, 159 P.3d 884 (2007); *Wierck v. Grinnell Mut. Reinsurance Co.*, 456 N.W.2d 191 (Iowa 1990); *Berglund v. State Farm Mut. Auto. Ins. Co.*, 121 F.3d 1225 (8th Cir. 1997) (Iowa law); *Christian Builders, Inc. v. The*

Cincinnati Ins. Co., 501 F. Supp. 2d 1224 (D. Minn. 2007) (Minnesota law); *American Best Food, Inc. v. Alea London, Ltd.*, 168 Wash. 2d 398, 229 P.3d 693 (banc 2010). Concerning Iowa law, compare *Johnson v. American Family Mut. Ins. Co.*, 674 N.W.2d 88 (Iowa 2004) (endorsing the "reasonable basis" test).

§2.6   c. Requirement of Blameworthy State of Mind

—In *Hollaway v. Direct Gen. Ins. Co.*, 497 S.W.3d 733 (Ky. 2016), the Supreme Court of Kentucky emphasized that to prevail on a third-party bad faith claim under Kentucky's Unfair Claims Settlement Practices Act, a plaintiff must show that the insured's actions were outrageous or with reckless indifference to the rights of others. The court noted that evidence of malevolent intent is required under Kentucky case law.

—In *Chiulli v. Liberty Mut. Ins., Inc.*, 97 Mass. App. 248, 146 N.E.3d 471 (2020), *review denied*, 485 Mass. 1102, 150 N.E.3d 1119 (2020), the appeals court held that the trial court erred when it found that insurer Liberty Mutual did not act willfully or knowingly when it violated Massachusetts' statutory settlement requirement under Mass. Gen. Laws ch. 93A. The court found that the insurer had a duty to offer settlement once the insured's liability became reasonably clear following closing arguments at trial. Instead, the insurer made its insured wait through Thanksgiving and Christmas, and internal documents showed that the delay was an intentional effort to use the insured's lack of funds to leverage a more favorable settlement. The court remanded for determination of whether a statutory penalty of 2 to 3 times the damages award would be proper.

—In *Pavia v. State Farm Mut. Auto. Ins. Co.*, 82 N.Y.2d 445, 626 N.E.2d 24, 605 N.Y.S.2d 208 (1993), the New York Court of Appeals adopted a new standard—"gross disregard"—in third-party cases. The court defined that phrase as "a deliberate or reckless failure to place on equal footing the interests of its insured with its own interests when considering a settlement offer"; or "a pattern of behavior evincing a conscious or knowing indifference to the probability that an insured would be personally accountable for a large judgment if a settlement offer within the policy limits were not accepted." 82 N.Y.2d at 453–54, 605 N.Y.S.2d at 211–12. For a case holding that a reasonable fact-finder could find that the insurer's conduct amounted to bad faith under the *Pavia* standard, see *Pinto v. Allstate Ins. Co.*, 221 F.3d 294 (2d Cir. 2000). See also *New England Ins. Co. v. Healthcare Underwriters Mut. Ins. Co.*, 146 F. Supp. 2d 280 (E.D.N.Y. 2001). Compare *Greenidge v. Allstate Ins. Co.*, 446 F.3d 356 (2d Cir. 2006) (affirming summary judgment for insurer; refusal to settle based on erroneous but reasonable policy interpretation does not subject insurer to bad faith liability; insurer had not been required to accept contingent settlement demand that involved agreeing to declaratory judgment action to determine applicable policy limits). Compare *General Motors Acceptance Corp. v. New York Cent. Mut. Fire Ins. Co.*, 116 A.D.3d 468, 983 N.Y.S.2d 513, 514 (2014), *leave to appeal denied*, 24 N.Y.3d 911, 1 N.Y.S.3d 6, 25 N.E.3d 343 (2014) (insurer's failure to make a policy limits settlement offer was "not prudent," but "'[a]n insurer does not breach its duty of good faith when it makes a mistake in judgment or behaves negligently'" (quoting *Federal Ins. Co. v. North Am. Specialty Ins. Co.* 83 A.D.3d 401, 402, 921 N.Y.S.2d 28 (2011))).

Prior to *Pavia*, the New York requirement of an "extraordinary" showing of "disingenuousness" or "dishonesty" on the insurer's part had been reiterated and discussed in *Crawford v. Hospital of Albert Einstein College of Medicine*, 159 A.D.2d 304, 552 N.Y.S.2d 582 (1990); *Roldan v. Allstate Ins. Co.*, 149 A.D.2d 20, 544 N.Y.S.2d 359 (1989); *General Star Nat'l Ins. Co. v. Liberty Mut. Ins. Co.*, 960 F.2d 377 (3d Cir. 1992) (New York law).

3. Application of Duty

§2.7   a. Failure To Settle

—Affirming a judgment for the insurer on the pleadings, the Alabama Supreme Court, in *Evans v. Mutual Assurance, Inc.*, 727 So. 2d 66 (Ala. 1999), held that no bad faith cause of action had ever accrued where the insurer, though it initially refused to settle and allowed the case to go to trial, had ultimately reached a postverdict settlement for more than the policy limits.

And affirming summary judgment in *Ross Neely Sys., Inc. v. Occidental Fire & Casualty Co.*, 196 F.3d 1347 (11th Cir. 1999), the Eleventh Circuit held that the insurer, defending under a reservation of rights, did not breach its enhanced duty of good faith by deciding not to settle, thereby risking an award of uncovered punitive damages. The court emphasized that at the time settlement offers were made, the risk at trial had seemed slight, and the decision not to settle had to be viewed in light of the information available to the insurer at the time.

—In *Jackson v. American Equity Ins. Co.*, 90 P.3d 136 (Alaska 2004), the Alaska Supreme Court held that the covenant of good faith does not broadly require a liability insurer to give its insured a pretrial assurance that it will cover an excess judgment against the insured if the insurer declines to accept a plaintiff's policy limits demand.

—The trial court erred, an Arizona Court of Appeals held in *Mora v. Phoenix Indem. Ins. Co.*, 996 P.2d 116 (Ariz. Ct. App. 2000), in denying an insurer's motion to intervene in the tort action against its insured in order to challenge the settlement negotiated by plaintiff and the insured. The court rejected the argument that the insurer had forfeited its right to intervene by breaching its good faith duty to settle. Distinguishing *Damron v. Sledge*, 105 Ariz. 151, 460 P.2d 997 (1969), the court reasoned that unlike a wrongful failure to defend, a failure to settle within policy limits is not such an egregious breach of obligation as to justify the insured's negotiation of a collusive settlement in violation of the policy's cooperation clause. See also *Quihuis v. State Farm Mut. Auto. Ins. Co.*, 235 Ariz. 536, 334 P.3d 719 (2014).

—For a discussion of the criteria, under California law, for determining whether or not an insurer acted unreasonably in rejecting a settlement offer, see *Walbrook Ins. Co. v. Liberty Mut. Ins. Co.*, 5 Cal. App. 4th 1445, 7 Cal. Rptr. 2d 513 (1992). Affirming a judgment for the primary insurer, and rejecting any rule that would approach a rule of strict liability for insurers who refuse settlement offers within policy limits, the court held that under the circumstances the primary insurer had reasonably assessed the likelihood and amount of liability, and had been understandably surprised by the size of the jury verdict. See also *Maslo v. Ameriprise Auto & Home Ins.*, 227 Cal. App. 4th 626, 173 Cal. Rptr. 3d 854 (2014), *as modified, review denied* (2014) (in claim under uninsured motorist policy, insurer allegedly rejected insured's payment demand without making settlement offer or conducting adequate investigation, refused insured's offer to mediate the claim, and caused insured to incur unnecessary costs and fees for arbitration when evidence of liability was clear; allegations sufficient to state claim for breach of implied covenant of good faith and fair dealing, even where liability of insurer under the policy was less than insured demanded); *Dorroh v. Deerbrook Ins. Co.*, 223 F. Supp. 3d 1081 (E.D. Cal. 2016), *aff'd*, ___ Fed. Appx. ___, 2018 WL 4566298 (9th Cir. 2018) (granting summary judgment in favor of insurer where insured attempted to settle without joining third-party claimant and settlement offer was beyond policy limits because it would have exposed insurer to potential liability from known third-party lienholder). (For a comparable discussion under New York law, see *General Star Nat'l Ins. Co. v. Liberty Mut. Ins. Co.*, 960 F.2d 377 (3d Cir. 1992).)

For a discussion of California law on the options available to excess insurers when presented with a settlement offer that has been approved by the insured and the primary insurer, see *Teleflex Med. Inc. v. National Union Fire Ins. Co.*, 851 F.3d 976 (9th Cir. 2017). The court rejected an excess insurer's motion to vacate judgment on a bad faith claim where the excess insurer delayed its response with respect to its obligation to accept the settlement or assume defense. The court emphasized that when an excess insurer is presented with a settlement offer that has been approved by the insured and the primary insurer, "[t]he excess insurer must (1) approve the proposed settlement, (2) reject it and take over the defense, or (3) reject it, decline to take over the defense, and face a potential lawsuit by the insured seeking contribution toward the settlement." *Id.* at 979.

Affirming summary judgment for the insurer, a California Court of Appeal, in *Finkelstein v. 20th Century Ins. Co.*, 11 Cal. App. 4th 926, 14 Cal. Rptr. 2d 305 (1992), emphasized that no cause of action for bad faith failure to settle ripens in the absence of a judgment in excess of policy limits. In the present case, the insured, certain that a jury verdict in excess of the $100,000 policy limits would ensue, but unable to convince the insurer to offer more than $75,000, voluntarily contributed some of his own money to effect a settlement of $85,000. The court emphasized the voluntariness of the insured's contribution and the absence of any duress on the insurer's part.

For a holding that a policy limits offer, because of its belated nature, did not preclude bad faith liability, see *Highlands Ins. Co. v. Continental Casualty Co.*, 64 F.3d 514 (9th Cir. 1995) (California law).

In 2016, the Advisory Committee to the Judicial Council of California considered and rejected a revision to the California Jury Instruction on bad faith failure to investigate, CACI No. 2334, pertaining to the reasonableness standard. See discussion in §4.28, *infra.*

—Applying Colorado law, the Tenth Circuit held, in *Trout v. Nationwide Mut. Ins. Co.*, 316 Fed. Appx. 797 (10th Cir.

2009), that the district court, in granting summary judgment in favor of the insurer, had erred reversibly in applying to a third-party claim the stricter first-party standard according to which the plaintiff would have had to show that the insurer not only acted unreasonably but with knowledge or reckless disregard of that unreasonableness.

—In *Harvey v. GEICO Gen. Ins. Co.*, 259 So. 3d 1 (Fla. 2018), *cert. denied*, 2018 WL 6681741 (Fla. 2018, the Supreme Court of Florida reversed an appellate court decision and reinstated a jury verdict against the insurer for $9.2 million. The insured was at fault in a fatal auto accident, and the claimant/estate of the decedent brought a wrongful death action against the insured after the insurer offered the policy limits to the claimant but failed to comply with a request for additional information. The court held, over a strong dissent, that the evidence supported the jury's finding of bad faith failure to settle where the insurer's claims adjuster failed to communicate with the claimant's attorney and the insured in critical ways. In addition, while the insurer offered the policy limits to the claimant, the insurer failed to comply with the claimant's demand to provide a statement from the insured about the insured's assets. Evidence indicated that such a statement would have persuaded the claimant to settle for the policy limits. The court was not persuaded by arguments that the insured's own conduct contributed to the failure to settle.

Reversing summary judgment in the claimant's bad faith action, the court in *Robinson v. State Farm Fire & Casualty Co.*, 583 So. 2d 1063 (Fla. Dist. Ct. App. 1991) held that the fact that the trial court had erred in reasoning that the insurer's bad faith liability for failure to settle had been precluded by the existence of a legitimate coverage dispute. (In an earlier lawsuit by the claimant against the insured, the trial court had found sufficient disputed factual issues to preclude summarily entering judgment finding coverage.) That coverage could not be found as matter of law was not dispositive of the insurer's liability for bad faith denial and failure to settle, the court held. See also *Perera v. United States Fid. & Guar. Co.*, 35 So. 3d 893 (Fla. 2010) (cause of action for bad faith may not be maintained where insurer's actions, because of existence of excess liability policy issued by another insurer, never resulted in insured's increased exposure to liability in excess of his total policy limits); *Macola v. Government Employees Ins. Co.*, 953 So. 2d 451 (Fla. 2006) (as matter of first impression, insurer's tender of policy limits to insured in response to insured's filing of civil remedy notice, after initiation of lawsuit against insured but before entry of excess judgment, does not preclude common-law cause of action against insurer for third-party bad faith); *Menchise v. Liberty Mut. Ins. Co.*, 932 So. 2d 1130 (Fla. Dist. Ct. App. 2006) (negligence is relevant to question of good faith by insurer with regard to settlement of claims, and genuine issues of material fact existed as to automobile liability insurer's good faith in responding to accident victim's settlement offer, where insurer had misplaced settlement offer and ignored some of its conditions without explanation); *John J. Jerue Truck Broker, Inc. v. Insurance Co. of N. Am.*, 646 So. 2d 780 (Fla. Dist. Ct. App. 1994) (existence of reasonable basis for disputing coverage does not preclude liability for violation of Florida Unfair Claim Settlement Practices statute); *Baranowski v. GEICO Gen. Ins. Co.*, 385 F. Supp. 3d 1267 (M.D. Fla. 2019), *aff'd*, 806 Fed. Appx. 971 (11th Cir. 2020) (granting insurer's motion for summary judgment where insurer acted diligently in contacting claimant's attorney with settlement offers, promptly responded to all of claimant's attorney's requests for information, and made frequent attempts to communicate with claimant's attorney, even though said attorney was not responsive or available; while insurer made some mistakes that were negligent, negligence without more did not amount to bad faith); *Feijoo v. Geico Gen. Ins. Co.* 137 F. Supp. 3d 1320 (S.D. Fla. 2015), *aff'd*, 678 Fed. Appx. 862 (11th Cir. 2017) (granting insurer's motion for summary judgment where insurer's decision to proceed to trial after pursing reasonable settlement could not be characterized as bad faith; negligence is relevant to bad faith claim only if negligence is cause of excessive judgment).

—Answering a question certified by a federal district court, the Georgia Supreme Court, in *Trinity Outdoor, LLC v. Central Mut. Ins. Co.*, 285 Ga. 583, 679 S.E.2d 10 (2009), held that an insurer may not be held liable for bad faith failure to settle a claim in the absence of a judgment against the insured in excess of policy limits.

Applying Georgia law, a federal district court in *Hulsey v. The Travelers Indem. Co. of Am.*, 460 F. Supp. 2d 1332 (N.D. Ga. 2006), denied summary judgment in an action by the driver of an insured vehicle who alleged that the insurer had negligently and in bad faith failed to honor a demand for the payment of policy limits by an injured passenger. The court held that there was a genuine issue of fact as to whether the insurer knew that the driver of the insured vehicle was a permissive driver prior to the expiration of the time-limited settlement demand. See also *Hughes v. First Acceptance Ins. Co. of Ga.*, 343 Ga. App. 693, 808 S.E.2d 103 (2017), *rev'd*, 305 Ga. 489, 826 S.E.2d 71 (2019) (administrator of insured's estate alleged that insurer negligently or in bad faith failed to settle in case that subsequently went to trial and resulted in $5.3 million judgment against insured's estate for injuries sustained by others in car accident caused by insured; court found that genuine issues of material fact existed as to whether insurer acted reasonably in failing to respond to time-limited offer to settled within policy limits where attorney for insurer admitted that offer-to-settle letters had been inadvertently placed in medical records and no follow-up occurred; lower court erred in finding that there must be evidence on record that insurer knew it could settle all claims against insured within policy limits because insurer may in good faith and without notification to other claimants settle part of multiple claims against insured even though such settlements deplete or exhaust policy limits). The Georgia Supreme Court reversed the opinion in *Hughes v. First Acceptance Ins. Co. of Ga.*, *supra*, concluding:

> [A]n insurer's duty to settle arises only when the injured party presents a valid offer to settle within the insured's policy limits. . . . [W]e conclude that the injured parties presented to the insurer a valid offer to settle within the insured's policy limits but that the offer did not include any deadline for accepting the offer. Based on the undisputed evidence, we conclude as a matter of law that the insurer did not act unreasonably in failing to accept the offer before it was withdrawn by the injured parties.

305 Ga. 489, 489–90, 826 S.E.2d 71, 73 (2019).

In *Kemper v. Equity Ins. Co.*, 396 F. Supp. 3d 1299 (N.D. Ga. 2019), *rev'd & remanded*, 823 Fed. Appx. 900 (11th Cir. 2020), the federal district court held that the insurer did not commit bad faith failure to settle when it sent the third-party claimant a settlement check for the $25,000 policy limits with a letter demanding that she hold the funds in escrow in the event medical providers placed a lien on the settlement. The court held that the insurer had complied with the "safe harbor" rule from *S. Gen. Ins. Co. v. Wellstar Health Sys., Inc.*, 315 Ga. App. 26, 726 S.E.2d 488 (2012), under which an insurer can properly require a claimant to placed funds in escrow to satisfy any potential lien. On appeal, however, the Eleventh Circuit reversed and remanded for trial, finding too many outstanding factual issues related to the plaintiff's failure-to-settle claim and the parties' conduct surrounding the escrow request to justify summary judgment for the insurer. The court noted that Ga. Code Ann. §9–11–67.1, passed after the accident at issue in *Kemper*, provides clarification on requirements for demand letters that "provides needed guidance to future parties embroiled in similar disputes." 823 Fed. Appx. at 901 n.1.

—In *Anastasi v. Fidelity Nat'l Title Ins. Co.*, 137 Haw. 104, 366 P.3d 160 (2016), the Supreme Court of Hawaii upheld the intermediate appellate court's denial of a title insurer's motion for summary judgment on its insured's bad faith claim. The court held that it was a question of fact whether the insurer unreasonably prolonged litigation over an allegedly forged warranty deed, rather than paying its insured's claim, in light of evidence that it knew for months that the deed had been forged.

—In *Haddick v. Valor Ins. Co.*, 198 Ill. 2d 409, 763 N.E.2d 299 (2001), the Illinois Supreme Court, affirming the reversal of dismissal, held that an insurer's duty to settle arises when the claimant makes a demand for the policy limits and when a finding of liability and recovery in excess of policy limits is reasonably probable. (The court rejected the insurer's contention that the duty arises only when a lawsuit is filed.) Accord *Rogers Cartage Co. v. Travelers Indem. Co.*, 2018 IL App. (5th) 160098, 103 N.E.3d 504 (2018), *appeal denied*, 108 N.W.3d 885 (Ill. 2018) (see discussions in §§2.38, 2.45). Compare *West Side Salvage, Inc v. RSUI Indem. Co.*, 215 F. Supp. 3d 728 (S.D. Ill. 2016), *aff'd on other grounds*, 878 F.3d 219 (7th Cir. 2017) (summary judgment in favor of insurer on bad faith claim for failure to settle underlying litigation; duty to settle arises when insurer knows claims will exceed policy limits and such knowledge overlaps in time with opportunity to settle in manner that resolves all claims against insured). And in *O'Neill v. Gallant Ins. Co.*, 769 N.E.2d 100 (Ill. Ct. App. 2002), an Illinois Court of Appeals affirmed jury awards of $710,063 in actual damages and $2.3 million in punitive damages in a case involving the insurer's refusal to settle an automobile accident liability claim for the $20,000 policy limits. The decision includes a detailed discussion of the evidentiary factors probative of insurance bad faith in the third-party context. See also *Powell v. American Serv. Ins. Co.*, 2014 IL App (1st) 123643, 7 N.E.3d 11, 379 Ill. Dec.

585 (2014) (affirming dismissal of claim of automobile insurer's bad faith refusal to settle claim; although complaint sufficiently alleged facts to establish reasonable probability of recovery in excess of policy limits, complaint failed to plead facts to establish reasonable probability of finding of liability against insured); *Iowa Physicians' Clinic Med. Found. v. Physicians Ins. Co. of Wisc.*, 547 F.3d 810 (7th Cir. 2008) (Illinois law; insurer of physician insured owed no duty to noninsured medical clinic operator which held medical malpractice policy on insured's behalf).

In *In re CFB Liquidating Corp.*, 581 B.R. 317 (Bkrtcy. N.D. Cal. 2017), *aff'd*, 591 B.R. 396 (N.D. Cal. 2018) (Illinois law), a federal bankruptcy court applying Illinois law reviewed at length a set of insurer actions that it determined constituted vexatious delay. The court applied the standard of 215 Ill. Comp. Stat. 5/155, which permits a court to award attorney's fees, costs, and a penalty amount for an insurer's "vexatious and unreasonable" delay in settling a claim. The court held that the standard for liability under §155 is "objectively unreasonable conduct that inures an insured." 581 B.R. at 331 (internal quotation marks omitted). The insurer at first agreed that no coverage issues remained concerning third-party asbestos claims. However, the insurer later retained new counsel who raised extensive new coverage issues (which the court held were estopped), made misrepresentations concerning evidence, and otherwise undertook conduct that the court found amounted to vexatious delay. The court awarded the insured's trustee in bankruptcy attorney's fees, costs, a $60,000 statutory penalty, and prejudgment interest. See §§2.70, 2.72.

—In *Nungesser v. Bryant*, 283 Kan. 550, 153 P.3d 1277 (2007), the Kansas Supreme Court held, as a matter of first impression, that an insured may not sue his or her liability insurer for negligent or bad faith failure to settle until the tort claim against the insured has been reduced to judgment.

In *Progressive Nw. Ins. Co. v. Gant*, 957 F.3d 1144 (10th Cir. 2020) (Kansas law), the Tenth Circuit predicted that the Kansas Supreme Court would hold that an insurer did not breach a duty to its insured by failing to investigate and discover whether the insured had more coverage with another insurer. The court affirmed summary judgment for the insurer on a claim of failure to settle.

—Applying Kentucky law in *Philadelphia Indem. Ins. Co. v. Youth Alive, Inc.*, 732 F.3d 645 (6th Cir. 2013), the Sixth Circuit affirmed the dismissal of the insured's counterclaims in a commercial excess liability insurer's action seeking a declaration of non-coverage. The insurer's interpretation of the insured's policies was not so obviously implausible as to give rise to a bad faith claim, the court held, nor did a bad faith claim arise from the insurer's conduct in refusing to settle claims pending the outcome of its declaratory judgment action.

—Under Louisiana law, the Fifth Circuit held in *Stanley v. Trinchard*, 500 F.3d 411 (5th Cir. 2007), summary judgment was precluded by fact issues as to the insurer's good faith in settling a civil rights action against its insured for policy limits without negotiating a full release for the insured, and as to whether insurer had acted in good faith in allegedly failing to advise the insured of the extent of its continued liability following the settlement.

In *Kelly v. State Farm Fire & Casualty Co.*, 169 So. 3d 328 (La. 2015), the Louisiana Supreme Court answered questions certified to it by the U.S. Court of Appeals for the Fifth Circuit. The Fifth Circuit affirmed an award of summary judgment for State Farm, but then on rehearing withdrew its opinion and certified the following question to the Louisiana high court: (1) "Can an insurer be found liable for a bad-faith failure-to-settle claim under [La. Rev. Stat. Ann. §22:1973(A)] when the insurer never received a firm settlement offer"? Under an automobile liability policy, State Farm had failed to respond to a letter from its insured submitting medical bills of an injured third party and proposing payment of policy limits. At trial, the insured was found liable for an amount far in excess of the policy limits.

State Farm argued that Louisiana's claims settlement practices statute did not impose bad faith because it had not received a "firm settlement offer."

The Louisiana Supreme Court answered in the affirmative. It approved the Fifth Circuit's holding in *Stanley v. Trinchard, supra*, that an insured's cause of action under §22:1973(A) is not limited by the prohibited acts listed in §22:1973(B), reasoning that §22:1973(A) codified a cause of action previously recognized by the courts. The court further held that a "firm settlement offer" is not required as a condition for finding an insurer acted in bad faith by failing to "make a reasonable effort to settle claims with the insured," as required by §22:1973(A).

The Louisiana high court rejected State Farm's argument that *Smith v. Audubon Ins. Co.*, 679 So. 2d 372 (La. 1996), compelled a different conclusion. In *Smith*, the court had stated that an insurer's failure to compromise litigation "just because the claimant offers to settle" is not itself proof of bad faith. The Fifth Circuit noted that *Smith* was decided before §22:1973 and its predecessor statute were enacted. It further noted that the factors listed in *Smith* as relevant to a determination of bad faith did not include receipt of a settlement offer. The *Kelly* court did say that the *Smith* factors should be applied to "measure whether an insurer has made a 'reasonable effort to settle claims'" under §22:1973(A). Based on the Louisiana court's response to its questions, the Fifth Circuit vacated its opinion affirming summary judgment for State Farm and remanded to the federal district court. *Kelly v. State Farm Fire & Casualty Co.*, 605 Fed. Appx. 420 (5th Cir. 2015) (unpublished).

Lest its opinion be taken to create too much latitude for bad faith claimants, the *Kelly* court stated in a footnote that

> we believe it is appropriate to reiterate that [La. Rev. Stat. Ann. §22:1973] should be strictly construed. A strict application of the statute does not contemplate gamesmanship, such as having unrealistic offers . . .

> presented through carefully ambiguous demands cou-
> pled with sudden-death timetables in order to "set up"
> the insurer for an excess liability judgment.

169 So. 3d 328, 344 n.34 (citations and internal quotation
marks omitted). For a discussion of the second certified
question, see §1.55, *supra.*

—Despite a large excess judgment, a Massachusetts Appeals Court held in *Mayer v. Medical Malpractice Joint
Underwriting Ass'n*, 40 Mass. App. Ct. 266, 663 N.E.2d 274
(1996), the insurer breached no duty in failing to settle
within policy limits, where defense counsel had repeatedly
advised the insurer that there was at least a 50 percent
chance that the insured would prevail in the underlying action; where this advice was grounded on the opinions of
three medical experts; and where the defense counsel had
further advised the insurer that any adverse verdict would
be well within policy limits. Compare *Hopkins v. Liberty
Mut. Ins. Co.*, 434 Mass. 556, 750 N.E.2d 943 (2001) (affirming judgment for claimant and multiplying damages and
awarding attorneys' fees pursuant to Massachusetts Unfair
Business Practices Act).

In *Rawan v. Continental Cas. Co.*, 483 Mass. 654, 136
N.E.3d 327 (2019), homeowners (claimants) brought a
claim for bad faith against an engineer's professional liability insurer after the engineer failed to design their home to
state building code standards. The insurance policy contained a consent-to-settle clause, and the insurer failed to
convince the insured to settle. After trial, the insurer paid
up to the policy limit and the insured paid the remainder of
the claim. The claimants then brought a bad faith claim
against the insurer for failure to settle. The court held that
a consent-to-settle provision in the insurance contract did
not violate the insurer's duty to effectuate a prompt, fair,
and equitable settlement under Mass. Gen. Laws Ann. ch.
176D §3(9)(f). However, the insurer must still conduct a reasonable investigation and engage in good faith settlement

attempts. The court affirmed summary judgment in favor of the insurer where the insurer had thoroughly investigated the underlying facts, informed the insured of the results of its investigation, encouraged mediation, explained the vulnerabilities to the insured, and encouraged the insured to settle. The court found that any deficiencies in the insurer's behavior did not cause harm to the claimants, especially because the judgment was paid in full by the insurer and the insured.

In *Chiulli v. Liberty Mut. Ins., Inc.*, 97 Mass. App. 248, 146 N.E.3d 471 (2020), *review denied*, 485 Mass. 1102, 150 N.E.3d 1119 (2020), the appeals court held that the trial court erred when it found that insurer Liberty Mutual did not act willfully or knowingly when it violated Massachusetts' statutory settlement requirement under Mass. Gen. Laws ch. 93A. The court found that the insurer had a duty to offer settlement once the insured's liability became reasonably clear following closing arguments at trial. The court rejected the insurer's argument that its liability had to be "clear" instead of "reasonably clear" before it was required to tender a settlement offer. The insurer made its insured wait through Thanksgiving and Christmas, and internal documents showed that the delay was an intentional effort to use the insured's lack of funds to leverage a more favorable settlement. The court remanded for determination of whether a statutory penalty of 2 to 3 times the damages award would be proper.

—In *Christian Builders, Inc. v. The Cincinnati Ins. Co.*, 501 F. Supp. 2d 1224 (D. Minn. 2007), a federal district court applying Minnesota law held that a liability insurer did not fail to evaluate the case fairly when it did not offer full policy limits in settlement of a wrongful death case despite the insured's clear liability, where it relied on the much lower settlement evaluation of a competent and experienced defense attorney. Nor, the court held, was the trial judge's refusal to remit the excess verdict on a posttrial motion evidence that the insurer's failure to offer the policy limits had been in bad faith.

—In *State Farm Mut. Auto. Ins. Co. v. Freyer*, 372 Mont. 191, 312 P.3d 403 (Mont. 2013), the Supreme Court of Montana explained that the determination whether an insurer acted in good faith in refusing a settlement offer on a third-party claim has to be made on a case-to-case basis, and the question is whether the insurer's grounds for contesting the third party's theories of liability were reasonable under the law as it existed during the relevant time period. See also *West for Lee v. United Servs. Auto. Ass'n*, 384 P.3d 58 (Mont. 2016) (granting summary judgment to automobile insurer who had reasonable grounds for conditioning settlement payment for policy limit on obtaining waiver of liens from TRICARE (government insurance program for military members), which provided medical insurance for injured third party).

—In *Princeton Ins. Co. v. Qureshi*, 380 N.J. Super. 495, 882 A.2d 993 (2005), a professional liability insurer had brought an action against insureds and their assignee seeking a declaratory judgment that the policy provided no coverage for a physician's professional corporation, and the assignee had counterclaimed alleging bad faith in refusing to settle a claim against the corporation for policy limits. Affirming summary judgment for the assignee, a New Jersey Superior Court, Appellate Division, held that the insurer had acted in bad faith by refusing to settle a claim against the corporation for policy limits unless the victim also settled a claim against the physician for a separate policy limit.

—Under New York law, it was held in *Greenidge v. Allstate Ins. Co.*, 446 F.3d 356 (2d Cir. 2006), that an insurer does not breach its duty of good faith when it makes a mistake in judgment or even when it behaves negligently, only when it demonstrates a gross disregard for its insured's interests and deliberately or recklessly fails to place on equal footing the interests of its insured with its own interests when considering a settlement offer. In the present case, the court held, the liability insurer did not breach its duty of good faith when it rejected the victims' offer to settle for a single policy limit of $300,000 if the insurer consented to a declaratory judgment action by the victims to determine whether injuries from lead paint triggered a second policy limit. See also *Doherty v. Merchants Mut. Ins. Co.*, 74 A.D.3d 1870, 903 N.Y.S.2d 836 (2010) (affirming summary judgment over strong dissent that carefully explains elements of insurers' settlement duties under New York law); *Kumar v. American Transit Ins. Co.*, 57 A.D.3d 1449, 869 N.Y.S.2d 715 (2008) (plaintiffs failed to establish that they lost actual opportunity to settle at time when all serious doubts about liability had been removed, or that insurer engaged in pattern of behavior evincing knowing indifference to probability that insureds would be held personally accountable for large judgment).

—Under Pennsylvania law, it was held in *Birth Ctr. v. St. Paul Cos.*, 727 A.2d 1144 (Pa. Super. Ct. 1999), an insurer's eventual payment of an excess verdict does not necessarily operate to extinguish a bad faith claim. The court wrote: "[W]here an insurer exposes its insured to a verdict in excess of the insured's policy limits without a real and substantial possibility of prevailing, an insurer cannot avoid all liability for bad faith simply by paying the excess judgment if the insured can prove it has suffered other legally cognizable damages . . . ." 727 A.2d at 1147. More recently, a federal district court interpreting Pennsylvania law cited *Birth Center, supra,* and other cases to hold that a contractual bad faith claim based on an insurer's handling of settlement of claims against its insured may be premised on negligence or unreasonableness and "does not require proof of recklessness or purposefulness." *McMahon v. Medical Protective Co.*, 92 F. Supp. 3d 367, 380, *recon. denied,* 2015 WL 4633698 (W.D. Pa. 2015) (after reviewing "somewhat tortuous history" of Pennsylvania law of insurer bad faith, adopting standards set forth in *DeWalt v. Ohio Casualty Ins. Co.*, 513 F. Supp. 2d 287 (E.D. Pa. 2007)). The *McMahon* court also predicted that "entry of an excess verdict is not a prerequisite for a third-party bad faith claim under Pennsylvania common law." 92 F. Supp. 3d at 383 (cited in *Wolfe v. Allstate Prop. & Ins. Co.*, 790 F.3d 487, 497 n.9 (3d Cir. 2015) (discussed in §§2.73 and 4.19A)). In *Wolfe, supra,* the Third Circuit held that under Pennsylvania law, an insurer has no duty to consider the possibility for punitive damages if a case goes to trial when making settlement offers because Pennsylvania public policy prohibits insuring for punitive damages.

In *Ironshore Specialty Ins. Co. v. Conemaugh Health Sys., Inc.*, 423 F. Supp. 3d 139 (W.D. Pa. 2019) (Pennsylvania law), an excess insurer brought a declaratory judgment action against the insured, arguing it was not liable for an excess judgment in a claim for medical malpractice. The insured counterclaimed for bad faith under Pa. Cons. Stat. §8371 for the insurer's handling of litigation in the medical malpractice case and for bringing the declaratory judgment action. The court, applying *Birth Center, supra,* stated that the insurer could not avoid a bad faith claim simply because it paid the excess judgment in the malpractice suit. The court refused to dismiss the counterclaim for bad faith where the insurer failed to engage in the settlement of the medical malpractice case, despite being given adequate warning by the insured that an excess judgment was likely, and the insured suffered damages by being forced to defend against the declaratory judgment action.

—In *Asermely v. Allstate Ins. Co.*, 728 A.2d 461 (R.I. 1999), the Rhode Island Supreme Court adopted what is in effect a standard of strict liability in third-party cases. The court wrote as follows: "[I]f it has been afforded reasonable notice and if a plaintiff has made a reasonable written offer to a defendant's insurer to settle within the policy limits, the insurer is obligated to seriously consider such an offer. If the insurer declines to settle the case within the policy limits, it does so at its peril in the event that a trial results in a judgment that exceeds the policy limits, including interest. If such a judgment is sustained on appeal or is unappealed, the insurer is liable for the amount that exceeds the policy limits, unless it can show that the insured was unwilling to accept the offer of settlement. The insurer's duty is a fiduciary obligation to act in the best interests of the insured. Even if the insurer believes in good faith that it has a legitimate defense . . . , it must assume the risk of miscalculation if the ultimate judgment should exceed policy limits." 728 A.2d at 464. In *DeMarco v. Travelers Ins. Co.*, 26 A.3d 585 (R.I. 2011), the Rhode Island Supreme Court amplified its explanation of the insurer's settlement duties in third-party cases, and, as a matter of first impression, applied that standard to a case involving multiple claimants with claims exceeding policy limits.

Distinguishing *Asermely, supra*, see *Imperial Casualty & Indem. Co. v. Bellini*, 947 A.2d 886 (R.I. 2008) (emphasizing that insurer is entitled, as in present case, to dispute claim that is "fairly debatable"); *Clauson v. New England Ins. Co.*, 254 F.3d 331 (1st Cir. 2001) (rule of *Asermely* was inapplicable in present case because insurer demonstrated that insured had been unwilling to accept offer of settlement).

—In *Tadlock Painting Co. v. Maryland Casualty Co.*, 473 S.E.2d 52 (S.C. 1996), the South Carolina Supreme Court, answering a certified question from the Fourth Circuit, gave first-time recognition to the tort of bad faith in connection with the handling of third-party claims. (As noted in book §1.33, South Carolina recognized the tort of first-party bad faith as long ago as 1983.)

—In *Johnson v. Tennessee Farmers Mut. Ins. Co.*, 205 S.W.3d 365 (Tenn. 2006), the Tennessee Supreme Court, reinstating a judgment on a jury verdict in favor of the insured, wrote in part as follows: "Bad faith refusal to settle is defined, in part, as an insurer's disregard or demonstrable indifference toward the interests of its insured. [Citation omitted.] This indifference may be proved circumstantially. [Citation omitted.] Bad faith on the part of the insurer can be proved by facts that tend to show 'a willingness on the part of the insurer to gamble with the insured's money in an attempt to save its own money or any intentional regard of the financial interests of the plaintiff in the hope of escaping full liability imposed upon it by its policy.' [Citation omitted.] If the claim exceeds the policy limits, then the insurer's conduct is subject to close scrutiny because there is a potential conflict of interest between the insurer and the insured.' [Citation omitted.]" 205 S.W.3d at 370.

—Affirming judgment on the pleadings for the insurer, the Fifth Circuit held, in *St. Paul Fire & Marine Ins. Co. v. Convalescent Servs., Inc.*, 193 F.3d 340 (5th Cir. 1999) (Texas law), that an insurer is not required to consider the possibility of an award of uncovered punitive damages in evaluating settlement offers.

A Texas Court of Appeals in May 1994 held that an excess insurer had no duty to accept a reasonable settlement offer until its excess coverage had been triggered by an agreement or determination of the primary insurer's liability for its policy limits. *Emscor Mfg., Inc. v. Alliance Ins. Group*, 879 S.W.2d 894 (Tex. Ct. App. 1994).

—In an *en banc* decision, the Washington Supreme Court held in *Matsyuk v. State Farm Fire & Casualty Co.*, 173 Wash. 2d 643, 272 P.3d 802 (2012), that the allegation that the tortfeasor's auto insurer had refused to effectuate an agreed liability settlement between the tortfeasor and the insured on behalf of the tortfeasor unless the insured released her claims as a PIP insured against the insurer stated a viable bad faith claim. See also *Miller v. Kenny*, 180 Wash. App. 772, 325 P.3d 278 (2014). In *Berkshire Hathaway Homestate Ins. Co. v. SQI, Inc.*, 132 F. Supp. 3d 1275 (W.D.Wash. 2015), *appeal dismissed* (9th Cir. 2017) (Washington law), the federal district court observed that Washington law concerning an insurer's duty to settle "contains almost no guidance" and that "lack of clarity in the law gives the court pause," but concluded that there was no insurer bad faith in this case because the insurer's failure to settle was grounded in a reasonable belief that no coverage existed under the policy in question. *Id.* at 1291–92 (citing *Tank v. State Farm Fire & Casualty Co.*, 105 Wash. 2d 381, 715 P.2d 1133 (1986)).

—In *State ex rel. State Auto Prop. Ins. Cos. v. Stucky*, 239 W. Va. 729, 806 S.E.2d 160 (2017), the court held that the insured could not maintain a bad-faith action against its liability insurer for failure to settle a third-party claim against the insured where the insurer defended its insured and paid a settlement within policy limits to the third-party claimants. The plaintiff insured had charged that the insurer delayed investigating its claim and defending and indemnifying the insured. The insurer had initially filed a declaratory judgment proceeding contesting coverage.

—In *Sta-Rite Indus. Inc. v. Zurich Re (U.K.) Ltd.*, 178 F.3d 883 (7th Cir. 1999), the Seventh Circuit concluded that under Wisconsin law no good faith duty is owed to an insured by an insurer who has only a nonexclusive right to associate in the settlement and defense of a claim.

—For an expression of the common view that an insurer cannot incur bad faith liability for a failure to settle in the absence of a duty to defend, see *International Surplus Lines Ins. Co. v. University of Wyo.*, 850 F. Supp. 1509 (D. Wyo. 1994) (Wyoming law).

§2.9 c. Failure To Defend

—In *Blackburn v. Fidelity & Deposit Co.*, 667 So. 2d 661 (Ala. 1995), the Alabama Supreme Court, reversing summary judgment, held that the test in bad faith failure to defend cases is not the "directed verdict rule" (since the duty to defend is broader than the duty to indemnify), but rather whether the insurer either failed to investigate the claim properly or failed to subject the results of that investigation to a fair review.

In *Aetna Casualty & Sur. Co. v. Mitchell Bros.*, 814 So. 2d 191 (Ala. 2001), it was held that although an insurer who undertakes the defense of its insured under a reservation of rights is normally subject to an enhanced duty of good faith, this enhanced duty is not imposed where it is the insured's chosen counsel who in fact controls the defense.

Breach of the enhanced duty of good faith that is owed by an insurer who undertakes the defense of its insured under a reservation of rights sounds in contract not in tort, the Alabama Supreme Court held in *Twin City Fire Ins. Co. v. Colonial Life & Accident Ins. Co.*, 839 So. 2d 614, 2002 WL 1353355 (Ala. 2002). See also *State Farm & Casualty Co. v. Myrick*, 611 F. Supp. 2d 1287 (M.D. Ala. 2009) (insurer did not breach its enhanced duty of good faith by maintaining during settlement negotiations that insureds' personal liability umbrella policy did not cover conversion claims and by refusing to contribute funds to settlement, where insurer challenged coverage on every claim and did not wrest control of ultimate settlement decision from insureds).

—Concerning conflicts of interest where a liability insurer defends under a reservation of rights, and the Alaska rule entitling an insured to select independent counsel at the insurer's expense, see *Great Divide Ins. Co. v. Carpenter ex rel. Reed*, 79 P.3d 599 (Alaska 2003); *CHI of Alaska v. Employers Reinsurance Corp.*, 844 P.2d 1113 (Alaska 1993) (extending holding of *Continental Ins. Co. v. Bayless & Roberts, Inc.*, 608 P.2d 281 (Alaska 1980)).

—Representing Arizona law's recognition of a cause of action for bad faith failure to defend, see *Jobe v. International Ins. Co.*, 933 F. Supp. 844 (D. Ariz. 1995).

—Also recognizing that under California law an insurer may incur liability for breach of the implied covenant of good faith and fair dealing by failing to defend an insured, see *Harper Constr. Co. v. Nat'l Union Fire Ins. Co.*, 377 F. Supp. 3d 1134 (S.D. Cal. 2019), *appeal filed* (9th Cir. 2020); *Public Serv. Mut. Ins. Co. v. Liberty Surplus Ins. Corp.*, 205 F. Supp. 3d 1161 (E.D. Cal. 2016), *reconsideration denied*, 2017 WL 3601381 (E.D. Cal. 2017); *Greenwich Ins. Co. v. Rodgers*, 729 F. Supp. 2d 1158 (C.D. Cal. 2010); *The Raisin Bargaining Ass'n v. Hartford Casualty Ins. Co.*, 715

F. Supp. 2d 1079 (E.D. Cal. 2010); *Allstate Ins. Co. v. Vavasour*, 797 F. Supp. 785 (N.D. Cal. 1992) (California law). But see *Marentes v. State Farm Mut. Auto. Ins. Co.*, 224 F. Supp. 3d 891 (N.D. Cal. 2016) (insurer had no duty to defend in absence of coverage even where insurer had undertaken defense of insured). For discussions of the scope of the duty to defend under California law, see *Ameron Int'l Corp. v. Insurance Co. of the State of Pa.*, 50 Cal. 4th 1370, 118 Cal. Rptr. 3d 95, 242 P.3d 1020 (2010); *Waller v. Truck Ins. Exch.*, 11 Cal. 4th 1, 44 Cal. Rptr. 2d 370 (1995); *Montrose Chem. v. Superior Court (Canadian Universal Ins. Co.)*, 6 Cal. 4th 287, 24 Cal. Rptr. 2d 467 (1993); *Gray v. Zurich Ins. Co.*, 65 Cal. 2d 263, 54 Cal. Rptr. 104 (1966); *Shade Foods, Inc. v. Innovative Prods. Sales & Marketing, Inc.*, 78 Cal. App. 4th 847, 93 Cal. Rptr. 2d 364 (2000); *Eigner v. Worthington*, 57 Cal. App. 4th 188, 66 Cal. Rptr. 2d 808 (1997); *Campbell v. Superior Court (Farmers Ins. Co.)*, 44 Cal. App. 4th 1308, 45 Cal. App. 4th 1232a, 52 Cal. Rptr. 2d 385 (1996); *Ticor Title Ins. Co. v. Employers Ins. Co.*, 40 Cal. App. 4th 1699, 48 Cal. Rptr. 2d 368 (1995); *Hartford Accident & Indem. Co. v. Superior Court*, 23 Cal. App. 4th 1774, 29 Cal. Rptr. 2d 32 (1994); *Amato v. Mercury Casualty Co.*, 18 Cal. App. 4th 1784, 23 Cal. Rptr. 2d 73 (1993), *after remand*, 51 Cal. App. 4th 1, 58 Cal. Rptr. 2d 784 (1996); *Marglen Indus., Inc. v. Aetna Casualty & Sur. Co.*, 4 Cal. App. 4th 414, 5 Cal. Rptr. 2d 659 (1992); *Love v. Fire Ins. Exch.*, 221 Cal. App. 3d 1136, 271 Cal. Rptr. 246 (1990); *Harper Constr. Co. v. Nat'l Union Fire Ins. Co.*, *supra*; *Staefa Control-Sys., Inc. v. St. Paul Fire & Marine Ins. Co.*, 847 F. Supp. 1460 (N.D. Cal. 1994) (California law); *Allstate Ins. Co. v. Salahutdin*, 815 F. Supp. 1309 (N.D. Cal. 1992).

For a discussion of California law on the options available to excess insurers when presented with a settlement offer that has been approved by the insured and the primary insurer, see *Teleflex Med. Inc. v. National Union Fire Ins. Co.*, 851 F.3d 976 (9th Cir. 2017). The court rejected an excess insurer's motion to vacate judgment on a bad faith claim where the excess insurer had delayed its response with respect to its obligation to accept the settlement or assume defense. The court emphasized that when an excess insurer is presented with a settlement offer that has been approved by the insured and the primary insurer, "[t]he excess insurer must (1) approve the proposed settlement, (2) reject it and take over the defense, or (3) reject it, decline to take over the defense, and face a potential lawsuit by the insured seeking contribution toward the settlement." *Id.* at 979.

In *Pulte Home Corp. v. American Safety Indem. Co.*, 14 Cal. App. 5th 1086, 223 Cal. Rptr. 3d 47 (2017), *reh'g denied, review denied* (2018) an insurer brought an appeal after a trial court awarded $1.4 million in compensatory and punitive damages to a general contractor/additional insured who had brought suit against the insurer to recover the costs of providing its own defense against a homeowner's construction defect lawsuit. A California appellate court affirmed the substantive ruling that the insurer's failure to defend was unreasonable and without proper cause, and therefore in bad faith, where (1) ambiguities in policy language should have been construed in favor of the reasonable expectations of the additional insured and any doubt as to whether there was a duty to defend should have been resolved in favor of the additional insured; (2) additional insured pleaded facts that arguably brought it within policy coverage; and (3) insurer was primarily looking out for its own interests, which was evidenced in testimony of the insurer's claims representatives and corporate counsel that the insurer routinely denied claims of additional insureds based on restrictive policy interpretations. The court remanded the case for recalculation of attorney's fees and punitive damages.

In *Swanson v. State Farm Gen. Ins. Co.*, 219 Cal. App. 4th 1153, 162 Cal. Rptr. 3d 477 (2013), a California Court of Appeal affirmed summary judgment, holding: (1) a liability insurer did not need to continue to pay insured's independent counsel after withdrawing its reservation of rights; and (2) the insurer did not waive its right to retake control of the defense by counsel of its choosing by failing to expressly reserve that right.

In *Amato v. Mercury Casualty Co.*, 53 Cal. App. 4th 825, 61 Cal. Rptr. 2d 909 (1997), a California Court of Appeal held, as a matter of first impression, that where an insurer tortiously breaches its duty to defend and the insured suffers a default judgment, the insurer is liable for that judgment even if it is later determined that the underlying claim was not covered by the policy. In *Blue Ridge Ins. Co. v. Jacobsen*, 25 Cal. 4th 489, 106 Cal. Rptr. 2d 535 (2001), the California Supreme Court held that an insurer who defends an insured under a reservation of rights may recover settlement payments when it is later determined that the policy did not cover the underlying claims. Concerning an insurer's right to seek reimbursement for costs incurred in defending claims that were not even potentially covered by the policy, see *Buss v. Superior Court (Transamerica Ins. Co.)*, 16 Cal. 4th 35, 65 Cal. Rptr. 2d 366 (1997).

In *Dalrymple v. United Servs. Auto. Ass'n*, 40 Cal. App. 4th 497, 46 Cal. Rptr. 2d 845 (1995), a California Court of Appeal emphasized that an insurer can erroneously dispute coverage without acting in bad faith, and held that in the present case, where the material facts were undisputed, the trial court should not have submitted the issue to a jury, but should have ruled as a matter of law that the insurer had had reasonable grounds for filing a declaratory judgment action. See also *Bernstein v. Consolidated Am. Ins. Co.*, 37 Cal. App. 4th 763, 43 Cal. Rptr. 2d 817 (1995). Compare *Century Sur. Co. v. Polisso*, 139 Cal. App. 4th 922, 43 Cal. Rptr. 3d 468 (2006) (existence of "genuine dispute" regarding existence of duty to defend does not justify insurer's refusal to do so); *Harper Constr. Co. v. Nat'l Union Fire Ins. Co., supra* (duty to defend extends to claims that are merely potentially covered in light of facts disclosed; summary judgment granted in favor of insurer on breach of duty to defend where government demanded that its contractor investigate and fix cracks in building that was recently built by contractor on government project; while insurer's duty to defend would be triggered under policy by initiation of suit, which was defined as civil legal proceeding, it was not triggered in this case because demand by government to investigate and fix damage was not arguably under definition of suit); *Saarman Constr., Ltd. v. Ironshore Specialty Ins. Co.*, 230 F. Supp. 3d 1068 (N.D. Cal. 2017) (defense of insured is excused only when complaint raises no single issue that could conceivably bring it within scope of coverage; insurer has duty to defend mixed actions if some claims are potentially covered even if action includes uncovered claims); *Perkins v. Allstate Ins. Co.*, 63 F. Supp. 2d 1164 (C.D. Cal. 1999) (California law; insurer was not entitled to summary judgment on bad faith claim where insurer had failed to investigate before refusing to defend, even if reasonable investigation would have revealed facts precluding coverage). But see *Durment v. Burlington Ins. Co.*, 820 Fed. Appx. 561 (9th Cir. 2020) (California law; insureds settled with claimant and assigned their claims against insurers to claimant in case in which insurers failed to defend insureds from amended complaint tendered on eve of trial; court held that claimant could not recover settlement amounts from insurers without establishing coverage; court stated general rule that insurer that breaches duty to defend is not liable for settlement costs outside scope of insurer's indemnification duty).

By assuming the defense of its insured under a reservation of rights, the insurer did not waive its right to deny coverage after the discovery process revealed undisputed facts negating coverage, the court held in *Ringler Assocs. v. Maryland Casualty Co.*, 80 Cal. App. 4th 1165, 96 Cal. Rptr. 2d 136 (2000). Also, the insurer was not required to obtain a declaratory judgment establishing that it had no duty to defend before withdrawing its defense (though such a course of action might have been prudent).

Concerning the circumstances under which a potential conflict of interest requires an employer to provide an insured with independent rather than staff counsel (per *San Diego Navy Fed. Credit Union v. Cumis Ins. Soc'y, Inc.*, 162 Cal. App. 3d 358, 208 Cal. Rptr. 494 (1984) and Cal. Civil Code §2860), see *Long v. Century Indem. Co.*, 163 Cal. App. 4th 1460, 78 Cal. Rptr. 3d 483 (2008); *Gray Cary Ware & Freidenrich v. Vigilant Ins. Co.*, 114 Cal. App. 4th 1185, 8 Cal. Rptr. 3d 475 (2004); *Gafcon, Inc. v. Ponsor & Assoc.*, 98 Cal. App. 4th 1388, 120 Cal. Rptr. 2d 392 (2002); *Frazier v. Superior Court*, 97 Cal. App. 4th 23, 188 Cal. Rptr. 2d 129 (2002); *Cybernet Ventures, Inc. v. Hartford Ins. Co. of the Midwest*, 168 Fed. Appx. 850 (9th Cir. 2006) (California law); *Citizens Ins. Co. of Am. v. Chief Digital Advisors*, ___ F. Supp. 3d ___, 2020 WL 6889174 (S.D. Cal. 2020); *Sovereign Gen'l Ins. Servs. v. National Casualty Co.*, 2008 WL 448041 (E.D. Cal. 2008). In *Citizens Ins. Co. of Am. v. Chief Digital Advisors*, *supra*, the federal district court denied the insurer's motion to dismiss the insured's claims of breach of contract and bad faith based on the insurer's failure to provide independent counsel. The court stated that the insured had properly alleged facts showing that counsel for the insurer could control the outcome of the coverage issue, and thus alleged an actual conflict of interest creating a duty to appoint independent counsel.

—In *Capstone Building Corp. v. American Motorists Ins. Co.*, 308 Conn. 760, 67 A.3d 961 (2013), the Connecticut Supreme Court undertook a detailed examination of an insurer's duty to defend, the consequences of a breach of that duty, and the standards for determining the reasonableness of the insured's subsequent settlement with the injured party. The court explained, *inter alia*, that a liability insurer has a duty to defend its insured if the pleadings allege a covered occurrence, even though facts outside the four corners of those pleadings indicate that the claim may be meritless or not covered.

—Applying the "reasonableness" standard applicable to

third-party claims under Colorado law, the Tenth Circuit, in *TPLC, Inc. v. United Nat'l Ins. Co.*, 44 F.3d 1484 (10th Cir. 1995), held that the insurer had not acted in bad faith in refusing to provide a defense based on an unsettled issue of law.

—See *Colony Ins. Co. v. G & E Tires & Serv., Inc.*, 777 So. 2d 1034 (Fla. Dist. Ct. App. 2000), concerning an insurer's right to reimbursement for costs incurred in connection with defense of claims where it is ultimately established there was no coverage.

In *Nationwide Mut. Fire Ins. Co. v. Beville*, 825 So. 2d 999 (Fla. Dist. Ct. App. 2002), it was held that failure of the insured to comply with a policy provision requiring notification of suits "as soon as practicable" was a "coverage defense" within the meaning of Florida's Claims Administration Statute, §627.426(2), which provides that an insurer is barred from asserting a "coverage defense" raised in a reservation of rights letter unless the insurer either obtains a non-waiver agreement from the insured or supplies independent counsel.

In *Travelers Indem. Co. of Ill. v. Royal Oak Enters., Inc.*, 344 F. Supp. 2d 1358 (M.D. Fla. 2004), the court held: (1) if a liability insurer acts negligently in carrying out its duty to defend, its conduct constitutes a breach of contract, entitling the insured to recover all naturally flowing damages; (2) if an insured establishes that the defense provided by the insurer was inadequate and that it was reasonable for the insured to retain its own attorneys, the insured is entitled to recover all reasonable costs and attorneys' fees incurred at the trial level, but an insurer is not required to pay the insured's expenses unless the insurer's actions "forced" the insured to engage his or her own attorneys; (3) under Florida law, a liability insurer does not breach its duty to defend by offering to defend only under a reservation of rights, but the insured may then reject defense and retain his or her own attorneys without jeopardizing the right to seek indemnification from the insurer for liability;

and (4) the mere existence of a conflict of interest is not enough to trigger an insurer's obligation to pay for independent counsel; there must be some evidence to suggest that the conflict actually affected counsel's representation in a way that could be said to elevate the insurer's interests over those of the insured.

Concerning the circumstances under which an insurer will be bound by a so-called *Coblentz* agreement, a negotiated final consent judgment entered against an insured which was not defended by its insurer, see *United States Fire Ins. Co. v. Hayden Bonded Storage Co.*, 930 So.2d 686 (Fla. Dist. Ct. App. 2006); *Chomat v. Northern Ins. Co. of New York*, 919 So. 2d 535 (Fla. Dist. Ct. App. 2006); *Wrangen v. Pennsylvania Lumbermans Mut. Ins. Co.*, 593 F. Supp. 2d 1273 (S.D. Fla. 2008). (Such agreements take their name from *Coblentz v. American Surety Co. of New York*, 416 F.2d 1059 (5th Cir. 1969).)

—In *Southern Guar. Ins. Co. v. Dowse*, 278 Ga. 674, 605 S.E.2d 27 (2004), the Georgia Supreme Court held that the release of an insured from liability as the result of a settlement reached with a third party following the insurer's refusal to defend did not relieve the insurer of its obligation to pay damages, though the insurer did not waive the right to contest the insured's assertion of coverage. See also *Transportation Ins. Co. v. Piedmont Constr. Group, LLC*, 301 Ga. App. 17, 686 S.E.2d 824 (2009) (trial court was justified in finding as matter of law that insurer had acted in bad faith in failing to defend insured, though existence of bad faith is ordinarily question for jury, where insurer offered in explanation only meritless reliance on business-risk clauses of CGL policy).

—In *Finley v. Home Ins. Co.*, 90 Haw. 25, 975 P.2d 1145 (1998), the Hawaii Supreme Court declined to adopt the rule that an insurer has an obligation to pay for independent counsel for the insured in cases where the insurer chooses to defend under a reservation of its right to contest its duty to indemnify the insured in the event of an adverse judgment. The court, thus rejecting the approach of *San Diego Navy Fed. Credit Union v. Cumis Ins. Soc'y, Inc., supra,* reasoned that "the best result is to refrain from interfering with the insurer's contractual right to select counsel and leave the resolution of the conflict to the integrity of retained defense counsel." 90 Haw. at 31–32, 975 P.2d at 1151–52. Concerning an "enhanced" good faith standard where an insurer defends under a reservaton of rights, see *Anastasi v. Fidelity Nat'l Title Ins. Co.,* 137 Haw. 104, 366 P.3d 160 (2016) (citing *Finley, supra*); *Delmonte v. State Farm Fire & Casualty Co.,* 90 Haw. 39, 975 P.2d 1159 (1999). And for a holding that the insurer's delay in agreeing to defend the insured raised a fact issue as to bad faith, see *CIM Ins. Corp. v. Masamitsu,* 74 F. Supp. 2d 975 (D. Haw. 1999). But see *Damon Key Leong Kupchak Hastert v. Westport Ins. Corp.,* 421 F. Supp. 3d 946 (D. Haw. 2019) (dismissing insured's bad faith claim where insurer's conduct in declining to defend against claim seeking sanctions from insured for contempt, which were clearly excluded under policy, was reasonable); *State Farm Fire & Casualty Co. v. GP West, Inc.,* 190 F. Supp. 3d 1003 (D. Haw. 2016) (granting summary judgment for insurer on claim of breach of covenant of good faith and fair dealing where insurer relied on governing law and reasonable interpretation of policy provisions in refusing to defend).

—In *Exterovich v. Kellogg,* 80 P.3d 1040 (Idaho 2003), the Idaho Supreme Court held that a liability insurer had a right to participate in an evidentiary hearing regarding damages after the insured city had reached a partial settlement on its liability and the trial court had found coverage. The insurer was a third-party defendant, the court reasoned, and even though it had initially denied a defense it could assert one after the court found coverage.

—It has been held that Illinois Insurance Code §155 (Ill. Rev. Stat. ch. 73, ¶ 767) applies not only to failures to pay claims (see supplement §1.27), but also to vexatious and unreasonable refusals to defend: *Richardson v. Illinois*

Power Co., 217 Ill. App. 3d 708, 577 N.E.2d 823 (1991). Applying Illinois law, the Seventh Circuit held, in *Transport Ins. Co. v. Post Express Co.*, 138 F.3d 1189 (7th Cir. 1998), that an insurer who defended under a reservation of rights and mishandled the defense was liable for the full amount of the judgment entered against its insured. See also *Rogers Cartage Co. v. Travelers Indem. Co.*, 2018 IL App. (5th) 160098, 103 N.E.3d 504 (2018), *appeal denied*, 108 N.W.3d 885 (Ill. 2018) (insurer may not justifiably refuse to defend unless it is clear from face of complaint that allegations do not bring case within potential coverage under policy; if insurer believes claim is not covered, it must either defend in underlying suit under reservation of rights or seek declaratory judgment that no coverage exists; insurer breached its duty to defend where it initially agreed to defend underlying action under reservation of rights and paid $1 million for defense in underlying action, but insurer subsequently used threat of negating coverage to prevent insured from settling at crucial time; insured ultimately settled for $7.5 million in claim related to clean up of two Superfund sites; see discussions in §§2.38, 2.45); *R. C. Wegman Construction Co. v. Admiral Ins. Co.*, 629 F.3d 724 (7th Cir. 2011) (Illinois law; insurer's duty of good faith includes duty to notify insured of potential conflict of interest and to reimburse reasonable expenses of new lawyer hired by insured following such notification).

—Holding that under Iowa law, an insurer's duty to defend its insured is measured by the first-party "fairly debatable" standard (rather than by the stricter third-party standard requiring protection of the insured's interests), see *North Iowa State Bank v. Allied Mut. Ins. Co.*, 471 N.W.2d 824 (Iowa 1991).

—In *Progressive Nw. Ins. Co. v. Gant*, 957 F.3d 1144 (10th Cir. 2020) (Kansas law), the Tenth Circuit held that the insurer did not breach its duty to defend by negligent hiring of defense counsel to handle the insured's wrongful death case. While the insurer was contractually obligated to provide competent counsel, the attorney's reputation for causing delays in litigation was not sufficient evidence of incompetence. The court noted that "in the highly competitive world of personal-injury litigation, complaints of allegedly unreasonable conduct of opposing counsel are hardly uncommon." *Id.* at 1152. Moreover, the insured failed to submit evidence of causation between counsel's conduct and the outcome of the litigation. The court also rejected the insured's claim that the insurer was vicariously liable for defense counsel's allegedly negligent misrepresentation, stating that the insured had a "steep hill to climb" to prevail on such a claim, and that vicarious liability is limited in Kansas to "those actions of the attorney in which the insurer was directly involved." *Id.* at 1154–55.

—Concerning a number of issues under Kentucky law relating to an insurer's duty to defend and its right to reimbursement following a defense under a reservation of rights, see *Travelers Prop. Casualty Co. of Am. v. Hillerich & Bradsby Co.*, 598 F.3d 257 (6th Cir. 2010).

—Louisiana's bad faith statute (La. Rev. Stat. Ann. §22:1220) does not provide a cause of action against an insurer that breaches its duty to defend. *Vaughan v. Franklin*, 785 So. 2d 79 (La. Ct. App. 2001).

—Holding that under Maryland law an insurer that refuses to perform its contractual duty to defend is subject to liability only for breach of contract, not for the tort of bad faith, see *Mesmer v. Maryland Auto. Ins. Fund*, 353 Md. 241, 725 A.2d 1053 (1999).

—Concerning Massachusetts law and the scope of the obligation of an insurer, when defending under a reservation of rights, to provide its insured with independent counsel, see *Hartford Casualty Ins. Co. v. A & M Assocs., Ltd.*, 200 F. Supp. 2d 84 (D. R.I. 2002) (Massachusetts law). In *Clarendon Nat'l Ins. Co. v. Philadelphia Indem. Ins. Co.*, 954 F.3d 397 (1st Cir. 2020) (Massachusetts law), the court held that the insurer of a property manager had no duty to defend against the claims of an insured property owner for liability for water damage to property where the allegations in the owner's underlying complaint "lie expressly outside the policy coverage and its purpose." *Id.* at 405 (internal quotation marks omitted).

—In *Twin City Fire Ins. Co. v. City of Madison*, 309 F.3d 901 (5th Cir. 2002) (Mississippi law), the Fifth Circuit, reversing summary judgment, held that fact issues were raised as to whether the insurer's reservation of rights letter had been adequately clear in explaining the insurer's conflict of interest. In the absence of such clarity, the court explained, an insurer may be estopped to deny coverage, and prejudice is demonstrated if the insured was induced to forego its right to hire independent counsel at the insurer's expense.

—Under Missouri law, it was emphasized in *Esicorp v. Liberty Mut. Ins. Co.*, 193 F.3d 966 (8th Cir. 1999), a cause of action for an insurer's breach of the duty to defend sounds only in contract, not in tort. For a case that analyzes multiple insurance contracts for breach of the duty to defend in the context of the insurers' refusal to defend the insured's third-party asbestos claims, see *Nooter Corp. v. Allianz Underwriters Ins. Co.*, 536 S.W.3d 251 (Mo. Ct. App. 2017).

—In *Merrick v. Fischer, Rounds & Associates, Inc.*, 305 Neb. 230, 939 N.W.2d 795 (2020), the Nebraska Supreme Court held that a liability insurer did not act in bad faith in declining to defend a lawsuit brought by an injured employee, because the employer's liability policy contained exclusions of coverage for workers' compensation and employer liability. The plaintiff employee, to whom the employer had assigned his claims against the insurer, failed to show the absence of a reasonable basis for the insurer's denial of benefits under the policy, and thus failed to demonstrate bad faith.

—See *Birsett v. General Accident Ins. Co.*, 226 A.D.2d 1027, 641 N.Y.S.2d 451 (1996), in which the court held that the record supported a finding that the insurer was sufficiently heedless of its obligations to the insured to justify an award in excess of policy limits. The insurer, relying on a clearly ineffective policy "cancellation," had refused to defend the insured in a personal injury action. Compare *Newmont v. American Home Assur. Co.*, 676 F. Supp. 2d 1146 (E.D. Wash. 2009) (analyzing New York law as not recognizing cause of action for bad faith breach of insurance contract).

—In *Roberts v. United States Fidelity & Guar. Co.*, 665 N.E.2d 664 (Ohio 1996), the Ohio Supreme Court refused to apply retroactively *Zoppo v. Homestead Ins. Co.*, 71 Ohio St. 3d 552, 644 N.E.2d 397 (1994), which eliminated any "intent" requirement and equated bad faith with unreasonableness. The court expressly left open whether *Zoppo* defines the standard that should be applied in future failure-to-defend cases. See also *Nationwide Mut. Ins. Co. v. Masseria*, 1999 WL 1313626, 1999 Ohio App. LEXIS 6119 (1999) (insurer's filing of declaratory judgment action seeking determination that it has no duty to defend may constitute bad faith if investigation was inadequate); *United Nat'l Ins. Co. v. SST Fitness Corp.*, 309 F.3d 914 (6th Cir. 2002) (Ohio law; insurer was not "volunteer" when it undertook insured's defense under reservation of rights and insurer was entitled to reimbursement of defense costs upon determination that it had no duty to defend or indemnify).

—Applying Oklahoma law, the Tenth Circuit, in *Automax Hyundai S. LLC v. Zurich Am. Ins. Co.*, 720 F.3d 798 (10th Cir. 2013), reversed summary judgment that had been granted on the grounds that the insured could not establish entitlement to coverage, and that the insurer had had at least a legitimate basis for denying coverage. The Tenth Circuit wrote (720 F.3d at 811):

> Yet the record suggests that Zurich may have misunderstood the duty in Oklahoma to defend an insured if the *facts* of the lawsuit reveal a mere possibility that a claim is covered, as well as the duty that, once an insured requests a defense, the insurer has to inquire into

the underlying facts. . . . It is possible that Zurich did not conduct the requisite investigation before denying Automax's claim. Such a scenario would suggest that Zurich did not have a reasonable basis. . . . [S]ummary judgment for Zurich is inappropriate at this time.

—Reiterating the position of the Oregon courts that a failure to defend can never amount to more than a breach of contract, see *Warren v. Farmers Ins. Co.*, 115 Or. App. 319, 838 P.2d 620 (1992).

—Texas law recognizes a breach of contract claim for failure to defend when the duty to defend exists under the contract. In *Lyda Swinerton Builders, Inc. v. Oklahoma Sur. Co.*, 903 F.3d 435 (5th Cir. 2018), the court affirmed that an insurer breached its duty to defend an additional insured general contractor who was sued for damages for work done by a subcontractor on a commercial office building, and the court affirmed the damages award of $655,600. The court used the 8-corners rule to determine whether the liability insurer had a duty to defend an insured against a third-party lawsuit. Under this rule, the court looks to the 4 corners of the petition and the 4 corners of the insurance policy to determine whether the matter could be potentially covered by the policy. The court found that the duty was triggered where the material deficiencies and other allegations in the petition potentially fell within the scope of coverage, which provided for defense in any suit against an insured for property damage.

Texas law does not recognize a tort cause of action for an insurer's bad faith refusal to defend. *Maryland Ins. Co. v. Head Indus. Coatings & Servs., Inc.*, 938 S.W.2d 27 (Tex. 1996); *United Servs. Auto. Ass'n v. Pennington*, 810 S.W.2d 777 (Tex. Ct. App. 1991); *HVAW v. American Motorists Ins. Co.*, 968 F. Supp. 1178 (N.D. Tex. 1997).

See *Texas Ass'n of County Government Risk Management Pool v. Matagorda County*, 52 S.W.3d 128 (Tex. 2000), for a holding that an insurer who defends under a reservation of rights is not entitled to the reimbursement of noncovered settlements. The *Matagorda* holding was followed, somewhat reluctantly, by a Texas court of appeals in *Excess Underwriters at Lloyd's v. Frank's Casing & Rental Tools, Inc.*, 93 S.W.3d 178, 2002 WL 1404705 (Tex. Ct. App. 2002), *rev. granted* 4/3/03. (The opposite conclusion to *Matagorda*'s is represented by the California Supreme Court's decision in *Buss v. Superior Court (Transamerica Ins. Co.), supra.*)

—In *Morrisville Water & Light Dept. v. United States Fidelity & Guar. Co.*, 775 F. Supp. 718 (D. Vt. 1991) (Vermont law), the court entered a declaratory judgment that the insurer was required to defend and indemnify the insured for claims concerning environmental clean-up pursuant to CERCLA, and held that genuine issues of material fact existed as to whether the insurer's denial of coverage and refusal to defend had been in bad faith. The court explained that under Vermont law, an insurer's legal duty is that of a fiduciary, and an insurer must take the insured's interests into account when determining whether a third party's claim is covered under a policy. 775 F. Supp. at 734.

—Under Washington law, the state supreme court held, in *Kirk v. Mt. Airy Ins. Co.*, 134 Wash. 2d 558, 951 P.2d 1124 (1998), the remedy for an insurer's bad faith refusal to defend is estoppel to deny coverage. See also *Truck Ins. Co. v. Vanport Homes, Inc.*, 147 Wash. 2d 751, 58 P.3d 276 (2002). (That holding represents an extension of *Safeco Ins. Co. of Am. v. Butler*, 118 Wash. 2d 383, 823 P.2d 499 (1992), which prescribed the same remedy in situations where an insurer conducts a bad faith defense under a reservation of rights.) See also *Ledcor Indus. (USA), Inc. v. Mutual of Enumclaw Ins. Co.*, 150 Wash. App. 1, 206 P.3d 1255 (2009).

In *American Best Food, Inc. v. Alea London, Ltd.*, 168 Wash. 2d 398, 229 P.3d 693 (banc 2010), the Washington Supreme Court wrote (168 Wash. 2d at 413, 229 P.3d at 700):

It cannot be said that the insurer did not put its own interest ahead of its insured when it denied a defense based on an arguable legal interpretation of its own policy. Alea failed to follow well established Washington State law giving the insured the benefit of the doubt as to the duty to defend and failed to avail itself of legal options such as proceeding under a reservation of rights or seeking declaratory relief. Alea's failure to defend based on a questionable interpretation of law was unreasonable and Alea acted in bad faith as a matter of law."

In *Osborne Constr. Co. v. Zurich Am. Ins. Co.*, 356 F. Supp. 3d 1085 (W.D. Wash. 2018) (Washington law), a general contractor brought an action against its subcontractor's insurer after the insurer failed to defend the general contractor as an additional insured on the subcontractor's policy. The court stated that the duty to defend is triggered if the insurance policy conceivably covers the allegations. The court held that the insurer breached its duty to defend where evidence in the insurer's own records showed the general contractor could arguably be considered an additional insured; a deductible requirement arguably applied to only the subcontractor, not the general contractor, as the additional insured; a demand for arbitration existed; and a sufficient request for defense was made by the general contractor. The court held that based on the failure to defend, the insurer was estopped from refusing to indemnify the general contractor from any liability in connection with claims for which it sought a defense.

—Holding that under Wisconsin law an insurer may incur liability for breach of the implied covenant of good faith and fair dealing by failing to defend an insured, see *Newhouse v. Citizens Sec. Mut. Ins. Co.*, 170 Wis. 2d 456, 489 N.W.2d 639 (Ct. App. 1992), *aff'd*, 176 Wis. 2d 824, 501 N.W.2d 1 (1993). But see *Novak v. American Family Mut. Ins. Co.*, 183 Wis. 2d 133, 515 N.W.2d 504 (Ct. App. 1994), rejecting the argument that public policy is violated by a policy provision permitting the insurer to abandon the defense of its insured once a policy-limits offer has been made and rejected.

—Also representing the rule that an insurer's decision to defend its insured under a reservation of rights does not always and necessarily create such a conflict of interest as to require the insurer to pay for separate counsel to represent the insured: *Midiman v. Farmers Ins. Exch.*, 76 Cal. App. 4th 102, 90 Cal. Rptr. 2d 85 (1999); *Dynamic Concepts, Inc. v. Truck Ins. Exch.*, 61 Cal. App. 4th 999, 71 Cal. Rptr. 2d 882 (1998); *Blanchard v. State Farm Fire & Casualty Co.*, 2 Cal. App. 4th 345, 2 Cal. Rptr. 2d 884 (1991); *Johnson v. Continental Casualty Co.*, 57 Wash. App. 359, 788 P.2d 598 (1990). On a related point, see *Kansas Bankers Sur. Co. v. Lynass*, 920 F.2d 546 (8th Cir. 1990) (South Dakota law; insurer's assertion of noncoverage was equivalent of reservation of rights, and insurer could not then insist on providing defense against insured's wishes).

§2.10 d. Improper or Ineffective Defense

—In *Lloyd v. State Farm Mut. Auto. Ins. Co.*, 189 Ariz. 369, 943 P.2d 729 (Ct. App. 1996), an Arizona Court of Appeals held that even in the absence of coverage, an insurer may be subject to liability for bad faith if it assumes the duty to defend and then defends ineffectively.

—Under Hawaii law, if an insurer assumes the defense and through its mishandling of the defense causes actual harm to the insured, a bad faith claim is cognizable despite a later declaration that the insurer had no duty to defend in the first place. *Delmonte v. State Farm Fire & Causalty Co.*, 90 Haw. 39, 975 P.2d 1159 (1999).

—In *Willis Coroon Corp. v. Home Ins. Co.*, 203 F.3d 449 (7th Cir. 2000) (Illinois law), the Seventh Circuit held that the insurer was estopped to assert coverage defenses because it had mishandled a defense it had undertaken under a reservation of rights. "When an insurer chooses to defend," the court wrote, "it must provide an effective defense, and it must not put its own interests ahead of those claiming to be its insureds." The insurer in the present case was also subject to statutory penalties and fees, the court held.

—In *Herbert A. Sullivan, Inc. v. Utica Mut. Ins. Co.*, 439 Mass. 387, 788 N.E.2d 522 (2003), the Massachusetts Supreme Judicial Court held that, although an insurer is under a duty of reasonable care in conducting an insured's defense, the insurer cannot be held vicariously liable for the malpractice of a hired attorney.

—In *Sapienza v. Liberty Mut. Fire Ins. Co.*, 389 F. Supp. 648 (D.S.D. 2019) (South Dakota law), insureds brought a breach of contract action against their insurer for inadequate defense after they lost a lawsuit with a neighbor and were forced to demolish their newly constructed house. The insureds hired their own defense attorney at the expense of the insurer. The insureds alleged that the insurer provided an inadequate defense by overriding the independent judgment of the defense counsel through instructions on how to handle the case and by refusing to hire independent experts to offer opinions on the sizing of the home. The insureds provided no details on whether the judgment of their attorney was hindered by the insurance company and no details on how they were harmed by lack of expert opinions. Noting that there is no South Dakota precedent on an insurer's liability for an inadequate defense, the court gave the insureds leave to amend their complaint to offer more detailed allegations.

—In *Safeco Ins. Co. of Am. v. Butler*, 118 Wash. 2d 383, 823 P.2d 499 (1992), the Washington Supreme Court engaged in an extended discussion of the elements of a cause of action for bad faith handling of an insurance claim when an insurer assumes an "enhanced obligation" by opting to defend under a reservation of rights. The court held, *inter alia*, that a showing of harm is an essential element of the cause of action, but that a rebuttable presumption of harm is recognized once the insured meets the burden of establishing bad faith. (The court rejected the argument that an insurer's improper handling of a reservation of rights defense is tantamount to self-dealing and should be treated as a breach of a true fiduciary duty.) Concerning an insured's remedy, the court held that where an insurer acts in bad faith in handling a claim under a reservation of rights, the insurer is estopped from denying coverage.

In the present case, the court affirmed the denial of summary judgment, holding that there were material facts in dispute as to whether Safeco acted in bad faith and whether those acts harmed the Butlers. The court rejected Safeco's argument that there could be no showing of harm because the injured party had signed an agreement not to execute his judgment against the insured. (The court reasoned an insurer guilty of bad faith is in no position to argue that the steps the insured took to protect himself should inure to the insurer's benefit.) As evidence of Safeco's bad faith, the insured alleged: (1) that Safeco waited two months before informing the insured of its decision to defend under a reservation of rights; (2) that Safeco delayed the insured's attorney's investigation; (3) that Safeco used that delay to enhance its position on the coverage issue; (4) that Safeco did not conduct a timely and thorough investigation; (5) that due to Safeco's delay, evidence was lost; (6) that Safeco attempted to use the insured's attorney to obtain statements for use in the coverage action; (7) that Safeco commingled information from the tort defense and coverage action files; and (8) that Safeco exhibited greater concern for its financial risk than the insured's interests.

In *Mutual of Enumclaw Ins. Co. v. Dan Paulson Construction, Inc.*, 161 Wash. 2d 903, 169 P.3d 1 (banc 2007), the Washington Supreme Court held that a liability insurer defending its insured under a reservation of rights did not successfully rebut the presumption of harm that arose from its bad faith in sending a subpoena and ex parte communications to the arbitrator who was resolving the underlying claim by a homeowner against the insured builder.

§2.11 e. Primary Insurer's Liability to Excess Insurer

—In *Federal Ins. Co. v. Travelers Casualty & Sur. Co.*, 834 So. 2d 140, 2002 WL 1998282 (Ala. 2002), addressing an issue of first impression under Alabama law, the Alabama Supreme Court declined to recognize any basis—either direct-duty or equitable subrogation—on which an excess insurer may sue a primary insurer for a bad faith refusal to settle.

—In this section of the book, it was noted that Arizona (by virtue of the holding in *Universal Underwriters Ins. Co. v. Dairyland Mut. Ins. Co.*, 102 Ariz. 518, 433 P.2d 966 (1967)) appeared to be the only jurisdiction whose courts had expressly rejected the equitable subrogation theory under which many courts permit an excess insurer to sue a primary insurer for a bad faith failure to settle a third party claim within primary policy limits. *Universal Underwriters* has now been overruled: *Hartford Accident & Indem. Co. v. Aetna Casualty & Sur. Co.*, 164 Ariz. 286, 792 P.2d 749 (1990). See also *Twin City Fire Ins. Co. v. Superior Court*, 164 Ariz. 295, 792 P.2d 758 (1990) (recognizing equitable subrogation theory, but declining to recognize cause of action based on any direct duty running from primary to excess insurer); *Leflet v. Redwood Fire & Casualty Ins. Co.*, 226 Ariz. 297, 247 P.3d 180 (Ct. App. 2011) (insured and insurer cannot join in *Morris* agreement that avoids primary insurer's obligation to pay policy limits and passes liability in excess of those limits on to other insurers); *AMHS Ins. Co. v. Mutual Ins. Co.*, 258 F.3d 1090 (9th Cir. 2001) (declining to extend equitable subrogation theory to relationship between co-insurers whose policies attach at same level).

—In several cases, California courts of appeal and federal courts applying California law have addressed significant issues relating to actions by the excess insurer against the primary insurer for bad faith failure to settle: *RLI Ins.*

Co. v. CNA Casualty of Calif., 141 Cal. App. 4th 75, 45 Cal. Rptr. 3d 667 (2006) (affirming summary judgment in favor of primary insurer; despite allegation that primary insurer had unreasonably refused offer to settle claim within its $1 million policy limit, excess insurer who had paid $1 million to settle tort claim could not maintain equitable subrogation action against primary insurer who had also paid $1 million, where tort claim did not go to trial and where no excess judgment was entered against insured); *United Servs. Auto. Ass'n v. Alaska Ins. Co.*, 94 Cal. App. 4th 638, 114 Cal. Rptr. 2d 449 (2001) (excess insurer that denies coverage of third-party claim waives right to challenge amount of settlement agreed to by primary insurer); *Diamond Heights Homeowners Ass'n v. National Am. Ins. Co.*, 227 Cal. App. 3d 563, 277 Cal. Rptr. 906 (1991) (reversing summary judgment in favor of excess insurer in action by insured: excess insurer was bound by reasonable settlement that invaded excess coverage even though settlement was finalized without excess insurer's consent; excess insurer's claims of bad faith and collusion were barred as a matter of law where excess insurer participated in settlement confirmation hearing and voiced objection, but failed to offer to take over insured's defense or to petition court for writ of mandate); *Continental Casualty v. Royal Ins. Co.*, 219 Cal. App. 3d 111, 268 Cal. Rptr. 193 (1990) (affirming judgment for excess insurer; since excess insurer stands in shoes of insured for purposes of equitable subrogation theory, trial judge correctly excluded as irrelevant evidence of excess insurer's own partial responsibility for loss of settlement opportunity); *Fortman v. Safeco Ins. Co. of Am.*, 221 Cal. App. 3d 1394, 271 Cal. Rptr. 117 (1990) (reversing summary judgment for primary insurer; since there was no evidence of collusion between insured and excess insurer, final entry of excess judgment against insured was not prerequisite to excess insurer's subrogation suit against primary insurer; primary insurer had rejected $125,000 settlement offer before trial, but five weeks into trial had finally agreed to contribute its $300,000 policy limits as part of settlement to which excess insurer had to contribute $1.25 million); *Sequoia Ins. Co. v. Royal Ins. Co. of Am.*, 971 F.2d 1385 (9th Cir. 1992) (California law; reversing summary judgment in favor of primary insurer: primary insurer's bad faith refusal to settle may properly be raised defensively by excess insurer in action by primary insurer to recover excess judgment); *American Alternative Ins. Corp. v. Hudson Specialty Ins. Co.*, 938 F. Supp. 2d 908 (C.D. Cal. 2013) (summary judgment on primary liability insurer's claim for equitable subrogation was precluded by existence of genuine issue of material fact as to whether excess liability insurer had unreasonably refused to settle underlying personal injury action within its policy limits); *Republic Western Ins. Co. v. Fireman's Fund Ins. Co.*, 241 F. Supp. 2d 1090 (N.D. Cal. 2003) (excess carrier had no duty to defend following primary insurer's wrongful failure to defend).

For an action by an excess insurer against the primary insurer for bad faith failure to defend, see *Public Serv. Mut. Ins. Co. v. Liberty Surplus Ins. Co.*, 205 F. Supp. 3d 1161 (E.D. Cal. 2016), *reconsideration denied*, 2017 WL 3601381 (E.D. Cal. 2017) (denying primary insurer's motion for summary judgment where excess insurer brought equitable indemnification claim against primary insurer and claim for breach of implied covenant of good faith and fair dealing for failure to defend; court declined to apply genuine dispute doctrine in third-party suit because primary insurer is obligated to defend suit in which there is potential for damages).

—The Delaware Supreme Court, in *Nationwide Mut. Ins. Co. v. Kesterson*, 575 A.2d 1127 (Del. 1990), relied on the reasoning of *Commercial Union Ins. Co. v. Ford Motor Co.*, 599 F. Supp. 1271 (N.D. Cal. 1984) (California law; see book), in holding that where an insurer has paid an excess judgment as the result of a suit for bad faith failure to settle, it would be inequitable to allow the insurer to recover from its insured's joint tortfeasor, in an action for equitable indemnity, that portion of its damages solely attributable to its own wrongful conduct.

—Affirming a judgment for the excess carrier, a Florida court, in *United States Fire Ins. Co. v. Morrison Assurance Co.*, 600 So. 2d 1147 (Fla. Dist. Ct. App. 1992), held (1) that the excess insurer could maintain an action against the primary insurer for failure to settle within policy limits without proving any underlying bad faith claim by the insured against the primary insurer (the insured had agreed that the settlement offer should be rejected); and (2) that a finding of bad faith liability was sufficiently supported by evidence that the primary carrier had failed to communicate the status of the case for 18 months, and had not advised the excess carrier as to settlement negotiations or of the possibility of an excess judgment. Also representing Florida's recognition of a cause of action for equitable subrogation between primary and excess insurers arising from the excess insurer's payment of a claim after the primary insurer's refusal to defend, see *Progressive Am. Ins. Co. v. Nationwide Ins. Co.*, 949 So. 2d 293 (Fla. Dist. Ct. App. 2007); *Galen Health Care, Inc. v. American Casualty Co.*, 913 F. Supp. 1525 (M.D. Fla. 1996). See also *Vigilant Ins. Co. v. Continental Casualty Co.*, 33 So. 3d 734 (Fla. Dist. Ct. App. 2010) (excess insurer had bad faith cause of action against primary liability carrier even though injured party in underlying products liability action released insured manufacturer); *Westchester Fire Ins. Co. v. Mid-Continent Cas. Co.*, 569 Fed. Appx. 753 (11th Cir. 2014) (in action brought by excess insurer, reversing federal district court ruling that primary insurer acted in bad faith when it failed to settle within policy limits; on appeal, Eleventh Circuit held there was no bad faith and no evidence of causal connection between failure to settle and excess carrier's obligation), *rev'g* 954 F. Supp. 2d 1374 (S.D. Fla. 2013)

Applying Florida law in *National Union Fire Ins. Co. v. Travelers Ins. Co.*, 214 F.3d 1269 (11th Cir. 2000), the Eleventh Circuit held that an excess insurer's duty to defend was triggered only by actual exhaustion of coverage under the primary policy, not by the primary insurer's mere "tendering" of its limits.

—In *Evanston Ins. Co. v. Stonewall Surplus Lines Ins. Co.*, 111 F.3d 852 (11th Cir. 1997), the Eleventh Circuit, applying Georgia and Wisconsin law, held that a third-level excess insurer could not assert a bad faith claim, as a subrogee of the insured, for the failure of the primary and first- and second-level excess liability insurers to notify the third-level insurer of its possible exposure, where the insured's attorney had agreed that the verdict would not exceed the limits of the second-level excess policy and had never complained of that insurer's handling of the settlement negotiations.

—In an anomalous decision issued in 1998, the Idaho Supreme Court apparently declined to recognize any cause of action by an excess against a primary insurer for bad faith failure to settle. *Stonewall Surplus Lines Ins. Co. v. Farmers Ins. Co.*, 132 Idaho 318, 971 P.2d 1142 (1998).

—Prior to 1994, a number of federal district court decisions applying Illinois law had appeared to adhere to the minority view that recognizes the existence of a direct duty running from primary to excess insurer, and that approach was also followed in *Schal Bovis, Inc. v. Casualty Ins. Co.*, 732 N.E.2d 1082 (Ill. App. Ct. 1999). In *Twin City Fire Ins. Co. v. Country Mut. Ins. Co.*, 23 F.3d 1175 (7th Cir. 1994), however, the Seventh Circuit rejected this approach and endorsed the more standard equitable subrogation theory. Discussing that issue and a number of other issues relative to the primary insurer's duty of good faith, see *Swedish-American Hosp. Ass'n of Rockford v. Illinois State Med. Inter-Insurance Exch.*, 916 N.E.2d 80, 2009 WL 3048427 (Ill. App. Ct. 2009); *Fox v. American Alternative Ins. Co.*, 757 F.3d 680 (7th Cir. 2014); *California Union Ins. Co. v. Liberty Mut. Ins. Co.*, 920 F. Supp. 908 (N.D. Ill. 1996). See also *Liberty Mut. Ins. Co. v. American Home Assurance Co.*, 384 F. Supp. 2d 940 (N.D. Ill. 2004) (as matter of first impression, "higher tier" excess insurer could not assert claim for bad faith failure to settle against "lower tier" excess insurer which participated in settlement negotiations but which, unlike primary insurer, did not exercise complete control over insured's defenses).

—In *PHICO Ins. Co. v. Aetna Casualty & Sur. Co. of Am.*, 93 F. Supp. 2d 982 (S.D. Ind. 2000) (Indiana law), a federal district court granted a primary insurer's motion for summary judgment, holding that the equitable doctrines of waiver, laches, and unclean hands barred an excess insurer from complaining of inadequacies in the defense conducted by the primary insurer. The excess insurer had failed to participate in the defense and had failed to make timely protests concerning assertedly improper defense decisions.

—In *West Am. Ins. Co. v. RLI Ins. Co.*, 698 F.3d 1069 (8th Cir. 2012), the Eighth Circuit predicted that under Kansas law, an excess insurer is subrogated to the rights of its insured for the purpose of asserting a claim that the primary insurer acted in bad faith in failing to settle within its policy limits. The primary insurer's agreement to arbitrate pursuant to a high/low agreement did not preclude the excess insurer, as subrogee of the insured, from asserting a claim for bad faith refusal to settle, the court held.

—In *National Sur. Corp. v. Hartford Casualty Ins. Co.*, 493 F.3d 752 (6th Cir. 2007), the Sixth Circuit predicted that under Kentucky law an excess insurer is permitted to recover against a primary insurer, under the doctrine of equitable estoppel, for injuries caused by the primary insurer's bad faith failure to settle claims against the insured. And even though an insured had an excess liability policy and was compensated for the entire excess verdict, the court continued, the insured still has a cause of action against the primary insurer for bad faith failure to settle within policy limits.

—Applying Louisiana law in *RSUI Indem. Co. v. American States Ins. Co.*, 768 F.3d 374 (5th Cir. 2014), the Fifth

Circuit held that the excess insurer had a subrogated claim against the primary insurer for any payment above the amount it otherwise would have been required to pay absent bad faith of primary insurer.

—In *Reliance Ins. Co. in Liquidation v. Chitwood*, 433 F.3d 660 (8th Cir. 2006) (Missouri law), the Eighth Circuit noted that Missouri courts have not recognized a direct duty of good faith between primary and excess insurers. Accord, *American Guarantee & Liability Ins. Co. v. United States Fid. & Guar. Co.*, 693 F. Supp. 2d 1038 (E.D. Mo. 2010), *aff'd*, 668 F.3d 991 (8th Cir. 2012).

—Applying New Jersey law, a federal district court, in *Employers Mut. Casualty Co. v. Key Pharmaceuticals*, 871 F. Supp. 657 (S.D. N.Y. 1994), held that the good faith settlement duty a primary insurer owes to an excess insurer was not "inherited" by the insured on the primary insurer's insolvency.

In *M & B Apartments, Inc. v. Teltser*, 745 A.2d 586 (N.J. Super. Ct. App. Div. 2000), affirming summary judgment, the court held that a second-layer excess insurer could have no liability to the third-layer excess insurer for refusal to settle where the policy clearly permitted such refusal where coverage was, as here, fairly debatable.

In *Bean v. Farmers Mut. Fire Ins. Co.*, 318 N.J. Super. 260, 723 A.2d 636 (1999), it was held that the direct duty of good faith that a primary insurer owes to an excess insurer under New Jersey law terminates if and when the excess insurer denies coverage.

And in *Charter Oak Fire Ins. Co. v. State Farm Mut. Auto. Ins. Co.*, 344 N.J. Super. 408, 782 A.2d 452 (Ct. App. Div. 2001), it was held that an excess insurer who had urged the primary insurer to tender its policy limits and not appeal a negligence judgment against the insured was equitably estopped from asserting a bad faith claim against the primary insurer.

—In *Allstate Ins. Co. v. American Transit Ins. Co.*, 977 F. Supp. 197 (E.D.N.Y. 1997), a federal district court predicted that the New York Court of Appeals would recognize that an excess insurer may maintain a malpractice claim against defense counsel hired by the primary carrier to defend the insured.

Under New York law, it was held in *AAA Sprinkler Corp. v. General Star Nat'l Ins. Co.*, 705 N.Y.S.2d 582 (App. Div. 2000), a primary insurer has no duty to place an excess insurer on notice of the likelihood of an excess judgment. A primary insurer must keep the insured informed, the court explained, but then the duty to inform the excess insurer falls solely on the insured. The court relied on *Monarch Cortland v. Columbia Casualty Co.*, 646 N.Y.S.2d 904 (App. Div. 1996).

And in *Federal Ins. Co. v. Liberty Mut. Ins. Co.*, 158 F. Supp. 290 (S.D.N.Y. 2001), the court granted summary judgment in favor of the primary insurer, reasoning that a finding of bad faith was precluded in connection with the primary's decision not to settle within policy limits by the fact that the amount of damages had been seriously contested, even though liability had been clear. See also *Indemnity Ins. Co. of N. Am. v. Transcontinental Ins. Co.*, 24 A.D.3d 121, 804 N.Y.S.2d 737 (2005) (affirming summary judgment; primary insurers could not be held liable for bad faith failure to accept settlement offer where they reasonably believed they had meritorious defense and reasonably determined that any adverse verdict would be within primary policy limits). Compare *Federal Ins. Co. v. North Am. Specialty Ins. Co.*, 83 A.D.3d 401, 921 N.Y.S.2d 28 (2011) (fact issue existed as to whether primary insurer deliberately and in bad faith had failed to assert anti-subrogation rule in order to allow insured to escape liability and thereby remove policy from layer of coverage that had to be exhausted before triggering excess coverage).

—A federal district court applying North Carolina law, in *United States Fire Ins. Co. v. Nationwide Mut. Ins. Co.*, 735 F. Supp. 1320 (E.D.N.C. 1990), declined to decide whether North Carolina law does or does not recognize either the equitable subrogation or the direct duty theory. In the present case, the court reasoned, the primary carrier had expressly undertaken a duty of good faith when it promised to keep the excess carrier informed as to the progress of the case.

—In *Greater N.Y. Ins. Co. v. North River Ins. Co.*, 85 F.3d 1088 (3d Cir. 1996), it was held that Pennsylvania law recognizes no "reverse" duty of good faith running from an excess insurer to a primary insurer.

—In *Royal Ins. Co. of Am. v. Reliance Ins. Co.*, 140 F. Supp. 2d 609 (D.S.C. 2001), the court declined to extend the South Carolina bad faith doctrine to permit an excess insurer's action against a primary insurer, and held that the present facts, involving the primary insurer's payment of its policy limits directly to the insured rather than to the excess insurer, did not support a right of equitable subrogation in the absence of evidence that, but for the direct payment, the claim could have been settled more cheaply.

—For discussions of the measures of damages recoverable by an excess insurer under Texas law, and of a primary insurer's affirmative defenses, see *National Union Fire Ins. Co. v. Insurance Co. of N. Am.*, 955 S.W.2d 120 (Tex. Ct. App. 1997), *aff'd*, *Keck, Mahin & Cate v. National Union Fire Ins. Co.*, 20 S.W.3d 120 (Tex. 2000).

In *Westchester Fire Ins. Co. v. Admiral Ins. Co.*, 152 S.W.3d 172 (Tex. App. 2004), an excess insurer brought an equitable subrogation claim against a primary professional medical liability insurer for negligent failure to settle within policy limits a claim against an insured nursing home. The trial court granted partial summary judgment and a directed verdict for the primary insurer and the excess insurer appealed. The court of appeal held: (1) the primary liability policy provided coverage for punitive damages, and such coverage was not void as against public policy; and (2) it was for a jury to decide the issue of whether the claimant made a settlement demand within the limits of the primary policy, and the issue of whether an ordinarily prudent insurer would have settled the underlying case.

—Concerning Utah law's recognition of a claim for equitable subrogation by an excess insurer against a primary insurer arising out of the excess insurer's payment of a claim to the insured or to a third party on behalf of the insured, see *Rupp v. Transcontinental Ins. Co.*, 627 F. Supp. 2d 1304 (D. Utah 2008).

—In *First State Ins. Co. v. Kemper Nat'l Ins. Co.*, 971 P.2d 953 (Wash. Ct. App. 1999), the court held that by operation of the doctrine of equitable subrogation, an excess insurer could state a claim under the Washington Consumer Protection Act against the primary insurer, in addition to a common-law bad faith claim.

—The following are additional cases endorsing a theory of equitable subrogation to allow an excess insurer to maintain a cause of action against a primary insurer for a bad faith failure to settle a third-party claim within primary coverage limits: *Sequoia Ins. Co. v. Royal Ins. Co. of Am., supra; United States Fire Ins. Co. v. Morrison Assurance Co., supra; Home Ins. Co. v. North River Ins. Co.*, 192 Ga. App. 551, 385 S.E.2d 736 (1989); *Great Am. Ins. Co. v. International Ins. Co.*, 753 F. Supp. 357 (M.D. Ga. 1990) (Georgia law); *Certain Underwriters of Lloyds v. General Accident Ins. Co. of Am.*, 909 F.2d 228 (7th Cir. 1990) (Indiana law); *Pacific Employers Ins. Co. v. P.B. Hoidale Co.*, 789 F. Supp. 1117 (D. Kan. 1992) (Kansas law); *Great Southwest Fire Ins. Co. v. CNA Ins. Cos.*, 557 So. 2d 966 (La. Ct. App. 1990); *St. Paul Ins. Co. v. AFIA Worldwide Ins. Co.*, 937 F.2d 274 (5th Cir. 1991) (Louisiana law); *Northfield Ins. Co. v. St. Paul Surplus Lines Ins. Co.*, 545 N.W.2d 57 (Minn. Ct. App. 1996); *Hartford Ins. Co. v. General Accident Group Ins. Co.*, 177 A.D.2d 1046, 578 N.Y.S.2d 59 (1991); *F.B. Washburn Candy v. Fireman's Fund*, 541 A.2d 771 (Pa. Super. Ct. 1988); *Greater N.Y. Ins. Co. v. North River Ins. Co., supra; American Centennial Ins.*

Co. v. Canal Ins. Co., 810 S.W.2d 246 (Tex. Ct. App. 1991), *writ of error granted*, Jan. 8, 1992; *General Star Indem. Co. v. Vesta Fire Ins. Corp.*, 173 F.3d 946 (5th Cir. 1999) (Texas law); *St. Paul Mercury Ins. Co. v. Lexington Ins. Co.*, 78 F.3d 202 (5th Cir. 1996) (Texas law); *Truck Ins. Exch. v. Century Indem. Co.*, 76 Wash. App. 527, 887 P.2d 455 (1995). See also *American States Ins. Co. v. Maryland Casualty Co.*, 628 A.2d 880 (Pa. Super. Ct. 1993) (umbrella insurer in breach of own duty to defend could not maintain bad faith action against primary insurer).

§2.12 f. Liability of Reinsurer

—It was held, in *Schreffler v. Pennsylvania Ins. Guar. Ass'n*, 586 A.2d 983 (Pa. Super. Ct. 1991), that the Pennsylvania Insurance Guarantee Association (I.G.A.) may not be held liable for bad faith failure to settle a claim against the insured of an insolvent insurer. The I.G.A. is immune from liability for actions taken under the Insurance Guarantee Act, including settlement of claims. (See §2.12 of the book for related holdings under California law; and concerning Florida law, see *Fernandez v. Florida Ins. Guar. Ass'n, Inc.*, 383 So. 2d 974 (Fla. Dist. Ct. App. 1980).)

Additional decisions standing for the immunity of insurance guaranty associations from bad faith liability have included *Garel v. Georgia Insurers' Insolvency Pool*, 191 Ga. App. 572, 382 S.E.2d 400 (1989); *Laris v. Parker*, 635 So. 2d 442 (La. Ct. App. 1994); *Barrett v. Massachusetts Insurers Insolvency Fund*, 412 Mass. 774, 592 N.E.2d 1317 (1992); *Bobby Kitchens, Inc. v. Mississippi Ins. Guar. Ass'n*, 560 So. 2d 129 (Miss. 1989); *Nevada Ins. Guar. v. Sierra Auto Ctr.*, 108 Nev. 1123, 844 P.2d 126 (1992); *Bentley v. North Carolina Ins. Guar. Ass'n*, 107 N.C. App. 1, 418 S.E.2d 705 (1992).

C. Insurer's Liability for Negligence

§2.13 1. In General

—In *Kazi v. State Farm Fire & Casualty Co.*, 70 Cal. App. 4th 1288, 83 Cal. Rptr. 2d 364 (1999), *review granted*, July 21, 1999, a California Court of Appeal, affirming summary judgment on a negligence cause of action, took the position that the tort of bad faith is the only tort cause of action that may be asserted in connection with an insurer's mishandling of a claim. Accord, *Cayo v. Valor Fighting & Mgmt. LLC*, 2008 WL 5170125 (N.D. Cal. 2008) (collecting authorities).

—In *Menchise v. Liberty Mut. Ins. Co.*, 932 So. 2d 1130 (Fla. Dist. Ct. App. 2006), the court noted, in reversing summary judgment in favor of the insured, that negligence is relevant to the question of an insurer's good faith with regard to the settlement of a claim. The evidence showed, *inter alia*, that the insurer had misplaced the settlement offer and ignored some of its conditions without explanation. Compare *Baranowski v. GEICO Gen. Ins. Co.*, 385 F. Supp. 3d 1267 (M.D. Fla. 2019), *aff'd*, 806 Fed. Appx. 971 (11th Cir. 2020) (although negligent conduct of insurer is relevant to determining bad faith, negligent conduct without more does not amount to bad faith); *Feijoo v. Geico Gen. Ins. Co.* 137 F. Supp. 3d 1320 (S.D. Fla. 2015), *aff'd*, 678 Fed. Appx. 862 (11th Cir. 2017) (negligence in carrying out good faith duty to insured is immaterial unless negligence is cause of excess judgment where question of negligence arises regarding insurer's decision to proceed to trial despite settlement offers).

—In *Hartford Casualty Ins. Co. v. New Hampshire Ins. Co.*, 417 Mass. 115, 628 N.E.2d 14 (1994), the Massachusetts Supreme Judicial Court announced the replacement of the bad faith standard in third-party cases with a pure negligence standard. The court noted what it believed to be a nationwide trend in that direction, and insisted that in practice, the negligence standard will not be significantly different from the bad faith standard as it had evolved in Massachusetts.

—In *Texas Farmers Ins. Co. v. Soriano*, 881 S.W.2d 312 (Tex. 1994), the Texas Supreme Court declined to decide whether Texas law should recognize the doctrine of third-party bad faith in addition to the negligence-based third-party doctrine recognized in *Stowers, G.A., Furniture Co. v. American Indem. Co.*, 15 S.W.2d 544 (Tex. Civ. App. 1929). Also declining to reach that issue, see *State Farm Lloyds Ins. Co. v. Maldonado*, 935 S.W.2d 805 (Tex. Ct. App. 1996), *aff'd in part and rev'd in part on other grounds*, 963 S.W.2d 38 (Tex. 1998). But see *Traver v. State Farm Mut. Auto. Ins. Co.*, 930 S.W.2d 862 (Tex. Ct. App. 1996), *rev'd on other grounds*, 980 S.W.2d 625 (Tex. 1998), expressly concluding that in the third-party context, Texas law recognizes only the *Stowers* duty. See also *Rocor Int'l, Inc. v. National Union Fire Ins. Co.*, 77 S.W.3d 253 (Tex. 2002); *Mid-Continent Casualty Co. v. Eland Energy, Inc.*, 795 F. Supp. 2d 493 (N.D. Tex. 2011). And in *Ford v. Cimarron Ins. Co.*, 230 F.3d 828 (5th Cir. 2000), it was held that the *Stowers* doctrine is also exclusive of any negligence cause of action against an insurer for the handling and settling of a third party's claim.

—Affirming partial summary judgment, the Supreme Court of Wyoming, in *Kirkwood v. Cuna Mut. Ins. Soc'y*, 937 P.2d 206 (Wyo. 1997), held that causes of action for negligent failure to pay and negligent infliction of emotional distress were included within the tort of bad faith and could not be separately maintained.

§2.14 2. Relationship to Liability for Bad Faith

—Jurisdictions recognizing the co-existence of third-party actions for negligence and for bad faith, and permitting insureds to pursue either remedy, are represented by the following decisions, in addition to those cited in the book: *State Farm Mut. Auto Ins. Co. v. Hollis*, 554 So. 2d 387

(Ala. 1989); *McCall v. Southern Farm Bureau Casualty Ins. Co.*, 255 Ark. 401, 501 S.W.2d 223 (1973); *Boston Old Colony Ins. Co. v. Gutierrez*, 386 So. 2d 783 (Fla. 1980); *Rector v. Husted*, 214 Kan. 230, 519 P.2d 634 (1974); *Gibson v. Western Fire Ins. Co.*, 210 Mont. 267, 682 P.2d 725 (1984); *American Fidelity & Casualty Co. v. L.C. Jones Trucking Co.*, 321 P.2d 685 (Okla. 1958); *Miles v. State Farm Mut. Ins. Co.*, 238 S.C. 374, 120 S.E.2d 217 (1961); *Aycock Hosiery Mills v. Maryland Casualty Co.*, 157 Tenn. 559, 11 S.W.2d 889 (1928); *Hamilton v. State Farm Ins. Co.*, 83 Wash. 2d 787, 523 P.2d 193 (1974); *Alt v. American Family Mut. Ins. Co.*, 71 Wis. 2d 340, 237 N.W.2d 706 (1976).

—In *Mutual Assurance, Inc. v. Schulte*, 970 So. 2d 292 (Ala. 2007), the Alabama Supreme Court explained that a lawful basis for a liability insurer's refusal to settle is a defense to a bad faith claim but not to a negligence claim. To defend against the latter, the insurer must establish that a reasonably prudent insurer would have relied on the same lawful basis in refusing to settle.

§2.15 3. Negligence and Bad Faith as Alternative Standards

—The following are additional cases representing the view that "bad faith" and "negligence" are essentially equivalent standards in evaluating an insurer's liability for nonsettlement of a third-party claim: *State Farm Mut. Auto. Ins. Co. v. Hollis*, 554 So. 2d 387 (Ala. 1989); *Miller v. Byrne*, 916 P.2d 566 (Colo. Ct. App. 1995); *Kemper v. Equity Ins. Co.*, 396 F. Supp. 3d 1299 (N.D. Ga. 2019) (Georgia law), *rev'd on other grounds*, 823 Fed. Appx. 900 (11th Cir. 2020); *Gray v. Grain Dealers Mut. Ins. Co.*, 871 F.2d 1128 (D.C. Cir. 1989) (North Carolina law).

—In *Shamblin v. Nationwide Mut. Ins. Co.*, 396 S.E.2d 766 (W. Va. 1990), the West Virginia Supreme Court announced the adoption of what it called a "hybrid negligence-strict liability" standard. See discussion of *Shamblin* in supplement §2.19.

4. Application of Duty

§2.16 a. In General: Failure To Settle

—In *Hughes v. First Acceptance Ins. Co. of Ga.*, 343 Ga. App. 693, 808 S.E.2d 103 (2017), *rev'd*, 305 Ga. 489, 826 S.E.2d 71 (2019) an administrator of the insured's estate alleged that the insurer negligently or in bad faith failed to settle a claim that subsequently went to trial and resulted in a $5.3 million judgment against the insured's estate for injuries sustained by others in a car accident caused by the insured. The court found that genuine issues of material fact existed as to whether the insurer acted reasonably in failing to respond to a time-limited offer to settled within policy limits where the attorney for the insurer admitted that the offer-to-settle letters were inadvertently placed in medical records and no follow-up had occurred. The Georgia Court of Appeals found that the lower court erred when it found that there must be evidence on the record that the insurer knew or reasonably should have known it could settle all claims against the insured within the policy limits, because an insurer may in good faith and without notification to other claimants settle part of multiple claims against the insured even though such settlements deplete or exhaust policy limits. The Georgia Supreme Court reversed the opinion in *Hughes v. First Acceptance Ins. Co. of Ga.*, *supra*. See discussion in §2.7.

—Addressing a choice-of-law question, a federal district court in Kansas, in *Mirville v. Allstate Indem. Co.*, 71 F. Supp. 2d 1103 (D. Kan. 1999), explained that under Kansas law the alleged negligent failure to settle would have been actionable (*Bolinger v. Nuss*, 449 P.2d 502 (Kan. 1969)), but under New York law, which was applicable here, it was not (*Pavia v. State Farm Mut. Auto. Ins. Co.*, 82 N.Y.2d 445, 626 N.E.2d 24, 605 N.Y.S.2d 208 (1993)). (The auto accident in question took place in Kansas, but the insurance contract had been formed in New York.) See also *Roberts v.*

Printup, 595 F.3d 1181 (10th Cir. 2010) (reversing summary judgment for insurer; listing factors courts consider in determining whether insurer was negligent, under Kansas law, in rejecting offer to settle within policy limits).

—In *Roberts v. Printup*, 422 F.3d 1211 (10th Cir. 2005) (Kansas law), the Tenth Circuit reversed summary judgment, holding that fact questions existed as to whether the automobile liability insurer had acted negligently by mishandling the claimant's time-sensitive settlement offer.

—In *Transcare N.Y., Inc. v. Finkelstein, Levine & Gittlesohn & Partners*, 23 A.D.3d 250, 804 N.Y.S.2d 63 (2005), the court affirmed the denial of the defendants' motion for summary judgment on a claim for negligent failure to settle, holding that summary judgment was precluded by the existence of and issue of material fact as to whether, *inter alia*, the insurer had made sufficient efforts to investigate the underlying claim and resolve the matter within policy limits.

§2.17 b. Failure To Defend

—In *Willcox v. American Home Assurance Co.*, 900 F. Supp. 850 (S.D. Tex. 1995), the court predicted that the Texas Supreme Court, if presented with the issue, would reject a negligence claim based solely on an insurer's breach of its duty to defend.

§2.18 c. Improper or Ineffective Defense

—A plaintiff has no claim for "malicious defense" when a defendant chooses trial rather than settlement, even if defendant had no hope of prevailing; and failing to accept a settlement offer, even if such conduct is completely unreasonable, is not grounds for the imposition of sanctions. *Triplett v. Farmers Ins. Exch.*, 24 Cal. App. 4th 1415, 29 Cal. Rptr. 2d 741 (1994).

—For a case recognizing the existence (and assignability

to the judgment creditor) of a cause of action to recover an excess judgment based on the insurer's failure to provide an adequate defense, see *Aaron v. Allstate Ins. Co.*, 559 So. 2d 275 (Fla. Dist. Ct. App. 1990).

D. Insurer's Liability Under Other Theories

§2.19 1. Strict or Absolute Liability

—In *Asermely v. Allstate Ins. Co.*, 728 A.2d 461 (R.I. 1999), the Rhode Island Supreme Court adopted what is in effect a standard of strict liability in third-party cases. The court wrote as follows: "[I]f it has been afforded reasonable notice and if a plaintiff has made a reasonable written offer to a defendant's insurer to settle within the policy limits, the insurer is obligated to seriously consider such an offer. If the insurer declines to settle the case within the policy limits, it does so at its peril in the event that a trial results in a judgment that exceeds the policy limits, including interest. If such a judgment is sustained on appeal or is unappealed, the insurer is liable for the amount that exceeds the policy limits, unless it can show that the insured was unwillling to accept the offer of settlement. The insurer's duty is a fiduciary obligation to act in the best interests of the insured. Even if the insurer believes in good faith that it has a legitimate defense . . . , it must assume the risk of miscalculation if the ultimate judgment should exceed policy limits." 728 A.2d at 464.

—In *Shamblin v. Nationwide Mut. Ins. Co.*, 396 S.E.2d 766 (W. Va. 1990), the West Virginia Supreme Court undertook a survey of the standards applied in other jurisdictions in assessing an insurer's possible liability for an excess judgment where a settlement offer within policy limits has been rejected. After weighing the policy arguments in favor of various standards, the court announced its adoption of a "hybrid negligence-strict liability standard." (Though the court's holding is quite explicit, its research and reasoning are somewhat dubious. In the course of its survey of the law of other jurisdictions, for example, the court makes the questionable characterization of California and New Jersey law as embodying a strict liability standard.) The court in *Shamblin* explained the newly announced West Virginia standard, and unusual allocation of the burden of proof, as follows (396 S.E.2d at 776):

> We believe that wherever there is a failure on the part of an insurer to settle within policy limits where there exists the opportunity to settle and where such settlement within policy limits would release the insured from any and all personal liability, the insurer has prima facie failed to act in the insured's best interest and that such failure to so settle prima facie constitutes bad faith towards its insured.

In *Shamblin* itself, the state supreme court affirmed an award of $1 million in compensatory damages, but reversed another $1.5 million in punitives, holding that the evidence had not supported a finding of the necessary level of willfulness and malice. See also *Strahin v. Sullivan*, 647 S.E.2d 765 (W. Va. 2007) (discussing and applying principles set forth in *Shamblin*).

§2.20 2. Breach of Fiduciary Duty

—See supplement §1.2 for a discussion of the tendency on the part of courts in a number of states to limit the availability of a cause of action for breach of fiduciary duty, and to back off from characterizing the relationship between insurer and insured as truly fiduciary in nature.

—See *Thompson v. Cannon*, 224 Cal. App. 3d 1413, 274 Cal. Rptr. 608 (1990), holding that no fiduciary duty is ordinarily owed to an insured by an independent adjuster hired by the insurer to adjust a disputed claim. (But see *Morrisville Water & Light Dept. v. U.S. Fidelity & Guar. Co.*, 775 F. Supp. 718 (D. Vt. 1991), explaining that under

Vermont law an insurer's legal duty *is* that of a fiduciary. *Morrisville* is discussed in supplement §2.9.)

—In *St. Paul Fire & Marine Ins. Co. v. A.P.I., Inc.*, 738 N.W.2d 401 (Minn. Ct. App. 2007), the court, emphasizing that the insurer–insured relationship is not *per se* fiduciary, held that erroneous instructions to that effect required reversal of the judgment and remand for a new trial (738 N.W.2d at 407).

> For [a] fiduciary duty to arise, first, the insured must come forward with facts showing arguable coverage or the insurer must become independently aware of such facts so that the insurer is obligated to defend or to further investigate the potential claim. [Citations omitted.] Second, the insurer must assume the duty to defend and the concomitant duty to reasonably settle . . . . Here, the district court's instructions did not limit the fiduciary duty to special circumstances . . . . This error carried into the court's instruction equating a breach of fiduciary duty with bad faith. The errors in the instructions on breach of fiduciary duty and bad faith require reversal of the judgment on those two claims and remand for a new trial.

—In *Graske v. Auto-Owners Ins. Co.*, 647 F. Supp. 2d 1105 (D. Neb. 2009), a federal district court held that under Nebraska law neither contributory negligence on the part of the insured nor reliance on the advice of counsel was an affirmative defense to the insured's claims against the insurer for breach of contract and breach of fiduciary duty based on the insurer's alleged failure to sufficiently investigate claims against the insured and to settle them for policy limits.

—In *Ironshore Specialty Ins. Co. v. Conemaugh Health Sys., Inc.*, 423 F. Supp. 3d 139 (W.D. Pa. 2019) (Pennsylvania law), an excess insurer brought a declaratory judgment action against the insured arguing it was not liable for an excess judgment in a claim for medical malpractice. The insured counterclaimed for breach of contract and breach of fiduciary duty for filing the declaratory lawsuit and for failure to participate in the settlement and defense of the malpractice suit. The court refused to dismiss the counterclaim for breach of fiduciary duty where the claim was not duplicative of the breach of contract claim, because the insured showed that it had no right to recoup losses under the contract for defending the declaratory judgment lawsuit, and success of the counterclaim did not depend on success of the breach of contract claim. In addition, the insured succeeding in pleading damages where it was forced to defend against the declaratory action, and it may have been forced to acquire additional insurance when it was unsure of the willingness of the insurer to cover prospective liabilities.

—In *Morden v. XL Specialty Ins.*, 177 F. Supp. 3d 1320 (D. Utah 2016), *aff'd in pertinent part*, 903 F.3d 1145 (10th Cir. 2018) (Utah law), the federal district court granted the insurer summary judgment on a claim of breach of fiduciary duty to its insured. The court quoted *Black v. Allstate Ins. Co.*, 100 P.3d 1163, 1169 (Utah 2004), for the rule that "an insurer bears such fiduciary responsibilities only where it 'controls the disposition of claims against its insured, who relinquishes any right to negotiate on his own behalf.'" 177 F. Supp. 3d at 1340. It was undisputed that the insurer did not appoint counsel for the insured, take part in its defense, or take any other action on behalf of the insured, which retained its own counsel.

—In *Mutual of Enumclaw Ins. Co. v. Dan Paulson Construction, Inc.*, 161 Wash. 2d 903, 169 P.3d 1 (banc 2007), the Washington Supreme Court noted that a liability insurer defending its insured under a reservation of rights has an enhanced obligation of fairness. But while that relationship is fiduciary, the court explained, it is something less than a true fiduciary relationship, which would require the insurer to place the insured's interests above its own.

3. Violation of Statutory Duty

§2.21 a. The Reinstatement of the California *Royal Globe* Action

As discussed in this section of the book and in previous supplements, a private third-party right of action under California's Unfair Claims Settlement Practices Statute (Cal. Ins. Code §§790.03 et seq.) was recognized by the state supreme court in 1979, in *Royal Globe Ins. Co. v. Superior Court*, 23 Cal. 3d 880, 153 Cal. Rptr. 842 (1979), but was subsequently repudiated by the supreme court in 1988, in *Moradi-Shalal v. Fireman's Fund Ins. Co.*, 46 Cal. 3d 287, 250 Cal. Rptr. 116 (1988). On October 8, 1999, legislation entitled the "Fair Insurance Responsibility Act of 2000," reinstating elements of the *Royal Globe* cause of action, was signed into law by California Governor Gray Davis. (The insurance industry immediately began discussing its intention to mount a referendum struggle to attempt to overturn the legislation.)

The act, which took effect on January 1, 2000, creates a private statutory third-party right of action to recover general, special, and punitive damages, with certain limitations: (1) The cause of action is limited to situations in which an individual brings the underlying claim for bodily injury, or for property damage resulting from a motor vehicle collision. (2) Bodily injury is defined to exclude emotional distress of any kind resulting from economic loss, and also to exclude emotional distress claims not accompanied by actual physical manifestations of the emotional distress. (3) A cause of action may not be asserted by a person injured in an auto accident who was driving while intoxicated at the time of the accident and was convicted of that offense. (4) An insurer who makes an honest mistake in judgment in connection with settlement of a claim cannot be considered to have violated its obligation to act in good faith. (5) As a condition of filing an action, plaintiff must have obtained a final judgment after trial, a judgment after default, or an arbitration award in an amount greater than a settlement offer rejected by plaintiff in the underlying action. (6) The act applies prospectively only, to events occurring on or after January 1, 2000, and to conduct of an insurer or its agents concerning accidents or losses that occur after that date. (7) The act exempts medical, legal, and health-care malpractice insurers when the failure to settle is due to the policyholder's refusal to settle the claim, and the consent of the policyholder is required for settlement. (These provisions are included in new Cal. Civ. Code §§2870 and 2871.)

In *PacifiCare Life & Health Ins. Co. v. Jones*, 27 Cal. App. 5th 391, 238 Cal. Rptr. 3d 150 (2018), *review denied* (2019) a California Court of Appeal upheld regulations issued by the California Insurance Commissioner to implement the unfair claims settlement practices statute, Cal. Ins. Code §790.03 and other sections of the Insurance Code. Insurer PacifiCare had obtained a trial court order granting it declaratory relief and enjoining enforcement of the regulations in question. The insurer sought relief from an order of the Insurance Commissioner finding it had engaged in more than 900,000 prohibited acts and practices and imposing penalties of more than $173 million. The appeals court reversed the trial court's rulings and remanded the matter for further proceedings. The court applied precedent from *Royal Globe Ins. Co. v. Superior Court, supra,* to hold that a violation of the unfair claims settlement statute could occur by an insurer's single knowing act. 238 Cal. Rptr. 3d at 154 (citing Cal. Code Regs., tit. 10, §2695.1(a)). The court also upheld the Commissioner's regulations defining the terms "knowingly committed" and "willful" or "willfully," according substantial deference to the regulations. Regulation 2695.2(1) provides that "knowingly" means "performed with actual, implied or constructive knowledge, including but not limited to, that which is implied by operation of law." *Id.* at 155 (internal quotation marks omitted). Regulation 2695.2(y) provides that "willful" or "willfully" is "simply a purpose or willingness to commit the act" and "does not require any intent to violate law, or to injure another, or to acquire any advantage." *Id.* (internal quotation marks omitted).

In addition, by a provision codified in new Cal. Code Civ. Proc. §1778, the act specifies that if the insurer requests or agrees to submit a claim to arbitration, the insurer will be conclusively deemed to have complied with its obligation of good faith.

Rejecting the existence of a private right of action under California's Unfair Competition Act (Business and Professions Code section 17200 et seq.) based on claims practices that violate the Unfair Claims Settlement Practices Statute, see *Textron Financial Corp. v. National Union Fire Ins. Co.*, 118 Cal. App. 4th 1061, 13 Cal. Rptr. 3d 586 (2004), *disapproved on other grounds by Zhang v. Superior Court (Cal. Cap. Ins. Co.)*, 57 Cal. 4th 364, 304 P.3d 163 (2013); *Maler v. Superior Court*, 220 Cal. App. 3d 1592, 270 Cal. Rptr. 222 (1990); *Safeco Ins. Co. v. Superior Court*, 216 Cal. App. 3d 1491, 265 Cal. Rptr. 585 (1990); *Zephyr Park v. Superior Court*, 213 Cal. App. 3d 833, 262 Cal. Rptr. 106 (1989). But see *contra, State Farm Fire & Casualty Co. v. Superior Court*, 45 Cal. App. 4th 1093, 53 Cal. Rptr. 2d 229 (1996).

§2.24 d. Private Statutory Actions in Other Jurisdictions

—Reiterating the principle that a general business practice of wrongful conduct is required to state a cause of action under the Connecticut Unfair Claims Settlement Practices Act (Conn. Gen. Stat. §38-61(6)), see *Quimby v. Kimberly Clark Corp.*, 28 Conn. App. 660, 613 A.2d 838 (1992). And holding that a general business practice may not be established by evidence of a pattern of conduct or a series of actions within a single insured's case, see

Lees v. Middlesex Ins. Co., 229 Conn. 842, 643 A.2d 1282 (1994).

In *Macomber v. Travelers Prop. & Casualty*, 261 Conn. 620, 804 A.2d 180 (2002), the court reasoned that acts prohibited by the Connecticut Unfair Insurance Practices Act are also unlawful acts within the meaning of the Connecticut Unfair Trade Practices Act, thus recognizing the standing of third-party claimants to sue for a wide range of unfair claims settlement practices. In *Carford v. Empire Fire & Marine Ins. Co.*, 94 Conn. App. 41, 891 A.2d 55 (2006), it was held that a third-party claimant's right to assert a private cause of action for violation of the Unfair Insurance Practices Act through the Unfair Trade Practices Act does not extend to third parties absent subrogation or a judicial determination of the insured's liability. See also *Tucker v. American Int'l Grp., Inc.*, 179 F. Supp. 3d 224 (D. Conn. 2016) (denying insurer's motion for summary judgment where subrogee plaintiff brought claims under CUTPA/CUIPA alleging insurer's failure to properly investigate, delay, and refusal to participate in alternative dispute resolution procedures; discussing interaction between CUIPA and CUTPA at some length); *Guillory v. Allstate Ins. Co.*, 476 F. Supp. 2d 171 (D. Conn. 2007) (insured sufficiently alleged that his homeowner's insurer violated Connecticut Unfair Trade Practices Act by alleging that insurer had failed to conduct reasonable investigation, gave no notice of scheduled examination under oath, failed to attempt good faith and prompt settlement, and failed to provide reasonable explanation for denial). Compare *Hartford Roman Catholic Diocesan Corp. v. Interstate Fire & Casualty Co.*, 199 F. Supp. 3d 559, *aff'd*, 905 F.3d 84 (2d Cir. 2018) (insured failed to show that insurer's delay in settling claims constituted a "general business practice," as required to establish a CUIPA/CUTPA claim; court reviewed insurer's handling of similar claims in wide range of jurisdictions and found delay in only about 9% to 11% of cases).

—No private right of action may be asserted under Delaware's Unfair Claim Settlement Practices Statute (18 Del. Code Ann. §2304(16)). *Yardley v. U.S. Healthcare, Inc.*, 698 A.2d 979 (Del. Super. Ct. 1996), *aff'd without op.*, 693 A.2d 1083 (Del. 1997).

—Resolving a split of authority, the Florida Supreme Court held, in a 1995 decision, that third-party claimants have standing to sue under Florida's Unfair Claim Settlement Practices Statute. *Auto-Owners Ins. Co. v. Conquest*, 658 So. 2d 928 (Fla. 1995). This holding was amplified in *State Farm Fire & Casualty Co. v. Zebrowski*, 673 So. 2d 562 (Fla. 1997), in which the state supreme court held that third-party claimants may bring direct actions under Fla. Stat. Ann. §624.155(1)(b)(1) only after the third-party claimant has obtained a judgment against the insured in excess of policy limits.

—Holding that there exists no private right of action under Georgia's unfair claims settlement practices statute (Ga. Code Ann. §33-6-34), see *Rodgers v. St. Paul Fire & Marine Ins. Co.*, 228 Ga. App. 499, 492 S.E.2d 268 (1997).

—Although no private right of action exists under Hawaii's Unfair Claims Settlement Practices Statute (Haw. Rev. Stat. §431:13-103), it was held in *Wailua Assocs. v. Aetna Casualty & Surety Co.*, 27 F. Supp. 2d 1211 (D. Hawaii 1998), that violations of the statute may be adduced to demonstrate an insurer's bad faith. In *Aquilina v. Certain Underwriters at Lloyd's Syndicate #2003*, 407 F. Supp. 3d 1016 (D. Haw. 2019), the federal district court confirmed that the Insurance Code, Haw. Stat. §431:13–102, does not provide a private right of action, but held in the first-party context that the Insurance Code did not preempt actions under the Unfair and Deceptive Acts or Trade Practices Act (UDAP) §480–2. The court also acknowledged the availability of a third-party bad faith action under common law.

—Reiterating that no private right of action is maintainable under Idaho's Unfair Claims Practices Statute, see *Simper v. Farm Bureau Mut. Ins. Co.*, 974 P.2d 1100

(Idaho 1999). Accord *Inland Group of Cos. v. Providence Washington Ins. Co.*, 985 P.2d 674 (Idaho 1999) (holding, however, that insured's expert was properly allowed to use statute to establish industry standard practices in Idaho).

—Holding that Indiana's unfair claims settlement practices statute (Ind. Code §27-4-1-4.5) does not support private claims, see *Neurological Resources, P.C. v. Anthem Ins. Co.*, 61 F. Supp. 2d 840 (S.D. Ind. 1999).

—Reiterating the position that Iowa's unfair claim settlement practices statute does not support a private right of action, see *Bates v. Allied Mut. Ins. Co.*, 467 N.W.2d 255 (Iowa 1991).

—Kentucky should be listed among those remaining states whose courts hold that the state's unfair claim settlement practices statute impliedly creates a private right of action against an insurer in favor of third-party claimants: *Wittmer v. Jones*, 864 S.W.2d 885 (Ky. 1993); *State Farm Mut. Auto. Ins. Co. v. Reeder*, 763 S.W.2d 116 (Ky. 1988), *rehearing denied*; *Phelps v. State Farm Mut. Auto. Ins. Co.*, 680 F.3d 725 (6th Cir. 2012). A single incident can support a cause of action under the Kentucky statute: a general business practice is not required. *Simpson v. Travelers Ins. Cos.*, 812 S.W.2d 510 (Ky. Ct. App. 1991). See also *Indiana Ins. Co. v. Demetre*, 527 S.W.3d 12, 26 (Ky. 2017) (although Unfair Claims Settlement Practices Act (UCSPA), Ky. Rev. Stat. Ann. §304.12-230, does not provide for private right of action, Ky. Rev. Stat. Ann. §446.070 "allows a person injured by a violation of any Kentucky statute to recover damages from the offender"; read together, the provisions create "'statutory bad faith cause of action'" (quoting *State Farm Mut. Auto. Ins. Co. v. Reeder, supra*); *Knotts v. Zurich Ins. Co.*, 197 S.W.3d 512 (Ky. 2006) (UCSPA applies to conduct that occurs both before and after commencement of litigation).

In *Shaheen v. Progressive Casualty Ins. Co.*, 114 F. Supp. 3d 444 (W.D. Ky. 2015), *aff'd*, 673 Fed. Appx. 481 (6th Cir. 2016), the federal district court granted summary judgment for the insurer, holding that the insurer did not act in bad faith under Kentucky's unfair claims practices statute when it refused to pay the coverage limits unless the third-party plaintiff (the estate of a decedent killed by a hit-and-run driver) released the insured from all other claims. The court first noted that it was "doubtful" that the insurer's conduct rose to the level of "outrageous" conduct required to support a finding of bad faith. Moreover, the court applied the reasoning of the Massachusetts high court in *Lazaris, infra*, to find that the insurer "did not violate its duties under the [Kentucky Unfair Claims Settlement Practices Act], because the claim would only be considered settled once the claimant had released its claims against the insured." 114 F. Supp. 3d at 451.

In *Merritt v. Catholic Health Initiatives, Inc.*, 612 S.W.3d 822 (Ky. 2020), the Kentucky Supreme Court held that a health care provider's foreign captive insurer was not subject to Kentucky's UCSPA. The insurance company was a subsidiary of the provider and insured only its owner's liabilities, rather than engaging in risk spreading. Moreover, the company was subject to the laws of the Cayman Islands, not Kentucky law.

—In *Theriot v. Midland Risk Co.*, 694 So. 2d 184 (La. 1996), the Louisiana Supreme Court held that Louisiana's bad faith statute (La. Rev. Stat. Ann. §22:1220) creates a right of action directly in favor of third-party claimants, but only as to those specific acts enumerated in the statute. See also *Kelly v. State Farm Fire & Casualty Co.*, 169 So. 3d 328 (La. 2015) (affirming rule in *Theriot, supra*); *Woodruff v. State Farm Ins. Co.*, 2000 WL 768849 (La. Ct. App. 2000); *Genusa v. Robert*, 720 So. 2d 166 (La. Ct. App. 1998); *Reed v. Recard*, 728 So. 2d 31 (La. Ct. App. 1998); *Venible v. First Fire Ins. Co.*, 718 So. 2d 586 (La. Ct. App. 1998); *Jeanpierre v. Mikaelian*, 709 So. 2d 915 (La. Ct. App. 1998); *Risinger v. State Farm Mut. Auto. Ins. Co.*, 711 So. 2d 293 (La. Ct. App. 1997). It was emphasized in *Vaughan v. Franklin*, 785 So. 2d 79 (La. Ct. App. 2001), that the statute does not provide a cause of action against an insurer that breaches its duty to defend. In *Kelly v. State Farm Fire, supra,* the Louisiana Supreme Court answered questions certified to it by the Fifth Circuit. The court approved the holding of the Fifth Circuit in *Stanley v. Trinchard,* 500 F.3d 411 (5th Cir. 2007), that a first-party insured's cause of action under La. Rev. Stat. Ann. §22:1973(A) is not limited by the acts enumerated in §22:1973(B). See discussion in §2.7, *supra.*

—Concerning a private right of action under Maine's unfair claims settlement practices statute (Me. Rev. Stat. Ann. tit. 24-A, §2436-A(1)(B)), see *School Union No. 37 v. United Nat'l Ins. Co.,* 617 F.3d 554 (1st Cir. 2010) (Maine law); *Anderson v. Virginia Sur. Co.,* 985 F. Supp. 182 (D. Me. 1998).

—Reasserting the existence of a third-party claimant's private right of action under the Massachusetts Unfair Claim Settlement Practices Statute (Mass. Gen. L. ch. 176D, §3(9)(f)), see *Rhodes v. AIG Domestic Claims, Inc.,* 961 N.E.2d 1067 (Mass. 2012); *Kapp v. Arbella Mut. Ins. Co.,* 426 Mass. 683, 689 N.E.2d 1347 (1998); *Clegg v. Butler,* 424 Mass. 413, 676 N.E.2d 1134 (1997); *Fundquest Inc. v. Travelers Casualty & Sur. Co.,* 715 F. Supp. 2d 202 (D. Mass. 2010); *Adams v. Rubin,* 964 F. Supp. 507 (D. Me. 1997) (Massachusetts law).

In *Lazaris v. Metropolitan Property & Casualty Ins. Co.,* 428 Mass. 502, 703 N.E.2d 205 (1998), the Massachusetts Supreme Judicial Court, overruling *Thaler v. American Ins. Co.,* 34 Mass. App. Ct. 639, 614 N.E.2d 1021 (1993), held that an insurer does not violate the unfair claims settlement practices statute by insisting on a release of the insured before paying the policy limits. See also *Premier Ins. Co. v. Furtado,* 428 Mass. 507, 703 N.E.2d 208 (1998).

In *O'Leary-Alison v. Metropolitan Property & Casualty Ins. Co.,* 752 N.E.2d 795 (Mass. App. Ct. 2001), the court recited the principle of Massachusetts law that an insurer's good faith (though mistaken) evaluation of a claim cannot subject it to bad faith liability. Accordingly, the court affirmed a judgment for the insurer despite the fact that it had refused to offer more than $20,000 to pay a claim that later resulted in a jury verdict of $125,000. The insurer's doubts about the value of the claim had been rational, the court held.

In *Bobick v. United States Fidelity & Casualty Ins. Co.*, 57 Mass. App. Ct. 1, 781 N.E.2d 8 (2003), summary judgment was reversed on a third-party claimant's statutory cause of action even though the insurer's pretrial settlement offer of $50,000 was only $10,000 less than the amount the claimant was awarded at trial. The question of the reasonableness of the settlement offer was inherently factual and could not be answered on the basis of posttrial hindsight, the court held, emphasizing the existence of evidence from which a trier of fact could have found that the insurer's investigation was inadequate. For another case that discusses the reasonableness of a settlement offer under the Massachusetts statute, see *Calandro v. Sedgwick Claims Mgmt. Servs.*, 264 F. Supp. 3d 321 (D. Mass. 2017), *aff'd*, 919 F.3d 26 (1st Cir. 2019) (third-party administrator hired by insurer to handle wrongful death claim that arose from death of nursing home resident made settlement offer that was within safe harbor provision of Mass. Gen. Laws Ann. ch. 93A, where settlement offered was reasonable in relation to injury actually suffered by claimant and offer was made within statutorily required time period; claimant was limited to recovering $1.9 million offered under safe harbor provision).

In *Calandro v. Sedgwick Claims Mgmt. Servs., Inc.*, 919 F.3d 26 (1st Cir. 2019), an administrator of an estate brought a claim under Massachusetts's Unfair Claim Settlement Practices Statute against the claims management firm that handled claims for a nursing home's liability insurer after the claimant's mother died in hospice following a fall at the nursing home. The court affirmed the lower court's finding that the claims management firm satisfied the requirements of the statute for an adequate investigation where it immediately hired a qualified claims investigator who gathered documents from the nursing home and sought witnesses, although some documents and witnesses were not located, and the claims investigator found that whether or to what extent the nursing home was liable for the death was not clear. In addition, the claims management firm made prompt and reasonable settlement offers at several points in time. The court noted that the claims management firm did not handle the claim in a model way, but stated that perfection is not the standard imposed by the statute.

In *National Union Fire Ins. Co. of Pittsburgh, Penn. v. West Lake Academy*, 548 F.3d 8 (1st Cir. 2008), the First Circuit held that the Massachusetts statute does not require an insurer to make a written offer of settlement as opposed to an oral offer.

And in *Rhodes v. AIG Domestic Claims, Inc., supra,* it was held that due process was not violated by an award of multiple damages against the tortfeasor's excess insurer in the amount of over $22 million, under the section of the unfair business practices act requiring damages for knowing or willful violations to be calculated by multiplying the amount of the underlying judgment.

In *Rawan v. Continental Cas. Co.*, 483 Mass. 654, 136 N.E.3d 327 (2019), homeowners (claimants) brought a claim for bad faith against an engineer's professional liability insurer after the engineer failed to design their home to state building code standards. The insurance policy contained a consent-to-settle clause, and the insurer failed to convince the insured to settle. After trial, the insurer paid up to the policy limit, and the insured paid the remainder of the claim. The claimants then brought a bad faith claim against the insurer for failure to settle. The court held that a consent-to-settle provision in the insurance contract did not violate the insurer's duty to effectuate a prompt, fair, and equitable settlement under Mass. Gen. Laws Ann. ch. 176D §3(9)(f). However, the insurer must still conduct a reasonable investigation and engage in good faith settlement attempts. The court affirmed summary judgment in favor of the insurer where the insurer thoroughly investigated the underlying facts, informed the insured of the results of its investigation, encouraged mediation, explained the vulnerabilities to the insured, and encouraged the insured to settle. The court found that any deficiencies in the insurer's behavior did not cause harm to claimants, especially because the judgment was paid in full by the insurer and the insured.

In *Chiulli v. Liberty Mut. Ins., Inc.*, 97 Mass. App. 248, 146 N.E.3d 471 (2020), *review denied*, 485 Mass. 1102, 150 N.E.3d 1119 (2020), the appeals court held that the trial court erred when it found that insurer Liberty Mutual did not act willfully or knowingly when it violated Massachusetts' statutory settlement requirement under Mass. Gen. Laws ch. 93A. The court found that the insurer had a duty to offer settlement once the insured's liability became reasonably clear following closing arguments at trial. The court rejected the insurer's argument that its liability had to be "clear" instead of "reasonably clear" before it was required to tender a settlement offer. The insurer made its insured wait through Thanksgiving and Christmas, and internal documents showed that the delay was an intentional effort to use the insured's lack of funds to leverage a more favorable settlement. The court remanded for determination of whether a statutory penalty of two to three times the damages award would be proper.

—It was reiterated in *Isagholian v. Transamerica Ins. Corp.*, 208 Mich. App. 9, 527 N.W.2d 13 (1994), that the Michigan Unfair Claim Settlement Practices Statute does not support a private right of action.

—Although no private right of action is available under Minnesota's unfair claims settlement practices statute (Minn. Stat. ch. 72A), an insured is not precluded from suing an insurer under the state's consumer protection statute (Minn. Stat. §§325F.68–325F.70). *Parkhill v. Minnesota Mut. Life Ins. Co.*, 995 F. Supp. 983 (D. Minn. 1998).

—Although no private right of action is available under Missouri's Unfair Trade Practices Act, Mo. Rev. Stat. §§375.930 *et seq.*, common-law third-party claims are not preempted. *Grisamore v. State Farm Mut. Auto. Ins. Co.*, 306 S.W.3d 570 (Mo. Ct. App. 2010). Insureds may also seek recovery for vexatious refusal to pay under Mo. Rev. Stat. §§375.420 and 375.296, which provide for statutory penalties and attorney's fees. In *Nooter Corp. v. Allianz Underwriters Ins. Co.*, 536 S.W.3d 251 (Mo. Ct. App. 2017), the court upheld a jury verdict finding that the insurer's failure to pay the insured's third-party asbestos claims was a vexatious refusal to pay under Mo. Rev. Stat. §§375.420 and 375.296. See also *Drury Co. v. Missouri United Sch. Inc. Counsel*, 455 S.W.3d 30 (Mo. Ct. App. 2014) (upholding award of actual damages, statutory penalty, and attorney's fees in connection with vexatious refusal to pay claim under §375.420); *Doe Run Resources Corp. v. Certain Underwriters at Lloyd's London*, 400 S.W.3d 463 (Mo. Ct. App. 2013) (insured provided substantial evidence that excess insurer acted recalcitrantly and vexatiously in handling insured's claim under §375.420).

—Concerning the Montana Unfair Claims Settlement Practices Act (Mont. Code Ann. §§33-18-242(6)(b) et seq. (1987)), it was held in *Lough v. Insurance Co. of N. Am.*, 789 P.2d 576 (Mont. 1990), that maintenance of a private cause of action does not require a prior judicial determination (in the form of an entry of judgment) of the insured's liability to the third-party claimant: a settlement of the underlying claim is sufficient to satisfy the statute. The Montana rule thus differs from that of the California cases discussed in book and supplement §2.22, and from that expressed by the West Virginia Supreme Court in *Grove v. Myers*, 382 S.E.2d 536 (W. Va. 1989) (see book), and *Berry v. Nationwide Mut. Fire Ins. Co.*, 381 S.E.2d 367 (W. Va. 1989).

Also concerning private rights of action under the Montana Unfair Claims Settlement Practices Act and the Unfair Trade Practices Act, (Mont. Code Ann. §§33-18-101 et seq.), see *Juedeman v. National Farmers Union*, 833 P.2d 191 (Mont. 1992), in which the state supreme court, affirming summary judgment, held that an auto insurer had not violated the statute's "leveraging" prohibition by conditioning its offer to settle a third party's personal injury claim upon a release of the insured's estate from any future claim for loss of consortium. The antileveraging provision applies only with respect to the manipulation of two separate coverages, the court explained, and here both claims fell under the same coverage. For other discussions and applications of the Montana statutes, see *Marshall v. Safeco Ins. Co. of Ill.*, 390 Mont. 358, 413 P.3d 828 (2018) (Uniform Trade Practices Act provides independent cause of action to insured or third-part claimant, once underlying claim has been settled); *Peterson v. St. Paul Fire & Marine Ins. Co.*, 239 P.3d 904 (Mont. 2010) (clarifying meaning of phrase "when liability is reasonably clear" for purposes of claims under Montana Unfair Trade Practices Act); *Jacobsen v. Allstate Ins. Co.*, 351 Mont. 464, 215 P.3d 649 (2009) (neither equitable nor insurance exception to "American rule" applied to permit recovery of attorneys' fees as element of damages for insurance bad faith, whether claim is brought under Unfair Trade Practice Act or under common law); *Brewington v. Employers Fire Ins. Co.*, 992 P.2d 237 (Mont. 1999) (Unfair Claims Practices Act does not preempt common-law bad faith cause of action on behalf of third-party claimants); *Dees v. American Nat'l Fire Ins. Co.*, 861 P.2d 141 (Mont. 1993) (affirming a $300,000 punitive damages award for an insurer's failure to conduct an adequate investigation of the cause of the insured's crop loss); *O'Fallon v. Farmers Ins. Exch.*, 859 P.2d 1008 (Mont. 1993) (holding, *inter alia*, that private right of action may be asserted against independent adjusters as well as insurers). See also *Ridley v. Guaranty Nat'l Ins. Co.*, 951 P.2d 987 (Mont. 1997), concerning an insurer's duty under the statute to pay amounts clearly owed to a third party even though other amounts may remain subject to dispute, and *Etter v. Safeco Ins. Co. of America*, 192 F. Supp. 2d 1071 (D. Mont. 2002). *Ridley* was subsequently clarified and applied in *Shilhanek v. D-2 Trucking, Inc.*, 315 Mont. 519, 2003 MT 122, 70 P.3d 721 (2003).

—For a case holding that no private right of action is provided by the Nebraska Unfair Insurance Trade Practices Act, see *McShane Constr. Co. v. Gotham Ins. Co.*, 867 F.3d 923 (8th Cir. 2017).

—Holding that a self-insured employer is not subject to the private right of action contemplated by New Mexico's unfair claims settlement practices statute (N.M. Stat. Ann. §§59A-16-1 et seq.), see *Kitchell v. Public Serv. Co.*, 972 P.2d 344 (N.M. 1998). In *Hovet v. Allstate Ins. Co.*, 135 N.M. 397, 89 P.3d 69 (N.M. 2004), it was held that a third-party claimant has a private right of action against a liability insurer for unfair claims practices in violation of the Insurance Code (NMSA §59A-16-30), but the action may be filed only after the conclusion of the underlying negligence litigation and after a judicial determination of fault. See also *Martinez v. Cornejo*, 146 N.M. 223, 208 P.3d 443 (Ct. App. 2008) (manager of insurer's adjusters was "insurer" Trade Practices and Frauds Act against whom third-party claimants could bring private actions for unfair claims settlement practices).

—Addressing an issue of first impression, a North Carolina Court of Appeals held, in *Wilson v. Wilson*, 121 N.C. App. 662, 468 S.E.2d 495 (1996), that North Carolina does not recognize a cause of action by third-party claimants against the insurer of an adverse party based on unfair and deceptive trade practices under N.C. Gen. Stat. §75–1.1. The court cited *Moradi-Shalal v. Fireman's Fund Ins. Co.*, 46 Cal. 3d 287, 250 Cal. Rptr. 116 (1988) (see §2.21), and noted that most states that have considered the issue have not allowed a third-party claim against the insurer of an adverse party. *Wilson v. Wilson, supra,* was distinguished in *Murray v. Nationwide Mut. Ins. Co.*, 472 S.E.2d 358 (N.C. Ct. App. 1996), in which it was held that the injured party in an automobile accident is an intended third-party beneficiary and may bring an action under North Carolina's unfair claims settlement practices statute (N.C. Gen. Stat. §58-63-15).

North Carolina is listed in the book as among those states requiring proof of a "general business practice" to support a statutory bad faith cause of action in first-party cases. See also *Belmont Land & Inv. Co. v. Standard Fire Ins. Co.*, 102 N.C. App. 745, 403 S.E.2d 924 (1991). For a discussion of the interrelation of N.C. Gen. Stat. ch. 75 and ch. 58, art. 3A, see *United States Fire Ins. Co. v. Nationwide Mut. Ins. Co.*, 735 F. Supp. 1320 (E.D. N.C. 1990) (chapter 58 does not create a private right of action, but a violation of N.C. Gen. Stat. §58.54.4 as a matter of law constitutes a violation of N.C. Gen. Stat. §75.1.1; there is no requirement, however, that plaintiff must prove a chapter 58 violation to prove a chapter 75 violation). See also *Gray v. North Carolina Ins. Underwriting Ass'n*, 352 N.C. 61, 529 S.E.2d 676 (2000) , *reh'g denied*, 544 S.E.2d 771 (2000); *Miller v. Nationwide Mut. Ins. Co.*, 112 N.C. 295, 435 S.E.2d 537 (Ct. App. 1993); *ABT Building Prods. Corp. v. National Union Fire Ins. Co. of Pittsburgh*, 472 F.3d 99 (4th Cir. 2006) (North Carolina law); *High Country Arts & Crafts Guild v. Hartford Fire Ins. Co.*, 126 F.3d 629 (4th Cir. 1997).

For a more recent case describing the relationship between North Carolina's Unfair Claim Settlement Practices (UCSP) statute, N.C. Gen. Stat. Ann. §58-63-15, and its Unfair and Deceptive Trade Practices Act (UDTPA), N.C. Gen. Stat. Ann. §75-1.1, see *Elliott v. American States Ins. Co.*, 883 F.3d 384 (4th Cir. 2018). The court explained that UDTPA §75-1.1 provides a private right of action, while the UCSP statute does not. The remedy for violation of a UCSP statutory provision is to bring an action under Section §75-1.1. Although establishing a violation of §58-63-15 requires establishing a general business practice, no such showing is required to establish a violation of §75-1.1 by reference to conduct prohibited by §58-63-15.

—North Dakota is listed in the book as among those states having rejected private enforcement of their unfair claim settlement practices statutes. In *Volk v. Wisconsin Mortgage Assurance Co.*, 474 N.W.2d 40 (N.D. 1991), however, the state supreme court referred to that question as still unresolved. (The court found it unnecessary to resolve the question in *Volk*, affirming summary judgment on the ground that even if the statute is privately enforceable, a general business practice is required and the plaintiff had failed to prove one.)

—Concerning Oklahoma's nonrecognition of private rights of action under the state unfair claims settlement practices statute and other consumer protection statutes, see *McWhirter v. Fire Ins. Exch., Inc.*, 878 P.2d 1056 (Okla. 1994); *Thompson v. State Farm Fire & Casualty Co.*, 34 F.3d 932 (10th Cir. 1994).

—In *Birth Ctr. v. St. Paul Cos., Inc.*, 567 Pa. 386, 787 A.2d 376 (2001), the Pennsylvania Supreme Court made clear that the cause of action created by Pennsylvania's bad faith statute (42 Pa. Cons. Stat. Ann. §8371) is not exclusive of a common-law cause of action for breach of the duty to settle, though one limited to contract-measure damages. See also *Wolfe v. Allstate Prop. & Ins. Co.*, 790 F.3d 487 (3d Cir. 2015) (discussed in §§2.73 and 4.19A); *Haugh v. Allstate Ins. Co.*, 322 F.3d 227 (3d Cir. 2003); *Ironshore Specialty Ins. Co. v. Conemaugh Health Sys., Inc.*, 423 F. Supp. 3d 139 (W.D. Pa. 2019) (Pennsylvania law); *United Nat'l Ins. Co. v. Indian Harbor Ins. Co.*, 160 F. Supp. 3d 828 (E.D. Pa. 2016); *Papurello v. State Farm Fire & Casualty Co.*, 144 F. Supp. 3d 746 (W.D. Pa. 2015); *McMahon v. Medical Protective Co.*, 92 F. Supp. 3d 367, *recon. denied*, 2015 WL 4633698 (W.D. Pa. 2015); *Empire Fire & Marine Ins. Co. v. Jones*, 739 F. Supp. 2d 746 (M.D. Pa. 2010).

—In *Asermely v. Allstate Ins. Co.*, 728 A.2d 461 (R.I. 1999), the Rhode Island Supreme Court recognized private statutory claims, under R.I. Gen. Laws §9-1-33(a), in the third-party as well as the first-party context. The unusual standard of strict liability that the court held applicable in the third-party context is discussed in §2.19.

—In *Rocor Int'l, Inc. v. National Union Fire Ins. Co.*, 77 S.W.3d 253 (Tex. 2002), the Texas Supreme Court addressed a number of issues relative to the scope of an insurer's duty to "attempt" settlement under Texas Insurance Code art. 21.21 and concerning the relationship of that duty to the common-law *"Stowers"* cause of action.

For Texas cases discussing the interrelation of the Texas Deceptive Trade Practices Act and Insurance Code art. 21.21 (discussed in this section of the book), see *Crown Life Ins. Co. v. Casteel*, 22 S.W.3d 378 (Tex. 1999); *Safeway Managing Gen. Agency v. Cooper*, 952 S.W.2d 861 (Tex. Ct. App. 1997); *Maryland Ins. Co. v. Head Indus. Coatings & Servs., Inc.*, 906 S.W.2d 218 (Tex. Ct. App. 1995); *Crum & Forster, Inc. v. Monsanto Co.*, 887 S.W.2d 103 (Tex. Ct. App. 1994); *Watson v. Allstate Ins. Co.*, 828 S.W.2d 423 (Tex. Ct. App. 1991); *Crawford & Co. v. Garcia*, 817 S.W.2d 98 (Tex. Ct. App. 1991); *Allied Gen. Agency, Inc. v. Moody*, 788 S.W.2d 601 (Tex. Ct. App. 1990); *Stewart Title Guar. Co. v. Sterling*, 772 S.W.2d 242 (Tex. Ct. App. 1989); *Aetna Casualty & Sur. Co. v. Joseph*, 769 S.W.2d 603 (Tex. Ct. App. 1989); *United Neurology, P.A. v. Hartford Lloyd's Ins. Co.*, 101 F. Supp. 3d 584 (S.D. Tex. 2015), *aff'd mem.*, 624 Fed. Appx. 225 (5th Cir. 2015).

In *Lyda Swinerton Builders, Inc. v. Oklahoma Sur. Co.*, 903 F.3d 435 (5th Cir. 2018), the court stated that defense costs incurred by the insured that were a result of the insurer's breach of its duty to defend were a claim within meaning of the Texas Prompt Payment Claims Act (Tex. Ins. Code §542.051–.061). In addition to defense costs, the insured would be entitled to 18-percent interest on the amount of the claim as a statutory penalty if the claim was successful on remand. The court explained that because it reversed the district court's judgment on the statutory claim, the interest would not stop accruing until the date judgment was entered by the trial court after it heard the case on remand. The court also reversed and remanded a claim related to extra-contractual damages under Chapter

541 of the Texas Insurance Code in light of *USAA Tex. Lloyds Co. v. Menchaca*, 545 S.W.3d 479 (Tex. 2018) (discussed in §1.56). The *Lyda Swinerton Builders* court stated that if the insured could establish that the insurer's misrepresentations caused it to be deprived of a benefit under the insurance contract, the insured could recover defense costs it incurred as actual damages under Chapter 541 without limitation from the independent-injury rule. In addition, the court stated that the insured could recover treble damages under Chapter 541 if the insurer knowingly committed the alleged acts.

—It was held by a Washington Court of Appeals, in *Neigel v. Harrell*, 82 Wash. App. 782, 919 P.2d 630 (1996), that insurers owe no settlement duties to third-party claimants under either the state Consumer Protection Act or the Unfair Claims Settlement Practices statute. The court cited and relied on the state supreme court's holding in *Tank v. State Farm Fire & Casualty Co.*, 715 P.2d 1133 (Wash. 1986). For a case that involves assignment of claims to a third party under Washington's Consumer Protection Act (Wash. Rev. Code Ch. 19.86) and the Insurance Fair Conduct Act (Wash. Rev. Code Ch. §48.30.010–.015), see *Gosney v. Fireman's Fund Ins. Co.*, 3 Wash. App. 2d 828, 419 P.3d 447 (2018), *review denied*, 191 Wash. 2d 1017 (2018) (see discussion in §4.28).

—For a discussion of accrual issues relative to the private statutory cause of action in West Virginia, see *Barefield v. DPIC Cos., Inc.*, 600 S.E.2d 256 (W. Va. 2004); *Rose ex rel. Rose v. St. Paul Fire & Marine Ins. Co.*, 599 S.E.2d 673 (W. Va. 2004); *Taylor v. Nationwide Mut. Ins. Co.*, 589 S.E.2d 55 (W. Va. 2003); *Robinson v. Continental Casualty Co.*, 406 S.E.2d 470 (W. Va. 1991). In *State ex rel. State Auto Prop. Ins. Cos. v. Stucky*, 239 W. Va. 729, 806 S.E.2d 160 (2017), the court held that the insured had no standing to assert a private right of action against its liability insurer under the West Virginia Unfair Trade Practices Act. The court stated that the statute was designed to protect plaintiffs seeking liability-related damages from the insured, and not the insured itself, but did not address whether such plaintiffs had a private right of action.

—In the following cases, the courts reiterated their jurisdictions' nonrecognition of any private right of action, express or implied, under the state's unfair claim settlement practices statute: *O.K. Lumber v. Providence Wash. Ins. Co.*, 759 P.2d 523 (Alaska 1988); *Schnacker v. State Farm Mut. Auto. Ins. Co.*, 843 P.2d 102 (Colo. Ct. App. 1992); *Hunt v. First Ins. Co.*, 82 Haw. 363, 922 P.2d 976 (1996); *Horning Wire Corp. v. Home Indem. Co.*, 8 F.3d 587 (7th Cir. 1993) (Illinois law); *Dietrich v. Liberty Mut. Ins. Co.*, 759 F. Supp. 467 (N.D. Ind. 1991) (Indiana law); *Johnson v. Federal Kemper Ins. Co.*, 74 Md. App. 243, 536 A.2d 1211 (1988); *City of Amsterdam v. Lam*, 703 N.Y.S.2d 606 (App. Div. 2000); *Rein Monroe Assocs. v. Royal Ins. Co. of Am.*, 175 A.D.2d 582, 572 N.Y.S.2d 247 (1991); *Telemaque v. New York Property Ins. Underwriting Ass'n*, 556 N.Y.S.2d 391 (App. Div. 1990); *Riordan v. Nationwide Mut. Fire Ins. Co.*, 756 F. Supp. 732 (S.D.N.Y. 1990) (although unfair claim settlement practices statute supports no private right of action, pattern of violations may satisfy requirements for cause of action under New York General Business Law §349 for "deceptive business practices"; see §1.34 concerning subsequent history following appeal to Second Circuit); *Tinlee Enterps., Inc. v. Aetna Casualty & Sur. Co.*, 834 F. Supp. 605 (E.D.N.Y. 1993) (distinguishing *Riordan v. Nationwide Mut. Fire Ins. Co., supra*, on its facts); *Dvorak v. American Family Life Ins. Co.*, 508 N.W.2d 329 (N.D. 1993) (declining to reach question of existence of private actions under North Dakota unfair claims settlement practices statute); *Farmer's Union Cent. Exch., Inc. v. Reliance Ins. Co.*, 675 F. Supp. 1534 (D.N.D. 1987) (North Dakota law; clarifying earlier opinion in same litigation, at 626 F. Supp. 583, apparently reasoning that breach of statutory duty can be probative of commission of common-law bad faith tort); *Gianfillippo v. Northland Ca-*

sualty Co., 861 P.2d 308 (Okla. 1993); *Walker v. Chouteau Lime Co.*, 849 P.2d 1085 (Okla. 1993).

—It should be noted that the N.A.I.C.'s 1990 amendments to the Model Unfair Trade Practices Act have added a provision to the Unfair Claim Settlement Practices portion of the Act expressly disclaiming the intent to contemplate enforcement by any private right of action.

§2.25 E. Liability of Attorneys and Other Agents and Employees

—See authorities discussed in §3.30.

II. ESTABLISHING BAD FAITH

A. Required Proof

§2.26 1. In General

—In *Camelot By the Bay v. Scottsdale Ins. Co.*, 27 Cal. App. 4th 33, 32 Cal. Rptr. 2d 354 (1994), a California Court of Appeal reversed a judgment for the insured for bad faith failure to settle, emphasizing that the danger of an excess judgment had never been presented. The insurer had justifiably refused to settle even though such refusal had exposed the insured to personal liability for claims not covered by the insurance policy. See also *Yan Fang Du v. Allstate Ins. Co.*, 697 F.3d 753 (9th Cir. 2012) (noting split of authority and not reaching question whether "genuine dispute doctrine" applies to duty to settle third-party claims); *State Farm Fire & Casualty Co. v. Yukiyo, Ltd.*, 870 F. Supp. 292 (N.D. Cal. 1994) (liability insurer's duty to settle is not enhanced by prospect of high attorney's fees). Similarly, it has been held that an insurer's settlement duties do not require the insurer to take into account the insured's possible exposure to uninsurable punitive damages. See, *e.g.*, *Soto v. State Farm Ins. Co.*, 83 N.Y.2d 718, 635 N.E.2d 1222, 613 N.Y.S.2d 352 (1994); *Magnum Foods,*

Inc. v. Continental Casualty Co., 36 F.3d 1491 (10th Cir. 1994) (Oklahoma law); *Wolfe v. Allstate Prop. & Ins. Co.*, 790 F.3d 487 (3d Cir. 2015) (discussed in §§2.73 and 4.19A) (Pennsylvania law); *St. Paul Fire & Marine Ins. Co. v. Convalescent Servs., Inc.*, 193 F.3d 340 (5th Cir. 1999) (Texas law). Compare *Landow v. Medical Ins. Exch.*, 892 F. Supp. 239 (D. Nev. 1995) (under Nevada law, insurer must consider emotional distress and damage to insured's business that will result from failure to settle and publicity of trial). But see, contra, *North Am. Van Lines v. Lexington Ins. Co.*, 678 So. 2d 1325 (Fla. Dist. Ct. App. 1996). In *Perera v. United States Fid. & Guar. Co.*, 35 So. 3d 893 (Fla. 2010), the Florida Supreme Court held that a cause of action for bad faith may not be maintained where the insurer's actions, because of the existence of an excess liability policy issued by another insurer, never resulted in the insured's increased exposure to liability in excess of his total policy limits.

—In *Kumar v. American Transit Ins. Co.*, 57 A.D.3d 1449, 869 N.Y.S.2d 715 (2008), a New York Supreme Court, Appellate Division, reversed summary judgment that had been entered in favor of the insureds, holding they had failed to establish that they had lost an actual opportunity to settle at a time when all serious doubts about liability had been removed, or that the insurer had engaged in a pattern of behavior evincing a knowing indifference to the probability that they would be held personally accountable for a large judgment. See also *General Motors Acceptance Corp. v. New York Cent. Mut. Fire Ins. Co.*, 116 A.D.3d 468, 983 N.Y.S.2d 513 (2014), *leave to appeal denied*, 24 N.Y.3d 911, 1 N.Y.S.3d 6, 25 N.E.3d 343 (2014) (automobile insurer did not act in bad faith toward insured driver or driver's excess insurer by failing to make policy limits settlement offer; automobile insurer's review of numerous medical documents, which included contradicting evaluations, provided justifiable basis for determination that passenger did not sustain serious injury causally related to collision as required to meet no-fault law's tort-recovery threshold); *Tokio Marine v. Macready*, 803 F. Supp. 2d 193 (E.D.N.Y. 2011) (New York law) (to prove bad faith claim against liability insurer, insured must establish that insurer's conduct constituted gross disregard of insured's interests, *i.e.*, that insurer engaged in pattern of behavior evincing conscious indifference to probability that insured would be held personally accountable for large judgment if policy limits settlement offer were not accepted).

—Concerning the entry of a final excess judgment—not simply the rejection of a reasonable settlement offer—as a prerequisite to the maintenance of a bad faith action, see *RLI Ins. Co. v. CNA Casualty of Calif.*, 141 Cal. App. 4th 75, 45 Cal. Rptr. 3d 667 (2006); *Cunningham v. Standard Guar. Ins. Co.*, 630 So. 2d 179 (Fla. 1994); *United Servs. Auto. Ass'n v. Jennings*, 707 So. 2d 384 (Fla. Dist. Ct. App. 1998), *aff'd*, 731 So. 2d 1258 (Fla. 1999); *Allstate Ins. Co. v. Campbell*, 334 Md. 381, 639 A.2d 652 (1994); *Jarvis v. Farmers Ins. Exch.*, 948 P.2d 898 (Wyo. 1997); *Sabins v. Commercial Union Ins. Cos.*, 82 F. Supp. 2d 1270 (D. Wyo. 2000) (Wyoming law). Compare *RLI Ins. Co. v. Scottsdale Ins. Co.*, 691 So. 2d 1095 (Fla. Dist. Ct. App. 1997) (no excess judgment in underlying action against insured was required for insured to assert bad faith failure-to-settle claims against primary and excess insurers). (Note that it was held in *Cunningham v. Standard Guar. Ins. Co.*, *supra*, that a stipulated judgment is the equivalent of a final judgment entered after trial for purposes of satisfying the preconditions for a third party's bad faith action.)

—In *Mid-Continent Ins. Co. v. Liberty Mut. Ins. Co.*, 236 S.W.3d 765 (Tex. 2007), the Texas Supreme Court explained that a liability insurer's common-law duty to its insured is limited to the *Stowers* duty to protect the insured by accepting a reasonable settlement offer within policy limits. That duty is not activated, the court continued, unless

(1) the claim is within the scope of coverage; (2) the demand is within policy limits; and (3) the terms of the

demand are such that an ordinarily prudent insurer would accept it, considering the likelihood and degree of the insured's potential exposure to an excess judgment. The court emphasized that a demand above liability policy limits, even if reasonable, does not trigger the *Stowers* duty.

—In *St. Paul Fire & Marine Ins. Co. v. Onvia, Inc.*, 165 Wash. 2d 122, 196 P.3d 664 (2008), the Supreme Court of Washington held that a third party has a cause of action for bad faith claims handling that is not dependent on the duty to indemnify, settle, or defend.

—See supplement §2.19 for a discussion of *Shamblin v. Nationwide Mut. Ins. Co.*, 396 S.E.2d 766 (W. Va. 1990), in which the West Virginia Supreme Court has come close to adopting a strict liability standard for failure-to-settle cases, and has placed an unusual burden of proof upon the insurer to establish the reasonableness of its conduct.

§2.27 2. Multiplicity of Factors

—For an articulation of Arizona law's eight-factor test for determining an insurer's bad faith in failing to settle a third-party claim, see *Lozier v. Auto Owners Ins. Co.*, 951 F.2d 251 (9th Cir. 1991) (Arizona law; affirming award in amount of $3.5 million *Damron* settlement between insured and victim). See supplement §2.63 for an explanation of the *Damron* settlement.

—For an articulation of Florida's multiple requirements of the duty of good faith in third-party claims, see *Feijoo v. Geico Gen. Ins. Co.* 137 F. Supp. 3d 1320 (S.D. Fla. 2015), *aff'd*, 678 Fed. Appx. 862 (11th Cir. 2017).

—For an enumeration of seven factors that Illinois courts have identified as probative of insurance bad faith in the third-party context, see *O'Neill v. Gallant Ins. Co.*, 769 N.E.2d 100 (Ill. Ct. App. 2002).

—In *McKinley v. Guaranty Nat'l Ins. Co.*, 144 Idaho 247, 159 P.3d 884 (2007), the Idaho Supreme Court listed seven factors to be considered by the trier of fact in determining whether an insurer acted in bad faith in failing to settle a claim against its insured. The court noted that two of the seven factors are entitled to particular emphasis: (1) the insurer's failure to communicate with the insured concerning any compromise offers; and (2) the amount of financial risk to which each party will be exposed in the event an offer is refused.

—For an enumeration of the eight factors that, according to the Tenth Circuit, are to be considered under Kansas law in determining whether an insurer's refusal to settle constituted a breach of its duty to act in good faith, see *Wade v. EMCASCO Ins. Co.*, 483 F.3d 657 (10th Cir. 2007).

—For a discussion of Kentucky's three-factor test to recover on a third-party bad faith claim, see *Hollaway v. Direct Gen. Ins. Co. of Miss., Inc.*, 497 S.W.3d 733 (Ky. 2016).

—Concerning New York law's multi-factor test, see *Pavia v. State Farm Mut. Auto. Ins. Co.*, 82 N.Y.2d 445, 626 N.E.2d 24, 605 N.Y.S.2d 208 (1993); *New England Ins. Co. v. Healthcare Underwriters Mut. Ins. Co.*, 295 F.3d 232 (2d Cir. 2002); *Pinto v. Allstate Ins. Co.*, 221 F.3d 294 (2d Cir. 2000).

B. Factors Suggesting Bad Faith

1. Failure To Advise Insured

§2.28 a. Potential for Excess Judgment

—Reiterating the principle that bad faith may be established by the single factor of an insurer's failure to warn its insured of the possibility of an excess judgment, see *Berges v. Infinity Ins. Co.*, 896 So. 2d 665 (Fla. 2004); *Mills v. State Farm Mut. Auto. Ins. Co.*, 27 So. 3d 95 (Fla. Dist. Ct. App. 2010); *Gourley v. Prudential Property & Casualty Ins. Co.*, 734 So. 2d 940 (La. Ct. App. 1999).

—In *Christian Builders, Inc. v. The Cincinnati Ins. Co.*, 501 F. Supp. 2d 1224 (D. Minn. 2007), a federal district court applying Minnesota law explained that although an insurer may be liable for bad faith if it fails to inform its insured of a potential conflict between its interests and those of the insured, it does not need to employ the words "conflict of interest": it is sufficient if the insurer advises the insured of the risk of an excess judgment, and that the insured would be liable for the excess portion of any judgment. In the present case, the court also held, the insurer had been under no duty to inform the insured of the estimated value of an excess verdict. When an insurer reasonably determines that there is only a remote chance that an excess verdict in any amount will be entered, Minnesota law does not require the insurer to give the insured an estimated dollar amount.

§2.29 b. Existence of Settlement Offers

—For additional cases emphasizing the failure of the insurer to inform the insured of the existence of settlement offers as a circumstance tending to establish the insurer's bad faith, see *Berges v. Infinity Ins. Co.*, 896 So. 2d 665 (Fla. 2004); *Odom v. Canal Ins. Co.*, 582 So. 2d 1203 (Fla. Dist. Ct. App. 1991); *Levier v. Koppenheffer*, 879 P.2d 40 (Kan. Ct. App. 1994); *Smith v. Blackwell*, 14 Kan. App. 2d 158, 791 P.2d 1343 (1989), *review granted*; *Lafauci v. Jenkins*, 844 So. 2d 19 (La. Ct. App. 2003); *Maryland Casualty Co. v. Dixie Ins. Co.*, 622 So. 2d 698 (La. Ct. App. 1993); *Keith v. Comco Ins. Co.*, 574 So. 2d 1270 (La. Ct. App. 1991), *cert. denied*, 577 So. 2d 16 (La. 1991); *Continental Casualty Co. v. Great Am. Ins. Co.*, 711 F. Supp. 1475 (N.D. Ill. 1989) (Michigan law); *Johnson v. Allstate Ins. Co.*, 262 S.W.3d 655 (Mo. Ct. A[1]pp. 2008); *Transcare N.Y., Inc. v. Finkelstein, Levine & Gittlesohn & Partners*, 23 A.D.3d 250, 804 N.Y.S.2d 63 (2005); and *Haugh v. Allstate Ins. Co.*, 322 F.3d 227 (3d Cir. 2003) (Pennsylvania law). Compare *Rodriguez v. American Ambassador Casualty*

Co., 4 F. Supp. 2d 1153 (M.D. Fla. 1998) (Florida law), *aff'd*, 170 F.3d 188 (11th Cir. 1999).

—In *Anguiano v. Allstate Ins. Co.*, 209 F.3d 1167 (9th Cir. 2000) (California law), the Ninth Circuit, reversing summary judgment, held there existed a genuine issue of material fact as to the insurer's bad faith in failing to inform its insured of settlement negotiations, even though the injured party's offers were defective in failing to account for an anticipated Medi-Cal lien on any settlement proceeds. The duty to communicate a settlement offer is particularly important, the court held, where, as in the present case, a conflict of interest exists between insurer and insured.

Because the insured's coverage had lapsed before the auto accident in question, the insurer had had no duty to inform the insured of settlement offers from the injured party, the court held in *Farmers Ins. Exch. v. Jacobs*, 75 Cal. App. 4th 373, 89 Cal. Rptr. 2d 222 (1999). Noncoverage was established in a declaratory judgment action after a wrongful death action, with the insurer defending the insured under a reservation of rights, had resulted in a $2.2 million judgment. (The court noted that the insurer had assumed an obligation as a volunteer to conduct the defense with due care, but the injured party had not asserted any negligence cause of action.)

—In *McKinley v. Guaranty Nat'l Ins. Co.*, 144 Idaho 247, 159 P.3d 884 (2007), the Idaho Supreme Court listed seven factors to be considered by the trier of fact in determining whether an insurer acted in bad faith in failing to settle a claim against its insured. The court noted that two of the seven factors are entitled to particular emphasis: (1) the insurer's failure to communicate with the insured concerning any compromise offers; and (2) the amount of financial risk to which each party will be exposed in the event an offer is refused.

—In *Kelly v. State Farm Fire & Casualty Co.*, 169 So. 3d 328 (La. 2015), the Louisiana Supreme Court held that an insured could bring a bad faith claim against an insurer that failed to disclose a letter from a third-party claimant proposing payment of policy limits. The court held that La. Rev. Stat. Ann. §22:1733(B)(1) made it bad faith to misrepresent or fail to disclose "pertinent facts," whether or not they "related to the insurance policy's coverage." 169 So. 3d at 344. See also discussion in §§1.55 and 2.7, *supra*.

—Concerning the scope of an insurer's qualified duty, under New York law, to inform its insured of settlement offers, see *Smith v. General Accident Ins. Co.*, 91 N.Y.2d 648, 697 N.E.2d 168, 674 N.Y.S.2d 267 (1998); *Redcross v. Aetna Casualty & Sur. Co.*, 688 N.Y.S.2d 817 (App. Div. 1999).

—In *State Farm Lloyds Ins. Co. v. Maldonado*, 935 S.W.2d 805 (Tex. Ct. App. 1996), *aff'd in part and rev'd in part*, 963 S.W.2d 38 (Tex. 1998), the court held that the duty of good faith required the insurer to inform the insured of a settlement offer exceeding policy limits where the offer contemplated that the insured was to pay the excess portion.

—In *Allstate Ins. Co. v. Miller*, 212 P.3d 318 (Nev. 2009), the Nevada Supreme Court wrote (212 P.3d at 318):

> [T]he covenant of good faith and fair dealing includes a duty to adequately inform the insured of settlement offers. This includes reasonable offers in excess of policy limits. Failure to adequately inform an insured of a settlement offer is a factor to consider in a bad-faith claim and, if established, can be a proximate cause of any resulting damages. We conclude that whether Allstate violated its duty to adequately inform [the insured] of the settlement opportunities that existed in this cases presented a question of fact for the jury.

§2.30 c. Extent of Policy Coverage

—In *Merrick v. Fischer, Rounds & Associates, Inc.*, 305 Neb. 230, 939 N.W.2d 795 (2020), the Nebraska Supreme Court held that an insurance broker had no duty to advise the company for which it procured insurance to purchase workers' compensation insurance. The company's employee, who was injured in the course of his employment, brought an action against the broker, claiming that he should have advised the company to purchase workers' compensation insurance. The court held that the duty of an insurance broker or agent to exercise reasonable care did not include volunteering information that an insured did not request about what type of coverage the insured should purchase.

2. Failure To Settle

§2.31 a. Improper Investigation or Evaluation of Claim

—Under California law, a federal district court explained in *Lincoln Gen. Ins. Co. v. Access Claims Administrators, Inc.*, 596 F. Supp. 2d 1351 (E.D. Cal. 2009), an insurer acts in bad faith if it ignores a policy-limits demand letter without exploring the details of the offer, or if it fails to seek clarification if the offer is unclear.

—In *Tucker v. American Int'l Grp., Inc.*, 179 F. Supp. 3d 224 (D. Conn. 2016) (Connecticut law), *rev'd on other grounds*, 305 Ga. 489, 826 S.E.2d 71 (2019) the federal district court denied the insurer's motion for summary judgment where the subrogee plaintiff brought claims under the Connecticut insurance trade practices statute alleging the insurer's failure to properly investigate, delay, and refusal to participate in alternative dispute resolution procedure. See §2.24 (discussing Connecticut statutory scheme).

—In *Hughes v. First Acceptance Ins. Co. of Ga.*, 343 Ga. App. 693, 808 S.E.2d 103 (2017), *rev'd*, 305 Ga. 489, 826 S.E.2d 71 (2019), an administrator of the insured's estate alleged that the insurer negligently or in bad faith failed to settle a claim that subsequently went to trial and resulted in a $5.3 million judgment against the insured's estate for injuries sustained by others in a car accident caused by the insured. The court found that genuine issues of material fact existed as to whether the insurer acted reasonably in failing to respond to a time-limited offer to settle within policy limits where the attorney for the insurer admitted that the offer-to-settle letters were inadvertently placed in medical records and no follow-up had occurred. The Georgia Supreme Court reversed the opinion in *Hughes v. First Acceptance Ins. Co. of Ga.*, *supra*. See discussion in §2.7.

—Addressing what it regarded as an issue of first impression under Idaho law, the Ninth Circuit, in *Morrell Constr., Inc. v. Home Ins. Co.*, 920 F.2d 576 (9th Cir. 1990), predicted "that the Idaho Supreme Court would not extend its bad faith cause of action to encompass failures to investigate or failures to initiate settlement negotiations before suit is filed." 920 F.2d at 581. (In so holding, the Ninth Circuit did, however, predict that Idaho would, in general, extend the insurance bad faith doctrine to the third-party context, having already recognized first-party bad faith in *White v. Unigard Mut. Ins. Co.*, 730 P.2d 1014 (Idaho 1986); see book §1.33.) On the issue of a presuit investigation duty, the Ninth Circuit noted a split of authority among the jurisdictions, and predicted that Idaho courts would prefer the no-duty rule of such cases as *Ramsey v. Interstate Insurers, Inc.*, 89 N.C. App. 98, 365 S.E.2d 172 (1988), *review denied*, 322 N.C. 607, 370 S.E.2d 248 (1988). And concerning the duty to initiate settlement negotiations, the court noted a similar split of authority. The court predicted that Idaho courts would disagree with such cases as *Alt v. American Family Mut. Ins. Co.*, 71 Wis. 2d 340, 237 N.W.2d 706 (1976) (see book), and adopt the no-duty approach of *Miller v. Kronk*, 35 Ohio App. 3d 103, 519 N.E.2d 856 (1987). The Ninth Circuit reasoned that an insurance policy *could* be drafted to affirmatively require presuit investigation and settlement negotiation initiation, if the insured so desired, but that such requirements would ordinarily have a price in the form of higher premiums.

—In *Haddick v. Valor Ins. Co.*, 198 Ill. 2d 409, 763 N.E.2d

299 (2001), the Illinois Supreme Court, affirming the reversal of dismissal, held that an insurer's duty to settle arises when the claimant makes a demand for the policy limits and when a finding of liability and recovery in excess of policy limits is reasonably probable. (The court rejected the insurer's contention that the duty arises only when a lawsuit is filed.)

—In *United Fire & Casualty Co. v. Shelly Funeral Home, Inc.*, 642 N.W.2d 648 (Iowa 2002), the Iowa Supreme Court held that where a claim was fairly debatable, the fact that an insurer conducted a "sub-par" investigation and evaluation was not enough, by itself, to create bad faith liability.

—For a Kansas case emphasizing the inadequacy of the insurer's investigation in affirming a bad faith judgment, see *Smith v. Blackwell*, 14 Kan. App. 2d 158, 791 P.2d 1343 (1989), *review granted*.

In *Progressive Nw. Ins. Co. v. Gant*, 957 F.3d 1144 (10th Cir. 2020) (Kansas law), the Tenth Circuit predicted that the Kansas Supreme Court would hold that an insurer did not breach a duty to its insured by failing to investigate and discover whether the insured had more coverage with another insurer. The court affirmed summary judgment for the insurer on a claim of failure to settle.

—In *Indiana Ins. Co. v. Demetre*, 527 S.W.3d 12 (Ky. 2017), the court affirmed a jury award of $925,000 in emotional distress damages and $2.5 million in punitive damages. The jury found that the insurer had delayed its investigation and settlement of a matter involving third-party claims against the insured for injury allegedly caused by leaking underground fuel storage tanks on land that he owned, and that the insurer filed a declaratory judgment action to avoid paying the insured's claims although the insurer had reason to know its action was unjustified. Although the insurer eventually provided coverage and a defense, the jury awarded damages for the insured's 4 years of anxiety and mental anguish. The court rejected the insurer's argument that defending the insured while asserting a reservation of rights and filing a declaratory judgment action on coverage, and eventually paying the claim, insulated the insurer from a bad faith action.

—In *Capitol Specialty Ins. Corp. v. Higgins*, 953 F.3d 95 (1st Cir. 2020), the court held that the Massachusetts federal district court did not err in concluding that a night club owner's liability insurer conducted an inadequate investigation of a claim against the owner by an underage exotic dancer who was severely injured in a car accident after becoming intoxicated at work. The court upheld a damages award of $5.4 million, including treble damages, for violation of Massachusetts' unfair claims settlement practices statute, Mass. Gen. Laws §176D 3(9)(d). In *Calandro v. Sedwick Claims Mgmt. Servs., Inc.*, 919 F.3d 26 (1st Cir. 2019), an administrator of an estate brought a claim under Massachusetts's Unfair Claim Settlement Practices Statute (Mass. Gen. Laws ch. 176D) against the claims management firm that handled claims for a nursing home's liability insurer after the claimant's mother died in hospice following a fall at the nursing home. The court affirmed the lower court's finding that the claims management firm satisfied the requirements of the statute for an adequate investigation where it immediately hired a qualified claims investigator who gathered documents from a nursing home and sought witnesses, although some documents and witnesses were not located, and the claims investigator found that whether or to what extent the nursing home was liable for the death was not clear. In addition, the claims management firm made prompt and reasonable settlement offers at several points in time. The court noted that the claims management firm did not handle the claim in a model way, but stated that perfection is not the standard imposed by the statute.

In *Rawan v. Continental Cas. Co.*, 483 Mass. 654, 136 N.E.3d 327 (2019), homeowners (claimants) brought a claim for bad faith against an engineer's professional liability insurer after the engineer failed to design their home to state building code standards. The insurance policy contained a consent-to-settle clause, and the insurer failed to convince the insured to settle. After trial, the insurer paid up to the policy limit and the insured paid the remainder of the claim. The claimants then brought a bad faith claim against the insurer for failure to settle. The court held that a consent-to-settle provision in the insurance contract did not violate the insurer's duty to effectuate a prompt, fair, and equitable settlement under Mass. Gen. Laws Ann. ch. 176D §3(9)(f). However, the insurer must still conduct a reasonable investigation and engage in good faith settlement attempts. The court affirmed summary judgment in favor of the insurer where the insurer thoroughly investigated the underlying facts, informed the insured of the results of its investigation, encouraged mediation, explained the vulnerabilities to the insured, and encouraged the insured to settle. The court found that any deficiencies in the insurer's behavior did not cause harm to claimants, especially because the judgment was paid in full by the insurer and the insured.

—In *Haugh v. Allstate Ins. Co.*, 322 F.3d 227 (3d Cir. 2003) (Pennsylvania law), the Third Circuit discussed the factors an insurer must consider—in addition to its insured objective liability—in deciding whether to accept a settlement offer. Those factors include the size of an adverse verdict, the strengths and weaknesses of the evidence and the persuasiveness and appeal of the witnesses on both sides, and the local history regarding similar cases.

—In *Johnson v. Tennessee Farmers Mut. Ins. Co.*, 205 S.W.3d 365 (Tenn. 2006), the Tennessee Supreme Court, reversing a judgment for the insurer, emphasized that ". . . the manner in which the insurer investigates the case 'has an important bearing upon the question of bad faith in refusing or failing to settle the claim.' [Citation omitted.] Ordinary care and diligence in investigation require the insurer to investigate the claim to such an extent that it can exercise an honest judgment regarding whether the claim should be settled. [Citation omitted.] Courts must review the facts that were known to the insurer and its agents and that should have been considered in deciding whether to settle." 205 S.W.3d at 370.

—In *Berkshire Hathaway Homestate Ins. Co. v. SQI, Inc.*, 132 F. Supp. 3d 1275 (W.D.Wash. 2015), *appeal dismissed* (9th Cir. 2017) (Washington law), the federal district court granted summary judgment for the insured on a bad faith claim based on alleged failure to conduct a reasonably prompt investigation, where the claim was based solely on the insurer's statement in an interrogatory response that its investigation was not yet complete and where the insurer had begin its investigation within a reasonable time under the circumstances.

§2.33 c. "Hard Line" Settlement Policy

—In *Bohna v. Hughes, Thorsness, Gantz, et al.*, 828 P.2d 745 (Alaska 1992), the Alaska Supreme Court affirmed the trial court's conclusion that an auto insurer had committed bad faith as a matter of law. The court wrote: "where an adverse verdict in excess of policy limits is likely, an insurance company has the duty to determine 'the amount of a money judgment which might be rendered against its insured,' and 'to tender in settlement that portion of the projected money judgment which [it] contractually agreed to pay.' [Citation omitted.]" 828 P.2d at 768. Here, the attorney hired by the insurer to defend the insured had estimated the verdict value of the case to be no less than $3 million, and the insurer's obligation for statutory unlimited attorney's fees to be no less than $162,680, and yet the insurer had never offered a specific dollar amount of more than $50,000. Also concerning the principle that an insurer is obligated to offer policy limits where liability and damages exceeding the policy limits are clear, see *Maloney v. Progressive Specialty Ins. Co.*, 99 P.3d 565 (Alaska 2004).

—In *Crackel v. Allstate Ins. Co.*, 92 P.3d 882 (Ariz. Ct. App. 2004), an Arizona Court of Appeals affirmed a judgment on a jury verdict finding a liability insurer liable for abuse of process based on the insurer's defense tactics in a case of clear liability. The jury found, *inter alia*, that the insurer had acted for the improper purpose of coercing the plaintiffs into abandoning certain of their claims and had refused to participate in good faith in a pretrial settlement conference.

—In *Haddick v. Valor Ins. Co.*, 198 Ill. 2d 409, 763 N.E.2d 299 (2001), the Illinois Supreme Court, affirming the reversal of dismissal, held that an insurer's duty to settle arises when the claimant makes a demand for the policy limits and when a finding of liability and recovery in excess of policy limits is reasonably probable. (The court rejected the insurer's contention that the duty arises only when a lawsuit is filed.) Accord *Rogers Cartage Co. v. Travelers Indem. Co.*, 2018 IL App. (5th) 160098, 103 N.E.3d 504 (2018), *appeal denied*, 108 N.W.3d 885 (Ill. 2018) (see discussions in §§2.38, 2.45). And in *O'Neill v. Gallant Ins. Co.*, 769 N.E.2d 100 (Ill. Ct. App. 2002), an Illinois Court of Appeals affirmed jury awards of $710,063 in actual damages and $2.3 million in punitive damages in a case involving the insurer's refusal to settle an automobile accident liability claim for the $20,000 policy limits. The decision includes a detailed discussion of the evidentiary factors probative of insurance bad faith in the third-party context.

—In *Chiulli v. Liberty Mut. Ins., Inc.*, 97 Mass. App. 248, 146 N.E.3d 471 (2020), *review denied*, 485 Mass. 1102, 150 N.E.3d 1119 (2020), the appeals court held that the trial court erred when it found that insurer Liberty Mutual did not act willfully or knowingly when it violated Massachusetts' statutory settlement requirement under Mass. Gen. Laws ch. 93A. The court found that the insurer had a duty to offer settlement once the insured's liability became reasonably clear following closing arguments at trial. The court rejected the insurer's argument that its liability had to be "clear" instead of "reasonably clear" before it was required to tender a settlement offer. The insurer made its insured wait through Thanksgiving and Christmas, and internal documents showed that the delay was an intentional effort to use the insured's lack of funds to leverage a more favorable settlement. The court remanded for determination of whether a statutory penalty of 2 to 3 times the damages award would be proper.

—Reinstating a judgment for the insured, a Pennsylvania court described the malpractice insurer's bad faith behavior as follows: "St. Paul's unrelenting decision to litigate . . . cannot be considered honest, objective and intelligent as its decision not to compromise was against the facts, the advice of trial counsel, the repeated admonitions of the court and the ardent appeals of its insured." *Birth Ctr. v. St. Paul Cos.*, 727 A.2d 1144 (Pa. Super. Ct. 1999). Compare *McMahon v. Medical Protective Co.*, 92 F. Supp. 3d 367, *recon. denied*, 2015 WL 4633698 (W.D. Pa. 2015) (denying insurer's motion for summary judgment on issue of whether insurer's alleged misrepresentations about how much it was willing to offer to settle dental malpractice claims against insured rose to the level of recklessness and therefore would support a finding of statutory bad faith).

§2.34 d. Nondisclosure of Policy Limits to Claimant

—For a Florida case stating the principle that an insurer's bad faith liability may be predicated on a refusal to disclose the policy limits to a third-party claimant, see *Powell v. Prudential Property & Casualty Co.*, 584 So. 2d 12 (Fla. Dist. Ct. App. 1991). Note, however, that it has been held in a California case that prior to the filing of suit, an insurer may not disclose policy limits to a third-party claimant without the insured's consent: *Griffith v. State Farm Ins. Cos.*, 230 Cal. App. 3d 59, 281 Cal. Rptr. 165 (1991) (relying provisions of the Insurance Information Privacy and Protection Model Act of the National Association of Insurance Commissioners (N.A.I.C.)). Compare *Smith v. Safeco Ins. Co.*, 50 P.3d 277 (Wash. Ct. App. 2002), *rev'd on other grounds*, 78 P.3d 1274 (Wash. 2003) (concealing policy limits sometimes benefits policyholder, and facts of particular case dictate whether insurer must disclose policy limits to third-party claimant before suit is filed).

§2.35 e. Ignoring Settlement Advice or Following Advice Not To Settle

—In *Christian Builders, Inc. v. The Cincinnati Ins. Co.*, 501 F. Supp. 2d 1224 (D. Minn. 2007), a federal district court applying Minnesota law held that a liability insurer did not fail to evaluate the case fairly when it did not offer full policy limits in settlement of a wrongful death case despite the insured's clear liability, where it relied on the much lower settlement evaluation of a competent and experienced defense attorney.

—In *Graske v. Auto-Owners Ins. Co.*, 647 F. Supp. 2d 1105 (D. Neb. 2009), a federal district court predicted that under Nebraska law an insurer's alleged good faith reliance on the advice of counsel was insufficient by itself to act as an affirmative defense to insured's bad faith claims for breach of contract and breach of fiduciary duty.

§2.36 f. Demand That Insured Contribute to Settlement

—Affirming summary judgment for the insurer, a California Court of Appeal, in *Finkelstein v. 20th Century Ins. Co.*, 11 Cal. App. 4th 926, 14 Cal. Rptr. 2d 305 (1992), emphasized that no cause of action for bad faith failure to settle ripens in the absence of a judgment in excess of policy limits. In the present case, the insured, certain that a jury verdict in excess of the $100,000 policy limits would ensue, but unable to convince the insurer to offer more than $75,000, had voluntarily contributed some of his own money to effect a settlement of $85,000. The court emphasized the voluntariness of the insured's contribution and the absence of any duress on the insurer's part. Compare *Shade Foods, Inc. v. Innovative Prods. Sales & Marketing, Inc.*, 78 Cal. App. 4th 847, 93 Cal. Rptr. 2d 364 (2000) (insurer could not reasonably condition settlement of its liability insurance obligation on insured's abandonment of right to reimbursement as third-party beneficiary of first-party coverage); *Aguerre, Inc. v. American Guar. & Liab. Ins. Co.*, 59 Cal. App. 4th 6, 68 Cal. Rptr. 2d 837 (1997) (affirming dismissal; liability insurer was not acting in bad faith in funding settlement with contribution from insured where insurer did not coerce contribution, and where contribution was small and in reasonable proportion to insured's punitive damages exposure).

—In *McMahon v. Medical Protective Co.*, 92 F. Supp. 3d 367, *recon. denied*, 2015 WL 4633698 (W.D. Pa. 2015), the federal district court granted summary judgment to the insurer on the issue of whether the insurer "invited" the insured to contribute her own funds to a dental malpractice settlement. The court found that questions by the insurer's attorney were "fairly mild and [did] not evince any overt pressure or insistence." *Id.* at 386–87. Given the high evidentiary burden for proving bad faith, the court granted summary judgment under claims of both contractual and statutory bad faith on that issue.

§2.37 g. Denial of Coverage

—See supplement §2.7 for a discussion of *Robinson v. State Farm Fire & Casualty Co.*, 583 So. 2d 1063 (Fla. Dist. Ct. App. 1991), representing the view that an insurer is not insulated from bad faith liability for refusal to settle by the fact that its belief in noncoverage initially may have had a reasonable (although mistaken) basis. Accord *Johansen v. California State Auto. Ass'n Inter-Insurance Bureau*, 15 Cal. 3d 9, 123 Cal. Rptr. 288 (1975); *John J. Jerue Truck Broker, Inc. v. Insurance Co. of N. Am.*, 646 So. 2d 780 (Fla. Dist. Ct. App. 1994); *Moses v. Halstead*, 477 F. Supp. 2d 1119 (D. Kan. 2007) (Kansas law); *Matagorda County v. Texas Ass'n of County Gov't Risk Management Pool*, 975 S.W.2d 782 (Tex. Ct. App. 1998), *aff'd*, 52 S.W.2d 128 (Tex. 2000); *Riggs v. Sentry Ins.*, 821 S.W.2d 701 (Tex. Ct. App. 1991). For cases representing the contrary view—reasonable coverage doubts *do* excuse a failure to settle—see *Associated Wholesale Grocers v. Americold*, 261 Kan. 806, 934 P.2d 65 (1997); *Snodgrass v. State Farm Mut. Auto. Ins. Co.*, 15 Kan. App. 2d 153, 804 P.2d 1012 (1991).

—In *Global Hawk Ins. Co. (RRG) v. Wesco Ins. Co.*, 424 F. Supp. 3d 848 (C.D. Cal. 2019) (California law), the court held that the insurer's denial of coverage for the insured did not amount to breach of the implied covenant of good faith and fair dealing where the insurer, under a mistaken belief that Texas law applied, believed that the *Stowers* doctrine gave it the right and obligation to settle a third-party claim for the policy limits even though it did not get a release of claims against the insured. The court held that while the denial of coverage would have likely been unlawful in California, breach of the implied covenant of good faith and fair dealing was precluded because the denial was based on a genuine dispute as to whether Texas law required it to accept the settlement offer.

§2.38 3. Failure To Defend

—Summary judgment on the insured's bad faith claim was precluded, the Eleventh Circuit held in *Perkins v. Hartford Ins. Group*, 932 F.2d 1392 (11th Cir. 1991), where the liability insurer's failure to investigate the incident underlying the claim against the insured raised a fact issue as to the insurer's bad faith in refusing to defend. Under

Alabama law, the court explained, when an insurer is uncertain what a third-party complaint is alleging, the insurer must either conduct an adequate investigation to assess its duty to defend, or accept the insured's defense, reserving the right to contest coverage later, based on facts developed at trial.

—In *Stalberg v. Western Title Ins. Co.*, 230 Cal. App. 3d 1229, 282 Cal. Rptr. 43 (1991), the court held that substantial evidence supported the finding that the insurer had breached the covenant of good faith by, *inter alia*, failing to perform any investigation of the third party's claims before denying coverage outright and refusing to defend the insured in a quiet title action. See also *Pulte Home Corp. v. American Safety Indem. Co.*, 14 Cal. App. 5th 1086, 223 Cal. Rptr. 3d 47 (2017), *reh'g denied, review denied* (2018) (any doubt as to whether there was duty to defend should have been resolved in favor of additional insured; affirming substantive ruling on award of punitive damages in favor of additional insured general contractor in construction defect case where insurer routinely denied claims of additional insureds based on restrictive policy interpretations); *Safeco Ins. Co. of Am. v. Parks*, 170 Cal. App. 4th 992, 88 Cal. Rptr. 3d 730 (2009) (insurer breaches duty of good faith if it ignores evidence that supports coverage). But see *Marentes v. State Farm Mut. Auto. Ins. Co.*, 224 F. Supp. 3d 891 (N.D. Cal. 2016) (granting summary judgment in favor of insurer on claim for breach of implied covenant of good faith and fair dealing because insurer had no duty to defend in absence of coverage even where insurer had undertaken defense of insured).

On the other hand, in *Lunsford v. American Guar. & Liability Co.*, 18 F.3d 653 (9th Cir. 1994) (California law), the Ninth Circuit held that an unjustified refusal to defend could not be the basis of bad faith liability, where the insurer had based its refusal on a reasonable, though mistaken, construction of the policy. Compare *Century Sur. Co. v. Polisso*, 139 Cal. App. 4th 922, 43 Cal. Rptr. 3d 468

(2006) (existence of "genuine dispute" regarding existence of duty to defend did not justify insurer's refusal to do so).

See also *Hillenbrand v. Insurance Co. of N. Am.*, 102 Cal. App. 4th 584, 125 Cal. Rptr. 2d 575 (2002) (affirming award of punitive damages on malicious prosecution cause of action where insurer had filed groundless declaratory judgment action to determine duty to defend).

—In *Pozzi Window Co. v. Auto-Owners Ins.*, 446 F.3d 1178 (11th Cir. 2006) (Florida law), the Eleventh Circuit, affirming a judgment for the insurer, listed as follows the factors in a bad faith determination in the liability insurance context: (1) efforts made by the insurer to resolve the coverage dispute promptly or in such a way as to limit any potential prejudice to the insured; (2) the substance of the coverage dispute, or the weight of legal authority on the coverage issue; (3) the insurer's diligence and thoroughness in investigating facts specifically pertinent to coverage; and (4) efforts made by the insurer to settle the liability claim in face of the coverage dispute.

—In *Transportation Ins. Co. v. Piedmont Constr. Group, LLC*, 301 Ga. App. 17, 686 S.E.2d 824 (2009), it was held that the trial court was justified in finding as a matter of law that the insurer acted in bad faith in failing to defend its insured, though the existence of bad faith is ordinarily a jury question, where the insurer offered in explanation only a meritless reliance on the business-risk clauses of the CGL policy.

—In *Apana v. TIG Ins. Co.*, 504 F. Supp. 2d 998 (D. Haw. 2007) (Hawaii law), a federal district court held that although the defendant commercial liability insurer had been under a duty to defend its insured in a personal injury action, the insurer's denial of coverage was not in bad faith because the denial had been based on an unsettled question of law regarding the applicability of CGL policy's "total pollution exclusion endorsement" in cases of personal injury resulting from relatively isolated inhalation or exposure to pollutants in the air. In *Damon Key Leong Kupchak*

Hastert v. Westport Ins. Corp., 421 F. Supp. 3d 946 (D. Haw. 2019), the federal district court dismissed the insured's bad faith claim where the insurer's conduct in declining to defend against a claim seeking sanctions from the insured for contempt, which were clearly excluded under policy, was reasonable.

—In *Rogers Cartage Co. v. Travelers Indem. Co.*, 2018 IL App. (5th) 160098, 103 N.E.3d 504 (2018), *appeal denied*, 108 N.W.3d 885 (Ill. 2018), the court held the insurer breached its duty to defend where it initially agreed to defend in the underlying action under a reservation of rights and paid $1 million for defense in the underlying action, but the insurer subsequently used the threat of negating coverage to prevent the insured from settling at a crucial time. The insured, a hauler of toxic and hazardous materials, lost an opportunity to settle for about $4 million in a lawsuit related to the clean-up of two Superfund sites and ultimately settled for $7.5 million.

—In *Talen v. Employers Mut. Casualty Co.*, 703 N.W.2d 395 (Iowa 2005), the Iowa Supreme Court reversed a judgment against the liability insurer for the majority shareholder of a bank holding company with respect to the conduct of business as an investment and financial adviser. The insurer did not act in bad faith by refusing to defend against a former bank employee's claims for breach of contract and defamation where the role in which the shareholder had been acting was an issue of disputed fact.

—In *Progressive Nw. Ins. Co. v. Gant*, 957 F.3d 1144 (10th Cir. 2020) (Kansas law), the Tenth Circuit held that the insurer did not breach its duty to defend by negligent hiring of defense counsel to handle the insured's wrongful death case. While the insurer was contractually obligated to provide competent counsel, the attorney's reputation for causing delays in litigation was not sufficient evidence of incompetence. The court noted that "in the highly competitive world of personal-injury litigation, complaints of allegedly unreasonable conduct of opposing counsel are hardly uncommon." *Id.* at 1152. Moreover, the insured failed to submit evidence of causation between counsel's conduct and the outcome of the litigation. The court also rejected the insured's claim that the insurer was vicariously liable for defense counsel's allegedly negligent misrepresentation, stating that the insured had a "steep hill to climb" to prevail on such a claim, and that vicarious liability is limited in Kansas to "those actions of the attorney in which the insurer was directly involved." *Id.* at 1154–55.

—Reiterating the principle that under Maryland law the tort of bad faith applies only to failures to settle, not to refusals to defend, the court, in *Mesmer v. Maryland Auto. Ins. Fund*, 353 Md. 241, 725 A.2d 1053 (1999), also emphasized that an insurer who refuses to defend is not subject to liability for failing to settle.

—Under Missouri law, it was held in *Millers Mut. Ins. Co. v. Shell Oil Co.*, 959 S.W.2d 864 (Mo. Ct. App. 1997), an insurer may have no further duty to defend one insured after exhausting its policy limits in the good faith settlement of a claim against another insured. In *Minden v. Atain Specialty Ins. Co.*, 788 F.3d 750 (8th Cir. 2015), the Eighth Circuit held that the insured failed to claim a "vexatious" failure to defend under Mo. Rev. Stat. §375.420 because the insurer had reasonable cause to believe there was no coverage, and therefore no duty to defend.

—In *Merrick v. Fischer, Rounds & Associates, Inc.*, 305 Neb. 230, 939 N.W.2d 795 (2020), the Nebraska Supreme Court held that a liability insurer did not act in bad faith in declining to defend a lawsuit brought by an injured employee, because the employer's liability policy contained exclusions of coverage for workers' compensation and employer liability. The plaintiff employee, to whom the employer had assigned his claims against the insurer, failed to show the absence of a reasonable basis for the insurer's denial of benefits under the policy, and thus failed to demonstrate bad faith.

—Affirming summary judgment, the Second Circuit emphasized in *Hugo Boss Fashions, Inc. v. Federal Ins. Co.*, 252 F.3d 608 (2d Cir. 2001), that overcoming New York law's presumption against bad faith liability requires more than an arguable difference of opinion and that here the insurer, before denying coverage, had "conducted a review of the coverage question, consulted with counsel, committed no overreaching, and did nothing more blameworthy than err."

—In *Nationwide Mut. Ins. Co. v. Masseria*, 1999 WL 1313620, 1999 Ohio App. LEXIS 6119 (1999), it was held that an insurer's filing of a declaratory judgment action seeking a determination that it has no duty to defend may constitute bad faith if its investigation was inadequate.

—Under Pennsylvania law, it was held in *Aetna Casualty & Sur. Co. v. Erickson*, 903 F. Supp. 832 (M.D. Pa. 1995), an insurer does not act in bad faith if its failure to defend is based on a reasonable, though incorrect, reading of the policy. See also *Post v. St. Paul Travelers Ins. Co.*, 691 F.3d 500 (3d Cir. 2012) (under Pennsylvania law, summary judgment is appropriate where there is no clear and convincing evidence that insurer's conduct was unreasonable and that it knew or recklessly disregarded its lack of reasonable basis; mere negligence or aggressive protection of insurer's interests is not bad faith); *USX Corp. v. Liberty Mut. Ins. Co.*, 444 F.3d 102 (3d Cir. 2006) (under Pennsylvania law, bad faith claim necessarily failed in light of determination that there was no potential coverage under policy); *Schuykill Stone Corp. v. State Auto. Mut. Ins. Co.*, 735 F. Supp. 2d 150 (D.N.J. 2010) (Pennsylvania law; even if there is evidence of questionable conduct giving appearance of bad faith, that evidence is not sufficient to establish bad faith refusal to defend if insurer had reasonable basis).

—In *Truck Ins. Co. v. Vanport Homes, Inc.*, 147 Wash. 2d 751, 58 P.3d 276 (2002), the Washington Supreme Court discussed failure to investigate and delay in responding to an insured as bases for a finding of bad faith in connection with a failure to defend. The court cited regulations promulgated pursuant to the Washington Consumer Protection Act that require an insurer to provide a prompt and reasonable explanation for the denial of a claim. See also *American Best Food, Inc. v. Alea London, Ltd.*, 168 Wash. 2d 398, 229 P.3d 693 (banc 2010) (insurer acted in bad faith as matter of law by refusing to defend based on questionable interpretation of law and failing to avail itself of options such as proceeding under reservation of rights or seeking declaratory relief); *Woo v. Fireman's Fund Ins. Co.*, 161 Wash. 2d 43, 164 P.3d 454 (2007) (reinstating judgment on jury verdict for insured on claim for bad faith failure to defend); *Farmers Ins. Co. v. Romas*, 88 Wash. App. 801, 947 P.2d 754 (1997) (insurer's filing of interpleader action and depositing policy limits with court clerk did not extinguish duty to defend); *Osborne Constr. Co. v. Zurich Am. Ins. Co.*, 356 F. Supp. 3d 1085 (W.D. Wash. 2018) (Washington law; duty to defend is triggered when insurance policy conceivably covers claims; insurer had no reasonable basis for its breach of duty to defend where it arguably covered additional insured, deductible arguably did not apply to additional insured, demand for arbitration was made, and sufficient request for defense was made; court held insurer was estopped from refusing to indemnify additional insured); *Chartis Specialty Ins. Co. v. Queen Anne HS, LLC*, 867 F. Supp. 2d 1111 (W.D. Wash. 2012) (when insurer fails to defend based on questionable interpretation of law, it acts in bad faith); *Absher Constr. Co. v. North Pacific Ins. Co.*, 861 F. Supp. 2d 1236 (W.D. Wash. 2012) (under Washington law, when insurer acts in bad faith by improperly refusing to defend, there is rebuttable presumption of harm and that coverage by estoppel is one appropriate remedy).

§2.38A 4. Other [NEW]

This section collects cases addressing factors suggesting bad faith other than failure to advise the insured, to settle, or to defend.

—In *Indiana Ins. Co. v. Demetre*, 527 S.W.3d 12 (Ky. 2017), the Kentucky Supreme Court held that defending an insured after asserting a reservation of rights and filing a declaratory judgment action did not preclude the insured from bringing a bad faith claim, even though the insurer eventually paid the insured's claim. Whether bad faith exists depends on whether the insurer's conduct was reasonable. In this case, the court upheld $925,000 in damages for emotional distress and $2.5 million in punitive damages to compensate for the insurer's lackluster handling of third-party liability claims against the insured and legal action against him.

—In *Marshall v. Safeco Ins. Co. of Ill.*, 390 Mont. 358, 413 P.3d 828 (2018), the Montana Supreme Court denied the defendant insurers' motion to dismiss a third-party claim that the insurers violated Montana's Uniform Trade Practices Act when they used the state's collateral source statute to reduce the compensation they paid to the third-party claimant for her injuries in an automobile accident. The defendants had insured the driver and the owner of the car involved in the accident, in which the insured was a passenger. The court held that whether the insurers had a reasonable basis in law for applying the collateral source rule was a question for the trial court.

III. INSURER'S DEFENSES TO LIABILITY FOR EXCESS JUDGMENT

A. Defenses Predicated on Insured's Conduct or Status

§2.39 1. Insured's Inaccurate or Inconsistent Statements

—See *St. Paul Fire & Marine Ins. Co. v. Tinney*, 920 F.2d 861 (11th Cir. 1991) (Alabama law), in which the Eleventh Circuit reversed summary judgment for the insurer with respect to the coverage issue, but held that the insured's notice of loss, while sufficient to constitute a "claim made" while the policy was still in effect, was so sketchy as to have provided the insurer with a sufficient basis for its "no coverage" position to preclude any finding of bad faith.

—Under Arizona law, the Ninth Circuit explained in *James River Ins. Co. v. Hebert Schenk, P.C.*, 523 F.3d 915 (9th Cir. 2008), a showing of either legal or actual fraud can allow an insurer to deny coverage due to a misrepresentation in an insurance application. "Legal fraud" occurs when (1) a question asked by the insurer seeks facts that are presumably within the insured's personal knowledge; (2) the insurer would naturally contemplate that the insured's answer represented the true facts; and (3) the answer was false. "Actual fraud," the court continued, occurs when an insurer's question calls for an opinion and the insured's answer was intended to deceive.

—See §1.24 concerning *Kransco v. American Empire Surplus Lines Ins. Co.*, 23 Cal. 4th 390, 97 Cal. Rptr. 2d 151 (2000), and the California Supreme Court's rejection of the "comparative bad faith" defense in both first- and third-party cases. (*Kransco* itself was a third-party case.) The court also rejected the proposition that the comparative *negligence* of an insured (here involving discovery misconduct) can operate to shield the insurer from full responsibility for its bad faith failure to settle. The court noted, however, that an insured's fraudulent conduct may be separately actionable, and that evidence of the insured's misconduct or breach of its express obligations may support a number of contract defenses to a bad faith action, by voiding coverage, by factually disproving the insurer's bad faith by showing that the insurer acted reasonably under the circumstances, or by forming the basis of a separate contract claim.

—In *Hartford Roman Catholic Diocesan Corp. v. Interstate Fire & Casualty Co.*, 199 F. Supp. 3d 559, *aff'd*, 905 F.3d 84 (2d Cir. 2018), the federal district court found no guidance in Connecticut law concerning the availability of a "reverse bad faith" affirmative defense for an insurer. The court applied the law articulated by the California Supreme

Court in *Kransco v. American Empire, supra*, and concluded that "Connecticut does not, and is not likely to, permit an affirmative defense of bad faith by insurers." *Hartford*, 199 F. Supp. 3d at 600.

§2.40 2. Insured's Failure To Cooperate With Insurer

—Under California law, it was held in *Safeco Ins. Co. of Am. v. Parks*, 170 Cal. App. 4th 992, 88 Cal. Rptr. 3d 730 (2009), where an insurer denies coverage due to a late notice of a claim, it may establish substantial prejudice and be excused from its obligations only by demonstrating that, if timely notice had been given, it would have undertaken the defense.

—In *Harvey v. GEICO Gen. Ins. Co.*, 259 So. 3d 1 (Fla. 2018), *cert. denied*, 2018 WL 6681741 (Fla. 2018, the Supreme Court of Florida reversed an appellate court decision and reinstated a jury verdict against the insurer for $9.2 million. The insured was at fault in a fatal auto accident, and the claimant/estate of the decedent brought a wrongful death action against the insured after the insurer offered the policy limits to the claimant but failed to comply with a request for additional information. The court held, over a strong dissent, that the evidence supported the jury's finding of bad faith failure to settle where the insurer's claims adjuster failed to communicate with the claimant's attorney and with the insured in critical ways. In addition, while the insurer offered the policy limits to the claimant, the insurer failed to comply with the claimant's demand to provide a statement from the insured about the insured's assets. The insurer argued that the insured was at fault for failing to provide such a statement to the claimant, which was critical to settling the claim within the policy limits. While the appellate court and a strong dissent in the high court agreed that the conduct of the claimant was a major factor in the failure to settle, the majority in the present case rejected the argument and placed full responsibility with the insurer.

—In *Kemper v. Equity Ins. Co.*, 396 F. Supp. 3d 1299 (N.D. Ga. 2019) (Georgia law), *rev'd & remanded*, 823 Fed. Appx. 900 (11th Cir. 2020), the federal district court held that the insurer did not commit bad faith or negligent failure to settle, noting that the only reason the parties failed to reach a settlement was the third-party claimant's "unreasonable refusal" to place the settlement funds in escrow to satisfy any potential liens by medical providers. On appeal, however, the Eleventh Circuit reversed and remanded for trial, finding too many outstanding factual issues related to the plaintiff's failure-to-settle claim and the parties' conduct surrounding the escrow request to justify summary judgment for the insurer. The court noted that Ga. Code Ann. §9–11–67.1, passed after the accident at issue in *Kemper*, provides clarification on requirements for demand letters that "provides needed guidance to future parties embroiled in similar disputes." 823 Fed. Appx. at 901 n.1. See also §2.7.

—For a discussion of Kansas law concerning the requirements of a noncooperation defense, including the requirement that the insurer demonstrate substantial actual prejudice, see *Johnson v. Westhoff Sand Co., Inc.*, 62 P.3d 685 (Kan. Ct. App. 2003).

—In *Rawan v. Continental Cas. Co.*, 483 Mass. 654, 136 N.E.3d 327 (2019), homeowners (claimants) brought a claim for bad faith against an engineer's professional liability insurer after the engineer failed to design their home to state building code standards. The insurance policy contained a consent-to-settle clause, and the insurer failed to convince the insured to settle. After trial, the insurer paid up to the policy limit and the insured paid the remainder of the claim. The claimants then brought a bad faith claim against the insurer for failure to settle. The court held that a consent-to-settle provision in the insurance contract did not violate the insurer's duty to effectuate a prompt, fair, and equitable settlement under Mass. Gen. Laws Ann. ch. 176D §3(9)(f). However, the insurer must still conduct a reasonable investigation and engage in good faith settlement attempts. The court affirmed summary judgment in favor of the insurer where the insurer thoroughly investigated the underlying facts, informed the insured of the results of its investigation, encouraged mediation, explained the vulnerabilities to the insured, and encouraged the insured to settle. The court found that any deficiencies in the insurer's behavior did not cause harm to claimants, especially because the judgment was paid in full by the insurer and the insured.

—In *Northwest Prosthetic & Orthotic Clinic, Inc. v. Centennial Ins. Co.*, 997 P.2d 972 (Wash. Ct. App. 2000), the court affirmed summary judgment for the insurer on the grounds that the insurer had been deprived of the opportunity to investigate the claim by the insured's actions in delaying its tender of the defense until the last minute, in failing to inform the insurer of imminent court dates, and in settling the case without informing the insurer that the settlement conference was taking place. See also *National Sur. Corp. v. Immunex Corp.*, 176 Wash. 2d 872, 297 P.3d 688 (2013) (summary judgment was precluded by genuine issue of material fact as to whether insurer had been prejudiced by insured's late notice of claim, as could relieve insurer of duty to defend); *Mutual of Enumclaw Ins. Co. v. T & G Constr., Inc.*, 199 P.3d 376 (Wash. 2008) (rejecting insurer's argument that it was released from obligation to indemnify by insured's failure to cooperate; insurer that had been defending insured was not prejudiced by insured's settlement without insurer's consent where insurer had refused to participate in settlement negotiations and where its intervention in proceeding on reasonableness of settlement had resulted in its reduction by $300,000).

—For a decision of the West Virginia Supreme Court reiterating the standard view that an insurer is not subject to liability for a failure to settle if the insured failed to cooperate in the defense, see *Charles v. State Farm Mut. Auto. Ins. Co.*, 452 S.E.2d 384 (W. Va. 1994).

§2.41 3. Insured's Failure To Demand That Insurer Accept Settlement Offer

—In *Delancy v. St. Paul Fire & Marine Ins. Co.*, 947 F.2d 1536 (11th Cir. 1991) (Georgia law), the Eleventh Circuit affirmed summary judgment, holding that the insurer could have incurred no liability for failure to settle a medical malpractice case where it had been the insured physician's consistent position that the third-party plaintiff had no case and would not prevail at trial. Accord *American Physicians Assurance Corp. v. Schmidt*, 187 S.W.3d 313 (Ky. 2006); *Bonner v. Automobile Club Inter-Insurance Exch.*, 899 S.W.2d 925 (Mo. Ct. App. 1995). Compare *Westchester Fire Ins. Co. v. General Star Indem. Co.*, 183 F.3d 578 (7th Cir. 1999) (Illinois law; insured's failure to make specific complaints about handling of case did not amount to "unequivocal consent" to taking case to trial where insured had repeatedly expressed desire for settlement); *Clausen v. New England Ins. Co.*, 83 F. Supp. 2d 278 (D. R.I. 2000) (Rhode Island law; insurer's liability was not limited to amount of settlement demand rejected by insured where insurer failed to prove that insured's rejection of demand had been unreasonable); *American States Ins. Co. v. State Farm Mut. Auto. Ins. Co.*, 6 F.3d 549 (8th Cir. 1993) (South Dakota law; rejecting "consent" defense to failure-to-settle claim where insured had not been fully informed and where his consent had not been unequivocal).

§2.42 4. Insured's Failure To Defend Following Insurer's Refusal To Defend

—Reversing summary judgment that had been granted on the grounds of workers' compensation exclusivity, a Florida appellate court held that the insurer, by refusing to defend

an action by its insured's employee, had given up the right
to control the settlement and therefore could not assert
defenses that the insured could have asserted against the
employee. *Wright v. Hartford Underwriters Ins. Co.*, 823
So. 2d 241 (Fla. Dist. Ct. App. 2002).

§2.43 5. Insured's Insolvency or Nonpayment of Excess Portion of Judgment

—In *Consolidated Am. Ins. Co. v. Mike Soper Marine
Servs.*, 942 F.2d 1421 (9th Cir. 1991) (California law), the
court held that having failed to defend its insured in bad
faith, and having failed to accept a reasonable settlement
offer, the insurer was liable for the full amount of an excess
judgment, notwithstanding the fact that, following the insurer's refusal to defend, the insured had received from the
third party a covenant not to execute any excess judgment
against him, in return for an assignment of the insured's
rights against the insurer. The Ninth Circuit reasoned that
the insured's interest had remained at risk at the time the
settlement offer was refused, even though the covenant not
to execute had already been signed. "A covenant not to
execute does not fully protect the insured," the court said.
"His credit may be impaired and he may be unable to enter
certain business transactions." 942 F.2d at 1426.

—In *Nunn v. Mid-Century Ins. Co.*, 244 P.3d 116 (Colo.
banc 2010), the Colorado Supreme Court held that an
insured driver suffered actual damages when he entered
into a stipulated judgment in excess of policy limits, as required in order for a passenger, as the insured's assignee,
to pursue a claim against the insurer for bad faith refusal
to settle.

—In *Fortner v. Grange Mut. Ins. Co.*, 286 Ga. 189, 686
S.E.2d 93 (2009), the Georgia Supreme Court held that an
automobile insurer that conditioned its acceptance of an
assignee's offer to settle on his signing a full release of the
insured with indemnification language, and dismissal of the

claim against the insured with prejudice, was not entitled to a safe harbor from bad faith liability.

—In *Economy Fire & Casualty Co. v. Collins*, 643 N.E.2d 382 (Ind. Ct. App. 1994), an Indiana court rejected the "payment rule" and endorsed the "judgment rule," according to which an insurer may be subject to liability for an entire excess judgment even though the insured may be judgment proof and lack the capacity to pay any part of the judgment.

—The Maine Supreme Court, in *Thurston v. Continental Casualty Co.*, 567 A.2d 922 (Me. 1989), stated its agreement with cases holding that an insured need not pay an excess judgment to recover damages. But the court modified that majority rule by insisting that, because of insolvency a nonpaying insured may not have been damaged in the full amount of the excess judgment, and the amount of the excess judgment is not necessarily the appropriate measure of damages. As in any other case, the court reasoned, an insured must prove the actual amount of economic harm caused by the insurer's breach of duty. The choice is not between collecting the entire excess judgment and no damages at all, the court continued, since there are other possible elements of damages—such as injury to credit rat-ing, injury to reputation, and expenses incurred in dealing with the existence of the judgment and settling the claim.

—In *J & J Farmer Leasing, Inc. v. Citizens Ins. Co. of Am.*, 680 N.W.2d 423 (Mich. Ct. App. 2004), a Michigan Court of Appeals held that a bad faith failure to settle claim was not precluded by an agreement by the parties to release the insured from the excess judgment in the underlying wrongful discharge suit. Distinguishing *Frankenmuth Mut. Ins. Co. v. Keeley*, 436 Mich. 372, 461 N.W.2d 666 (1990), the court held that an insurer found liable for a bad faith failure to settle is required to pay the excess judgment to the extent the insured would have been able to pay, regardless of the existence of a release from the underlying prevailing party.

—In *Pinto v. Allstate Ins. Co.*, 221 F.3d 294 (2d Cir. 2000)

(New York law), the Second Circuit reasoned that "[t]o allow an insurer to escape liability because its insured lacks the ability to pay an excess judgment would introduce a perverse and undesirable incentive into personal liability actions, discouraging rather than encouraging settlement." 221 F.3d at 403. The court also rejected the argument that a release from liability extinguishes an assigned bad faith claim.

—In *Logan v. Allstate Ins. Co.*, 169 Ohio App. 3d 754, 865 N.E.2d 57 (2006), an Ohio Court of Appeals cited *Carter v. Pioneer Mut. Casualty Co.*, 67 Ohio St. 2d 146, 423 N.E.2d 188 (1981) (see book) for the proposition that Ohio law applies the "judgment rule" rather than the "payment rule." According to the "judgment rule," the court explained, an entry of judgment against an insured's estate in excess of policy limits is sufficient damage alone to sustain a recovery from the insurer if it is adjudicated that there was a breach of duty by the insurer in defending the insured's estate.

—Under Texas law, according to a federal district court in *Willcox v. American Home Assurance Co.*, 900 F. Supp. 850 (S.D. Tex. 1995), an insurer's liability cannot exceed the policy limits where the third party and the insured have signed a covenant not to execute the excess portion of a judgment. See also *In re Davis*, 253 F.3d 807 (5th Cir. 2001) (insured whose bankruptcy relieved him of liability for excess judgment could not state *Stowers* claim for insurer's failure to settle).

—For additional cases representing the majority view that the actual payment of an excess judgment is not a prerequisite to a cause of action against a wrongfully nonsettling insurer, see *Industrial Chem. & Fiberglass Corp. v. North River Ins. Co.*, 908 F.2d 825 (11th Cir. 1990) (Alabama law); *Medical Mut. Liab. Ins. Soc'y v. Evans*, 91 Md. App. 421, 604 A.2d 934, *rev'd on other grounds*, 330 Md. 1, 622 A.2d 103 (1993); *Calo v. State Farm Mut. Auto. Ins. Co.*, 227 A.D.2d 432, 642 N.Y.S.2d 906 (1996); *Gray v. Grain Dealers Mut. Ins. Co.*, 871 F.2d 1128 (D.C. Cir. 1989) (North

Carolina law); *Logan v. Allstate Ins. Co.*, *supra*; *Campbell v. State Farm Mut. Auto. Ins. Co.*, 840 P.2d 130 (Utah Ct. App. 1992); *Rupp v. Transcontinental Ins. Co.*, 627 F. Supp. 2d 1304 (D. Utah 2008) (Utah law).

§2.45 7. Insured's Collusion With Claimant

—In *Safeway Ins. Co. v. Guerrero*, 106 P.3d 1020 (Ariz. 2005), the Arizona Supreme Court reinstated the trial court's dismissal of a liability insurer's claim for intentional interference with contractual relations against a plaintiff's attorney who, the insurer alleged, had "stepped outside the legal boundaries for *Damron/Morris* agreements and purposefully implemented a scheme to 'manufacture' a bad faith claim in order to generate a multi-million dollar recovery instead of collecting on a $15,000 motor vehicle policy." The Arizona Supreme Court held that the attorney's negotiation of the *Morris* agreement in question had not been "improper conduct" that would give rise to liability for intentional interference with contractual relations, even if the attorney had been aware that the insurer's failure to settle within policy limits was not in bad faith. The attorney's profit motive was not improper, the court added, nor was the attorney's threat of multi-million dollar liability in the event of a trial against the insured, given the severity of the claimant's injuries.

—Collusive assistance in the procurement of a judgment not only constitutes a breach of the cooperation clause but also is a breach of the covenant of good faith and fair dealing, the court held in *Span, Inc. v. Associated Int'l Ins. Co.*, 227 Cal. App. 3d 463, 277 Cal. Rptr. 828 (1991). Fact issues had been raised as to collusion, the court held, reversing summary judgment in an action against an excess insurer. See also *Andrade v. Jennings*, 54 Cal. App. 4th 307, 62 Cal. Rptr. 2d 787 (1997); *Pengilly Masonry, Inc. v. Aspen Ins. UK, Ltd.*, 674 F. Supp. 2d 1150 (E.D. Cal. 2009) (under California law, cognizable claim of collusion in settlement agreement requires evidence that injured party had no substantial claim or chance of recovery and that parties permitted judgment in injured party's favor that was disproportionate to injuries). Compare *Safeco Ins. Co. of Am. v. Parks*, 170 Cal. App. 4th 992, 88 Cal. Rptr. 3d 730 (2009) (collusion instruction was not warranted even though tortfeasor had assigned her bad faith claim to personal injury judgment creditor before arbitration occurred; although arbitration award was large, it was reasonable given judgment creditor's severe injuries).

In *Xebec Dev. Partners, Ltd. v. National Union Fire Ins. Co.*, 12 Cal. App. 4th 501, 15 Cal. Rptr. 726 (1993), *disapproved on other grounds, Essex Ins. Co. v. Five Star Dye House, Inc.*, 38 Cal. 4th 1252, 45 Cal. Rptr. 3d 362, 137 P.3d 192 (2006), a California Court of Appeal held that the jury should have been permitted to consider the full merits of the third party's underlying claims against the insured, to determine whether the insured's settlement of those claims was reasonable and not collusive for purpose of using that settlement to measure damages for the insurer's breach of the duty to defend.

—In *Rogers Cartage Co. v. Travelers Indem. Co.*, 2018 IL App. (5th) 160098, 103 N.E.3d 504 (2018), *appeal denied*, 108 N.W.3d 885 (Ill. 2018), the court held that the settlement offer was not the product of collusion between the insured and the underlying claimants. The insured, a hauler of toxic and hazardous materials, settled for $7.5 million in lawsuit related to the clean-up of two Superfund sites. The insured did not conceal settlement negotiations from the insurer, and where the insured did not disclose every detail, the court found the insurer was not prejudiced by any lack of disclosure. In addition, the court found that the settlement was reasonable and there was no evidence the insurer was baited into rejecting one deal so the insured could reach a different settlement. The fact that some of the settlement money could come back to the insured does not make it per se collusive.

—In *Patrons Oxford Ins. Co. v. Harris*, 905 A.2d 819 (Me. 2006), the Supreme Judicial Court of Maine explained that, in connection with an insured's settlement of a tort claim without the permission of a liability insurer providing a defense under a reservation of rights, the insured's mere lack of cooperation with his or her liability insurer is not dispositive on the issue of fraud or collusion as defenses to the ability of the insured's judgment creditor to "reach and apply" the liability policy to the judgment.

—In *Fireman's Fund Ins. Co. v. Imbesi*, 361 N.J. Super. 539, 826 A.2d 735 (2003), the court refused to enforce against a liability insurer a $4.15 million settlement between the insured employer and its former employee after the insurer had denied coverage and refused to defend the employer against the employee's sexual harassment claims. Although the insurer had not been justified in denying coverage and refusing to defend, the court held, the settlement was unreasonable, collusive, and unenforceable where the employee had relied on naked allegations, the employer and the participating insurers had failed to mount a challenge to her valuation of the case, and the settlement terms disproportionately burdened the nonparticipating insurer. See also *New Jersey Eye Ctr., P.A. v. Princeton Ins. Co.*, 394 N.J. Super. 557, 928 A.2d 25 (2007) (ophthalmologist breached his obligations to malpractice insurer when he agreed to settle medical malpractice claims without insurer's consent).

—In *Woo v. Fireman's Fund Ins. Co.*, 161 Wash. 2d 43, 164 P.3d 454 (banc 2007), the Washington Supreme Court explained that once the trial determines that a settlement is reasonable, the burden is on the insurer to prove collusion, and held that the insurer in the present case failed to provide any such evidence at trial. "In contrast," the court wrote, "[the insured] cited testimony of [the plaintiff's attorney] who stated unequivocally that the settlement was 'devoid of any bad faith, collusion, or fraud.' Woo challenged the list of cases cited by Fireman's in which the insured escaped liability, noting that he did not, and noted that Fireman's never provided any suggestions regarding what a reasonable settlement would have been. Finally,

Woo pointed to extensive evidence that he mounted a vigorous defense prior to settling. . . ." 161 Wash. 2d at 69, 164 P.3d at 467. See also *Gosney v. Fireman's Fund Ins. Co.*, 3 Wash. App. 2d 828, 419 P.3d 447 (2018), *review denied*, 191 Wash. 2d 1017 (2018) (if amount of covenant judgment is deemed reasonable, it becomes presumptive measure of damages in bad faith action unless insurer can rebut presumption by showing collusion or fraud; trial court did not err in jury instruction on definition of collusion) (see discussion in §4.28).

—In *State Farm Fire & Casualty Co. v. Winsor*, 5 F. Supp. 2d 1258 (D. Wyo. 1998), a federal district court applying Wyoming law granted the insurer's motion for summary judgment on a bad faith claim involving a collusive settlement and stipulated judgment entered into without the insurer's consent.

B. Defenses Predicated on Claimant's Conduct

1. Claimant's Failure To Propose Settlement Within Policy Limits

§2.46 a. Absence of Demand as Precluding Insurer's Bad Faith

—It was held in *Heredia v. Farmers Ins. Exch.*, 228 Cal. App. 3d 1345, 279 Cal. Rptr. 511 (1991) that the insurer could not be subjected to liability for an excess judgment because the settlement offer it had rejected had been beyond the policy limits: the third-party plaintiff had demanded the policy limits plus the insurer's continued defense of the insured (in order to prevent the other defendants from mounting an "empty chair" defense). See also *Dorroh v. Deerbrook Ins. Co.*, 223 F. Supp. 3d 1081 (E.D. Cal. 2016), *aff'd*, ___ Fed. Appx. ___, 2018 WL 4566298 (9th Cir. 2018) (granting summary judgment in favor of 7insurer where insured attempted to settle without joining third-party claimant and settlement offer was beyond policy limits because it would have exposed insurer to potential liability from known third-party lienholder). Compare *Aguilar v. Gostischef*, 220 Cal. App. 4th 475, 163 Cal. Rptr. 3d 187 (2013) (evidence supported finding that accident victim's pretrial settlement offer of $700,000 to driver's insurer was reasonable and in good faith so that victim was entitled to award of costs in light of verdict that exceeded that amount); *Reid v. Mercury Ins. Co.*, 220 Cal. App. 4th 262, 162 Cal. Rptr. 3d 894 (2013) (affirming summary judgment; insurer could not be liable for bad faith failure to settle where there had been no settlement offer from third party and where insurer had done nothing to foreclose possibility of settlement); *Boicort v. Amex Assurance Co.*, 78 Cal. App. 4th 1390, 93 Cal. Rptr. 2d 763 (2000) (reversing summary judgment; absence of settlement offer within policy limits did not preclude insurer's liability for bad faith where insurer had refused to disclose policy limits to claimant and had failed to ask insured for permission to disclose that information). See also *Howard v. American Nat'l Fire Ins. Co.*, 187 Cal. App. 4th 498, 115 Cal. Rptr. 3d 42 (2010) (insurer does not breach duty to settle if it had no opportunity to do so; in single insurer case, opportunity to settle is typically shown by proof that injured party made reasonable settlement offer within policy limits and insurer rejected it); *Yan Fang Du v. Allstate Ins. Co.*, 697 F.3d 753, (9th Cir. 2012) (stating that under present facts it was unnecessary to resolve split of authority as to whether breach of good faith duty to settle can be found in absence of settlement demand).

—See *Wierck v. Grinnell Mut. Reinsurance Co.*, 456 N.W.2d 191 (Iowa 1990), representing the view that a finding of bad faith depends on proof of the existence of a settlement offer for a specific amount within policy limits. "It is an extraordinary thing to require an insurer to pay more than the policy limits. A bad faith claim cannot be based on settlements never presented to the liability insurance carrier. It is thus incumbent on the person claiming bad faith to show that a settlement offer was extended to and was in bad faith rejected by the insurer. . . . This is a matter of set amounts, and the burden of showing the amounts is upon the person claiming bad faith." 456 N.W.2d at 195.

—In *State Farm Fire & Casualty Co. v. Metcalf*, 861 S.W.2d 751 (Mo. Ct. App. 1993), the Missouri Court of Appeals reversed a judgment for the insureds' assignees on the ground that there had been a failure of proof as to the existence of a policy-limits settlement offer or other opportunity to settle for that sum. In a separate opinion concurring in the result, Judge Shrum argued that because the insurer had refused to defend and had denied coverage, it should have been estopped from relying upon the absence of a policy-limits offer, or upon the absence of an apparently futile demand by the insured that the claim be settled within policy limits.

—In *CBLPath, Inc. v. Lexington Ins. Co.*, 73 A.D.3d 829, 900 N.Y.S.2d 462 (2010), the court explained that, under New York law, proof that a demand for settlement was made is a prerequisite to proving a bad faith failure to settle. Additionally, the plaintiff must show that the insured lost an actual opportunity to settle the claim at a time when all serious doubts about the insured's liability had been removed. Accord, *Tokio Marine v. Macready*, 803 F. Supp. 2d 193 (E.D.N.Y. 2011) (New York law).

—In *Mid-Continent Ins. Co. v. Liberty Mut. Ins. Co.*, 236 S.W.3d 765 (Tex. 2007), the Texas Supreme Court explained that a liability insurer's common-law duty to its insured is limited to the *Stowers* duty to protect the insured by accepting a reasonable settlement offer within policy limits. That duty is not activated, the court continued, unless (1) the claim is within the scope of coverage; (2) the demand is within policy limits; and (3) the terms of the demand are such that an ordinarily prudent insurer would accept it, considering the likelihood and degree of the insured's potential exposure to an excess judgment. The court emphasized that a demand above liability policy limits, even if reasonable, does not trigger the *Stowers* duty.

§2.47 b. Absence of Demand as Factor in Determination of Bad Faith

—Also holding that the lack of a formal policy limits settlement demand does not preclude an insurer's liability for bad faith failure to settle, but is only one factor for the jury's consideration: *Powell v. Prudential Property & Casualty Ins. Co.*, 584 So. 2d 12 (Fla. Dist. Ct. App. 1991); *Berglund v. State Farm Mut. Auto. Ins. Co.*, 121 F.3d 1225 (8th Cir. 1997) (Iowa law); *City of Hobbs v. Hartford Fire Ins. Co.*, 162 F.3d 576 (10th Cir. 1998) (New Mexico law); *Hartford Ins. Co. v. Methodist Hosp.*, 785 F. Supp. 38 (E.D.N.Y. 1992) (New York law). See also *Howard v. American Nat'l Fire Ins. Co.*, 187 Cal. App. 4th 498, 115 Cal. Rptr. 3d 42 (2010) (liability insurer breached duty to settle although there was never demand within insured's policy limits where demand of $1.85 million had been well within limits of multiple insurers on risk); *Allstate Ins. Co. v. Miller*, 212 P.3d 318 (Nev. 2009) (liability insurer can be liable for bad faith failure to settle even where demand exceeded policy limits if insured was willing and able to pay amount of proposed settlement beyond policy coverage); *Moratti v. Farmers Ins. Co. of Wash.*, 162 Wash. App. 495, 254 P.3d 939 (2011) (because it was liability insurer's own representation that prevented formal demand letter, insured's assignee's failure to make demand did not bar bad faith claim).

§2.48 c. Insurer's Affirmative Duty To Initiate Settlement Negotiations

—In *Yan Fang Du v. Allstate Ins. Co.*, 697 F.3d 753 (9th Cir. 2012), the Ninth Circuit, applying California law, affirmed a judgment on a jury's verdict in favor of the insurer, writing in part: "The bad faith claim asserted here is that the case would have been settled within policy limits had [the insurer] initiated earlier settlement negotiations. [The insurer] contends that if there was a duty to initiate settlement talks, it did so in a timely fashion in view of the circumstances. The record supports [that] contention." 697 F.3d at 758–59.

—See *Morrell Constr., Inc. v. Home Ins. Co.*, 920 F.2d 576 (9th Cir. 1990) (Idaho law), in which the Ninth Circuit predicted that the Idaho Supreme Court would not hold that the third-party bad faith doctrine imposes upon insurers a noncontractual duty to initiate settlement negotiations before a third party files suit. The court noted the existence of a split of authority on the issue among the states, but predicted that Idaho courts would prefer the position of such cases as *Miller v. Kronk*, 35 Ohio App. 3d 103, 519 N.E.2d 856 (1987), over that of *Alt v. American Family Mut. Ins. Co.*, 71 Wis. 2d 340, 237 N.E.2d 706 (1976). (The Ninth Circuit in *Morrell* similarly predicted that Idaho courts would impose on insurers no duty of presuit investigation: see supplement §2.31.)

—For a discussion, relative to an action under the Massachusetts unfair claims settlement practices statute, of an insurer's duty to attempt a policy-limits settlement despite the claimant's hard-line position, see *Metropolitan Property & Casualty Ins. Co. v. Choukas*, 47 Mass. App. Ct. 196, 711 N.E.2d 933 (1999). See also *Rhodes v. AIG Domestic Claims, Inc.*, 961 N.E.2d 1067 (Mass. 2012) (insurer's statutory duty to make prompt and fair settlement offer does not depend on claimant's willingness to accept such offer, and even excessive demands on part of claimant do not relieve insurer of duty to extend prompt and equitable offer once liability and damages are reasonably clear).

—The Texas Supreme Court has rejected the view that an insurer has a duty to initiate settlement negotiations. *American Physicians Ins. Exch. v. Garcia*, 876 S.W.2d 842 (Tex. 1994). (The *Garcia* decision contains a useful collection of citations from other jurisdictions that are arguably at odds with the Texas Supreme Court's conclusion, though the court makes an attempt to harmonize them (876 S.W.2d at 850 n.17).) See also *Birmingham Fire Ins. Co. v. American Int'l Adjusting Co.*, 947 S.W.2d 592 (Tex. Ct. App. 1997) (applying rule of *Garcia* to situation involving action by excess insurer against primary insurer).

§2.49 2. Claimant's Failure To Allow Reasonable Time for Insurer's Consideration of Settlement Offer

—Applying California law, the Second Circuit, in *Schwartz v. Liberty Mut. Ins. Co.*, 539 F.3d 135 (2d Cir. 2008), affirmed a judgment on a jury verdict for the insured in a diversity action against his excess insurers to recover amounts he had paid to settle a securities fraud class action. Evidence that the excess insurers had participated in and monitored the progress of unsuccessful settlement negotiations presented jury questions, the court held, as to whether the insurers had had an adequate opportunity to evaluate a mid-trial settlement offer, and as to whether the settlement amount was reasonable.

—In *Southern Gen. Ins. Co. v. Holt*, 262 Ga. 267, 416 S.E.2d 274 (1992), the court held that an insurer's obligation to protect the interests of its insured prohibits the insurer from relying on its own internal scheduling procedures in an attempt to justify failure to give appropriate consideration to a settlement offer of limited duration. Compare *Baker v. Huff*, 323 Ga. App. 357, 747 S.E.2d 1 (2013) (liability for excess judgment cannot be based on insurer's failure to accept time-limited offer to settle within policy limits where offer imposed unreasonably short period of time to respond); *Kingsley v. State Farm Mut. Auto. Ins. Co.*, 353 F. Supp. 2d 1242 (N.D. Ga. 2005) (liability insurer's failure to respond to time-limited settlement offer does not constitute bad faith per se).

—Two decisions by the Kansas Supreme Court have addressed distinguishable situations involving settlement offers of limited duration. In *Glenn v. Fleming*, 247 Kan. 296, 799 P.2d 79 (1990), the court affirmed summary judgment on the ground that the settlement offer had been premature, conditional, and left open for only two weeks. The court subsequently distinguished that set of facts from those in *Hawkins v. Dennis*, 258 Kan. 329, 905 P.2d 678 (1995), where although the offer had been left open for only seven days, there existed the additional factor of the insurer's negligence in taking an adamant noncoverage position without investigation.

—In *Rogers v. Government Employers Ins. Co.*, 598 So. 2d 670 (La. Ct. App. 1992), a Louisiana Court of Appeals held that in setting a five-day limit for the acceptance of a settlement offer, the third-party claimant did not give enough time to act, precluding a finding of bad faith.

—In *La Vaud v. Country-Wide Ins. Co.*, 29 A.D.3d 745, 815 N.Y.S.2d 680 (2006), a New York court explained that to establish a prima facie case of bad faith refusal to settle, the insured must demonstrate that the insurer's conduct constituted a gross disregard of the insured's interests. In the present case, the court held, no prima facie case was established by evidence that the defendant automobile insurer had failed to respond to a time-restricted demand for settlement within full policy limits.

§2.50 3. Claimant's Ineffective Settlement Offer

—In *Williams v. Geico Casualty Co.*, 301 P.3d 1220 (Alaska 2013), the Alaska Supreme Court wrote (301 P.3d at 1226):

> We have not directly addressed how an insurer should handle multiple insureds. Other jurisdictions have utilized two different approaches. The first is that the insurer should seek to release all insureds, but if it cannot, then it ought to seek to settle on behalf of one. [Citation

omitted.] The second approach requires an insurer to seek release of all insureds; when a settlement cannot be reached the insurer must file a declaratory action to determine what coverage is owed. [Citation omitted.] [¶] We are persuaded that the latter approach is the better one. . . . [S]eeking a settlement to the benefit of one insured while leaving others open to liability could cause unfairness. Further, the latter approach avoids a potential bad faith claim by an insured who was unprotected and efficiently adjudicates the rights and duties of the insurer and the insured.

In *Whitney v. State Farm Mut. Auto. Ins. Co.*, 258 P.3d 113 (Alaska 2011), the Alaska Supreme Court held that an automobile liability insurer did not breach its legal duty to settle with an injured bicyclist when it rejected an offer to settle for amounts that exceeded the policy limits.

—It was held *McReynolds v. American Commerce Ins. Co.*, 225 Ariz. 125, 235 P.3d 278 (2010), that an insurer's prompt good faith filing of an interpleader as to all known claimants, with payment of policy limits into the court and a continued defense of the insured as to each pending claim, acts as a safe harbor for an insurer against a bad faith claim when multiple claimants are involved and the expected claims are in excess of the applicable policy limits.

—In *Strauss v. Farmers Ins. Exch.*, 26 Cal. App. 4th 1017, 31 Cal. Rptr. 2d 811 (1994), a California Court of Appeal, affirming summary judgment, held that the insurer could not have incurred bad faith liability for refusing a policy-limits settlement offer that would have released only one of three insureds and left two others bereft of coverage. Accord *Lehto v. Allstate Ins. Co.*, 31 Cal. App. 4th 60, 36 Cal. Rptr. 2d 814 (1994). Compare *Country Mut. Ins. Co. v. Anderson*, 628 N.E.2d 499 (Ill. App. Ct. 1993) (insurer did not commit bad faith by agreeing to policy limits settlement that resulted in complete release of named insured but left additional insured uncovered and undefended), with *Shell Oil v. National Union Fire Ins. Co.*, 44 Cal. App. 4th 1633,

52 Cal. Rptr. 2d 580 (1996) (insurer's disbursement of policy limits to indemnify one insured constituted actionable breach of duties to defend and indemnify coinsured). And in *Schwartz v. State Farm Fire & Casualty Co.*, 88 Cal. App. 4th 1329, 106 Cal. Rptr. 2d 523 (2001), it was held that an excess insurer, before paying one insured's claim, must consider other insureds' rights even before their primary insurance has been exhausted.

—It was held in *Williams v. Infinity Ins. Co.*, 754 So. 2d 573 (Fla. Dist. Ct. App. 1999), affirming dismissal of a bad faith claim, that an insurer has no duty to settle with one claimant to the exclusion and detriment of other potential claimants. The insurer had acknowledged coverage but had refused to pay the policy limits to two claimants because that would have prejudiced three other claimants, instead tendering the policy limits on the condition that the amount satisfy the claims of the claimants' entire estate.

In *Shin Crest PTE, Ltd. v. AIU Ins. Co.*, 605 F. Supp. 2d 1234 (M.D. Fla. 2009), a federal district court held that a commercial general liability insurer did not act in bad faith at the mediation of a products liability claim against an insured retailer by failing to offer the policy limits in exchange for the release of all claims against both the retailer and the insured manufacturer even though the eventual post-mediation settlement exhausted policy limits without releasing claims against the manufacturer. The manufacturer's liability was not clear at the time of the mediation, the court explained, the manufacturer denied any product defect, and that denial was supported by the opinion of a defense expert. At the time of the settlement, the court added, the insurer had unsuccessfully attempted to obtain a release of the manufacturer, and the insurer had an obligation to settle the claim against the retailer in the absence of any possibility of a release as to both insureds.

See also *General Security Nat. Ins. Co. v. Marsh*, 303 F. Supp. 2d 1321 (M.D. Fla. 2004) (explaining factors relevant to determining reasonableness of decisions made in settling multiple claims). Compare *Contreras v. U.S. Security Ins. Co.*, 927 So. 2d 16 (Fla. Dist. Ct. App. 2006) (reversing judgment on directed verdict for insurer; as matter of first impression, automobile insurer could be held liable for bad faith arising out of its refusal to accept offer, made by estate of deceased pedestrian, to settle with insured owner of automobile but not with its driver, who was covered as permissive user of automobile; when estate refused to include driver, insurer had duty to protect owner from excess judgment). *Farinas v. Florida Farm Bureau Gen. Ins. Co.*, 850 So. 2d 555 (Fla. Dist. Ct. App. 2003) (reversing summary judgment; jury question was raised as to whether insurer had acted reasonably in exhausting policy limits in settling with only three of multiple claimants).

In *Berges v. Infinity Ins. Co.*, 896 So. 2d 665 (Fla. 2004), the Florida Supreme Court addressed the question whether an offer to settle a claim on behalf of a minor prior to court approval is invalid as a matter of law. Court approval, the court held, is not a prerequisite to a valid settlement offer, and the evidence supported a jury finding of bad faith and an award of the amount of the excess judgment plus interest.

—Concerning Georgia law relative to the allocation of insufficient policy limits among multiple insureds, see *Miller v. Georgia Interlocal Risk Management Agency*, 232 Ga. App. 231, 501 S.E.2d 589 (1998). And see *Cotton States Mut. Ins. Co. v. Brightman*, 276 Ga. 683, 580 S.E.2d 519 (2003), holding that it was sufficiently proven that negotiations would have led to settlement had the insurer responded to a conditional offer with a counteroffer in an attempt to protect its insured from excess liability. The insurer unsuccessfully contended that it had been precluded from accepting the claimant's offer because this offer included a condition beyond its control (the payment of policy limits by another insurer). See also *ACCC Ins. Co. v. Carter*, 621 F. Supp. 2d 1279 (N.D. Ga. 2009) (insurer did not act in bad faith in paying policy limits without conditioning payment on release of its insured). Compare

Fortner v. Grange Mut. Ins. Co., 286 Ga. 189, 686 S.E.2d 824 (2009) (insurer that conditioned its acceptance of assignee's offer to settle on assignee's signing a full release of insured with indemnification language and dismissing claim against insured with prejudice was not entitled to safe harbor from liability for bad faith).

—In *Capitol Specialty Ins. Corp. v. Higgins*, 953 F.3d 95 (1st Cir. 2020), the court held that the Massachusetts federal district court did not err in concluding that a night club owner's liability insurer conducted an inadequate investigation of a claim against the owner by an underage exotic dancer who was severely injured in a car accident after becoming intoxicated at work, but that a damages award based on a $7.5 million settlement amount reached without participation of the insurer and without judicial review was improper. The court upheld a damages award based on a $1.8 million award, with damages trebled damages for willful conduct, for violation of Massachusetts' unfair claims settlement practices statute, Mass. Gen. Laws §176D 3(9)(d).

—Under Missouri law, it was held in *Purscell v. Tico Ins. Co.*, 959 F. Supp. 2d 1195 (W.D. Mo. 2013), summary judgment was appropriate where the insured had not made a sufficiently definite demand upon the insurer to settle claims arising from an auto accident. The insured's attorney had sent a letter requesting that "this matter" be settled within policy limits, but it was unclear whether "this matter" referred only to claims of the accident victims in the vehicle with which the insured's car had collided, or whether "this matter" also concerned a possible wrongful death claim on behalf of the insured's passenger.

—In *Greenidge v. Allstate Ins. Co.*, 446 F.3d 356 (2d Cir. 2006) (New York law), the Second Circuit, affirming a grant of summary judgment, held that the insurer had not been required to accept a contingent settlement demand that involved agreeing to a declaratory judgment action to determine the applicable policy limits .

In *In re September 11 Litigation*, 723 F. Supp. 2d 534 (S.D.N.Y. 2010), the court held that, under New York law, an insurer has discretion to settle, in good faith, one or more claims against it even if doing so may jeopardize the ability of later recovering or settling plaintiffs to collect on their claims. An insurer has no duty to pay out claims ratably or to consolidate them.

—In *DeMarco v. Travelers Ins. Co.*, 26 A.3d 585 (R.I. 2011), the Rhode Island Supreme Court explained that when an insurer is faced with multiple claimants with claims that in the aggregate exceed the policy limits, the insurer has a fiduciary duty to engage in timely and meaningful settlement negotiations in an attempt to bring about the settlement of as many claims as possible, and must negotiate as if there were no policy limits applicable to the claims. In the present case, the court held, a passenger who had been injured while riding in the insured's vehicle and who had obtained a judgment against the insured, was entitled to pre-judgment and post-judgment interest from the insurer who had rejected his settlement offer at the policy's $1 million limit, even though the accident had involved multiple claims with claims exceeding policy limits.

—Under Texas law, it was held in *Texas Farmers Ins. Co. v. Soriano*, 881 S.W.2d 312 (Tex. 1994), an insurer may satisfy its *Stowers* duty by settling with one claimant even though the insured is left exposed to another claim. See also *AFTCO Enters., Inc. v. Acceptance Indem. Ins. Co.*, 321 S.W.3d 65 (Tex. App. 2010); *Carter v. State Farm Mut. Auto. Ins. Co.*, 33 S.W.3d 369 (Tex. App. 2000); *Travelers Indem. Co. v. Citgo Petroleum Corp.*, 166 F.3d 761 (5th Cir. 1999).

The insured had no claim based on the insurer's failure to settle, the Texas Supreme Court held in *Trinity Universal Ins. Co. v. Bleeker*, 966 S.W.2d 489 (Tex. 1998), because the claimants' offers had not included hospital liens and would not therefore have amounted to full releases of the insured's liability.

§2.51 4. Claimant-Assignee's Failure To Cooperate With Insurer

—In *Baranowski v. GEICO Gen. Ins. Co.*, 385 F. Supp. 3d 1267 (M.D. Fla. 2019), *aff'd*, 806 Fed. Appx. 971 (11th Cir. 2020), the federal district court granted the insurer's motion for summary judgment where the insurer acted diligently in contacting the claimant's attorney with settlement offers, responded promptly to all of the claimant's attorney's requests for information, and attempted many times to communicate with the claimant's attorney. In evaluating the totality of the circumstances to determine whether the insurer could have settled within the policy limits, the court noted the unresponsiveness on the part of claimant's attorney to communication attempts by the insurer, and it noted that the claimant's attorney failed to specify what changes he wished to see in the settlement offer before he filed the bad faith lawsuit.

§2.52 C. Defense Predicated on Insurer's Conduct: Lack of Causation Between Insurer's Conduct and Excess Judgment

—In *Howard v. American Nat'l Fire Ins. Co.*, 187 Cal. App. 4th 498, 115 Cal. Rptr. 3d 42 (2010), the court explained that, in most cases, an excess judgment is needed to establish liability and damages for a wrongful refusal to settle. But an insured may also recover, despite the lack of an excess judgment, if the insurer's misconduct went beyond a simple failure to settle within policy limits, or the insured suffered consequential damages apart from an excess judgment.

—In *Macola v. Government Employees Ins. Co.*, 953 So. 2d 451 (Fla. 2006), the Florida Supreme Court held, as a matter of first impression, that an insurer's tender of policy limits to an insured in response to the insured's filing of a civil remedy notice, after initiation of a lawsuit against the insured but before the entry of an excess judgment, does not preclude the maintenance of a common-law cause of action against the insurer for third-party bad faith. The Florida Supreme Court so held in answering questions certified by the Eleventh Circuit, and upon receiving the answers, the Eleventh Circuit reversed summary judgment that had been granted by the United States District Court for the Middle District of Florida. See *Macola v. Government Employees Ins. Co.*, 483 F.3d 1229 (11th Cir. 2007).

—In *Perera v. United States Fid. & Guar. Co.*, 35 So. 3d 893 (Fla. 2010), the Florida Supreme Court held that a cause of action for bad faith may not be maintained where the insurer's actions, because of the existence of an excess liability policy issued by another insurer, never resulted in the insured's increased exposure to liability in excess of his total policy limits.

—Answering a question certified by a federal district court, the Georgia Supreme Court, in *Trinity Outdoor, LLC v. Central Mut. Ins. Co.*, 285 Ga. 583, 679 S.E.2d 10 (2009), held that an insurer may not be held liable for bad faith failure to settle a claim in the absence of a judgment against the insured in excess of policy limits.

See *Cotton States Mut. Ins. Co. v. Brightman*, 276 Ga. 683, 580 S.E.2d 519 (2003), concerning the "difficult issue" of the sufficiency of proof, under Georgia law, that negotiations would have led to settlement had the insurer responded to a conditional offer with counteroffers in an attempt to protect its insured from excess liability. Concerning this issue, see also *Kingsley v. State Farm Mut. Auto. Ins. Co.*, 353 F. Supp. 2d 1242 (N.D. Ga. 2005).

—In *Wade v. EMCASCO Ins. Co.*, 483 F.3d 657 (10th Cir. 2007), the Tenth Circuit, applying Kansas law and citing *Hawkins v. Dennis*, 258 Kan. 329, 905 P.2d 678 (1995), held that there must be a causal link between the insurer's conduct and the excess judgment against the insured: an insured may recover under a bad faith claim only for those excess judgment losses directly and naturally resulting from the breach. If, for example, the court explained, a claimant arbitrarily withdraws an initial settlement offer and later rejects an identical proposal from the insurer, the claimant's conduct is the legal cause of the failure to settle.

—Applying Massachusetts law, the First Circuit, in *Peckham v. Continental Casualty Co.*, 895 F.2d 830 (1st Cir. 1990), held that the trial judge had properly submitted the issue of proximate causation to the jury. The court also held that the evidence had supported a finding that although the insurer had committed a breach of duty in delaying a policy limits offer contingent on resolution of a coverage issue pending before the state supreme court, the effect of that breach had been "cured" by a belated offer. The court also reasoned that the jury could have found for the insurer on the proximate causation issue by inferring from the evidence that the claimants' attorney would have rejected a policy limits offer even had one been made in a more timely fashion. See also *Rhodes v. AIG Domestic Claims, Inc.*, 961 N.E.2d 1067 (Mass. 2012) (causal link was sufficiently established by showing that insurer had failed to initiate settlement process once merits of claim were clear); *RLI Ins. Co. v. General Star Indem. Co.*, 997 F. Supp. 140 (D. Mass. 1998) (notwithstanding substandard performance by primary liability insurer in handling claim by brain-damaged child, child's representatives would not have agreed to settlement of claim for $1 million policy limits, and thus it could not be found that primary insurer's performance was cause of need for umbrella insurer to contribute to ultimate settlement).

—In *Alexander Mfg., Inc. v. Illinois Union Ins. Co.*, 665 F. Supp. 2d 1185 (D. Or. 2009), the court explained that, under Oregon law, an insured may prove the causation element of a claim for negligent or bad faith failure to settle a claim within policy limits through evidence that the injured party would have accepted such a settlement if one had been offered. In the present case, neither party carried its burden on summary judgment with regard to either causation or damages, the court held, and those issues required resolution by a trier of fact.

—Concerning Texas law relative to excess judgment/ causation issues, see *Archer v. The Med. Protective Co. of Fort Wayne, Ind.*, 197 S.W.3d 422 (Tex. App. 2006); *Wheelways Ins. Co. v. Hodges*, 872 S.W.2d 776 (Tex. App. 1994); *Allstate Ins. Co. v. Kelly*, 680 S.W.2d 595 (Tex. App. 1984).

§2.53 D. Statute of Limitations

—Under Arizona law, a third-party bad faith failure-to-settle claim accrues not when an excess judgment is entered, but only at the time the underlying action becomes final and non-appealable. *Taylor v. State Farm Mut. Auto. Ins. Co.*, 185 Ariz 174, 913 P.2d 1092 (1996).

—Under Arkansas law, the Eighth Circuit held, in *Carpenter v. Automobile Club Interinsurance Exch.*, 58 F.3d 1296 (8th Cir. 1995), a claim for bad faith and negligence in failing to settle accrued at the time the insured was held liable in the underlying tort action, not on the earlier date when the insurer failed to respond to settlement letters.

—In *Archdale v. American Int'l Specialty Lines Ins. Co.*, 154 Cal. App. 4th 449, 64 Cal. Rptr. 3d 632 (2007), a California Court of Appeal, affirming and reversing summary judgment in parts, held, *inter alia*: (1) a 4-year statute of limitations applied to a contract claim against the insurer, which had been assigned to the claimant, for rejecting a reasonable settlement offer within the tortfeasor's policy limits; (2) the tortfeasor's claim against the insurer for emotional distress and punitive damages, which sounded in tort, was barred by a 2-year statute of limitations; and (3) the 4-year statute of limitations on the contractual claim was tolled pending the entry of a final judgment in the underlying action following appeals by the insurer and the tortfeasor.

—Denying the insurer's motion for summary judgment, a

federal district court in *Vanderloop v. Progressive Casualty Ins. Co.*, 769 F. Supp. 1172 (D. Colo. 1991) held that under Colorado law, a cause of action for bad faith failure to settle accrues only when excess liablity is finally established; *i.e.*, when judgment on appeal becomes final. (The limitations period that begins to run at that time is the 2-year limitations period for tort actions.)

—In *Chandler v. American Fire & Casualty Co.*, 377 Ill. App. 3d 253, 879 N.E.2d 396 (2007), in an action by an insured's judgment creditors for bad faith failure to settle after a judgment against the insured, the court held that the claim arose, and the 5-year limitations period began to run, no later that the date of the judgment against the insured and, thus, before the date of the insurer's rejection of the post-judgment settlement demand.

—In *Amdahl v. Stonewall Ins. Co.*, 484 N.W.2d 811 (Minn. Ct. App. 1992), a Minnesota Court of Appeals, affirming the denial of a motion to dismiss, held that in an action against a liability insurer for bad faith failure to settle a claim, the statute of limitations does not begin to run until the appellate process is complete and final judgment has been entered.

—Concerning a number of issues, under New York law, relating to the running of the statute of limitations and accrual of causes of action alleging breaches of an insurer's duties to indemnify, defend, and settle, see *Roldan v. Allstate Ins. Co.*, 149 A.D.2d 20, 544 N.Y.S.2d 359 (1989).

—In *Haugh v. Allstate Ins. Co.*, 322 F.3d 227 (3d Cir. 2003) (Pennsylvania law), the Third Circuit explained that while the 2-year limitations period may have run on a cause of action created by Pennsylvania's bad faith statute (42 Pa. Cons. Stat. Ann. §8371) that claim was not exclusive of a common-law claim for breach of the duty to settle, which is subject to a 4-year statute of limitations. See also *Sikirica v. Nationwide Ins. Co.*, 416 F.3d 214 (3d Cir. 2005) (Pennsylvania law; 2-year statute of limitations on insured's statutory bad faith claim against its comprehensive liability insurer began to run when insurer provided clear notice of its denial of coverage and refusal to defend); *United Nat'l*

Ins. Co. v. Indian Harbor Ins. Co., 160 F. Supp. 3d 828 (E.D. Pa. 2016) (same).

—In *Moratti v. Farmers Ins. Co. of Wash.*, 162 Wash. App. 495, 254 P.3d 939 (2011), it was held that an action for bad faith in the handling of an insurance claim is a tort claim subject to a 3-year statute of limitations, and such a claim accrues when the underlying judgment against the insured becomes final.

IV. THIRD-PARTY JUDGMENT CREDITOR'S RIGHT OF ACTION

A. Right To Direct Suit for Excess Judgment Against Insurer

§2.54 1. In General

—The following are additional cases representing the standard view that there is no nonstatutory basis upon which a judgment creditor can sue the insurer directly for the excess portion of a judgment: *Hicks v. Alabama Pest Servs., Inc.*, 548 So. 2d 148 (Ala. 1989); *Leal v. Allstate Ins. Co.*, 199 Ariz. 250, 17 P.3d 95 (Ct. App. 2000); *Old Republic Ins. Co. v. Ross*, 180 P.3d 427 (Colo. banc 2008); *Cassidy v. Millers Casualty Co.*, 1 F. Supp. 2d 1200 (D. Colo. 1998) (Colorado law); *Hipsky v. Allstate Ins. Co.*, 304 F. Supp. 2d 284 (D. Conn. 2004) (Connecticut law); *Simmons v. Puu*, 105 Hawaii 112, 94 P.3d 667 (2004); *Hettwer v. Farmers Ins. Co.*, 797 P.2d 81 (Idaho 1990); *State Farm Mut. Auto. Ins. Co. v. Estep*, 873 N.E.2d 1021 (Ind. 2007); *Menefee v. Schurr*, 751 N.E.2d 757 (Ind. Ct. App. 2001); *Dimitroff v. State Farm Mut. Auto. Ins. Co.*, 647 N.E.2d 339 (Ind. Ct. App. 1995); *Bates v. Allied Mut. Ins. Co.*, 467 N.W.2d 255 (Iowa 1991); *Langsford v. Flattman*, 864 So. 2d 149 (La. 2004); *Bellah v. State Farm Fire & Casualty Ins. Co.*, 546 So. 2d 601 (La. Ct. App. 1989); *Murrell v. Williamsburg Local Sch. Dist.*, 92 Ohio App. 3d 92, 634 N.E.2d 263 (1993); *Pasipanki v. Morton*, 61 Ohio App. 3d 184, 572 N.E.2d 234

(1990); *Hoar v. Aetna Casualty & Sur. Co.*, 968 P.2d 1219 (Okla. 1998); *Colony Ins. Co. v. Burke*, 698 F.3d 1222 (10th Cir. 2012) (Oklahoma law); *Johnson v. Beane*, 664 A.2d 96 (Pa. 1995); *Marks v. Nationwide Ins. Co.*, 762 A.2d 1098 (Pa. Super. Ct. 2000); *Johnson v. Viking Ins. Co.*, 706 F. Supp. 720 (D.S.D. 1989) (South Dakota law); *P.G. Bell Co. v. United States Fidelity & Guar. Co.*, 853 S.W.2d 187 (Tex. Ct. App. 1993); *Caserotti v. State Farm Ins. Co.*, 791 S.W.2d 561 (Tex. Ct. App. 1990); Lasewicz v. Joyce Van Lines, Inc., 830 F. Supp. 2d 286 (S.D. Tex. 2011) (Texas law); *Vickers v. Gray & Co.*, 761 F. Supp. 37 (E.D. Tex. 1991), *aff'd without op.* (5th Cir. Oct. 13, 1992) (Texas law); *Larocque v. State Farm Ins. Co.*, 660 A.2d 286 (Vt. 1995); *Dussault ex rel. Walker-Van Buren v. American Int'l Group, Inc.*, 123 Wash. App. 863, 99 P.3d 1256 (2004). An insurer owes no duty of good faith to a third-party claimant even where the third party also happens to be a policyholder: *Pixton v. State Farm Mut. Auto. Ins. Co.*, 809 P.2d 746 (Utah App. Ct. 1991); *Elmore v. State Farm Mut. Auto. Ins. Co.*, 504 S.E.2d 893 (W. Va. 1998); *Herrig v. Herrig*, 844 P.2d 487 (Wyo. 1992).

—In *Williams v. State Farm Mut. Auto. Ins. Co.*, 886 So. 2d 72 (Ala. 2003), the court granted summary judgment on an accident victim's action for bad faith failure to pay. The court distinguished *Howton v. State Farm Mut. Auto. Ins. Co.*, 507 So. 2d 448 (Ala. 1987), where it was held that a third-party accident victim may sue a tort-feasor's liability insurer directly only where "the insurer undertakes a new and independent obligation directly with a nonparty to the insurance contract in its efforts to negotiate a settlement of the third party's claim." 507 So. 2d at 450.

—For discussions of the unique Florida third-party-standing rule of *Thompson v. Commercial Union Ins. Co.*, 250 So. 2d 259 (Fla. 1971), as clarified by *Fidelity & Casualty Co. v. Cope*, 462 So. 2d 459 (Fla. 1985), see *Camp v. St. Paul Fire & Marine Ins. Co.*, 616 So. 2d 12 (Fla. 1993); *State Farm Mut. Auto. Ins. Co. v. Marshall*, 618 So. 2d

1377 (Fla. Dist. Ct. App. 1993); *Martin v. State Farm Mut. Auto. Ins. Co.*, 808 N.E.2d 47 (Ill. App. Ct. 2004); *Herrig v. Herrig, supra.* (The Florida rule allows a third party to sue an insurer directly for bad faith failure to settle without an assignment, but specifies that the third party's claim is not a separate and distinct one, but is merely derivative of the insured's. Accordingly, there are no damages, and no bad faith action may be maintained, once the injured party has released the tort-feasor from all liability or the excess judgment has been satisfied.)

—Under Kansas law, the Tenth Circuit held in *Moses v. Halstead*, 581 F.3d 1248 (10th Cir. 2009), a judgment creditor is not required to obtain an assignment of rights from the debtor in order to bring a claim against the debtor's insurer for negligent or bad faith failure to settle. The court cited *Nichols v. Marshall*, 491 F.2d 177 (10th Cir. 1974), for the proposition that "under longstanding garnishment law in Kansas, once judgment has entered, the judgment creditor takes the place of the judgment debtor and may take that which the latter could enforce." 491 F.2d at 184.

—In *Railsback v. Mid-Century Ins. Co.*, 680 N.W.2d 652 (S.D. 2004), the South Dakota Supreme Court reversed summary judgment that had been granted in favor of a liability insurer on a claim by an automobile accident victim who alleged that the insurer had misrepresented the policy limits during settlement negotiations. The court held inapplicable the prohibition against a direct action by an injured third party and emphasized that an insurer owes a duty not to knowingly cause or further a third-party claimant's misunderstanding of the policy limits to his or her detriment.

§2.55 a. Garnishment

—Concerning the rule that a judgment creditor, in obtaining a writ of garnishment against a tort-feasor's insurance company, is ordinarily limited to recovering no more than the policy limits, see *St. Paul Fire & Marine Ins. Co. v.*

Nowlin, 542 So. 2d 1190 (Ala. 1988); *Safeway Ins. Co. v. Thompson*, 688 So. 2d 271 (Ala. Civ. App. 1996); *Metropolitan Property & Casualty Ins. Co. v. Crump*, 237 Ga. App. 96, 513 S.E.2d 33 (1999). Compare *Moses v. Halstead*, 581 F.3d 1248 (10th Cir. 2009) (Kansas law; judgment creditor may proceed by garnishment against tortfeasor's insurer for unpaid balance of judgment in excess of policy limits where insurer failed to settle within policy limits by virtue of negligence or bad faith).

—In *Greer v. Eby*, 309 Kan. 182, 432 P.3d 1001 (2019), the Supreme Court of Kansas reversed a garnishment order that had been granted in favor of the judgment creditor and her insurer where the garnishee/insurer met its burden to prove its policy defense. The garnishee/insurer successfully proved its policy defense by showing that (1) its insured breached its duties under the insurance contract by failing to give the garnishee/insurer notice of the excess judgment lawsuit, and (2) the lack of notice prejudiced the garnishee/insurer. The lower courts had ruled that the garnishee/insurer failed to show prejudice because it was notified that such a lawsuit was likely and it had even offered to pay a settlement amount, but the Supreme Court of Kansas held that the prejudice element was met because the insured failed to notify the garnishee/insurer of the actual lawsuit. The garnishee/insurer was prejudiced when the lawsuit resulted in default judgment against the insured, who did not respond to the claim. The court stated that the garnishee/insurer never had a chance to defend against the suit and to challenge the allegations that its insured's negligence caused the accident.

—In *Allen v. Bryers*, 512 S.W.3d 17 (Mo. 2016), *as modified*, (Mo. banc 2017), *cert. denied*, ___ U.S. ___, 138 S. Ct. 212 (2018), the garnishment court exceeded its authority in awarding an amount in excess of the policy limit where the insurer wrongfully refused to defend the insured, but the garnishment court did not make a finding on whether the insurer acted in bad faith when it refused to defend.

§2.56 b. Judgment Creditor as Third-Party Beneficiary

—For additional cases representing recognition of a judgment creditor's standing as a third-party beneficiary, see *Low v. Golden Eagle Ins. Co.*, 101 Cal. App. 4th 1354, 125 Cal. Rptr. 2d 155 (2002); *Harper v. Wausau Ins. Corp.*, 56 Cal. App. 4th 1079, 66 Cal. Rptr. 2d 64 (1997); *Hand v. Farmers Ins. Exch.*, 23 Cal. App. 4th 1847, 29 Cal. Rptr. 2d 258 (1994); *Cain v. Griffin*, 849 N.E.2d 507 (Ind. 2006); *Donald v. Liberty Mut. Ins. Co.*, 18 F.3d 474 (7th Cir. 1994) (Indiana law); *Campbell v. American Int'l Group, Inc.*, 976 P.2d 1102 (Okla. Civ. App. 1999). Compare *GDF Int'l, S.A. v. Associated Electric & Gas Ins. Servs. Ltd.*, 2003 WL 926790 (N.D. Cal. 2003) (rejecting argument that liability provisions normally give claimants third-party beneficiary status and discussing limited situations in which Cal. Ins. Code section 11580 permits judgment creditor to bring direct action against liability insurer); *Ristow v. Threadneedle Ins. Co.*, 220 Wis. 2d 644, 583 N.W.2d 452 (Ct. App. 1998) (declining, per *Kranzush v. Badger State Mut. Casualty Co.*, 103 Wis. 2d 56, 307 N.W.2d 256 (1981), to recognize bad faith cause of action by third-party claimant against insurer who allegedly breached settlement agreement). (Note that *Harper v. Wassau Ins. Corp.*, *supra*, as well as *Shaolian v. Safeco Ins. Co.*, 71 Cal. App. 4th 268, 83 Cal. Rptr. 2d 702 (1999), stand for the proposition that an injured third party may sue a tortfeasor's insurance company for bad faith if the "med-pay" provision of a liablility policy provides no-fault coverage.)

In *Hughes v. Mid-Century Ins. Co.*, 38 Cal. App. 4th 1176, 45 Cal. Rptr. 2d 302 (1995), the court affirmed the dismissal of a judgment creditor's bad faith action against the tortfeasor's insurer, holding that the underlying judgment in the underlying action was not "final" in the relevant sense because the time to appeal that judgment had not expired. The judgment creditor had attempted to bring his bad faith action, the court explained, before achieving the status of judgment creditor enjoying third-party-beneficiary status and rights under the policy.

§2.57 2. Effect of Direct Action Statutes

—For a holding that California's direct action statute (Cal. Ins. Code §11580) applies to any judgment based on property damage, see *People ex rel. City of Willits v. Certain Underwriters at Lloyd's of London*, 97 Cal. App. 4th 1125, 118 Cal. Rptr. 2d 868 (2002). At issue was an action by the State of California against the insured's excess umbrella liability insurer to recover for property damage caused by pollution at a manufacturing plant. See also *Howard v. American Nat'l Fire Ins. Co.*, 187 Cal. App. 4th 498, 115 Cal. Rptr. 3d 42 (2010); *Gray v. Begley*, 182 Cal. App. 4th 1509, 106 Cal. Rptr. 3d 729 (2010); *Travelers Casualty & Sur. Co. v. Superior Court*, 126 Cal. App. 4th 1131, 24 Cal. Rptr. 3d 571 (2005); *GDF Int'l, S.A. v. Associated Electric & Gas Ins. Servs. Ltd.*, 2003 WL 926790 (N.D. Cal. 2003).

B. Assignment of Excess Liability Action by Insured

§2.60 2. Assignability of Claim to Judgment Creditor

—The general rule upholding the assignability of bad faith claims has been endorsed in the following cases: *Denham v. Farmers Ins. Co.*, 213 Cal. App. 3d 1061, 262 Cal. Rptr. 146 (1989); *Aaron v. Allstate Ins. Co.*, 559 So. 2d 275 (Fla. Dist. Ct. App. 1990) (claim for excess judgment was assignable under theory that insurer provided inadequate defense); *Feijoo v. Geico Gen. Ins. Co.* 137 F. Supp. 3d 1320 (S.D. Fla. 2015), *aff'd*, 678 Fed. Appx. 862 (11th Cir. 2017) (Florida law); *Fortner v. Grange Mut. Ins. Co.*, 286 Ga. 189, 686 S.E.2d 93 (2009); *Southern Guar. Ins. Co. v. Dowse,*

278 Ga. 674, 605 S.E.2d 27 (2004); *Southern Gen. Ins. Co. v. Ross*, 227 Ga. App. 191, 489 S.E.2d 53 (1997); *Cuson v. Maryland Casualty Co.*, 735 F. Supp. 966 (D. Haw. 1990) (Hawaii law); *Brocato v. Prairie State Farmer's Ins. Ass'n*, 166 Ill. App. 3d 986, 520 N.E.2d 1200 (1988); *In re New Era, Inc.*, 135 F.3d 1206 (7th Cir. 1998) (Illinois law); *Pistalo v. Progressive Casualty Ins. Co.*, 953 N.E.2d 152 (Ind. Ct. App. 2012); *Allstate Ins. Co. v. Axsom*, 696 N.E.2d 482 (Ind. Ct. App. 1998) (assignability extends to punitive damages claims); *Associated Wholesale Grocers v. Americold*, 261 Kan. 806, 934 P.2d 65 (1997); *Glenn v. Fleming*, 247 Kan. 296, 799 P.2d 79 (1990) (overruling *Heinson v. Porter*, 244 Kan. 667, 772 P.2d 778 (1989)); *Wade v. EMCASCO Ins. Co.*, 483 F.3d 657 (10th Cir. 2007) (Kansas law); *Medical Mut. Liab. Ins. Soc'y v. Evans*, 330 Md. 1, 622 A.2d 103 (1993); *Kaplan v. Harco Nat'l Ins. Co.*, 708 So. 2d 89 (Miss. Ct. App. 1998) (assignability extends to punitive damages claims); *Stephen R. Ward v. United States Fed. Guar. Co.*, 681 F. Supp. 389 (S.D. Miss. 1988) (Mississippi law; endorsing minority view that assignability extends to punitive damages claims); *Rupp v. Transcontinental Ins. Co.*, 627 F. Supp. 2d 1304 (D. Utah 2008) (Utah law); *Bird v. Best Plumbing Group, LLC*, 175 Wash. 2d 756, 287 P.3d 551 (Wash. banc 2012); *St. Paul Fire & Marine Ins. Co. v. Onvia, Inc.*, 165 Wash. 2d 122, 196 P.3d 664 (2008); *Hamblin v. Castillo Garcia*, 6 Wash. App. 2d 78, 441 P.3d 1283 (2019) (assignability extends to damages for emotional distress and may include provision to allow insured to be compensated from global settlement agreement). But see *Quick v. National Auto Credit*, 65 F.3d 741 (8th Cir. 1995), holding that under Missouri law, a car lessee's action against the car lessor for bad faith failure to settle was not assignable. Also representing the minority nonassignability rule, see *Cash v. State Farm Fire & Casualty Co.*, 125 F. Supp. 2d 474 (M.D. Ala. 2000) (Alabama law); *Terrell v. Lawyers Mut. Liab. Ins. Co.*, 507 S.E.2d 923 (N.C. Ct. App. 1998); *Horton v. New S. Ins. Co.*, 468 S.E.2d 856 (N.C. Ct. App. 1996).

—In *Nunn v. Mid-Century Ins. Co.*, 244 P.3d 116 (Colo. banc 2010), the Colorado Supreme Court held that an insured driver suffered actual damages when he entered into a stipulated judgment in excess of policy limits, as required in order for a passenger, as the insured's assignee, to pursue a claim against the insurer for bad faith refusal to settle.

—In *Fortner v. Grange Mut. Ins. Co.*, *supra*, the Georgia Supreme Court held that an insurer who conditioned its acceptance of assignee's offer to settle on his signing a full release of insured with indemnification language and dismissing claim against insured with prejudice was not entitled to safe harbor from liability for bad faith action.

—In *O'Neill v. Gallant Ins. Co.*, 769 N.E.2d 100 (Ill. Ct. App. 2002), the Illinois Court of Appeals for the Third District validated *compelled* assignments of bad faith settlement claims, overruling its own earlier decision to the contrary in *Roundtree v. Barringer*, 92 Ill. App. 3d 903, 416 N.E.2d 675 (1981), and agreeing with a decision by another Illinois Court of Appeals in *Phelan v. State Farm Mut. Auto. Ins. Co.*, 114 Ill. App. 3d 96, 448 N.E.2d 579 (1983). (The disagreement between the *Roundtree* and *Phelan* courts was discussed in §2.60 of the book.)

—In *Johnson v. Beane*, 664 A.2d 96 (Pa. 1995), the Pennsylvania Supreme Court held (1) that a judgment creditor cannot maintain a garnishment action against the judgment debtor's insurer for bad faith failure to settle in the absence of an actual assignment of the bad faith claim from the judgment debtor to the judgment creditor; and (2) that when an injured party is fully compensated for a particular loss by his or her underinsured motorist carrier, the injured party may not bring a "bad faith garnishment" action against the tort-feasor's liability insurer for failure to settle.

—Under Rhode Island law, the state supreme court held in *Mello v. General Ins. Co. of Am.*, 525 A.2d 1304 (R.I. 1987), ". . . an insured may assign its bad-faith claim against its insurer to the injured claimant for the limited purpose of recovering the difference between the judgment received against the insured and the insurance-policy limits." 525 A.2d at 1306. See also *DeMarco v. Travelers Ins. Co.*, 26 A.3d 585 (R.I. 2011) (injured passenger's execution of general release contemporaneously with insured driver's execution of assignment documents following judgment for passenger in excess of policy limits did not extinguish passenger's right to pursue claims against insurer for amount of judgment).

§2.63 5. Prejudgment Assignment by Insured

—Reversing summary judgment for the insured, an Arizona court, in *State Farm Mut. Auto. Ins. Co. v. Peaton*, 168 Ariz. 184, 812 P.2d 1002 (1991), held that the insured had breached the cooperation clause of his auto insurance policy by settling the case with the injured party, and assigning his claims against the insurer, at a time when the insurer had not breached any of its contractual obligations to the insured. The court explained that an insured may enter into a *"Damron* agreement"—an assignment to an injured third party of all claims against an insurer for bad faith—only after the insurer has done something in violation of contract that places the insured in jeopardy. (Such agreements derive their name in Arizona from *Damron v. Sledge*, 105 Ariz. 151, 460 P.2d 997 (1969).) See also *Parking Concepts, Inc. v. Tenney*, 207 Ariz. 19, 83 P.3d 19 (2004); *United Servs. Auto. Ass'n v. Morris*, 154 Ariz. 113, 741 P.2d 246 (1987); *Associated Aviation Underwriters v. Wood*, 98 P.3d 572 (Ariz. Ct. App. 2004); *Waddell v. Titan Ins. Co.*, 88 P.3d 1141 (Ariz. Ct. App. 2004); *Himes v. Safeway Ins. Co.*, 66 P.3d 74 (Ariz. Ct. App. 2003).

—In *Smith v. State Farm Mut. Auto. Ins. Co.*, 5 Cal. App. 4th 1104, 7 Cal. Rptr. 2d 131 (1992), it was held: (1) a judgment against the insured is a necessary condition to the insured's right to assign a bad faith cause of the action to the claimant; (2) that condition is not satisfied by a stipulated judgment with a covenant not to execute; but (3) the insured's liability was sufficiently adjudicated by his conviction for manslaughter with gross negligence. The *Smith* holding that a stipulated judgment is inadequate to support an assignment was subsequently followed by a federal district court in *Somerset South Properties, Inc. v. American Title Ins. Co.*, 873 F. Supp. 355 (S.D. Cal. 1994), and by a state court of appeal in *Safeco Ins. Co. of Am. v. Superior Court*, 71 Cal. App. 4th 782, 84 Cal. Rptr. 2d 43 (1999), but was rejected as too rigid by another court of appeal, in *McLaughlin v. National Union Fire Ins. Co.*, 21 Cal. App. 4th 486, 26 Cal. Rptr. 2d 520 (1993). The *McLaughlin* court wrote: "The countervailing policy concerns explored in *Critz* [*v. Farmers Ins. Group*, 230 Cal. App. 2d 788, 41 Cal. Rptr. 401 (1964)], namely those in favor of settlement and equalization of insured's and insurer's strategic advantages, are also important. Each case develops its own dynamic and has its own mix of procedures and circumstances which should be evaluated to determine whether the problems of collusion and prejudice are substantially diminished in that case." 21 Cal. App. 4th at 507–08, 26 Cal. Rptr. 2d at 530. Accord *Pruyn v. Agricultural Ins. Co.*, 36 Cal. App. 4th 500, 42 Cal. Rptr. 2d 295 (1995). For a related discussion, citing *Smith* with approval and relying on the particularly collusive nature of the present facts for the conclusion that a stipulated judgment was inadequate, see *Wright v. Fireman's Fund Ins. Co.*, 11 Cal. App. 4th 998, 14 Cal. Rptr. 2d 588 (1992). Distinguishing *Smith* on the ground that in the present case the stipulated judgment had been approved as a good faith settlement under Cal. Code Civ. Proc. §877.6, see *Roman v. Unigard Ins. Group*, 26 Cal. App. 4th 177, 31 Cal. Rptr. 2d 501 (1994). See also *Sanchez v. Truck Ins. Exch.*, 21 Cal. App. 4th 1778, 26 Cal. Rptr. 2d 812 (1994).

In *Finkelstein v. 20th Century Ins. Co.*, 11 Cal. App. 4th 926, 14 Cal. Rptr. 2d 305 (1992), a California Court of Appeal, affirming summary judgment for the insurer, emphasized that no cause of action for bad faith failure to settle ripens in the absence of a judgment in excess of policy limits. In the present case, the insured, certain that a jury verdict in excess of the $100,000 policy limits would ensue, but unable to convince the insurer to offer more than $75,000, had voluntarily contributed some of his own money to effect a settlement of $85,000. The court emphasized the voluntariness of the insured's contribution and the absence of any duress on the insurer's part.

In 2002, the California Supreme Court, in *Hamilton v. Maryland Casualty Co.*, 27 Cal. 4th 718, 117 Cal. Rptr. 2d 318 (2002), clarified an important issue concerning assignments following stipulated judgments. The court wrote (27 Cal. App. 4th at 721–22):

> A liability insurer agrees to defend its insured against a personal injury lawsuit. After the insurer refuses a settlement demand within the policy limits, the claimant and the insured, without the insurer's participation, agree on a settlement. Under the settlement agreement, a stipulated judgment in excess of the policy limits is entered, the claimant agrees not to execute the judgment against the insured, and insured assigns to the claimant the insured's cause of action for breach of the insurer's duty to accept a reasonable settlement demand. The trial court approves the settlement as made in good faith pursuant to Code of Civil Procedure section 877.6.
>
> In a subsequent action by the claimant, as the insured's assignee, against the insurer for breach of contract, is the amount of the stipulated judgment presumptively binding on the insurer as to the damages suffered by the insured as a result of the alleged contract breach? We conclude it is not: a defending insurer cannot be bound to a settlement to which it has not agreed and in which it has not participated. . . . In this circumstance, we further conclude, the claimant may

not maintain an action for breach of the duty to settle because, in light of the settlement before trial and the covenant not to execute against the insured, the stipulated judgment is insufficient to prove that the insured suffered any damages from the insurer's breach of its settlement duty.

The court emphasized that the situation is different in a situation where the insurer denies coverage and repudiates its obligation to defend. In such a case, the policyholder may make a reasonable noncollusive settlement without the insurer's consent and seek reimbursement for the settlement amount in a bad faith action. (See *Samson v. Transamerica Ins. Co.*, 30 Cal. 3d 220, 178 Cal. Rptr. 343 (1981).) In *Mercado v. Allstate Ins. Co.*, 340 F.3d 824 (9th Cir. 2003), the court reasoned that the *Hamilton* holding should be extended to tort as well as contract claims. See also *Wolkovitz v. Redland Ins. Co.*, 112 Cal. App. 4th 154, 5 Cal. Rptr. 3d 95 (2003) (bankruptcy court's allowance of $26 million personal injury claim against bankruptcy estate of insured debtor, pursuant to settlement agreement between bankruptcy trustee and claimant, did not constitute judicial determination of insured's liability to claimant).

In *Durment v. Burlington Ins. Co.*, 820 Fed. Appx. 561 (9th Cir. 2020) (California law), the insurers failed to defend the insureds from an amended complaint that was tendered on the eve of trial. The insureds then settled with the claimant and assigned their claims against insurers to the claimant. The court stated that a breaching insurer is generally liable for a post-breach judgment only to the extent of coverage, and it rejected the argument that the duty to indemnify applied only to judgments, not to settlements. The court held that the claimant could not recover settlement amounts from the insurers without establishing coverage.

—In *Carford v. Empire Fire & Marine Ins. Co.*, 94 Conn. App. 41, 891 A.2d 55 (2006), a Connecticut Appellate Court held, as a matter of first impression, that victims had no cause of action against the tortfeasor's insurer for violation of the Unfair Insurance Practices Act prior to a judicial determination of the insured's liability.

—Also distinguishing *Fidelity & Casualty Co. v. Cope*, 462 So. 2d 459 (Fla. 1985), discussed in the book, see *Camp v. St. Paul Fire & Marine Ins. Co.*, 616 So. 2d 12 (Fla. 1993). See §2.54 of this supplement for discussion of Florida law and the *Camp* decision. See also *United Servs. Auto. Ass'n v. Jennings*, 731 So. 2d 1258 (Fla. 1999); *Cunningham v. Standard Guar. Ins. Co.*, 630 So. 2d 179 (Fla. 1994).

—In *Weber v. Indemnity Ins. Co. of N. Am.*, 345 F. Supp. 2d 1139 (D. Hawaii 2004), the court predicted that the Hawaii Supreme Court would reject the California approach of *Hamilton v. Maryland Casualty Co.*, *supra*, according to which stipulated judgments and assignments of rights between an insured and a third-party claimant are enforceable only in situations where an insurer has failed to defend the insured. Hawaii law would permit enforcement of such a stipulated judgment, the court held, where the insurer has breached its obligations by committing the tort of bad faith failure to settle.

—In *Guillen v. Potomac Ins. Co. of Ill.*, 203 Ill. 2d 141, 785 N.E.2d 1 (2003), the Illinois Supreme Court held that an insurer who had wrongfully refused to defend its insured was obligated to pay the $600,000 for which the insured had settled the claim in return for a covenant not to execute. The court rejected the insurer's argument that such a settlement does not create a "legal obligation" and is inherently collusive, but the court did hold that the assignee has the burden of proving that the settlement was reasonable as part of its prima facie case.

—In *Nungesser v. Bryant*, 283 Kan. 550, 153 P.3d 1277 (2007), the Kansas Supreme Court, addressing an issue of first impression, held that an insured may not sue his or her liability insurer for a negligent or bad faith failure to settle until the tort claim against the insured has been reduced to judgment.

—Answering a question of first impression under Ohio law, a federal district court, in *Romstadt v. Allstate Ins. Co.*, 844 F. Supp. 361 (N.D. Ohio 1994), *aff'd*, 59 F.3d 608 (6th Cir. 1995), granting summary judgment, held that the insured's assignee could not maintain a bad faith action against the insurer, where the amount of damages had never been determined by a factfinder, but instead, the insured and the third-party claimant had entered into an agreed judgment and an assignment of the bad faith claim in exchange for a release and satisfaction of judgment as to any claim in excess of policy limits. The court reasoned that the bad faith claim was fatally flawed due to the absence of an essential element—the insured's exposure to an excess judgment.

—In *State Farm Fire & Casualty Co. v. Gandy*, 925 S.W.2d 696 (Tex. 1996), the Texas Supreme Court announced rules designed to eliminate collusive prejudgment assignments. The court held that the assignment of a bad faith claim for failure to defend, given in exchange for a covenant not to execute, is invalid if (1) it is made prior to the adjudication of the claim in a fully adversarial trial, (2) the insurer has tendered a defense, and (3) the insurer has accepted coverage or has made a good faith effort to adjudicate coverage issues. (The opinion contains a useful collection of authorities from other jurisdictions concerning collusive assignments.) See also *Stroop v. Northern County Mut. Ins. Co.*, 133 S.W.3d 844 (Tex. App. 2004); *First Gen. Realty Corp. v. Maryland Casualty Co.*, 981 S.W.2d 495 (Tex. Ct. App. 1998).

—Under Virginia law, a federal district court held in *Spence-Parker v. Maryland Ins. Group*, 937 F. Supp. 551 (E.D. Va. 1996), the attorneys' failure to inform the judge that their settlement was not adversarial in nature constituted constructive fraud and entitled the insurer to have the consent judgment set aside.

—The principle that an insurer is liable for no-personal-liability settlements in excess of policy limits has been recognized by the Washington Supreme Court in both the failure-to-settle and the failure-to-defend situation. See *Truck Ins. Co. v. Vanport Homes, Inc.*, 147 Wash. 2d 751, 58 P.3d 276 (2002); *Besel v. Viking Ins. Co. of Wis.*, 146 Wash. 2d 730, 49 P.3d 887 (2002).

—In *Strahin v. Sullivan*, 647 S.E.2d 765 (W. Va. 2007), construing *Shamblin v. Nationwide Mut. Ins. Co.*, 396 S.E.2d 766 (W. Va. 1990), the West Virginia Supreme Court of Appeals held that the insured did have a claim for failure to settle within policy limits that could be assigned to the claimant where the insured had assigned his rights against the insurer prior to trial and was never actually exposed to personal liability for a judgment in excess of policy limits.

—In *Gainsco Ins. Co. v. Amoco Prod. Co.*, 53 P.3d 1051 (Wyo. 2002), the Wyoming Supreme Court held that the inclusion of a covenant not to execute in a settlement agreement did not bar the assignee from pursuing a bad faith claim against the insurer. The court also held, however, that in the present case the decision of the insurer (who was defending under a reservation of rights) to reject a proposed settlement had not been objectively unreasonable, and that the insured and the claimant had failed to carry their burden of proving that their settlement amount had been reasonable.

V. DAMAGES

§2.64 A. Factors Affecting Recovery

—Concerning the duty to mitigate, see *State Farm Mut. Auto. Ins. Co. v. Schlossberg*, 82 Md. App. 45, 570 A.2d 328 (1990), holding that the insurer was not entitled to present evidence on the insured's failure to mitigate based on the insured's failure to assign his bad faith cause of action to the third-party judgment creditor and thus insulate himself from any damages resulting from the excess verdict. (The court also held that damages were correctly calculated simply as the difference between the insurance coverage and the jury verdict, and the trial judge had therefore acted correctly in fixing the amount of damages without a jury.)

—Reiterating (somewhat reluctantly) the position of the Oregon courts that a failure to defend can never amount to more than a breach of contract, see *Warren v. Farmers Ins. Co.*, 115 Or. App. 319, 838 P.2d 620 (1992).

—Applying Pennsylvania law that an insurer that violates its contractual duty of good faith in failing to settle can be liable for nominal damages, and insured need not claim compensatory damages to prevail, see *Wolfe v. Allstate Prop. & Ins. Co.*, 790 F.3d 487 (3d Cir. 2015).

B. Compensatory and Consequential Damages

1. Amount of Excess Judgment

§2.65 a. Failure To Settle

—Under Idaho law, the state supreme court explained in *McKinley v. Guaranty Nat'l Ins. Co.*, 144 Idaho 247, 159 P.3d 884 (2007), in a third-party action where the insurer unreasonably denies a settlement or payment, the insured may recover contract damages up to the policy limits and then tort damages for the excess. If the cause of action is based on delay and not denial, however, the court continued, the insurer has already paid the policy limits and contract damages are therefore unavailable.

—In *Pacific Employer's Ins. Co. v. P. B. Hoidale Co.*, 796 F. Supp. 1428 (D. Kan. 1992) (Kansas law), the court rejected the argument that a primary insurer who had negligently or in bad faith failed to initiate settlement negotiations was liable not for the full amount of the excess judgment, but only for that part of the judgment in excess of the amount for which the claim could reasonably have been settled.

—Where the insurer's bad faith liability had been decided by default, it was held in *State Farm Mut. Auto. Ins. Co. v. Schlossberg*, 82 Md. App. 45, 570 A.2d 328 (1990), that the trial judge had correctly denied the insurer a jury trial on the issue of damages. The damages to be awarded were a fixed sum determinable by mathematical computation, the court explained—the difference between the excess judgment and the policy limits, plus interest and costs—and there were no "facts" for a jury to decide.

—In *Rawan v. Continental Cas. Co.*, 483 Mass. 654, 136 N.E.3d 327 (2019), homeowners (claimants) brought a claim for bad faith against an engineer's professional liability insurer. The insurance policy contained a consent-to-settle clause, and the insurer failed to convince the insured to settle. After trial, the insurer paid up to the policy limit and the insured paid the remainder of the claim. The claimants then brought a bad faith claim against the insurer for failure to settle. The court held that the consent-to-settle provision in the insurance contract did not violate the insurer's duty to effectuate a prompt, fair, and equitable settlement under Mass. Gen. Laws Ann. ch. 176D §3(9)(f). The court stated that in situations with unreasonable insureds who refuse to settle, the insured should be held to account at trial and suffer the possibility of large damages awards.

In *Calandro v. Sedgwick Claims Mgmt. Servs.*, 264 F. Supp. 3d 321 (D. Mass. 2017), *aff'd*, 919 F.3d 26 (1st Cir. 2019) the court found that a third-party administrator hired by the insurer to handle a wrongful death claim that arose from the death of a nursing home resident made a settlement offer that was within the safe harbor provision of Mass. Gen. L. ch. 93A, because the settlement offered was reasonable in relation to the injury actually suffered by the claimant and the offer was made within the statutorily required time period. In this subsequent action, the safe harbor provision limited the claimant to recovering the $1.9 million offered under the provision.

—In *J & J Farmer Leasing, Inc. v. Citizens Ins. Co. of Am.*, 680 N.W.2d 423 (Mich. Ct. App. 2004), a Michigan Court of Appeals held that a bad faith failure to settle claim was not precluded by an agreement by the parties to release the insured from the excess judgment in the underlying wrongful discharge suit. Distinguishing *Frankenmuth Mut. Ins. Co. v. Keeley*, 436 Mich. 372, 461 N.W.2d 666 (1990), the court held that an insurer found liable for a bad faith failure to settle is required to pay the excess judgment to the extent the insured would have been able to pay, regardless of the existence of a release from the underlying prevailing party.

—In *Bird v. Best Plumbing Group, LLC*, 175 Wash. 2d 756, 287 P.3d 551 (Wash. banc 2012), the Washington Supreme Court engaged in a careful explanation of nine factors that a court must consider to determine if a settlement is reasonable, in situations where an injured party has entered into a stipulated judgment against the insured in exchange for a covenant not to execute on that judgment and an assignment of the insured's bad faith claim against the insurer. When such a "covenant judgment" has been entered into, the Court emphasized, the settling parties have the burden of proving the reasonableness of the settlement. (This issue under Washington law had previously been addressed in similar terms in *Chaussee v. Maryland Casualty Co.*, 60 Wash. App. 504, 803 P.2d 1339 (1991).) See also *Hamblin v. Castillo Garcia*, 6 Wash. App. 2d 78, 441 P.3d 1283 (2019) (trial court did not abuse its discretion by finding that settlement amount of $1.5 million was reasonable under factors from *Chaussee v. Maryland Casualty Co.*, *supra*, but appellate court remanded to modify 1 provision of agreement that guaranteed insured 10 percent of total amount of any global settlement to compensate insured for emotional distress resulting from insurer's bad faith; court found provision unreasonable under *Chaussee* because it invaded funds intended to compensate injured; where insured assigns all bad faith claims to injured plaintiff through covenant judgment settlement agreement, equitable principles do not permit guaranteed fixed percentage of global settlement to compensation insured for emotional distress); *Gosney v. Fireman's Fund Ins. Co.*, 3 Wash. App. 2d 828, 419 P.3d 447 (2018), *review denied*, 191 Wash. 2d 1017 (2018) (if amount of covenant judgment is deemed reasonable, it becomes presumptive measure of damages in bad faith action unless insurer can rebut presumption by showing collusion or fraud; see discussion in §4.28). For a comparable discussion under Missouri law, see *Hyatt Corp. v. Occidental Fire & Casualty Co.*, 801 S.W.2d 382 (Mo. Ct. App. 1990) (insurer may not complain of manner or amount of settlement absent collusion or bad faith). See also *Fireman's Fund Ins. Co. v. Imbesi*, 361 N.J. Super. 539, 826 A.2d 735 (2003); *Crawford v. Infinity Ins. Co.*, 139 F. Supp. 2d 1226 (D. Wyo. 2001) (Wyoming law).

§2.66 b. Refusal To Defend

—Under Alaska law, it was held in *United States v. CNA Financial Corp.*, 214 F. Supp. 2d 1044 (D. Alaska 2002), damages for bad faith breach of the duty to defend include the full amount of the settlement between the insured and the claimant.

—In *Amato v. Mercury Casualty Co.*, 53 Cal. App. 4th 825, 61 Cal. Rptr. 2d 909 (1997), a California Court of Appeal held, as a matter of first impression, that where an insurer tortiously breaches its duty to defend and the insured suffers a default judgment, the insurer is liable for that judgment even if it is later determined that the underlying claim was not covered by the policy.

—Holding that under Maryland law an insurer who refuses to perform its contractual duty to defend is subject to liability only for breach of contract and for contract-measure damages, not for the tort of bad faith, see *Mesmer v. Maryland Auto. Ins. Fund*, 353 Md. 241, 725 A.2d 1053 (1999).

—In *The Burlington Ins. Co. v. Northland Ins. Co.*, 766 F. Supp. 2d 515 (D.N.J. 2011), a federal district court held that under New Jersey law, where an insurer has wrongfully refused coverage and a defense to its insured, and the insured is therefore obliged to defend him- or herself in an action later held to be covered by the policy, the insurer is liable for the amount of the judgment obtained against the insured, or the amount of a good faith and reasonable settlement.

—In *Birsett v. General Accident Ins. Co.*, 226 A.D.2d 1027, 641 N.Y.S.2d 451 (1996), the court held that the record supported a finding that the insurer had been sufficiently heedless of its obligations to the insured to justify an award in excess of policy limits. The insurer, relying on a clearly ineffective policy "cancellation," had refused to defend the insured in a personal injury action.

—Under Texas law, according to a federal district court, in *Willcox v. American Home Assurance Co.*, 900 F. Supp. 850 (S.D. Tex. 1995), the damages recoverable on a contract claim for breach of the duty to defend do not include damages in excess of the policy limits. The insured's damages are generally limited to policy limits, expenses incurred in defending the suit (including attorney's fees and costs), and fees and costs incurred in the suit to enforce the judgment or settlement against the insurer. (Note that Texas law does not recognize a tort cause of action for bad faith refusal to defend: *United Servs. Auto. Ass'n v. Pennington*, 810 S.W.2d 777 (Tex. Ct. App. 1991).)

Texas law recognizes a breach of contract claim for failure to defend when the duty to defend exists under the contract. In *Lyda Swinerton Builders, Inc. v. Oklahoma Sur. Co.*, 903 F.3d 435 (5th Cir. 2018), the court affirmed that an insurer breached its duty to defend an additional insured general contractor who was sued for damages for work done by a subcontractor on a commercial office building, and the court affirmed the damages award of $655,600. In response to the insurer's argument that some of the defense costs claimed were unnecessary, the court stated that because the insurer breached its duty to defend, it could not object to defense expenditures that were supported by the record and not patently unreasonable. The court also reversed and remanded a claim related to extra-contractual damages under Chapter 541 of the Texas Insurance Code in light of *USAA Tex. Lloyds Co. v. Menchaca*, 545 S.W.3d 479 (Tex. 2018) (discussed in §1.56). The court in *Lyda Swinerton Builders* stated that if the insured could establish that the insurer's misrepresentations caused it to be deprived of a benefit under the insurance contract, the insured could recover defense costs it incurred as actual damages under Chapter 541 without limitation from the independent-injury rule. In addition, the court stated that the insured could recover treble damages under Chapter 541 if the insurer knowingly committed the alleged acts.

—In *Newhouse v. Citizens Sec. Mut. Ins. Co.*, 501 N.W.2d 1 (Wis. 1993), the Wisconsin Supreme Court concluded that "when an insurance company fails to follow the proper procedure of requesting a bifurcated trial on the issues of coverage and liability and an excess judgment is rendered against the insured before the coverage issue is finally determined, the excess judgment is a natural and proximate [result] of the insurance company's breach of its duty to defend for which it is liable." 501 N.W.2d at 7.

§2.68 3. Other Financial Losses

—Under Florida law, it was held in *Swamy v. Caduceus Self Ins. Fund, Inc.*, 648 So. 2d 758 (Fla. Dist. Ct. App. 1994), an insured may not recover damages for harm to his or her professional reputation caused by an excess judgment.

—Affirming an award of damages for lost profits in a

Pennsylvania failure-to-settle case, see *Birth Ctr. v. St. Paul Cos.*, 727 A.2d 1144 (Pa. Super. Ct. 1999).

§2.69 4. Emotional Distress

—In *Pershing Park Villas Homeowners Ass'n v. United Pac. Ins. Co.*, 219 F.3d 895 (9th Cir. 2000) (California law), the Ninth Circuit, affirming a judgment in favor of the insured, held, *inter alia*, that an insured may recover for all emotional distress incident to an insurer's bad faith denial of coverage and failure to defend if the insurer's conduct, as in the present case, also caused substantial financial loss.

—In *Goodsen v. American Standard Ins. Co. of Wisc.*, 89 P.3d 409 (Colo. 2004), the Colorado Supreme Court overruled *Farmers Group v. Trimble*, 768 P.2d 1243 (Colo. Ct. App. 1988) (a third-party case), to the extent that *Trimble* held that emotional distress damages may be recovered for the bad faith breach of an insurance contract only where the emotional distress has resulted from substantial property or economic loss. Emotional distress is a foreseeable result of an insurer's bad faith delay in paying a claim, the Colorado Supreme Court held, even where the claim is ultimately paid in full.

—In *Berglund v. State Farm Mut. Auto. Ins. Co.*, 121 F.3d 1225 (8th Cir. 1997) (Iowa law), the Eighth Circuit predicted that the Iowa Supreme Court would permit recovery of damages for emotional distress in cases involving an insurer's failure to exercise good faith in representing an insured against a third party.

—In *Indiana Ins. Co. v. Demetre*, 527 S.W.3d 12 (Ky. 2017), the court affirmed a jury award of $925,000 in emotional distress damages and $2.5 million in punitive damages. The jury found that the insurer had delayed its investigation and settlement of a matter involving third-party claims against the insured for injury allegedly caused by leaking underground fuel storage tanks on land that he owned, and that the insurer filed a declaratory judgment action to avoid paying the insured's claims although the insurer had reason to know its action was unjustified. Although the insurer eventually provided coverage and a defense, the jury awarded damages for the insured's 4 years of anxiety and mental anguish. The court rejected the insurer's argument that defending the insured while asserting a reservation of rights and filing a declaratory judgment action on coverage, and eventually paying the claim, insulated the insurer from a bad faith action.

The Kentucky Supreme Court held that the plaintiff was not required to provide expert medical or scientific proof to support his claim for emotional distress damages. Such proof is required for a standalone claim of intentional or negligent infliction of emotional distress, but when a claim for emotional distress damages is one of several damages claims, the court does not impose a heightened evidence requirement. Instead, "Kentucky has long recognized that 'damages for anxiety and mental anguish are recoverable in an action for statutory bad faith' provided there is 'clear and satisfactory' evidence from which 'the jury could infer that anxiety or mental anguish in fact occurred.'" 527 S.W.3d at 39 (quoting *Motorists Mut. Ins. Co. v. Glass*, 996 S.W.2d 437, 454 (Ky. 1997)). In a footnote, the court declined to revisit the rule from *Motorists* that harm from emotional distress need not be "severe" to be compensable. *Id.* at 40 n.30.

—In *Capitol Specialty Ins. Corp. v. Higgins*, 953 F.3d 95 (1st Cir. 2020), the court held that the Massachusetts federal district court did not err in concluding that a night club owner's liability insurer conducted an inadequate investigation of a claim against the owner by an underage exotic dancer who was severely injured in a car accident after becoming intoxicated at work. The court upheld a damages award based on a $1.8 million award, with damages trebled damages for willful conduct, for violation of Massachusetts' unfair claims settlement practices statute,

Mass. Gen. Laws §176D 3(9)(d), holding that damages for emotional distress, mental anguish, and "fear of financial ruin" were recoverable.

—In *Rinehart v. Shelter Gen. Ins. Co.*, 261 S.W.3d 583 (Mo. Ct. App. 2008), it was held that in an insured's action against an automobile insurer for bad faith failure to settle third parties' personal injury claims, the trial court did not err in admitting testimony by the insured concerning the financial pressure that had motivated his agreement with the third parties to pursue a bad faith claim. The court rejected the argument that his testimony ran afoul of the general prohibition on injecting a litigant's financial condition to influence the jury. The court wrote (261 S.W.3d at 590):

> Rinehart's explanatory comments regarding the agreement were relevant to prove his emotional distress as a part of the damages on his bad faith claim. His petition alleged that he "suffered mental agony, distress, anxiety, and worry as a result of being faced with a substantial judgment against him." Rinehart's testimony about the financial pressure he felt from the judgment . . . was necessary to explain the factors causing him emotional distress as a direct result of Shelter's failure to pay the claims of the accident victims.

—In *Jacobsen v. Allstate Ins. Co.*, 351 Mont. 464, 215 P.3d 649 (2009), the Montana Supreme Court clarified that a claim for emotional distress damages "parasitic" to an underlying tort may go to the jury without any requirement that the plaintiff show serious or severe emotional distress. That requirement applies only to independent claims for the negligent or intentional infliction of emotional distress.

—In *Hamblin v. Castillo Garcia*, 6 Wash. App. 2d 78, 441 P.3d 1283 (2019), the court analyzed a provision of a covenant judgment agreement that guaranteed the insured 10 percent of the total amount of any global settlement to compensate the insured for emotional distress that resulted from the insurer's bad faith failure to settle. The court found the provision unreasonable under *Chaussee v. Md. Cas. Co.*, 60 Wash. App. 504, 803 P.2d 1339 (1991), because the provision potentially invaded funds intended to compensate the injured. The appellate court stated that an insured may pursue emotional distress damages that result from an insurer's bad faith conduct, but when the insured assigns all bad faith claims as part of a covenant judgment agreement, a guaranteed and fixed percentage of the global settlement is not reasonable.

—Emotional distress, if proven, has sometimes been recognized as a recoverable measure of damages in a tort action for breach of the covenant of good faith, even if plaintiff suffered no other type of harm. See, *e.g., Campbell v. State Farm Mut. Auto. Ins. Co.*, 840 P.2d 130 (Utah Ct. App. 1992); *Gary v. American Casualty Co.*, 753 F. Supp. 1547 (W.D. Okla. 1990). Compare *Continental Ins. Co. v. Superior Court (Bangerter)*, 37 Cal. App. 4th 69, 43 Cal. Rptr. 2d 374 (1995) (insured may not recover for emotional distress in absence of economic loss); *Torres v. Automobile Club of S. Cal.*, 36 Cal. App. 4th 972, 43 Cal. Rptr. 2d 147 (1995) (emotional distress is not compensable unless severe or accompanied by other substantial damage); *Greer v. Burkhardt*, 58 F.3d 1070 (5th Cir. 1995) (Mississippi law; emotional distress damages are not available in action for bad faith failure to defend).

But concerning an independent claim for the intentional infliction of emotional distress in connection with an insurer's bad faith failure to settle, it was held in *Southern Gen. Ins. Co. v. Holt*, 200 Ga. App. 759, 409 S.E.2d 852 (1991), *aff'd in relevant part*, 262 Ga. 267, 416 S.E.2d 274 (1992), that the trial court had erred in denying the insurer's motion for a directed verdict. The court held: (1) The insurer's conduct was not sufficiently egregious; (2) The insured's distress was not sufficiently severe; and (3) Awarding damages for the intentional infliction of emotional distress after awarding punitive damages for bad faith would result in an impermissible double recovery.

On the other hand, a California Court of Appeal decision (*subsequently ordered depublished* by the state supreme court and hence not citable), reversed the dismissal of a third-party claimant's cause of action for the intentional infliction of emotional distress in connection with an insurer's failure to settle, although aware of the insured's clear liability and the third party's severe injuries and financial distress. (Following the insurer's refusal to settle, a jury awarded the third party $650,000—within policy limits.) *Weiner v. Fireman's Fund Ins. Co.*, 284 Cal. Rptr. 340 (1991), *ordered depublished*, Oct. 3, 1991.

§2.70 5. Attorney's Fees

—In *Williams v. Geico Casualty Co.*, 301 P.3d 1220 (Alaska 2013), the Alaska Supreme Court held that public policy was not violated by an award of attorney's fees to an automobile insurer that had commenced a declaratory judgment action seeking a determination of its obligations. The Court explained that the actions of the insureds and their assignees had precipitated the protracted and complex litigation, and that the insurer had consistently offered settlements within applicable policy limits.

—The California Supreme Court, in *Essex Ins. Co. v. Five Star Dye House, Inc.*, 38 Cal. 4th 1252, 45 Cal. Rptr. 3d 362, 137 P.3d 192 (2006), held that injured third party to whom the insured had assigned his claims against his liability insurer was entitled to recover attorney's fees incurred in recovering policy benefits wrongfully withheld. The court disapproved *Xebec Development Partners, Ltd. v. National Union Fire Ins. Co.*, 12 Cal. App. 4th 501, 15 Cal. Rptr. 2d 726 (1993).

In *Howard v. American Nat'l Fire Ins. Co.*, 187 Cal. App. 4th 498, 115 Cal. Rptr. 3d 42 (2010), the court addressed a number of attorneys' fees issues, holding, *inter alia*, that the trial court had properly characterized attorneys' fees, which were incurred postjudgment in hiring an attorney to obtain an appeal bond, explore bankruptcy, and negotiate with victims, as costs incurred to mitigate the damages caused by the insurer's failure to defend, settle, and indemnify, and properly ordered reimbursement.

In *Pulte Home Corp. v. American Safety Indem. Co.*, 14 Cal. App. 5th 1086, 223 Cal. Rptr. 3d 47 (2017), *reh'g denied, review denied* (2018), the court reversed an award of $471,313.21 in *Brandt* fees awarded to a general contractor who brought suit against its insurer for failure to defend in a construction defect case and remanded for recalculation of fees. The court determined that the trial court should have calculated the *Brandt* fees based on the insured's original contingency fee agreement rather than the modified agreement, where the modified agreement appeared to be manipulated to maximize recovery of *Brandt* fees. The court explained that under *Brandt v. Superior Court*, 37 Cal. 3d 813, 693 P.2d 796 (1985), attorney's fees may be recovered in a bad faith action, but only those expended in enforcing the benefits due under the contract, not those expended to obtain an amount in excess of the amount due under the contract. In this case, which involved a contingency fee agreement, the court was required to use the rule from *Cassim v. Allstate Ins. Co.*, 33 Cal. 4th 780, 94 P3d 513 (2004) to parse out the percentage of the legal work expended to obtain contract recovery from the percentage used on the punitive damages award. The court further explained that while the law allows calculation of *Brandt* fees based on a modified fee agreement, the trial court had discretion to disregard a fee agreement that was manipulated to maximize recovery of *Brandt* fees.

—In *Bernhard v. Farmers Ins. Exch.*, 915 P.2d 1285 (Colo. 1996), the Colorado Supreme Court held that attorney's fees expended in securing a judgment for the bad faith breach of an insurance contract are not recoverable in the absence of a contractual provision. (The court expressed disagreement with the reasoning of the California

Supreme Court in *Brandt v. Superior Court*, 37 Cal. 3d 813, 210 Cal. Rptr. 211 (1985).)

—In *Allstate Ins. Co. v. Regar*, 942 So. 2d 969 (Fla. Dist. Ct. App. 2006), it was held that the assignee of a third-party bad faith claim is entitled to attorneys' fees under F.S.A. §627.428, a statute that requires an insurer to pay the fees of a named or omnibus insured or a named beneficiary. Since the entire cause of action was assigned, the court reasoned, the assignee stands in the shoes of the insured and is entitled to all remedies to which the insured would otherwise be entitled.

—See *Mobil Oil Corp. v. Maryland Casualty Co.*, 288 Ill. App. 3d 743, 681 N.E.2d 552 (1997), for discussion of a number of issues concerning entitlement to and calculation of attorney's fees under the Illinois vexatious refusal to settle statute (Ill. Ins. Code §155). (The court affirmed a fee award in the amount of $442,762.) See also *Rogers Cartage Co. v. Travelers Indem. Co.*, 2018 IL App. (5th) 160098, 103 N.E.3d 504 (2018), *appeal denied*, 108 N.W.3d 885 (Ill. 2018) (see discussions in §§2.38, 2.45).

In *In re CFB Liquidating Corp.*, 581 B.R. 317 (Bkrtcy. N.D. Cal. 2017), *aff'd*, 591 B.R. 396 (N.D. Cal. 2018) (Illinois law), a federal bankruptcy court applying Illinois law awarded attorney's fees, costs, and a $60,000 penalty amount under 215 Ill. Comp. Stat. 5/155 because it found the insurer had committed "vexatious and unreasonable" delay in settling asbestos claims. The court reviewed the factors applicable in determining an appropriate attorney's fee to award. The court rejected the insurer's argument that it should take into account the fees the insurer paid its own counsel. The court noted that the $60,000 penalty amount available under §155 was "relatively meaningless" given the facts of the case but concluded that $60,000 was the maximum penalty allowed under the statute. The court also awarded prejudgment interest under the Illinois Interest Act, 815 Ill. Comp. Stat. Ann. 205/2. See §§2.7, 2.72.

—Under Indiana law, it was held in *Allstate Ins. Co. v.*

Axsom, 696 N.E.2d 482 (Ind. Ct. App. 1998), attorney's fees are not recoverable in bad faith actions.

—In *Nooter Corp. v. Allianz Underwriters Ins. Co.*, 536 S.W.3d 251 (Mo. Ct. App. 2017), the court upheld a jury verdict finding that the insurer's failure to pay the insured's third-party asbestos claims was a vexatious refusal to pay. Under Mo. Rev. Stat. §375.420, the court granted the insured's motion for attorney's fees. See also *Drury Co. v. Missouri United Sch. Inc. Counsel*, 455 S.W.3d 30 (Mo. Ct. App. 2014) (upholding award of actual damages, statutory penalty, and attorney's fees in connection with vexatious refusal to pay claim under §375.420).

—In *Jacobsen v. Allstate Ins. Co.*, 351 Mont. 464, 215 P.3d 649 (2009), the Montana Supreme Court held that attorneys' fees are not a recoverable element of damages in connection with a claim for insurance bad faith.

—Concerning Tennessee law and the availability of attorneys' fees in litigation establishing an insurer's bad faith failure to defend, see *Forrest Constr., Inc. v. The Cincinnati Ins. Co.*, 728 F. Supp. 2d 955 (M.D. Tenn. 2010).

—In *Woo v. Fireman's Fund Ins. Co.*, 161 Wash. 2d 43, 164 P.3d 454 (2007), involving a suit by a dentist against his professional and general liability insurer to recover for breach of the duty to defend, bad faith, and violation of Washington Consumer Protection Act, the court wrote: "Attorney fees are recoverable at trial, and if the plaintiff prevails on appeal, under the CPA. In a duty to defend action, an insured is entitled to fees on appeal . . . because the insurer 'compels the insured to assume the burden of legal action, to obtain the full benefit of his insurance contract.' *Olympic Steamship Steamship Company, Inc. v. Centennial Ins. Co.*, 117 Wash. 2d 37, 811 P.2d 673 (Wash. 1991)." In *Schreib v. American Family Mut. Ins. Co.*, 129 F. Supp. 3d 1129 (W.D. Wash. 2015), a federal district court applying Washington law held that *Olympic Steamship* fees are recoverable only when an insurer has wrongfully denied *coverage*, as opposed to failing to pay all or part of a *claim*. Attorney's fees and costs are available to a prevailing party under Washington's Consumer Protection Act (Wash. Rev. Code Ch. 19.86.090) and the Insurance Fair Conduct Act (Wash. Rev. Code Ch. 48.30.015). See *Gosney v. Fireman's Fund Ins. Co.*, 3 Wash. App. 2d 828, 419 P.3d 447 (2018), *review denied*, 191 Wash. 2d 1017 (2018) (awarding $400,812.50 in attorney's fees and $4,800 in costs to decedent's estate; decedent was killed by insured's pizza delivery driver).

—In *Allied Processors, Inc. v. Western Nat'l Mut. Ins. Co.*, 629 N.W.2d 329 (Wis. Ct. App. 2001), the court affirmed a contingent attorneys' fee award as an element of damages for bad faith failure to settle. The court held that expert fees were also recoverable. Concerning the nonrecoverability of attorneys' fees expended in coverage (as opposed to bad faith) litigation, see *Reid v. Benz*, 629 N.W.2d 262 (Wis. 2001).

C. Punitive Damages

§2.71 1. In General

—For cases representing the prevailing rule that punitive damages are recoverable in the third-party insurance bad faith context, although some subjective elements of blameworthiness is usually required in addition to the bad faith itself, see *Patrick v. Maryland Casualty Co.*, 217 Cal. App. 3d 1566, 267 Cal. Rptr. 24 (1990); *O'Neill v. Gallant Ins. Co.*, 769 N.E.2d 100 (Ill. Ct. App. 2002); *Indiana Ins. Co. v. Demetre*, 527 S.W.3d 12 (Ky. 2017); *Capitol Specialty Ins. Corp. v. Higgins*, 953 F.3d 95 (1st Cir. 2020) (Massachusetts law); *Sloan v. State Farm Mut. Auto. Ins. Co.*, 85 P.3d 230 (N.M. 2004); *Jessen v. National Excess Ins. Co.*, 108 N.M. 625, 776 P.2d 1244 (1989); *Georgetown Realty, Inc. v. Home Ins. Co.*, 313 Or. 97, 831 P.2d 7, *on remand*, 113 Or. App. 641, 833 P.2d 1333 (1992); *In re Mt. Hawley Ins. Co.*,

427 S.C. 159, 829 S.E.2d 707 (2019); *National Fire Ins. Co. v. Valero Energy Corp.*, 777 S.W.2d 501 (Tex. Ct. App. 1989); *Hampton v. State Farm Mut. Auto. Ins. Co.*, 778 S.W.2d 476 (Tex. Ct. App. 1989); *Campbell v. State Farm Mut. Auto. Ins. Co.*, 432 Utah Adv. Rep. 44, 2001 WL 1246676 (Utah 2001); *Berry v. Nationwide Mut. Fire Ins. Co.*, 381 S.E.2d 367 (W. Va. 1989); *Allied Processors, Inc. v. Western Nat'l Mut. Ins. Co.*, 629 N.W.2d 329 (Wis. Ct. App. 2001).

In *Sloan v. State Farm Mut. Auto. Ins. Co.*, *supra*, the New Mexico Supreme Court, answering a certified question from the Tenth Circuit, explained that evidence of negligence is an insufficient basis for a punitive damages instruction in a third-party bad faith case, but that bad faith conduct typically involves a culpable mental state and, except in rare cases, a punitive damages instruction should be given. (Following the New Mexico Supreme Court's answer, the Tenth Circuit ordered the trial judge in the present case to reinstate a punitive damages claim. See *Sloan v. State Farm Mut. Auto. Ins. Co.*, 360 F.3d 1220 (10th Cir. 2004).)

—For cases representing the minority position that punitive damages are not available, because a bad faith cause of action sounds only in contract, see *Associated Wholesale Grocers v. Americold*, 261 Kan. 806, 934 P.2d 65 (1997); *Guarantee Abstract & Title Co. v. Interstate Fire & Casualty Co.*, 232 Kan. 76, 652 P.2d 665 (1982); *Georgetown Realty, Inc. v. Home Ins. Co.*, 102 Or. App. 611, 796 P.2d 651 (1990); *Canyon Country Store v. Bracey*, 781 P.2d 414 (Utah 1989).

—Concerning constitutional limits on the size of punitive damages awards, the Supreme Court held on April 7, 2003, that ". . . few awards exceeding a single-digit ratio between punitive and compensatory damages, to a significant degree, will satisfy due process." *State Farm Mut. Auto. Ins. Co. v. Campbell*, 538 U.S. 408, 425 (2003). The court reversed a decision of the Utah Supreme Court that had reinstated a

$145 million punitive damages award, in addition to $1 million in compensatory damages, in a case involving an insurer's bad faith refusal to accept a policy limits settlement offer on a claim against its insured. The majority opinion stated that the present case was "neither close nor difficult" under the three "guideposts" for excessiveness as set forth in *BMW of N. Am., Inc. v. Gore*, 517 U.S. 559 (1996). (In that earlier decision, the court had not mentioned any specific ratio as a constitutional limit.) On remand, the Utah Supreme Court reduced the punitive damages award from $145 million to $9 million (not following the Supreme Court's suggestion by way of dictum that $1 million would be the appropriate amount in the present case). *Campbell v. State Farm Mut. Auto. Ins. Co.*, 98 P.3d 409 (Utah 2004). See also, *e.g., Goddard v. Farmers Ins. Co. of Or.*, 344 Or. 232, 179 P.3d 645 (banc 2008) (punitive damages award that in 4:1 ratio to actual and potential harm to plaintiff from insurer's bad faith failure to settle comported with due process and was warranted; jury's award of over $20 million, in 16:1 ratio, was constitutionally excessive where, although insurer's actions were repeated, were directed at a financially vulnerable victim, were not limited to that victim alone, and involved intentional malice and deceit, those actions did not cause physical harm or involve reckless disregard for health and safety of others).

Concerning the inclusion of postjudgment interest in the amount of damages to be multiplied in calculating punitive damages, see *Anderson v. National Union Fire Ins. Co.*, 476 Mass. 377, 67 N.E.3d 1232 (2017). The plaintiffs brought actions under the consumer protection statute (Mass. Gen. Laws Ann. ch. 93A) and the unfair claims practices statute (Mass. Gen. Laws Ann. ch. 176D) alleging that the defendants' primary and excess insurers engaged in egregious and deliberate behavior to deprive them of fair compensation for injuries sustained when the plaintiffs were struck by a bus while crossing a street. The Superior Court had held that the insurers' behavior was willful and egregious and required the maximum penalty permitted under Mass. Gen. Laws Ann. ch. 93A, §9(3). The Superior Court included postjudgment interest in the "amount of judgment" to be multiplied under ch. 93A, §9(3), and the appeals court affirmed. The Supreme Judicial Court held that postjudgment interest is not an element of compensatory damages. The court vacated the judgment and held that the amount of damages to be multiplied for a willful and knowing violation under ch. 176D or ch. 93A does not include postjudgment interest. *Cf. Capitol Specialty Ins. Corp. v. Higgins, supra* (Massachusetts law; holding that trial court erred in awarding prejudgment interest on treble damages and remanding for recalculation of prejudgment interest based on actual damages).

2. Breach of Duty to Settle

§2.72 a. Particular Cases—Punitive Damages Allowed

—The following cases are among those in which courts have awarded punitive damages for bad faith failure to settle or have affirmed such awards: *Carrier Express, Inc. v. Home Indem. Co.*, 860 F. Supp. 1465 (N.D. Ala. 1994) (Alabama law); *O'Neill v. Gallant Ins. Co.*, 769 N.E.2d 100 (Ill. Ct. App. 2002); *Berglund v. State Farm Mut. Auto. Ins. Co.*, 121 F.3d 1225 (8th Cir. 1997) (Iowa law); *Chiulli v. Liberty Mut. Ins., Inc.*, 97 Mass. App. 248, 146 N.E.3d 471 (2020), *review denied*, 485 Mass. 1102, 150 N.E.3d 1119 (2020); *Capitol Specialty Ins. Corp. v. Higgins*, 953 F.3d 95 (1st Cir. 2020) (Massachusetts law); *Johnson v. Allstate Ins. Co.*, 262 S.W.3d 655 (Mo. Ct. App. 2008); *Jessen v. National Excess Ins. Co.*, 108 N.M. 625, 776 P.2d 1244 (1989); *Farmers Ins. Co. v. Soriano*, 844 S.W.2d 808 (Tex. Ct. App. 1992); *Allied Processors, Inc. v. Western Nat'l Mut. Ins. Co.*, 629 N.W.2d 329 (Wis. Ct. App. 2001). Compare *Goddard v. Farmers Ins. Co. of Or.*, 202 Or. App. 79, 120 P.3d 1260

(2005) (punitive damages award of over $20 million was constitutionally excessive).

—In *In re CFB Liquidating Corp.*, 581 B.R. 317 (Bkrtcy. N.D. Cal. 2017), *aff'd*, 591 B.R. 396 (N.D. Cal. 2018) (Illinois law), a federal bankruptcy court applying Illinois law awarded attorney's fees, costs, and a $60,000 penalty amount under 215 Ill. Comp. Stat. 5/155 because it found the insurer had committed "vexatious and unreasonable" delay in settling asbestos claims. The court noted that the $60,000 penalty amount available under §155 was "relatively meaningless" given the facts of the case but concluded that $60,000 was the maximum penalty allowed under the statute. The court also awarded prejudgment interest under the Illinois Interest Act, 815 Ill. Comp. Stat. Ann. 205/2. See §§2.7, 2.70.

—In *Chiulli v. Liberty Mut. Ins., Inc.*, *supra*, the appeals court remanded for determination of whether a statutory penalty of 2 to 3 times the damages award would be proper where it held that the trial court erred in finding that insurer Liberty Mutual did not act willfully or knowingly when it violated Massachusetts' statutory settlement requirement under Mass. Gen. Laws ch. 93A. The court found that the insurer had a duty to offer settlement once the insured's liability became reasonably clear following closing arguments at trial. Instead, the insurer made its insured wait through Thanksgiving and Christmas, and internal documents showed that the delay was an intentional effort to use the insured's lack of funds to leverage a more favorable settlement.

—In July 1996, a Salt Lake City jury assessed $145 million in punitive damages against an auto insurer who had refused a $50,000 policy limits settlement offer, thereby exposing its insured to liability for an excess judgment in the amount of $253,000. The bad faith trial followed a reversal of summary judgment in *Campbell v. State Farm Mut. Auto. Ins. Co.*, 840 P.2d 130 (Utah Ct. App. 1992), in which a Utah Court of Appeals held, *inter alia*, that the insured's bad faith cause of action was not necessarily vitiated by the fact that the insurer had ultimately paid the excess judgment. (Other aspects of that opinion are referred to in §§2.43 and 2.69.) In 2001, the jury award was upheld by the Utah Supreme Court. *Campbell v. State Farm Mut. Auto. Ins. Co.*, 432 Utah Adv. Rep. 44, 2001 WL 1246676 (Utah 2001).

§2.73 b. Particular Cases—Punitive Damages Not Allowed

—In *Hulsey v. The Travelers Indem. Co. of Am.*, 460 F. Supp. 2d 1332 (N.D. Ga. 2006), the court granted summary judgment on a claim for punitive damages by the driver of an insured vehicle who alleged negligent and bad faith failure to honor a demand for payment of the policy limits by an injured passenger. The insured failed to show by clear and convincing evidence, the court held, that the insurer's actions demonstrated willful misconduct, malice, fraud, wantonness, oppression, or such an entire lack of care as would raise the presumption of a conscious indifference to consequences. See also *Hughes v. First Acceptance Ins. Co. of Ga.*, 343 Ga. App. 693, 808 S.E.2d 103 (2017), *rev'd on other grounds*, 305 Ga. 489, 826 S.E.2d 71 (2019) (claimant failed to point to specific evidence on record showing type of willful or wanton conduct that supports punitive damages; conclusory argument that trier of fact could conclude that insurer acted with such conscious indifference failed).

—In *Soto v. State Farm Ins. Co.*, 83 N.Y.2d 718, 635 N.E.2d 1222, 613 N.Y.S.2d 352 (1994), the New York Court of Appeals held that no cause of action exists whereby an insurer may be forced to reimburse an insured for the punitive damages portion of an excess judgment, even though the insurer's failure to settle the claim within policy limits was in bad faith. Accord *PPG Indus., Inc. v. Transamerica Ins. Co.*, 20 Cal. 4th 310, 84 Cal. Rptr. 2d 455

(1999); *Lira v. Shelter Ins. Co.*, 913 P.2d 514 (Colo. 1996). The court in *Soto* based this dubious conclusion on the principle that New York law precludes insurance coverage for punitive damages. Distinguishing *Soto*, see *Ansonia Assocs. Ltd. v. Public Serv. Mut. Ins. Co.*, 692 N.Y.S.2d 5 (App. Div. 1999).

—In *Wolfe v. Allstate Prop. & Ins. Co.*, 790 F.3d 487 (3d Cir. 2015), the Third Circuit considered the issue as a matter of first impression under Pennsylvania law. After an extensive discussion of cases, including *Lira*, *PPG*, and *Soto*, *supra*, the court held that "in light of Pennsylvania's public policy against insuring punitive damages," "an insurer has no duty to consider the potential for the jury to return a verdict for punitive damages when it is negotiating a settlement of the case." Therefore, the Third Circuit concluded, the trial court erred in allowing evidence of a punitive damages award against the insured to be presented to the jury in the insured's bad faith action against the third-party insurer for failure to settle the underlying claim pretrial because the award was not relevant to the insurer's settlement actions. *Id.* at 495 (distinguishing *Carpenter v. Automobile Club Interins. Exch.*, 58 F.3d 1296 (8th Cir. 1995)).

—See supplement §2.19, for discussion of *Shamblin v. Nationwide Mut. Ins. Co.*, 396 S.W.2d 766 (W. Va. 1990), reversing an award of $1.5 million in punitives for failure of the evidence to show the necessary level of willfulness and malice on the insurer's part.

3. Breach of Duty To Defend

§2.74 a. Particular Cases—Punitive Damages Allowed

—On June 15, 1993, a Superior Court jury in Orange County, California, awarded $4.6 million, including $4 million in punitive damages, against the Aetna Insurance Company for bad faith failure to defend an insured in a business dispute, and for refusal to pay the legal fees the insured had incurred when forced to hire its own defense attorneys. *Americana Sav. Bank v. Aetna Casualty & Sur. Co.*, No. 651102. According to plaintiff's attorney Thomas M. Robins, of the Los Angeles firm of Frandzel & Share, his client made a pretrial settlement demand of $1.5 million, but was offered only $100,000.

And in October 1993, Orange County Superior Court Judge C. Robert Jameson awarded $60 million, including $57 million in punitive damages, for the bad faith of Truck Insurance Exchange, a Farmers' subsidiary, in failing to defend an insured in a 1989 patent infringement and unfair competition lawsuit brought by a competitor. *Surgin Surgical Instrumentation, Inc. v. Farmers Group, Inc.*, No. 662216 (Daniel J. Callahan, attorney for plaintiff). During the trial, a former assistant vice-president for Farmers testified that Farmers and Truck Insurance had engaged in a pattern of discovery abuse that included the shredding of documents the companies had denied possessing. Judge Jameson's ruling described Truck Insurance's conduct as "despicable, vile, malicious, fraudulent, and oppressive," according to an account in the *Los Angeles Daily Journal* of November 16, 1993.

Other notable jury awards of punitive damages in California have included *Walker v. Farmers Ins. Exch.*, 153 Cal. App. 4th 965, 63 Cal. Rptr. 3d 507 (2007) (punitive damages award of $1.5 million rather than jury's $8.3 million was warranted in elderly insured's action against condominium insurer for bad faith in denial of defense in underlying personal injury action); *International Paper v. Affiliated FM*, No. 974350 (San Francisco County Super. Ct. Nov. 2, 2001) ($68 million against insurer who abandoned policyholder to own defense against nationwide class action); *Fresno Unified Sch. Dist. v. Coregis Ins. Co.*, No. 99AS00773 (Sacramento County Super. Ct. Oct. 6, 2000) ($13 million against insurer who denied coverage relative to discrimination suits against school district even though policy had been marketed for protection against exactly such litigation); *Hanstad v. Truck Ins. Exchange*, No. LC031514 (Los Angeles County Super. Ct. May 10, 2000) ($40 million in action by contractor who proved that insurer had failed to defend him in bankruptcy after client sued him for defective work); *Earnest v. Truck Ins. Exchange*, No. 707368 (Orange County Super. Ct. Apr. 3, 2000) ($30 million against insurer who refused to defend policyholder for property contamination in purported reliance on exclusion that did not apply to relevant time period).

In *Pulte Home Corp. v. American Safety Indem. Co.*, 14 Cal. App. 5th 1086, 223 Cal. Rptr. 3d 47 (2017), *reh'g denied*, *review denied* (2018), the court reversed a $500,000 punitive damages award to an additional general contractor who brought suit against its insurer for failure to defend in a construction defect case. The court affirmed that the additional insured was entitled to punitive damages where testimony of the insurer's claims representatives and corporate counsel showed that the insurer routinely issued policies to additional insureds knowing the additional insureds would expect a defense, but the insurer routinely denied claims for defense of additional insureds based on restrictive policy interpretations. The court remanded the case for recalculation of punitive damages award after it reversed the *Brandt* fees (attorney's fees) award. The court directed the trial court to maintain the 1-to-1 ratio of compensatory damages to punitive damages.

In *Century Sur. Co. v. Polisso*, 139 Cal. App. 4th 922, 43 Cal. Rptr. 3d 468 (2006), a California Court of Appeal held that a punitive damages award in a 3.2:1 ratio to compensatory damages was not so grossly disproportionate as to violate due process, given the reprehensibility of the insurer's conduct, in refusing to defend insureds against a third-party lawsuit that indisputably stated claims for covered losses under a CGL policy. The insurer's five-year "intentional and malicious" course of conduct, the court explained, had caused severe emotional and economic harm to the insureds.

—In *Indiana Ins. Co. v. Demetre*, 527 S.W.3d 12 (Ky. 2017), the Kentucky Supreme Court upheld an award of $925,000 damages for emotional distress and $2.5 million in punitive damages to compensate for the insurer's lackluster handling of third-party liability claims against the insured and legal action against him. See also §§2.31 and 2.38A.

§2.75 b. Particular Cases—Punitive Damages Not Allowed

—In *Pacific Group, U.S. v. First State Ins. Co.*, 841 F. Supp. 922 (N.D. Cal. 1993), *rev'd on other grounds*, 70 F.3d 524 (9th Cir. 1995) (California law), a federal district court granted an excess insurer's motion for judgment notwithstanding the verdict after a jury had awarded $21 million in punitive damages for the insurer's refusal to defend. The court held that the evidence failed to show the oppression, fraud, or malice necessary to support an award of punitive damages under California law. According to the court's reading of the evidence, the insurer had drawn the erroneous—though nonfraudulent and nonmalicious—conclusion (based upon an admittedly inadequate investigation of the claim) that it was not required to drop down and defend. (The court also noted that the $21 million award had been excessive in relation to the insurer's $62 million net worth.)

—Reversing a judgment for the insured, in light of serious debate about the applicability of the CGL policies in question to the facts of the case, the Eleventh Circuit, in *Pozzi Window Co. v. Auto-Owners Ins.*, 446 F.3d 1178 (11th Cir. 2006), emphasized that under Florida law, in order for punitive damages to be awarded in a third-party bad faith action, the insurer's conduct against the insured's

interests must have been so egregious as to have constituted an independent tort.

—Reluctantly following *Farris v. United States Fidelity
& Guar. Co.*, 284 Or. 453, 587 P.2d 1015 (1978) (discussed
in this section of book), an Oregon Court of Appeals, in
Warren v. Farmers Ins. Co., 115 Or. App. 319, 838 P.2d 620
(1992), held that an insurer's breach of its contractual duty
to defend cannot be the basis of an award of tort damages
for failure to settle.

—It was held by the South Carolina Supreme Court, in
BP Oil Co. v. Federated Mut. Ins. Co., 329 S.C. 631, 496
S.E.2d 35 (1998), that the insured was not entitled to punitive damages where the insurer's refusal to defend had
been only unreasonable, not willful or reckless.

§2.76 4. Nonrecoverability by Judgment Creditor

—See *Southern Gen. Ins. Co. v. Holt*, 262 Ga. 267, 416
S.E.2d 274 (1992), in which the Georgia Supreme Court
held that an insured who had assigned his claim for compensatory damages for his insurer's bad faith failure to settle
had forfeited his right to sue for punitive damages based on
the same claim. The court declined to create an exception
to the rule that a party must have a valid claim for compensatory damages in order to recover punitive damages.

3

Pretrial Procedures

I. PLAINTIFF'S PRELIMINARY STEPS

I. PLAINTIFF'S PRELIMINARY STEPS

G. Determining Parties

§3.24 1. Plaintiffs

—Under Arizona law, a federal district court held in *Smith v. Allstate Ins. Co.*, 202 F. Supp. 2d 1061 (D. Ariz. 2002), a passenger injured in an automobile accident as the result of the driver's negligence was a third-party claimant to whom the insurer owed no duty of good faith, notwithstanding the fact that the passenger (the driver's wife) was a co-insured under the liability policy. The court cited decisions from four other jurisdictions in support of the conclusion that an insured is a third-party claimant when seeking benefits based on a co-insured's liability coverage: *Wilson v. Wilson*, 121 N.C. App. 662, 468 S.E.2d 495 (1996); *Rumley v. Allstate Indem. Co.*, 924 S.W.2d 448 (Tex. Ct. App. 1996); *Sperry v. Sperry*, 990 P.2d 381 (Utah 1999); and *Herrig v. Herrig*, 844 P.2d 487 (Wyo. 1992).

—Under Florida law, it was held in *Blue Cross & Blue Shield v. Halifax Ins. Plan, Inc.*, 961 F. Supp. 271 (M.D. Fla. 1997), subrogated health insurers have standing to sue other insurers for violations of Florida's Unfair Claim Settlement Practices Act (Fla. Stat. Ann. §624.155).

—Under Illinois law, the Seventh Circuit held in *Iowa Physicians' Clinic Med. Found. v. Physicians Ins. Co. of Wisc.*, 547 F.3d 810 (7th Cir. 2008), a physician's insurer owed no duty to the noninsured medical clinic operator which held a medical malpractice policy on the insured physician's behalf.

—It was held by an Indiana court, in *County Line Towing, Inc. v. Cincinnati Ins. Co.*, 714 N.E.2d 285 (Ind. Ct. App. 1999), that since, under the circumstances, there was no basis for treating a corporation's sole shareholder and CEO as the corporation's alter ego, the CEO lacked standing to sue the corporation's insurer for bad faith. See also *G & S Holdings LLC v. Continental Casualty Co.*, 697 F.3d 534, 2012 WL 4120549 (7th Cir. 2012) (owners and affiliates of insured metal processor were not real parties in interest with respect to claims arising from insurer's failure to timely pay processor for damage caused by explosion, and thus owners and affiliates lacked prudential standing to bring claims against insurer for breach of contract, promissory estoppel, bad faith and negligent claims handling, and breach of fiduciary duty).

—See *Roach v. Atlas Life Ins. Co.*, 769 P.2d 158 (Okla. 1989), for a discussion by the Oklahoma Supreme Court of the principle that an insurer's duty of good faith and fair dealing runs to the beneficiary of a life insurance policy. See also *Ellis v. Liberty Mut. Ins. Co.*, 208 P.3d 934 (Okla. Civ. App. 2008) (citing *Roach v. Atlas Life Ins. Co.*, *supra*, and emphasizing that there must be either contractual or statutory relationship between insurer and party asserting bad faith claim); *Colony Ins. Co. v. Burke*, 698 F.3d 1222 (10th Cir. 2012) (Oklahoma law; there is no duty for insurance company to deal fairly and in good faith with injured third party).

In *Townsend v. State Farm Mut. Auto Ins. Co.*, 860 P.2d 236 (Okla. 1993), the Oklahoma Supreme Court held that "class 2" insureds (nonnamed but permissive users and occupants) under an uninsured motorist policy have standing to assert bad faith claims against the insurer.

In *Rednour v. JC & P Partnership & Acceptance Ins. Co.*, 996 P.2d 487 (Okla. Ct. Civ. App. 1999), the court affirmed summary judgment on the ground that only a party to an insurance contract has standing to assert a bad faith claim. In the present case, plaintiff was a nonparty "incidental beneficiary" who had been injured in a fall on premises insured by defendant, and who believed that payment of his medical expenses had been unreasonably delayed. On the standing question, the court distinguished cases involving life insurance policies and uninsured motorist policies. Both of those types of insurance are designed to protect others, the court reasoned, whereas "[t]he primary purpose behind a business owner's purchase of liability insurance is the protection of assets."

In *May v. Mid-Century Ins. Co.*, 151 P.3d 132 (Okla. 2006), the Oklahoma Supreme Court held that a condominium unit owner had no enforceable contractual rights against the association's property insurer and therefore could not assert a bad faith tort claim against the insurer for failure to pay for fire losses, even if the condominium owner was a third-party beneficiary and the policy allowed the insurer to bring a subrogation action. The court emphasized that the policy gave the insurer the exclusive choice to settle covered losses directly with the unit owners or with the association, and placed no obligation on the owner to make payment directly to the owner.

—Under Pennsylvania's bad faith statute, it was held in *Belmont Holdings Corp. v. Unicare Life & Health Ins. Co.*, 2000 WL 1763668 (E.D. Pa. 2000), an employer, despite being the "policyholder," lacked standing to assert a claim on behalf of its employees against a group health insurer.

—In *Kleckley v. Northwestern Nat'l Casualty Co.*, 2000 WL 19329 (S.C. 2000), the South Carolina Supreme Court explained that only contracting parties have standing to sue an insurer for bad faith. The court therefore affirmed dismissal of an action by an injured restaurant patron who had attempted to sue the restaurant's liability insurer. The court rejected the argument that plaintiff was a person directly entitled to benefits rather than a third party claiming through an insured and was thus the equivalent of a contracting party.

—Holding that independent insurance agents have standing to sue for an insurer's violation of Tex. Ins. Code art. 21.21, §4, see *Tweedell v. Hochheim Prairie Farm Mut. Ins. Ass'n*, 962 S.W.2d 685 (Tex. Ct. App. 1998), *review granted*, July 1, 1999. Compare *United Neurology, P.A. v. Hartford Lloyd's Ins. Co.*, 101 F. Supp. 3d 584 (S.D. Tex. 2015), *aff'd mem.*, 624 Fed. Appx. 225 (5th Cir. 2015) (owner of building for which tenant had purchased insurance coverage had no standing to bring contractual or bad faith claims against insurer because owner was not in privity with tenant, was not a third-party beneficiary under the policy, and had no special relationship with insured).

—Two Utah decisions have addressed the standing of nonparties to an insurance contract to sue for bad faith: *Sperry v. Sperry, supra* (affirming dismissal; named insured under auto insurance policy was "third party" who lacked standing to sue for bad faith in connection with insurer's handling of her wrongful death action against co-insured); *Cannon v. Travelers Indem. Co.*, 994 P.2d 824 (Utah Ct. App. 2000) (though expressly entitled to medical benefits, injured person was not designated in policy as "insured" and therefore lacked standing to sue for extracontractual damages in connection with insurer's handling of claim under medical payments provision of homeowner policy).

—In *Goff v. Penn Mut. Life Ins. Co.*, 229 W. Va. 568, 729 S.E.2d 890 (W. Va. 2012), the West Virginia Supreme Court held that upon the death of the insured, a primary beneficiary of a life insurance policy has standing to bring a statutory bad faith claim against the insurer under the unfair claim settlement practices section of the Unfair Trade Practices Act.

—Under Wisconsin law, also, life insurance beneficiaries have standing to sue an insurer for bad faith. *Estate of Plautz by Pagel v. Time Ins. Co.*, 189 Wis. 2d 136, 525 N.W.2d 342 (1994). And in *Meleski v. Schbohm LLC*, 341 Wis. 2d 716, 817 N.W.2d 887 (Ct. App. 2012), it was held that the plaintiff, who had been injured on the insured's property, could file a bad faith claim against the insurer after the insurer had refused to pay the plaintiff's medical bills.

§3.25 a. Spouse

—An Arizona Court of Appeals held that the spouse of an insured had no standing to bring a bad faith action against a health insurer for nonpayment of claims. *Fobes v. Blue Cross & Blue Shield, Inc.*, 176 Ariz. 692, 861 P.2d 692 (Ct. App. 1993). The court adopted the reasoning of *Hatchwell v. Blue Shield*, 198 Cal. App. 3d 1027, 244 Cal. Rptr. 249 (1988) (discussed in this section of the book).

—Concerning California law on a number of issues concerning the standing of the wife of a named insured to make claims under a CGL policy, and to receive benefits and bad faith damages, see *Century Sur. Co. v. Polisso*, 139 Cal. App. 4th 922, 43 Cal. Rptr. 3d 468 (2006).

—In *United Fire Ins. Co. v. McClelland*, 780 P.2d 193 (Nev. 1989), the Nevada Supreme Court reversed an award of $73,000 in emotional distress damages awarded to the wife in connection with a group accident and health insurer's denial of her husband's claims for medical treatment.

The state supreme court agreed with the insurer's argument on appeal that the wife had no standing to sue, since she was neither a contracting party nor a claimant.

—See *Vecchiarelli v. Continental Ins. Co.*, 216 A.D.2d 909, 628 N.Y.S.2d 892 (1995), for the holding that a homeowner's insurer owes no tort duty to the spouse of its insured.

—An Ohio Court of Appeals, in *Gillette v. Estate of Gillette*, 837 N.E.2d 1283 (Ohio Ct. App. 2005), held as a matter of first impression that the named insured's wife could not assert a bad faith claim regarding an allegedly unreasonable delay in resolving a claim for benefits under a policy's liability section, but could assert a bad faith claim regarding a claim for benefits under medical payments and family compensation sections. With respect to the liability claim, the court explained, the wife stood in the shoes of a third-party claimant who was not owed any contractual duty by the insurer. With respect to the latter claims, however, the wife was a first-party claimant because the insurer had agreed to provide medical payments benefits and family compensation benefits to her, as an insured, for her own losses and expenses.

—Under Texas law, it was held in *Bates v. Jackson Nat'l Life Ins. Co.*, 927 F. Supp. 1015 (S.D. Tex. 1996), beneficiaries of life insurance policies lack standing to sue insurers for bad faith handling of claims.

—In *Liberty Mut. Ins. Co. v. Shores*, 147 P.3d 456 (Utah Ct. App. 2006), a Utah Court of Appeals held that, under the circumstances, a named insured was a third-party claimant not entitled to sue her automobile insurer for bad faith in the handling of a claim against her spouse. The named insured was attempting to assert claims in her capacity as an injured party seeking to recover against an insured, the court explained, not in her capacity as an insured in her own right.

§3.26 b. Personal Representative of Insured's Estate

—In *Georgia Casualty & Sur. Co. v. White*, 582 So. 2d 487 (Ala. 1991), the Alabama Supreme Court held: (1) a bad faith cause of action that was filed after the insured's death, for the insurer's insistence on settling a claim for uninsured motorist benefits for less than the claim's admitted value, did not survive the insured's death, because the cause of action did not relate back to fraud claims filed before the insured's death, which involved distinct conduct; but (2) the death of insured did not affect his claim that insurer refused in bad faith to pay the total amount allowed by stacking coverages, even though stacking issue had been resolved by the state supreme court only after the insured's death, where the extent of liability and extent of injury had been determined previously.

—In *Guarantee Trust Life Ins. Co. v. Estate of Casper*, 2018 CO 43, 418 P.3d 1163 (Colo. 2018), the Supreme Court of Colorado considered the operation of the survival statute, Colo. Rev. Stat. §13-201101(1), with regard to bad faith claims. The insured died after the jury reached its verdict but before the final order was entered, and the insured's estate was substituted for the insured. The court held that the survival statute did not bar the estate's recovery or limit its damages for a claim for bad faith breach of insurance contract or for a claim under the bad faith statute (Colo. Rev. Stat. §10-3-116).

—Reversing summary judgment, an Oklahoma Court of Appeals, in *Clements v. ITT Hartford*, 973 P.2d 902 (Okla. Civ. App. 1998), held that a claim for bad faith denial of uninsured motorist benefits survived the insured's death. The court explained that Oklahoma's survival statute (Okla. Stat. tit. 12, §1051) creates a more expansive standard than the common law, providing for the survival of causes of action for "injury to the person . . . or personal estate."

§3.27 c. Corporation and Shareholders

—Also representing the standard view that a duty of good faith is owed to shareholders only if they are named insureds under the policy, see *Warfield v. Fidelity & Deposit Co.*, 904 F.2d 322 (5th Cir. 1990) (Texas law). But see *Stephen R. Ward v. United States Fidelity & Guar. Co.*, 681 F. Supp. 389 (S.D. Miss. 1988) (Mississippi law). And holding that former officers and directors of a professional corporation lack standing to sue the corporation's insurer for bad faith, see *Republic Indem. Co. of Am. v. Schofield*, 47 Cal. App. 4th 220, 54 Cal. Rptr. 2d 637 (1996).

—Under Pennsylvania's bad faith statute, it was held in *Belmont Holdings Corp. v. Unicare Life & Health Ins. Co.*, 2000 WL 1763668 (E.D. Pa. 2000), an employer, despite being the "policyholder," lacked standing to assert a claim on behalf of its employees against a group health insurer.

2. Defendants

§3.29 a. Insurer

—In *Gatecliff v. Great Republic Life Ins. Co.*, 821 P.2d 725 (Ariz. 1991), the Arizona Supreme Court reversed summary judgment, holding that there existed issues of fact relating to a parent insurer's liability (under an alter ego theory, an instrumentality theory, or a direct liability theory), for a subsidiary insurer's breach of contract and bad faith in connection with the cancellation of a group health policy.

Holding that the Arizona Property and Casualty Insurance Guaranty Fund is not subject to liability for bad faith, see *Bills v. Arizona Property & Casualty Ins. Guar. Fund*, 984 P.2d 574 (Ariz. 1999).

—A number of California decisions stand for the potential bad faith liability of the State Compensation Insurance Fund, a self-supporting workers' compensation carrier created by the state legislature: *Tricor Cal., Inc. v. State Compensation Ins. Fund*, 30 Cal. App. 4th 230, 35 Cal. Rptr. 2d 550 (1994); *Security Officers Serv., Inc. v. State Compensation Ins. Fund*, 17 Cal. App. 4th 887, 21 Cal. Rptr. 2d 653 (1993); *Maxon Indus., Inc. v. State Compensation Ins. Fund*, 16 Cal. App. 4th 1387, 20 Cal. Rptr. 2d 730 (1993); *Courtesy Ambulance Serv. v. Superior Court*, 8 Cal. App. 4th 1504, 11 Cal. Rptr. 2d 161 (1992).

Concerning the test under California law for determining whether parent and subsidiary insurance companies are "alter egos," and therefore whether the parent company can be sued for bad faith, see *Wady v. Provident Life and Accident Ins. Co.*, 216 F. Supp. 2d 1060 (C.D. Cal. 2002).

In *Martin v. Pacificare of Cal.*, 198 Cal. App. 4th 1390, 130 Cal. Rptr. 3d 714 (2011), the court held that a statute providing that healthcare service providers "are each responsible for their own acts of omissions" precluded a service plan's bad faith liability for a medical group's denial of coverage, and statute barred vicarious liability claims.

In *Chu v. Old Republic Home Protection Co., Inc.*, ___ Cal. App. 5th, ___ Cal. Rptr. 3d ___, 2021 WL 302868 (2021), the court held that home services protection companies are not subject to tort liability for bad faith, as they are not insurance companies. Although such companies are governed by one section of the Insurance Code, the court concluded based on a review of the legislative history that they are not treated as insurance companies for liability purposes.

—Concerning the statutory immunity from suit of the Florida Medical Malpractice Joint Underwriting Association, see *Florida Medical Malpractice Joint Underwriting Ass'n v. Indemnity Ins. Co. of N. Am.*, 689 So. 2d 1040 (Fla. 1996). In *Citizens Prop. Ins. Corp. v. Perdido Sun Condo. Ass'n*, 164 So. 3d 663 (Fla. 2015), the Florida Supreme Court resolved a split among the appellate districts, holding that Citizens Property Insurance Corporation, a state-created property insurer, was immune from first-party bad faith claims brought under Fla. Stat. §624.155. The court concluded that the "willful torts" exception to the insurer's immunity did not refer to statutory bad faith claims. The court stated that a bad faith claim could be elevated to willful tort, depending on the facts of the case, but concluded that the insured did not plead a willful tort claim.

—In *Adams v. UNUM Life Ins. Co. of Am.*, 508 F. Supp. 2d 1302 (N.D. Ga. 2007) (Georgia law), a federal district court held: (1) The insurer's parent corporation was not liable on an alter ego theory in connection with the insured's breach of contract claims; (2) joint venturer liability was not applicable to the insured's claims for breach of contract and bad faith; (3) the insured was not a third-party beneficiary with respect to a general services agreement between the insurer and the parent corporation; and (4) a statute (West's Ga. Code Ann. §33-4-6(a)), providing for bad faith claims against an insurer, did not authorize a bad faith claim against the parent corporation as the administrator of the insurance plan.

—In *Sandalwood Estates Homeowners' Ass'n, Inc. v. Empire Indem. Ins. Co.*, 665 F. Supp. 2d 1355 (S.D. Fla. 2009), the court held that an insured could not proceed with a statutory bad faith claim against the insurer's parent corporation under Florida law arising from the processing of claims, absent evidence of a contractual relationship between the insured and the corporation.

—According to the Hawaii Supreme Court's decision in *Mendes v. Hawaii Ins. Guar. Ass'n*, 87 Haw. 14, 950 P.2d 1214 (1998), the Hawaii Insurance Guaranty Association is statutorily immune from bad faith claims.

—The requirements of Kentucky's Unfair Claims Settlement Practices Act do not apply to self-insured entities. *Davidson v. American Freightways, Inc.*, 25 S.W.3d 94 (Ky. 2000). See also *Merritt v. Catholic Health Initiatives, Inc.*, 612 S.W.3d 822 (Ky. 2020) (holding that health care provider's captive insurer was not subject to Kentucky's UCSPA, where insurance company was provider's subsidiary and insured only its owner's liabilities, rather than engaging in risk spreading).

—Under Massachusetts law, it was held in *Wheatley v. Massachusetts Insurers Insolvency Fund*, 925 N.E.2d 9, 456 Mass. 594 (2010), an insurer's insolvency fund was a "person engaged in the business of insurance" subject to consumer action under the unfair business practices act for alleged unfair claims settlement practices.

In *Lemos v. Electrolux N. Am., Inc.*, 78 Mass. App. Ct. 376, 937 N.E.2d 984 (2010), it was held that a "captive insurer" was engaged in the business of insurance for purposes of the assertion of a claim for unfair settlement practices. (The court explained that "captive" insurance companies are separate insurance companies formed to bear the risks of the parent company.)

—In *Dombroski v. Wellpoint, Inc.*, 119 Ohio St. 3d 506, 895 N.E.2d 538 (2008), the Ohio Supreme Court held that alleged bad faith in denying the insured's claim was not fraud, an illegal act, or a similarly unlawful act, as required to satisfy the second prong of the test for piercing the corporate veil, and thus parent and sister corporations could not be held liable.

In *William Powell Co. v. Nat'l Indem. Co.*, 141 F. Supp. 3d 773 (S.D. Ohio. 2015) (Ohio law), the court dismissed the insured's bad faith claim against two entities that were third-party claims administrators after the court found that the insured lacked privity with the defendants. The court noted that Ohio does not provide bad faith claims where the parties are not in privity with each other, and the court declined to extend the duty of good faith to third-party claims administrators.

—In *Oliver v Farmers Ins. Group of Cos.*, 941 P.2d 985 (Okla. 1997), the Oklahoma Supreme Court held that management companies and insurer associations may be named as defendants in bad faith actions.

Oklahoma's State Insurance Fund is protected by the sovereign immunity provision of the state's Government Tort Claims Act and could therefore not be sued for bad faith failure to make timely payment of a workers' compensation claim. *Fehring v. State Ins. Fund*, 19 P.3d 276 (Okla. 2001).

—The Rhode Island Insurers' Insolvency Fund, like a solvent insurer, has a duty to participate in settlement negotiations and to protect insureds from excess liability. *Rhode Island Insurers' Insolvency Fund v. Benoit*, 723 A.2d 303 (R.I. 1999).

§3.30 b. Individuals

—For additional cases holding that individual agents and employees are not normally subject to liability for bad faith, or for conspiring with the insurer to commit bad faith (though they may be individually liable for other torts), see *Sanchez v. Lindsey Morden Claims Servs., Inc.*, 72 Cal. App. 4th 249, 84 Cal. Rptr. 2d 799 (1999); *Cooper v. Equity Gen. Ins. Co.*, 219 Cal. App. 3d 1252, 268 Cal. Rptr. 692 (1990); *Minnesota Mut. Life Ins. Co. v. Ensley*, 174 F.3d 977 (9th Cir. 1999) (California law); *Thiele v. State Farm Mut. Auto. Ins. Co.*, 973 F. Supp. 1091 (N.D. Ind. 1997) (Indiana law); *Butler v. Nationwide Mut. Ins. Co.*, 712 F. Supp. 528 (S.D. Miss. 1989) (Mississippi law); *Hauff v. Petterson*, 755 F. Supp. 2d 1138 (D.N.M. 2010); *Island House Inn, Inc. v. State Auto Ins. Cos.*, 150 Ohio App. 3d 522, 782 N.E.2d 156 (2002); *Lyons v. Lindsey Morden Claims Management, Inc.*, 985 S.W.2d 86 (Tex. Ct. App. 1998); *Amica Mut. Ins. Co. v. Schettler*, 768 P.2d 950 (Utah Ct. App. 1989). See also *Villa v. McFerren*, 35 Cal. App. 4th 733, 41 Cal. Rptr. 2d 719 (1995) (psychiatrist who allegedly conspired to deny insured disability benefits was not subject to liability for conspiracy to commit bad faith); *Riccatone v. Colorado Choice Health Plans*, 315 P.3d 203 (Colo. Ct. App. 2013) (neither third-party administrators of employer's self-funded health care plan nor advisor to plan owed participants common-law duty of good faith); *Cary v. United of Omaha Life Ins. Co.*, 43 P.3d 655 (Colo. Ct. App.

2001) (because of absence of privity of contract, insured under health and disability plan had no bad faith cause of action against plan's third-party administrator); *Aquilina v. Certain Underwriters at Lloyd's Syndicate #2003*, 407 F. Supp. 3d 1016 (D. Haw. 2019) (Hawaii law; dismissing bad faith first-party tort claim based on failure to allege contractual relationship between insureds and agents); *Shobe v. Kelly*, 279 S.W.3d 203 (Mo. Ct. App. 2009) (claims adjuster could not be held personally liable as she functioned solely as agent of insurer, did not personally control settlement, did not have individual authority to settle claims, and did not represent that she had such authority); *Logsdon v. Fifth Third Bank*, 100 Ohio App. 3d 333, 654 N.E.2d 115 (1994) (where auto loan borrower failed to purchase insurance and lender was forced to do so to cover collateral, insurer had no good faith duty to borrower); *Wathor v. Mutual Assistance Adm'rs*, 87 P.3d 559 (Okla. 2004) (no duty of good faith was owed to insureds by health plan's third-party administrator); *Miller v. Mill Creek Homes, Inc.*, 195 Or. App. 310, 97 P.3d 687 (2004) ("captive" agent—agent who generally sold only one company's policies—was not insureds' agent and he thus lacked relationship with insureds that would have made him potentially liable to them for economic damages resulting from negligence); *McLaren v. AIG Domestic Claims, Inc.*, 853 F. Supp. 2d 499 (E.D. Pa. 2012) (insured failed to allege facts sufficient to demonstrate that claims administrator was insurer's alter ego); *Givens v. Mullikin*, 75 S.W.3d 383 (Tenn. 2002) (insurer may be vicariously liable for tortious conduct of attorney whom insurer appoints to defend insured); *Lakeside FBBC, LP v. Everest Indem. Ins. Co.*, ___ F. Supp. 3d ___, 2020 WL 1814405 (W.D. Tex. 2020) (Texas law; Texas Prompt Payment of Claims Act, Tex. Ins. Code §§542.051–.061, applies only to insurers and not to insurance adjusters); *Barefield v. DPIC Cos., Inc.*, 600 S.E.2d 256 (W. Va. 2004) (defense attorney hired by insurer was not subject to state's Unfair Trade Practices Act). *Cf. Merrick v. Fischer, Rounds &*

Associates, Inc., 305 Neb. 230, 939 N.W.2d 795 (2020) (insurance broker had no duty to inform insured company that it should purchase workers' compensation insurance; broker's or agent's duty of reasonable care did not encompass volunteering information that insured did not request).

Compare *C.P. ex rel. M.L. v. Allstate Ins. Co.*, 996 P.2d 1216 (Alaska 2000) (insurer's salaried claims adjusters owe duty of due care to insureds in connection with adjustment of claims and may be personally liable for failure to exercise reasonable care to avoid interfering with insured's rights under liability policy to receive defense and indemnity); *McNeill v. State Farm Life Ins. Co.*, 116 Cal. App. 4th 597, 10 Cal. Rptr. 3d 679 (2004) (insured could assert fraud claim against agent who allegedly intentionally misrepresented total premiums that would be required under life insurance policy); *Tran v. Farmers Group, Inc.*, 104 Cal. App. 4th 1202, 128 Cal. Rptr. 2d 728 (2002) (attorney-in-fact for interinsurance exchange may be sued for breach of fiduciary duty and bad faith); *Jones v. AIG Risk Mgmt., Inc.*, 726 F. Supp. 2d 1049 (N.D. Cal. 2010) (putative agents of insurer were not parties where they were not named as parties, and contract specified that coverage was being provided by insurer only, even though one putative agent allegedly played role in the handling of the claim); *Macey v. Allstate Prop. & Casualty Ins. Co.*, 220 F. Supp. 2d 1116 (N.D. Cal. 2002) (California law; recognizing that "special duty" arises, *inter alia*, where agent misrepresents nature, extent, or scope of coverage being offered); *Cary v. United of Omaha Life Ins. Co.*, 68 P.3d 462 (Colo. 2003) (duty of good faith extended to third-party administrator who acted as claims handler for self-insured employer); *Scott Wetzel Serv., Inc. v. Johnson*, 821 P.2d 804 (Colo. 1991) (independent adjuster hired by self-insured employer may be subject to bad faith liability in connection with handling of workers' compensation claim); *Jordan v. City of Aurora*, 876 P.2d 38 (Colo. Ct. App. 1993) (applying *Scott Wetzel* holding retroactively); *Lance v. Employers Fire Ins. Co.*, 66 F. Supp. 2d 921 (C.D. Ill. 1999) (Illinois law; remanding to state court and rejecting argument that agent had been fraudulently joined as defendant, court discusses unsettled nature of Illinois law concerning direct claims against agents); *Winburn v. Liberty Mut. Ins. Co.*, 933 F. Supp. 664 (E.D. Ky. 1996) (Kentucky law; granting motion to remand to state court; insurance agent was not fraudulently joined as defendant to defeat diversity since Kentucky law recognizes potential first-party bad faith liability of agent even for conduct performed within scope of employment, and since insured made colorable claim that agents are "persons" within meaning of state unfair claims settlement practices act); *Twin City Fire Ins. Co. v. City of Madison*, 309 F.3d 901 (5th Cir. 2002) (Mississippi law; insured under liability policy could state cause of action for bad faith claims handling against insurer's affiliates and their individual employees); *Fillinger v. Northwestern Agency, Inc.*, 938 P.2d 1347 (Mont. 1997) (insurance agents are subject to liability under Montana's unfair claim settlement practices statute, Mont. Code Ann. §§33-18-201 et seq.); *O'Fallon v. Farmers Ins. Exch.*, 859 P.2d 1008 (Mont. 1993) (insurance adjusters are subject to liability under Montana's unfair claim settlement practices statute); *Wangler v. Lerol*, 670 N.W.2d 830 (N.D. 2003) (*"Miller-Shugart* agreement," under which insured stipulated to liability and assigned rights against insurer to claimant, did not preclude negligence action against agent who allegedly failed to procure requested coverage); *Al's Café, Inc. v. Sanders Ins. Agency*, 2003 PA Super. 110, 820 A.2d 745 (2003) (recognizing that agent/broker's duty of reasonable care includes duty to ascertain whether selected insurer is reputable and financially sound); *Londo v. McLaughlin*, 402 Pa. Super. 527, 587 A.2d 744 (1991) (reversing dismissal: broker who advised insured to misrepresent smoking history on policy application had good faith duty to inform insured of possible consequence of noncoverage); *Banker v. Valley Forge Ins.*

Co., 401 Pa. Super. 367, 585 A.2d 504 (1991) (reversing dismissal: broker was subject to bad faith liability for failure to correct insured's misunderstanding in connection with an ill-advised change of coverage); *Liberty Mut. Ins. Co. v. Garrison Contractors, Inc.*, 966 S.W.2d 482 (Tex. 1998) (insurance company employees are "persons" within meaning of Texas unfair claims settlement practices statute (Tex. Ins. Code art. 21.21, §16); *William H. McGee & Co. v. Schick*, 792 S.W.2d 513 (Tex. Ct. App. 1990) (insurer's managing agent, who issued policies, collected premiums, and paid claims, was subject to statutory bad faith liability under Tex. Ins. Code art. 21.21; affirming awards of compensatory and punitive damages, attorney's fees, interest, and penalties); *Thomas v. Ohio Casualty Group of Ins. Cos.*, 3 F. Supp. 2d 764 (S.D. Tex. 1998) (Texas law; upholding potential liability of insurance agent for misrepresentation of fact or action outside scope of authority); *French v. State Farm Ins. Co.*, 156 F.R.D. 159 (S.D. Tex. 1994); *Herman v. Millicovsky*, 834 F. Supp. 182 (S.D. Tex. 1992) (Texas law; noting that Texas law permits private actions against adjusters under Tex. Ins. Code art. 21.21); *AAS-DMP Mgmt., L.P. Liquidating Trust v. Acordia Northwest, Inc.*, 63 P.3d 860 (Wash. Ct. App. 2003) (identifying factors that may create "special relationship" between broker and insured); *Taylor v. Nationwide Mut. Ins. Co.*, 589 S.E.2d 55 (W.Va. 2003) (insurance company's employee claims adjuster could be held personally liable for violations of West Virginia Unfair Trade Practices Act).

II.   INSURER'S PRELIMINARY STEPS

§3.37 C. Declaratory Relief Action

—Affirming summary judgment, a Texas Court of Appeals held that the insured's bad faith allegations in connection with the handling of an underinsured motorist claim had been a compulsory counterclaim in the insurer's prior declaratory judgment action, which had resulted in a finding of noncoverage. The insured's bad faith claim was barred by res judicata and collateral estoppel, the court held, because the coverage action and the bad faith action were based on the same transaction. *Miller v. State & County Mut. Fire Ins. Co.*, 1 S.W.3d 709 (Tex. Ct. App. 1999).

III. ARBITRATION

§3.40 B. Policy-Required Arbitration

—Concerning the split of authority as to whether bad faith claims are encompassed by mandatory arbitration provisions, see, *e.g.*, *Dyess v. American Hardware Ins. Group, Inc.*, 709 So. 2d 447 (Ala. 1997); *Zolezzi v. Pacificare of Cal.*, 105 Cal. App. 4th 573, 129 Cal. Rptr. 2d 526 (2003); *Mansdorf v. California Physicians Serv., Inc.*, 87 Cal. App. 3d 412, 151 Cal. Rptr. 388 (1978); *Rios v. Allstate Ins. Co.*, 68 Cal. App. 3d 811, 137 Cal. Rptr. 441 (1977); *Guaranty Nat'l Ins. Co. v. Williams*, 982 P.2d 306 (Colo. 1999); *Dale v. Guaranty Nat'l Ins. Co.*, 948 P.2d 545 (Colo. 1997); *Lovey v. Regence BlueShield of Idaho*, 139 Idaho 37, 72 P.3d 877 (2003); *Nealy v. State Farm Mut. Auto. Ins. Co.*, 695 A.2d 790 (Pa. Super. Ct. 1997); *In re Terra Nova Ins. Co.*, 992 S.W.2d 741 (Tex. Ct. App. 1999); *Escalante v. Century Ins.*, 49 Wash. App. 375, 743 P.2d 832 (1987); *Long v. Great W. Life & Annuity Co.*, 957 P.2d 823 (Wyo. 1998).

IV. SETTLEMENT

§3.41 A. Plaintiff

—Also representing the rule in some jurisdictions that an insurer in a possible excess judgment situation is under no good faith duty to initiate settlement negotiations, see *Morrell Constr., Inc. v. Home Ins. Co.*, 920 F.2d 576 (9th Cir.

1990) (Idaho law); *American Physicians Ins. Exch. v. Garcia*, 876 S.W.2d 842 (Tex. 1994). *Morrell* is discussed in supplement §§2.31, 2.48. The *Garcia* decision contains a useful collection of citations from other jurisdictions that are arguably at odds with the Texas Supreme Court's conclusion, though the court makes an attempt to harmonize them (876 S.W.2d at 850 n.17).

—For a discussion of California law on the options available to excess insurers when presented with a settlement offer that has been approved by the insured and the primary insurer, see *Teleflex Med. Inc. v. National Union Fire Ins. Co.*, 851 F.3d 976 (9th Cir. 2017). The court rejected an excess insurer's motion to vacate judgment on a bad faith claim where the excess insurer delayed its response with respect to its obligation to accept the settlement or assume defense. The court emphasized that when an excess insurer is presented with a settlement offer that has been approved by the insured and the primary insurer, "[t]he excess insurer must (1) approve the proposed settlement, (2) reject it and take over the defense, or (3) reject it, decline to take over the defense, and face a potential lawsuit by the insured seeking contribution toward the settlement." *Id.* at 979.

§3.42 B. Defendant

—For additional cases recognizing the relevance and admissibility on the issue of bad faith of evidence of the insurer's conduct even after suit has been filed, see *National Ins. Ass'n v. Sockwell*, 829 So. 2d 111 (Ala. 2002); *National Sec. Fire & Casualty Co. v. Coshatt*, 690 So. 2d 391 (Ala. Civ. App. 1996); *Tucson Airport Auth. v. Certain Underwriters at Lloyd's*, 186 Ariz. 45, 918 P.2d 1063 (Ct. App. 1995); *Continental Casualty Co. v. Royal Ins. Co.*, 219 Cal. App. 3d 111, 268 Cal. Rptr. 193 (1990) (excess liability case); *Home Ins. Co. v. Owens*, 573 So. 2d 343 (Fla. Dist. Ct. App. 1990); *Norman v. American Nat'l Fire Ins. Co.*, 198 Ill. App. 3d 269, 555 N.E.2d 1087 (1990); *Gooch v. State*

Farm Mut. Auto. Ins. Co., 712 N.E.2d 38 (Ind. Ct. App. 1999); *Verne R. Houghton Ins. Agency, Inc. v. Orr Drywall Co.*, 470 N.W. 2d 39 (Iowa 1991); *Knotts v. Zurich Ins. Co.*, 197 S.W.3d 512 (Ky. 2006); *Graham v. Gallant Ins. Co.*, 60 F. Supp. 2d 632 (W.D. Ky. 1999) (Kentucky law); *Federated Mut. Ins. Co. v. Anderson*, 991 P.2d 915 (Mont. 1999); *UTI Corp. v. Fireman's Fund Ins. Co.*, 896 F. Supp. 362 (D.N.J. 1995) (New Jersey law); *Journal Publishing Co. v. American Home Assurance Co.*, 771 F. Supp. 632 (S.D.N.Y. 1991) (New Mexico law); *Ingalls v. Paul Revere Life Ins. Co.*, 561 N.W.2d 273 (N.D. 1997); *Goddard v. Farmers Ins. Co.*, 173 Or. App. 633, 22 P.3d 1224 (2001), *aff'd in relevant part*, 344 Or. 232, 179 P.3d 645 (2008); *Zimmerman v. Harleysville Mut. Ins. Co.*, 860 A.2d 167 (Pa. Super. Ct. 2004); *O'Donnell v. Allstate Ins. Co.*, 734 A.2d 901 (Pa. Super. Ct. 1999); *Rottmund v. Continental Assurance Co.*, 813 F. Supp. 1104 (E.D. Pa. 1992) (Pennsylvania law; Pennsylvania's bad faith statute (Pa. Cons. Stat. §8371) applied to postlitigation conduct occurring after statute's effective date even though original denial of claim occurred before effective date); *American Nat'l Prop. & Casualty Co. v. Stutte*, 105 F. Supp. 3d 849 (E.D. Tenn. 2015) (Tennessee law; in case of first impression in Tennessee, federal district court held that insurer's obligation to act in good faith based on Tennessee's bad faith statute, Tenn. Code Ann. §56–7-105, does not end following 60-day waiting period for insured to file suit, but only insofar as insurer's postlitigation conduct relates to claim or refusal to pay, not to litigation process).

Some courts, however, have disagreed. Applying Oklahoma law, the Tenth Circuit, in *Timberlake Constr. Co. v. U.S. Fidelity & Guar. Co.*, 71 F.3d 335 (10th Cir. 1995), held that "while evidence of an insurer's litigation conduct may, in some rare instances, be admissible on the issue of bad faith, such evidence will generally be inadmissible, as it lacks probative value and carries a high risk of prejudice." The court added that "[a]llowing litigation conduct to serve as evidence of bad faith would undermine an insurer's right to contest questionable claims and to defend itself against such claims." 71 F.3d at 341. See also *Howard v. State Farm Mut. Auto. Ins. Co.*, 450 S.E.2d 582 (S.C. 1994), reversing a judgment for the insured on the ground that evidence of the insurer's litigation conduct was irrelevant and should not have been admitted. Accord, *Parsons v. Allstate Ins. Co.*, 165 P.3d 809 (Colo. Ct. App. 2007); *Blanchard v. Mid-Century Ins. Co.*, 933 N.W.2d 631, 2019 S.D. 54 (S.D. 2019); *Sinclair Oil Corp. v. Republic Ins. Co.*, 967 F. Supp. 462 (D. Wyo. 1997) (Wyoming law).

In *California Physicians' Serv. v. Superior Court* (Landa), 9 Cal. App. 4th 1321, 12 Cal. Rptr. 2d 95 (1992), a California Court of Appeal rejected the notion that a cause of action in tort can be stated for the filing of bad faith or malicious defensive pleadings. The court thus disagreed with the trial court, which, in overruling the insurer's demurrer, had reasoned that since an insurer's duty of good faith continues after litigation is initiated, the interposition of defenses that are patently untenable constitutes bad faith. Defensive pleading, the court of appeal held, is communication protected by the absolute litigation privilege. The court distinguished *White v. Western Title Ins. Co.*, 40 Cal. 3d 870, 221 Cal. Rptr. 509 (1985) (discussed in book §3.42), as having involved postlitigation conduct not embodied in court documents. (At the same time, the court of appeal raised questions as to *White*'s current vitality.) Also distinguishing *White*, in holding that the litigation privilege protected an insurer against fraud claims in connection with its alleged concealment of policy limits and of the existence of policies, see *California Dredging Co. v. I.N.A.*, 18 Cal. App. 4th 572, 22 Cal. Rptr. 2d 461 (1993). See also *Old Republic Ins. Co. v. FSR Brokerage, Inc.*, 80 Cal. App. 4th 666, 95 Cal. Rptr. 2d 583 (2000) (absolute litigation privilege protected fraud allegations against insured brought by insurer after paying all benefits due under policy). And invoking the attorney-client privilege to similarly limit the admissibility of evidence of bad faith litigation conduct, see *Palmer v. Farmers Ins. Exch.*, 861 P.2d 895 (Mont. 1993).

—In *Mutual of Enumclaw Ins. Co. v. Dan Paulson Construction, Inc.*, 161 Wash. 2d 903, 169 P.3d 1 (banc 2007), the Washington Supreme Court held that a liability insurer defending its insured under a reservation of rights did not successfully rebut the presumption of harm that arose from its bad faith in sending a subpoena and ex parte communications to the arbitrator who was resolving the underlying claim by a homeowner against the insured builder. A liability insurer may defend under a reservation of rights while seeking a declaratory judgment that it has no duty to defend, the court explained, but it must avoid seeking adjudication of factual matters disputed in the underlying litigation, because advocating a position adverse to its insured's interests constitutes bad faith.

For refusals to apply the duty of good faith to insurer conduct following settlement or the entry of judgment, see *Ridgeway v. U.S. Life Credit Life Ins. Co.*, 793 A.2d 972 (Pa. Super. Ct. 2002); *Mid-Century Ins. Co. of Texas v. Boyte*, 80 S.W.3d 546 (Tex. 2002).

V. THE COMPLAINT

A. General Considerations

§3.44 a. Choice of Forum

—A federal district court denied an insurer's motion to dismiss for forum non conveniens in *Connex R.R. LLC v. AXA Corp. Solutions Assurance*, 209 F. Supp. 3d 1147 (C.D. Cal. 2016). The court held that there was a strong local interest in litigating the bad faith claim in the district court rather than allowing the matter to be litigated in France. The factors important to the court's decision included the following: The insurer failed to fulfill its contract obligations in California, bad faith claims for tort and punitive damages against an insurer are fundamental to California public policy, and France would not provide remedies for plaintiff's claims of bad faith.

Denying the insured's motion for remand to California state court, a federal district court, in *Basel v. Allstate Ins. Co.*, 757 F. Supp. 39 (N.D. Cal. 1991), held that the insured's action against the insurer for bad faith refusal to settle a claim for property damage under a homeowner's policy was not a "direct action" against the insurer, within the meaning of 28 U.S.C. §1332(3), so as to preclude the exercise of federal diversity jurisdiction. The court expressed its disagreement with the contrary holding in *Chavarria v. Allstate Ins. Co.*, 749 F. Supp. 220 (C.D. Cal. 1990).

—Two decisions by federal district courts in Texas have addressed the fraudulent or nonfraudulent nature of the joinder of individual defendants in an effort to defeat diversity jurisdiction and bar removal: *Herman v. Millicovsky*, 834 F. Supp. 182 (S.D. Tex. 1992) (granting motion to remand: joinder of individual adjusters as defendants was not fraudulent); *Arzehgar v. Dixon*, 150 F.R.D. 92 (S.D. Tex. 1993) (denying motion to remand: joinder of individual employees of insurer as defendants was fraudulent).

B. Causes of Action

§3.48 1. Breach of Covenant of Good Faith and Fair Dealing (Bad Faith)

—In *Virgin v. State Farm Fire & Casualty Co.*, 218 Cal. App. 3d 1372, 267 Cal. Rptr. 704 (1990), a California Court of Appeal reversed the dismissal of a first-party bad faith action that had been filed against the insurer before the insurer's formal denial of the claims at issue. The timing defect was a matter in abatement, the court reasoned, that should have been ignored since it had been cured (by the insurer's subsequent denial of the claims) by the time the insurer had moved to dismiss.

In *Citizens Ins. Co. of Am. v. Chief Digital Advisors*, ___ F. Supp. 3d ___, 2020 WL 6889174 (S.D. Cal. 2020), the federal district court denied the insurer's motion to dismiss the insured's claims of breach of contract and bad faith based on the insurer's failure to provide independent counsel. The court stated that the insured had properly alleged facts showing that counsel for the insurer could control the outcome of the coverage issue, and thus alleged an actual conflict of interest creating a duty to appoint independent counsel.

—In *Powell v. Infinity Ins. Co.*, 282 Conn. 594, 922 A.2d 1073 (2007), the Connecticut Supreme Court, affirming summary judgment, held that the doctrine of res judicata barred the assertion of claims for bad faith and violation of the Connecticut Unfair Trade Practices Act and Unfair Insurance Practices Act where, in an earlier action, the insured had obtained a favorable judgment on a contract claim for uninsured motorist benefits. "We conclude," the court wrote, "that the plaintiffs' claims in the present case are precluded because they grew out of the same transaction or nucleus of facts, entailed the presentation of the same evidence and involved infringement of the same rights as those implicated in the prior action." 922 A.2d at 1076.

—In *Aquilina v. Certain Underwriters at Lloyd's Syndicate #2003*, 407 F. Supp. 3d 1016 (D. Haw. 2019) (Hawaii law), the federal district court dismissed the complaint of insureds alleging fraudulent and misleading conduct by insurers, agents, and brokers. The court held that the complaint, *inter alia*, failed to satisfy the Fed. R. Civ. P. 9(b) requirement to plead fraud with particularity, as well as the Fed. R. Civ. P. 8(a) requirements prohibiting impermissible group pleading. The court granted leave to amend the complaint, noting that the circumstances of the case were "concerning." The plaintiff property owners alleged that certain surplus line insurers, agents, and brokers fraudulently schemed to steer the plaintiffs to purchase homeowner's insurance policies that contained exclusions for lava-related damage, resulting in lack of coverage for devastating damage from the 2018 eruption of the Kilauea Volcano.

In *Damon Key Leong Kupchak Hastert v. Westport Ins. Corp.*, 421 F. Supp. 3d 946 (D. Haw. 2019) (Hawaii law), the court dismissed the insured's bad faith claim where the insurer's conduct in declining to defend against a claim seeking sanctions from the insured for contempt, which were clearly excluded under policy, was reasonable. The court noted that the insured's allegations of bad faith conduct were "conclusory assertions, unadorned with any factual enhancement." *Id.* at 957.

—In *Selective Ins. Co. of S.C. v. Sela*, 353 F. Supp. 3d 847 (D. Minn. 2018), the federal district court held that Federal Rules of Civil Procedure 8 and 15 applied to pleading a claim for bad faith in federal court, rather than Minn. Stat. Ann. §604.18 subdiv. 4(a). The court concluded that the state statute, which contained barriers to pleading bad faith not found in the federal rules, was not applicable to an action in federal court.

—In *Aiello v. Geico Gen. Ins. Co.*, 379 F. Supp. 3d 1123 (D. Nev. 2019), the federal district court, applying Nevada law, dismissed the plaintiff insured's bad faith claim against her insurer under an uninsured motorist policy, with leave to amend. The court concluded that the plaintiff alleged only that her insurer failed to pay her damages, without alleging that the insurer "denied coverage with an actual or implied awareness that there was no reasonable basis supporting its decision." *Id.* at 1128.

—In *McDonough v. State Farm Fire & Casualty Co.*, 365 F. Supp. 3d 552 (E.D. Pa. 2019), the federal district court dismissed the insured's statutory bad faith claim based on the insured's failure to allege specific facts indicating that the insurer had no reasonable basis for offering settlement below policy limits. "A plaintiff must plead specific facts as evidence of bad faith and cannot rely on conclusory statements." *Id.* at 557 (internal quotation marks omitted). The court granted the insured leave to amend its complaint. Accord *Clapps v. State Farm Ins. Cos.*, 447 F. Supp. 3d 293 (E.D. Pa. 2020) (Pennsylvania law; dismissing bad faith claim under Pa. Cons. Stat. §8371, with leave to amend, where complaint stated mere conclusory allegations with no factual detail).

§3.49 2. Breach of Fiduciary Relationship

—See supplement §1.2 for discussion of the arguable judicial trend away from the "fiduciary" characterization of the relationship between insurer and insured.

—In *Henry v. Associated Indem. Corp.*, 217 Cal. App. 3d 1405, 266 Cal. Rptr. 578 (1990), a California Court of Appeal affirmed the dismissal of an insured's cause of action for breach of fiduciary duty. Reasoning that the complaint suggested the existence of nothing more than an arm's-length business relationship, the court discounted as "merely dicta" the 1986 suggestion by the California Supreme Court (in *Frommoethelydo v. Fire Ins. Exch.*, 42 Cal. 3d 208, 228 Cal. Rptr. 160 (1986)) that a cause of action could be stated against an insurer for breach of fiduciary duty. (And, indeed, the California Supreme Court does seem to have subsequently backed off from its *Frommoethelydo* remarks —see supplement §1.2.)

A result similar to that in *Henry v. Associated Indem. Corp.*, *supra*, was also reached in *Love v. Fire Ins. Exch.*, 221 Cal. App. 3d 1136, 271 Cal. Rptr. 246 (1990).

One commentator, in light of the slant of California cases relating to fiduciary duty in the insurance context, has warned of a "guarded prognosis" for the tort of breach of fiduciary duty in commercial contexts in general. Heeseman, "Claims Limited in Breach of Fiduciary Duty," *Los*

Angeles Daily Journal, June 20, 1990. (Note, however, that a fiduciary duty certainly arises relative to claim denials in situations where an employer acts in the dual role of administrator and funding source of a disability plan. See *Nord v. The Black & Decker Disability Plan,* 296 F.3d 823 (9th Cir. 2002) (California law).)

—In *Aquilina v. Certain Underwriters at Lloyd's Syndicate #2003,* 407 F. Supp. 3d 1016 (D. Haw. 2019) (Hawaii law), the federal district court dismissed claims of insureds alleging fraudulent and misleading conduct by agents and brokers dealing in surplus lines homeowner's insurance, including a claim for breach of fiduciary duty. The court held that the insureds failed to allege the existence of a special or fiduciary relationship, noting that the defendant agents acted for the insurers, but granted leave to amend the complaint.

—In *Mutual of Enumclaw Ins. Co. v. Dan Paulson Construction, Inc.,* 161 Wash. 2d 903, 169 P.3d 1 (banc 2007), the Washington Supreme Court noted that a liability insurer defending its insured under a reservation of rights has an enhanced obligation of fairness, But while that relationship is fiduciary, the court explained, it is something less than a true fiduciary relationship, which would require the insurer to place the insured's interests above its own.

§3.51 4. Intentional or Negligent Infliction of Emotional Distress

—Three decisions by California Courts of Appeal have involved significant discussions and applications of the tort of intentional infliction of emotional distress in contexts involving nonpayment of claims made by injured third parties under liability policies: *Moukalled v. Fire Ins. Exch.,* 221 Cal. App. 3d 769, 271 Cal. Rptr. 588 (1988), *ordered not to be published in official reports* (reversing dismissal of cause of action by claimant); and *Continental Ins. Co. v. Superior Court (Shea),* 221 Cal. App. 3d 1520, 271 Cal.

Rptr. 266 (1990) (ordering trial court to sustain insurer's demurrer); *Krupnick v. Hartford Accident & Indem. Co.*, 28 Cal. App. 4th 185, 34 Cal. Rptr. 2d 39 (1994).

The *Moukalled* case (noncitable because ordered depublished) involved a three-count third-party complaint (for violation of the unfair claim settlement practices statute, intentional infliction of emotional distress, and negligence), arising from the handling of plaintiff's claim for injuries sustained in an unprovoked attack by the insured's doberman pinscher. The insurer was aware that the claim was unquestionably covered by the policy, and that delay in payment would prevent the claimant from obtaining treatment necessary to minimize permanent injuries and scarring. Nonetheless, the insurer refused to make any medical payments whatsoever pending a "thorough investigation." According to the court, the insurer engaged in a series of disingenuous delaying tactics, and thus "undertook a course of conduct to cause Moukalled severe emotional distress and financial hardship so as to minimize Moukalled's ultimate recovery."

Continental Ins. Co. v. Superior Court (Shea), supra, involved a different result in a somewhat similar factual setting: the liability insurer's refusal to make advance payments needed by the severely injured claimant, despite the insurer's knowledge of the claimant's extreme financial distress, to coerce his acceptance of a cheap settlement. In holding that these facts would not support a cause of action for intentional infliction of emotional distress, the court reasoned as follows (221 Cal. App. 3d at 1525, 271 Cal. Rptr. at 268):

> As alleged in the complaint, the gravamen of plaintiffs' action is the refusal by defendants to make a requested advance payment in anticipation of settlement. The question is whether defendants' alleged knowledge of facts revealing plaintiffs' particular emotional and financial vulnerability imposes upon defendants a duty

actively to alleviate plaintiffs' plight. We hold that it does not. Since it is an insurer's "conduct, not its state of mind, that must be outrageous" [citation omitted], the reasons why defendants failed to act are immaterial. Defendants' failure to act, where the law does not require defendants to act, will not support an intentional tort.

In *Krupnick v. Hartford Accident & Indem. Co., supra.*, the court of appeal, affirming summary judgment, rejected the use of a claim for the negligent infliction of emotional distress as a method by which a third-party claimant may bring an action directly against the insurer relating to the insurer's conduct in settlement negotiations. The court emphasized the claimants' lack of any preexisting relationship with the insurer such as might create a duty of care.

—Applying District of Columbia law, a federal district court, in *Nugent v. UNUM Life Ins. Co. of Am.*, 752 F. Supp. 2d 46 (D. D.C. 2010), granted summary judgment on a cause of action for the intentional infliction of emotional distress, explaining that although "a cause of action that could be considered a tort independent of contract performance is a viable claim, even in the insurance contract . . . the tort must exist in its own right independent of the contract, and any duty upon which the tort is based must flow from considerations other than the contractual relationship" (752 F. Supp. 2d at 53). The court cited *Choharis v. State Farm Fire & Casualty Co.*, 961 A.2d 1080 (D.C. 2008) for that proposition and stated that in the present case the allegations involved only conduct such as "harassment," and the questioning of the insured's veracity, which "are not in and of themselves sufficiently egregious to constitute a stand alone tort." *Id.* There was no claim for defamation, for example, the court emphasized.

—In *Young v. Allstate Ins. Co.*, 119 Hawaii 403, 198 P.3d 666 (2008), the Hawaii Supreme Court, reversing summary judgment, held that a claim for intentional infliction of emotional distress was adequately stated by an automobile accident victim's allegations concerning the liability insurer's low-ball settlement offers. Although the insurer promised to treat the victim fairly, it appealed a modest arbitration award, and the victim ultimately received an award six times greater.

—In *McKinley v. Guaranty Nat'l Ins. Co.*, 144 Idaho 247, 159 P.3d 884 (2007), the Idaho Supreme Court, affirming summary judgment, held that the insured had failed to raise factual issues concerning a claim of intentional infliction of emotional distress. While the insurer could have acted more expeditiously, the court reasoned, its delay in settling claims arising out of an accident with multiple victims was not reckless nor beyond the bounds of decency. The insurer had needed time to investigate, the court held, and had sought to settle within four months of the accident.

—In *Setzer v. Farmers Ins. Co.*, 185 Fed. Appx. 748 (10th Cir. 2006) (Oklahoma law), the Tenth Circuit, affirming the dismissal of a claim by an automobile accident victim, held that the insurer's obtaining of medical records beyond the scope of the victim's authorization was not "outrageous" or "highly offensive to a reasonable person."

§3.52 5. Fraud or Deceit

—*In McNeill v. State Farm Life Ins. Co.*, 116 Cal. App. 4th 597, 10 Cal. Rptr. 3d 679 (2004), a California Court of Appeal held that an insured could assert a fraud claim against the agent who allegedly intentionally misrepresented the total premiums that would be required to be paid under a policy of life insurance.

—In *Macomber v. Travelers Prop. & Casualty*, 261 Conn. 620, 804 A.2d 180 (2002), the Connecticut Supreme Court reversed the dismissal of a third party's fraud and statutory bad faith claims in connection with an insurer's failure to disclose the cost and value of a structured settlement annuity. The court reasoned that acts prohibited by the Connecticut Unfair Insurance Practices Act are also unlawful acts within the meaning of the Connecticut Unfair Trade

Practices Act, thus recognizing the standing of third-party claimants to sue for a wide range of unfair claims settlement practices.

—In *Aquilina v. Certain Underwriters at Lloyd's Syndicate #2003*, 407 F. Supp. 3d 1016 (D. Haw. 2019) (Hawaii law), the federal district court dismissed the claims of insureds alleging fraudulent and misleading conduct by agents and brokers dealing in surplus lines homeowner's insurance. The court held that the complaint, *inter alia*, failed to satisfy the Fed. R. Civ. P. 9(b) requirement to plead fraud with particularity, as well as the Fed. R. Civ. P. 8(a) requirements prohibiting impermissible group pleading. The court granted leave to amend the complaint, however, noting that the circumstances of the case were "concerning." The plaintiff property owners alleged that certain surplus line insurers, agents, and brokers fraudulently schemed to steer the plaintiffs to purchase homeowner's insurance policies that contained exclusions for lava-related damage, resulting in lack of coverage for devastating damage from the 2018 eruption of the Kilauea Volcano.

—Applying Kansas law and affirming summary judgment, the Tenth Circuit held in *Wade v. EMCASCO Ins. Co.*, 483 F.3d 657 (10th Cir. 2007), that a purported fraud claim based on the allegation that the insurer had intentionally misrepresented that appointed counsel would vigorously defend the insured against a negligence claim was in reality just a claim that the insurer had breached its duty to defend.

—In *Cooper v. Berkshire Life Ins. Co.*, 148 Md. App. 41, 810 A.2d 1045, *cert. denied*, 373 Md. 407, 818 A.2d 1105 (Md. 2003), a Maryland appellate court reversed summary judgment on fraud and negligent misrepresentation claims brought by an insured against the issuer of a life insurance policy and the insurer's agents, holding that the insurer could be liable for misrepresenting the financial assumptions underlying an "illustration" of a "disappearing premium" that was attached to the policy. On this theory, the insured could seek to prove that the "illustration" did not correctly reflect financial information known to the insurer at the time it was written. However, the court held, the insurer could not be found liable on the theory that its agents had misrepresented to the insured that the premium —as "illustrated"—was *guaranteed* to disappear within ten years, because such an oral representation was contrary to the policy's written explanation that the 10-year payment term was only *contingent*. The agents themselves, however, might be subject to liability for such misrepresentations— even though they were contrary to the policy's terms—if the insured were able to show that his reliance had been reasonable based on a relationship of trust and confidence.

—In *Mooneyham v. Progressive Gulf Ins. Co.*, 910 So. 2d 1223 (Miss. Ct. App. 2005), a Mississippi Court of Appeals affirmed a judgment on a directed verdict for the insurer, holding that the insurer had no fiduciary or other special relationship with the victim and had therefore owed no duty to disclose during settlement negotiations that the victim would need to pay all medical expenses out of the $500 settlement amount.

—Concerning South Carolina law's recognition of a tort action against an insurer for its adjuster's fraudulent procurement of a release, see *Gaskins v. Southern Farm Bureau Casualty Ins. Co.*, 581 S.E.2d 169 (S.C. 2003).

—In *Railsback v. Mid-Century Ins. Co.*, 680 N.W.2d 652 (S.D. 2004), the South Dakota Supreme Court reversed summary judgment that had been granted in favor of a liability insurer on a claim by an automobile accident victim who alleged that the insurer had misrepresented the policy limits during settlement negotiations. The court held inapplicable the prohibition against a direct action by an injured third party and emphasized that an insurer owes a duty not to knowingly cause or further a third-party claimant's misunderstanding of the policy limits to his or her detriment.

In *Landon v. American Family Mut. Ins. Co.*, 293 F. Supp. 3d 879 (D.S.D. 2017), the court denied the insurer's motion to dismiss the insured's claim for first-party bad faith, rejecting the insurer's argument that the plaintiff had to comply with the requirements of Fed. R. Civ. P. 9(b) for pleading fraud. The court applied the holding of another 2017 case, *Haney v. American Family Mut. Ins. Co.*, 223 F. Supp. 3d 921 (D.S.D. 2017), that Rule 9(b) heightened pleading standards "do not apply to first-party bad faith claims under South Dakota law." 293 F. Supp. 3d at 884 (internal quotation marks omitted). See also §1.52.

—In two decisions filed in 2011, federal district courts applying Texas law granted insurers' motions for summary judgment, emphasizing that the rule requiring that fraud be pled with particularity applies to all averments of fraud, including those made in connection with claims under the Texas Insurance Code and the Deceptive Trade Practices Act. *Luna v. Nationwide Prop. & Casualty Ins. Co.*, 798 F. Supp. 2d 821 (S. D. Tex. 2011); *SHS Investment v. Nationwide Mut. Ins. Co.*, 798 F. Supp. 2d 811 (S.D. Tex. 2011). But see *Ramirez v. Allstate Vehicle & Prop. Ins. Co.*, ___ F. Supp. 3d ___, 2020 WL 5806436 (S.D. Tex. 2020) (Texas law; holding insureds stated bad faith claims under Texas common law and unfair claims practices statutes by alleging misrepresentations by insurer concerning covered loss and failure to conduct reasonable investigation; insureds' complaint was sufficient under Fed. R. Civ. P. 9(b) standard for pleading fraud or misrepresentation; see also §1.26).

§3.53 6. Breach of Contract

—In *Citizens Ins. Co. of Am. v. Chief Digital Advisors*, ___ F. Supp. 3d ___, 2020 WL 6889174 (S.D. Cal. 2020), the federal district court denied the insurer's motion to dismiss the insured's claims of breach of contract and bad faith based on the insurer's failure to provide independent counsel. The court stated that the insured had properly alleged facts showing that counsel for the insurer could control the outcome of the coverage issue, and thus alleged an actual conflict of interest creating a duty to appoint independent counsel.

—In *St. Paul Ins. Co. v. Rakkar*, 838 S.W.2d 622 (Tex. Ct. App. 1992), a Texas Court of Appeals affirmed an award of $60,000 for breach of contract even though the insured had not sought or obtained jury findings on the breach of contract claim. The trial court is not required to submit jury questions on undisputed facts, the court explained, and every element of the breach of contract claim had been undisputed, except the question whether the insured had intentionally burned down his house, and that question had been answered in the negative by the jury in connection with the insured's bad faith claim. (The court also affirmed an award of extracontractual and punitive damages for breach of the duty of good faith.)

In *In re Allstate Tex. Lloyds*, 202 S.W.3d 895 (Tex. App. 2006), it was held that severance of contract and bad faith claims was not required by insurer's offer to settle the contract claim. Prejudice is not presumed merely because contract and bad faith claims are joined in the same action, the court explained, and an insurer seeking severance bore the burden of showing prejudice. In the present case, the trial court had ordered bifurcation of the trial as to evidence regarding the bad faith claims that would prejudice the contract claim.

§3.54 7. Declaratory Relief

—See *Kunkel v. Continental Casualty Co.*, 866 F.2d 1269 (10th Cir. 1989) (federal law), in which the Tenth Circuit affirmed a district court judgment declaring the amount of coverage potentially available to an accountant under a policy of malpractice insurance, rejecting the argument that the declaratory judgment action had been untimely. The district court properly exercised jurisdiction under the Declaratory Judgment Act (28 U.S.C. §2201), the court held, even though the fact of coverage remained uncertain because it depended upon (1) the outcome of a collateral action charging the accountant with securities law violations, and (2) a determination that any liability he might incur was not excepted from the terms of the policy.

E. Alleging Damages

§3.58 2. Punitive Damages

—In federal court, under the liberal federal pleading rules, a plaintiff may "include a 'short and plain' prayer for punitive damages that relies entirely on unsupported and conclusory averments of malice or fraudulent intent, [and] need not plead evidentiary facts to support . . . the mental state required to impose punitive damages." *Clark v. Allstate Ins. Co.*, 106 F. Supp. 2d 1016 (S.D. Cal. 2000). The court denied a motion to strike a punitive damages allegation, rejecting the argument that the complaint's allegations were inadequate because they did not establish entitlement to punitive damages under California substantive law.

—Reversing the denial of the insurer's motion to strike a claim for punitive damages, a Florida court held in *State Capital Ins. Co. v. Mattey*, 689 So. 2d 1295 (Fla. Dist. Ct. App. 1997), that an insurance company has a substantive right not to be subjected to financial worth discovery until the trial court has made an affirmative finding that there is a reasonable evidentiary basis for a punitive damages claim.

VI.   DEFENDANT'S RESPONSIVE PLEADINGS

§3.61 B. Answer: Sample Form

—The uncertainty, under California law, concerning whether an insurer who denies coverage on one ground waives other grounds for denial was clarified by a 1995 decision by the California Supreme Court. In *Waller v. Truck Ins. Exch.*, 11 Cal. 4th 1, 44 Cal. Rptr. 2d 370 (1995), the court rejected the "automatic waiver rule" of *McLaughlin v. Connecticut Gen. Life Ins. Co.*, 565 F. Supp. 434 (N.D. Cal. 1983), and held that under the correct rule, "waiver" requires the intentional relinquishment of a right, and to establish the affirmative defense of waiver, an insured has the burden of proving the insurer's intent to relinquish. (The court disapproved *Alta Cal. Regional Ctr. v. Fremont Indem. Co.*, 25 Cal. App. 4th 455, 30 Cal. Rptr. 2d 841 (1994), to the extent that decision relied on the automatic waiver rule of *McLaughlin.*) "Of the 33 sister states to consider the issue," the California Supreme Court noted, "32 agree with the California rule. [Citations omitted.] Only one state has held that an insurer waives coverage defenses not stated in its initial denial letter. (*Armstrong v. Hanover Insurance Company* (1971) 130 Vt. 182, 289 A.2d 669, 672)." 11 Cal. 4th at 32, 44 Cal. Rptr. 2d at 387.

See supplement §1.20 for discussion of *State Farm Mut. Auto. Ins. Co. v. Superior Court (Johnson Kinsey, Inc.)*, 228 Cal. App. 3d 721, 279 Cal. Rptr. 116 (1991), holding that an "advice of counsel" defense in a bad faith action is not "new matter" that must be affirmatively pleaded.

In the following cases, courts have discussed whether an insurer may attempt to justify the nonpayment of claim based on after-acquired information not possessed at the time of the original denial.

—In *Schultz v. Geico Casualty Co.*, 429 P.3d 844 (Colo. 2018), the Supreme Court of Colorado reaffirmed the "well-established principle" that an insurer cannot not rely on information it did not have at the time it made its coverage decision to show that its decision was reasonable. *Id.* at 848–49.

—In *Selective Ins. Co. of S.C. v. Sela*, 353 F. Supp. 3d 847 (D. Minn. 2018) (Minnesota law), the federal district court stated that "whether [insurer] had a reasonable basis for denying [insured's] claim must be assessed based on the circumstances existing at the time that [the claim was denied]. What happened *after* [insurer] denied [insured's] claim is irrelevant." *Id.* at 865–66.

—Under Montana law, it was held in *EOTT v. Certain Underwriters at Lloyd's*, 59 F. Supp. 2d 1072 (D. Mont. 1999), that an insurer may assert as a defense a legal *theory* omitted from its original denial letter (unless the omission prejudiced the insured), but may not rely on *facts* that were unknown to the insurer at the time it denied coverage.

—In *Lindenberg v. Jackson Nat'l Life Ins. Co.*, 912 F.3d 348 (6th Cir. 2019), *cert. denied*, ___ U.S. ___, 140 S. Ct. 635 (2019) (Tennessee law), the court rejected the insurer's "*post hoc* explanation" for its conduct in a bad-faith breach of contract case, raised in the course of litigation, where the insurer failed to allege any basis for its defense in either its interpleader complaint or its motion to dismiss.

C. Cross-Complaints

§3.63 2. Cross-Complaint for Rescission of Policy

—It was held in *Koral Indus., Inc. v. Security Conn. Life Ins. Co.*, 788 S.W.2d 136 (Tex. Ct. App. 1990), that where a jury found that the insurer had been entitled to rescind a policy of life insurance on the basis of the insured's intentional misrepresentations relating to his medical history, it would be inconsistent to permit recovery by the insured on causes of action for common-law and statutory bad faith. The court accordingly reversed a judgment based on a jury verdict for the insured.

D. Defense Motions

§3.67 2. Change of Venue

—Neither an action for nonpayment of benefits under the Texas workers' compensation act, nor a related bad faith cause of action, is removable to federal district court under 28 U.S.C. §1445(c): for purposes of the removal statute, both claims "arise under" the workers' compensation laws of the state of Texas. *Almanza v. Transcontinental Ins. Co.*, 802 F. Supp. 1474 (N.D. Tex. 1992); *Allsup v. Liberty Mut. Ins. Co.*, 782 F. Supp. 325 (N.D. Tex. 1992); *Watson v. Liberty Mut. Fire Ins. Co.*, 715 F. Supp. 797 (W.D. Tex. 1989). But see, *contra, Patin v. Allied Signal, Inc.*, 865 F. Supp. 365 (E.D. Tex. 1994).

§3.68 E. Petition To Remove: Sample Form

—See supplement §3.44 for discussion of *Basel v. Allstate Ins. Co.*, 757 F. Supp. 39 (N.D. Cal. 1991), holding that a bad faith action is not a "direct action" against an insurer, within the meaning of 28 U.S.C. §1332(c), so as to preclude the exercise of federal diversity jurisdiction.

VII. DISCOVERY BY PLAINTIFF

§3.69 A. Production of Documents

—See *Bacher v. Allstate Ins. Co.*, 211 F.3d 52 (3d Cir. 2000) (federal law; discovery order seeking information about prior bad faith actions against defendant was not reviewable under "collateral order doctrine" prior to final judgment in bad faith action where discovery order neither related to "highly sensitive" information such as trade secrets nor involved issues of privilege); *American Protection Ins. Co. v. Helm Concentrates, Inc.*, 140 F.R.D. 448 (E.D. Cal. 1991) (federal law; insured was not entitled to discover information as to reserves established on claims at issue in first-party bad faith action); *Champion Int'l Corp. v. Liberty Mut. Ins. Co.*, 128 F.R.D. 608 (S.D.N.Y. 1989) (federal law; similar claim files of other insureds held discoverable); *Ex parte Union Sec. Life Ins. Co.*, 727 So. 2d 1 (Ala. 1998) (setting aside trial court's order requiring production of documents relating to consumer complaints in overly broad geographic area); *Ex parte Finkbohner*, 682 So. 2d 409 (Ala. 1996) (insured was entitled to discovery of files pertaining to prior bad faith actions against insurer); *State Farm Mut. Auto. Ins. Co. v. Superior Court (Miel)*, 167 Ariz. 135, 804 P.2d 1323 (1991) (trial court abused its discretion in ordering overbroad and unduly burdensome discovery of insurer's other claims documents); *Viking Ins. Co. v. Jester*, 310 Ark. 317, 836 S.W.2d 371 (1992) (discovery sanctions for insurer's failure to obey court order requiring production of entire auto accident claim file properly included striking of insurer's answer, declaring default against insurer as to liability, and awarding fees and costs to insured); *Glenfed Dev. Corp. v. National Union Fire Ins. Co.*, 53 Cal. App. 4th 1113, 62 Cal. Rptr. 2d 195 (1997) (insurers' claims manuals are discoverable); *Lipton v. Superior Court*, 48 Cal. App. 4th 1599, 56 Cal. Rptr. 2d 341 (1996) (evidence of reserves and correspondence with reinsurers may be discoverable in bad faith litigation); *Fireman's Fund Ins. Co. v. Superior Court*, 233 Cal. App. 3d 1138, 286 Cal. Rptr. 50 (1991) (trial court abused its discretion in ordering discovery of defendant's communication with reinsurer—"highly sensitive commercial information"—without first conducting *in camera* inspection for relevance); *Silva v. Basin Western, Inc.*, 47 P.3d 1184 (Colo. 2002) (noting in *dictum* that in litigation between insured and insurer, unlike personal injury actions by third parties, insured may be entitled to discovery of information concerning reserves and settlement authority); *Allstate Indem. Co. v. Ruiz*, 899 So. 2d 1121 (Fla. 2005) (in first-party bad faith action holding producible in discovery all materials in insurer's underlying claim and related litigation file that were created up to and including date of resolution of underlying disputed matter that pertain in any way to coverage, benefits, liability, or damages); *State Farm Mut. Auto. Ins. Co. v. Cook*, 744 So. 2d 567 (Fla. Dist. Ct. App. 1999) (insurer was entitled to protective order staying production of internal manuals relative to bad faith claim until coverage issue was resolved); *Allstate Ins. Co. v. American S. Home Ins. Co.*, 680 So. 2d 1114 (Fla. Dist. Ct. App. 1996) (trial court erred in ordering discovery of excess carrier's claim and litigation files); *State Farm Fire & Casualty Co. v. Martin*, 673 So. 2d 518 (Fla. Dist. Ct. App. 1996) (discovery of claim file is not permitted until coverage question is resolved); *General Accident Fire & Life Ins. Co. v. Boudreau*, 658 So. 2d 1006 (Fla. Dist. Ct. App. 1994) (insured was entitled to discovery of everything in claim file up to date of judgment in underlying case); *Superior Ins. Co. v. Holden*, 642 So. 2d 1139 (Fla. Dist. Ct. App. 1994) (trial judge abused discretion in ordering production of claim file while coverage issues remained unresolved); *Dunn v. National Sec. Fire & Casualty Co.*, 631 So. 2d 1103 (Fla. Dist. Ct. App. 1993) (error in denying insured's request for discovery of claim file required reinstatement of claim for punitive damages); *Continental Casualty Co. v. Aqua Jet Filter Sys., Inc.*, 620 So. 2d 1141 (Fla. Dist. Ct. App. 1993) (third-party claimant was entitled to obtain litigation file of attorney who represented insured in underlying litigation); *International Indem. Co. v. Saia Motor Freight Line*, 223 Ga. App. 544, 478 S.E.2d 776 (1996) (trial court did not abuse discretion in ordering discovery of claim file); *Cedillo v. Farmers Ins. Co.*, 163 Idaho 131, 408 P.3d 886 (2017) (holding plaintiff could not prevail in her challenge to trial court's withholding certain portions of her claim file from discovery because she failed to argue that she was prejudiced as a result); *Paramount Ins. Co. v. Eli Constr. Gen. Contractor*, 159 A.D.2d 447, 553 N.Y.S.2d 127 (1990) (discoverable documents include reports by independent investigators and adjusters made before rejection of claim); *Stern v. Aetna Casualty & Sur. Co.*, 159 A.D.2d 1012, 552 N.Y.S.2d 730 (1990) (insured is entitled to discovery of entire claim file, including portions predating commencement of litigation, if defendant's witness reviewed entire file in preparation for deposition); *Bloom v.*

Mutual of Omaha Ins. Co., 557 N.Y.S.2d 614 (App. Div. 1990) (modifying trial court's discovery order to protect agent's business files other than files concerning other policy cancellations, because those related to agent's "alleged history of filing incorrect or fraudulent applications"); *Berg v. Nationwide Mut. Ins. Co., Inc.*, 44 A.3d 1164, 2012 PA Super 88 (2012) (summary denial of automobile insured's request for unredacted insurer's claims log, or, alternatively, for in camera review of claims log, was abuse of discretion); *Saldi v. Paul Revere Life Ins. Co.*, 224 F.R.D. 169, 2004 WL 1858403 (E.D. Pa. 2004) (Pennsylvania law; in action alleging wrongful termination of disability benefits, permitting extremely broad discovery relative to insurer's business practices, policies, and procedures as relevant to allegations that insurer followed pattern and practice of terminating payments on valid claims in order to increase profits); *Bartlett v. John Hancock Mut. Life Ins. Co.*, 538 A.2d 997 (R.I. 1998) (staying discovery in bad faith action pending resolution of underlying breach of contract claims); *Kessel v. Bridewell*, 872 S.W.2d 837 (Tex. Ct. App. 1994) (insured was entitled to discover adjusters' personnel records to determine whether employees who mishandled claim had been disciplined); *State Farm Mut. Auto. Ins. Co. v. Engelke*, 824 S.W.2d 747 (Tex. Ct. App. 1992) (extremely broad discovery order upheld, covering other lawsuits and complaints, claims manuals, training manuals, and advertisements); *Alpha Life Ins. Co. v. Gayle*, 796 S.W.2d 834 (Tex. Ct. App. 1990) (issuing writ ordering trial judge to vacate order compelling discovery of unredacted copies of similar claim files; privacy interests of other insureds required masking of names and addresses); *State Farm Mut. Auto. Ins. Co. v. Stephens*, 425 S.E.2d 577 (W. Va. 1992) (discovery order was unduly burdensome that asked for information on every bad faith claim filed against insurer since 1980).

See also Burman, *Confidential Insurer-Reinsurer Communications*, 27 Rutgers L.J. 727 (1996).

§3.70 1. Attorney-Client Privilege and Work Product Rule

—The following cases address a variety of discovery issues, in bad faith actions, relating to the attorney-client privilege and the work product rule: *Allstate Ins. Co. v. Levesque*, 263 F.R.D. 663 (M.D. Fla. 2010) (under "sword and shield" doctrine, party who raises claim that will necessarily require proof by way of priviliged communication, cannot insist that communication is privileged in connection with discovery proceedings); *Nationwide Mut. Fire Ins. Co. v. Smith*, 174 F.R.D. 250 (D. Conn. 1997) (federal law; predenial conversations between fire experts retained by insurer were discoverable over work-product objection, and insureds were entitled to discover information relating to other fire claims that expert had investigated); *Ferrara & DiMercurio, Inc. v. St. Paul Mercury Ins. Co.*, 173 F.R.D. 7 (D. Mass. 1997) (federal law; advice of insurer's counsel was not protected because counsel's opinion was directly at issue); *Video Warehouse, Inc. v. Boston Old Colony Ins. Co.*, 160 F.R.D. 83 (S.D. W. Va. 1994) (federal law; memo prepared for response to Insurance Commission was not protected work product); *Allendale Mut. Ins. Co. v. Bull Data Sys., Inc.*, 152 F.R.D. 132 (N.D. Ill. 1993) (federal law; documents containing ordinary insurance information did not come under protection of work product rule simply because investigator happened to be a lawyer); *Stout v. Illinois Farmers Ins. Co.*, 150 F.R.D. 594 (S.D. Ind. 1993) (federal law; work product rule did not protect documents produced by insurer between date of fire loss and denial of claim, in absence of evidence during that period of "identifiable resolve" to litigate); *Catino v. The Travelers Ins. Co., Inc.*, 136 F.R.D. 534 (D. Mass. 1991) (federal law; no attorney-client privilege protected communications between insurer and attorney hired by insurer to represent insured against the insured's assignee, but documents prepared in anticipation of case brought by assignee against insurer were protected from discovery by assignee); *Eureka Fin. Corp. v. Hartford Accident & Indem. Co.*, 136 F.R.D. 179 (E.D. Cal. 1991) (federal law; counsel waived any privileges by making improper blanket objection to discovery; allegedly privileged materials must be specifically identified); *Auto Owners Ins. Co. v. Totaltape, Inc.*, 135 F.R.D. 199 (M.D. Fla. 1990) (federal law; ordering insurer to produce certain interoffice memos, phone messages, claims file, and claims manual: insurer made insufficient showing that materials had been prepared "in anticipation of litigation"); *Central Constr. Co. v. Home Indem. Co.*, 794 P.2d 595 (Alaska 1990) (trial court should have granted motion to compel *in camera* review of insurer's attorney-client communications pursuant to "crime or fraud" exception to attorney-client privilege embodied in Alaska Evid. Rule 503(d)(1)); *State Farm Mut. Auto. Ins. Co. v. Lee*, 13 P.3d 1169 (Ariz. 2000) (attorney-client privilege is waived by even implicit invocation of advice-of-counsel defense); *Safeway Ins. Co. v. Superior Court*, 1995 WL 77870 (Ariz. Ct. App.) (where insurer expressly disavowed intent to rely on advice-of-counsel defense, no finding of implied waiver of attorney-client privilege could be based merely on one employee's deposition testimony that denial decision had been based in part on advice of counsel); *Zurich Am. Ins. v. Superior Court (Watts Indus.)*, 155 Cal. App. 4th 1485, 66 Cal. Rptr. 3d 833 (2007) (a document is not discoverable if (1) it contains discussion of legal advice or strategy of counsel; (2) insurer did not waive privilege by distributing it within corporation beyond those with "need to know"; (3) document was treated as confidential); *2,022 Ranch, LLC v. Superior Court*, 113 Cal. App. 4th 1377, 7 Cal. Rptr. 3d 197 (2003) (factual claim file information was not protected from discovery merely by virtue of fact that in-house claims adjusters were attorneys); *State Farm Fire & Casualty Co. v. Superior Court (Taylor)*, 54 Cal. App. 4th 625, 62 Cal. Rptr. 2d 834 (1997) (evidence of insurer's discovery abuses supported application of crime/fraud exception to dispel attorney-client privilege); *State Farm Fire & Casualty Co. v. Superior Court*, 216 Cal. App. 3d 1222, 265 Cal. Rptr. 372 (1989) (attorney-client privilege was not waived by virtue of fact that insurer communicated with both insured and its coverage counsel through same claims adjuster); *Freedom Trust v. Chubb Group of Ins. Cos.*, 38 F. Supp. 2d 1170 (C.D. Cal. 1999) (California law; Cal. Evid. Code §956, establishing a "crime-fraud" exception to attorney-client privilege, does not apply to tort of insurance bd faith); *Munoz v. State Farm Mut. Auto. Ins. Co.*, 968 P.2d 126 (Colo. Ct. App. 1998) (erroneous disclosure of insurer's protected documents did not prejudice trial); *Hutchinson v. Family Farm Casualty Ins. Co.*, 273 Conn. 33, 867 A.2d 1 (2005) (extending attorney-client privilege's crime/fraud exception to bad faith cases, but holding that to invoke that exception insured must make showing of probable cause to believe that insurer had used its attorneys to facilitate bad faith conduct); *Loftis v. Amica Mut. Ins. Co.*, 175 F.R.D. 5 (D. Conn. 1997) (Connecticut law; work product doctrine, though not attorney-client privilege, protected from discovery letter from outside counsel to insurer containing after-the-fact assessment of insurer's handling of claim); *Robarge v. Patriot Gen. Ins. Co.*, 42 Conn. Supp. 164, 608 A.2d 722 (Super. Ct. 1992) (questions put to deponent concerning circumstances of meeting involving insurer's agents and employees concerning investigation, adjustment, and defense of underlying claim did not seek discovery of "documents and tangible things" but rather sought discovery of "facts" that were not protected by work product rule); *Tackett v. State Farm Fire & Casualty Ins. Co.*, *supra* (where insurer makes factual representations that implicitly rely on advice of counsel as justification for denial, insurer cannot shield itself from disclosure of complete advice of counsel relevant to handling of claim and implicitly waives attorney-client privilege); *Genovese v. Provident Life & Accident Ins. Co.*, 74 So. 3d 1064 (Fla. 2011) (answering certified question; attorney-client privileged communications are not discoverable in action for first-party bad faith); *Allstate Indem. Co. v. Ruiz*, 899 So. 2d 1121 (Fla. 2005) (work product protection that may otherwise be afforded to documents prepared in anticipation of litigation of underlying coverage dispute does not automatically operate to protect such documents from discovery in ensuing or accompanying bad faith action; when underlying claim has been resolved, all files pertaining to that dispute are discoverable in first-party case as in common-law third-party bad faith cases); *United Servs. Auto. Ass'n v. Jennings*, 731 So. 2d 1258 (Fla. 1999) (third-party claimant was entitled to discover claim file for underlying tort action even though third-party claim was brought pursuant to stipulated judgment not excess judgment after trial); *Progressive Express Ins. Co. v. Scoma*, 975 So. 2d 461 (Fla. Dist. Ct. App. 2007) (attorney-client privilege precluded insured's judgment creditor from obtaining discovery of automobile liability insurer's confidential communications with attorney hired to represent insured in tort action; judgment creditor did not acquire insured's statutory rights under privilege even if she stood in his shoes as third-party beneficiary and had independent statutory right to sue insurer for bad faith failure to settle); *Florida Farm Bureau Gen. Life Ins. Co. v. Copertino*, 810 So. 2d 1076 (Fla. Dist. Ct. App. 2002) (work product doctrine protects claims file and litigation memos in situation where third-party claimant is alleging that insurer improperly exhausted insured's coverage limits in settling with other claimants); *State Farm Mut. Auto. Ins. Co. v. LaForet*, 591 So. 2d 1143 (Fla. Dist. Ct. App. 1992) (insured's bare assertion of need and undue hardship were insufficient to justify production of work product documentation in claim file: showing of need must consist of specific reasons and explanations); *General Accident Ins. Co. v. American Mut. Ins. Co.*, 562 So. 2d 414 (Fla. Dist. Ct. App. 1990) (trial judge erred in disregarding issue of possible work product privilege in ordering production of primary insurer's claim file); *Colonial Penn Ins. Co. v. Mayor*, 538 So. 2d 100 (Fla. Dist. Ct. App. 1989) (coverage must be established before entire claim file becomes discoverable); *Western States Ins. Co. v. O'Hara*, 357 Ill. App. 3d 509, 828 N.E.2d 842 (2005) (under common interest exception to attorney-client privilege doctrine, when insured asserts bad faith in connection with insurer's settlement with third party, insured may discover communications between insurer and attorney retained by insurer to give advice regarding that third-party claim); *Hartford Fin. Servs. Group, Inc. v. Lake County Park & Recreation Bd.*, 717 N.E.2d 1232 (Ind. Ct. App. 1999) (trial court erred in entering discovery order entitling plaintiff in first-party bad faith action access to insurer claim file); *Burr v. United Farm Bureau Mut. Ins. Co.*, 560 N.E.2d 1250 (Ind. Ct. App. 1990) (trial judge erred in ruling that work product privilege automatically protected all claim file documents dated after litigation counsel was hired; to invoke privilege, insurer should have been required to establish that specific documents were prepared in anticipation of litigation, rather than ordinary course of insurer's claims investigation activities); *Hicks v. Somers*, 567 So. 2d 1137 (La. Ct. App. 1990), *review denied*, 568 So. 2d 1044 (holding that *Hodges v. Southern Farm Bureau Casualty Ins. Co.*, 433 So. 2d 125 (La. 1983), does not permit blanket discovery of files of insurer's attorney unless same attorney also represented insured; declining to follow contrary holdings of *Cantrelle Fence & Supply Co. v. Allstate Ins. Co.*, 550 So. 2d 1306 (La. Ct. App. 1989), and *McHugh v. Chastant*, 503 So. 2d 791 (La. Ct. App. 1987), which "misread" *Hodges*); *Dixie Mill Supply Co. v. Continental Casualty Co.*, 168 F.R.D. 554 (E.D. La. 1996) (Louisiana law; insurer did not waive attorney-client privilege by chosing to defend bad faith case); *Dunn v. State Farm Fire & Casualty Co.*, 927 F.2d 869 (5th Cir. 1991) (Mississippi law; attorney-client privilege extended to all communications between insurer and attorneys retained for purpose of ascertaining legal obligations to insured: privilege was not waived with respect to investigative tasks performed by attorneys, provided tasks related to rendition of legal services); *State ex rel. Tracy v. Dandurand*, 30 S.W.3d 831 (Mo. 2000) (insurer waived attorney-client privilege with respect to documents provided to its retained expert designated for trial); *Holmgren v. State Farm Mut. Auto. Ins. Co.*, 976 F.2d 573 (9th Cir. 1992) (Montana law; opinion work product was discoverable where insurer's mental impressions were at issue and need for material was compelling); *California State Auto. Ass'n Inter-Ins. Bureau v. Eighth Judicial Dist. Court*, 788 P.2d 1367 (Nev. 1990) (denying insurer's petition for writ to vacate trial court's order compelling discovery of claim file; insurer's failure to raise privilege issues in opposition to motion to compel discovery had prevented trial judge from making any reviewable factual findings concerning validity of insurer's privilege arguments); *Evans v. United Serv. Auto. Ass'n*, 541 S.E.2d 782 (N.C. Ct. App. 2001) (endorsing "case-by-case" approach, but stating that documents prepared by insurer before denial of claim are generally not protected as work product or by attorney-client privilege because they are not prepared in anticipation of litigation); *Boone v. Vanliner Ins. Co.*, 91 Ohio St. 3d 209, 744 N.E.2d 154 (2001) (abrogating attorney-client privilege in cases alleging bad faith denial of coverage); *Stewart v. Siciliano*, 985 N.E.2d 226 (Ohio Ct. App. 2012) (insured was entitled to discovery of insurer's claims file, which contained otherwise privileged attorney-client communications, but trial court had to conduct in camera review before ordering its discovery); *Whitacre v. Nationwide Ins. Co.*, 2012-Ohio-4557, 2012 WL 4712518 (Ohio Ct. App. 2012) (attorney-client privilege did not protect entire contents of claims file, and work product doctrine did not prevent non-policy holder from taking depositions of insurer's claims representative, or preclude trial court from allowing discovery of insurer's claims file); *Unklesbay v. Fenwick*, 167 Ohio App. 3d 408, 855 N.E.2d 516 (2006) (claims file materials showing insurer's lack of good faith in processing, evaluating, or refusing to pay claim were unworthy of protection afforded by attorney-client or work-product privilege); *Garg v. State Auto. Mut. Ins. Co.*, 155 Ohio App. 3d 258, 800 N.E.2d 757 (2003) (claim file documents were not protected from discovery despite fact they were created prior to denial of claim); *Mid-American Nat'l Bank & Trust Co. v. Cincinnati Ins. Co.*, 74 Ohio App. 3d 481, 599 N.E.2d 699 (1991) (insurer waived attorney-client privilege when it disclosed portion of contents of independent counsel's opinion); *Allied World Assurance Co. v. Lincoln Gen. Ins. Co.*, 280 F.R.D. 197 (M.D. Pa. 2012) (work product privilege was inapplicable to communications between excess insurer and primary insurer's retained defense counsel concerning defense of insureds, and attorney-client privilege did not attach to communications among primary insurer's attorney, the insurer, and the insureds); *In re Mt. Hawley Ins. Co.*, 427 S.C. 159, 829 S.E.2d 707 (2019) (discussed in this section; holding that an insurer's denial of bad faith or assertion of good faith in its answer does not, without more, place privileged communication "at issue," thereby waiving the privilege); *Dakota, Minn. & Eastern R.R. Corp. v. Acuity*, 771 N.W.2d 623 (S.D. 2009) (where insurer unequivocally delegates its initial claims function and relies exclusively on outside counsel to conduct investigation and determination of coverage, attorney-client privilege does not protect communications between insurer and that outside counsel); *In re Texas Farmers Ins. Exch.*, 990 S.W.2d 737 (Tex. Ct. App. 1999), *petition for mandamus denied*, 12 S.W.3d 807 (Tex. 2000) (work product rule but not attorney-client privilege protected file of attorney hired as investigator to conduct examinations under oath of fire insurance policyholders); *Aetna Casualty & Sur. Co. v. Blackman*, 810 S.W.2d 438 (Tex. Ct. App. 1991) (insurer who had failed to segregate materials on basis of whether they had been used by expert witness in forming mental impressions and opinions was precluded from claiming any privilege against disclosure of any material in possession of expert); *Cedell v. Farmers Ins. Co. of Washington*, 176 Wash. 2d 686, 295 P.3d 239 (banc 2013) (insurer may overcome presumption of discoverability of attorney-client communications in first-party bad faith litigation by showing that its attorney was not involved in quasi-fiduciary tasks of investigating or evaluating or processing insured's claim, but instead was providing insurer with counsel as to its own potential liability); *Leahy v. State Farm Mut. Auto. Ins. Co.*, 3 Wash. App. 2d 613, 418 P.3d 175 (2018) (holding trial court did not abuse its discretion when it denied underinsured motorist (UIM) plaintiff-insured discovery of documents in insurer's claim file based on attorney-client privilege and work product doctrine; UIM plaintiff faces higher bar for discovering privileged information; trial court followed proper procedure by reviewing documents in camera); *Barry v. USAA*, 989 P.2d 1172 (Wash. Ct. App. 1999) (in bad faith action relating to underinsured motorist claim, all communications between insurer and its lawyer were privileged; distinguishing situations where attorney first represented insured in action against tortfeasor and later handles insurer's defense to underinsured motorist claim); *State of W. Va. v. Madden*, 215 W. Va. 705, 601 S.E.2d 25 (2004) (discussing principles, modeled on federal rules, governing crime-fraud exception to attorney-client privilege and work-product doctrine and holding such principles fully applicable in context of first-party bad faith litigation). *State ex rel. Medical Assurance, Inc. v. Recht*, 583 S.E.2d 80 (W. Va. 2003) (addressing issues relative to application of privilege in bad faith actions by third-party claimants and holding that insured's protections were not lost merely because materials had been shared with insurer).

In *In re Mt. Hawley Ins. Co.*, *supra*, the Supreme Court of South Carolina addressed the question of when the attorney-client privilege is deemed waived by an insurer in bad faith litigation. A narrow question was certified to the state high court by the U.S. Court of Appeals for the Fourth

Circuit: "Does South Carolina law support application of the 'at issue' exception to attorney-client privilege such that a party may waive the privilege by denying liability in its answer?" 427 S.C. at 162, 829 S.E.2d at 709. The South Carolina high court answered "no," and noted that it found little authority supporting "the untenable proposition that the mere denial of liability in a pleading constitutes a waiver of the attorney-client privilege." *Id.* The court then reviewed three approaches to attorney-client privilege in the insurance bad faith context from different states: (1) a "substantial minority" approach extending the crime-fraud exception to the privilege to include any tort, including insurance bad faith, with the result that the entire pre-denial claim file is discoverable; (2) on the other extreme, upholding the privilege absent a party's direct, express reliance on a privileged communication in making a claim or defense; and (3) a middle-ground approach involving a case-by-case analysis of the facts, as set out in a case from the Supreme Court of Arizona, *State Farm Mut. Auto. Ins. Co. v. Lee*, *supra*. The *Lee* court held that the insurer impliedly waived the attorney-client privilege when it took the position that its interpretation of the policy at issue and handling the claim depended on its subjective interpretation of the law, as guided by advice from counsel. The *Mt. Hawley* court found that approach to be reasonable and adopted the *Lee* framework. The court concluded that this approach "is the most consistent with South Carolina's policy of strictly construing the attorney-client privilege and requiring waiver to be 'distinct and unequivocal.'" *Id.* at 177, 829 S.E.2d at 717. The court noted, however, that the approach could place insurers in a difficult situation in responding to insureds' allegations of subjective bad faith.

§3.71 2. Discovery of Similar Claims Files

—Cases ruling on the discoverability of similar claims files have included the following: *Champion Int'l Corp. v.*

Liberty Mut. Ins. Co., 128 F.R.D. 608 (S.D.N.Y. 1989) (federal law; similar claim files of other insureds held discoverable); *Ex parte O'Neal*, 713 So. 2d 956 (Ala. 1998) (although insured was entitled to interrogatory answers regarding other lawsuits, undue burden was placed on insurer by questions asking for names of other insureds whose claims had been handled by particular adjuster); *Underwriters at Lloyd's London v. Narrows*, 846 P.2d 118 (Alaska 1993) (trial court abused discretion in failing to determine willfulness of insurer's initial noncompliance with discovery order relating to other claims files before granting extreme sanction of striking insurer's answer); *State Farm Mut. Auto. Ins. Co. v. Superior Court (Miel)*, 167 Ariz. 135, 804 P.2d 1323 (1991) (trial court abused discretion in ordering overbroad and burdensome production of other claims documents); *Hawkins v. Allstate Ins. Co.*, 152 Ariz. 490, 733 P.2d 1073, *cert. denied*, 484 U.S. 874 (1987) (see also book §§1.9, 1.66; holding admissible evidence of insurer's handling of other similar claims); *Pollock v. Superior Court*, 93 Cal. App. 4th 817, 113 Cal. Rptr. 2d 453 (2001) (psychotherapist-patient privilege would be impermissibly violated by granting plaintiff's request for names of other claimants whose psychiatric disability claims had been denied by defendant insurer; distinguishing *Colonial Life & Accident Ins. Co. v. Superior Court*, 31 Cal. 3d 785, 183 Cal. Rptr. 810 (1982)); *National Sec. Fire & Casualty Co. v. Dunn*, 751 So. 2d 777 (Fla. Dist. Ct. App. 2000) (overly broad discovery order relative to similar claims files violated attorney-client privilege and work product doctrine in absence of showing of compelling need, and order failed to give proper consideration to privacy rights of other insureds); *Bloom v. Mutual of Omaha Ins. Co.*, 557 N.Y.S.2d 614 (App. Div. 1990) (modifying trial court's discovery order to protect agent's business files other than files concerning other policy cancellations since those related to agent's "alleged history of filing incorrect or fraudulent applications"); *Humphreys v. Caldwell*, 888 S.W.2d 469

(Tex. 1994) (insurer failed to adequately prove harassment and burden in objecting to discovery of files concerning all lawsuits defended in previous five years); *Alpha Life Ins. Co. v. Gayle*, 796 S.W.2d 834 (Tex. Ct. App. 1990) (issuing writ ordering trial judge to vacate order compelling discovery of unredacted copies of similar claim files; privacy interests of other insureds required masking of names and addresses); *West Virginia ex rel. W. Va. Fire & Casualty Co. v. Karl*, 505 S.E.2d 210 (W. Va. 1998) (insurer would be required to produce similar claims files redacted to protect identities of other insureds, per approach of *Colonial Life & Accident Ins. Co. v. Superior Court, supra*, discussed in book §3.72).

§3.75 C. Interrogatories: Sample Interrogatory

—Concerning the insurer's duty to update interrogatory answers, see *Polk v. Dixie Ins. Co.*, 897 F.2d 1346 (5th Cir. 1990) (Mississippi law). In *Polk*, an action involving an insurer's arson defense to a claim for the loss of an automobile by fire, the insured unsuccessfully argued on appeal that the trial judge had abused his discretion in permitting a defense witness to offer evidence of an arson motive on the insured's part that had not been disclosed in interrogatory answers seven months previously.

§3.81 D. Depositions

—In *State Farm Mut. Auto. Ins. Co. v. Schlossberg*, 82 Md. App. 45, 570 A.2d 328 (1990), a Maryland Court of Appeals affirmed a default judgment that had been entered against the insurer on the ground of a "wholesale" failure to comply with discovery. The court acknowledged that at one point in the dispute the trial judge had abused his discretion in entering an order compelling discovery without giving the insurer a reasonable opportunity to contest. That error was subsequently rendered harmless, however, the court reasoned, when following the insurer's noncompliance with the discovery order, the trial judge had entered a default judgment only conditionally, and had given the insurer a chance to cure its noncompliance—a chance of which the insurer had "willfully and contumaciously" failed to take advantage.

—For a second case involving imposition of sanctions against an insurer for noncompliance with discovery orders, see *Allstate Tex. Lloyds v. Johnson*, 784 S.W.2d 100 (Tex. Ct. App. 1989). The court of appeals held that the trial judge had not abused his discretion in ordering that all of Allstate's pleadings be struck, that Allstate be prohibited from engaging in further discovery, and that Allstate pay the insured's costs in deposing a totally uncooperative Allstate adjuster. The adjuster had invoked, through Allstate's counsel, completely unfounded claims of privilege and had refused to answer many questions on the basis of spurious objections.

VIII. DISCOVERY BY DEFENDANT

§3.84 A. Production of Documents

—In *Midkiff v. Shaver*, 788 S.W.2d 399 (Tex. Ct. App. 1990), a Texas Court of Appeals issued a writ vacating a trial court order compelling the insureds to provide discovery of their full medical histories in connection with their claim for $45,000 in emotional distress damages for the insurer's nonpayment of a claim for water damage to the insured's building. Since the insureds were alleging only the ordinary emotional response to the insurer's alleged breach of duty, the court of appeals held, the trial judge had abused his discretion in ordering discovery of medical records beyond those dealing with the particular symptoms allegedly caused by the insurer's conduct in the present case.

C. Interrogatories and Depositions

§3.86 1. Basic Guidelines

—See *Jones v. State Farm Fire & Casualty Co.*, 129 F.R.D. 170 (N.D. Ill. 1990) (federal law), in which the court rejected the argument that the insurer was not entitled to depose the insured because the insured had already given the insurer a 61-page statement and submitted to a 106-page examination under oath, in connection with his fire insurance claim. The court reasoned that there was no reason to assume that the deposition would cover areas already covered, and that the insured could make a motion for a protective order under Rule 30(d), if and when the need arose, to ensure that the deposition was limited to new areas of inquiry.

4

Trial and Posttrial Procedures

II. POSTTRIAL PROCEDURES §4.37

I. TRIAL

§4.5   B. Motion To Bifurcate Issues

—In *Shade Foods, Inc. v. Innovative Prods. Sales & Marketing, Inc.*, 78 Cal. App. 4th 847, 93 Cal. Rptr. 2d 364 (2000), the court discussed the "undeniable advantages" of conducting separate trials on liability and coverage, but held that given the "highly unusual circumstances" of the present case the trial judge had not abused his discretion in ordering a consolidated trial.

—In *Novell v. American Guar. & Liab. Ins. Co.*, 15 P.3d 775 (Colo. Ct. App. 1999), a Colorado Court of Appeals rejected the argument that the trial court had abused its discretion denying the insurer's motion to bifurcate the case into separate trials for breach of contract and bad faith claims. The court noted that bifurcation would have involved a significant duplication of evidence and attorneys' fees.

—Under Florida law, an insured's claim, under Fla. Stat. Ann. §624.155(1)(b)(1), for failing to settle a claim in good faith does not accrue before the conclusion of the underlying litigation for the contractual uninsured motorist insurance benefits. *Cunningham v. Standard Guar. Ins. Co.*, 630 So. 2d 179 (Fla. 1994); *Blanchard v. State Farm Mut. Auto. Ins. Co.*, 575 So. 2d 1289 (Fla. 1991); *Imhof v. Nationwide Mut. Ins. Co.*, 634 So. 2d 617 (Fla. 1994); *Maryland Casualty Co. v. Alicia Diagnostic, Inc.*, 961 So. 2d 1091 (Fla. Dist. Ct. App. 2007); *Vanguard Fire & Casualty Co. v. Golmon*, 955 So. 2d 591 (Fla. Dist. Ct. App. 2006); *Hartford Ins. Co. v. Mainstream Constr. Group, Inc.*, 864 So. 2d 1270 (Fla. Dist. Ct. App. 2004); *Liberty Mut. Ins. Co. v. Farm, Inc.*, 754 So. 2d 865 (Fla. Dist. Ct. App. 2000); *State Farm Mut. Auto. Ins. Co. v. Cook*, 744 So. 2d 567 (Fla. Dist. Ct. App. 1999); *General Star Indem. Co. v. Anheuser-Busch Cos.*, 741 So. 2d 1259 (Fla. Dist. Ct. App. 1999); *Allstate Ins. Co. v. Baughman*, 741 So. 2d 624 (Fla. Dist. Ct. App. 1999); *Doan v. John Hancock Mut. Ins. Co.*, 727 So. 2d 400 (Fla. Dist. Ct. App. 1999); *State Farm Mut. Auto. Ins. Co. v. Oteiza*, 595 So. 2d 1095 (Fla. Dist. Ct. App. 1992). In *Blanchard*, the state supreme court therefore held that the insured did not impermissibly split his cause of action by not asserting his bad faith claim in his original state court action under Fla. Stat. Ann. §627.727. After obtaining a favorable resolution of that claim, the insured had then filed a diversity action in federal district court under Fla. Stat. Ann. §624.155, which provides Florida's civil remedy for first-party bad faith. (The supreme court in *Blanchard* overruled a contrary holding in *Schimmel v. Aetna Casualty & Sur. Co.*, 506 So. 2d 1162 (Fla. Dist. Ct. App. 1987).) *Blanchard* was subsequently followed in the third-party case *XL Specialty Ins. Co. v. Skystream, Inc.*, 988 So.2d 96 (Fla. Dist. Ct. App. 2008), but was distinguished in *Clough v. Government Employees Ins. Co.*, 636 So. 2d 127, 130 (Fla. Dist. Ct. App. 1994), where the court wrote:

> While *Blanchard* does hold that in ordinary circumstances, an insured must obtain a judgment in excess of policy limits before prosecuting a first party bad faith claim, it is clear that it is the establishment of the fact that such damages were incurred and not their precise amount which forms the basis for a subsequent first party cause of action for bad faith. There is no sound reason for refusing to allow parties to stipulate to damages in excess of available policy limits in the underlying litigation and then pursuing a bad faith claim wherein, at the appropriate point, the precise amount of such damages can be determined.

In *State Farm Mut. Auto. Ins. Co. v. Tranchese*, 49 So. 2d 809 (Fla. Dist. Ct. App. 2010), the court held that the insurer was entitled to have a bad faith claim abated pending a final determination of coverage and damages for the underlying uninsured motorist claim, and that the insured was not entitled to discovery related to the insurer's business practices until after the obligation to provide coverage and damages had been determined.

—The Iowa Supreme Court, in *Handley v. Farm Bureau Mut. Ins. Co.*, 467 N.W.2d 247 (Iowa 1991), held that the trial court had abused its discretion in denying the insurer's motion to sever claims against it for underinsured motorist coverage, and for bad faith failure to pay benefits, from a wrongful death action against the negligent driver. The court reasoned that even though the negligence of the other driver had been established, and evidence of insurance therefore would not prejudice the jury's liability decision, it was likely that evidence of insurance would cause the jury to return a larger verdict against the other driver.

—Granting a writ of supervisory control, the Montana Supreme Court held that the trial court had abused its discretion in denying the insured's motion to impanel only one jury to hear, *seriatim*, bifurcated contract and bad faith claims. The method the insured sought, the court held, would avoid relitigation and would serve the interests of judicial economy, fairness, and clarity. *Malta Pub. Sch. Dist. v. Montana Seventeenth Judicial Dist. Court*, 938 P.2d 1335 (Mont. 1997).

—In *Eizen Fineburg & McCarthy, P.C. v. Ironshore Specialty Ins. Co.*, 319 F.R.D. 209 (E.D. Pa. 2017) (Pennsylvania law), the court denied the insurer's motion to bifurcate the insured's statutory and common-law bad faith claims from the insured's breach of contract claim. The court found that a verdict in favor of the insurer on the breach of contract claim would not necessarily obviate the need to try the bad faith claims because some of the conduct alleged as bad faith was conduct that was separate from the contract claim. The court found that litigating the claims together would not prejudice the insurer with extra cost or privilege issues during discovery.

—In *Bartlett v. John Hancock Mut. Life Ins. Co.*, 538 A.2d 997 (R.I. 1998), the Rhode Island Supreme Court held that discovery on a bad faith claim should be stayed pending resolution of underlying coverage issues. See also *Imperial Casualty & Indem. Co. v. Bellini*, 746 A.2d 130 (R.I. 2000) (trial and motion judges, confronted with a bad faith claim filed simultaneously with a breach of contract claim, must sever the two claims and allow discovery only insofar as it is relevant to the contract claim, and defer discovery in the bad faith claim until complaining party has proven underlying breach of contract claim).

—In *State Farm Mut. Auto. Ins. Co. v. Wilborn*, 835 S.W.2d 260 (Tex. Ct. App. 1992), the court granted the insurer's petition for writ of mandamus, ordering the trial court to vacate its denial of the insurer's motion for separate trials on an uninsured motorist claim and a bad faith claim. Since the bad faith claim was based on a settlement offer, and since evidence of settlement offers would be inadmissible relative to the uninsured motorist claim, severance of the two claims was necessary to avoid prejudice, the court explained. Accord *Texas Farmers Ins. Co. v. Stem*, 927 S.W.2d 76 (Tex. Ct. App. 1996); *F.A. Richard & Assocs. v. Millard*, 856 S.W.2d 765 (Tex. Ct. App. 1993); *United States Fire Ins. Co. v. Millard*, 847 S.W.2d 668 (Tex. Ct. App. 1993). Compare *Liberty Mut. Fire Ins. Co. v. Akin*, 927 S.W.2d 627 (Tex. 1996) (trial court did not abuse discretion under circumstances in refusing to sever contract and bad faith claims).

—Affirming a judgment and awards of compensatory and punitive damages on a bad faith cause of action relating to the insurer's nonpayment of a claim under a homeowner's policy, the West Virginia Supreme Court of Appeals, in *Berry v. Nationwide Mut. Fire Ins. Co.*, 381 S.E.2d 367 (W. Va. 1989), rejected the insurer's argument, *inter alia*, that the trial judge had abused his discretion in denying a motion to bifurcate the issues of breach of contract and punitive damages. Noting that the insurer rested its argument on *Jenkins v. J.C. Penney Casualty Ins. Co.*, 280 S.E.2d 252 (W. Va. 1981), where it was held that an implied statutory cause of action may not be maintained until the underlying claim is resolved, the court emphasized the important distinction between third-party cases such as *Jenkins*, and the first-party context of the present case. The court acknowledged that bifurcation could have been ordered under W. Va. R. Civ. P. 42(c), but that such an order is purely permissive on the part of the trial judge. "In this case," the court concluded, "there is no showing that the appellant has been prejudiced by the circuit court's refusal to try the issues of breach of contract and punitive damages separately." 381 S.E.2d at 373. See also *Light v. Allstate Ins. Co.*, 506 S.E.2d 64 (W. Va. 1998) (bifurcation of contract and bad faith claims is not mandatory in first-party cases arising under unfair claims settlement practices statute). Compare *Smith v. Westfield Ins. Co.*, 932 F. Supp. 770 (S.D. W. Va. 1996) (bad faith claim must be severed from claim for underinsured motorist benefits, and bad faith claim must be stayed pending resolution of contract claim). Other aspects of the *Berry* decision are discussed in supplement §§1.66, 2.24, 4.34.

—In *Dahmen v. American Family Mut. Ins. Co.*, 635 N.W.2d 1 (Wis. Ct. App. 2001), it was held that the trial judge had erred in denying the insurer's motion to bifurcate claims for underinsured motorist benefits and bad faith, and to stay discovery on the bad faith claim. The court noted that on the bad faith claim, but not on the UIM claim, the insured would be entitled to discover work product and attorney-client information. The risk of jury confusion and prejudice from a consolidated trial would be substantial, the court emphasized, and the interests of judicial economy and possible settlement would not be enhanced.

E. Presenting Evidence

1. Plaintiff's Examination of Witnesses

c. Expert Witnesses

§4.15 (1) Attorney

—For an opinion deploring the misuse, in a first-party bad faith case, of overbroad expert legal testimony that had invaded the province of the judge, see *Kyle v. United Servs. Auto. Ass'n*, 30 Cal. Rptr. 2d 163 (Cal. Ct. App. 1994). (Note that the California Supreme Court ordered depublication of the Kyle opinion on August 11, 1994. While the opinion is thus no longer citable, it still appears in the bound volume of the California Reporter, and may be valuable for its reasoning and argument.) For another opinion unfavorable to the use of expert testimony concerning claims-handling standards and practices, see *Thompson v. State Farm Fire & Casualty Co.*, 34 F.3d 932 (10th Cir. 1994) (Oklahoma law).

—There was no error in the admission of expert attorney

testimony concerning applicable standards of insurer good faith, a Colorado Court of Appeals held in *Southerland v. Argonaut Ins. Co.*, 794 P.2d 1102 (Colo. Ct. App. 1990), affirming a judgment for a workers' compensation claimant and awards of $60,000 in compensatory damages and $25,000 in punitives. The evidence supporting the jury finding of bad faith included evidence of repeated late and inadequate payments, failure to supply requested information, and a general attitude of noncooperation. With respect to the challenged expert testimony by an attorney, who assessed the insurer's conduct against the legal standard of good faith and standards in the insurance industry, the court first rejected the argument that only persons with experience in the insurance industry can qualify as experts on the industry's operations. The court acknowledged that the attorney-expert may have misstated the applicable legal standard of good faith, appearing to equate the standard to mere reasonableness and omitting any element of willfullness or reckless disregard. But any error in that regard was either harmless or waived, the court reasoned, because the jury was subsequently instructed by the court on the correct standard, and because counsel for the insurer had failed to bring out the correct standard in the form of an objection or on cross-examination. See also *Novell v. American Guar. & Liab. Ins. Co.*, 15 P.3d 775 (Colo. Ct. App. 1999); *Klein v. State Farm Mut. Auto. Ins. Co.*, 948 P.2d 43 (Colo. Ct. App. 1997).

—Applying Kansas law, a federal district court, in *Moses v. Halstead*, 477 F. Supp. 2d 1119 (D. Kan. 2007), held that even though most of the facts were not so complicated as to require the testimony of an expert witness, the testimony of an attorney concerning the process of handling an insurance defense case and the applicable standard of care would be helpful to the Court. The insurer's motion to strike the expert testimony was therefore overruled.

—*Cf. Peterson v. Western Nat'l Mut. Ins. Co.*, 946 N.W.2d 903, 915 (Minn. 2020) (in considering insured's claim for bad faith failure to investigate, rejecting insurer's defense that it relied on opinion of its litigation attorney that insurer could prevail in a jury trial when it declined coverage under underinsured motorists policy; relevant inquiry was not "[w]hether an insurer may possibly convince a jury at trial," but rather "whether a reasonable insurer, having conducted a full investigation and a fair evaluation that considers and weighs all of the facts before it, would have denied the insured the benefits of the insurance policy in the first place"; insurer could not "hide behind the advice of outside litigation counsel").

—In *Nooter Corp. v. Allianz Underwriters Ins. Co.*, 536 S.W.3d 251 (Mo. Ct. App. 2017), the court relied on the expert testimony of two attorneys in upholding a jury verdict finding that the insurer's failure to pay the insured's third-party asbestos claims was a vexatious refusal to pay under Mo. Rev. Stat. §§375.420 and 375.297. One attorney testified that the insurer's conduct fell short of the customs and practices in the insurance industry and provided specific examples of conduct in letters sent by the insurer. The other attorney was corporate counsel for the insured.

—In a failure-to-settle case, a Pennsylvania court held that there was no error in admitting evidence that three different trial judges in the underlying medical malpractice action had expressed the opinion that the insurer should settle within policy limits. Holding that the judges' opinion statements were relevant in determining whether the insurer's decision not to settle had been objective and intelligent, the court noted with approval that the trial court had not allowed plaintiff to call the judges as live witnesses and had instructed the jury on the limited purpose of the evidence. *Birth Ctr. v. St. Paul Cos.*, 727 A.2d 1144 (Pa. Super. Ct. 1999), *appeal granted*, Mar. 1, 2000.

—In *Gosney v. Fireman's Fund Ins. Co.*, 3 Wash. App. 2d 828, 419 P.3d 447 (2018), *review denied*, 191 Wash. 2d 1017 (2018) the court held that the trial court did not err in limiting the scope of expert attorney testimony where the attorney's testimony at trial was contrary to his deposition testimony, and where the testimony at trial was not based on new information gleaned at trial.

§4.16 (2) Claims Expert

—An insurer's proffered testimony by a claims handling expert should have been admitted as relevant to the issue of the insurer's bad faith in interpreting a contractual provision, it was held in *Amerigraphics v. Mercury Casualty Co.*, 182 Cal. App. 4th 1538, 107 Cal. Rptr. 3d 307 (2010). The testimony would have provided evidence that the insurer's incorrect interpretation of the provision was at least reasonable under industry standards.

In *Hangarter v. Provident Life & Accident Ins. Co.*, 373 F.3d 998 (9th Cir. 2004) (California law), the Ninth Circuit held that the district court did not err in admitting expert testimony regarding bad faith issues even though the district court had failed to hold a formal *Daubert* hearing. Although the district court had mistakenly believed that *Daubert* and *Kumho* did not apply to the witness's nonscientific testimony, it had nonetheless performed its gatekeeping function by making a reliability determination after probing the expert's knowledge and experience. Nor, the Ninth Circuit held, was the rule against expert opinions on ultimate issues violated by the expert's testimony that the insurer had deviated from industry standards in terminating the insured's disability benefits.

—In *American Family Mut. Ins. Co. v. Allen*, 102 P.3d 333 (Colo. banc 2004), the Supreme Court of Colorado held that in a first-party bad faith action, expert testimony is not required to establish the insurer's standard of care when a statute (here, the Unfair Claims Practices Act, C.R.S.A. §§10-3-1101 et seq.) provides valid, though not conclusive, evidence of the standard of care and when that standard is within the common knowledge and experience of the average juror. Accord *Fisher v. State Farm Mut. Auto. Ins. Co.*,

419 P.3d 985 (Colo. Ct. App. 2015), *aff'd*, 418 P.3d 501 (Colo. 2018); *TBL Collectibles, Inc. v. Owners Ins. Co.*, 285 F. Supp. 3d 1170 (D. Colo. 2018) (discussed in this section). See also *Gustafson v. American Family Mut. Ins. Co.*, 901 F. Supp. 2d 1289 (D. Colo. 2012) (in context of third-party bad faith claim, expert testimony is not required to establish reasonableness of insurer's conduct where standard of care does not entail specialized knowledge beyond that of average juror).

In *TBL Collectibles, Inc. v. Owners Ins. Co.*, *supra*, the federal district court applying Colorado law granted the insured's motion to exclude testimony of the insurer's expert, an insurance law attorney, to the extent the court found the testimony to be irrelevant. The court denied the motion to dismiss the expert's testimony regarding Colorado insurance regulations pertaining to the reasonableness of an insurer's delay or denial of claims payment.

In *O'Sullivan v. Geico Casualty Co.*, 233 F. Supp. 3d 917 (D. Colo. 2017), the court denied in part and granted in part the insurer's motion to strike the insured's claims expert who was to testify on a bad faith claim related to the insurer's obligation to reform an existing uninsured motorist policy. The court allowed testimony on the relevant industry standards for handling such a claim, and it allowed the expert's opinion on ways the insurer departed from industry standards. The court did not allow the expert to offer an opinion on whether the insurer's overall process was reasonable or contrary to its duty of good faith and fair dealing.

In *Wahlert v. Am. Standard Ins. Co. of Wis.*, 173 F. Supp. 3d 1187 (D. Colo. 2016), the court noted that the claims practices consultant hired as an expert by the plaintiff presented as unknowledgeable and unqualified when the consultant attempted to show a pattern on the part of the insurer by criticizing how the insurer handled similar cases and made broad assertions without offering specific facts to support them.

—In *Jefferson Ins. Co. v. Dunn*, 224 Ga. App. 732, 482 S.E.2d 383 (1997), a Georgia Court of Appeals explained that expert testimony regarding the standards, practices, and customs of the insurance business were relevant to whether the defendant insurer had acted in bad faith in denying coverage and failing to settle a third-party claim. The court found no error in a series of evidentiary rulings relative to such testimony that recognized its relevance and admissibility in general, but sustained objections where the testimony had threatened to invade the province of the jury. See also *Butler v. First Acceptance Ins. Co.*, 652 F. Supp. 2d 1264 (N.D. Ga. 2009) (Georgia law; attorney who specialized in personal injury law was not qualified to offer expert testimony relating to standard of care applicable to insurance claims adjuster who receives time-limited demand letter).

—In *Nassen v. National States Ins. Co.*, 494 N.W.2d 231 (Iowa 1992), *cert. denied*, 507 U.S. 1031 (1993), the Iowa Supreme Court held that the trial court had properly admitted expert testimony that the defendant nursing home insurer had been engaging in "cash flow underwriting" and "postclaim underwriting." Such testimony was admissible to provide the basis for the expert's opinion that the insurer had been using a fraudulent underwriting technique. The admissibility of such testimony was not governed by the Rule of Evidence concerning whether conduct on a particular occasion was in conformity with habit or practice, but rather by Rules pertaining to the bases upon which an admissible expert opinion may be formed.

—In *King v. GEICO Indem. Co.*, 712 Fed. Appx. 649 (9th Cir. 2017) (unpublished) (Montana law), the court held that the trial court did not abuse its discretion by admitting the insured's expert's testimony where the expert did not address an ultimate issue of law, but rather testified about how the claim was handled in relation to industry standards.

—Affirming a judgment for the insurer, the New Mexico

Supreme Court, in *Shamalon Bird Farm v. United States Fidelity and Guar. Co.*, 111 N.M. 713, 809 P.2d 627 (1991), held that the trial court had not abused its discretion in excluding the proposed testimony of a plaintiff's expert witness. The court explained that the expert's deposition showed that although he had worked as an insurance adjuster, he had never handled a claim like the one at issue (under a business interruption policy), and had received no training in the area. The expert's lack of preparation for his deposition, and his inability to explain the basis of his opinions, also meant, the court added, that the insurer would have been deprived of a reasonable opportunity to prepare its trial cross-examination. See also *Garcia v. Metropolitan Life Ins. Co.*, 859 F. Supp. 2d 1229, 2012 WL 1660606 (D. N. Mex. 2012) (granting motion to exclude testimony of insured's bad faith expert in action involving cancellation of disability insurance benefits where expert's deposition testimony indicated that she was not qualified to render medical opinions and that she had no experience with claims handling in New Mexico).

—In *Furr v. State Farm Mut. Auto. Ins. Co.*, 128 Ohio App. 3d 607, 716 N.E.2d 250 (1998), an Ohio Court of Appeals, affirming awards of compensatory and punitive damages in a bad faith action involving a claim for uninsured motorist benefits, held that the trial court had not abused its discretion in permiting plaintiff's expert, an insurance lawyer, to present opinions concerning casualty insurance, uninsured motorist insurance, reserves, bad faith claims, the Ohio Administrative Code, and an insurer's duty to its insured in connection with the processing and investigation of claims.

—An Oklahoma Court of Appeals, in *Hall v. Globe Life & Accident Ins. Co.*, 968 P.2d 1263 (Okla. Civ. App. 1998), *cert. denied*, held that the trial court in a bad faith action involving a life insurance claim did not abuse its discretion in permitting expert testimony concerning insurance investigations, the central issue in the case.

—Affirming a judgment for the insurer in a bad faith action involving a dispute over underinsured motorist benefits, an appellate court in Pennsylvania held that the trial judge had not abused his discretion in disallowing expert testimony on how claims are properly managed and evaluated, and as to whether the insurer had a reasonable basis for denying the insured's claim in the present case. The court expressed the view that bad faith is ordinarily a concept that does not require specialized knowledge, and held that this was true in the present case. *Bergman v. United States Servs. Auto. Ass'n*, 742 A.2d 1101 (Pa. Super. Ct. 1999). But see *Mohney v. American Gen. Life Ins. Co.*, 116 A.3d 1123, 2015 PA Super 113, *appeal denied*, 130 A.3d 1291 (Pa. 2015) (vacating judgment for insurer and remanding for new trial on issue of bad faith; ruling that trial court abused its discretion in excluding insured's claims expert because "[t]he issue in question, involving the standards in the insurance industry for the training of claim adjusters in applying legal precedent when deciding insurance claims, is sufficiently complex" to permit expert testimony).

—In *Crow v. United Benefit Life Ins. Co.*, 2001 WL 285231 (N.D. Tex. 2001) (Texas law), the court excluded expert testimony on the grounds that it would have invaded the province of both the jury and the court. In her proposed testimony, the expert would have defined the standard of good faith and fair dealing and listed 19 actions taken by the insurer that breached that standard. The case involved the insurer's denial of authorization and payment for medical treatment. See also *Southland Lloyds Ins. Co. v. Cantu*, 399 S.W.3d 558, 2011 WL 1158244 (Tex. App. 2011) (affirming judgment for insureds; independent insurance adjuster's testimony on estimated cost to repair home was sufficiently relevant and reliable to be admissible expert testimony).

§4.17 d. Plaintiff

—In *Rinehart v. Shelter Gen. Ins. Co.*, 261 S.W.3d 583 (Mo. Ct. App. 2008), it was held that in an insured's action against an automobile insurer for bad faith failure to settle third parties' personal injury claims, the trial court did not err in admitting testimony by the insured concerning the financial pressure that had motivated his agreement with the third parties to pursue a bad faith claim. The court rejected the argument that his testimony ran afoul of the general prohibition on injecting a litigant's financial condition to influence the jury. The court wrote (261 S.W.3d at 590):

> Rinehart's explanatory comments regarding the agreement were relevant to prove his emotional distress as a part of the damages on his bad faith claim. His petition alleged that he "suffered mental agony, distress, anxiety, and worry as a result of being faced with a substantial judgment against him." Rinehart's testimony about the financial pressure he felt from the judgment . . . was necessary to explain the factors causing him emotional distress as a direct result of Shelter's failure to pay the claims of the accident victims.

§4.19A   g. Insured's Damages [NEW]

In *Wolfe v. Allstate Prop. & Ins. Co.*, 790 F.3d 487 (3d Cir. 2015), the Third Circuit held that the federal district court erred in allowing evidence of a punitive damages award against the insured to be presented to the jury in the insured's bad faith action against the insurer for failure to settle an underlying claim because the punitive damages award was not relevant to the insurer's settlement actions. The court based its reasoning on Pennsylvania public policy that forbids insuring for punitive damages. See discussion in §2.73, *supra*.

§4.20   2. Defense Witnesses

—Several cases have given different answers to the question whether an insurer, in attempting to justify its denial of a claim, can rely on evidence that does not meet judicial requirements for admissibility—*e.g.*, polygraph test results, or hearsay. See *Conti v. Republic Underwriters Ins. Co.*, 782 P.2d 1357 (Okla. 1989) (insurers may rely on inadmissible evidence); *Amica Mut. Ins. Co. v. Schettler*, 768 P.2d 950 (Utah Ct. App. 1989) (insurers may not rely on types of evidence not meeting criteria for admissibility in court); *Industrial Indem. Co. of the Northwest v. Kallevig*, 114 Wash. 2d 907, 792 P.2d 520 (1990) (trial judge did not abuse discretion in prohibiting insurer from introducing evidence of insured's refusal to submit to polygraph test to establish reasonable basis for denial of claim).

I. Sample Jury Instructions

3. Bases of Liability

§4.28 a. Bad Faith

—In *Government Employees Ins. Co. v. Gonzalez*, 403 P.3d 1153 (Alaska 2017), the Supreme Court of Alaska concluded that the trial court should have allowed plaintiff's jury instruction that the "fact that an insurer ultimately pays benefits due under the contract does not relieve it from liability for negligence or bad faith if, in its handling of the claim, it unreasonably delayed payment of those benefits or otherwise breached its obligation of good faith and fair dealing." *Id.* at 1160–61. However, the court held that no prejudice arose from failure to give the instruction because the jury found the underinsured motorist (UIM) insurer acted in bad faith when it delayed paying plaintiff's claim. The court upheld an award of nominal damages of $2, punitive damages of $450,000, and attorney's fees for an UIM insurer's bad faith delay in paying the plaintiff's claim. The court held that the actual harm suffered by plaintiff included her post-lawsuit recovery of a claim award of $83,487.50 in UIM benefits plus interest, and that such actual amount resulted in a "reasonable single-digit ratio" of actual to punitive damages under *State Farm Mut. Auto. Ins. Co. v. Campbell, supra. Gonzalez*, 493 P.3d at 1165.

—In *McCoy v. Progressive West Ins. Co.*, 171 Cal. App. 4th 785, 90 Cal. Rptr. 3d 74 (2009), a California Court of Appeal held that the defendant automobile insurer had not been entitled to a separate jury instruction on the "genuine dispute doctrine," where the jury was correctly instructed that the insured was required to prove that the insurer had unreasonably failed to properly investigate the claim, and had unreasonably failed to pay policy benefits.

The Judicial Council of California reviewed changes proposed by its Advisory Committee to California Jury Instructions (CACI) dealing with insurance bad faith. On December 11, 2015, the Judicial Council approved changes to CACI No. 2332 (and related instructions) defining bad faith failure to investigate to mean that the insurer "acted unreasonably, that is, without proper cause." See Judicial Counsel of Calif. Civil Jury Instructions (CACI), at 162–64 (June 2016 Supp.) (as approved at June 2016 Judicial Council Meeting). The prior version of the instruction had defined bad faith as acting either unreasonably or without proper cause, and the new version essentially combines the two concepts into one test. See *Revising California's Jury Instructions on Insurance Bad Faith: The Nature of the Tort of Insurance Bad Faith, Legal Solutions Blog*, THOMSON REUTERS, http://blog.legalsolutions. thomsonreuters.com/practice-of-law/revising-californias-jury-instructions-on-insurance-bad-faith-the-nature-of-the-tort-of-insurance-bad-faith/.

The Advisory Committee had also proposed adding a second reasonableness inquiry to CACI No. 2334, on bad faith refusal to settle, requiring a showing that the insurer acted unreasonably in failing to accept a settlement demand, in addition to the existing element that the settlement demand must have been reasonable. However, the Advisory Committee later dropped that proposal. On June 24, 2016, the Judicial Council accepted the revised proposal for CACI No. 2334. See CACI, at 165–71. As updated, CACI No. 2334 does not contain the second reasonableness test, but the Directions for Use include a statement that the need for such an additional element "is a plausible, but unsettled, requirement" under California law. See *id.* at 166; see also *Revising California's Jury Instructions on Insurance Bad Faith: Are the Twin Goals of Accuracy and Understandability in Conflict?*, *Legal Solutions Blog*, THOMSON REUTERS, http://blog.legalsolutions.thomson-reuters.com/practice-of-law/revising-californias-jury-instructions-on-insurance-bad-faith-are-the-twin-goals-of-accuracy-and-understandability-in-conflict.

—Under North Dakota law, the Eighth Circuit held in *Moore v. American Family Mut. Ins. Co.*, 576 F.3d 781 (8th Cir. 2009), that where there was some evidence from which the jury could infer that the insurer had committed prohibited acts with a frequency indicating a general business practice, the trial court did not commit plain error in giving an instruction that permitted the jury to consider as evidence of bad faith the insurer's violations of statutes prohibiting unfair settlement practices.

—In *Johnson v. United Parcel Serv., Inc.*, 946 N.W.2d 1 (S.D. 2020), a workers' compensation insurer unreasonably terminated medical payments paid to an employee. The insurer terminated its payments after consulting with an attorney who told the insurer it could terminate the payments after a neurologist determined that the employee's former employment no longer contributed to her condition. The lower court determined that termination of the payments was unreasonable as a matter of law, but sent the question of whether the insurer knew it was unreasonable to the jury. The lower court prevented the insurer from presenting evidence to support its advice-of-counsel defense. It instructed the jury that it could not conclude that the insurer misunderstood its legal duties. It also instructed the jury not to consider the advice the insurer received from the attorney in considering whether the insurer knew there was no reasonable basis to terminate the payments. The Supreme Court of South Dakota held that the lower court erred in excluding evidence of the advice-of-counsel defense and erred in the jury instructions. The court found that such evidence was critical for the jury's determination of whether the insurer knew there was no reasonable basis for terminating payments, and it was critical for the jury to use in determining punitive damages.

—In *USAA Tex. Lloyds Co. v. Menchaca*, 545 S.W.3d 479 (Tex. 2018), the Texas Supreme Court reviewed and clarified Texas precedent on whether an insured can recover policy benefits as actual damages for an insurer's statutory violation absent a finding that the insured had a contractual right to the benefits under the insurance policy. In the case under review, a jury answered "no" when asked whether the insurer failed to comply with the terms of the insurance policy in denying to pay damages to the insured after her home was damaged by a hurricane. However, the jury answered "yes" when asked whether the insurer engaged in unfair or deceptive practices in violation of the Texas Insurance Code, including whether the insurer refused to pay the claim for damages without conducting a reasonable investigation. The jury awarded the insured $11,350 as actual damages, which the jury calculated by using the difference between what the insurer should have paid under the policy and the amount actually paid. The Texas Supreme Court remanded the case for a new trial based on the irreconcilable and fatal conflict in the jury's answers. The opinion includes some guidance on how to formulate jury instructions to avoid irreconcilable conflicts in similar cases. See discussion in §1.56.

—In *Gosney v. Fireman's Fund Ins. Co.*, 3 Wash. App. 2d 828, 419 P.3d 447 (2018), *review denied*, 191 Wash. 2d 1017 (2018) the decedent's estate brought several claims after the personal representative was assigned legal rights to the claims under a covenant agreement. The claims included a tort claim for bad faith failure to defend or settle and claims under Washington's Consumer Protection Act (CPA) and the Insurance Fair Conduct Act (IFCA). The personal representative reached a covenant agreement for

$10,800,289 related to an accident in which the decedent was killed by the insured's pizza delivery driver. The court addressed several issues related to jury instructions. One such issue was whether the omission of instructions related to the amount due to the decedent's estate was proper. The court found that the omission was proper because the amount due is the amount of the covenant agreement as a matter of law where the amount was reasonable and the assignee did not seek additional damages. Second, the court found that the trial court did not err in instructing the jury that a single violation of Wash. Admin. Code §284-30-330 constitutes bad faith under the CPA. Third, the court found that the jury instruction provided on the definition of collusion was within the discretion of the trial court.

—In *Berry v. Nationwide Mut. Fire Ins. Co.*, 381 S.E.2d 367 (W. Va. 1989) (also discussed in supplement §§1.66, 2.24, 4.5, 4.34), the court approved the following instruction concerning an insurer's liability for first-party bad faith (381 S.E.2d at 373 n.6):

> The court further instructs the jury that should you find that the Plaintiffs are entitled to recover against the Defendant . . . under the Contract of Insurance between the parties, then you may consider the claim of the Plaintiffs which is based upon an insurer's duty to deal fairly and in good faith with its policy holders. The law implies in every homeowner's contract of insurance a covenant of good faith and fair dealing. It is a duty required by West Virginia law. The duty requires an insurance company to deal in good faith and fairly with its insureds in handling its insureds' claims.
>
> The duty of an insurance company towards its insured is analogous to that of a fiduciary in that it must assess claims as a result of an appropriate and careful investigation and its conclusion should be the result of the weighing of probabilities in a fair and honest way. The insured has a right to receive the benefits of the

agreement and for the insurer to fulfill its obligation not to impair the right of its insured to receive the benefits of the ageement. It must give at least as much consideration to the insured's interest as it does to its own.

Therefore, if you find from a preponderance of the evidence submitted in this case that Defendant . . . failed to conduct an appropriate and reasonable investigation, failed to weigh the probabilities of any investigation in a fair and honest way or failed to give at least as much consideration to the Plaintiffs' interests as it did to its own, then you may find that the Defendant breached its duty of good faith and fair dealing and your verdict may be for [the plaintiffs].

6. Damages

§4.34 b. Punitive Damages

—*Berry v. Nationwide Mut. Fire Ins. Co.*, 381 S.E.2d 367 (W. Va. 1989), contains an extensive discussion of the standards for recovery of punitive damages under West Virginia law, and of an insured's entitlement to, and the wording of, punitive damages instructions. The discussion occurs in the course of the court's affirmance of a judgment for the insured and of awards of $75,000 for breach of contract, $50,000 for breach of the duty of good faith and fair dealing, and $500,000 in punitive damages. The case involved nonpayment of a claim under a homeowner's policy. The court approved a punitive damages instruction that read as follows (381 S.E.2d at 373 n.6):

> You are further instructed that punitive damages may be awarded in your discretion if you find that the insurance company's actions evidenced an intentional, reckless or willful failure to determine whether or not there was any lawful basis for its refusal to pay its insured at the time of its refusal. That is to say, were its

acts done with such malice as implied a spirit of mischief or criminal indifference to the civil obligations affecting the rights of its insured. . . .

The court cited *Hayseeds, Inc. v. State Farm Fire & Casualty Co.*, 352 S.E.2d 73 (W. Va. 1986) (see book §§1.16, 1.36, 1.59, 2.24), for the definition of the required level of malice (381 S.E.2d at 374 (quoting *Hayseeds*, 352 S.E.2d at 80–81)):

> By "actual malice" we mean that the [insurance] company actually knew that the policyholder's claim was proper, but willfully, maliciously and intentionally denied the claim. We intend this to be a bright line standard, highly susceptible to summary judgment for the defendant [insurance company] . . . . Unless the policyholder is able to introduce evidence of intentional injury—not negligence, lack of judgment, incompetence, or bureaucratic confusion—the issue of punitive damages should not be submitted to the jury.

The *Berry* court held that the facts of the present case clearly suggested that the insurer had known plaintiff's claim was valid, and that there was therefore ample evidence to have presented a jury question on punitive damages, based upon the insurer's willful, malicious, and intentional denial of the claim.

§4.36A K. Motions After Verdict [NEW]

This section addresses post-verdict procedures during trial.

—In *Shreve v. State Farm Fire & Casualty Co.*, 247 So. 3d 1175 (La. Ct. App. 2018), *writ denied*, 255 So. 3d 574 (La. 2018) the court affirmed a JNOV on a bad faith claim under La. Stat. Ann. §22:1973 and dismissed $140,000 in noncontractual damages and $25,000 in attorney's fees. The court held that reasonable persons could not have found that the insurer acted in bad faith toward the insured when handling the claim where the insured did not discover a crack in the foundation of their home until almost 3 years after the alleged damage occurred, the insurer hired an engineer to evaluate the crack within 2 weeks of the claim, the insurer's engineer found the crack to be from a source not covered under the policy, and the insurer hired a second engineer who confirmed its first engineer's report when it was faced with a conflicting report from insured's engineer.

Appendices

583

I. Jurisdictions With Statutes Specifically Prohibiting Unfair Claims Settlement Practices*

State	Statute
Alabama	Ala. Code §27-12-24 (2018)
Alaska [2]	Alaska Stat. §21.36.125 (2018)
Arizona [2]	Ariz. Rev. Stat. Ann. §20-461 (2018)
Arkansas	Ark. Code Ann. §§23-66-205, 23-66-206 (2018)
California	Cal. Ins. Code §§790.02, 790.03 (2018)
Colorado	Colo. Rev. Stat. §§10-3-1103, 10-3-1104 (2018)
Connecticut	Conn. Gen. Stat. §§38a-815, 38a-816 (2018)
Delaware [2]	Del. Code Ann. tit. 18, §§2303, 2304 (2018)
District of Columbia	D.C. Code §31-2231.17 (2018)
Florida [1]	Fla. Stat. §§626.9521, 626.9541, 626.9631, 626.9743, 626.9744 (2018)
[1][2]	Fla. Stat. §624.155 (2018)
Georgia [2]	Ga. Code Ann. §§33-6-1 to 33-6-37 (2018)

(1) Statute specifically states that the existence of the statute does not relieve insurer from liability under other laws or from civil liability.

(2) Statute specifically states that no private right of action is created.

*This list is provided as a general reference. Each state's statutory scheme is unique. Some states may have other statutes addressing claims practices for specific types of insurance (*e.g.*, health care, workers comp, motor vehicle) that are not included here.

Hawaii	Haw. Stat. §§431:13-101 to 431:13-204 (2018)
Idaho	Idaho Code Ann. §41-1329 (2018)
Illinois	215 Ill. Comp. Stat. 5/154.5 to 5/154.8 (2018)
Indiana (1)(2)	Ind. Code §§27-4-1-1 to 27-4-1-19 (2018)
Iowa	Iowa Code §507B.4 (2018)
Kansas	Kan. Stat. Ann. §§40-2403 to 40-2404 (2018)
Kentucky	Ky. Rev. Stat. Ann. §304.12-230 (2018)
Louisiana	La. Rev. Stat. Ann. §§22:1964, 22:1973 (2018)
Maine (1)(2)	Me. Rev. Stat. tit. 24, §§2164-D, 2436-A (2018)
Maryland (1)(2)	Md. Code Ann., Ins. §§27-301 to 27-306 (2018)
Massachusetts (1)	Mass. Gen. Laws ch. 176D, §3 (2018)
Michigan	Mich. Comp. Laws §§500.2006, 500.2026 (2018)
Minnesota	Minn. Stat. §72A.19, 72A.20 (2018)
Mississippi	none; see App. II
Missouri (1)	Mo. Rev. Stat. §§375-1000 to 375-1018 (2018)

---

(1) Statute specifically states that the existence of the statute does not relieve insurer from liability under other laws or from civil liability.

(2) Statute specifically states that no private right of action is created.

Montana	Mont. Code Ann. §33-18-201 to 33-18-245 (2018) (specifically states that no cause of action for bad faith is available under common law; statute provides only cause of action)
Nebraska	Neb. Rev. Stat. §§44-1536 to 44-1544 (2018)
Nevada [1][2]	Nev. Rev. Stat. §§686A.300 to 686A.325 (2018)
New Hampshire	N.H. Rev. Stat. Ann. §§417:3, 417:4
New Jersey	N.J. Stat. Ann. §§17B:30-2, 17B:30-13.1 (2018) (life insurance, health insurance, and annuity); §§17:29B-3, 17:29B-4 (2018) other insurance)
New Mexico [1]	N.M. Stat. Ann. §§59A-16-3, 59A-16-20, 59A-16-30 (2018)
New York [1]	N.Y. Ins. Law §§2601, 2401–2409 (2018)
North Carolina [2]	N.C. Gen. Stat. §§58-63-10, 58-63-15 (2018)
North Dakota [1]	N.D. Cent. Code §§26.1-04-02, 26.1-04-03, 26.1-04-18 (2018)
Ohio	Ohio Rev. Code Ann. §3901.041 & Ohio Admin. Code §3901-1-07
Oklahoma	Okla. Stat. tit. 36, ch. 1, art. 12a-1, 1250.1 to 1250.17 (2018)

(1) Statute specifically states that the existence of the statute does not relieve insurer from liability under other laws or from civil liability.

(2) Statute specifically states that no private right of action is created.

Oregon	Or. Rev. Stat. §746.230 (2018)
Pennsylvania	40 Pa. Cons. Stat. §§1171.4, 1171.5 (2018)
Puerto Rico	P.R. Laws Ann. tit. 26, §§2716a, 2716b, 2716c (2018)
Rhode Island (2)	R.I. Gen. Laws §§27-9:1-1 to 27-9:1-9
South Carolina	S.C. Code Ann. §§38-59-10 to 38-59-50 (2018)
(2)	S.C. Code Ann. §§38.59-200 to 38-59-270 (health care only) (2018)
South Dakota	S.D. Codified Laws §58-33-67 (2018)
Tennessee (1)	Tenn. Code Ann. §§56-8-101 to 56-8-113 (2018)
Texas	Tex. Ins. Code Ann. §§542.001 to 542.014 (2018)
(1)	Tex. Ins. Code Ann. §§542.051 to 542.061 (2018)
(1)	Tex. Ins. Code Ann. §§541.060, 541.151 (2018)
Utah (2)	Utah Code Ann. §31A-26-303 (2018) Utah Code Ann. §31A-26-301.6 (2018) (health care claims)
Vermont	Vt. Stat. Ann. tit. 8, §§4723–4724 (2018)
Virginia (1)(2)	Va. Code Ann. §38.2-510 (2018)

---

(1) Statute specifically states that the existence of the statute does not relieve insurer from liability under other laws or from civil liability.

(2) Statute specifically states that no private right of action is created.

Washington	Wash. Admin. Code §§284-30-300 to 284-30-400 (2018) (implementing Wash. Rev. Code §48.30.10 (2018))
West Virginia [2]	W. Va. Code §§33-11-1 to 33-11-10 (2018)
Wisconsin	Wis. Admin. Code Ins. §6.11 (2018)
Wyoming	Wyo. Stat. Ann. §26-13-124 (2018)

---

(2) Statute specifically states that no private right of action is created.

II. Jurisdictions With No Statute Specifically Naming Unfair Claims Settlement Practices

State	Statute
State	*Statute*
Mississippi	Miss. Code Ann. §§83-5-33, 83-5-35, 83-5-45 (2018)
Ohio	Ohio Rev. Code Ann. §§3901.20, 3901.21 (pattern settlement only; (but see administrative regulations, listed in App. I)
Washington	Wash. Rev. Code §48.30.10 (2018) (but see administrative regulations, listed in App. I)
Wisconsin	Wis. Stat. §628.34 (2018) (but see administrative regulations, listed in App. I)

III. Jurisdictions With Statutes Providing for Recovery of Attorney's Fees, Damages, and/or Interest in Suits Against Insurers to Recover Benefits Under Insurance Policies[†]

State	*Statute*
Arkansas [3], [4]	Ark. Code Ann. §§23-79-208, 23-79-209 (2018)
Colorado [3][4][6]	Colo. Rev. Stat. §10-3-1116 (2018)
Delaware [3]	18 Del. Code Ann. §4102 (2018) (for property insurance cases)
Florida [3][4][6]	Fla. Stat. §624.155 (2018)
Georgia [3][4]	Ga. Code Ann. §33-4-6 (2018)
Idaho [3]	Idaho Code Ann. §41-1839 (2018)
Illinois [3][4]	215 Ill. Comp. Stat. 5/155 (2018)
Kansas [3]	Kan. Stat. Ann. §40-256 (2018)
Kentucky [3][5]	Ky. Rev. Stat. Ann. §304.12-235 (2018)
Louisiana[3][4]	La. Rev. Stat. §22:1892 (2018)
Maine [3][4][5][6]	Me. Rev. Stat. tit. 24-A, §§2436, 2436-A (2016)

---

[3] Attorney's fees

[4] Damages or penalty

[5] Interest

[6] Statute provides it does not limit or prohibit any claim or action by insured against insurer.

[†] This list is provided as a general reference. Each state's statutory scheme is unique. Some states may have other statutes addressing fees, damages, and interest available for claims under specific types of insurance coverage (*e.g.*, health care, workers comp, motor vehicle) or against specific types of insurers (*e.g.*, unauthorized or alien) that are not included here. Also not included are general civil liability statutes. Many states address fees, damages, and interest via court opinions (common law).

Maryland (3)(4)(5)(6)	Md. Code Ann., Ins. §3-1701 (2018)
Minnesota (3)(4)(5)	Minn. Stat. §604.18 (2018)
Missouri (3)(4)(5)	Mo. Rev. Stat. §375.420 (2018)
Montana (4)	Mont. Code Ann. §33-18-242 (2018)
Nebraska (3)	Neb. Rev. Stat. §44-359 (2018)
Nevada (4)	Nev. Rev. Stat. §686A.310.2 (2018)
New Hampshire (3)	N.H. Rev. Stat. Ann. §491:22-b (2018)
New Mexico (3)(4)	N.M. Stat. Ann. §59A-16-30 (2018)
(3)	·N.M. Stat. Ann. §39-2-1 (2018) (first-party insured only)
North Carolina (3)	N.C. Gen. Stat. §6-21.1 (2018)
Oklahoma (3)	Okla. Stat. Ann. tit. 36, ch. 1, §1219 (2018)
(3)(5)	Okla. Stat. Ann. tit. 36, ch. 1, §3629 (2018)
Pennsylvania (3)(4)(5)	42 Pa. Cons. Stat. §8371 (2018)
Rhode Island (3)(4)	R.I. Gen. Laws §9-1-33 (2018)
South Carolina (3)	S.C. Code Ann. §38-59-40 (2018)
South Dakota (3)(6)	S.D. Codified Laws §§58-12-3, 58-33-46.1 (2018)
Tennessee (4)	Tenn. Code Ann. §56-7-105(a) (2018)
(3)	Tenn. Code Ann. §56-7-105(b) (2018)

(3) Attorney's fees

(4) Damages or penalty

(5) Interest

(6) Statute provides it does not limit or prohibit any claim or action by insured against insurer.

Texas (3)(5)(6)	Tex. Ins. Code Ann. §542.060, 542.061 (2018)
(3)(4)	Tex. Ins. Code Ann. §541.152 (2018)
Virginia (2)(3)	Va. Code Ann. §38.2-209 (2018)
Washington (3)(4)(6)	Wash. Rev. Code §48.30.015 (2018) (excludes health plans)
Wyoming (3)(5)	Wyo. Stat. Ann. §26-15-124 (2018)

---

(3) Attorney's fees

(4) Damages or penalty

(5) Interest

(6) Statute provides it does not limit or prohibit any claim or action by insured against insurer.

Bibliography

Adler & Mann, *Good faith: A new look at an old doctrine*, 28 Akron L. Rev. 31 (1994).

Annotation, *Excess carrier's right to maintain action against primary liability insurer for wrongful failure to settle claim against insured*, 10 A.L.R.4th 879 (1998).

Aromando, *The surety's liability for bad faith: claims for extracontractual damages by an obligee under the payment bond*, 47 Me. L. Rev. 389 (1995).

Baker, *Liability insurance conflicts and defense lawyers: from triangles to tetrahedrons*, 4 Conn. Ins. L.J. 101 (1998).

Barker, *Evidentiary sufficiency in insurance bad faith suits*, 6 Conn. Ins. L.J. 81 (1999).

Bauman, *Emotional distress damages and the tort of insurance bad faith*, 46 Drake L. Rev. 717 (1998).

Beaver, *The standard of review in ERISA benefits denial cases after* Firestone Tire and Rubber Co. v. Bruch: *revolution or deja vu?* 26 Tort & Ins. L.J. 1 (1990).

Boothby, *Comparative bad faith: will the courts allow insurance carriers to introduce a unicorn into insurance bad faith litigation?*, 18 Thomas Jefferson L. Rev. 121 (1996).

Bourhis, *Insult to Injury: Insurance, Fraud, and the Big Business of Bad Faith* (Berrett-Koehler, 2005).

Bowdre, *Enhanced obligation of good faith: a mine field of unanswered questions after* L & S Roofing Supply Co., 50 Ala. L. Rev. 755 (1999).

Brown, *Conflicts of interest between insurer and insured: when is independent counsel necessary?* 22 J. Legal Prof. 211 (1998).

Brown, *Extra-contractual damages stemming from a first-party insurer's bad-faith breach: will Minnesota adopt the tort or contract theory of recovery?* 26 Wm. Mitchell L. Rev. 525 (2000).

Burton, *Good faith in Articles 1 and 2 of the U.C.C.: the practice view*, 35 Wm. & Mary L. Rev. 1533 (1994).

Cady, Andrews, Cuppett & Loss, *The law of insurance company claim misconduct in West Virginia*, 101 W. Va. L. Rev. 1 (1998).

Chandler, *Reconsidering the duty to settle*, 42 Drake L. Rev. 741 (1993).

Chinonis, *Implied covenant of good faith: a two-way street in franchising*, 11 DePaul Bus. L.J. 229 (1998).

Clann, Brown & Sydow, *Judicial interpretation of insurance contracts in maritime law: the duty of good faith in handling claims*, 66 Tul. L. Rev. 479 (1991).

Comment, *Bad faith breach of insurance contract: Idaho's misapplication of tort law*, 28 Idaho L. Rev. 457 (1991).

Comment, *Bad faith denial of insurance claims: whose faith, whose punishment? An examination of punitive damages and vicarious liability*, 65 Tul. L. Rev. 395 (1990).

Comment, *"Constructive denial," "debatable reasons," and bad faith refusal to pay an insurance claim—the evolution of a monster*, 22 Cumb. L. Rev. 349 (1991).

Comment, *Defining "duty" in the duty-to-settle doctrine as applied to third-party insurance claims in Georgia*, 8 Ga. St. U. L. Rev. 809 (1992).

Comment, *Section 1–208: "Good faith" and the need for a uniform standard*, 73 Marq. L. Rev. 639 (1990).

Comment, *Small employers and group health insurance: should ERISA apply?*, 52 La. L. Rev. 971 (1992).

Comment, *There ought to be a law: the insurer's duty to particularize grounds for denial of claims*, 18 W. St. U. L. Rev. 825 (1991).

Crosky, *Bad faith in California: Its history, development and current status*, 26 Tort & Ins. L. J. 561 (1991).

Distelhorst, *A business ethics approach to contractual good faith and fair dealing: briefly modeled in selected managed healthcare contexts*, 26 Ohio N.U. L. Rev. 57 (2000).

Duckworth, *The tort of bad faith arising from workers' compensation matters—a rumbling volcano*, 39 Drake L. Rev. 87 (1989).

Durbin & Loy, *Current status of good faith law in Oklahoma*, 24 Okla. City U. L. Rev. 155 (1999).

Egler, *The individual life insurance sales practice case: a litigation primer*, 50 Fed'n Ins. & Corp. Couns. Q. 1 (1999).

Fenton, *The tort of bad faith in Iowa workers' compensation law*, 45 Drake L. Rev. 839 (1997).

Fischer, *Broadening the insurer's duty to defend: how* Gray v. Zurich Insurance Co. *transformed liability insurance into litigation insurance*, 25 U.C. Davis L. Rev. 141 (1991).

Fussner, *Overview of bad faith litigation in Missouri*, 62 Mo. L. Rev. 807 (1997).

Gabel & Feldhaus, *Erosion of the exclusive remedy doctrine at the hands of bad faith: the right cause but the wrong effect*, 6 J. Legal Stud. Bus. 1 (1998).

Goldberg, Segalla & Cohen, *Can the puzzle be solved: Are punitive damages awardable in New York for first-party bad faith?*, 44 Syracuse L. Rev. 723 (1993).

Gray, *Conflicts and waiver of privilege in the insurance relationship*, 10 Ins. L.J. 75 (1998).

Grenier, *The ERISA shield around HMOs cannot be justified*, 12 Regent U.L. Rev. 283 (1999).

Haley & Wolkin, *Bad faith and the financial institution bond*, 25 Tort & Ins. L.J. 715 (1990).

Harman, *The good faith gamble in franchise agreements: does your implied covenant trump my express term?* 28 Cumb. L. Rev. 473 (1998).

Horstman, Nahrstadt, & Hengsbach, *Punitive and other damages for emotional distress in third party bad faith actions*, 50 Fed'n Ins. & Corp. Couns. Q. 47 (1999).

Jerry, *Consent, contract, and the responsibilities of insurance defense counsel*, 4 Conn. Ins. L.J. 153 (1998).

Jeter, *Is* Universe Life Insurance Co. v. Giles *a reasonable alternative to the "no reasonable basis" standard of bad faith liability?*, 51 Baylor L. Rev. 175 (1999).

Kahn & Nemirow, *Unauthorized settlement agreements in a reservation of rights context*, 34 Tort & Ins. L.J. 799 (1999).

Kaplan, *Discoverability of claim files in bad faith litigation*, For the Defense, Feb. 1991, at 9.

Kennedy, *Good faith principles judicially imposed in dealings between primary and excess insurers and reinsurers*, 26 Tort & Ins. L.J. 590 (1991).

Kornblum & Bailey, *Using insurance experts in bad faith cases: should I or shouldn't I?* Trial, Feb. 2000, at 30.

Kornblum, Ferry, & Lee, *Environmental claims and bad faith: contract obligations that mature into extra-contractual lawsuits*, 52 Ohio St. L.J. 1245 (1991).

Lessman, *Third party bad faith refusals to settle in* Nielsen v. Boos, 43 S.D. L. Rev. 680 (1998).

Linstrom, *Unfair claims settlement practices: A summary of California law*, 15 Whittier L. Rev. 691 (1994).

Macintosh, *Gilmore spoke too soon: Contract rises from the ashes of the bad faith tort*, 27 Loy. L.A. L. Rev. 483–540 (1994).

Main, *Bad faith in the workers' compensation context: a cause in search of an action*, 30 Tulsa L.J. 507 (1995).

McGuire & McMahon, *Bad faith, excess liability and extracontractual damages: counsel for the excess carrier looks at the issues*, 72 U. Det. Mercy L. Rev. 49 (1994).

McIlwain, *Clear as mud: an insurer's rights and duties where coverage under a liability policy is questionable*, 27 Cumb. L. Rev. 31 (1996).

Miller & Lewis, *The impact of the good faith requirement upon the parties*, 26 Tort & Ins. L.J. 602 (1991).

Nielsen, *Advice of counsel in insurance bad faith litigation: a substantive framework for pleading, discovery and proof*, 25 Tort & Ins. L.J. 533 (1990).

Note, *At-will employment: time for good faith and fair dealing between employers and employees*, 28 Willamette L. Rev. 681 (1992).

Note, *Borrowing* Foley v. Interactive Data Corp. *to finance lender liability claims*, 41 Hastings L.J. 1383 (1990).

Note, *Can punitive damages withstand a due process challenge after* Bankers Life & Casualty Co. v. Crenshaw *and* Browning-Ferris Industries of Vermont v. Kelco Disposal? 18 Fordham Urb. L.J. 121 (1990).

Note, *Constitutional defenses against punitive damages: down but not out*, 65 Ind. L.J. 141 (1989).

Note, *"Contracting around" the good faith covenant to avoid lender liability*, 1991 Colum. Bus. L. Rev. 359.

Note, *A counter-revolution in insurance bad faith:* Moradi-Shalal v. Fireman's Fund Ins. Cos., 18 W. St. U. L. Rev. 847 (1991).

Note, *Excess carriers are equitably subrogated to insured's cause of action against primary carriers for breach of* Stowers *duty*, 23 Tex. Tech. L. Rev. 643 (1992)

Note, *The implied covenant of good faith and fair dealing in Alaska: One court's license to override contractual expectations*, 11 Alaska L. Rev. 35 (1994).

Note, *The injured third party in California: extending bad faith for full compensation*, 26 Val. U. L. Rev. 843 (1992).

Note, *The insurance company or the insured: where does defense counsel's loyalty really lie?*, 70 U. Det. Mercy L. Rev. 215 (1992).

Note, *Insurer bad faith: the need for an exception to the attorney-client privilege*, 11 Rev. Litig. 111 (1991).

Note, *The insurer's duty of good faith and fair dealing in the context of litigation*, 60 Geo. Wash. L. Rev. 1931 (1992).

Note, *Limitations on a first-party breach of good faith and fair dealing action accrues at denial of claim*, 33 S. Tex. L. Rev. 329 (1992).

Note, *The need for revisiting the imposition of bad faith liability*, 15 U. Puget Sound L. Rev. 203 (1991).

Note, *Reservations of rights in insurance contracts*, 32 Ariz. L. Rev. 387 (1990).

Note, *Stowers Doctrine Catch-22 resolved for Texas insurers*, 26 Tex. Tech. L. Rev. 169 (1995).

Note, *Third-party claimants may not pursue a cause of action against insurers*, 25 Tex. Tech. L. Rev. 985 (1994).

Oberdorf, *Bad faith insurance litigation in Pennsylvania: recurring issues under section 8371*, 33 Duq. L. Rev. 45 (1995).

Ochoa & Wistrich, *Unraveling the tangled web: choosing the proper statute of limitations for breach of the implied covenant of good faith and fair dealing*, 26 Sw. U. L. Rev. 1 (1996).

Paine & Sourial, *Recent developments in California insurance law: enforceability of stipulated judgments against insurance carriers*, 22 Pepp. L. Rev. 1017 (1995).

Parker, *The development of first-party extracontractual insurance litigation in Oklahoma: an analytical examination*, 31 Tulsa L.J. 57 (1995).

Perritt, *Implied covenant: anachronism or augur*, 20 Seton Hall L. Rev. 683 (1990).

Potter & Gable, *The emerging bad faith cause of action takes on the exclusive remedy doctrine*, 48 Mercer L. Rev. 63 (1996).

Quinn, *The ethical habitat of adjusters: principles, problems, and practicalities*, 10 Environmental Claims J. 91 (1998).

Quinn, *Insurer bad faith—sic et non—Texas style*, 19 Ins. Litig. Rep. 485 (1997).

Reichert, *Good faith and fair dealing developments*, 27 Colo. Law. 115 (1998), 27 Colo. Law. 73 (1998).

Richmond, *Insured's bad faith as shield or sword: Litigation relief for insurers?*, 77 Marq. L. Rev. 41 (1993).

―――, *An overview of insurance bad faith law and litigation*, 25 Seton Hall L. Rev. 74 (1994).

―――, *Reimbursing insurers' defense costs: restitution and mixed actions*, 35 San Diego L. Rev. 457 (1998).

―――, *Trust me: Insurers are not fiduciaries to their insureds*, 88 Ky. L.J. 1 (1999).

―――, *Walking a tightrope: the tripartite relationship between insurer, insured, and insurance defense counsel*, 73 Neb. L. Rev. 265 (1994).

Shidlofsky, *The changing face of first-party bad faith claims in Texas*, 50 SMU L. Rev. 867 (1997).

Silver & Syverud, *The professional responsibilities of insurance defense lawyers*, 5 Duke L.J. 255 (1995).

Smith, *Understanding the tort of third-party bad faith in Wyoming*, 26 Land & Water L. Rev. 635 (1991).

Stern, *Bad faith suits against HMOs: finally, a breakthrough*, 20 Whittier L. Rev. 313 (1998).

Sukel & Pipkin, *Discovery and admissibility of reserves*, 34 Tort & Ins. L.J. 191 (1998).

Sutherland, *One client, one defense: Revisiting CHI with the Alaska rules of professional conduct*, 11 Alaska L. Rev. 1 (1994).

Symposium on the Law of Bad Faith in Contract and Insurance, 72 Tex. L. Rev. 1203–1702 (1994).

Syverud, *The duty to settle*, 76 Va. L. Rev. 1113 (1990).

Thomas, *Utmost good faith in reinsurance: a tradition in need of adjustment*, 41 Duke L.J. 1548 (1992).

Van den Dungen, *Good faith, unconscionable conduct and imaginary community standards—Section 51AC of the Trade Practices Act and the insurance industry*, 10 Ins. L.J. 1 (1998).

Vance & Matherne, *Legal ethics—defense counsel's responsibilities to insured and insurer,* 6 U.S.F. Mar. L.J. 157 (1993).

Wencl & Strickland, *Allstate's "customer service" charade,* Trial, Sep. 1999, at 42.

Widiss, *Obligating insurers to inform insureds about the existence of rights and duties regarding coverage for losses,* 1 Conn. Ins. L.J. 67 (1995).

Williams, *A new twist in insurance litigation:* Stowers *suits by excess carriers against primary carriers,* 33 S. Tex. L. Rev. 1 (1992).

Willis, *The substantive law of lender liability,* 26 Tort & Ins. L.J. 742 (1991).

Wood, *Assignments of rights and covenants not to execute in insurance litigation,* 75 Tex. L. Rev. 1373 (1997).

Young, *The work product doctrine: functional considerations and the question of the insurer's claim file,* 64 U. Chi. L. Rev. 1425 (1997).

Table of Cases by Jurisdiction

Colorado

Feijoo v. Geico Gen. Ins. Co.
137 F. Supp. 3d 1320 (S.D. Fla.
2015), aff'd, 678 Fed. Appx.
862 (11th Cir. 2017): §§2.7,
2.13, 2.27, 2.60

Fernandez v. Florida Ins. Guar.
Ass'n, Inc., 383 So. 2d 974
(Fla. Dist. Ct. App. 1980):
§2.12

Fidelity & Casualty Co. v. Cope,
462 So. 2d 459 (Fla. 1985):
§§2.54, 2.63

Florida Farm Bureau Gen. Life
Ins. Co. v. Copertino, 810 So.
2d 1076 (Fla. Dist. Ct. App.
2002): §3.70

Florida Medical Malpractice
Joint Underwriting Ass'n v.
Indemnity Ins. Co. of N. Am.,
689 So. 2d 1040 (Fla. 1996):
§3.29

Florida Physicians Union, Inc.,
The v. United Healthcare of
Fla., 837 So. 2d 1133 (Fla.
Dist. Ct. App. 2003): §1.33

Fortune v. First Protective Ins.
Co., 302 So. 3d 485 (Fla. Dist.
Ct. App. 2020): §§1.10, 1.33

Freeman v. Cohen, 969 So. 2d
1150 (Fla. Dist. Ct. App. 2007):
§2.2

Fridman v. Safeco Ins. Co. of
Ill., 185 So. 3d 1214 (Fla.
2016) : §§1.33, 1.56

Galen Health Care, Inc. v.
American Casualty Co.,
913 F. Supp. 1525 (M.D. Fla.
1996): §2.11

General Accident Fire & Life
Ins. Co. v. Boudreau, 658 So.
2d 1006 (Fla. Dist. Ct. App.
1994): §3.69

General Accident Ins. Co. v.
American Mut. Ins. Co.,
562 So. 2d 414 (Fla. Dist. Ct.
App. 1990): §3.70

General Security Nat. Ins. Co. v.
Marsh, 303 F. Supp. 2d 1321
(M.D. Fla. 2004): §2.50

General Star Indem. Co. v.
Anheuser-Busch Cos., 741 So.
2d 1259 (Fla. Dist. Ct. App.
1999): §4.5

Genovese v. Provident Life &
Accident Ins. Co., 74 So. 3d
1064 (Fla. 2011): §3.70

Greene v. Well Care HMO, Inc.,
778 So. 2d 1037 (Fla. Dist. Ct.
App. 2001): §1.33

Hartford Ins. Co. v. Mainstream
Constr. Group, Inc., 864 So. 2d
1270 (Fla. Dist. Ct. App. 2004):
§4.5

Harvey v. GEICO Gen. Ins. Co.,
259 So. 3d 1 (Fla. 2018), cert.
denied, 2018 WL 6681741 (Fla.
2018: §§2.4, 2.7, 2.40

Hogan v. Provident Life &
Accident Ins. Co., 665 F. Supp.
2d 1273 (M.D. Fla. 2009):
§§1.2, 1.10, 1.55, 1.66

Home Ins. Co. v. Owens, 573 So.
2d 343 (Fla. Dist. Ct. App.
1990): §3.42

Imhof v. Nationwide Mut. Ins.
Co., 634 So. 2d 617 (Fla.
1994): §4.5

John J. Jerue Truck Broker, Inc.
v. Insurance Co. of N. Am.,
646 So. 2d 780 (Fla. Dist. Ct.
App. 1994): §§1.20, 2.7, 2.37

Kafie v. Northwestern Mut. Life
Ins. Co., 834 F. Supp. 2d 1354
(S.D. Fla. 2011): §1.10

New Mexico

Whitacre v. Nationwide Ins. Co.,
2012-Ohio-4557, 2012 WL
4712518 (Ohio Ct. App. 2012):
§3.70

William Powell Co. v. Nat'l
Indem. Co., 141 F. Supp. 3d
773 (S.D. Ohio. 2015): §§1.2,
3.29

Wilson v. Ohio Casualty Ins. Co.,
185 Ohio App. 3d 276, 923
N.E.2d 1187 (2009): §1.19A

Zoppo v. Homestead Ins. Co.,
71 Ohio St. 3d 552, 644 N.E.2d
397 (1994): §§1.9, 2.9

Oklahoma

Adair State Bank v. American
Casualty Co., 949 F.2d 1067
(10th Cir. 1991): §1.38

Allison v. UNUM Life Ins. Co. of
Am., 381 F.3d 1015 (10th Cir.
2004): §§1.29, 1.32

Alsobrook v. National Travelers
Life Ins. Co., 852 P.2d 768
(Okla. Ct. App. 1992): §1.66

American Fidelity & Casualty
Co. v. L.C. Jones Trucking
Co., 321 P.2d 685 (Okla. 1958):
§2.14

Automax Hyundai S. LLC v.
Zurich Am. Ins. Co., 720 F.3d
798 (10th Cir. 2013): §2.9

Bailey v. Farmers Ins. Co., Inc.,
137 P.3d 1260 (Okla. Civ. App.
2006): §1.20

Bannister v. State Farm Mut.
Auto. Ins. Co., 692 F.3d 1117
(10th Cir. 2012): §1.33

Barnes v. Oklahoma Farm
Bureau Mut. Ins. Co., 11 P.3d
162 (Okla. 2000): §§1.33, 1.59,
1.66

Berry v. Banner Life Ins. Co.,
718 Fed. Appx. 259 (5th Cir.
2018): §1.19A

Brashier v. Farmers Ins. Co.,
925 P.2d 20 (Okla. 1996),
overruled, Barnes v.
Oklahoma Farm Bureau Mut.
Ins. Co., 11 P.3d 162 (Okla.
2000): §1.59

Campbell v. American Int'l
Group, Inc., 976 P.2d 1102
(Okla. Civ. App. 1999): §2.56

Capstick v. Allstate Ins. Co.,
998 F.2d 810 (10th Cir. 1993):
§1.66

City Nat'l Bank & Trust Co. v.
Jackson Nat'l Life Ins. Co.,
804 P.2d 463 (Okla. Ct. App.
1990): §§1.18, 1.20

Clements v. ITT Hartford,
973 P.2d 902 (Okla. Civ. App.
1998): §3.26

Coblentz v. Oklahoma Farm
Bureau Mut. Ins. Co., 915 P.2d
938 (Okla. Ct. App. 1995):
§1.20

Colony Ins. Co. v. Burke,
698 F.3d 1222 (10th Cir.
2012): §§2.54, 3.24

Conover v. Aetna US
Healthcare, 320 F.3d 1076
(10th Cir. 2003): §1.29

Conti v. Republic Underwriters
Ins. Co., 782 P.2d 1357 (Okla.
1989): §4.20

Cooper v. National Union Fire
Ins. Co., 921 P.2d 1297 (Okla.
Ct. App. 1996): §1.66

DeAnda v. AIU Ins., 2004 OK 96,
98 P.3d 1080 (Okla. 2004):
§1.28

Ironshore Specialty Ins. Co. v. Conemaugh Health Sys., Inc., 423 F. Supp. 3d 139 (W.D. Pa. 2019): §§1.33, 2.7, 2.20, 2.24

Johnson v. Beane, 664 A.2d 96 (Pa. 1995): §§2.54, 2.60

Johnson v. State Farm Life Ins. Co., 695 F. Supp. 2d 201 (W.D. Pa. 2010): §§1.33, 1.36

Keefe v. Prudential Property & Casualty Ins. Co., 203 F.3d 218 (3d Cir. 2000): §1.11

Kilmer v. Connecticut Indem. Co., 189 F. Supp. 2d 237 (M.D. Pa. 2002): §§1.11, 1.16

Klinger v. State Farm Mut. Auto. Ins. Co., 115 F.3d 230 (3d Cir. 1997): §§1.9, 1.66

Kramer v. State Farm Fire & Casualty Ins. Co., 603 A.2d 192 (Pa. Super. Ct. 1992): §1.26

Kunji Harrisburg, LLC v. Axis Surplus Ins. Co., 447 F. Supp. 3d 303 (E.D. Pa. 2020): §§1.19A–1.20, 1.33

Liberty Mut. Ins. Co. v. Paper Mfg. Co., 753 F. Supp. 156 (E.D. Pa. 1990): §1.33

Lincoln Benefit Life Co. v. Bowman, 221 F. Supp. 3d 617 (E.D. Pa. 2016): §1.10

Londo v. McLaughlin, 402 Pa. Super. 527, 587 A.2d 744 (1991): §§1.17, 3.30

Margolies v. State Farm Fire & Casualty Co., 810 F. Supp. 637 (E.D. Pa. 1992): §1.33

Marks v. Nationwide Ins. Co., 762 A.2d 1098 (Pa. Super. Ct. 2000): §2.54

Martin v. Lancaster Battery Co., 530 Pa. 11, 606 A.2d 444 (1992): §1.28

McDonough v. State Farm Fire & Casualty Co., 365 F. Supp. 3d 552 (E.D. Pa. 2019): §§1.33, 3.48

McGuigan v. Reliance Standard Life Ins. Co., 256 F. Supp. 2d 345 (E.D. Pa. 2003): §1.29

McLaren v. AIG Domestic Claims, Inc., 853 F. Supp. 2d 499 (E.D. Pa. 2012): §3.30

McMahon v. Medical Protective Co., 92 F. Supp. 3d 367, 380, recon. denied, 2015 WL 4633698 (W.D. Pa. 2015): §§2.7, 2.24, 2.33, 2.36

Metropolitan Grp. Prop. & Casualty Ins. Co. v. Hack, 312 F. Supp. 3d 439 (M.D. Pa. 2018): §§1.9, 1.26, 1.33

Mishoe v. Erie Ins. Co., 762 A.2d 369 (Pa. Super. Ct. 2000): §1.26

Mohney v. American Gen. Life Ins. Co., 116 A.3d 1123, 2015 PA Super 113, appeal denied, 130 A.3d 1291 (Pa. 2015): §§1.9, 1.10, 4.16

Moy v. Schreiber Deed Sec. Co., 572 A.2d 758 (Pa. Super. Ct. 1990): §1.37

Nealy v. State Farm Mut. Auto. Ins. Co., 695 A.2d 790 (Pa. Super. Ct. 1997): §§1.33, 3.40

Nguyen v. Healthguard of Lancaster, Inc., 282 F. Supp. 2d 296 (E.D. Pa. 2003): §1.29

Northwestern Mut. Life Ins. Co., The v. Babayan, 430 F.3d 121 (3d Cir. 2005): §§1.9, 1.18

Rhode Island

Betco Scaffolds Co. v. Houston United Casualty Ins. Co., 29 S.W.3d 341 (Tex. Ct. App. 2000): §1.10

Birmingham Fire Ins. Co. v. American Int'l Adjusting Co., 947 S.W.2d 592 (Tex. Ct. App. 1997): §2.48

Carter v. State Farm Mut. Auto. Ins. Co., 33 S.W.3d 369 (Tex. Ct. App. 2000): §2.50

Caserotti v. State Farm Ins. Co., 791 S.W.2d 561 (Tex. Ct. App. 1990): §2.54

Caton v. Leach Corp., 896 F.2d 939 (5th Cir. 1990): §1.42

Central Sav. & Loan Ass'n v. Stemmons N.W. Bank, 848 S.W.2d 232 (Tex. Ct. App. 1992): §1.45

Chicago Title Ins. Co. v. Alford, 3 S.W.3d 164 (Tex. Ct. App. 1999): §1.20

Childers v. Pumping Sys., Inc., 968 F.2d 565 (5th Cir. 1992): §1.45

Coca-Cola Bottling Co. v. Coca-Cola Co., 769 F. Supp. 599 (D. Del. 1991): §1.45

Coffman v. Scott Wetzel Servs., Inc., 908 S.W.2d 516 (Tex. Ct. App. 1995): §1.19

Coleman v. Federal Sav. & Loan Ins. Corp., 762 S.W.2d 243 (Tex. Ct. App. 1988): §1.45

Coleman v. Lumbermens Mut. Casualty Co., 786 S.W.2d 445 (Tex. Ct. App. 1990): §1.28

Columbia Universal Life Ins. Co. v. Miles, 923 S.W.2d 803 (Tex. Ct. App. 1996): §1.23

Commonwealth Lloyds Ins. Co. v. Downs, 853 S.W.2d 104 (Tex. Ct. App. 1993): §1.14

Commonwealth Lloyd's Ins. Co. v. Thomas, 825 S.W.2d 135 (Tex. Ct. App. 1992): §§1.16, 1.33, 1.58, 1.66

Coors, Adolph, Co. v. Rodriguez, 780 S.W.2d 477 (Tex. Ct. App. 1989): §1.45

Crawford & Co. v. Garcia, 817 S.W.2d 98 (Tex. Ct. App. 1991): §2.24

Crim Truck & Tractor Co. v. Navistar Int'l Trans. Corp., 823 S.W.2d 591 (Tex. 1992): §1.2

Crow v. United Benefit Life Ins. Co., 2001 WL 285231 (N.D. Tex. 2001): §4.16

Crowder v. Tri-C Resources, Inc., 393 S.W.2d 821 (Tex. Ct. App. 1991): §1.45

Crown Life Ins. Co. v. Casteel, 22 S.W.3d 378 (Tex. 1999): §2.24

Crum & Forster, Inc. v. Monsanto Co., 887 S.W.2d 103 (Tex. Ct. App. 1994): §2.24

Dallas Fire Ins. Co. v. Texas Contractors Sur. & Casualty Agency, 159 S.W.3d 895 (Tex. 2004): §1.38

Davis, In re, 253 F.3d 807 (5th Cir. 2001): §2.43

Dear v. Scottsdale Ins. Co., 947 S.W.2d 908 (Tex. Ct. App. 1997): §2.2

Dixon v. State Farm Fire & Casualty Co., 799 F. Supp. 691 (S.D. Tex. 1992): §1.16

Utah

West Virginia

Mills v. Regent Ins. Co., 152 Wis. 2d 294, 449 N.W.2d 294 (Ct. App. 1989): §1.10

Newhouse v. Citizens Sec. Mut. Ins. Co., 176 Wis. 2d 824, 501 N.W.2d 1 (1993): §2.66

Newhouse v. Citizens Sec. Mut. Ins. Co., 170 Wis. 2d 456, 489 N.W.2d 639 (Ct. App. 1992), aff'd, 176 Wis. 2d 824, 501 N.W.2d 1 (1993): §2.9

Novak v. American Family Mut. Ins. Co., 183 Wis. 2d 133, 515 N.W.2d 504 (Ct. App. 1994): §2.9

Plautz, Estate of, by Pagel v. Time Ins. Co., 189 Wis. 2d 136, 525 N.W.2d 342 (1994): §3.24

Reid v. Benz, 629 N.W.2d 262 (Wis. 2001): §2.70

Ristow v. Threadneedle Ins. Co., 220 Wis. 2d 644, 583 N.W.2d 452 (Ct. App. 1998): §2.56

Roehl Transp., Inc. v. Liberty Mut. Ins. Co., 784 N.W.2d 542 (Wis. 2010): §2.2

Samuels Recycling Co. v. CNA Ins. Cos., 223 Wis. 2d 233, 588 N.W.2d 385 (Ct. App. 1998): §1.20

Schlussler v. American Family Mut. Ins. Co., 157 Wis. 2d 516, 460 N.W.2d 756 (Ct. App. 1990): §1.10

Sta-Rite Indus. Inc. v. Zurich Re (U.K.) Ltd., 178 F.3d 883 (7th Cir. 1999): §2.7

State Farm Fire & Casualty Co. v. Walker, 157 Wis. 2d 459, 459 N.W.2d 605 (Ct. App. 1990): §§1.16, 1.23

Stewart v. Farmers Ins. Group, 321 Wis. 2d 391, 773 N.W.2d 513 (Wis. App. 2009): §1.59

Tang v. C.A.R.S. Protection Plus, Inc., 734 N.W.2d 169 (Wis. Ct. App. 2007): §1.11

Trible v. Tower Ins. Co., 168 N.W.2d 148 (Wis. 1969): §§1.18, 1.19A, 1.66

Trinity Evangelical Lutheran Church v. Tower Ins. Co., 251 Wis. 2d 212, 641 N.W.2d 504 (Ct. App. 2002), aff'd, 661 N.W.2d 789 (Wis. 2003): §1.62

Trinity Evangelical Lutheran Church & School-Friestadt v. Tower Ins. Co., 661 N.W.2d 789 (Wis. 2003): §§1.18, 1.19A, 1.33, 1.66

United Capital Ins. Co. v. Bartolotta's Fireworks Co., 200 Wis. 2d 284, 546 N.W.2d 198 (Ct. App. 1996): §2.2

Wyoming

Ahrenholtz v. Time Ins. Co., 968 P.2d 946 (Wyo. 1998): §1.33

Anderson v. South Lincoln Special Cemetery Dist., 972 P.2d 136 (Wyo. 1999): §1.42

Andrews v. Southwest Wyo. Rehab. Ctr., 974 P.2d 948 (Wyo. 1999): §1.42

Cathcart v. State Farm Mut. Auto. Ins. Co., 123 P.3d 579 (Wyo. 2005): §§1.9, 1.33

Cenex, Inc. v. Arrow Gas Serv., 896 F. Supp. 1574 (D. Wyo. 1995): §1.45